A New Approach to the Economics of Health Care

A Conference Sponsored by the
American Enterprise Institute for Public Policy Research

A New Approach to the Economics of Health Care

Edited by Mancur Olson

American Enterprise Institute for Public Policy Research
Washington and London

The conference out of which this volume grew was organized when Robert Helms was director of AEI's Center for Health Policy Research. I am deeply grateful to him for his tireless cooperation in organizing the conference and in the early stage of the work on this volume. When Helms moved to the government, Jack Meyer succeeded him at AEI and offered the same complete and cordial cooperation in the late stage of the editing of this volume. Again, I am most grateful to him. Rosemary Gibson, Susan Khoury, William Knight, Adele Krokes, Gretchen Erhardt, and Natalie McPherson gave invaluable help, in both the conference and the book, for which I am far more thankful than they may realize. Whatever mistakes remain are mine alone.

M.O.

Library of Congress Cataloging in Publication Data
Main entry under title:

A New approach to the economics of health care.

(AEI symposia ; 81E)
Includes bibliographical references.
1. Medical economics—United States—Congresses. 2. Medical care, Cost of—United States—Congresses. 3. Medical policy—United States—Congresses. 4. Medical economics—Congresses. I. American Enterprise Institute for Public Policy Research. II. Series. [DNLM: 1. Health services—Economics—United States. W 74 N5314]
RA410.53.N47   338.4'73621'0973   81–14980
ISBN 0–8447–2212–X   AACR2
ISBN 0–8447–2213–8 (pbk.)

AEI Symposia 81E

Printed in the United States of America

Contributors

Richard Arnould
Associate Dean
College of Commerce and Business Administration
University of Illinois

Graham Atkinson
Chief—Institutional Analysis
Maryland Health Services Cost Review Commission

Christopher Clague
Professor of Economics
University of Maryland

Harold A. Cohen
Executive Director
Maryland Health Services Cost Review Commission

Jack Cook
President
Health Systems Research Corporation

Robert W. Crandall
Senior Fellow
The Brookings Institution

A. J. Culyer
Professor of Economics
University of York
England

David Eisenstadt
Antitrust Division
Department of Justice

Alain C. Enthoven
Marriner S. Eccles Professor of Public and Private Management
Stanford University

H. E. Frech III
Professor of Economics
University of California, Santa Barbara

Warren Greenberg
Visiting Professor of Managerial Economics
University of Maryland

Glenn M. Hackbarth
Research Associate
Duke University

Clark C. Havighurst
Professor of Law
Duke University

J. Rogers Hollingsworth
Professor of History
University of Wisconsin-Madison

Paul L. Joskow
Professor of Economics
Massachusetts Institute of Technology

Alfred Kahn
Adviser to the President on Inflation

David I. Kass
Economist
Federal Trade Commission

Alvin K. Klevorick
Professor of Economics
Yale University

Thomas R. McCarthy
Assistant Professor of Economics and Management
Oakland University

Alan Maynard
Senior Lecturer in Economics
University of York
England

Jack A. Meyer
Resident Fellow
American Enterprise Institute

Joseph P. Newhouse
Senior Economist
The Rand Corporation

Wallace E. Oates
Professor of Economics
University of Maryland

Mancur Olson
Distinguished Professor of Economics
University of Maryland

Mark V. Pauly
Professor of Economics
Northwestern University

Paul A. Pautler
Economist
Federal Trade Commission

Uwe E. Reinhardt
Professor of Economics and Public Affairs
Princeton University

Carl J. Schramm
Director, Center for Hospital Finance and Management
Johns Hopkins University

Laurence S. Seidman
Professor of Economics
Swarthmore College

Frank A. Sloan
Professor of Economics
Vanderbilt University

Ingemar Ståhl
Professor of Economics
Lund University, Sweden

Paul Starr
Assistant Professor of Sociology
Harvard University

Bruce Steinwald
Professor of Economics
Vanderbilt University

William D. White
Assistant Professor of Economics
University of Illinois at Chicago Circle

Alan Williams
Professor of Economics
University of York
England

Richard Zeckhauser
Professor, John F. Kennedy School of Government
Harvard University

Christopher Zook
Consultant
Bain and Company

*This conference was held at
the Washington Hilton Hotel
in Washington, D.C., on September 25–26, 1980.*

Contents

FOREWORD   xv
William J. Baroody, Jr.

INTRODUCTION   1
Mancur Olson

PART ONE
THE PROBLEM: INHERENT DIFFICULTIES COMPOUNDED BY MISTAKEN PRINCIPLES

The Impossibility of Finding a Mechanism to Ration Health Care
Resources Efficiently   29
Robert W. Crandall

The Long-Lost Free Market in Health Care: Government and
Professional Regulation of Medicine   44
H. E. Frech III

Paying the Piper and Calling the Tune: The Relationship between
Public Financing and Public Regulation of Health Care   67
Mark V. Pauly

Failures to Control Health Costs: Departures from First
Principles   87
Richard Zeckhauser and Christopher Zook

Commentary
    William D. White 117
    Paul Starr 119

PART TWO
EXPERIENCE ABROAD: IS IT SO DIFFERENT?

Alternative Systems of Health Care Provision: An Essay on Motes and Beams 131
A. J. Culyer, Alan Maynard, and Alan Williams

Health Insurance and Cost Containment Policies: The Experience Abroad 151
Uwe E. Reinhardt

Can Equality and Efficiency Be Combined? The Experience of the Planned Swedish Health Care System 172
Ingemar Ståhl

Commentary
J. Rogers Hollingsworth 196
Joseph P. Newhouse 202

PART THREE
REGULATION: CAN IT IMPROVE INCENTIVES?

Regulation: Incentives Rather Than Command and Control ... 211
Graham Atkinson and Jack Cook

Alternative Regulatory Mechanisms for Controlling Hospital Costs 219
Paul L. Joskow

A Design for Resolving the Conflicts Resulting from Separate Regulation of Hospital Rates and Hospital Capacity 258
Harold A. Cohen and Carl J. Schramm

Regulatory Approaches to Hospital Cost Containment: A Synthesis of the Empirical Evidence 273
Bruce Steinwald and Frank A. Sloan

Commentary
Thomas R. McCarthy 308
Christopher Clague 312

PART FOUR
The Health Professions: "The Dog That Didn't Bark?"

Physician and Medical Society Influence on Blue Shield Plans:
Effects on Physician Reimbursement 319
  David I. Kass and Paul A. Pautler

The Effects of Provider-Controlled Blue Shield Plans: Regulatory
Options 337
  Richard Arnould and David Eisenstadt

Provider-Influenced Insurance Plans and Their Impact on
Competition: Lessons from Dentistry 359
  Warren Greenberg

Enforcing the Rules of Free Enterprise in an Imperfect Market:
The Case of Individual Practice Associations 375
  Clark C. Havighurst and Glenn M. Hackbarth

Commentary
  Alvin K. Klevorick   405
  Wallace E. Oates   411

PART FIVE
One Step toward the New Approach

A Brief Outline of the Competition Strategy for Health Services
Delivery System Reform 419
  Alain C. Enthoven

Health Care Competition: Are Tax Incentives Enough? 422
  Jack A. Meyer

Consumer Choice Health Plan and the Patient Cost-Sharing
Strategy: Can They Be Reconciled? 448
  Laurence S. Seidman

Supply-Side Economics of Health Care and Consumer Choice
Health Plan 465
  Alain C. Enthoven

CONCLUSION

Health Care Economics: Paths to Structural Reform 491
  Alfred E. Kahn

Foreword

This volume is one of a series of studies and conference proceedings on health care financing and regulation published by AEI's Center for Health Policy Research. In response to intense discussion in the 1970s of national health insurance, AEI presented analyses of the impact of existing and proposed government programs and regulations in health policy. The Institute published a legislative analysis on compulsory health insurance proposals and the proceedings of a conference entitled *National Health Insurance: What Now, What Later, What Never?* These and other analyses concentrated on assessing the potential of national health insurance, hospital cost containment, and other government initiatives for solving the real problems in health policy rather than attacking the symptoms of the problems.

This volume bridges the debates of the 1970s and 1980s, thus laying the groundwork for future research by the Institute. Indeed, in the past twenty years, the health policy debate has undergone significant change. The 1960s were characterized by the emergence of government-financed health insurance for special groups with the enactment of the Medicare and Medicaid entitlement programs. The 1970s witnessed a sharp increase in federal and state expenditures for health care, along with a variety of new government regulations. In this decade, public policy concerns, which had previously focused primarily on access and quality, began to center on the problem of controlling rising health care expenditures.

In the 1980s health care costs are looming ever larger in tight state and federal budgets despite government efforts to limit cost escalation. Medicare and Medicaid expenditures have been doubling every four years. There is still concern that sectors of the population do not have access to adequate health care even though some segments of society have what health observers have called "overinsurance."

As we enter the 1980s, a new approach to health care economics is emerging. Health policy analysts are beginning to think of the health care sector more as an economic system. The focus of the health policy debate is on changing the incentives in medical care delivery and financing to encourage a more efficient allocation of resources, reflecting cost-conscious consumer and provider choices. It is becoming evident that fundamental structural changes in medical care delivery and financing can lower the cost of health care for both public beneficiaries and private insurance enrollees.

In the introduction, Mancur Olson presents a fresh perspective on what he considers to be two lingering problems in health care: overspending and the unmet health care needs of certain sectors of the population. The contributors to the volume address the nature of medical markets at home and abroad, along with the effects of government regulatory policies and the role of the health professions in the functioning of the market.

This book takes a step further and ventures into an analysis of the more market-oriented approach to health care delivery and financing that has taken root among many health policy observers and analysts. Although interest in market reform is growing, there has been limited independent investigation of the issues at stake. The Institute remains dedicated to the commitment of providing analysis of health policy issues to promote informed debate and wise public policy choices. We believe that this volume will make a substantial contribution to the new direction in health policy.

We are indebted to Mancur Olson for devoting substantial effort to assembling a distinguished cadre of authors and discussants. His thoughtful, creative approach has woven together divergent views on health care issues confronting us today. We would also like to thank Dr. Robert B. Helms, deputy assistant secretary for planning and evaluation at the U.S. Department of Health and Human Services and former director of the Center for Health Policy Research, who helped provide the conceptual framework for the conference.

WILLIAM J. BAROODY, JR.
President
American Enterprise Institute

Introduction

Mancur Olson

Although the authors of the papers and commentaries in this volume have diverse opinions and ideologies, their work in the aggregate seems to offer a unified and fresh perspective on health care policy. This perspective in turn provides a vision of a new class of proposals for practical policy that could in my judgment greatly improve the efficiency and availability of health care, not only in the United States but in other countries as well. To be sure, the unity may be evident only if it is already in the mind's eye—the differences of opinion among the contributors are often fundamental, and I would not expect all the authors to agree on the unified perspective that I claim to see. I hope the reader will give each of the papers the careful study that it deserves and then form his own judgment about what perspective is best. But first let us try to reach the new perspective that allegedly allows us to see the unity implicit in the diversity.

There is a hint about the new perspective in popular debates about health policy in the United States. One common complaint is that government programs and private insurance together do not cover everyone or all types of care, and there is some demand for measures or for a system that would catch what now falls between the cracks. Another common complaint is that expanded government health programs in combination with the favorable tax treatment of health insurance premiums paid by employers have led to stupendous increases in the costs of health care. This in turn leads to demands for limits on expenditures or for changes and cutbacks in government intervention in the health care sector. Although these two complaints sometimes come from different quarters, they also often come from the same sources, as when the Carter administration sought limitations in the rate of inflation of health costs partly in the hope that lower costs would eventually make national health insurance financially feasible. There is no inconsistency in being concerned simultaneously about unmet needs for medical care and about the increasing costs of the care that is received.

Although there is no inconsistency in the two complaints, there is something at least faintly paradoxical in their both being common at the same time in the same society. If government programs and expenditures for health care have proliferated and the buying of health insurance has been subsidized to the point where our society is spending far too much on health care, then why, at the same time, are there some types of health care or some people for whom far too little is spent? If we believe that Jones spends far too much of his income on clothing, we will be a little surprised if at the same time he has no shoes. If social concerns and egalitarian impulses have generated huge government expenditures and there are tax subsidies for health insurance to boot, resulting by common consent in overspending, how is it that these concerns, impulses, and expenditures have left some people or types of care out altogether? There is no logical difficulty in spending too much on medical care in some cases and too little in other cases, but it does require explanation. A few readers might deny that there is anyone who deserves care now who does not get it, but they should agree that there is an uneven level of lavishness in our spending for health care, and this too needs an explanation.

Tax Subsidy and Overinsurance

Let us look first at the complaint about overinsurance for which tax subsidies are supposed to be responsible and return later to explicit government expenditures on health programs. The complaint about this alleged overinsurance appears to have been inspired particularly by the work of Martin Feldstein,[1] one of this country's most respected economists and a leading student of health care policy, but by now this complaint is quite general. Overinsurance is frequently blamed for the explosion in the costs of health care in the United States. There is undoubtedly justification for criticizing tax subsidies that in effect make income received in the form of health insurance tax free, whereas income received in most other forms is taxable. There can be no doubt that this subsidy, taken by itself, does encourage overspending (technically, more spending than is "Pareto-optimal") on health care.

But this subsidy should not be taken by itself—it might be overwhelmed by other factors, and I hypothesize that this is actually the case. First, there is the paradox already described—the underspending

---

[1] Martin Feldstein, "The Welfare Loss of Excess Health Insurance," *Journal of Political Economy,"* vol. 81 (1973), pp. 251–80; idem., "The High Cost of Hospitals—and What to Do about It," *Public Interest*, no. 49 (Summer 1977), pp. 40–54; and Feldstein and Bernard Freedman, "Tax Subsidies: The Rational Demand for Insurance and the Health Care Crisis," *Journal of Public Economics*, vol. 7 (1977), pp. 155–78.

of those who are not covered by insurance or government programs should have a countervailing effect on aggregate health expenditures. Second, it is often overlooked in discussions of the tax subsidy that the considerable public and charitable expenditures to provide medical care for those who cannot afford it, and the fact that many patients get away with not paying their debts for the medical care they receive, act as a *disincentive* to the purchase of insurance, in much the same way as the existence of social security makes it optimal for an individual to make smaller private provision for retirement than would otherwise be appropriate. Perhaps one reason this influence is overlooked is that most of those who discuss the matter in print probably enjoy relatively high levels of education and income and are accordingly more familiar with the incentive effects of explicit taxes than with the incentive effects of those subsidies that are directed mainly at the less fortunate. The health insurance tax subsidy is, as Feldstein has pointed out, particularly important for workers covered under collective-bargaining contracts and seems most significant in states having a good deal of manufacturing employment.[2] It is not obvious that all factory workers should be completely insensitive to the likelihood that their health costs in any major emergency would be paid by the government or absorbed as bad debts by providers if they did not have sufficient insurance. Many health insurance policies also have upper limits on reimbursements that imply that the insured is not fully covered for catastrophic health care expenses, and the widespread willingness at all income levels to accept such policies probably owes something to the conviction that in such an event the insured would probably not have to pay all the costs. Thus public and charitable support for many of those who cannot pay medical bills, whether because of prior poverty or because of the costliness of their affliction, must by itself work to induce individuals to spend less than socially efficient amounts on medical insurance. If there is the maximizing behavior that economists usually find, the argument I am making must have some force; and if there is no maximizing behavior, then the tax subsidy does not matter either.

Possibly the quantitative significance of the two factors I have just mentioned is small; we will not know until there is an adequate empirical study of the matter. We must also ask whether the quantitative significance of the tax subsidy is sufficient to explain the colossal increases in health costs; the evidence I have seen on that point is by no means compelling. There are many, many tax subsidies, and—alas!—apparently more with each passing year, but most of them do not seem to

---

[2] Feldstein, "Welfare Loss of Excess Health Insurance," p. 255, and "High Cost of Hospitals," p. 451.

produce such sweeping effects. Home-produced food, for example, usually escapes income tax, but the change in the amount of gardening as tax rates rise is not large enough to strike the eye; the services that spouses and other family members provide for one another are not taxed, but even so there is the widespread feeling that family life needs more encouragement; capital gains are taxed at less than half the rate of tax on other income, but almost no one argues that there is too much investment; depletion allowances inefficiently subsidize domestic oil production, but almost no one thinks we have too much oil. In each of the foregoing cases there are other aspects of the matter that I have left out, so the analogies are not compelling. But as we have seen and shall see, the argument that tax subsidies largely explain the overspending on health care also leaves out a good deal.

When we return to direct government expenditure on health programs we see not only the aforementioned paradox that a willingness to expand the function of government should be combined with a tendency to leave some people and problems out altogether but also another puzzling element. Almost everyone agrees that egalitarian or humanistic feelings (combined with a readiness to accept bigger government) helped explain programs such as Medicare and Medicaid and other efforts to help the aged and the poor obtain medical care. Yet these programs have also been designed and administered in such a way as to generate vastly increased incomes for physicians and some other relatively well-to-do providers. It is ironic that the same programs should have been designed to have both markedly egalitarian and notably inegalitarian consequences, and we should not be satisfied with any explanation of U.S. health care policy that does not encompass both these realities.

From this perspective, the familiar slogans from the ideological debates do not seem nearly sufficient. On the one hand, those who are primarily concerned with the gaps in medical coverage and attribute them to callousness or laissez-faire prejudice must explain how the functions of government and insurance have increased so much and how they have led to overspending. On the other hand, those who attribute the difficulties in the health area to soft-heartedness and faith in big government must explain why coverage is so uneven and why prosperous groups such as physicians are the most notable beneficiaries of the new programs. Something else must be operating besides the forces depicted in the ideological slogans and beyond the incentives described in economists' discussions of the tax subsidy for health insurance.

Fee-for-Service versus Prepaid Group Practice

Whatever else is operating should help to explain how there can be overspending in some areas and not in others and ideally also why the same system has both egalitarian consequences and special benefits for prosperous providers. Fee-for-service arrangements naturally enter the discussion here, especially now that much is being made of the advantages of prepaid group practice. It would seem that such arrangements should be among the suspects, for they are consistent with excessive care and costs in cases where the patient or his third-party payer has money, and consistent also with too little care or no care for those without resources. Exploitation of fee-for-service is also consistent with the high incomes of physicians.

In fact, fee-for-service arrangements taken by themselves cannot really resolve any of our paradoxes. If there is competition among physicians and other providers of medical care, those who provide more services or more expensive services than are appropriate will have *some* tendency to lose business to those who serve their patients' interests better. To be sure, the patient is often not well enough informed to know whether he is getting unnecessary services or not. If fee-for-service leads to a sufficient excess of services, however, there will be a greater demand for second opinions as well as a market for individuals who provide the disinterested information patients need to make wise choices about medical care. If there is medical-care insurance in a competitive market, the insurers who monitor service levels best will be able to offer better value for premiums, so that competition among insurers will also limit abuse of fee-for-service arrangements. As Paul Joskow and Mark Pauly point out in their contributions to this volume, competition among insurers tends to bring about optimal amounts of coinsurance that will balance the greater "moral hazard" that comes from fuller coverage, against the reduction in risk that fuller coverage also provides. By the same logic, competition among insurers should provide an optimal degree of surveillance of fee-for-service providers. Finally, in a competitive market there is also the opportunity to form prepaid groups, and if abuse of fee-for-service institutions is sufficiently serious, these groups will take more business away from fee-for-service providers. (The reader's observations and experience may run counter to the conclusions drawn in this paragraph, and we shall soon see that this is because another factor is involved.)

The aforementioned constraints that a competitive market places on abuse of fee-for-service arrangements are not by any means so confining that they rule out all abuse or necessarily prevent abuse from being commonplace. Nor do they rule out some problems that can come from the *interaction* of fee-for-service arrangements with some other institutions we shall discuss later. Yet it is important to note that incentives under fee-for-service are just as good on balance as those in prepaid group practice. To the extent competitive pressures and consumer ignorance allow, the fee-for-service physician can provide unnecessarily costly services. Equally, to the extent that competitive pressures and consumer ignorance allow, the prepaid group can provide less service or poorer service than the consumer has paid for. Thus there is no inherent superiority of prepaid group practice over fee-for-service, and fee-for-service in a competitive environment cannot explain the uneven levels of service or the high incomes of providers that are observed.

The Subtle Subsidy

The main source of the unevenness in health care expenditures in this country is probably often overlooked because it is both subtle and familiar. Usually when an individual in this country has health insurance or receives government-financed care, he has "freedom of choice" about which physicians or other providers to use. When hospital care is needed, the physician may act as the patient's agent in choosing the hospital, but again (except when a physician is denied hospital privileges) the physician-agent has freedom of choice. At first glance this freedom seems only proper and natural—no more than the freedom we have when we decide at what store we will buy our clothing or food in a market economy. When there is a third-party payer, however, this so-called freedom of choice is profoundly different from the freedom we enjoy in other sectors of a market economy. It is the *freedom to choose the most expensive of the available alternatives without having to pay extra for it.*

As Jack Meyer, for example, points out in his contribution to this volume, the system of insurance reimbursement takes away the incentive to choose less costly providers and thus also takes away the incentives of providers to engage in price competition. If charging less will not affect the cost to the individual consumer or the likelihood of winning his patronage, then why charge less? Indeed, the patient (or his physician) will have an incentive to seek the best and most comfortable care, since it does not cost him any extra money; the providers will have an incentive to compete with one another in providing more costly care even if the extra dollars spent are worth only pennies to the patient. The situation is usually much the same for those whose medical care is paid for by the government; thus even the poorest people often have an incentive to choose the most costly care.

To be sure, the real world is complex and this nation is diverse, so the situation is not quite as simple as I have just described it. The individual obviously does have an incentive to take the cost of health care into account when he pays the bills himself. There are often certain stipulations about how much the provider may charge—the physician's fee, for example, must be "usual, customary, and reasonable," and the hospital may bill only for legitimate costs of providing the care. The definitions of what is usual, customary, and reasonable, however, are mainly in the hands of providers who have an incentive to make the usual fees high. Similarly, a hospital's costs may be high because of lavishness and even waste yet consist only of "legitimate" or allowable expenditures. What is considered customary or reasonable in the long run also depends largely on what is commonplace. Thus the regulations that ostensibly limit fees and costs have much less effect than do the incentives for overspending.

The incentive to seek more costly health care—if the extra costs buy anything of value at all—generally holds for both physicians and hospitals when care is covered by insurance and to a considerable extent is also true of Medicare and Medicaid. This is the main reason, in my judgment, for the overspending on health care. With this huge incentive for overspending for insured patients, it is easy to see why the tax exemption of employer-provided health insurance seemed so important. In fact, the overinsurance due to the tax subsidy is partially offset, or perhaps more than offset, by the underinsurance, or total lack of insurance, of others. Some types of expenditures for medical care, and some people, are not covered by third-party payers.

Those who must pay for their own health care will usually spend less than those who do not have to pay for it, and if they are poor, they will spend very much less or even forgo the medical care. As third-party payers spend more and more on health care, prices rise, and it then benefits individuals to buy less of the care they must pay for themselves. *Thus we have an explanation of the unevenness of medical expenditure— of the widespread complaints about current needs and demands for a more comprehensive system cheek-by-jowl with the complaints about overspending on health care.* The tax subsidy for health insurance is miscast as the villain in the overspending drama, but it does add to the *unevenness* of the provision of medical care that is emphasized here.

This unevenness cannot be attributed simply to callousness or laissez-faire ideology or explained by the growth of government or egalitarianism, but it is exactly what should be expected from the familiar structure of incentives I have just outlined. Because the system that has just been described obviously increases payments to providers, it can also explain the paradoxical tendency for egalitarian public policies to increase the incomes of prosperous physicians, drug companies, and other providers. It can also explain excess hospital beds and duplicative equipment, since these need not cause any problem for the hospital that can compete as well or better with more costly facilities.

7

Who Sought the Subtle Subsidy?

This arrangement, whereby we as consumers have an incentive to choose ever more costly care and providers have an incentive to offer it, must itself be explained. Why would such a wasteful and expensive system be adopted? Who is responsible for proposing and supporting it?

As a hardened economist, I believe that those who profit from the arrangement are the ones who sought it. This belief grows not only out of the lore of my craft but also out of the history of the arrangement at issue, which goes back to a time when the government did not have much to do with the health care system.

Let us begin with hospitals. The main features of the system of hospital insurance in this country were worked out by Blue Cross in the depression of the 1930s. Blue Cross was created by hospitals and by the American Hospital Association (AHA). Of the thirty-nine Blue Cross plans that were established in the 1930s, twenty-two obtained all the initial funds from hospitals and five obtained part of their funds from hospitals.[3] The AHA promulgated seven "standards which should characterize group hospitalization plans," and one of these "standards" is our old friend, "freedom of choice of hospital and physician subscriber."[4] The AHA along with various state hospital groups also sought enabling legislation for the Blue Cross plans that exempt them from the general insurance laws of the state, give them status as benevolent and charitable institutions, relieve them of the obligation to maintain the reserves required of commercial insurers, and exempt them from taxes. The New York United Hospital Fund, with the support of the AHA, persuaded the New York legislature to pass the first such enabling legislation, and by 1945 similar laws had been adopted in thirty-five states.[5] In many states Blue Cross plans are exempt from state taxation, and the Internal Revenue Service has also exempted them from federal income taxes.

The result of this legislative effort is that Blue Cross has tax advantages and sometimes also other legal advantages over its commercial competitors. The situation varies from state to state, but in many states these advantages are quite significant. The combination of these advantages and the symbiotic relationship between hospitals and Blue Cross helped give Blue Cross plans a dominant position in the market for medical insurance in most of the United States. In 1945 Blue Cross

---

[3] Sylvia A. Law, *Blue Cross—What Went Wrong?* (New Haven, Conn., and London: Yale University Press, 1974), pp. 6–7. I have drawn heavily on this book in preparing this part of the introduction.

[4] Ibid., p. 8.

[5] Ibid., p. 9.

claimed 61 percent of the hospital insurance market.[6] This percentage subsequently diminished substantially, but in most communities the Blue Cross plan remained very much larger than any competitor.

Because most other insurance companies had a relatively small share of the market, hospitals could refuse to deal with one of them if its policies were unacceptable; these other insurance companies did not have the market power of Blue Cross. Because of this and Blue Cross's relationship with hospitals, Blue Cross plans in a number of states were also able to work out what is in effect a two-price system for hospital care, whereby patients with Blue Cross insurance would be billed less for hospital care than commercially insured or self-insured patients. Notably this was done through agreements that stipulated that the Blue Cross would pay the "costs" of the hospital care provided to its subscribers, with the provision that the hospital's losses from bad debts and charity care should not be counted as costs. The hospital would accordingly have to add enough to its charges to commercially insured and self-paying patients to cover not only the costs of their treatment but also the whole burden of bad debts and charity. In the state of Maryland before the advent of state rate regulation there, this often meant about a 15 percent cost reduction and a corresponding competitive advantage for Blue Cross over its competitors.

There is no doubt in my mind that the encouragement of health insurance by hospitals through Blue Cross plans helped an enormous number of people. Presumably hundreds of thousands if not millions of families had insurance they would not have had otherwise. The value of spreading risk through this insurance must have made an important contribution to the well-being of a large number of people. It must also have enabled some people to obtain hospital care that they needed very badly but could not have afforded otherwise. The hospitals' promotion of a dominant insurance firm in each area may also possibly have achieved certain economies of scale that would not have been achieved otherwise. Possibly the existence of a dominant firm also lessened the problem of adverse risk selection. Thus the purpose here is not to argue that hospital promotion of Blue Cross plans was a bad thing—on balance it may have been a good thing.

The point is rather that through Blue Cross the hospitals were able to ensure that all or almost all insurers gave their customers so-called freedom of choice about which hospitals to patronize. That is, in effect they created a system whereby almost everyone who was insured could choose the most costly hospital without paying extra, thereby tending to eliminate price competition among hospitals.

---

[6] Ibid., p. 11.

At this point an alert economist with an awareness of the multiplicity of ways in which competition can increase efficiency might ask: Why didn't some clever entrepreneur in a commercial insurance company contract only with hospitals of above-average efficiency? By offering subscribers a choice among only these hospitals, the insurance company could have offered better value to subscribers and thus drawn business away from Blue Cross and other competitors. The less efficient hospitals would then have lost business, and this in turn would have improved efficiency in the industry.

Why, indeed, didn't something like the process just described occur regularly? What plausible explanation is there, except that the same cartel-like practices and lobbying power that gave rise to Blue Cross and to the special legislation that favored it, kept insurers from making such competitive arrangements? If an insurance company faced a boycott by its customers or was persistently criticized by hospitals and physicians, it could not profit from introducing a plan that generated competition among providers.

Significantly, the AHA permitted health insurance plans to license the Blue Cross name and insignia only if the plans met certain "standards." One of these standards was that the health insurance plan had to have "written agreements with at least 75 percent of the nonfederal short-term hospitals registered by the American Hospital Association containing at least 75 percent of these hospitals' beds in the plan's service area."[7] This requirement ensured that no Blue Cross plan could select only the most efficient hospitals in its area. Its effect was to reduce competitive pressure on less efficient hospitals.

Capturing the Public Sector

It is interesting to see how the insurance arrangement that eliminated price competition among providers for insured patients spread from the private sector to the public sector. In 1961 the Kennedy administration came into office committed to a social-security type of hospital insurance program for the aged. Initially, the hospital industry, like the American Medical Association, opposed any such program. In January 1962 the House of Delegates of the AHA changed its policy and supported a social-security type of health program *on condition that the actual administration of the program be entrusted to Blue Cross.*[8] The Department of Health, Education, and Welfare (HEW), presumably seeing an opportunity to obtain AHA support and to avoid hospital boycotts of

[7] Ibid.
[8] Ibid., p. 32.

10

patients covered by the proposed social-security scheme, appointed a task force to consider the use of Blue Cross and other insurers in the administration of health insurance for the aged. After the task force had made its report, legislation was introduced that provided for a "fiscal intermediary." In the 1965 Social Security Act, a "fiscal intermediary" is defined as an organization or agency nominated by "any group or association of providers of services." The secretary of HEW is empowered to negotiate reimbursement arrangements with such fiscal intermediaries; under these arrangements the fiscal intermediary determines the amounts of payments to the providers, subject to review by the secretary. Thus, as a fiscal intermediary, Blue Cross would apply the same reimbursement arrangement to Medicare that it had applied to those who were insured through the private sector. (By 1968 Blue Cross was also involved in the administration of Medicaid in twenty-three states.)

The American Hospital Association/Blue Cross Association "Principles of Payment for Hospital Care" stipulates that "payments to different hospitals for the same service may differ." So it was to be under Medicare. As Robert Ball of HEW explained to the House Ways and Means Committee in 1965, the "main," indeed the "overwhelming" principle was that "per diem costs will differ depending on the hospital from place to place, and we will reimburse whatever it [the costs] turns out to be."[9] At the time Ball spoke, most observers had not even the faintest idea how much the costs would ultimately "turn out to be," but no one with an understanding of the significance of the elimination of price competition and of buyers' incentives to seek better value can be surprised at the result.

Physicians and the Subtle Subsidy

Mark Pauly, a contributor to the present volume, and M. A. Redisch have shown elsewhere[10] that some hospitals can be regarded as essentially physicians' cooperatives—that is, institutions that are essentially controlled by the physicians who practice in them. We should accordingly expect the hospital industry would sometimes support insurance arrangements and government policies that are favorable to physicians. We have already seen that, according to the AHA, one of the seven standards that should characterize group hospitalization plans is "freedom of choice of hospital and physician by subscriber." Organizations

---

[9] Ibid., p. 62.

[10] Mark Pauly and M. A. Redisch, "The Not-for-Profit Hospital as a Physicians' Cooperative," *American Economic Review*, vol. 62, no. 1 (March 1973), pp. 87–99.

of physicians have also worked directly to obtain insurance arrangements and government policies that take away most of the patient's incentive to seek better value in physicians' services and that curtail price competition among physicians.

In his contribution to this volume and in an earlier article with Lawrence Goldberg,[11] Warren Greenberg argues that physicians have used their organized power to eliminate insurance arrangements that policed the provision of unnecessary services to insured patients and that encouraged price competition among physicians. Part of the argument is drawn from the record of an unsuccessful antitrust suit against the Oregon State Medical Society. This record shows that for a time in Oregon there were commercial insurance companies with policies far different from those with which we are familiar now. These commercial insurance companies regularly examined the services that physicians provided or proposed to provide to insured patients and refused to pay for services the companies deemed unnecessary. They also sometimes questioned the physicians' fees they were asked to pay. These practices naturally reduced the costs of the insurance companies and made it possible for them to offer insurance with lower premiums and thereby to gain more business. Thus their policies were exactly what would be expected in a free market. These practices naturally also made the incomes of physicians in Oregon lower than they might have been and encouraged price competition among physicians as well. The Oregon State Medical Society opposed the practices of the insurance companies in various ways and in particular urged member physicians essentially to boycott the offending insurance companies. The Oregon State Medical Society also created the Oregon Physicians' Service (the Oregon Blue Shield insurance plan) to compete with the offending insurance companies. By encouraging partiality toward their own insurance company and resistance to the offending commercial insurance companies, the organized physicians were able to eliminate cost-cutting and competition-inducing insurance practices.

There is also evidence that forces similar to those that operated in Oregon were operating in other states. In the early 1970s the Aetna insurance company endeavored to use policies somewhat similar to those used by the insurance companies in Oregon but was ultimately persuaded to change its policies because of the opposition of physicians and the American Medical Association. Moreover, in his contribution to this volume, Greenberg shows that the very Blue Shield plans established largely by physicians operate one way when they insure dental work and

---

[11] Warren Greenberg and Lawrence Goldberg, "The Effect of Physician-Controlled Health Insurance," *Journal of Health, Politics, and Law*, vol. 2, no. 1 (Spring 1977), pp. 48–78.

quite differently when they insure patients for physicians' fees. When the plans insure patients for dental work, they monitor the extent of dental service and the fees in much the same way commercial insurance companies in Oregon once monitored physicians. Greenberg argues that insurance plans organized by dentists do not have the legal and other advantages that Blue Shield enjoys in the medical area, and accordingly have not been able to control competitive forces to such an extent.

The papers in this volume by David Kass and Paul Pautler and by Richard Arnould and David Eisenstadt also provide evidence that physician influence in Blue Shield plans raises the costs of medical care. They compare several Blue Shield plans that appear to have different degrees of physician representation or that have different advantages in the insurance market. Then they relate these differences to variations in physicians' fees under the several plans. Each of these two papers brings a large amount of data to bear on the problem through the use of modern statistical techniques. The results of the tests in these two papers are what would be expected from the foregoing, but they are not strong enough to be compelling. There is as well an alternative specification that leads to different results.[12] I conjecture, along with some others, that the influence of organized physicians on *all* Blue Shield plans is so pervasive that the variation among these plans in the extent of physician influence is not large enough to generate variations in physicians' fees that are dramatic enough to produce really definitive statistical results. Every Blue Shield plan has at least one physician on its board. Moreover, if a Blue Shield plan eliminates the incentive for an insured patient to seek better value in physicians' care and eliminates price competition among providers, then it must be profoundly influenced by physicians—no other group's interests are served by this arrangement.

Conspicuous Controversies and Unobtrusive Power

The physicians, hospitals, and other organized providers (such as unionized hospital workers and pharmaceutical companies) have profited disproportionately from Medicare and Medicaid. We have explained the most important reason for this, but we have not yet resolved the paradox of why this occurred as a result of an egalitarian impulse to broaden the coverage of social insurance. To explain the paradox fully we must also explain how the Medicare program was passed in the first place. We must explain not only why the providers' lobbies succeeded

---

[12] William J. Lynk, "Regulatory Control of the Membership of Blue Shield Board of Directors," unpublished (March 1980).

in determining how the Medicare program was to be administered, but also why the same powerful organized physicians failed to prevent the passage of Medicare legislation.

The reasons this occurred are illuminated by the theory of public or collective goods. As I argued in *The Logic of Collective Action*,[13] it does not follow that because some group, such as the consumers of medical care, would in the aggregate gain from collective action that it will therefore organize to act collectively. The argument is too elaborate to be set out here, but one aspect of it may be immediately comprehensible. Each individual consumer finds that any sacrifice he would make to achieve an objective that he shares with a large group will accrue mostly to others in the group. Because the individual who might pay dues to a lobby working for less expensive medical care would bear the whole cost of his dues contribution, but would share any gains his contribution might earn with everyone else in the group, he will be better off if he does not pay such dues. If others in the group obtain favorable policies, he will benefit from the policies anyway. Thus, in general, large groups having common interests will not organize to serve those common interests. Those groups that are able to organize can do so because they are small or because they have coercive power (as in a union shop or a picket line) or other "selective incentives." Because selective incentives are discussed in detail in *The Logic of Collective Action*, I will not describe them here, except to point out that physicians are richly endowed with these incentives and thus relatively well organized, both in this country and abroad.

Just as organizational power is a collective or public good to a group, so is most information about public affairs. If the typical individual citizen were to devote much time to studying the government's health policy and then work to improve it, the fruits of his labors would be shared with the whole society rather than accruing mainly to him. The individual is, moreover, extremely unlikely to cast a tie-breaking vote in any national election. Because of this general logic relating to collective goods, then, the typical citizen will usually obtain information about the government's health policy only to the extent that this is essentially costless or worth gathering because of its intrinsic interest.

Because some of the providers have selective incentives that enable them to organize, and because the typical citizen has no incentive to gather detailed information on health policy, the details of health policy are mainly determined by providers. The inefficient arrangements for third-party reimbursement mentioned earlier fall in this category.

[13] Mancur Olson, Jr., *Logic of Collective Action: Public Goods and the Theory of Groups* (Cambridge, Mass.: Harvard University Press, 1971).

When momentous policy controversies arise, however, there is a possibility that the typical citizen will hear of these controversies and perhaps arrive at an opinion about them. If an issue becomes a major part of a presidential campaign, for example, ordinary citizens may learn of it because the drama and uncertainty of such campaigns can attract the interest of voters who would otherwise remain rationally ignorant. The campaign may even have entertainment value.

When a matter of health care policy or any other public policy does receive this degree of attention, the perceived interests of larger numbers of constituents will usually triumph over the interests of smaller numbers of them. Because professional providers such as physicians are far less numerous than the consumers of health care, and even less numerous than consumers over age sixty-five, it is not surprising that Medicare was passed despite the opposition of physicians. Nor is it surprising that the same Medicare program eventually came to be administered in a way that is extremely favorable to providers and bad for the more numerous consumers and taxpayers. Now we have an explanation of our paradox of egalitarian legislation providing disproportionate gains for relatively well-off providers.

In another publication, *The Rise and Decline of Nations*,[14] I explore the logic of this argument more carefully and give other examples. One of these is the contrast between the high nominal rate of progression of the income tax and the quite different incidence of the loopholes. The degree of progression of regular tax brackets and the different incidence of the loopholes are the products of the same political system, and might be supposed to have much the same incidence. The main reason they do not is that the former is a product of a major controversy in which the more numerous low- and middle-income voters prevailed, whereas the latter is much influenced by discreet lobbying efforts in which small groups of often wealthy individuals and firms have relatively greater influence.

The general considerations that have just been set out naturally apply to other countries as well. This leads to the prediction that similar paradoxes occur in other countries also. This appears to be the case. As Uwe Reinhardt points out in his contribution to this volume and in another paper,[15] the West German system, for example, has channeled vast amounts of additional income to providers at the same time that the breadth of social insurance has increased. I hypothesize that one

[14] Mancur Olson, *The Rise and Decline of Nations* (New Haven, Conn.: Yale University Press, forthcoming).

[15] Uwe F. Reinhardt, "Health Insurance and Cost-Containment Policies: The Experience Abroad," *American Economic Review*, vol. 70, no. 2 (1980), pp. 149–56.

reason that health costs have increased rapidly as a percentage of national income in most Western democracies since World War II is that efforts to broaden the coverage of social insurance have been passed for humanitarian and egalitarian reasons, and that providers in most of these countries have managed to have these programs implemented in ways that increase the incomes of providers. In his contribution, Ingemar Ståhl documents an increase in coverage coinciding with an increase in health care costs in Sweden. To some extent, this argument fits the health care situation in the United Kingdom, discussed in this volume by Anthony Culyer, Alan Maynard, and Alan Williams, especially when unionized workers in the National Health Service are taken into account, but less clearly. One reason may be the historically deep division in Britain between general practitioners and hospital-based consultants described in this volume by Hollingsworth, which presumably makes physicians less powerful than they would otherwise be.

Regulation with Unchanged Incentives

The overspending that the so-called freedom of choice leads to has been made all the more serious as Medicare and government programs have expanded the use of this device and increased the amount of money that could be misspent. Naturally this overspending eventually provoked efforts to control the level of expenditures. Because the government, as Mark Pauly points out in his chapter in this book, is paying a large part of the bill, political leaders, who had to suffer the criticism for rising taxes and social insurance contributions and for the curtailments of other public expenditure made necessary by health spending, have been among those who are seriously concerned about the explosion in the costs of health care, and most especially of hospital care. No doubt the increasingly obvious excess capacity and duplication of facilities have also helped generate interest in measures that might limit the escalation of the costs of medical care. Thus various kinds of regulation have been introduced in efforts to limit inflation in the cost of health care.

There is a widespread tendency to lump all types of regulation together, and to debate the merits of "regulation" or "government" generally as compared with "markets," with all "markets" also thought to be much the same. I will argue that this ideological approach is inadequate, especially in the health area. The incentives that face the regulators vary dramatically with the institutional arrangements, and the rules that the regulators promulgate in turn can vary dramatically from one situation to another. Similarly, the word "market" is used to cover such diverse phenomena in the health area that the term sometimes is more of a slogan than an analytical category. Thus in what follows we must make finer distinctions.

Let us just consider two types of regulation that have a similar inspiration and structure. These are the certificate-of-need (CON) program and the professional standards review organization (PSRO) undertakings for utilization review (UR). The inspiration of both of these types of regulation, as I see it, is the belief that the incentives for overspending can be countervailed simply by creating bodies of specialized and representative officeholders, or members of respected professions, that have the authority to disapprove wasteful spending or utilization. The specialized knowledge and concern for the public interest of those who are appointed or elected to office or the professional ethics of the professionals will, it is believed, ensure that waste is prevented, and perhaps bring the blessing of rational planning as well. There is no mechanism to ensure that these regulators will not be influenced by the providers, and there is no arrangement to ensure that they are held responsible for (or are likely to lose their posts because of) the level of health insurance premiums or of government expenditures on health care.

As the papers in this volume by Bruce Steinwald and Frank Sloan, by Paul Joskow, and by Harold Cohen and Carl Schramm show, history has not been kind to the faith that inspired CON and utilization review. Indeed, this is an understatement. A large number of studies have shown that the certificate-of-need program has had little or no effect or merely substituted excessive expenditures of one type for excessive expenditures of another kind. Utilization review also appears to have failed. I suspect that anyone who understands the so-called freedom-of-choice arrangements that physicians and hospitals have worked out for themselves, and who still believes that professional review will prevent excessive costs, will believe anything.

Some of the reasons that the CON and UR schemes fail to achieve their objectives and do little more than waste resources and delay decision making are evident from the more general discussions of regulation and markets in the papers in this volume, such as that by Richard Zeckhauser and Christopher Zook. Another reason schemes of this sort fail emerges from my general line of argument as well as from some direct observations. That is, providers with an incentive to preserve or increase overspending or overuse are organized and heard, whereas taxpayers and insurance-premium payers (which are larger groups without selective incentives) are not. Thus the health systems agencies and similar bodies are mainly influenced by (and are often merely representatives of) the providers. The economist knows that there would be some shortcomings of CON and UR even if they were handled only by wise and disinterested guardians, but in practice it is usually the foxes that are put in charge of the chicken coops.

From personal observation in the state of Maryland, where I served two terms as vice-chairman of the Health Services Cost Review Commission, I can testify to the almost total absence of pressures from consumers and taxpayers and to the ubiquitousness of pressures from providers and communities or suppliers connected with them. My interactions with health systems agencies and similar bodies in Maryland suggested that this was a particularly severe problem in certificate-of-need decisions. The astonishing examples of subservience to provider interests in CON decisions that Harold Cohen and Carl Schramm describe in their paper in this volume are very much in keeping with my earlier observations of the CON process in Maryland.

The Vague Distinction

There is a danger in going directly from the abject failure of CON and UR regulation to sweeping judgments about the way that "regulations" and "markets" will work or fail to work. This danger arises often in discussions of the ceilings or "caps" that the government has sometimes proposed placing on hospital costs, in discussions of state rate-setting schemes for hospitals, and in discussions of other proposals. One problem in such discussions is that it is sometimes assumed that in the absence of new government intervention, there is a free market in health care in the United States today, or something resembling a free market, so that the familiar arguments about the relative merits of regulation and markets can be used with slight modification. In fact, as H. E. Frech shows in his contribution to this book, in general there is not a free market in health care in the United States today. Not only has there been an increase in government regulation in recent years, but there has also been the long-standing professional cartelization, so that Frech writes of the "long-lost" free market.

In view of this, and the aforementioned breadth and vagueness of the word "regulation," there is in my judgment a danger of confusion. The "market" outcome is not an efficient or competitive outcome. Thus it is obviously possible that proposals that are described as "regulation" might in fact move the allocation, at least in the short run, in the direction of what would be generated by a competitive market. This does not mean that the regulatory proposals would be the best choice in the long run, but it is nonetheless important because slogans and stereotypes often obscure the need for a careful analysis of the special patterns of

18

incentives in the health care system in the United States (and many other countries) today.

A careful analysis must take into account the systematic incentive for overspending of most of those covered by third-party payers. As long as someone else pays the bill, the user has an incentive, other things being equal, to choose the most costly care, as long as the extra dollars add even pennies to the value. On top of this there is the widespread use of retrospective reimbursement for hospital costs. Under this system a hospital can have a reason to spend money on "allowable" items that may not add as much as a few pennies to the quality of care, such as higher pay for administrators and other employees who would have remained on the job even with lower pay, or duplicative facilities, or whatever. If, as is often the case, an overwhelming proportion of the hospital's patients are covered by third-party payers, the hospital will be reimbursed for almost all of its unnecessary expenditures as well as its necessary expenditures, as long as these are in "allowable" categories. Elsewhere I have called this arrangement "the more you spend, the more you get" system.[16] When a hospital is in a strong enough market position so that it does not have to worry about the fraction of patients that are not covered under the system, this system can add substantially to overspending. The status of physicians at a hospital often rises as the quality and facilities of the hospital expand, and the pay of administrators may increase as well. These motives can have a substantial effect when a hospital receives eighty or ninety cents more or less automatically by spending a dollar.

It is widely supposed that governments have a similarly dramatic tendency to overspend. Here it is important to distinguish efficiency in general from overspending; a government can underspend and still waste some of its resources, or overspend and still fail to get as much out of its budget as it should. Governments may regularly be inefficient, but this does not mean that they always overspend, much less overspend on a heroic scale. Without arguing that government on the average is on target, I would nonetheless conclude that no proof or model I have read in the literature of economic theory or of public choice succeeds in showing that governments will systematically overspend by very large amounts. As for those who are certain that there is such a tendency, do they feel that there is a great deal of overspending on both social programs and defense? On both the environment and police? And how many feel that the United States and Britain overspent on defense in

---

[16] U.S., Congress, House, "Testimony," *Hearings before Subcommittee on Health, Committee on Ways and Means*, 94th Congress, 2d session, August 3, 1976, pp. 114–27.

the mid-1930s? More than a few politicians have lost their jobs because of dissatisfaction of citizens with taxes, inflation, and regulation, and this limits public spending to some extent, at least in the long run.

My hypothesis is that in the United States today the incentive to hold down expenditures on health care, or at least expenditures on hospital care, is less strong than the incentive to hold down government spending in general. In much of the health care system, it pays to choose the more costly care if it is worth just a little more than the next best care; for most governments, it pays to spend only when the gains are perceived to be larger, or more easily visible, or more strategically placed than the extra taxes or the resulting inflation.

There is support for my hypothesis in the findings reported in this volume by Paul Joskow and others on the apparent tendency of state rate regulation to reduce hospital costs. The state rate regulators surely do not achieve the ideally efficient levels of expenditure that a purely competitive industry would achieve in the long run, nor in my judgment do they even come close. But they do not have the tremendous incentives to overspend that the hospitals in the states with rate setting had before rate setting began. They may, in other words, come closer to what a competitive market would achieve than the bizarre "market" arrangements that they replace.

It is not only that the rate setting may eliminate the freedom-of-choice incentives for overspending but also that the incentives the rate setters themselves face may sometimes be far different from those facing those who control CON and UR. If hospital rates rise faster in a state with a rate-setting commission than in the rest of the nation, the rate-setting commission is likely to be in trouble; it would seem manifestly to have failed to fulfill its function. A health systems agency administering CON regulations, by contrast, is not likely to be in trouble as long as the providers are happy; health insurance premiums and taxes may rise to stellar heights, but the insurance commissioner or the governor or someone else is responsible for that. There is, I think, also some evidence that the incentives facing the regulator or other government decision makers matter in the relatively low level of spending on health care in Great Britain, especially as compared with the United States and West Germany, for example. In Britain the money for the National Health Service comes directly out of the treasury. Though there are many other sources of inefficiency in the National Health Service, the politicians who decide how much should be spent on health have to face the complaints if other types of government expenditures are curtailed or taxes are raised because more is given to the National Health Service. They also share in the blame for inadequacies of the health system. Thus, though they do not have the information or incentive to make optimal decisions, overall costs and benefits are weighed in some fairly sane way. In the United States, by contrast, the "market" system is not unlike the situation of a government that is financed by foreign aid and can get more money simply by increasing expenditures.

As I am one of the first practitioners of state rate regulation, the reader may well ask whether the views I have just expressed are influenced by my personal experience. Although that experience certainly provided relevant observations and possibly introduced biases, these observations and possible biases have never made, and do not now make me an *advocate* of state regulation of rates. Regulation of hospital rates would have no place whatever in my ideal system for organizing health care. I think that in the long run rate-setting bodies will probably be captured by the industry they regulate, however strong the initial efforts to guard against this. They also lack the detailed information about each hospital's needs and possible savings that good hospital administrators in a competitive environment would have. Thus the moral of this story is *not* that there should be regulation of hospital rates—we should use our voices to advocate other measures instead, to which I shall soon turn. The moral is rather that the words "market" and "regulation" are so vague in their application to the current health care system that they are more likely to mislead than to illuminate. There is very little in the U.S. health care system that should be called a market. The way regulation works also depends on the incentives the regulators face, and regulation can also, as Graham Atkinson and Jack Cook point out in their contribution to this book, be used to improve incentives rather than for command and control.

A Summary of the Argument So Far

I have argued that the twin complaints about overspending on health care and about unmet needs or unevenness of care are not adequately explained by any of the conventional analyses of the U.S. health care system. The growth of the role of government cannot explain the unevenness of medical expenditures, and the tax subsidy for health insurance is not sufficient to explain either overspending or unmet needs. The effect of modern egalitarian sentiment accounts for some of the extra spending, but not for the tendency for new health programs to make already prosperous providers still better off. Nor can fee-for-service arrangements account for the twin complaints; they are on balance as efficient as those under prepaid group practice.

The single most important source of overspending and unevenness of care is the requirement of freedom of choice for most patients covered by third-party payers, which eliminates price competition among providers and gives patients an incentive to choose more costly care even when the gains to the patient are negligible. In the case of hospitals this is often compounded by a system of retrospective reimbursement, which implies that the more a hospital spends, the more it will get. Although the cartelistic and lobbying power of providers is not sufficient to block egalitarian health proposals when they become so controversial that the rational ignorance of voters is overcome, it is sufficient to require that the new government programs adopt the freedom-of-choice methods and institutions that the providers have required in the private sector. The social losses from these arrangements are then multiplied. The skyrocketing increases in the prices of medical care caused by the arrangements just described make those types of health care that are not covered by third-party payers so expensive that less is purchased, and for the poorest of those without third-party coverage some of the care may be prohibitively expensive, so the unevenness of medical care is also explained.

Governmental or professional regulations that attempt to countervail the incentives for overspending under the aforementioned arrangements, like the requirement that there be certificates of need or professional standards review organizations for utilization review, are abysmal failures, among other reasons because the system of regulation is in reality controlled by organized providers. The incentives for overspending in the existing health care system in the United States are far greater than any that may characterize government in general. It follows that *government agencies that are held responsible for both the costs and the quality of medical care may well choose allocations that are closer to the perfectly competitive ideal than the existing "market" would*, and this may help explain some cost reductions in hospital costs due to state rate-setting bodies. Accordingly, slogans or ideologies built around the words "regulation" and "markets" are inadequate substitutes for careful economic analysis. Rate-setting bodies and federal agencies setting expenditure caps are not consistent with maximum efficiency, however, and may in the long run also be captured by the regulated industry, so that they would have no role in "first-best" systems.

Policy Implications

As Robert Crandall makes clear in his contribution to this volume, some difficulties and losses are inherent in the use of insurance, and some kind of insurance or prepayment is needed to finance medical care. There are also some other difficulties in attaining an ideally efficient system for organizing health care. Thus we should be wary of any solution that looks too easy or promises too much. Nonetheless, I submit that the somewhat eccentric diagnosis I have offered here suggests that the main disease is definitely curable—there is a large tumor but not an invasive malignancy. If our diagnosis is correct, we also know exactly where the surgery is needed.

All that really must be cut out to allow the patient to function with normal efficiency is the arrangement that eliminates, for patients with third-party payers, price competition among providers and the incentive of patients to seek value as well as quality and convenience in care. If different insurance companies can compete on an equal basis, and none of them is blocked from making deals with *individual* providers rather than cartels of providers, then these insurance companies will try to give good value to those whom they insure. They will have policies akin to those once offered by commercial health insurance companies in Oregon or akin to those available now for dental care.

The lower the price of the care, the lower the premiums an insurance company can charge; the better the quality of care that the insurance premium from a given company buys, the greater the willingness of individuals, employers, and unions to pay that premium. Thus insurance companies competing for business will have an incentive to take into account the patients' desires for lower premiums and for quality and convenience. Similarly, providers who must compete in terms of both price and quantity for insured patients will have an incentive to offer the level of quality of care that maximizes the demand for their service and to offer this quality of care at a competitive (marginal cost) price. As a number of the authors in this volume point out, the competition among insurance companies will deal optimally with "moral hazard"— that is, the tendency for insurance to generate increased demand because it lowers the price to the insured. Insurance companies that choose optimal coinsurance rates and an optimal degree of monitoring of claims will be able to offer better value to customers than those that do not; thus there would then be no point in legislating particular arrangements for coinsurance. Individuals having different preferences with respect to convenience and quality of care will tend to choose different insurance packages and purchase access to different sets of providers or to wider or narrower sets of providers. If there is no cartel discrimination against insurance companies that deal with efficient subsets of providers and that police claims aggressively, then of course an insurance company should be permitted to offer a policy that allows the insured patient whatever right he has now to choose *any* provider, however costly, without extra charge—though the excess premium the insurance company would need for this plan might mean that few would choose it. The individual would have *true* freedom to choose—he would be free to buy any medical care or insurance he was willing to pay for, but he would not, as is so generally true now, be effectively denied the opportunity to purchase insurance from firms that were free to seek out less costly providers.

If the government were also free in practice to deal with less costly providers and to encourage competition among them, it too would have reason to seek better value in buying access to medical care. Governments, as I have argued earlier, are under pressure both to maximize services and to reduce taxes. Thus to the extent they are not constrained by cartelistic and lobbying pressure from providers, they will seek better value in the medical care they buy. Voucher systems or other plans that would give those entitled to publicly financed care a share of any savings that resulted from not selecting more costly care would also encourage efficiency, and take into account variations in preferences as well. When the cost of medical care is reduced, the political resistance to efforts to deal with any unmet or inadequately met needs diminishes, and the paradox with which we began will be at least partly resolved. It would take us far afield here to go into this important matter, and the ways that remaining needs could best be met, or the shortcomings of some existing proposals for dealing with unmet needs. But it is clear that the high cost of medical care partly explains the unevenness of its provision and that a government that encourages competition among providers and shops for value (or encourages those with its entitlements to do so) can do more for those who slip through the interstices of the present system.

Note that the "prepaid group practice" and "health maintenance organization" labels have not been mentioned in this policy prescription. All of the kinds of benefits described previously could be achieved without the prepaid group practice that is normally associated with health maintenance organizations. As I argued earlier, fee-for-service arrangements are not inherently less efficient than prepaid group practice; thus an efficient health care system in my judgment need not encourage prepaid group practice. The elimination of cartelization among providers, so that insurance companies could deal with providers individually and avoid so-called freedom-of-choice rules, and equality of treatment of different insurance companies, would be sufficient to bring the benefits of competition and shopping for value to the insured, even though all providers are paid on a fee-for-service basis. Because this is a point that is sometimes not appreciated, it is worth emphasizing. The relatively slow expansion of prepaid group practice in recent years when there have been some government efforts to encourage it, suggests that *possibly* there is a substantial preference for fee-for-service care, and this makes it all the more fortunate that a competitive health system with insurance does not require prepaid group practice. Of course, this is no reason to prohibit or discourage prepaid group practice; consumers ought to be free to choose this method just as they should be free to choose fee-for-service care. If providers are prohibited from behaving as a cartel and all insurance plans are treated equally, those for whom prepaid group practice is preferred will in the long run buy that and those for whom fee-for-service is best on balance will choose that.

Having, I hope, established that there is nothing *inherently* superior about prepaid group practice, we can now see the main attraction of prepaid group practice in the *existing* U.S. health care system. In my judgment, this is that *it is practically the only existing alternative to the so-called freedom-of-choice rule for those who want health insurance.* When a family buys its medical insurance by making regular prepayments to a group practice, it is buying insurance without also purchasing the right to go to any physician or hospital, however costly, without paying extra, and thus without eliminating price competition among providers. Undoubtedly, this is the reason that organized medicine started resisting prepaid group practice so early and so ferociously. The prepaid group practice has an incentive to provide efficient care to make possible a prepayment level that will attract customers, and also an incentive to provide care of a quality that will attract customers; it has an incentive to be competitive, and its existence introduces an element of competition into the market for insured patients. A prepaid group practice has the same incentive to compete and to offer a level of cost and quality appealing to buyers that insurance companies free to deal with subsets of fee-for-service providers would have. I am not the first to treat prepaid group practices as only *one* of the kinds of insurance arrangements that permits price competition, and as valuable for that reason rather than because of any inherent superiority over fee-for-service. This central aspect of the matter nonetheless does not usually receive the emphasis it deserves.

If this analysis is correct, it follows that Alain Enthoven's Consumer Choice Health Plan, summarized in this volume, is a most constructive contribution to the debate. I hope readers will examine that plan carefully, along with Jack Meyer's and Laurence Seidman's valuable if differing assessments of it, and then ponder Enthoven's rejoinder. There is another valuable and resonant analysis of this matter (and also summary comments on many of the other papers in this volume) in Alfred Kahn's concluding essay. Whatever plan is finally judged best, there is no doubt that Enthoven's plan is one of those that would encourage price competition in the provision of medical care and offer an alternative to the arrangements I have criticized here.

If I am also correct in emphasizing the need for insurance plans made by insurers who are free to bargain with subsets of the fee-for-service providers and to police claims vigorously, there is also a compelling case for applying the antitrust laws more vigorously to physicians, hospitals, and the anticompetitive insurance arrangements they have created. As Clark Havighurst and Glenn Hackbarth argue in this book, the "individual practice associations" that have often been established by medical societies are more likely to restrain trade than to foster competition. At the least they do not meet what I believe is the urgent need for *competitive* fee-for-service insurance alternatives to prepaid group practice arrangements. Prepaid group practice arrangements are not expanding fast enough to bring about the degree of price competition that the U.S. health care system so desperately needs. Thus there is in my judgment a need not only for antitrust action that would make insured fee-for-service medicine competitive, but also for legislative changes directed to the creation of a competitive medical environment. Just as governments had to establish efficient systems of property rights and laws allowing corporations with limited liability before a modern and efficient economy was possible, so also in my judgment a price-competitive medical environment can only be established by government policies that are designed to create efficient markets.

It would be fun to explore alternative ways of making the health system in the United States, or that in other countries, price competitive, but that would lead us away from the papers that, I like to think, embody or contribute to the new approach of this volume. To be sure, several papers in this volume argue for different approaches. No small effort has been made to ensure that fundamentally different points of view are expressed in this volume. Many of the authors of papers in this book will probably not agree with the arguments I have put forth in this introduction. What we have, then, is in part a sequence of debates, some of which are rather spirited. Nonetheless, perhaps because of my preconceptions, I see them as debates about and contributions to a new approach to the economics of health care. Whether they are that or something else, they will, I hope, prove to be as useful to the reader as they have been to me.

Part One

The Problem: Inherent Difficulties
Compounded by Mistaken Principles

The Impossibility of Finding a Mechanism to Ration Health Care Resources Efficiently

Robert W. Crandall

To a student of regulation, it is ironic that in the past decade we have reached a consensus that we spend too much on private medical care while over the same period the Congress has designed a raft of new health safety regulatory programs that treat compliance costs as free lunches. Moreover, during this decade traditional price-quantity-entry regulation has fallen into considerable disfavor just as various people seek to impose more of it upon the health care sector of the economy. We do not have to be students of the health care industry to recognize that traditional rate-setting regulation in the health care sector is more problematic than in other markets and that the deficiencies in health safety regulation reflect many of the societal forces preventing us from developing rational devices for allocating resources to the health care sector.

This chapter presents a novice's view of (1) the problems involved in finding a set of institutions that will lead to efficient use of the complex services rendered, (2) the inevitability of insurance, (3) the locus of decision making, (4) the recent experience with regulatory decision making in the health safety area, and (5) price or quantity regulation in the health care sector. Since this chapter attempts to provide an outsider's view of the problems of this industry, little attempt is made to incorporate the existing literature on the economics of the health care industry. Instead, a more general literature is drawn upon for potential insights into the problem of optimal allocation of resources in health care.

The Need for Prepayment or Insurance

Three aspects of the health care problem stand out as major determinants of market performance: (1) the individual is exposed to the possibility of enormous expenditures for treatment of a large number of low-probability illnesses, (2) the probability of incurring large medical expenses generally increases with age after infancy,[1] and (3) health care services are so diverse and complex that contractual arrangements for the future delivery of services are difficult to draw up and enforce. Even if people are willing to pay the actuarial value of treatment of a given disease or disorder, they will be unable to afford the treatment if all medical expenses are handled through spot transactions. Moreover, most would undoubtedly wish to save for unhealthy as well as rainy days. The obvious solution: insurance contracts that combine the spreading of risk in each year with the transferral of expenditures from early to later life. Thus, insurance and "third-party" payment become a necessity unless the provision of insurance is integrated with the supply of the medical service.

The necessity of purchasing at least part of one's health care through some insurance instrument is only part of the problem for the individual, who must also contend with the complexity of the contract and of the service to be rendered. The question of health care costs is further complicated by the buyer's inability to understand his choices. Consider the types of insurance that a person typically buys: life insurance, which is a low-yielding form of saving combined with a quantum of insurance; casualty insurance on an automobile and fire casualty insurance on a home and its contents;[2] and implicit insurance (through expressed and implied warranties) on a large number of other risks that come with durables that are purchased. In each case, the individual is paying today to offset the risk of some adverse occurrence in the future. Defining the risk, however, is a major problem for the buyer. Even in the case of life insurance, the Federal Trade Commission has told us, the average policy holder cannot understand what he is buying.[3]

If the buyer is considering accident insurance, for example, he may not understand what constitutes an accident or the damages from that accident. He may not understand distinctions that are drawn between damage and normal wear and tear. Furthermore, he may not know

---

[1] For data on the distribution of health care costs by age group, see Robert M. Gibson, Marjorie Smith Mueller, and Charles R. Fisher, "Age Differences in Health Care Spending, Fiscal Year 1976," *Social Security Bulletin* (August 1977), pp. 3–14.

[2] For analyses of the property insurance industry, see Paul Joskow, "Cartels, Competition, and Regulation in the Property Liability Insurance Industry," *Bell Journal of Economics* (Autumn 1973), pp. 375–427; and Dennis Smallwood, "Competition Regulation and Product Quality in the Automobile Insurance Industry," in Almarin Phillips, ed., *Promoting Competition in Regulated Industries* (Washington, D.C.: Brookings Institution, 1975).

[3] Federal Trade Commission, *Life Insurance Cost Disclosure: A Report to the Federal Trade Commission*, July 1979.

whether a policy covers current replacement cost, depreciated replacement cost, or depreciated historical cost. As for life insurance, the policyholder may not know how much an ordinary life contract earns on the premium paid over and above that required for simple term insurance. Calculating this rate of return is sufficiently complicated to keep most consumers from making completely well-informed choices among contracts. (Nevertheless, they have been able to conclude that whole ordinary life policies are not good investments, as the trend toward term insurance attests.)

The problems are no less difficult for the insurer, who has the difficult task of both writing the insurance and policing the claims. Obviously, life insurance presents few problems in this regard, but every form of casualty insurance is burdened with moral hazard problems and even fraud.[4] In the case of automobile insurance, the imposition of large deductibles on collision coverage is far from a complete solution. Another form of casualty insurance, workmen's compensation, is beset with similar problems. When is a "back injury" an injury, for example, and how can one be sure that it is employment related? The failure of the workmen's compensation market has led to federal regulation of worker safety. Although students of regulation might favor experience-rated compensation over detailed workplace government regulation, apparently the workmen's compensation programs do not work well because they do not provide the proper incentives for accident prevention.[5]

Moral hazard is an issue for service contracts as well. Consider why such contracts are not generally available for most durables after their limited warranties expire. It is simply that insured consumers are more likely to abuse their durables. For expensive durables, however, one might still expect the market for insurance to be greater than it is. New houses have traditionally not been insured in this fashion despite sizable potential losses from defects. Builders might have specific warranty obligations under various state laws, but after some period of time, this warranty expires (or the builder might disappear before the claim materializes). Why has a market for insuring against major defects—which might cost the average householder as much as the most expensive

---

[4] For two analyses of the moral hazard problem in health care insurance, see Kenneth J. Arrow, "Uncertainty and the Economics of Medical Care," *American Economic Review* (December 1963), pp. 941–69; and Mark V. Pauly, "Overinsurance and Public Provision of Insurance: The Roles of Moral Hazard and Adverse Selection," *Quarterly Journal of Economics* (February 1974), pp. 44–54.

[5] For an analysis of workmen's compensation and alternatives to it, see James Robert Chelius, *Workplace Safety and Health: The Role of Workers' Compensation* (Washington, D.C.: American Enterprise Institute, 1977).

medical therapy—not developed?[6] The answer is, as we have already seen, that drawing up the terms of the insurance contract and policing claims are extremely difficult to do. When is a cracked foundation the result of a building defect, and when is it the result of subsequent activities in the vicinity of the house? Are the cosmetic damages in the areas around the defect related to the defect or to the owner's negligence of the property? How can the costs of repairing the defect be monitored? (Consider the difficulties this problem has caused for automobile casualty insurers.) In fact, one of the first attempts to offer a homeowner's warranty has had considerable problems in controlling claims and in defining the risk.[7] The transactions costs required to control claims may well make the premiums too large to be attractive compared with self-insurance.

Service contracts on other durables are available, past their initial warranty periods, but at premiums considerably above the actuarial value to a careful consumer.[8] Automobiles can be leased. Household appliances can be purchased with service contracts, but this market seems to work poorly. The difficulties in controlling claims, defining the extent of the coverage, and preventing abuse of the product undoubtedly interfere with a successful market for such a service. If other insurance markets work poorly because of these problems, medical insurance will surely experience similar difficulties.

The fundamental question, then, is whether or not any contract will be able to define precisely the full limits to coverage. Can a contract for health care, for example, possibly specify how much therapy is to be provided for each and every type of illness or injury under every circumstance? Of course it cannot; therefore, the best it can do is to place dollar limits on various covered procedures and even to place limits (with or without coinsurance) on total coverage. But it cannot specify when a physician may order therapy for a given malady or to what extent expenses on diagnosis should be covered because circumstances will vary for each case. Nor can a health care contract limit expensive discre-

---

[6] One reason might be that consumers do not believe that such defects are likely to be important in determining the resale value of their homes. See John Weicher, "Protecting New Home Buyers: Housing Quality Values and Warranties," mimeographed (December 5, 1980).

[7] The Home Owners Warranty Corporation has offered a new-home warranty since 1974 at a rate that has proved to be noncompensatory. As a result of rising claims, it recently announced a major increase in rates. Existing evidence does not indicate how much of the increase has been caused by the traditional problems in policing casualty insurance claims.

[8] For evidence on this relationship, see "Service Contracts: A Poor Insurance Buy," *Consumer Reports* (November 1980), p. 684.

tionary surgery except, perhaps, to specify that additional opinions are to be obtained before the surgery is authorized. Given the problem of defining the extent of coverage with precision, the consumer's range of choice among contracts will be minimized by the insurer's inability to specify differences in the terms of a contract and to enforce them.

Medical insurance fails in a second less important function: that is, it does not provide a means of shifting the time profile of medical outlays. As we have said, the average person finds his medical expenses rising with time. Some mechanism is therefore needed to allow each person in his earlier, productive years to spread his medical expenses more evenly over time. Otherwise, he may be forced to assume a rising burden in later years. Most medical insurance plans are structured to spread this expense evenly over the insured population, but they do not allow an individual to contract for long-term coverage. Rather, group plans generally operate on a year-to-year basis and are structured so that younger, healthier families implicitly subsidize older plan members. Participation in these health plans is dependent on continued association with an employer. These programs adjust rates according to changes in the experience of the insured population. Moreover, younger participants should logically be less likely to participate or should choose the "low option" because they have lower expected health care outlays than other members of the plan. Finally, the rate is likely to reflect the age mix of those currently covered, not an estimate of the constant annual premium required to amortize a life-long health plan. If one is lucky enough to be old while most members of his group are young, his rate will be low. If, on the other hand, he is old at a time when the age mix of the covered population is much older, he will probably pay higher rates. This system is not conducive to efficient choices of insurance.[9]

Because most of us purchase our insurance through a tax-subsidized employer program and because meaningfully different coverages for different tastes and age groups within the employee group are not available, we cannot opt for more limited coverage, perhaps with coinsurance from the first dollar, than is available through the average plan provided by the employer's carrier. Although some alternative health maintenance organization plans may be available, in general the range of choice is rather narrow. Moreover, because insurers find it difficult to explain and enforce differences in coverage, they are unlikely to be motivated

---

[9] It is not clear why employers have not offered insurance plans that are structured to reflect differences in the cost of insurance across age and family sizes within their employee groups. The difficulty of finding other nondeferred types of compensation with similar tax treatment may be one reason. Another might be the egalitarian appearance of "equal" coverage at "equal" rates for all employees.

to offer many different programs to the same employee group. The result is a tendency toward rather comprehensive programs that offer the insured little incentive to economize on claims.

Clearly, other mechanisms can be used by consumers to adjust the time profiles of their expenditure flows. Financial institutions exist for income earners of young to middle age to set aside income for later health care requirements. The problem is that existing health insurance contracts do not provide the right age-dependent or family-size-dependent vector of prices. Calabrizi[10] would probably explain this situation as an attempt by insurers to maintain the appearance of equity (the second-order decision) in the mechanism chosen to allocate resources to health care (the first-order decision). Whatever the motive, the structure of health insurance contracts available through employers not only shifts the burden from old to young, but it also provides the wrong market signals.

The Decision to Commit Resources

If medical care is so complicated that different insurance contracts to cover this care cannot be understood by consumers and cannot provide enforceable limits to the application of resources for each case, few decisions to use resources in medical diagnosis or treatment will be made by the consumer or by the insurance company. Thus it is left to the physician to make such decisions or at least to guide the consumer's decision. Many have complained that these decisions are made without a budget constraint, since the third-party insurance carrier will pay (within some rough limits) for any procedure deemed appropriate by the physician.[11] Presumably, this system gives the physician incentive to continue to apply resources until their marginal value is virtually zero, not their market price.

Economists and others intent on reform generally respond to this problem by indicting third-party payment and by suggesting a substitute. Since prepayment and spreading of risks through insurance instruments are obvious requisites for consumers, the only solution, it is said, is to integrate the provision of the medical services and the insurance. Health maintenance organizations (HMOs) or prepaid group practices are therefore recommended as more efficient substitutes for third-party payment. Unfortunately, such solutions invite problems of a different sort.

---

[10] Guido Calabrizi and Phillip Bobbitt, *Tragic Choices* (New York: W. W. Norton and Company, 1978).

[11] For a theoretical presentation of this issue, see Pauly, "Overinsurance and Public Provision of Insurance."

First, if the problem of third-party payment is that resources are overcommitted to medical care, the danger of integrating insurance and medical care is that the incentives will be reversed. Resources may become undercommitted as the group practice or HMO finds that its interests and the interests of the patients diverge. In the absence of reliable information—a hallmark of the medical care sector—the consumer may not be able to react quickly enough to this behavior by changing vendors. He is unlikely to change vendors in any case because of the importance of a continuing patient-doctor relationship. Even if he were so disposed, the economies of scale in HMOs may be so large that effective competition among them may be possible only in large metropolitan areas.

Second, it is unrealistic to expect medical doctors to wish to engage in the sale of insurance. Not only are they ill-equipped to deal with questions that arise in insurance, but they may find that insurance goals are inconsistent with their medical ethics, in that their role is to provide healing, not to ration resources through insurance contracts. Cynics may argue that the reluctance of physicians to engage in insurance functions is rooted in self-interest, since the development of HMOs might increase competition among physicians. This argument is far too simplistic.

If physicians became part of integrated insurance and medical delivery institutions, they would have to be given instructions on what values to assign to healing or saving lives. Would these values be specified in the insurance contract? Would different values be offered at different insurance rates? If so, would the same physician have to offer a given type of therapy to one patient but deny it to another because the latter chose the "low option"? What would he do if the therapy was required to prevent imminent death? It is unrealistic to expect physicians to participate willingly in the sale and enforcement of insurance contracts.

We must also ask whether a single organization can sell insurance and offer medical services efficiently. The literature on industrial organization[12] and simple observation suggest that the advantages of specialization in business firms are considerable, and that diversification leads to problems. Firms selling steel, for example, rarely succeed in fabricating that steel. Oil companies do not make good mass merchandisers. Thus few large companies diversify to any extent outside their principal markets. General Motors has decided to forswear the automobile casualty insurance market despite the fact that excessive insur-

---

[12] Charles Berry, "Corporate Growth and Diversification," *Journal of Law and Economics* (October 1971), pp. 371–86; and Ronald Coase, "The Nature of the Firm," *Economica* (November 1937), pp. 386–405.

ance costs must reduce the demand for motor vehicle services. Can we be sure, then, that integration of insurance and medical delivery systems can work efficiently?

Experience in other sectors with integration of this variety is not encouraging. Given the problem of servicing claims and of fraud in general, casualty insurance companies might be expected to provide the repairs that arise from claims, particularly in the automobile casualty market. In fact, this type of integration has been limited despite the obvious opportunities available. Even Sears does not formally integrate the two.[13] Apparently, the business of repairing cars is not one that casualty insurers are eager to undertake. In the case of home warranties, the movement is obviously away from integration. The initial objective of the Home Owners Warranty Corporation was to provide third-party insurance coverage as a substitute for the builder's warranty after two years. If other businesses are unwilling to integrate into the sale of casualty insurance, why should we expect doctors to do so?

Lessons from "Social" Regulatory Experience

Perhaps the most wasteful institution in the civilian economy today is the new health safety environmental regulatory agency. It is wasteful because it operates without a budget constraint and without clear instruction from Congress. As a result, it cannot possibly reach sensible decisions in mandating the use of society's scarce resources. A brief reflection upon our sorry experience in this regard is instructive to anyone who would prescribe alternative structures for the health care sector.

The number of statutes prescribing some form of regulation of risks to health and safety has grown at a staggering rate. The Clean Air Act Amendments of 1977, the Federal Water Pollution Control Act, and the amendments to it in 1977, the Occupational Safety and Health Act (OSH Act), the Toxic Substances Control Act, the Federal Insecticide, Fungicide, and Rodenticide Act, and the National Highway Traffic Safety Act are but a few of the recent examples. In each statute, a regulatory agency is instructed to protect the public health and safety, but the criteria for such protection vary somewhat from statute to statute. In no case has Congress suggested that precise cost-benefit analysis should guide the decisions. More important, the statute never defines the value that an agency should attach to reducing risk of morbidity or death. Congress is unwilling to admit that trade-offs must be made

---

[13] Sears did consider such an integration in the 1950s, but it found the opposition from other repair garages so great that it decided to abandon the idea rather than pursue the plan before state insurance commissions.

36

between guns-butter and human health or safety. Agency decisions simply mirror this reluctance. One cannot find a case in which an administrator justified a decision to set a standard at, say, 5 parts per million rather than 4 parts per million by saying that the reduction of the last 1 part per million cost more than the expected savings in human life are worth. He would not justify his decisions in this fashion because he would not want to answer to the uninformed and emotional public reaction that would argue we should not "trade lives for dollars." As a result, decisions can be and often are inconsistent and wasteful of society's resources.

Because Congress has not squarely confronted the issue of how resources should be allocated by regulators, it finds itself legislating in a piecemeal fashion, often instructing an agency to carry regulation to the maximum "feasible" level (OSH Act) for any significant health risk, or even requiring that regulations be set so as to assure absolute protection for all risks with an adequate margin of safety (the Clean Air Act). Neither instruction reflects a logical approach to the problems of protecting the public interest because Congress will not openly and explicitly provide an agency with the guidance it needs in determining the value of extending life or human health. The statutes Congress devises often address health risks that are stochastic in nature and that may have long lead times. Therefore, Congress is not ducking the problem of deciding whether clearly identifiable individual lives are to be saved from a specific threat such as a mine disaster. Rather, it is providing instructions for an agency to set, for example, maximum allowable levels of suspected carcinogens that might affect individuals in twenty or thirty years. If you or I contract cancer, we will not be able to ascribe it to someone's regulatory decision. The regulator or the congressman will have retired from political office and may even have expired by the time we contract the dread disease.

Some contend that continuing concern over the inefficiency of the current health care market points to a need for government regulation. If physicians, hospitals, and medical insurers cannot stem the wasteful flow of resources into the health sector, some argue, a government agency will have to do it. Our experience with health safety regulation augurs poorly for the success of any such venture. If regulators confronted with impersonal decisions in the health safety area cannot admit that resources trade for lives, how can regulators of institutions providing highly personal and often critical health care be expected to behave rationally and coldheartedly? Nor can we expect self-regulation by a consortium of doctors to provide the desired results. Only the consumer can make binding decisions on the allocation of his resources between health care and other goods and services. Even if the consumer were to make these decisions himself, however, it is not certain that a societal institution could be found to enforce them. The individual who has chosen self-insurance and who has exhibited a high rate of time preference in his consumption patterns is not likely to be spurned by the society at large when he appears penniless at the door of a hospital for a kidney transplant.

Nonprofit Institutions

Before discussing various forms of government regulation of the health care sector, we should consider briefly the problems created by the economic system operating in the health care industry. To predict the outcome of any constraint placed on an economic organization, one needs to know that organization's goals or objectives. Most of us understand the objective function of physicians. At least we are willing to conclude that we do on the basis of annual statistics on income levels of the various professions, although we may not understand all the additional constraints imposed by medical ethics, teaching, research or hospital affiliation, and peer pressure.

The major problem for an economist, however, is the lack of a profit motive at the hospital level. If hospitals in general are nonprofit institutions but are effectively controlled by physicians, can one predict how hospital management might respond to an external societal control? If, for instance, hospitals were limited by a total-cost constraint, how would they allocate their resources to meet this limitation on total costs? Would they be more likely to reduce amenities for physicians or for patients? Would they economize on variable oulays or on capital equipment? Economists have considerable difficulty demonstrating how a rate-of-return constraint ought to be structured so as to keep regulated utilities from misallocating capital and variable inputs.[14] Regulated utilities are profit-oriented firms, however, and we assume that they are profit maximizers. What do medical care institutions maximize? This question must be answered before definitive policy judgments can be made on the choice of control instruments.

Regulation: Price or Quantity?

The imposition of regulation on the medical sector is said to be a means of limiting the excessive cost of health care. Presumably this regulation

---

[14] A lengthy literature on this issue has developed since the classic article by Harvey Averch and Leland L. Johnson, "Behavior of the Firm under Regulatory Constraint," *American Economic Review* (December 1962), pp. 1052–69. See also, Elizabeth E. Bailey, *Economic Theory of Regulatory Constraint* (Lexington, Mass.: Lexington Books, 1973).

is intended to reduce the excessive flow of resources into the health care sector and to prevent exploitation of market power by vendors of medical services. These vendors are usually defined as physicians who have the power to affect fees even though they may be in competition with numerous fellow practitioners.

Obviously, price controls are useful only to limit the prices of services that are not elastic in supply. Doctors' fees are the most obvious candidates for controls, but other resources temporarily fixed in supply may also be targets. Hospital or nursing home fees can and have been regulated.

Price controls in the health care sector are unlikely to work for very long for the same reason that they do not work elsewhere in a civilian economy. Clever businessmen find ways of redefining products and services or of introducing new ones at a rate with which the controllers cannot cope. Health care involves such a complicated set of changing services that "innovation" to avoid or frustrate regulation would quickly undermine the entire regulatory scheme. No one who has examined a week's hospital bill can fail to be impressed with how difficult price control would be over time if applied universally to this sector.

Nor are price controls addressed to the principal problem in this sector. The physician-controlled, insurance-based medical sector generates excessive demand for resources that are generally supplied competitively to physicians and to hospitals. If medical equipment and supplies or other inputs are monopolized, there are other societal approaches to controlling or eliminating monopoly power. The problem of controlling the cost of health care seems to be one of controlling quantity, not the price of individual inputs.

If it is the quantity of resources flowing into the health care sector that needs to be restricted, more direct controls can "work." Hospital beds can be limited by regulatory fiat, and the number of practicing physicians can be limited (although controlling the hours of work or the intensity of effort may be more difficult). Health planning agencies or regulatory commissions might even control the supply of gauze and clamps. But how would they know where to set the optimal quantity? If the quantity of resources in the health care sector is controlled but the demand is unchanged because prices, income levels, insurance coverage, and consumers' health needs are unaffected, the inevitable result will be queueing for services or a reduction in their quality. The reduction of quality is a common result of excessively strict regulation of public utilities.[15] It would surely occur in the case of health care.

---

[15] For evidence on the effects of regulation on service quality, see Andrew S. Carron and Paul W. MacAvoy, *The Decline of Service in the Regulated Industries* (Washington, D.C.: American Enterprise Institute, 1980).

Given consumer impatience with queues and the physician's distaste for making difficult choices among patients in queues, one can safely predict that quantitative controls on resources will operate to reduce the quality of health care services as the system strives to continue to serve the (excessive) demands created by the system. The quantitative controls do not address the problem of excessive demand; they cannot, therefore, solve the problem.

The dismal conclusion is that if excessive demands created artificially by the current system are a major source of resource misallocation, no intervention on the supply side will work short of the intervention of the omniscient social planner. We shall have to address the real source of market failure, not the symptoms of it.

Control over price or quantity will not put a stop to resource misallocation in health care because it will not address the fundamental problem. If physicians, hospital administrators, or nursing home managers are not cost minimizers (for a given vector of services), imposing controls upon them is unlikely to move them closer to the optimum. Past experience in public utility regulation suggests that while rate and entry regulation may limit the power of monopolies to set prices (although it most often does not), this success is purchased at the expense of inefficiency in production. Public utility commissions rarely attempt to dictate the choice of production technique because they realize that such a task is beyond their capability. It is difficult enough simply to estimate the firm's cost of capital.

If current or prospective regulators of health care services were able to identify efficient technologies and prescribe them for the regulated institutions under their purview, they would be bordering on omniscience. The most sophisticated recent literature on optimal economic planning typically focuses on output levels or prices, but it leaves choice of technique to the enterprises being controlled by the plan.[16] Although some regulators in the health care sector occasionally stumble on the correct decision in prescribing specific resource combinations, they probably proceed on hunch more often than on science in limiting the number of CAT scanners or physicians per hospital.

The Pessimism in Perspective

In our attempts to correct the sources of market failure in the health care sector, we cannot hope to get closer than nth best solutions in many cases. The crux of the problem lies in the complexity of the service and

---

[16] See Martin Weitzman, "Prices versus Quantities," *Review of Economic Studies* (December 1974), pp. 477–91.

the need for insurance. Other services are plagued with similar problems, as we can readily see from the Better Business Bureau's files on auto repair establishments and the refusal of most of these establishments to accept personal checks for payment. The same reasons appear to be the cause of poor performance in casualty insurance markets. The problems arising in the health care sector are probably more serious because medical care is a superior good that we consume at increasing rates with rising incomes and because demand may be price elastic in the relevant range. Were information costless, one could imagine how entrepreneurs in the insurance business might strive to design a health care package that would specify precise limits to every conceivable type of therapy in every circumstance. They might even design elaborate coinsurance provisions to discourage excessive consumption of health care services. Overconsumption would probably still occur, however. The casualty being insured in the health care market is not as identifiable as other casualties, nor is there a completely inelastic demand for health care. Lowering the price of the service to the consumer must, ceteris paribus, increase demand. It is the nature of an insurance contract that the price for incremental service is lower than it would have been without the contract. What should concern us is how price elastic the demand function is in the relevant range. If it is considerably more elastic as the price per unit of service falls toward zero, coinsurance becomes important. If it is elastic throughout, major misallocation will result from any coinsurance.

Even if insurance did not intervene in the consumer's decision to purchase medical care, the current system of nonproprietary institutions might generate substantial waste. Without effective competition among these institutions—particularly among hospitals—resources might be allocated poorly, and allocations might reflect doctors' preferences more than those of the patients. All the current horror stories about over-investment in sophisticated equipment might still be told. Integration of physician and hospital services into a single organization might be an appropriate solution for this problem. HMOs without prepaid insurance—group practices with extensive clinical facilities—would provide an appropriate incentive for decision makers to minimize the cost of providing a given quality and quantity of service. Unfortunately, identifying the nonproprietary hospital as the villain would clearly be a difficult political and public relations task given the current reputation of proprietary hospitals.

If integrated services were to substitute for the current nonprofit hospitals without federal regulations on the breadth of service offerings, the minimum efficient scale of operation might be much smaller than apparently has been the case with HMOs. Nevertheless, it would be surprising if the minimum efficient scale in the provision of inpatient and outpatient services through what we now call a hospital turned out to be lower than the minimum efficient scale in running an insurance program.

In the current unintegrated situation the chances are obviously greater for a gradual move toward integration of physicians' services and hospital-like facilities than for a shift from a nonproprietary to a proprietary form of hospitals. Society will tolerate some extension of a physician's income-maximizing activity far more readily than it will allow a hospital system to dispense healing for profit. But we must not expect too much from HMOs, for we may find that it is as difficult to integrate various aspects of health care as it was for Henry Ford to own and operate a railroad. (Apparently he could not cope with an alien institution—government regulation.)

Conclusion

The current form of health care payment is without doubt a major cause of resource misallocation. Part of the problem stems from the extremely complex nature of medical services, which makes it impossible to write and enforce contractual arrangements with precision. Our recent experience with health safety regulation suggests that a politically responsive agency would not be successful in limiting the flow of resources to the health care sector, but it is doubtful that integration of physicians, hospitals, and insurance into organizations such as HMOs would proceed at a very rapid pace. Since the economy is generally organized to reflect specialization, physicians are neither willing to offer insurance contracts to patients nor likely to be efficient in performing such a service. They may, however, offer comprehensive services through an integrated organization that does not offer insurance. Finally, neither price nor quantity control is likely to be successful in regulating the health care sector. Quantitative controls on resource flows would probably do no more than assure the continuation of excessive demand and service degradation.

What types of reform can work? A first step would be to revise the form of health insurance contracts by experimenting with coinsurance and by repealing the tax preference provided for employer health insurance. Consumers must be shown that such reforms can save them money by reducing everyone else's demand for services. A move away from employer-funded programs would also heighten the worker's interest in more efficient insurance and delivery systems. Changing the tax law to treat all compensation of labor in the same manner would obviously reduce the attractiveness of employer-funded health insurance, but the political obstacles to such a change may be insuperable. These changes would not improve the functioning of the health care sector drastically, but then drastic improvement in this area does not seem possible.

The Long-Lost Free Market in Health Care: Government and Professional Regulation of Medicine

H. E. Frech III

Most observers believe that on a cost/benefit basis the U.S. medical care industry does not perform very well. In particular, we spend far more for health care than do the residents of most other nations, yet our health status, as measured by such indexes as life expectancy and workdays lost, is below that of most industrial nations. Further, the costs of medical care are rising rapidly (for example, the average cost of a hospital day has risen by 189 percent in the last ten years), but health status has not risen noticeably in the same period. This poor performance has led to legal and regulatory changes and to pressure for more such changes, which is based largely on the argument that the free market has failed and that we thus need more regulation. But the premise of this argument is wrong.

Medical care is, in fact, so heavily regulated that it may be the most completely regulated sector of the economy. Many health occupations are licensed, with resulting control over entry, education, experience, and the tasks that workers perform. Other aspects of the delivery of health services are indirectly regulated by groups that dominate the licensure process. Besides being under considerable control of these licensing groups, hospitals are regulated in many ways: state agencies set minimum input levels, state and local agencies approve investments, and Medicare and Medicaid agencies decide which costs will be reimbursed. Further, potential entrants into the health care sector usually must secure permission of regulators. In many states health maintenance organizations (HMOs) are hindered or effectively prohibited (unless

Thanks are due for comments on earlier versions of this chapter to Richard Zeckhauser, Lee Benham, Paul B. Ginsburg, Donald Winkler, W. Douglas Morgan, Charles E. Phelps, Ronald L. Williams, John M. Marshall, and Stuart Altman.

44

they meet strict federal regulations).[1] Profit-seeking firms, too, are discouraged directly or indirectly by regulation and in some states are forbidden altogether. We can add to this list health insurance rates, which are regulated in many states, as well as other aspects of insurance that are regulated even more widely. We should also note the regulatory and tax advantages for nonprofit Blue Cross hospital insurance and Blue Shield physician insurance.

Outside of the realm of direct regulation, the government intervenes a great deal in the medical care industry, most importantly in health insurance. Through Medicare and Medicaid the government provides complete health insurance (covering a large proportion of medical costs) for millions of consumers. The tax deductibility of health insurance creates a large subsidy to the purchase of complete health insurance. Close in importance is governmental subsidy of biomedical research—a multibillion-dollar enterprise. Until recently, the government subsidized the construction of hospitals except for those seeking a profit.

These various governmental interventions clearly show that it is a serious mistake to describe the current health care industry as a free market or unregulated system. The industry is far from a laissez-faire or perfectly competitive system. Thus the use of market elements and competition in medical care should not be rejected on the basis of the poor performance of the current American system. Rather, medical care has been so closely regulated that the weaknesses of the current medical care system might be taken as evidence against extensive regulation.

At the same time, standard economic arguments about the efficiency of free competitive markets cannot be used to reject new regulation. In normal circumstances, industries in such markets will operate optimally without government interference, and regulation may only make them perform worse. Since the health care system is already heavily regulated and contains many monopolistic elements, it does not follow that intervention is bound to make matters worse. Given the regulated and partly monopolistic nature of the health care industry, the arguments for and against any existing or proposed regulatory measure must be more subtle and more sophisticated than in the case of most other industries.

Regulation and Market Allocation: Alternative Decentralized Schemes

On the matter of choosing between regulation and market allocation, some confusions must be cleared up before progress can be made. First,

[1] An HMO contracts to provide medical services in return for a prepaid premium. It combines the functions of insurer and health services provider. The Kaiser prepaid group practice is the best-known example.

both the regulated and unregulated markets will be imperfect. Although a model of perfect competition or perfect governmental allocation can be a useful and interesting benchmark, the ultimate comparison must be between *two imperfect alternatives*.

The second point is that any relevant choice will have market and regulatory features. It will be a mixed system, as all known economies in history have been, in which a continuum of choice will be available. On this point, it is especially important to avoid emotionalism. Fear of a completely free market should not inhibit us from considering inclusion of some market features, any more than fear of a completely centralized system should hinder consideration of regulatory elements. Regulatory and market elements cannot be mixed, however, in a random fashion.

The regulation chosen must be compatible with the market elements, and vice versa. Establishing appropriate regulations requires some understanding of the requirements for reasonable operation of both the market and political or bureaucratic orders. Price controls are good examples of regulations that are not always compatible with market and regulatory operation. Prices are the signals providing both the information about relative values and the incentives for the efficient allocation of resources. Direct price controls hamper the market's key allocative system, especially in competitive industries. From the regulatory viewpoint, price controls are incompatible with the realities of centralized decision making in that the amount of detailed information about demand and supply conditions needed for proper and rapid adjustment of prices typically exceeds what is possible to obtain.

Third, any possible system will be largely decentralized. That is, the information required for centralized decision making in medical care is so great that key decisions in any practical system will continue to be made by individual physicians or by a small, local group of physicians. What policy makers do in altering the regulatory framework and other interventions is to change the incentive and informational structure under which decisions are actually made. Thus, the real choice is between various decentralized systems, regardless of the centralized appearance of organization charts. Before looking at proposed alternatives, however, we must closely examine the incentives created and the information made available both for market participants and for political actors.

The last general consideration is the problem of producer influence over regulation. The political economy of regulation seems to cause provider interests to dominate consumer interests.

In recent years there has been a revolution in the way scholars view regulation. The prevailing view once was that regulation serves consumer groups by reducing monopolistic exploitation or by compensating for market imperfection. The current view is that by and large regulation benefits producer groups, mainly by preventing competition and by increasing the ability of such groups to exploit consumers monopolistically.[2] This latter view is based on the idea that government is controlled by self-interested groups or coalitions. Although producer interest groups usually have the strongest interest in dominating regulation, this simplistic model breaks down in some cases and a more general analysis of coalition formation becomes necessary. In the health care field, however, the evidence is reasonably persuasive that medical care regulation has often aided providers by directly reducing competition and by aiding private activities of producers.

This new conception of regulation has important implications for regulatory policy. First, regulation will promote subtle and unintended costs as a result of its anticompetitive side effects. Second, providers will have more opportunities to influence regulation in order to serve their own interests. It is important that designers of regulatory systems reduce these opportunities. These two considerations will be recurrent themes of this chapter.

The choice between regulatory and market elements must be made on the basis of careful examination of the actual imperfect alternatives. Too often casual arguments have been used to reject alternatives.

Rationales for Regulation

Three main characteristics of the health care industry are popularly said to prevent the efficient operation of markets and thus to be the cause of existing or expanded extensive governmental intervention: consumer ignorance of medical technology; the provision of medical care for the poor; and distorted incentives introduced by third-party payment for medical care. Each of these factors and its implications for regulatory policy will be discussed in turn, with emphasis on the importance of considering existing regulatory and monopolistic elements in formulating new regulations.

Consumer Ignorance. It is widely believed that since consumers know little about medical care, they cannot make intelligent choices. Thus, the argument goes, the regulatory system should see to it that consumers

---

[2] For only a few references in a large and growing literature see Walter Adams and Horace M. Grey, *Monopoly in America: Government as Promoter* (New York: Macmillan, 1955), chap. 3; George J. Stigler, "The Theory of Regulation," *Bell Journal of Economics*, vol. 2 (Spring 1971), pp. 3–21; and William A. Jordan, "Producer Protection, Prior Market Structure and the Effects of Government Regulation," *Journal of Law and Economics*, vol. 15 (April 1972), pp. 151–76.

have no choice and so will not hurt themselves. This argument is used to support regulations that constrain consumer choice, generally in the name of protecting the quality of medical care.

Specifically, consumers are said to be ignorant of differences in the technical quality or effectiveness of medical care. No doubt the effort to reduce consumer uncertainty about quality partly motivated the formation of strong medical societies and some of the ethical concepts behind professional standards.[3] Since direct measurement of medical care quality has been thought to be too difficult for regulators to carry out, regulations have focused on inputs, particularly manpower inputs. Also largely in the name of quality, restrictions have been placed on certain ways of providing medical care (for example, the use of profit-seeking firms, prepaid group practice, and the delegation of tasks to nonphysician workers).

Although these regulations may be beneficial, the mere statement that consumers' medical knowledge is imperfect is *not* a sufficient basis for the case. There are incentives to develop mechanisms for providing enough relevant information to consumers, without requiring technical knowledge.

Market responses to consumer ignorance. On the other side, poor consumer information can be overcome by the use of manufacturers' brand names, so that consumers may know something about the expected quality of a Chevrolet automobile or a Sony television, for example. The brand name capital has value for the seller. Protecting the value of one's reputation provides strong incentives for providing reliable quality products. Consumer information can also be made available through advertising, which increases the importance of brand names. At the same time, the existence of a brand name certifies some of the informational content of the advertising.

The reputations of retailers also serve to certify the quality of merchandise. Both retailers and manufacturers have guarantee programs wherein much of the quality risk is shifted to the manufacturer. The medical parallel of these programs is the health maintenance organization, which, in a sense, attempts to guarantee conditions of health for the body.

Another significant market response has been the development of an entire industry to provide information on quality of consumer goods. The automotive press, for example, provides skilled tests on cars and

---

[3] See Kenneth J. Arrow, "Uncertainty and the Welfare Economics of Medical Care," *American Economic Review*, vol. 53 (December 1963), pp. 941–73; and Richard Zeckhauser, "Ethics, Patient Behavior and the Organization of Medical Care" (unpublished paper, Kennedy School of Government, Harvard University, March 27, 1974).

publishes the results. For products in general there are several independent certifying agencies.

Providing further incentives for maintaining quality and honesty is the law of product liability and fraud. The medical malpractice activity may be the busiest area of litigation on product (service) liability. Despite some failings, malpractice litigation supplies information and protects quality in medical care.[4]

Suppression of consumer information by regulation. The striking aspect of the current medical care system is the efforts of regulators and the medical profession to reduce consumer information. Primarily through informal regulation of "ethical" practices based on the licensure power, the medical profession has prevented advertising and, until recently, has prohibited the testimony of physicians against others in malpractice suits. The incentive for suppressing consumer information is clear: If consumers have poor information about alternative sources of care, an individual provider will be able to raise prices somewhat without losing many of his patients to a competitor. Perhaps most important, a provider who desires to expand will expect little gain from reducing his prices if very few consumers are informed about his and other prices, levels of quality, and so on. Recent research by Lee Benham, for example, shows that restricting advertising raises prices of eyeglasses.[5] Also, recent work by Mark Pauly and Mark Satterthwaite shows physician pricing to be sensitive to consumer information.[6]

Another effective means of suppressing consumer information has been the medical profession's resistance to HMOs partly through licensure and partly through state laws that restrict or even outlaw HMOs. HMOs would perform as department stores of medicine certifying the quality of medical care and providing information and incentives to maintain reputations for quality and honesty.

Informational advantages of consumers over providers. Providers are not better informed than consumers, for all relevant information. There is important knowledge which is vital for many rational medical decisions to which only the consumer has access. This information is the *consumer's scale of values*, which plays a vital role in three types of

[4] See H. E. Frech III, "The Economics of Medical Malpractice: Commentary," in Simon Rottenberg, ed., *The Economics of Medical Malpractice* (Washington, D.C.: American Enterprise Institute, 1978), pp. 280–88.

[5] Lee Benham, "The Effect of Advertising on the Price of Eyeglasses," *Journal of Law and Economics*, vol. 15 (October 1972), pp. 337–52.

[6] Mark V. Pauly and Mark A. Satterthwaite, "The Pricing of Primary Care Physician's Services: A Test of the Role of Consumer Information" (Working Paper no. 26, Economics Department, Northwestern University, March 1979), pp. 21–22.

decisions: (1) the weighing of medical care against other goods valued by the consumer (for example, leisure and housing); (2) the consumer's evaluation of risk; and (3) the evaluation of different medical procedures of which the main results are symptomatic relief, rather than cures.

Only the consumer knows how much he would be willing to sacrifice for a certain amount of comfort or reduction in the risk of disease. The problem of attitude toward risk is very subtle. Many medical procedures are risky, and in some cases the worst possible outcomes are far worse than the initial problem. Surgery is an obvious example, since the risk of serious complications is present even in relatively minor surgery. Whether or not dangerous treatments are worth the risks involved cannot be decided on the basis of medical technology alone. It is necessary to assess the risky prospects subjectively, and only the consumer can do this for himself.

In the case of medical procedures directed toward symptomatic relief, consumer preferences play a significant role, since variations in the use of such procedures over a wide range of intensity apparently have a small effect on health.[7] Much of the benefit of medical care is assessable only by highly subjective standards because it occurs in the form of comfort and symptomatic relief and thus is known only to the consumer. As a result, consumer tastes and decisions are extremely important to the medical care industry.

The main point here is that consumer ignorance of medical technology does not mean that consumers should be prevented from exercising choice in the marketplace. The market can and does develop substitutes for detailed technical knowledge. Many current regulations directly and indirectly suppress important consumer information, however. The quality of consumer information can be improved without endangering other aspects of the medical care system, as it has been since the recent Supreme Court decision allowing medical advertising.

Medical Care for the Poor. It is widely held that most Americans are willing to provide financial support for health care for the poor.[8] There-

---

[7] For two examples of a rich literature see Richard Auster, Irving Leveson, and Debara Saracheck, "The Production of Health: An Exploratory Study," *Journal of Human Resources*, vol. 4 (Fall 1969), pp. 411–36, and Lee Benham and Alexandra Benham, "The Impact of Incremental Medical Services on Health Status, 1963–1970," in Ronald Andersen, Joanna Pravits, and Odin N. Anderson, eds., *Equity in Health Services: Empirical Analyses in Social Policy* (Cambridge, Mass.: Ballinger, 1975), pp. 217–27. As an exception to the usual finding, incremental medical care seems to have an important effect on perinatal mortality. See Ronald L. Williams, "Explaining a Health Care Paradox," *Policy Sciences*, vol. 6 (1975), pp. 91–101, and "Outcome-Based Measurements of Medical Care Output" (Ph.D. diss., University of California, Santa Barbara, 1974).

[8] See Mark V. Pauly, *Medical Care at Public Expense* (New York: Praeger, 1971).

fore, there may be a role for governmental subsidy of health insurance for the poor as a result of the free-rider problem confronting private charity.[9]

The problem of supporting medical care for the poor appears to be related entirely to questions of taxation and of mixing public and private charity. There also exists, however, a semiprivate system of cross-subsidization by which some services and some groups are charged prices higher than costs in order to subsidize other facilities, services, and groups. This system of cross-subsidization has arisen because some services are priced higher than cost and thus earn monopoly rents. These rents are then used to pay for subsidized services or individuals. To maintain the rents, competition must be prevented or attenuated.

"Cream skimming" and the argument against competition. The impulse to protect monopoly rents finds its expression in arguments against "cream skimming," which is the provision of profitable services rather than a mixture of profitable and unprofitable ones. The argument is most often applied to hospitals and health insurers. Of course, cream skimming is merely rational decision making by independent business firms. The fact that it is possible is prima facie evidence of noncompetitive behavior on the part of the existing firms. Otherwise, price would be competed down to approximately marginal cost in all services. For cream skimming to be possible, prices must be discriminatory and monopolistic.

The current regulatory system provides for a significant amount of cross-subsidization. Historically, the poor have gained significantly from this practice through the receipt of free care, hence the relevance of the charitable motive in preserving some of the anticompetitive elements of current regulation. The argument for cross-subsidization forms part of the traditional rationale for the two main types of hospital regulations: barriers against profit-seeking hospitals, and entry restrictions generally. New hospitals, especially profit-seeking ones, are thought to be especially likely to offer only profitable services. This new competition deprives existing providers of revenues, thereby jeopardizing their ability to offer unremunerative services.

The argument for regulation of health insurance may be less familiar than the one advocating hospital regulation. Blue Cross and Blue Shield insurers have many regulatory advantages over their ordinary commercial competitors.[10] Protected by regulation, these firms widely practice

---

[9] For each potential donor, the benefits of charitable activity are approximately the same whether or not he contributes. There is an incentive for each donor to "free ride" on the contribution of others. This behavior can lead to an undersupply of private charity.

[10] See H. E. Frech III, "Market Power in Health Insurance: Effects on Insurance and Medical Markets," *Journal of Industrial Economics*, vol. 28 (September 1979), pp. 55–72;

a form of cross-subsidization called community rating. In this scheme, the insurer *purposely* charges identical prices to differing risks. The regulatory advantages are defended partly because they allow these insurers to charge higher than competitive rates for good risks to subsidize those with a higher risk of using insurance benefits. Commercial insurers who experience-rate (that is, set price in relation to expected losses for different risk classes, on the basis of group experience) are charged with cream skimming.

Cross-subsidization and the poor. Although the poor were among the major beneficiaries of cross-subsidization in the hospital industry in the past, they do not seem to benefit very much from this practice now. Recent work by Silver indicates that the quantity of charity care provided by the typical voluntary hospital is now limited,[11] largely because of the extent of governmental (Medicare and Medicaid) and private financing for hospital services delivered to the poor. Services that are subsidized appear to be those favored by hospital administration and medical staffs. Laboratory, x-ray, and pharmacy services and the daily room charge are thought to be priced above their cost, whereas obstetric care, the emergency room, intensive care, and underused services are operated at a loss.[12] This situation may be one particularly unfortunate result of cross-subsidization in that many hospitals may prefer to subsidize services that are rarely used. This approach is widely believed to increase costs and to reduce the quality of medical care.

Furthermore, in the case of community rating of health insurance, it is not clear that poor consumers benefit. Some recent research indicates that for any given health status, lower-income individuals are less likely to consume medical care.[13] Indeed, some calculations of Rosett

---

"Blue Cross, Blue Shield and Health Care Costs: A Review of the Economic Evidence," in Mark V. Pauly, ed., *National Health Insurance: What Now, What Later, What Never?* (Washington, D.C.: American Enterprise Institute, 1980), pp. 250–63; and Nancy T. Greenspan and Ronald J. Vogel, "Taxation and Its Effect on Public and Private Health Insurance and Medical Demand," *Health Care Financing Review*, vol. 1 (Spring 1980), pp. 42–43.

[11] Laurens H. Silver, "The Legal Accountability of Nonprofit Hospitals," in Clark C. Havighurst, ed., *Regulating Health Facilities Construction* (Washington, D.C.: American Enterprise Institute, 1974), pp. 183–200.

[12] See Clark C. Havighurst, "Regulation of Health Facilities and Services by 'Certificate of Need,' " *Virginia Law Review*, vol. 59 (October 1973), p. 1191.

[13] See Richard N. Rosett and Lien-Fu Huang, "The Effect of Health Insurance on the Demand for Medical Care," *Journal of Political Economy*, vol. 81 (March/April 1973), pp. 281–305; "Redistribution of Income through Blue Cross Community-Rated Premiums" (Discussion Paper no. 72–9, Economics Department, University of Rochester, June 1972); Joseph P. Newhouse and Charles E. Phelps, "New Estimates of Price and Income Elasticities of Medical Care Services," in Richard N. Rosett, ed., *The Role of Health Insurance in the Health Services Sector: Proceedings of a Conference* (New York: National Bureau of Economic Research, 1976), pp. 261–312.

and Huang show that community rating redistributes from the poor to the rich and from blacks to whites.[14]

Problems with regulatory cross-subsidization. Even if the poor were a significant beneficiary of cross-subsidization, many other problems would have to be dealt with. First, the system requires monopoly pricing, with its related inefficiency, on some services and to some groups. A more efficient way to support medical care for the poor is to use a broadly based tax such as the income tax. This point has been made forcefully by Pauly in arguing that community rating of health insurance is inefficient.[15]

Second, regulatory cross-subsidization systems are largely unaccountable to the legislature and to the public.

The third point is that those who regulate virtually any sector of the economy favor their sector's growth and thus will be protective of the size of the industry and will favor high gains from monopoly pricing to finance the services they favor. The resulting price discrimination increases the resources used by the industry. This process has been noted in other regulated sectors. According to Noll, "regulatory policy might accurately be characterized as maximizing the size of the regulated industry."[16]

Protection of cross-subsidization in the health care industry underlies much of the regulatory and professional objection to profit-seeking firms in health care. The argument is that profit-seeking firms are more likely to supply only profitable services. It has been shown, however, that the bias against profit-seeking firms leads to inefficiently operated firms.[17]

Insurance and Supply-limiting Regulation. The last feature of the medical care system widely believed to require regulation is extensive third-party payment for medical care. This common view is presented with clarity by Grosse:

[14] Rosett and Huang, "Community-Rated Premiums," pp. 5–6.

[15] Mark V. Pauly, "The Welfare Economics of Community Rating," *Journal of Risk and Insurance*, vol. 31 (September 1970), pp. 407–18.

[16] Roger G. Noll, *Reforming Regulation: An Evaluation of the Ash Council Proposals* (Washington, D.C.: Brookings Institution, 1974), p. 16.

[17] For a study of inefficiency of nonprofit health insurers see H. E. Frech III, "The Property Rights Theory of the Firm: Empirical Results from a Natural Experiment," *Journal of Political Economy*, vol. 84 (January 1976), pp. 143–52. For an analysis of the relative inefficiency of nonprofit hospitals, see Kenneth W. Clarkson, "Some Implications of Property Rights in Hospital Management," *Journal of Law and Economics*, vol. 15 (October 1972), pp. 363–84. A good general survey is Louis De Alessi, "The Economics of Property Rights: A Review of the Evidence," *Research in Law and Economics*, vol. 2 (July 1980), pp. 1–47.

> The growth of government and insurance payment for health services has reduced the resistance to cost increases that might otherwise have limited utilization. Without the apparent blank check, hospital administrations would probably have been slower to introduce cost-generating services or hospital beds for which no clear need existed. Because, to the individual family, the use of many expensive health services comes largely prepaid, limitation of use has only modest financial benefits. To the providers of care, government and insurers ask only that services be performed and that the charges be based on cost or community practice. Expensive decisions of physicians to specialize and expensive decisions of hospitals to add resources result in costs to the community which few individual consumers have any interest in fighting at the time when they have a perceived need for service. . . . One of the ways movements toward efficiency may be achieved is for the community to control the quantities of the various health care services which will be permitted or encouraged to function in that community.[18]

The economic theory behind this statement is that if the effect of health insurance is to increase demand for medical care beyond the optimal amount, then the supply ought to be reduced to prevent the consumption of excessively high quantity and quality.

This type of regulation would be eschewed in a typical competitive industry or even in a typical monopolistic industry. In the competitive case, the market would supply the optimal quantity and quality, so that intervention would only create problems. In the second case, the economic argument against limiting supply is even stronger. Since a monopolist supplies less than the optimal quantity, a governmental proposal to reduce supply would only make the problem worse. The distinctive feature of this system of medical care is extensive government-subsidized third-party insurance that leads to a large oversupply of medical care. Only in the framework of this excessive insurance, caused largely by government policy, does a supply-limiting policy make any sense.

Suppression of market responses by regulation. In addition, regulation has been used to retard and impede market responses to the problems of third-party payment. Two innovations that might help to reduce these problems—the HMO and direct control efforts by insurers—have been retarded indirectly by licensure and directly by hostile regulation.

---

[18] Robert N. Grosse, "The Need for Health Planning," in Clark C. Havighurst, ed., *Regulating Health Facilities Construction* (Washington, D.C.: American Enterprise Institute, 1974), p. 28.

54

The HMO limits supply by professionally allocating medical care on a nonprice basis. It avoids the dangers of choosing an inappropriate supply of care and of ignoring consumer tastes by competing with others and with fee-for-service medicine for customers. HMOs still have a rationing problem because they cannot adjust perfectly to variations in demand among their memberships. (Thus I would argue that HMOs should be allowed to select certain population groups.)

Another market response to the subsidy or moral hazard of insurance gaining more attention is claim review and monitoring by insurance companies, which are approximately halfway between fee-for-service medicine and the HMO idea. In a free market, such cost control by insurers would probably be an effective means of competition. As discussed by Havighurst, there are several techniques by which insurers might compete in terms of cost control:

> First, retrospective review of claims allows utilization to be examined and compared to norms, and charges which are out of line can be flagged and questioned. Second, various types of sanctions could be imposed where abuses have occurred, ranging from disallowances of a patient's claims for indemnification, leaving him to pay the provider to various arrangements whereby the provider would end up bearing the cost: . . . not too long ago a major insurer undertook to assist its insureds in resisting suits by physicians to recover charges which the insurer had disallowed as unnecessary expenditures. Third, more extreme cost-control measures include requirements for obtaining the insurer's prior approval for certain expenditures for hospitalization, diagnostic tests, or surgery; of course, the medical profession reacts strongly against efforts to control costs in this manner, as was demonstrated when HEW recently attempted to introduce pre-admission certification under Medicaid and Medicare.[19]

In an insurance cost control scheme, the insurer plus the participating providers form a kind of loosely knit HMO. If competition of this sort were allowed, a continuum of insurance plans could be expected in the market. At one extreme, there would be the HMO, which would undertake strict insurer control of the supply of medical care. Intermediate would be insurers practicing less strict control of insurable expenditures.

---

[19] Clark C. Havighurst, testimony in U.S. Congress, Senate Subcommittee on Antitrust and Monopoly of the Committee on the Judiciary, Hearings: *Competition in the Health Services Market*, pts. 1–3, 93rd Cong., 2d sess., May 14, 15, 17, 29, 30; July 10, 1974, 3 vols., pp. 1074–75. The intermediate case resembles the Foundation for Medical Care (FMC) idea that a local medical society forms an organization to control utilization and fees. The main difference is that these medical foundations are local monopolies. An insurer-based approach would involve competition of many insurers.

At the other extreme would be insurers with virtually no controls on use.

Further, the approach of supply-limiting regulation will also run into serious problems in determining how severely to restrict the supply of medical care and in rationing the care of those who desire it. These problems will be discussed fully in the following section.

The Effects of Regulation

This section brings out some of the less obvious effects of selected regulations. In many cases, the subtle effects of a given regulation have to be examined in relation to the entire regulatory framework.

Occupational Licensure. Occupational licensure in health care was sought by the professions concerned, first by the physicians, and recently by many other health care professions.[20] The stated goal of licensure has been to raise quality and to provide information, since any licensed physician has had to possess certain minimum qualifications. The professions have sought licensure in part to reduce the number of professionals. As the head of the American Medical Association Council on Medical Education has pointed out: "With the reduction of medical schools from 160 to eighty, there occurred a marked reduction in the number of medical students and medical graduates. We had anticipated this and felt that this was a desirable thing."[21] Supply restrictions and the prevention of competition within the profession create some of the costs of regulation. At this point, let us briefly discuss the benefits of this kind of regulation.

Information, quality, and licensure. Licensure was instituted to protect consumers from dishonest and incompetent practitioners. It was to raise the standards for entry into the profession and to provide valuable assurance to the public that each professional had the required skill and knowledge. Two issues are intertwined here, information and quality.

The argument that licensure benefits the public by raising quality is faulty. If consumers choose a lower quality level than they really desire, they lack adequate information. If licensure raises quality above the level that consumers actually prefer, a cost will result, not a benefit. Licensure undoubtedly raises the average quality of licensed profes-

---

[20] The material in this section is drawn largely from H. E. Frech III, "Occupational Licensure and Health Care Productivity: The Issues and the Literature," in John Rafferty, ed., *Health Manpower and Productivity: The Literature and Required Future Research* (Lexington, Mass.: Lexington Books, 1974), pp. 119–42.

[21] A. D. Bevan, "Cooperation in Medical Education and Medical Service," *Journal of the American Medical Society*, vol. 90 (1928), p. 1176.

sionals, but since their number is restricted, the average quality of medical care actually received may be reduced. The argument has been made forcefully by a hospital administrator:

> It's easy to sit behind a desk in Chicago and frame ideals about the quality of care. But, a supposedly non-qualified doctor can put on a tourniquet and give the usual drugs for shock to tide the patient over until an American-trained doctor gets there. And that's better than having the patient die.[22]

The assertion that licensure would reduce the extent of fraud and dishonesty is difficult to discuss a priori, for the connection between the two is not obvious. There has been, however, an interesting empirical study of the impact of licensure on prices and fraud in the television repair industry, in which repairmen are licensed in some states and not in others. Licensure was found to raise prices substantially for repairs but to have no effect on the incidence of fraud.[23]

On the other side of the ledger are the costs of occupational licensure. These costs have been considerable especially in health care, but many of them have been indirect and difficult to perceive.

Restriction of supply. An obvious cost of licensure arises from the restriction of the supply of the licensed occupation. In raising the cost of those inputs licensure increases the cost of services to consumers and eventually leads to substitution of other inputs. The most striking example is probably the substitution of other inputs for physician time. It has been estimated that the licensure restriction directly raises physician incomes by about 25 percent over the free-entry income.[24] If we ignore substitution possibilities and the effect of high wages on physician hours of work, this figure indicates that the costs of physician services are about 15 percent higher than they would be if entry into the existing type of medical schools were free.[25] Since without licensure medical education would probably be less costly, this 15 percent understates the cost increase due to licensure.

Rapidly proliferating and tightening licensure for the allied health occupations has had similar effects, in that the average skill level of hospital employees has declined in recent years, probably because the

---

[22] Quoted by R. Stevens and J. Vermeulen, "Foreign-Trained Physicians and American Medicine" (unpublished paper, Yale University, June 1971), p. III–8.

[23] See J. J. Phelan, *Regulation of the Television Repair Industry in Louisiana and California: A Case Study* (Washington, D.C.: Federal Trade Commission, November 1974), pp. 31–32.

[24] Frech, "Occupational Licensure," pp. 122–23.

[25] See Cotton M. Lindsay, "Measuring Human Capital Returns," *Journal of Political Economy*, vol. 79 (November/December 1971), pp. 1195–1215.

more skilled professions have obtained strict licensing. However, separate licensure may sometimes be a device to allow nonphysician manpower to practice separately from physicians. This is pro-competitive.

By limiting the number of medical schools, licensure has given the remaining medical schools great power to select their entrants, and to discriminate against groups such as women, blacks, and especially Jews.

Since educational requirements have become a convenient way of limiting entry into licensed occupations, detailed specifications have evolved for educational programs. Many observers believe that this trend has prevented innovation and efficency in education.

Reduction of competition within the medical care industry. The sanction of losing one's license has been used to discipline professionals in order to reduce competition within medicine. Consumer information has been reduced as a result. Virtually all professions try to limit consumer information wherever competition is involved, commonly by restricting advertising. Benham and Benham have provided fascinating evidence on the impact of advertising limitations and strong professional organizations on consumer interests.

Benham found that in states where advertising of eyeglasses was legally prohibited, prices were almost double the prices ($18.00 more) in states where advertising was least restricted.[26] More recently, Benham and Benham investigated the connection between powerful professional organizations and eyeglass prices[27] and found that as membership in the Optometrist Association rose from 43 to 91 percent of all optometrists, eyeglass prices rose by about $12.00. Organized medicine has been similarly opposed to HMOs and insurer cost controls. Organized medicine's resistance to HMO-type practice by means of licensure and other regulations is recounted by Kessel, Rayack, and Barton,[28] who note that many state laws and regulations hinder the development of HMOs. Other research indicates that strict insurance regulation applied to HMOs and the common requirement by state law that any physician be allowed to join any HMO appear to have been importantly responsible for slowing the growth of HMOs.[29]

[26] Benham, "Advertising," pp. 337–52.

[27] See Lee Benham and Alexandra Benham, "Regulating through the Professions: A Perspective on Information Control," *Journal of Law and Economics*, vol. 18 (October 1975), pp. 421–48.

[28] See Reuben A. Kessel, "Price Discrimination in Medicine," *Journal of Law and Economics*, vol. 1 (October 1958), pp. 20–53; Elton Rayack, *Professional Power and American Medicine: The Economics of the American Medical Association* (New York: World, 1967); and David M. Barton, "Alternative Institutional Arrangements for Medical Care Insurance" (Ph.D. diss., University of Virginia, 1974), pp. 74–141.

[29] Robert E. Schlenker, Jean N. Quale, and Richard McNiel, Jr., "Socioeconomic and

That the medical profession has also fought insurer cost controls in many ways has come to light in two interesting antitrust cases. The Blue Shield and medical society of Oregon were sued in 1948 for using boycott and predatory pricing against private health insurers. In defense, they submitted a list of insurer cost controls as evidence of "unethical interference." In reviewing the case, Havighurst notes that this "could now be regarded as evidence of monopolistic intent and not as involving a cognizable ethical issue."[30] In a related case, Blue Shield and the Medical Society of Ohio were sued by the state of Ohio under antitrust law. In the words of the complaint, the defendants were charged with "fixing, raising and stabilizing prices for physician services . . . [using] acts of boycott, coercion and intimidation directed at insurance companies and other parties who attempted to utilize or introduce methods aimed at curbing rapidly rising fees."[31] This case was settled out of court.

Restrictions on manpower substitution. Occupational licensure has restricted the substitution of different manpower inputs by establishing narrow specifications for job content and entry requirements.[32] The incentives for each occupation to restrict entry and to circumscribe the right of others to perform certain tasks are obvious, but the costs incurred in the inefficient use of manpower inputs are somewhat less obvious. A particularly subtle cost arises from the restriction of upward occupational mobility. If it were not for occupational licensure, a worker might gradually upgrade his skills with experience. Instead, licensure creates a rigid caste system.

Despite its subtlety, the cost of licensure has been recognized by the American Medical Association (AMA) House of Delegates, which has called for wider rights of physicians to delegate tasks. The AMA statement is especially interesting, since the medical profession was one of the pioneers in occupational licensure:

> . . . there is need to avoid the problems of overspecialization and fractionalization of services entailed by occupational li-

---

Legal Factors Associated with HMO Presence: An Examination of State Data," Report HSRC-HMO-2 (Minneapolis, Minn.: InterStudy, October 1973), p. 29.

[30] Havighurst, testimony in U.S. Congress, "Competition in Health," p. 1076. For more on this case, which involved the creation of Oregon Blue Shield, see Lawrence G. Goldberg and Warren Greenberg, "The Emergence of Physician-Sponsored Health Insurance: A Historical Perspective," in *Competition in the Health Care Sector: Past, Present, and Future* (Germantown, Md.: Aspen Systems, 1978), pp. 231–54.

[31] State of Ohio v. Ohio Medical Indemnity, Inc., and The Ohio State Medical Association, complaint by Office of Attorney General, July 9, 1975, p. 7. Civil Action 6, C-Z-75-478, filed in the Southern district of Ohio, eastern division.

[32] See Ruth Roemer, "Licensing and Regulation of Medical and Medical-Related Practitioners in Health Service Teams," *Medical Care*, vol. 9 (January/February 1971), pp. 42–54.

censure systems and the resultant controls on entry into occupations and scope of permissible functions. . . . *There seems
to be a growing body of opinion that occupational licensure has
outlived its usefulness as a method assuring quality health services.*

*Proliferation in mandatory occupational licensure laws
tends to foster a "craft union" approach to health care and may
lead to unwarranted increase in cost of services. . . .*

*Current occupational licensure laws tend to inhibit inno-
vation in the education and use of allied manpower and restrict
the avenues available for entry into or upward mobility in a
health career. . . .*[33]

Of course, the association is speaking of licensure for professions other
than its own.

There are also disputes among different specialities within the medical profession. Here, hospital privileges are often at stake. But, the
medical profession's control of hospitals is largely, if indirectly, based
on licensure. Many observers believe that exclusion from hospital rights
is used in an anticompetitive manner. Dr. Charles E. Letourneau, president of the College of Legal Medicine, has explained the loss of hospital
privileges among general practitioners:

> Yes, typically this happens when a horde of surgical specialists
> moves into an area only to discover there's not enough surgery
> around. I've seen it affect four or five hospitals in the same
> community. Board-certified men tried to freeze out the com-
> petition completely, although local G.P.'s have been there for
> thirty years doing good work.[34]

Since hospital rights are often associated with specialty certification, it
is not surprising that entrance requirements unrelated to quality are
used by some specialty boards. The most common requirement is to
exclude foreign medical graduates from even being considered *unless
they are leaving the country.*[35]

Closely related to these restrictions on occupational mobility are
restrictions on geographical mobility of licensed professionals. These
are most serious for nonphysician manpower and foreign-trained physicians.

Health Insurance Regulation. The main effect of health insurance reg-

---

[33] American Medical Association, "Licensure of Health Occupations," adopted by the
House of Delegates, December 1970. Italics in the original.

[34] Quoted in Rayack, *American Medical Association*, p. 224.

[35] For information on this and other restrictions on foreign-trained physicians, see Rosemary Stevens and Jean Vermeulen, "Foreign Trained Physicians and American Medicine"
(unpublished paper, Yale University, June 1971), p. III–18.

ulation is that it favors the nonprofit insurers who are heavily influenced by medical providers—Blue Cross for hospitals and Blue Shield for physician services.[36] Regulations having such an effect include reserve requirements, taxation, and rate regulation. The regulatory advantages arise from the nonprofit nature of the firms and from special enabling acts for Blue Cross and Blue Shield firms. In states with relatively strict health insurance regulation, for example, Blue Cross plans have a larger share of the market. The cost advantage that regulation bestows on the "Blue" plans has several undesirable consequences.

First, it gives the firms the power to increase the completeness of insurance held by consumers. Since these firms are nonprofit organizations, the major way in which they can benefit the medical providers that influence them is to raise the completeness of insurance. This action increases the demand for medical care, which raises the rents earned by suppliers, and also reduces incentives for consumers to search, thereby further isolating individual providers from the competition of other providers.

Supply-limiting Regulation. In recent history, hospital supply has been limited through the efforts of local health-planning associations and other informal groups.[37] In response to the rapid inflation caused by expanding health insurance, this type of regulation has been expanding rapidly in geographic terms and in terms of the powers held by planning agencies, as expressed in the certificate-of-need law and in the similar review called for by Public Law 92–603, Section 1122. The intent of the certificate-of-need law is to prohibit hospitals from adding to the supply of beds or from making certain other capital investments without the permission of some health-planning agency. Entry into the industry also requires permission. The agency having responsibility for the first review is usually the local areawide health-planning agency. Section 1122 requires that investments exceeding $100,000 and changes in bed size or services be approved by a state-designated agency for reimbursement under Social Security programs. By 1979, forty-seven states had enacted certificate-of-need laws.[38]

---

[36] See H. E. Frech III, "Blue Cross, Blue Shield, and Health Care Costs," and Greenspan and Vogel, "Taxation and Health Insurance," pp. 42, 43.

[37] See Sol S. Shalit, "Barriers to Entry in the American Hospital Industry" (Ph.D. diss., University of Chicago, September 1970), pp. 30–41; Symond R. Gottlieb, "A Brief History of Health Planning in the United States," in Clark C. Havighurst, ed., *Regulating Health Facilities Construction* (Washington, D.C.: American Enterprise Institute, 1974), pp. 7–26; and J. Joel May, "The Impact of Health Planning on the Hospital Industry" (paper presented at the American Economic Association Meetings, San Francisco, California, December 1974), pp. 16–23.

[38] Frank A. Sloan, "Regulation and the Rising Cost of Hospital Care" (unpublished paper, Vanderbilt University, undated), p. 25.

FIGURE 1
THE IMPACT OF INSURANCE AND REGULATION ON THE PRICE AND
QUANTITY OF HEALTH CARE

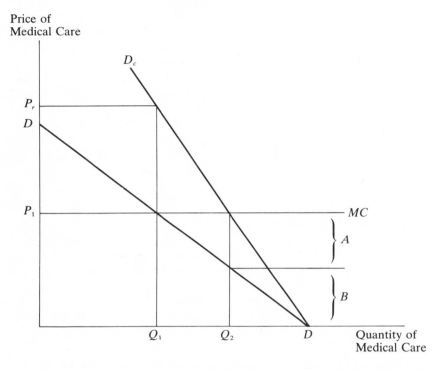

As we have seen, the rationale for this type of regulation is based on the special characteristics of health insurance. Nonetheless, there are serious problems in determining how much to restrict supply and in rationing the care. The following section discusses these problems in the context of a simple economic model and then presents the results of recent empirical research on the impact of supply-limiting regulation.

The theoretical rationale. The model employed here (see figure 1) ignores the dimension of quality, for which the argument is exactly parallel in that insurance induces consumers to demand excessive quality as well as excessive quantity. Thus, ideal regulation ought to reduce quality from the high levels supplied in the unrestricted market to the same extent that it reduces quantity.

The first step is to develop a theoretical benchmark for the optimal quantity of medical care. That requires the demand curve of consumers with insurance that has no moral hazard or subsidy effect. Thus, let us take the demand of well-informed consumers with idealized insurance (with no adverse incentives) as the ideal, which is acceptable except for those with low incomes. The rest of society would like to subsidize their consumption of medical care. Thus, the benchmark results from adding the demand curve of well-informed middle- and upper-class consumers to an appropriately subsidized demand curve for poorer individuals. This ideal demand curve leads to the optimal quantity of medical care, Q_1. It is also the competitive equilibrium.

Now let us shift from this ideal insurance to actual insurance of the coinsured type that pays a certain portion of medical expenses. Under the simplifying assumption that the realistic insurance has the same income effect on demand increase of illness as ideal insurance, we can ignore the income effect on demand in the event of illness. In such a situation, realistic insurance merely raises the demand curve by rotating it about its intersection with the quantity axis. This action gives demand curve DcD. The coinsured and idealized demand curves are related as follows. The vertical distance between DcD and DD is that part of the price paid by the insurer, and the distance between DD and the quantity axis is the part paid by consumers. For example, at Q_2, the amount of the price paid by the insurer is A, while B gives the consumer out-of-pocket expenditure. The introduction of realistic insurance leads to a new equilibrium quantity of Q_2. According to Grosse's argument, this is too much medical care and supply-limiting regulation might be worthwhile.

Determination of the optimal quantity of care. The rationale makes supply-limiting regulation look useful. But, the regulators have to resolve some difficult problems. First, to what level should the regulators limit the supply of medical care? If they have the demand curves to look at, the problem is easily solved. In actuality, however, the hypothetical ideal demand curve is not known. It depends on the health status, tastes, and incomes of consumers. As recent discussion shows, there is no general agreement on even a crude way to estimate the ideal level of supply of medical care.[39]

Price and nonprice rationing. Even if regulators could calculate the optimal level of services for a given market area, they face serious problems in deciding how to ration the medical services. Two options

---

[39] See Havighurst, "Regulation by 'Certificate of Need,' " pp. 1224–31; Joseph P. Newhouse and Jan P. Acton, "Compulsory Health Planning Laws and National Health Insurance," in Clark C. Havighurst, ed., *Regulating Health Facilities Construction* (Washington, D.C.: American Enterprise Institute, 1974), p. 222; Richard A. Posner, "Certificates of Need for Health Care Facilities: A Dissenting View," in Clark C. Havighurst, ed., *Regulating Health Facilities Construction* (Washington, D.C.: American Enterprise Institute, 1974), p. 117.

are available, price or nonprice rationing. The planners could allow price rationing by simply limiting supply and by allowing the price to rise enough to clear the market. This is what past supply-limiting regulation has done, both in the case of physicians and other licensed occupations and hospitals. Although this approach can lead to the optimal quantity of medical care, such a combination of third-party payment, regulatory supply determination, and market-clearing prices drastically reduces the risk-spreading benefits of insurance.

In this situation, consumers pay Q_1 times P_1 if they are ill. It will be convenient to define this total payment, if sick, as the financial risk. Compare this financial risk with that under coinsurance, but with no supply limitation. In that situation, the consumers pay B per unit, while the insurer pays A. Consumer financial risk is then B times Q_2. In fact, the financial risk will be greater with regulation if the arc elasticity of the coinsured demand curve is less than one. Most estimates of this demand elasticity indicate that it is substantially below unity.

If consumers desire to purchase insurance in the unregulated case, they will desire to add more insurance to offset the increase in risk caused by the regulation of supply. This reaction will lead to another round of price increases and financial risk increases. The spiral of more and more complete insurance and higher and higher prices will be restrained only by wealth effects reducing demand for health care and possibly for health insurance and/or some other interventions.

Another problem is caused by the nonprofit structure of most health care firms. The supply restriction leads to large monopoly rents for health care providers. In the case of profit-seeking firms, these monopoly rents are only a transfer and pose no efficiency problems. If the firms are nonprofit organizations, however, the potential for waste cannot be ignored. Among others, Feldstein and Taylor argue that hospitals respond to higher demand for their product by raising the quality *in their own eyes* of the services they supply.[40] This approach can be seriously wasteful for two reasons. First, the hospital's ideas about high quality are likely to differ from those of consumers. Hospitals may invest in little-used sophisticated equipment and services that may actually reduce the quality of medical care from consumers' views. Specialized surgery units are an example of this duplication of facilities, which actually reduces quality since it leads to poorer chances of survival. Also, in-

[40] See Martin Feldstein, "Quality Change and the Demand for Medical Care" (unpublished paper, Economics Department, Harvard University, undated), pp. 41, 42, and Martin Feldstein and Amy K. Taylor, *The Rapid Rise of Hospital Costs*, Staff Report, Executive Office of the President, Council on Wage and Price Stability (January 1977), pp. 20–38, 66–68.

surance leads consumers to demand medical care of too high a quality level. Supply-limiting regulation with price rationing exacerbates the problem.

As an alternative to price rationing, regulators could ration the medical services in some nonprice manner. This practice has many advantages. It preserves the reduction in financial risk, which is the main reason for the purchase of medical insurance. Second, it reduces the monopoly rents earned by providers. This approach has not been widely used in the past, probably because it is extremely difficult for the regulators to know how to ration the medical care among competing consumers. Appropriate rationing of health services is based on the interplay of consumer preferences and the available supply of medical resources. Rationing by the regulators is likely to substitute professional preferences for those of consumers, and thus may introduce a new and significant dimension of risk. Consumers will receive the wrong amount and mix of medical services in terms of their own preferences. Thus, even if financial risk is lowered by nonprice rationing, the risk in terms of consumer values may be quite large.

Fortunately, one does not have to be content with speculation about all aspects of supply-limiting regulation. Even though the expansion of this regulation is relatively recent, excellent empirical research is available on some impacts of such regulation on hospitals.

The impact of supply-limiting regulation: empirical evidence. Most researchers have found that supply-limiting regulation does little to the growth rate of overall costs, although there is a great deal of evidence that such regulation leads to slower growth in hospital beds and more rapid growth in investment in hospital beds. Frank Sloan calls this finding a "consensus" of researchers.[41]

Joel May, for example, examined the impact of local health planning agencies on hospital behavior in 144 metropolitan areas. In 1970, areas with such planning agencies had 13 percent fewer hospital beds, but 9 percent more plant, and 16 more nonplant assets per bed. Further, they used 8 percent more employees per bed.[42]

Salkever and Bice used similar statistical techniques, but they focused on investment over the period 1968–1972. They compared states that had certificate-of-need laws with those that did not have them. The states with such supply-restricting laws were found to have experienced from 3 to 9 percent slower growth in hospital beds, but 10 to 20 percent more rapid growth in investment per bed. The net result was no change

[41] Sloan, "Regulation and Hospital Care," p. 1.
[42] May, "Health Planning," p. 35.

in total investment owing to certificate-of-need controls, but a marked change in the composition of investment.[43]

Sloan used more recent data that allowed more time for the full effects of certificate-of-need regulation to be reflected in hospital costs. He found a small, but statistically significant, reduction in the growth of hospital costs, due to the regulation. Sloan also found small effects of state controls of the rates that hospitals can charge third-party insurers, which is far rarer than certificate-of-need laws.[44]

My interpretation of these results is an adaptation of Feldstein's, and it is also similar to Noll's conjecture on the effect of supply-limiting regulation.[45] The regulatory supply restriction allows hospitals to charge higher prices. Since they are legally nonprofit firms and are subject to cost-based reimbursement, the only effective way of raising prices is to raise costs by upgrading the "style of medical care" to a level considered better in quality or more sophisticated by the hospitals and medical staff.

Conclusions

Current regulation of the U.S. medical care system is partly responsible for its poor performance. Regulation of this industry is inherently difficult because its output is complex and because the influence of providers over regulation is strong. Regulatory reform to improve incentives, to make the system more responsive to consumer preferences, and to reduce the anticompetitive effects of existing regulation could be highly beneficial. Whether one considers adding to or reducing regulation, cognizance of the existing highly regulated and partly monopolistic nature of the market is necessary for accurate analysis. Further, it seems possible to mitigate the anticompetitive effects of some regulation by vigorous antitrust enforcement.[46]

[43] David S. Salkever and Thomas W. Bice, *Hospital Certificate-of-Need Controls: Impact on Investment, Costs and Use* (Washington, D.C.: American Enterprise Institute, 1979), p. 75. For similar results on the impact of regulation on the composition of hospital costs, see Frank A. Sloan and Bruce Steinwald, "Effects of Regulation on Hospital Costs and Input Use," *Journal of Law and Economics*, vol. 23 (April 1980), pp. 81–109.

[44] Sloan, "Regulation and Hospital Care," pp. 18, 21.

[45] Martin Feldstein, "Hospital Cost Inflation: A Study of Nonprofit Price Dynamics," *American Economic Review*, vol. 61 (December 1971), pp. 853–72; Roger G. Noll, "The Consequences of Public Utility Regulation of Hospitals," in *Controls on Health Care* (Washington, D.C.: Institute of Medicine, National Academy of Sciences, 1975), pp. 25–48.

[46] Antitrust activity in the medical care industry is growing rapidly. This has been partly due to the influence of William S. Comanor as head of the Bureau of Economics of the Federal Trade Commission since mid-1978. For more on the potential of antitrust activity see H. E. Frech III, "Medical Monopoly: The Potential for Antitrust Policy," *Fourth Annual Program on Antitrust in the Health Care Field, Conference Course Book*, Washington, D.C., National Health Lawyers' Association, January 7, 8, 1981.

Paying the Piper and Calling the Tune: The Relationship between Public Financing and Public Regulation of Health Care

Mark V. Pauly

Regulation in the medical care industry often takes a form similar to the pattern typical of public utility regulation—control of prices, entry, and sometimes returns. But the reason that public utilities ought to be regulated is generally not the same for hospitals. The ideal case for public utility regulation is the decreasing-cost firm, whereas empirical evidence suggests that above a fairly small size, neither hospitals nor physician practices have significantly decreasing costs. Thus the normative case for medical care regulation and the criteria that define the ideal outcome will obviously be different for the medical care industry.

Regulators and regulated firms might also be expected to behave differently in the medical care industry because of a significant distinction between the industry and other regulated industries. For the medical care industry, government not only functions as regulator, but it also functions as a *purchaser* of a major share of industry output. (In FY 1977, for example, 40 percent of personal health care expenditures were paid by public sources, as were 55 percent of hospital expenditures.) It is very likely that government's interests as payer will influence its behavior as regulator, even though the two roles are often performed by separate bureaucracies, or at different levels of government. Moreover, in its role of specifying the kind of care it will pay for, government as payer probably affects the behavior of government as regulator.

What form will such behavior take? What are the positive consequences of permitting those who finance medical care in the public sector to have a say (directly or indirectly) in its regulation? Should public payers have representation or influence on health planning and regulating bodies? What is the ideal normative outcome of the planning-regulation process, and how far away from ideal outcomes are actual outcomes likely to be? Are there institutional arrangements that will lead to improvements (somehow defined) in actual outcomes?

These are the questions to be addressed in this chapter. Much of the discussion will be concerned with hospital regulation, because that is where the bulk of regulation has occurred up to the present, but it will also consider at some length the use of regulation to permit governmental exercise of its inherent monopsony power in physician and hospital service markets.

These questions are important for public policy. The usual criticism of hospital regulation (by economists and others) has generally struck one of three themes, the dominant one being that hospital regulation has been ineffective in reducing hospital cost. Some current revisionism hints that "mature" rate regulation may be finally working, but certificate of need (CON) still appears to be a waste of regulatory resources. A second theme is that regulation in this industry, as in many others, tends to be "captured" by the regulated industry, and is either rendered ineffective or (worse) is used to yield monopoly benefits (for example, prevention of competition) to industry members. A third complaint is that even if (or when) regulation becomes effective in controlling costs, the resulting excess demand for care will lead to intolerable and/or inefficient queues or other forms of nonprice rationing.

This chapter presents a view different from each of these. It assumes (and offers some reasons for assuming) that when the public regulator is also the payer, regulation eventually can contain hospital and health care costs. Whether this task is accomplished by rate regulation or CON is not important. Some reasons are also offered for supposing that when the public regulator is also the payer, full industry capture is unlikely. Finally, though the importance of rationing inefficiencies is not denied, this chapter argues that there is a good chance of even more severe, even more adverse consequences of effective, noncaptured regulation *if public sector decision makers rationally respond to the incentives they face.* These arguments do not support a benign tolerance for regulation as a second best but politically feasible long-term substitute for market forces; they offer strong evidence for the desirability of moving toward a market solution as quickly as possible.

What Is Regulation?

Regulation is here taken to mean public-utility-style regulation—that is, regulation of entry and/or prices. In particular, this discussion will be concerned with certificate-of-need regulation and rate regulation, but it will also deal with the potential impact of fee regulation on the physician market. This type of regulation, which generally applies to all users of medical care, should be distinguished from the public regulation of the type of care provided only to public insurance beneficiaries, such as utilization review, price ceilings for government-provided care, and so forth. These sorts of practices will be referred to as "public control," and are of interest for their interactions with regulation.

Regulation can be thought of as representing a kind of public good, a set of circumstances applicable to everyone. Perhaps the easiest way to understand this concept is to suppose that the regulator determines the "style" or "quality" of care (or at least the maximum thereof). This "style" or "quality" is analogous to what economists call a public good, a good which all must consume or experience equally, and which has a resource cost. This discussion largely ignores the interaction between quality and quantity, and simply assumes that higher style means higher total cost as well as cost per unit.

The public payer exerts influence at two levels. The government that pays the bills is the same government that writes and comments on the rules within which the regulatory agency itself operates. In addition, the public agency which pays bills may also pay for some of a regulator's budget, may give it grants, and can select or dismiss it.

A Normative Theory of Hospital Regulation

In selecting the level of this public good, how ought the government to behave? What is the ideal level of quality or style, and is government regulation required or useful for achieving it?

The traditional rationale for regulation based on decreasing cost, as we have said, does not generally apply to the health care industry. But if this rationale does not apply, it does not follow that there is no rationale for regulation, for it is relatively easy to develop such a rationale and to indicate what it says about ideal outcomes, as follows.

Let D in figure 1 be a particular individual's demand curve for some aspect of quality of medical care (for example, the number of laboratory tests or nursing hours per hospital stay, or the number of minutes per physician visit). MC is the minimal marginal cost per unit of quality. Then (considerations of risk aversion aside) the optimal amount of quality is q^*. But if insurance of the cost coverage type reduces the user price of quality to P_I, the amount of quality demanded increases to q_I, and a welfare loss is suffered as the individual consumes quality worth less than its cost. This loss may be offset by risk-reduction benefits.

Suppose, however, that regulation could constrain quality closer to q^*. Then the consumer might be able to enjoy the benefits of risk reduction without (as much) moral hazard. (Note also that prices or

FIGURE 1
EFFECT OF INSURANCE ON THE DEMAND FOR QUALITY

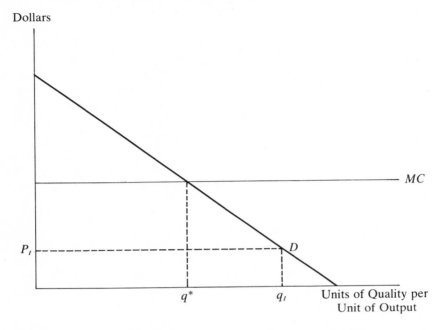

profits would generally have to be limited if supply is restricted to avoid having gains transferred to providers.) If all consumers had identical demands for quality, q^* would be the optimal target for regulation. If they had different demands—but regulation mandated a uniform level for all—then there would need to be a trade-off between quality at more appropriate levels on average and imperfect satisfaction of the demands of nonaverage individuals. The question of whether quality is or must be the same for everyone will be considered in the section, "Does Limiting Moral Hazard Have to Be a Public Good?" The main point here is that public regulation can be viewed as a collective measure to deal with the moral hazard inherent in current methods of financing in the United States. This discussion ignores the question of why the private sector has not provided such limits, or whether it is possible to locate q^* and limit quality without doing more harm than good. This latter question will be treated later. For the present, let us consider how closely regulation, given that it exists, would approximate this ideal.

For physicians' services, the same definition of optimality would apply. This analytical problem is made more complex because the physicians' market may be characterized by monopoly power and monopoly rents and because the long-run supply curve may slope upward, raising

70

the possibility of monopsonistic behavior by a large purchaser. Let us consider the "easier" hospital problem first and then turn to the issue of physicians' services.

Positive Models of Medical Care Regulation

What actual outcome is likely to be achieved by regulation? In particular, what is likely to be the influence of public payers on regulatory outcomes, and will such influence lead to better outcomes? How will actual outcomes compare with the ideal outcomes described in the preceding section? Three possible positive models of regulation are available to answer these questions: an industry capture model, a public choice model, and a political economy model.

The industry capture model suggests that the regulatory process is often created for, or comes to be captured by, the industry it regulates. Regulation then operates to maximize the well-being of firms in the industry. The theory is somewhat vague when it comes to identifying "firms in the industry": those firms in the industry in the (sometimes distant) past when regulation began; actual and potential entrants; or firms which have been in the industry for a certain period of time? To avoid this imprecision, it may be necessary to identify a set of dominant firms that really represent the industry, although the theory of which firms are or come to be dominant firms in the regulatory sense is far from complete.

In the case of hospitals, there is the added difficulty of identifying the interest of not-for-profit firms. Maximization of net money rents is not a plausible interest. One plausible alternative is the maximization of the net money rents of physicians who give orders in the hospital and from whom it obtains patients. Another plausible alternative is the maximization of the utility of the hospital administration via income-in-kind, in the form of the characteristics of hospital inputs and outputs. The most plausible alternative of all is that hospital behavior will maximize some combination of money rents for physicians and income-in-kind for administrators.

The presence of a large public payer probably makes total industry capture less likely in this industry than in others. For the moment, let us assume that a public purchaser of any service is interested in keeping down the amount paid out to providers, while providers are interested in larger revenues. With high public payment in the medical care industry, it follows that full capture is unlikely.

If we reject the total industry capture model, we still need a positive model of the behavior of the public payer qua regulator in order to predict what will happen. Such considerations lead naturally to a second

71

model in which regulation is not subject to the parochial and pecuniary interests of a powerful industry, but instead serves the preferences of voter-taxpayer-consumers to whom public officials are ultimately responsible. Such a model is more in line with arguments favoring public regulation. Since the tenure, salary, and budget of the regulator or bureaucrat are determined by politicians, and since those politicians must receive voter approval, regulatory behavior can be expected to reflect voter preferences. Even if the regulator is responsive to voter interests, however, the outcome will probably still be far from ideal.

Let us illustrate this point by means of a simple public choice model in which providers and bureaucrats are taken to be a negligible fraction of the voting public. The remainder of the population is divided into two groups: beneficiaries of public insurance and nonbeneficiaries who generally purchase private insurance and who pay the (net) taxes for the public insurance. These persons will be called "taxpayers," and the model assumes that there are more taxpayers than public beneficiaries. If the level of quality that all taxpayers desire for themselves *and* for the public beneficiaries is the same given the cost shares paid, then a public choice equilibrium in which the regulator satisfies voter preferences will coincide with the ideal. The regulator will, in satisfying those preferences, be giving correct signals with respect to the level of quality. He can achieve this level by limiting inputs to those that will produce the desired quality level and by setting prices to yield revenues equal to costs.

In this model, "consumer representatives" on regulatory boards will have the same preferences as the public insurer, so that, the "accountability" issue discussed by Marmor and Monroe[1] will be irrelevant. Regardless of whether representatives are accountable in some political sense to constituencies or whether such representatives are simply a random sample from the population, they will make the proper tradeoffs between costs and benefits. If they are subject to election, their reason for reflecting voter preferences is obvious. If they are randomly selected and concern themselves only with their private costs and benefits, they will still be making the proper choice by balancing the benefits from quality against *their own* higher insurance premiums and medical care outlays that regulatory decisions imply.

Another model would be one in which consumer-voter-taxpayers preferred different levels of uniform quality for everyone. Then even if the public payer took the broader view, and even if he had perfect

---

[1] T. Marmor and J. Monroe, "Representing Consumer Interests: Imbalanced Markets, Health Planning, and the HSAs," *Health and Society*, vol. 58 (Spring 1980), pp. 125–65.

information, the level of quality that would be a majority rule equilibrium need not be optimal. The level will reflect the preferences of the voter having median preferences for quality, so that minorities having more intense preferences on either side will find their views ignored. The public official who tried to do the optimal thing would find himself, or his legislative patron, voted out of office.

Even in this "almost ideal" case, a kind of nonoptimality arises if there is no technical reason for uniform quality to prevail for all. Is there any particular reason, for example, why the standard of four beds per thousand under which health systems agencies (HSAs) must plan, and the level of access and probability of admission delay that it implies, need apply to all groups of consumers? Different groups may have different preferences for availability versus cost. The point to be noted here is that the public-good nature of regulation may to some extent be an artificial constraint.

A third model is one in which homogeneous taxpayers desire a less expensive style of care for beneficiaries than for themselves. The style could be differentiated by convenience (waiting and travel time), by amenities (personal doctor), or possibly by clinical quality (number of tests to be run, indications for surgery). Considerable evidence indicates that when separate choice is possible, what is chosen for public beneficiaries represents a different "class" of care than what taxpayers choose for themselves. Public nursing home care, county hospitals, and the Veterans Administration (VA) system all seem to represent a style that is different from what taxpayers choose for themselves. The point is not that such "two-class" medicine is right or proper, but that such an outcome is commonly generated by the democratic political process. Development of a framework in which these different preferences can be taken into account is plausible, even when actual regulated quality must be uniform.

To understand the problem facing decision makers in the public sector, consider a simple geometric example, as shown in figure 2. Suppose that a uniform level of quality has to be decided, that the supply schedule S_1 is taken by all to be competitive, and that taxpayers are identical. Finally, suppose that D_T is the demand curve of a taxpayer for quality for himself, and that D_B is his demand curve for quality for a tax-supported public beneficiary.

The public payer must decide what level of quality he would like regulation to achieve. If he pays attention only to taxpayers' evaluation of the quality level for the beneficiaries of public insurance and the taxes that they pay for that insurance, he will in following voter preferences select quality level q_0. If he pays attention only to taxpayers' preferences

FIGURE 2
CHOICE OF QUALITY AS A PUBLIC GOOD

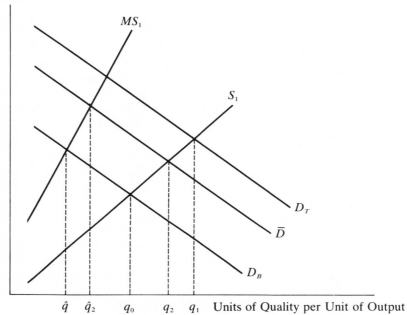

Dollars

MS_1

S_1

D_T

$\bar{D}$

D_B

$\hat{q}$ $\hat{q}_2$ q_0 q_2 q_1 Units of Quality per Unit of Output

for quality for themselves, he will choose the level represented by q_1. Since quality must be the same for all, however, a single level must be chosen.

If the public payer took a broad perspective in which he considered the interests of taxpayers in quality for themselves *and* for beneficiaries, he would choose a quality intermediate between q_0 and q_1, at quality q_2, obtained by constructing $\bar{D}$ as a weighted average of the demand curves for beneficiaries and voter-consumers. (Note that the preferred level of quality would vary directly with the ratio of taxpayers to beneficiaries.) If q_2 is chosen, however, taxpayers as consumers will be frustrated if they could otherwise have purchased quality for themselves at a price equal to marginal cost. Thus even if the public representative is doing the best he can, he is likely to be criticized for being at once too lavish for beneficiaries and too stingy for taxpayer-consumers. Public insurers, however, will probably concentrate on the costs and benefits for public beneficiaries rather than take the broader view. There are several reasons for this supposition. On one hand, the public budget is likely to be much more visible and quantifiable to the public payer than are the consequences for consumer-voter utility of various quality levels. The budget is measured, it is projected and published, and it visibly rises and causes political outcry. A higher level of payment to providers is obviously undesirable. The interests of taxpayers (as consumers) in quality are less clear, and the link between cost-containment regulation and actual quality achieved is imprecise.

From the consumer-voter-taxpayer's point of view, there are similar informational problems. The consumer knows (or hopes) that lower budgets for Medicare and Medicaid will somehow save him tax dollars. But the implications of regulation for quality are difficult for him to discern. It is easy for the bureaucrat to claim that cost savings will not come out of "real" quality, that budgets can be cut by eliminating fat and waste in the industry, or that delivering a smaller number of services (for example, less surgery) really represents higher quality.

Finally, the public payer's own objective function may be consistent with reduction in or control of payments to providers. While it has been hypothesized that bureaus prefer higher budgets and use their monopoly positions to get them,[2] this objective is supposedly desired because rewards are tied to the employees and resources *under the public official's control.* Automatic payments to providers of medical care are essentially uncontrolled distributions of largess, however, and may be thought by the bureau to represent a charge against resources that might otherwise be available for purposes it desires. Far from being maximized by the bureau, the Medicare and Medicaid budget *for payments to providers* may in fact be a target for minimization.

Thus there are two reasons for the public payer to keep down resource use by providers:

- It fits his private objectives better.
- Voters can monitor the total budget (tax funds) that a bureau receives better than they can monitor how it is divided between real medical services and objectives of the bureau.

Both the objective function of the bureau and the constraint against which it maximizes will favor restraint on payment to providers. In this sense, such behavior seems to reflect optimization by a monopoly bureau against a distorted voter demand curve, as suggested by Denzau and Mackay.[3] Even though provider payments may represent real services

[2] William Niskanen, *Bureaucracy and Representative Government* (Chicago: Aldine, 1974). Niskanen does analyze the case in which the public agency can behave as a *discriminating* monopsonist, but not the cases in which it either buys inputs competitively or as a non-discriminating monopsonist.

[3] A. Denzau and R. Mackay, "A Model of Benefit and Tax Share Discrimination by a Monopoly Bureau," *Journal of Public Economics*, vol. 9 (June 1980), pp. 341–69.

to patients (even if at excessive levels) and bureaucratic programs may not represent real benefits, bureau behavior may reduce the former and increase the latter.

For these reasons, the public payer will probably favor a level of quality more like q_0 than q_2. *If* consumer representatives were truly representative, they would favor somewhat higher levels than q_0. They would favor either q_1 if they too took a narrow view of representing consumers only as consumers, or q_2 if they took a broader view. (Note, however, that their preferred level would still be lower than the current, moral-hazard-determined level.) The significant point here is that the quality level favored by the public payer may be overly restrictive. The tendency to restrict quality is present even if the bureau is highly responsive to voter preferences (but is narrow or myopic in its outlook), and the tendency is reenforced by plausible private motivations and incentives for public officials.

The final theory of regulation to be discussed is what Noll has called the political economy theory.[4] This theory hypothesizes that decisions are not made exclusively in the regulated industry's interest, and are not even based exclusively on the politician-bureaucrat's interpretation of the voter's interest. Instead, decisions are the outcome of a process of give-and-take between industry and regulator, who fully recognize the pressures that can be brought to bear. The outcome represents the mixed interests of regulators and those being regulated, while consumer or voter interests are only weakly acknowledged.

Some considerations this theory raises are evident from the possibility for "narrow" behavior by the public payer. The political economy theory emphasizes the weakness of the link between voter preferences and regulator behavior. The extent of this weakness may be affected by the presence of the public payer. One often cited reason that the regulator comes to terms with the regulated industry is the asymmetry of information, in that the regulated industry generally has better access to information and better resources to present favorable information than either the regulator or any interested consumers. The presence of a large public payer in principle changes this situation somewhat, since the payer itself either has or can obtain information of value for regulatory as well as reimbursement purposes. Medicare cost reports, if they were reliable, would be of use to regulators. The real problem in the hospital industry is not that hospitals have data that regulators want,

[4] Roger Noll, "The Consequences of Public Utility Regulation of Hospitals," in Ruth Hanft and Paul Rettig, eds., *Controls on Health Care* (Washington, D.C.: The Institute of Medicine of the National Academy of Sciences, 1975).

but rather that the kind of data regulators would need to act sensibly—measures of output, measures of benefit, and measures of marginal cost—are things that no one, not even hospitals, has been able to collect and use.

A second reason for a weak link between regulation and the consumer-voter-taxpayer is the difference in the concentration of interests. The industry, it may be alleged, represents a highly concentrated interest whose advocates are paid for their advocacy, whereas the interest of consumers is diffuse, for the level of concern per consumer is low and advocacy is difficult to finance. The presence of a public payer does change the situation by introducing the interests of budget restraint (of taxpayer qua taxpayer). To some extent, the public payer also represents the interests of public beneficiaries. The one to be left out as a user of medical care, however, is the private consumer-patient.

HSA boards must by law have a majority of consumer representatives. In addition to the predictable problems of making sure that these persons represent consumers efficiently, there is the added difficulty that the funding and rules under which they operate—the standards, guidelines, and criteria of appropriateness—must come from the public payer. A possible consequence, given the conditions of the job of consumer representative and advancement in it, is self-selection of consumer representatives. Representatives will come to be those whose views roughly correspond to the view of the public payer. In addition, the kind of prevention of ostensible "duplication and waste" that is the mission of HSAs will attract persons who, for whatever reasons, think that providers should be constrained. The aura of professional planning helps to contribute to this tendency. While HSAs vary considerably, many have clearly taken this view, rather than advocating the interests of middle-class consumers.

One final aspect of the relation between regulation, public payment, and industry behavior should be considered. Although full-industry capture seems implausible for the medical care industry in the presence of a large public payer, there can be beneficial collusion with a *part* of the industry. Increasing rents for some part of the industry can accompany lower expenditures; then at least some hospitals would be satisfied and the regulator would be pleased to keep the budget down. The only loser would be some consumers, who would have to pay more for care at a set of possibly less convenient or less desirable hospitals. One possibility is that the larger, higher-quality teaching hospitals might emerge as the winning subset. These hospitals, the regulator, and the public payer can all gain from using regulatory power to close or restrict smaller, less sophisticated, but possibly cheaper or more convenient hospitals. Alternatively, limitation of hospital inputs, as through CON, can permit physicians with access to the remaining inputs to recoup monopoly rents through higher fees for physicians' services, even when the hospital itself does not charge more or is not permitted to do so.

Health, Regulation, Public Payment, and Monopsony Power

Thus far I have dealt with the public insurer who takes medical care prices as given and who considers quality to be uniform and to be determined only by regulation. Neither of these assumptions is really plausible, because the government will probably recognize its monopsony power in two ways:

- Its own purchasing decisions will affect price.
- In regulation of the entire market, input prices will be affected by decisions which affect the total amount of outputs and inputs if the supply is not perfectly elastic.

Let us first analyze these problems within highly simplified models and then draw out some implications for practical policy. Again, we will have two possible models of governmental behavior—one in which the two interests of the taxpayer are considered and balanced, and one in which the budget cutters hold sway.

In terms of figure 2, the relevant notional marginal cost curve for the government now becomes MS_1, a curve marginal to the true supply curve S_1.[5] If the government takes the "balancing" viewpoint, it selects level $\hat{q}_2$; if it concentrates only on the level for its beneficiaries, it sets even lower level $\hat{q}$. The main point is that regardless of which approach holds, recognition of monopsony by government implies a reduction in the quality level it prefers. Note also that in either case, the reduction is excessive compared with the optimal level discussed in the section "A Normative Theory of Hospital Regulation." Even if all demands for quality were identical, the presence of monopsony would still introduce a different quality level preferred by the public sector and those that individuals would choose privately if they could pay for different levels of quality.

Even if the bureaucrat takes the larger view, "two class" medicine will arise if public controls are available for limiting the quality of care for public beneficiaries. The reason is that he will naturally behave like a monopsonist for public beneficiaries, but may find it more difficult to do so for private beneficiaries.

---

[5] The precise position of MS_1 depends upon the assumptions the public payer makes about how its decisions affect prices.

FIGURE 3
ILLUSTRATION OF EFFICIENCY ASPECTS OF MONOPSONY BEHAVIOR

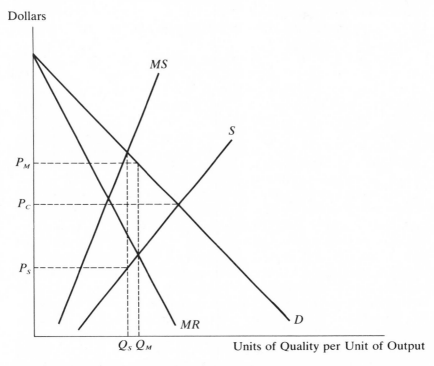

The "Broader View" Monopsonist. A somewhat different diagram will help to illustrate the efficiency issues surrounding monopsony. Let S in figure 3 be the supply curve of some type of medical service with an upward-sloping long-run supply curve. (I will ignore the question of short-run quasi rents.) Let D be the broad view (weighted average) demand curve for that service. The monopoly price would be P_M, the competitive price P_C, and the monopsony price P_S.

Welfare is maximized when the sum of consumer and producer surpluses is maximized, and this maximization of course occurs at the competitive price P_C. The movement down from P_M to P_C increases welfare, but the movement from P_C to P_S reduces welfare. The lower price reduces welfare in the sense that producers could compensate monopsonistic consumers to maintain the higher price and producers could still be better off. Of course, the different solutions also involve different distributions of real income between consumers and producers if compensation is not paid.

While P_C seems attractive as a target (and is in fact the optimal solution described in the section "A Normative Theory of Hospital Regulation"), is there any reason to prefer P_S? McMenamin[6] argues that health care suppliers are on average wealthier than beneficiaries (of public programs), and that these higher incomes may represent monopoly rents.

As a justification for monopsony behavior, "picking on the rich doctors" may not be as attractive as it might seem. First, measured purely in terms of current income, it is not obvious that health care suppliers overall have higher incomes than taxpayers. Physicians may, but do registered nurses, medical technicians, and licensed practical nurses? Second, if price falls to P_C, at that point suppliers are earning competitive returns. While physicians may have higher-than-average current incomes, these incomes would be the returns only for the investment (and lower-than-average levels of past consumption) that they have made in human capital. It would probably be difficult to make a convincing case for a social welfare function that places lower weights on individuals because of their profession (medicine) or their preference for investment in human capital.

A case can be made, of course, for enforcing the movement from P_M to P_C. Whether such a movement is of practical importance depends on the extent of monopoly power in the medical industry and its source. The evidence of the existence of monopoly rents for physicians' services is conflicting and inconclusive. There could probably be substantial short-run reductions in physician fee levels without causing a serious reduction in quantity or quality, even in a competitive market. A more realistic model than one depicting pure competition or pure monopoly might be one of monopolistic competition in which the welfare effects of mandated price reductions, and even the meaning of a "competitive" level, are ambiguous. What we can say is that quality or access will decline as price is reduced (at least in the long run).

For hospital services or inputs to hospital services, the results are even less definitive. Direct monopoly rents by nonprofit hospitals are implausible. Hospitals may be burning up would-be monopoly profits in excessive quality, but then the implications of reducing price are to reduce quality. Surely there is no evidence that price reductions will only result in a reduction in slack or inefficiency.

There may also be some classes of hospital employees who earn monopoly rents. There is some evidence that registered nurses, for

[6] Peter McMenamin, "On the Welfare Economics of Government Subsidized Demand for Health Care," Working Paper OR–1, U.S. Department of Health and Human Services, Health Care Financing Administration, Office of Research Demonstration and Statistics, September 1980.

example, may recently have obtained differential rent[7] and that all classes of hospital employees receive philanthropic surpluses.[8] Nonetheless, should we allow social policy to cut medical costs by reducing the incomes of nurses and orderlies? And will limits on public payments to hospitals, on hospital rates, or on hospital capital investment necessarily have this effect? One can argue that limits on capital investment will indeed prompt excessive substitution of labor for capital[9] and will bid up rents for hospital-specific occupations that substitute for capital.

If rents were earned by physicians in their hospital practices, then it is possible for a reduction in hospital inputs to cause an increase in physician fees and an increase in rents. We cannot be sure of the outcome, because there will also be a substitution of physician for hospital inputs if hospital inputs are reduced. The main point is that it will not be easy for the public sector to use its monopsony power appropriately with respect to hospitals.

The Narrow Monopsonist. There are some problems in achieving optimality even if the public payer had an idealized broad perspective. If the payer takes the narrower focus, problems are likely to be more severe. The payer intent on reducing outlays has no incentive to stop pushing provider prices down just because the competitive level is reached. An overuse of market power is likely, once the possibility of exercising it is opened.

Influence over regulation extends the payer's monopsony power. If a bureau tries to reduce the prices it pays by controls on its payments, providers can respond by shifting to the private market. Regulation provides a way of controlling the entire market, however, and thus limits the ability of providers to avoid monopsony. But since the exercise of monopsony by government is not necessarily socially beneficial (or just), the use of regulation to extend monopsony is not necessarily a good thing.

The basic message for policy is that endorsing government exercise of monopsony power, either in its role as payer or in its role as regulator, is potentially dangerous. Government monopsony *could* be beneficial if the evidence for monopoly were strong and the evidence that the government would stop at the competitive level existed. But the former

---

[7] See Victor Fuchs, "The Earnings of Allied Health Personnel—Are Health Workers Underpaid?" *Explorations in Economic Research*, vol. 3 (Summer 1976), pp. 123–41.

[8] M. S. Feldstein, *The Rising Cost of Hospital Care* (Washington, D.C.: Information Resources Press, 1971).

[9] Philip Held and Mark Pauly, "Charging the Victim: An Evaluation of Reimbursement Policy in the U.S. End Stage Renal Disease Program," unpublished paper, Department of Economics, Northwestern University, November 1980.

is weak and the latter is nonexistent, so that perhaps one should search for alternative devices. At least we should be cautious about permitting the exercise of such power.

Does Limiting Moral Hazard Have to Be a Public Good?

Up to this point the public good nature of regulation has been taken as given. It is useful, however, to ask whether control of moral hazard *must* be accomplished in this way, and to investigate the consequences of requiring the maximum level of resource intensity or quality to be determined publicly when such determination is unnecessary.

Pure Public Goods. Some decisions regulatory bodies make do seem to be necessarily universal. Decisions on the existence or nonexistence of certain specialized and uncommon types of facilities are of a pure public-good character. Although the *existence* of a facility may be a public good, however, the *use* of the facility need not be, for different groups can be entitled to use it in different amounts. The public payer, for example, might desire a lower-than-average level of use for its beneficiaries. The critical question then is whether differing levels of use can be achieved.

Impure Public Goods and Externalities. Most medical regulatory activity affects most resident and providers, but not in the same way, because regulation is not really a pure public good. People who live close to a particular provider, or who typically use that provider, will be more affected by limits on the output or fees of that provider than persons who rarely use it; regulation is not consumed or experienced "equally." In a similar way, public beneficiaries will be more affected by controls on their own benefit levels than by the controls (if any) on benefit levels of others.

Some spillover effects between providers or between groups of beneficiaries, however, are likely. In part, these spillovers are artificial. They arise from the presence of community rating in private insurance and from the federal tax financing of Medicare and Medicaid. In either case, the level of quality (and cost) in one area affects the well-being of people in other areas. There may also be spillovers between quality levels. An increase in quality for one set of consumers may cause physicians or hospitals to change the quality they provide to other consumers, or in other areas. Such a spillover is to be expected if physicians follow the "norms" hypothesis, and treat all patients in a similar way.[10]

[10] See J. Harris, "The Aggregate Coinsurance Rate and the Supply of Innovations in the Hospital Sector," unpublished paper, Department of Economics, Massachusetts Institute

In this "impure" case, results may be worse than in cases of pure public goods. If no regulation exists, the presence of externalities means that independent actions will not lead to optimality. For example, if the public payer uses control of benefits to lower the quality or style for public beneficiaries, the style for all will be lowered. High style chosen by a set of private insureds will increase the taxes of persons in other parts of the country who must pay for at least a higher style for public beneficiaries.

Regulation does not, however, provide an obvious solution to such externalities. Ideal regulation is ideal, but the usual positive theory of collective choice for such impure public goods concludes that at least some projects would be carried forward to an excessive extent.[11] Vote trading, deal swapping, and pork barreling all lead to excessive levels for projects favored by a dominant group. These observations would be especially applicable to the behavior of consumer representatives.

How does the presence of public regulation affect these predictions? The result would seem to be a kind of imposed "publicness." General federal planning standards mean that in some sense improvements for one area have an opportunity cost in terms of project approvals for other areas. There is also larger scope for an alliance of payer-regulators and a subgroup of providers.

These observations lead to two major conclusions. First, the existence of public payment may help to explain why the pork barreling that some analysts forecasted for hospital regulation has not occurred, at least not in an obvious way. Second, the presence of public influence is likely to lead to aggregate underprovision in the impure public good–political economy case, just as in the pure public good case, although there may be areas of overprovision within that aggregate underprovision.

Spillovers. If spillovers do exist, there *may* still be a need for regulation, as imperfect as that regulation is likely to be. The critical questions are: To what extent are spillovers actually present? Do the spillovers *need* to be there? Perhaps the spillover problem is not of great importance, since the norms hypothesis has not been definitively tested. Perhaps the importance of quality spillovers is small—ordering quality à la carte is possible. At least, there may be organizational structures that minimize

---

of Technology, July 1979; Joseph Newhouse and M. S. Marquis, "The 'Norms' Hypothesis and the Demand for Medical Care," *Journal of Human Resources, Supplement,* (1978), pp. 159–82; M.V. Pauly, "Overinsurance: The Conceptual Issues," in M.V. Pauly, ed., *National Health Insurance: What Now, What Later, What Never?* (Washington, D.C.: American Enterprise Institute, 1980).

[11] James Buchanan and Gordon Tullock, *The Calculus of Consent* (Ann Arbor: University of Michigan Press, 1962), chap. 9–10.

spillovers. The impact of quality on federal expenditures might then be handled by placing controls only on the public insurance rather than by imposing such standards on all through regulation. Here again, some organizational structures may be able to control public beneficiary quality or style with minimal spillovers.

Conclusions and Remedies

The main conclusion of this discussion is that public payer influence on health care regulation is likely to pull too far in the direction of quality reduction. This tendency must be set against the incentives in current insurance to overprovide quality. To get a horse that is galloping north to go west, it may be necessary to pull strongly to the south, even though the south is not the intended direction of travel. The problem for us is that we do not know which way is west, so that we do not know whether all the current pushing and pulling will result in the right vector. It would be comforting to have a system that automatically sends the horse in the right direction.

Another obvious conclusion is that in practice governments are unlikely to achieve the optimal result described in the section "A Normative Theory of Regulation." We know that actual governments are always imperfect, but it is nonetheless useful to investigate the form imperfection is likely to take. The relevant questions are whether some ways of organizing regulation are better than others, and (more fundamentally) whether some regulation is better than existing or alternative market arrangements without regulation.

The preceding analysis is consistent with three alterations—in political-procedural, analytical, and organizational arrangements—which might improve systems of regulation. The political implication is that the influence of keepers of the public purse on regulation may be detrimental unless they can be induced to take the "wide view." Given current incentives and current kinds of information, even a well-meaning public payer will find it difficult to take such a view. Some method of opening to voter scrutiny regulatory decisions on the trade-off between cost saving and quality would be useful. Rather than have the issue shunted off to the Health Resources Administration or to the Health Care Financing Administration as a technical problem in regulatory procedure, planning standards or reimbursements should be determined by Congress, which is presumably subject to direct voter control.

But Congress's time for addressing such issues is limited. Congress may even be aware of the choices being made at present and either approves of them and/or wants to keep them concealed. This is, of course, the dilemma of the policy analyst—if government is made endogenous, the theory that explains why government behaves imperfectly can also be made to show that the same government will not be eager to accept advice on how to improve itself. Nevertheless, it still seems worthwhile to present the arguments in the hope that they may lead to some change.

A second change, which would complement the first, would involve an explicit attempt to assemble information for the task of trading off costs and benefits. This task is the essence of regulation. Health regulation is not a matter of determining some technically knowable standards, based on the techniques of a legitimate science known as health planning, nor is it based on some measurable and valid health needs. There are no such standards, there is no such science, and there are no such needs. The job of evaluation cannot be avoided by trying to cloak it in a false professionalism.

Up to the present, there has been no serious attempt to measure these benefit or cost changes in order to assist in making decisions. If decisions are to be made rationally by the Congress or anyone else, such information is surely needed. We need to know what cost savings regulations accomplish (not just what they squeeze from one compartment to another), what reductions they bring about in things people value—comfort, dignity, convenience, even the probability of life and death—and what values people attach to these things.

The organizational change would be different. It would not try to improve the collective decision-making process but would try to let the government off the hook of controlling moral hazard by letting someone else do it. Market choices by consumers of whatever *private* regulators and regulations they prefer could substitute for imposed public regulation. There are many ways of increasing the efficiency of such market choices, ranging from removal of existing distortive influences such as professional collusion and nonneutral taxation through organizational forms such as health maintenance organizations and health alliances. The idea is that there can be differences in quality levels (at least for large markets) so that consumers can choose the quality of style they most prefer and insurance premiums can reflect the cost consequences of their choices.

One final point can be made in favor of the competitive strategy. If both normative considerations and political exigencies will lead to a different style of care for public beneficiaries, then obviously beneficiaries should not be included in all competitive plans. It will be efficient for some plans to exclude such beneficiaries (unless they pay an additional charge) on the grounds that the style of care appropriate for them, given the relevant trade-offs and the amount that government is paying on their behalf, will differ from the style of care appropriate for plan members.

Does this then raise the specter of "two class" medicine? I think not. What a competitive system would involve is not "two class" but "dozen class" medicine, with different styles of care for many different preferences and resources. The object then would be to mix public beneficiaries with nonbeneficiaries having similar preferences. A voucher arrangement is a logical way to do this, for example, one that permitted (and perhaps encouraged with partial matching) those public beneficiaries who wished to do so to obtain "rich taxpayer style" care. Our goal should be anonymity, not uniformity, in a way that best satisfies the values people place on equity for others and free choice for themselves.

Failures to Control Health Costs: Departures from First Principles

Richard Zeckhauser and Christopher Zook

Recent government efforts to control health care costs through direct regulation have met with little success. Medical costs remain high and are increasing, despite the institution of a complicated, economically inefficient, and hard-to-manage collection of regulatory programs. Some studies suggest those programs may actually have increased total system costs. At best, they have had little measurable effect. Was the original diagnosis of the health cost problem incorrect? Was the wrong treatment applied? Or, was the correct treatment applied in an ineffective or weak fashion? Answers to these questions are needed to shape health care policy in the 1980s.

We argue that the traditional methods of government regulation cannot be expected to succeed when applied to medical care. The present approach to regulating health care providers developed (1) without a clear understanding of the problem at hand, but with a strong sense that "something" had to be done to contain medical costs; and (2) without careful assessment of such important alternatives as private-sector regulation by insurance companies and other nongovernmental third-party payers, or without careful use of incentives by the government. To set the problem in the proper analytic perspective, we examine the a priori reasons to regulate any private market and the common arguments as to why traditional regulation should play a major role in the health care sector. We then identify the conditions that favor traditional regulation and show that the health sector for the most part does not possess these characteristics. Thus, only if some special, compelling arguments for regulation could be made would we pursue that course as our primary approach to containing health care costs. We come to the opposite conclusion, both on an a priori basis and through a review of experience,

Glen Elliott, David Ellwood, Nancy Jackson, Elena Nightengale, and participants at the AEI Conference gave us helpful comments.

that health care should be one of the *last* candidates for traditional regulation and one of the first areas in which to develop appropriate incentives.

Reasons for Government Intervention into Private Markets

Market failures or imperfections—most often externalities, anticompetitive behavior, inadequate information—and/or a concern for distributional equity traditionally have justified American government interference into private economic transactions. Notable market failings do exist in the medical care sector and provide a reason why current outcomes may deviate substantially from an ideal outcome. This raises the questions (addressed in concluding sections) of whether government participation can be expected to improve matters and if so, of what relative advantages would be offered by traditional regulatory versus incentive-based approaches.[1]

Externalities. Externalities of consumption and production historically have justified government intervention into private activities. When an economic activity confers unintended costs or benefits upon a third party, that activity is typically occurring at a nonoptimal level. Since private decisions generally do not account for such public costs and benefits, collective action is often taken to alter the private calculus and to increase social welfare.

Three principal types of externality can be identified. *Real externalities* are epitomized by the spillover problem that arises when the factory's smoke dirties the laundry's wash. The policy issue in this typical case is how to induce optimal behavior—through allocation of property rights, externally imposed taxes, or administrative fiat. Two public health examples will illustrate how government can respond to a recognized externality. Every individual who is vaccinated against infectious disease presents his neighbor with an external benefit; hence certain inoculations are mandatory. Every drunken driver raises the probability of injury for all other unsuspecting drivers and pedestrians; therefore the government prohibits this activity and devotes resources

---

[1] Market failures can be thought of as special cases in which transaction costs defeat an efficient allocation of resources. In choosing a mode of organization in such circumstances, the objective should be to minimize the sum of transaction costs plus misallocation costs. (Both are zero in the hypothetical, perfectly competitive market.) In choosing among allocation procedures in which the government is a participant, transaction costs may be a major consideration. For example, considerable resources may be expended attempting to influence government decisions. We are indebted to Christopher DeMuth for discussions on this subject, which we expect to be a fruitful area for future inquiry.

to curtailing it. Real externalities, however, are not a primary cause for government regulation in medical care.

Pecuniary externalities occur whenever a change in behavior alters the market demand or supply curve. Thus actions by one participant affect the prices faced by others in the market. Although government intervention prompted by pecuniary externalities may be politically valid, it cannot be justified on the grounds of market failure, since pecuniary externalities merely reflect the working of the market system and entail no loss of efficiency.

Much of the escalation in medical care costs has been due to the pecuniary externality by which new insurance, entitlement, and expenditure programs have bid up the prices of factors of production already in the health care sector. Such insurance-induced increases in costs undoubtedly have played a major role in promoting government regulation of health care.

Financial externalities arise whenever one individual's consumption of a good reduces the real income of other individuals, because the individual is charged less than the full resource cost of the good and the others must pay the difference. This situation provides an incentive for excessive consumption, a phenomenon that is referred to as "moral hazard." Such undercharging at the time of consumption is a central fact of American medical care. Each individual's use of health services, which is turned into a common property resource through insurance, leads to higher payments for all, paid either directly as insurance premiums, or indirectly through taxes or a reduction in funds available for other public purposes. Rather than altering incentives for this type of excessive consumptive behavior, government intervention has directly regulated inputs (certificates of need), clinical practices (professional standard review organizations), or facility location and expansion (health systems agencies). Financial externalities do lead to inefficiency, since individuals will be "demanding services" that they value at less than the cost of producing them.

Inadequate Information. The unregulated market may deviate from the social ideal because market participants have incomplete or distorted information. Such information asymmetry creates an "agency" problem between the doctor and the patient,[2] and provides a potential justification for government intervention.

The patient entering the physician's office with a painful swelling can often be persuaded to follow any regimen suggested by the physician,

---

[2] Kenneth Arrow, "Uncertainty and the Welfare Economics of Medical Care," *American Economic Review,* vol. 53 (December 1963), pp. 941–73.

from returning home and taking aspirin to subjecting himself to a costly battery of diagnostic tests. This would still be true, though perhaps for a slightly smaller percentage of individuals, if the patient had to pay the full cost of the tests. The doctor (supplier), not the patient (consumer), determines the outcome. The solution is not to provide the patient with complete information. He would not know how to process it, or even how to assess whether it is correct. However, several approaches to correcting the imbalance of information have proved useful. Information can be provided at points of frequent or important decisions. Examples of measures that have been tried (but were not necessarily effective) include second-opinion programs in surgery, public dissemination of findings suggesting that radical mastectomy is not necessary in many cases of breast cancer, and the requirement that pharmacists and drug manufacturers provide package inserts and other labeling about over-used drugs. Incentives also can be imposed on providers to act in a more cost-effective manner when entering a range of "flat-of-the-curve medicine," that is, where further resource expenditures yield little medical gain; this is an alleged benefit of prospective reimbursement for common procedures. Difficult problems arise, however, when potential gains in diagnostic accuracy or therapeutic effectiveness are traded off against dollars, even when incentives are in no way perverse.

Collusive or Anticompetitive Behavior. Government often intervenes in monopoly and oligopoly to prevent the "unfair application of market power." The extreme case would be natural monopoly, as in the telephone industry, or the regional monopoly that results from economies of scale in electric utilities. The market power rationale applies in only limited fashion to the medical care sector, where there are more than 7,000 hospitals, more than 380,000 physicians, and countless specialized clinics and care centers. In small communities, a hospital or even a physician may exercise market power. More broadly, medical associations can restrict competition, most easily through restrictions on behavior, such as ruling out the advertising of prices. Where anticompetitive behavior is observed, the natural question is whether traditional antitrust remedies are appropriate, since competition does seem to be a possibility, or whether we should move immediately to regulation.[3] For instance, modern technology and a more competitively oriented regulatory environment are reducing the monopoly power of the tele-

---

[3] The Federal Trade Commission recently issued an order against the American Medical Association limiting its ability to ban the advertising of prices by its members. (The order survived a challenge in the Second Circuit Court.) Here the traditional antitrust approach of barring impediments to information flow was favored over a regulatory approach such as trying to set prices.

phone company. Might there be an equivalent potential for promoting competition in the medical care market?

The absence of competition may be attributed to widespread insurance, to the nonprofit character of most hospitals, and to government regulation that has suppressed the few competitive forces that remain. In medical care the absence of strong competition or incentives to be efficient is not due primarily to oligopoly or monopoly, but to political and institutional barriers. Attempts to close even the smallest, most inefficient health care facilities repeatedly encounter this institutional barrier to competition. Shutting down large-scale facilities is more difficult still, since their political support is likely to be proportionally stronger, as recent attempts to close highly inefficient medical facilities in New York City have shown. And although it is generally easier to deny permission for new facilities than to remove them once they are in place, political pressures have often thwarted efforts to prevent hospitals from adding unjustified facilities, the primary purpose of the certificate-of-need program.

Distributional Equity. Considerations of distributional equity sometimes justify government intervention in the marketplace. Dollars determine the allocation of goods in free markets. Proponents of intervention often argue that the distribution of wealth should not determine the availability of goods such as adequate housing, medical care, or education.[4] Difficult social choices arise in defining the level at which such goods should be guaranteed by public programs. In medical care, where prices of many services at the margin have been driven near zero with insurance, we may have gone too far.

Summary of the justification for government intervention. Suppose that an appropriate price structure for medical-care services were established. Even then, traditional economic justifications for government regulation might remain. Given the natural and appropriate use of insurance, the health care consumption of one individual will always impose externalities on others. Information in the health care sector is transmitted imperfectly and will always be principally in the hands of expert providers, not consumers. Yet, these economic justifications may have played a relatively small role in the actual motivation for government participation in the field of health care. Pecuniary externalities, the general belief that there was a crisis of costs in the health sector,

---

[4] It is important to recognize the inefficiency inherent in this mode of redistribution and the fact that it may injure the interests of the poor if the overall level of resource transfers is limited. See A. Hylland and R. J. Zeckhauser, "Distributional Objectives Should Affect Taxes But Not Program Choice or Design," *Scandinavian Journal of Economics*, vol. 81 (June 1979), pp. 264–84.

and the wish to assure the equitable distribution of medical care have all helped to justify and structure regulatory interventions.

Certainly, our present pricing structure for medical care is far from appropriate, at least in the sense that prices do not guide resource allocation decisions toward efficiency. It is the exception rather than the rule when the present system rewards either providers or consumers for conserving resources. We believe that much government regulation has developed as a means for coping with the warped incentives attendant upon the present system—which is itself largely an outgrowth of government programs. What, then, has been the record of these regulatory programs?

Regulatory Responses to Hospital Costs

Primarily as a result of Medicare and Medicaid, hospital expenditures by the federal government have grown from $0.4 billion in 1964 to $7.6 billion in 1968, $14.5 billion in 1972, and about $45 billion in 1980. In part, this trend represents a direct transfer of economic burden from the private to the public sector. But it is also symptomatic of an unprecedented growth in total medical expenditures (public plus private), from 4.5 percent of GNP in 1955 to 5.9 percent in 1965 and almost 9 percent in 1980.

Hospital costs are a particular concern. Since 1970, total hospital expenditures have doubled in inflation-adjusted dollars. Moreover, the share of all medical expenses devoted to hospital care has grown from 31 percent in 1950 to over 45 percent today. Fiscal incentives are especially scarce in this sector; at present 94 percent of hospital revenues are received from third-party payers, rather than from the patient receiving the care.

From the individual's perspective, the full extent of these health care costs has been masked by the fact that they are increasingly covered by taxes. The share of personal health expenses paid by federal and state governments has risen from less than 25 percent in 1966 to 33 percent in 1971 and 40 percent today. The public share of hospital revenues is still higher, 55 percent.

Although the individual cannot see the pie being sliced up, an increasing proportion of his tax dollar is going into health care. Fully 13 percent of the federal budget is now devoted to health care expenditures, up from 4 percent in 1963. When taxes, insurance payments, and direct expenditures are totaled, the average American today commits more than a month of his yearly labor to securing medical protection.

Growth in expenditures, prices, and federal budget commitment to health care raised political anxiety and led to legislation for traditional forms of regulation in health service delivery. These programs included case-by-case medical record review by a committee deciding on "appropriate" practice (professional standards review organizations, or PSROs), hospital investment constraints with case-by-case government review (certificate of need), local federally funded planning committees (health systems/agencies), and additional doctor inputs into each surgery decision (second-opinion programs). Complete revenue control for each of the 7,000 hospitals in the United States, a particularly emphatic form of regulation, has also been proposed in Congress, the last time with presidential support.

To evaluate these public policies it is essential to know their effect on utilization (if any), their net marginal benefits, and their performance relative to other alternatives.[5]

The professional standard review organization (PSRO) program was introduced in 1972 in an effort by the Department of Health, Education, and Welfare (HEW) to reduce marginally useful hospital admissions, days, and procedures through case-by-case record review and identification of deviations from "standard practice." In this classic form of command-and-control regulation, hospitals that do not meet certain standards are denied payments under Medicaid and Medicare. The costs of this sort of review run to about twenty dollars per record; the program's effectiveness remains unclear.

Studies of PSRO programs in Utah[6] and New Mexico[7] have shown no effect on utilization in spite of high administrative costs. Studies in Colorado apparently show a large effect on admissions. The Colorado results (unlike Utah or New Mexico), however, contain a flaw in method, failing to adjust for secular declines in overall admissions that were already under way before the PSRO program.[8] Adjustments for these effects make the results more ambiguous as to PSRO effectiveness. A 1977 HEW review of 172 PSROs over 1974–1976 also found that physician record review had little impact on utilization and suggested that utilization was not reduced by even the amount needed to cover direct administrative costs (1.5–2.0 percent).[9]

---

[5] See also Steinwald and Sloan, this volume, for a further evaluation of the empirical evidence. They, too, find few positive effects from existing regulatory approaches.

[6] Paul A. Bonner, "On Site Concurrent Hospital Utilization Review: An Evaluation of Impact on Utilization Patterns and Expenditures" (Ph.D. diss., Harvard School of Public Health, 1976).

[7] Robert H. Brook and Kathleen N. Williams, "Evaluation of the New Mexico Peer Review System, 1971–1973," Supplement to *Medical Care,* vol. 14 (December 1976).

[8] U.S. Congress, Congressional Budget Office, *Expenditures for Health Care: Federal Programs and Their Effects,* 1977.

[9] Mark R. Chassin, "The Containment of Hospital Costs: A Strategic Assessment," Supplement to *Medical Care,* vol. 16 (October 1978).

Evidence of positive PSRO impact on utilization came from study of the Massachusetts Medicaid program from 1974 to 1977.[10] This study estimated that Medicaid utilization rates decreased by 5 percent relative to their non-Medicaid groups because of a two-year program of PSRO review. A close look at the data, however, indicates that the Medicaid group's average length of stay was merely brought closer to the average level of the population from a much higher level in the prereview period. It is possible that small changes in insurance rate redesign might have achieved these relatively small reductions in utilization at a fraction of the administrative cost and deadweight efficiency loss.

Certificate of need (CON) is a state-administered program of hospital investment control begun in 1972 that requires that any single capital expenditure above some threshold, often $100,000, be approved by the state department of public health. This sort of case-by-case input control requires explicit trade-offs between a new pediatric ward in a small community hospital versus diagnostic equipment for a big city hospital center. CON also encounters more fundamental problems:

- CON may tend to prevent entry of new types of providers whose long-run costs will be lower than those of existing suppliers.

- CON may freeze existing service configurations by making change through new investment more difficult.

- CON fosters a maze of special exceptions and political "end runs" through the state legislature, in part because of the exceedingly difficult trade-offs it creates.

The major study of CON is by Salkever and Bice,[11] who use state hospital cost data from 1968 to 1972. They found no evidence that CON reduced aggregate investment. CON may, however, have an unintended influence on the mix of investment by type, size, and location. For instance, Britton[12] found that large, powerful, and more sophisticated hospitals in Massachusetts were more successful in obtaining equipment under CON than were other hospitals. As Chassin suggests in a study of hospital cost containment programs, "The available data, therefore, support the hypothesis that CON legislation will not control total investment in hospitals."[13] Using current data, more recent research by Policy Analy-

---

[10] A. Fulchario et al., "Can the PSRO's Be Cost Effective?" *New England Journal of Medicine,* vol. 299 (September 1978), pp. 574–80.

[11] D. S. Salkever and T. W. Bice, "The Impact of Certificate of Need Controls on Hospital Investment," *Milbank Memorial Fund Quarterly,* vol. 54 (Spring 1976), pp 185–213; *Hospital Certificate-of-Need Controls: Impact on Investment, Costs, and Use* (Washington, D.C.: American Enterprise Institute, 1979).

[12] Charles Britton, "Certificate of Need Legislation in Health Care Delivery" (Ph.D. diss., Massachusetts Institute of Technology, Sloan School of Management, 1975).

[13] Chassin, "The Containment of Hospital Costs," p. 26.

sis, Inc.,[14] and by Joskow[15] confirms the insignificant effect of CON programs on hospital costs or revenues. Investment controls of this type can distort the mix of investment, politicize decisions to acquire capital equipment, and entail nontrivial administrative cost.

Less thorough evaluation has been made of the more than 200 health systems agencies that are currently "planning" health facilities distribution, or of the second-opinion-in-surgery programs. Experience suggests, however, that these traditional forms of direct regulation through the setting of standards or through case-by-case outcome review are unlikely to be very effective.

We have focused here on methods to regulate the quantity, type, or use of medical inputs. Another form of public intervention is rate setting by state governments; in general it is applied to reimbursement to hospitals under Medicaid and Medicare (although a few programs apply to all insurance payments by providers). Recent evidence indicates that hospital cost inflation is moderated by rate setting.[16] However, attempts to use rate setting to control hospital costs while preserving economic efficiency will encounter several difficult problems:[17]

- defining the unit for pricing (day, disease, treatment)
- adjusting prices in the future to reflect new conditions, particularly if regulation drives prices further out of step from resource costs
- monitoring quality responses to pricing while avoiding pyramiding regulation[18]

We next examine circumstances under which regulation is and is not likely to be effective. In many ways the poor performance of regulation

---

[14] Policy Analysis, Inc., *Evaluation of the Effect of Certification of Need Progress* (Cambridge, Mass.: 1980).

[15] Paul Joskow, "Alternative Regulatory Mechanisms for Controlling Hospital Costs," this volume.

[16] Brian Biles, Carl J. Schramm, and J. Graham Atkinson, "Hospital Cost Inflation under State Rate-Setting Programs," *New England Journal of Medicine*, vol. 303 (September 18, 1980), pp. 664–68; and Harold Cohen and Carl Schramm, "A Design for Resolving the Conflicts Resulting from Separate Regulation of Hospital Rates and Hospital Capacity," this volume.

[17] For a more detailed analysis, see Katherine Bauer, "Hospital Rate Setting—the Way to Salvation?" in M. Zubkoff, I. E. Raskin, and R. S. Hanft, eds., *Hospital Cost Containment; Selected Notes for Future Policy* (New York: PRODIST, 1978), pp. 224–69; or Fred Hellinger, "The Effects of Certificate of Need Legislation on Hospital Investment," *Inquiry*, vol. 13 (June 1976), pp. 187–93.

[18] For instance, a prospective rate of $1,000 for angiography and evaluation in the hospital could result in larger numbers of short visits, in out-of-hospital billing for certain diagnostic tests, or some other change in the type of visit initially defined as "admission for angiograph" but in response to the set rate redefined by the provider to increase cash flow. The complexity of defining the service provided by the hospital or predicting patient costs based on some fixed, observable variable that cannot be manipulated or redefined by the provider, is a major problem for this form of government intervention.

in medicine should not be surprising. Both empirical data and economic logic suggest that incentives, not command-and-control regulation, should be the predominant public interventions in the field of health care.

Conditions Most Favorable to "Traditional" Modes of Regulation

Experience is gradually teaching us that traditional forms of government regulation—such as those in effect at present in the medical care sector—can function well under certain conditions, but very poorly under others. Deregulation of the natural gas, airline, and trucking industries reflects an awakening to the importance of fit between the economic situation and regulatory approach.

On the basis of an examination of these experiences and economic logic, we can define the economic conditions that seem to favor regulation. These are discussed in turn below.

The fact that these conditions are seldom found in medical care raises doubts about the effectiveness of direct regulation there. The principal reason for regulatory failure in medical care may well be this "mismatch," not poor implementation or weak sanctions. Our review of the economic characteristics of the health care industry suggests that carefully tailored financial incentives could be far more effective than regulation.

Natural Monopoly. Natural monopolies are conducive to direct regulation. They arise when, for example, there is a single proprietary resource, an insuperable entry barrier, or extremely pronounced economies of scale. In such situations, the unregulated market would tend toward excessive prices and suboptimal output. Regulation can be exceedingly complex, however, even in the case of a single economic unit in a relatively well-defined situation producing one commodity (electricity, phone communications, postage).

The medical care industry is by no means a natural monopoly. There are at present 7,000 hospitals, many of small size relative to their regional market, and more than 380,000 physicians, most of whom practice privately. Barriers to entry are characteristically low; almost any group of clinicians can easily set up a business. Finally, there is relatively little formal collusion, although certain practices such as restrictions on advertising, whatever their initial motivation, may produce collusive results.

The Industry Produces One or a Few Homogeneous Products. Traditional government regulation is likely to be more effective when it is dealing with a single product or a few items that can be standardized for rate setting, or quality regulation. Examples are mileage standards, auto inspection requirements, electricity, and gasoline. Yet even homogeneous product regulations such as these can easily stir up definitional issues the resolution of which consumes resources and clouds decisions. For instance, oil price regulation becomes much more complex when the product is broken down into old oil, new oil, and stripper oil.

Few services compare with medicine in diversity and heterogeneity. First, the number of different tests and relatively standard procedures in a hospital runs into the hundreds. Medical care is a sequence of actions carried out through time and is difficult to standardize. Second, each disease typically requires specialized resources and treatment modes. Even within a narrow diagnostic category there may be substantial differences in the expected cost of illness and the required treatment (a problem plaguing proposals for prospective reimbursement by diagnosis). Third, the most complex, difficult to characterize cases consume the majority of medical resources. In the typical hospital, the high-cost 12 percent of patients account for more resources (on an annual basis) than the other 88 percent.[19] These high-cost patients would be almost impossible to classify and regulate using broad standards.

The complexity of the medical product has also made it relatively easy for institutions to adapt to regulation in a manner that works against the original intent of the regulation. Constrained by the capital controls imposed through certificate-of-need regulation, hospitals can emphasize services. If per diem reimbursement rates are fixed, such institutions can push up lengths of stay and occupancy rates. When subjected to the scrutiny of PSROs, doctors may be slightly more assiduous in recording ambiguous symptoms. There is a strong judgment component in any medical decision; moreover, the condition of patients changes continuously. The regulator, not being present when decisions are made, is at a strong disadvantage. He cannot determine to what extent the regulated decision maker has changed his actions in a manner that frustrates the intent of the regulatory action.

Low Elasticities Favor Traditional Regulation. Direct regulation is more likely to be the preferred alternative if incentives, reward, and penalty structures have little effect on behavior. Debate over government regulation can often be reduced to disagreement over the empirical magnitude of elasticities of supply and demand—those who believe elasticities are low tend to favor direct regulation.

---

[19] Christopher J. Zook and Francis D. Moore, "The High Cost Users of Medical Care," *New England Journal of Medicine,* vol. 302 (May 1, 1980), pp. 996–1002.

If the demand for oil was perfectly inelastic over several years, arguments for rationing would be greatly strengthened. If the supply of housing (including its quality) was found to be inelastic, arguments for rent controls would be more persuasive. If price and profit responses in the economy were weak, wage and price control might hold more policy promise. In general, the higher the elasticities, the greater the potential for workable financial incentives. The higher the elasticities, the greater the likelihood that inflexible regulation will create deadweight efficiency losses in the economy.

As we argue in a later section of this chapter, the medical care sector appears to be characterized by substantial long-run elasticities of demand and supply. The industry will react to financial incentives.

Large Arenas with a Few Poor Performers Can Be Regulated. Traditional regulatory approaches are favored where the problem is the existence of a few poor performers. Minimum standards and case-by-case review are more likely to succeed in changing the behavior of a small number of extreme cases than a multitude of average performers. Common examples are university accreditation, auto safety regulation, SEC rules to prevent stock swindles, and regulations to prevent the selling of contaminated foods. Examples also exist in health care in the licensing of nursing homes and the policing of hospital incompetence and dangerous practice.

The "large arena with a few poor performers" argument is not the rationale for major government initiatives in health care, however. Here the problem is that all segments and providers seem to be characterized by excessive utilization and high (and rising) costs. The regulatory objective has been to foster the cost-effective use of resources by the majority, not to control a small, extreme group of severe offenders.

Traditional Regulation Is More Likely to Succeed When There Is a Single Measurable Objective. Traditional regulation is difficult when the activity being regulated, or the variable being set, involves difficult trade-offs among conflicting values. This problem is relatively insignificant in, say, rate-of-return regulation of the telephone industry, but appears in its most extreme form in health care. Few decisions occur at the "flat of the curve" where additional inputs of medical resources would add no value. Rather, the relevant question is that difficult one of "how much is enough?"

The number of X-rays to order for a particular category of patient or the choice of kidney dialysis or transplantation for a patient with renal failure cannot be made efficiently on a mass or average basis. The "appropriate" balance of cost and expected outcome in one case may not be right in another. Where such value trade-offs exist (especially if important clinical variables are not observable by the regulator), it may be more expedient to ensure that the correct incentives are in place, rather than to specify each individual outcome.

Summary: The Characteristics of the Health Care Sector Are Not Conducive to Effective Regulation. In general, regulation of the medical care sector has not been successful, although there are strong reasons for some form of public intervention to control costs and to correct for market failure, including a number that have been created or exacerbated by the public sector itself.[20] We conclude that this failure reflects the use of command-and-control regulation inappropriate to the structure of the industry.

The comparative advantages of regulation versus incentives, which are based on our reading of economic theory and regulatory history, are summarized in table 1. These advantages, it should be stressed, are comparative; absolute advantage would be determined by the particular case. This summary does show, however, that medical care has few of the economic characteristics that are conducive to traditional outcome regulation:

- With 7,000 hospitals and 380,000 physicians, the industry is far from being a natural monopoly.
- The problem is pervasive, not confined to a few extremely poor performers.
- Medical care comprises a complex array of goods and services that are difficult to standardize. Moreover, these resources are heavily concentrated on a small fraction of patients with the most complex conditions.
- Regulatory objectives in health care involve complex value/cost trade-offs along a poorly understood production function, in contrast to a single-valued target such as rate of return.
- Elasticities of supply and demand are often significant.

The point that clinical decisions, choices regarding personal health maintenance, and hospital input decisions are sensitive to financial and other incentives is central to our argument. Indeed, many arguments in public health policy that first seem ideological could actually be resolved if we knew the value of elasticities regarding utilization, personal habits, and

---

[20] Penny Feldman and Richard J. Zeckhauser, "Some Sober Thoughts on Health Care Regulation," in Paul MacAvoy, ed., *Regulating American Business* (San Francisco: Institute for Contemporary Studies, 1978), pp. 93–123.

TABLE 1

COMPARATIVE ADVANTAGES OF REGULATION VERSUS INCENTIVES IN THE HEALTH CARE SECTOR

Regulation Favored	Incentives Favored
Few providers	Many providers
Simple product	Complex product
Single or few products	Many products
Low elasticities	High elasticities
Good information on costs and quantities	Poor information, hard to interpret
Weak potential for detrimental adaptation to regulation	Strong potential for detrimental adaptation
Few poor performers in large arena	Most performers displaying similar behavior
Single, clear objective	Multiple, subtle objectives

SOURCE: The authors.

clinical decisions. The following section reviews the empirical evidence on patient and provider responses to the financial incentives.

Incentives for the Efficient Use of Medical Resources as the Alternative to Regulation

Broad Potential Application and the Capability of Precise Targeting. Incentives for cost-effective use of health services can be applied in or out of the hospital through insurance premium design or copayment provisions, on the provider or on the patient. Most evidence on the potential effects of financial incentives is derived from studies of valuations in coinsurance rates or of comparative insurance systems; but "rifle-shot" incentives designed to deal with specific problems may be still more effective.

Evidence from broad-based studies of insurance rates suggests that incentives can be effective in health care and that the opportunity may be especially great to apply incentives at specific leverage points. Appropriate pricing schemes can channel the patient facing a complex procedure to a specialized cost-effective facility, can direct the chronic alcoholic to outpatient care rather than to inpatient warehousing in the local hospital, and can give providers incentives to monitor and educate severe diabetics rather than send them home, only to have them reappear in more acute form in a readmission. Such incentives are likely to be significantly more efficient than any broad system of coinsurance that

100

is based primarily on age and income status and that reimburses at "cost."

The effectiveness of a more tactical approach depends, first, on identifying areas where large quantities of resources are consumed and where incentives can be usefully applied. Public policy should be redirected toward design of incentive programs for cost-effective use of those concentrations of medical resources.

We first examine evidence on the overall effect of insurance rates on utilization of medical care resources and then discuss several specific areas of medical care utilization where incentives have seldom been applied but seem to offer substantial promise.

Effect of Insurance Incentives on Utilization. Comparisons of insurance plans show that financial incentives can have a profound impact on medical markets. High price elasticities would suggest that financial incentives could be used to influence levels of utilization as well as the mix of utilization across competing or substitute modes of care. This observation is important because the current hospital-oriented, cost-reimbursed system (92 percent of persons have hospital insurance) encourages substitution of the highest-priced mode of care for lower-cost modes. Inpatient stays for surgery that can be done on an ambulatory basis and hospital admission for alcoholic problems are two of many such instances. Incentives, rather than regulation, should be the alternative of greatest *comparative* advantage if elasticities are high.

Feldstein[21] summarized early studies of demand elasticities and found that the evidence supported an elasticity of demand for inpatient services between 0.5 and 0.7. Many of these studies contained a downward bias because of their failure to adjust for increasing hospital quality (positively correlated with price) and to define properly net price facing the consumer. Research since the Feldstein survey has confirmed the relationship between financial incentives and medical care utilization.

A study by Newhouse and Schwartz[22] also found substantial price effects, especially for ambulatory services. They estimated that a 100 percent decrease in the price (from zero insurance to complete insurance) would raise demand by 120 percent; a 75 percent decrease in price (to 25 percent coinsurance) would raise demand by 60 percent. A more

---

[21] Martin Feldstein, "Econometric Studies of Health Economics," in M. D. Intriligator and D. Kendrik, eds., *Frontiers of Quantitative Economics II* (New York: Elsevier North Holland, 1974).

[22] Joseph Newhouse, Charles Phelps, and William Schwartz, "Policy Options and the Impact of National Health Insurance," *New England Journal of Medicine*, vol. 290 (June 13, 1974), pp. 1345–59.

recent study of the California Medicaid experience by Helms, New-house, and Phelps[23] found that when a one-dollar coinsurance fee was included for physician visits, the quantity demanded declined by 8 percent while hospital visits increased. Other work by Newhouse on the effects of deductibles on demand for hospital care[24] and on the important Rand Health Insurance Experiment has also shown large decreases in demand in response to fairly small increases in net price.[25] For instance, an increase in the deductible for hospitalization from fifty to two hundred dollars reduced demand by 15 percent. Cross-elasticities of demand— how much the price of one service affects the utilization of another— are equally important although more difficult to study. Conceivably, further subsidization of ambulatory care might reduce total costs, for example, if it had a sufficient effect in reducing hospitalizations.

Dental care shows even higher price elasticities than medical care. Research by Manning and Phelps[26] found strong price-demand associations in the 1971 National Opinion Research Center Survey of people's use of dental facilities. In that study, price elasticities of demand ranged from 0.65 for white adult males to 1.40 for children.

These various data are typical of findings from studies of the effects of coinsurance and deductibles on the demand for health services. The studies have generally used individual panel data on which demand equations can be estimated, separating price effects from those of other intervening variables.[27] Another approach would compare actuarial premium differences between comparable plans over similar populations, with the principal difference being attributable to insurance structure. Although it is difficult to find the perfect natural experiment, the consistency of results across available studies suggests that the findings are likely to be robust. In general, comparative studies show that insurance plans with contrasting financial incentives generate highly different patterns of utilization.

---

[23] Jay Helms, Joseph P. Newhouse, and C. E. Phelps, "Copayment and Demand for Medical Care: The California Medicaid Experience," *Bell Journal of Economics,* vol. 9 (Spring 1978), pp. 192–208.

[24] Joseph P. Newhouse et al., "The Effect of Deductibles on the Demand for Medical Care Services," *Journal of the American Statistical Association,* vol. 75 (September 1980), pp. 525–53.

[25] Joseph Newhouse et al., "Some Interim Results from a Controlled Trial in Health Insurance" (mimeo), Rand Corporation, 1981.

[26] Willard G. Manning, Jr., and Charles E. Phelps, "The Demand for Dental Care," *Bell Journal of Economics,* vol. 10 (Autumn 1979), pp. 503–25.

[27] For problems in these econometric estimates, see Joseph Newhouse and C. Phelps, "On Having Your Cake and Eating It Too: Econometric Problems in Estimating the Demand for Health Services," *Journal of Econometrics,* vol. 13, no. 3 (August 1980), pp. 365–90.

A survey by Luft[28] examined research on health maintenance organizations. HMOs provide "full service" health care for a fixed yearly fee with low but positive coinsurance rates. HMOs are private organizations with explicit cash flow objectives and therefore have strong cost-reducing incentives. Luft examined over forty studies since 1950 comparing such prepaid plans to plans using fee for service, and concluded that, for a comparable offering of coverage, there was a per capita cost difference that averaged 13 percent and was as high as 40 percent for some particular pairwise comparisons. Cost differences arose primarily in the frequency of hospitalization, as opposed to length of stay or cost per day. This apparent elasticity of hospitalization frequencies is an important observation that we will return to later as one area for focused incentives.

Christianson and McClure[29] compared six HMOs in the Minneapolis/St. Paul area with a Blue Cross fee-for-service plan. They, too, found large differences in the cost per enrollee. The HMOs were always lower-priced than Blue Cross, with pairwise differences as high as 50 percent. Variation occurred primarily in hospital days per capita, although this variable was not broken down into days per stay, first admissions, or readmissions.

Gaus[30] reports similar results in his study of prepaid group practices offered to Medicaid recipients. Huge differences between the prepaid alternative and traditional insurance were found in the number of hospital days per enrollee (340 days per 1,000 persons in the group practice versus 885 days in fee for service). Services offered and population served were also apparently similar. Another example is offered by Enthoven's study of Medicare reimbursement in Washington State, where the Group Health Cooperative of Puget Sound received on average $202 per diem from Medicare, versus $356 for the fee-for-service sector. He concludes that "Medicare pays more to doctors who charge more and more to hospitals that cost more."[31] These examples demonstrate the large effect that financial incentives placed on the provider of health care can have upon utilization and cost.

---

[28] Harold Luft, "How Do Health Maintenance Organizations Achieve Their Savings?" *New England Journal of Medicine,* vol. 298 (June 15, 1978), pp. 1336–43.

[29] J. B. Christianson and Walter McClure, "Competition in the Delivery of Medical Care," *New England Journal of Medicine,* vol. 301 (October 11, 1979), pp. 812–18.

[30] C. R. Gaus, B. S. Cooper, and C. G. Hirschman, "Contrast in HMO and Fee for Service Performance," *Social Security Bulletin,* vol. 39 (May 1976), p. 314.

[31] Alain C. Enthoven, "Consumer Choice Health Plan I: Inflation and Inequality in Health Care Today: Alternatives for Cost Control and an Analysis of Proposals for National Health Insurance," *New England Journal of Medicine,* vol. 298 (June 1978), pp. 650–58.

Areas Where Precise Incentives Should Be Considered. The ideal insurance scheme, balancing risk spreading and incentives, would tailor financial reimbursement provisions to each type of clinical situation. This has been demonstrated theoretically.[32] It also follows from considering the wide range of illnesses and medical treatments. It may be best to pay for future care of an accident victim with a new spinal cord injury through a longitudinal form of prospective reimbursement, for instance, while financing the occasional (and random) broken bone by traditional forms of insurance using coinsurance and deductibles.

A system that finances different conditions in specialized ways might offer several advantages. First, the financial burden on the patient could be systematically less in cases where financial incentive structures would be deemed morally wrong (mental illness) or ineffective (pancreatic cancer). Incentives to be cost effective with resources in such cases might better be applied to the clinician. Second, selective reimbursement encourages the clustering of highly complex procedures in facilities that could reap economies of scale because of learning advantages as well as physical factors. Third, patients could be channeled along cost-effective routes; in some instances this could mean using the family physician, in others a highly specialized care facility.

Redesign of insurance incentives could begin in several areas of high-cost utilization where resources concentrate on relatively few types of patients or procedures. In any one year the high-cost 12 percent of patients in a hospital account for over 50 percent of hospital charges and the high-cost 20 percent account for nearly 70 percent. A close inspection of these high-cost patients' records[33] indicated that their utilization was much more often characterized by repeated hospitalizations for treatment of the same disease (often over many years) than by single, costly "intensive care" episodes. These repeated admissions tended to be more costly than first admissions. Consequently (1) many high-cost patients can be characterized as predictable recidivists, returning for treatment of the same disease or its sequelae; (2) better long-term care management may be able to avert future costly hospital readmissions; and (3) incentives targeted on predictable groups of future users at high risk (for example, the heavy smoker) may be worth exploring. These

---

[32] Richard J. Zeckhauser, "Medical Insurance: A Case Study of the Tradeoff between Risk Spreading and Appropriate Incentives," *Journal of Economic Theory,* vol. 2, no. 1 (March 1970), pp. 10–26.

[33] Steven A. Schroeder, Jonathan A. Showstack, and Edith A. Roberts, "Frequency and Clinical Description of High Cost Patients in 17 Acute Care Hospitals," *New England Journal of Medicine,* vol. 300 (June 7, 1979), pp. 1306–9; and Zook and Moore, "The High Cost Users of Medical Care."

remain preliminary hypotheses that suggest new directions to be explored carefully.

We have identified three areas of resource utilization where reasonable opportunities to use low-cost alternatives may exist or where adverse health events could be prevented. Each would require specialized incentives. The first, incentives to reduce harmful habits, is directed to reducing illness incidence or severity. The second, incentives to reduce the frequency of hospitalization where lower-cost alternatives exist (especially for repeated hospitalization for the same disease), is directed to pre-admission behaviors and alternatives. The third, incentives to channel patients to providers with a threshold level of success or experience with complex procedures (for example, abdominal aortic aneurysm repair), is directed to hospital practice.

Incentives to reduce unhealthy personal habits. The link between illness and the personal habits of excessive drinking, smoking, and overeating to the point of obesity has become clearer during the past few years; yet health insurance schemes have made few attempts to introduce incentives to reduce habit frequency or severity.

One study[34] examined the association between the costs of hospital care for single illnesses and the presence of a habit of smoking, alcoholism, or obesity with potential relationship to the existing illness. The data for the study were gathered through case-by-case record retrieval in a sample of five Boston hospitals. Findings indicate that high-cost patients were disproportionately persons with a potentially harmful personal habit, as noted by the doctor in the medical record (table 2).

Regression analysis on these data has suggested that the presence of a severe habit, such as smoking or overeating, increased one-year costs to hospital patients in the sample by $1,129, five-year costs by $2,988, and ten-year costs for the same disease by $3,882. If the severe habit was alcoholism, the increases were still large. The higher cost was most often due to more repeated hospitalizations for the same disease rather than more days per stay or higher cost per day.

These results show a strong positive relationship between unhealthy personal habits and medical expenditures. The cost-sharing nature of insurance and the magnitude of this association provide reason in themselves for public concern with incentives to reduce the incidence of these behaviors. To date, relatively few attempts have been made to alter this kind of behavior, and except for employer-provided programs, financial incentives have hardly been tried at all. Most efforts have taken the form of voluntary community programs. Yet, even these have achieved

[34] Zook and Moore, "The High Cost Users of Medical Care."

TABLE 2

PATIENTS WITH POTENTIALLY HARMFUL HABITS RELATED TO THEIR
CURRENT ILLNESSES, IN A SAMPLE OF BOSTON HOSPITALS
(percent)

Category of Use	Adult Teaching Hospital	Veterans Hospital[a]	Suburban Community Hospital	Tax-Supported Municipal Hospital
All patients				
Percentage of all patients	22	50	22	18[b]
Percentage of all single stays	24	49	24	24
Percentage of total billings	27	59	33	26
Percentage of most costly 20% of patients	31	69	39	36
Percentage of most costly 20% of patients over 18 years of age	31	69	41	40
High-cost utilization modes				
Cost-intensive stays	40	76	44	33
Prolonged hospitalizations	30	61	26	29
Repeated hospitalizations for the same disease	27	58	42	33

NOTE: Habits classified as potentially harmful include illness associated with alcohol abuse, drug abuse, obesity, heavy smoking, and intentional or self-conscious noncompliance with a treatment regimen recommended by the physician. All data are based on page-by-page review of hospital medical record notes. The children's hospital data in the original study are excluded, since many categories of habit are inapplicable.
[a] Includes only the general medical/surgical patient populations.
[b] If obstetrics is excluded, this statistic rises to 25 percent.
SOURCE: Christopher J. Zook and Francis D. Moore, "The High Cost Users of Medical Care," *New England Journal of Medicine*, vol. 302 (May 1, 1980), pp. 996–1002.

reassuring success to date, offering hope for greater success in stronger programs.

Such voluntary community programs for risk factor management have only recently been attempted in several small pilot projects. Experimental results from the Multiple Risk Factor Intervention Trial by HEW (MRFIT), the North Karelia (Finland) Project,[35] and the Stanford Heart Disease Prevention Program for Risk Factor Modification[36] showed reductions in smoking, hypertension, and serum cholesterol

[35] P. Puska et al., "Community Control of Acute Myocardial Infarction in North Karelia," *Practical Cardiology*, vol. 4 (January 1978), p. 94.

[36] J. W. Farquhar et al., "Community Education for Cardiovascular Health," *The Lancet*, vol. 1, no. 2 (June 4, 1977), pp. 1192–95.

levels in small, defined populations. The Stanford project was a community educational campaign approach that resulted in a 20–35 percent improvement in health care knowledge in the experimental versus the control community, a 20–40 percent decline in cholesterol consumption, a 7–24 percent smoking decrease, and a reduction in coronary heart disease of 15–20 percent during the two years of the study.[37] These community programs show that a significant portion of unhealthy behavior can be altered.

The American record on habit modification has not been impressive. No decline in drinking or the use of drugs is apparent. Per capita consumption of alcohol by volume is at its highest level since 1860. In spite of the explosion in knowledge of smoking-health links since the 1964 report of the U.S. surgeon general, the subsequent requirement for health warning labels on cigarettes and in advertisements for them, and the elimination of television advertising of cigarettes in 1974, the proportion of young women smoking cigarettes has increased steadily (although there has been a decline in the number of older women and male smokers and in cigarette consumption per capita).

Early success in voluntary social-psychological/informational programs such as MRFIT is most promising for stronger financial incentives, including an array of forms of reward including taxation, altered insurance premiums, or required attendance in courses (backed by dollar penalties). The enormous costs of life-style-related illness and their uneven distribution across population groups demand a strong program to gather data, perhaps through small controlled experiments or pilot projects, and then to incorporate the results in the finance of health care services.

Incentives to reduce frequency of hospital admission. Studies of contrasting insurance plans,[38] cost groups of patients,[39] and geographic areas[40] have shown a consistently greater variation in rates of hospital admission per capita than in days per admission or cost per day. If admission rates are a highly elastic component of medical expenditure, this may be an important area in which to introduce incentives to substitute low-cost alternatives for high-cost hospitalization, especially if quality of care and the probability of future hospital admission are similar. The benefits could be very large, since hospital costs represent an increasing share of the nation's rising health care bill.

[37] Lester Breslow, "Risk Factor Intervention for Health Maintenance," *Science,* vol. 200 (May 26, 1978), pp. 908–12.

[38] Luft, "How Do Health Maintenance Organizations Achieve Their Savings?"

[39] Zook and Moore, "The High Cost Users of Medical Care."

[40] Marian Gornick, "Medicare Patients: Geographic Differences in Hospital Discharge Rates and Multiple Stays," *Social Security Bulletin* (June 1977), pp. 22–41.

107

Health insurance at present offers strong incentives to the patient to seek hospitalization and to the hospital to admit patients. (As Harris[41] has shown, low-intensity hospitalization tends to be more profitable than complex tertiary care.) By contrast, reimbursement for follow-up care or long-term chronic assistance is relatively shallow. This reimbursement differential is likely to provide an explanation of the findings of Miller and Goldstein[42] that even a relatively simple program of follow-up care for diabetics reduced their admission rate to the hospital by 50 percent, and the findings of Shepard et al.[43] that follow-up programs for hypertensives can yield reduced hospitalization. Other studies[44] also confirm that follow-up and chronic care can, in some patient/diagnostic categories, reduce readmission rates.

We do not mean to imply that financial incentives are not now used at all, only to stress that their potential is unmet. The Senate Finance Committee recently approved a number of measures designed to use incentives to increase the efficiency of medical resources used for the care of persons on public insurance programs. Reimbursement, for instance, has been restricted for conditions (such as detoxification) which do not require acute hospital facilities, but which were often billed to Medicare and Medicaid at these high rates. By contrast, reimbursement has been liberalized for some types of outpatient care that were being performed on an inpatient basis primarily because the patient payments required were lower. Such substitutability among services is often high[45] and should be considered in insurance design.[46]

[41] Jeffrey E. Harris, "Pricing Rules for Hospitals," *Bell Journal of Economics,* vol. 10 (Spring 1979), pp. 224–43.

[42] Leona Miller and Jack Goldstein, "More Efficient Care of Diabetic Patients in a County Hospital Setting," *New England Journal of Medicine,* vol. 286 (June 29, 1972), p. 1388.

[43] D. S. Shepard et al., "Cost Effectiveness of Interventions to Improve Compliance with Anti-hypertensive Therapy" (abstract), *Preventive Medicine,* vol. 8, no. 2 (February 1979), p. 229.

[44] Robert Brook, Francis Appel, Charles Avery, Morton Orman, and Robert Stevenson, "Effectiveness of Inpatient Follow Up Care," *New England Journal of Medicine,* vol. 285 (December 30, 1971), pp. 1509–19; R. Forrester, "Improving Care of the Chronically Ill," *Hospitals* (January 16, 1975), pp. 57–62; and Drummand Rennie, "Home Dialysis and the Costs of Uremia," *New England Journal of Medicine,* vol. 298 (February 16, 1978), pp. 399–400.

[45] Karen Davis and Louise B. Russell, "The Substitution of Hospital Outpatient Care for Inpatient Care," *Review of Economics and Statistics,* vol. 54 (May 1972), pp. 109–20.

[46] One potential problem for the use of financial incentives derives from the dominance of nonprofit institutions in the health care sector. At present, only 14 percent of hospitals are proprietary, for-profit institutions, and their share is declining. Nonprofit institutions are more likely to have revenue levels as a major objective, with cost reduction and margin increase as relatively less important goals. Consider the case of two treatments, one high-technology treatment costing $100 and one low-technology treatment costing $50. If reimbursement were set at $105 for the former mode and $70 for the latter, one would expect nonprofit and for-profit hospitals to differ on which method is preferable.

Incentives to channel patients to hospitals with the greatest comparative advantage in particular procedures. The present reimbursement system for hospital costs does not differentially reward institutions with different skills and competences for assuming the care of particular types of patients. The distribution of patients across hospitals is unlikely to be close to optimal, a tentative conclusion that is reinforced by the observation that most hospitals perform a relatively similar mix of procedures and treat a similar mix of illnesses. The high costs of unexpected medical complications suggest that even small percentage changes in their incidence through the rechanneling of patients with especially risky treatment courses could yield large benefits in terms of resource savings and alleviation of human suffering.

The patient data of the Moore-Zook study (where twenty-two separate categories of unexpected medical events were studied in the records of 2,238 patients) showed a strong association between high medical costs and unexpected complications while receiving hospital treatment. Figure 1 shows that the incidence of these events was many times greater among high-cost than low-cost patients (both per day and per stay). Regression analysis of billing, controlling for disease category, age, sex, surgery, secondary diagnosis, employment, marital status, habits, and stage of treatment (proxied by the previous number of hospitalizations for the same disease), confirmed this strong association between costs and unanticipated clinical problems arising during treatment. Regression analysis of correlates with billing suggested that on average an unexpected event was associated with a bill that was nearly $2,000 higher. Other studies[47] confirm both the frequency and the high costs of such events.

Cost-based reimbursement has the unfortunate effect of rewarding relatively high-cost hospitals and discouraging an accurate accounting of true costs in the hospital. Tying reimbursement more closely to a reasonable level of expected cost (possibly including cost of readmission within a short period after discharge) would give hospitals greater incentive to reduce their own costs; at the same time, the nonspecialized hospital would have less incentive to assume the care of patients requiring difficult procedures in which it has a cost disadvantage when

---

[47] Richard Wenzel, "Hospital Acquired Infections," *American Journal of Epidemiology,* vol. 103 (March 1976), p. 251; Nathan Couch, Nicholas Tilney, and Francis D. Moore, "The Cost of Misadventure in Colonic Surgery," *American Journal of Surgery,* vol. 135 (1978), pp. 641–46; Sandra Polakerety, Mary Dunne, and John Cook, "Nosocomial Infection: The Hidden Cost in Health Care," *Hospitals* (1978), pp. 101–106; David Feingold, "Hospital-Acquired Infections," *Journal of the American Medical Association,* vol. 283 (1970), pp. 1384–91; and H. Beatty and R. Petersdorf, "Iatrogenic Factors in Infectious Disease," *Annals of Internal Medicine,* vol. 65 (1966), p. 641.

FIGURE 1

Unexpected Adverse Events during Indexed Hospitalization of Patients Ranked by Billing Percentile

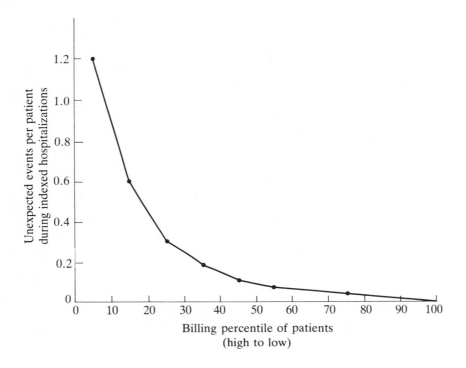

total recuperative cost and follow-up visits are included (and probably a quality disadvantage). This approach might be particularly valuable in areas like cardiac surgery, where both cost and outcome are strongly affected by hospital experience.

Recent studies of surgical mortality[48] show a strong negative correlation between the volume of an operation performed and mortality. Hospitals more experienced in a given procedure have lower unit costs and better health outcomes than other hospitals. This result is not surprising, since the influence of experience on costs has been documented in a wide range of industries and activities. (The original studies of experience curves were conducted in the aircraft industry.) But it is a

[48] H. S. Luft, J. P. Bunker, and A. C. Enthoven, "Should Operations Be Regionalized? The Empirical Relation between Surgical Volume and Mortality," *New England Journal of Medicine,* vol. 301 (December 20, 1979), pp. 1364–69.

finding that may have major implications for efficient health care system design, moving toward more specialized hospitals or services. Such a move would probably be encouraged by forms of prospective reimbursement that gave the providing agency a long-term interest in cost-effective treatment of patients with known, possibly repetitive conditions (such as a spinal cord injury or cystic fibrosis).

Personal habits, hospital admission decisions, and unexpected complications are but a few of the many areas in which incentives could be applied in lieu of traditional regulation. The question that remains, however, is who should take the initiative.

Who Should Oversee Performance in the Health Sector?

If we start from the premise that economic activity should reside in the private sector unless the government will clearly do a superior job, we highlight a fundamental question: Why should government, rather than private insurers or employers, regulate health care? Why, for example, can Blue Cross not refuse to reimburse a hospital that builds extra beds? Why should an employer who finances most of his employees' health coverage not be the one to determine whether he will pay for coronary bypass surgery? Although the government is often assumed to be the appropriate overseer, this may not always be the case.

Seven basic reasons are commonly given for relying on the government to regulate the behavior of health care providers. Upon inspection, however, none of these arguments is obviously compelling in many important cases.

1. The public is more accepting of the government as a regulator. Its motive is to protect the public interest, not to make money. Insurance companies and employers are suspect.

2. Traditional market forces are not at work in the health care sector.

• Insurance companies, many of them nonprofit or mutual companies, all of them subject to regulation, may have insufficient incentives to hold down costs. Indeed their rewards may increase with their volume of expenditures. Incentives are so distorted that they would not want to regulate to public purposes.

• Hospitals, the principal institutions that would be regulated, are 86 percent nonprofit. Hence many traditional economic theorems may not apply to them. Even if third-party payers applied regulations and incentives that would induce profit-making hospitals to behave appropriately, those with different incentives might not.

3. The government now has a strong financial interest in the outcome. It cannot be a free rider on the regulatory efforts of others. The government sponsors the Medicaid and Medicare programs, as well as a host of grants to provide factor inputs. Moreover, since insurance premiums and medical expenditures are partly tax deductible, and medical benefits are not taxed, the government has a share in any private insurance transactions. Therefore, private payers would have an inadequate incentive to hold down costs.

4. There are some aspects of behavior affecting health care costs that private actors cannot control. For example, they cannot pursue speeders, tax unhealthful foods, or keep unsafe products off the market. Government, with broader jurisdiction, can choose the extent to regulate through control of individual behavior.

5. The significant size of many institutions within the industry favors the government as principal actor. An insurer who attempted to regulate the behavior of a large provider would be in a bilateral monopoly situation, for example. It is not clear the outcome would be desirable. In theory at least, the government might not have to bargain and could set appropriate prices and quantities.

A simpler argument along the same lines is that the government is already the largest player. It can simply use monopsony power to hold down prices.

6. The government is already so involved in the health care sector that it must become more involved. That is, there must be pyramiding intervention. In recent years, for example, courts and legislatures have limited the ability of insurers to compete by mandating that certain services be provided as part of any health care plan and by requiring that different classes of individuals be charged the same rates even though their experiences might be demonstrably different. Competition to hold down rates is thus discouraged, and the government must regulate to make sure that even uneconomic customers are served.

The arguments above are predominantly economic and efficiency oriented, and follow from the traditional microeconomic framework. Since many other factors have contributed to the growth of government regulation in the health care sector, numerous other arguments could probably be made for the government as opposed to private parties as controllers of costs and utilization. The most common of these is:

7. Limiting demand through pricing and financial incentives is undesirable or immoral. Yet that is the mechanism that private-sector organizations would employ. (The argument that such mechanisms would hurt the poor is less compelling, given that the government already provides coverage for them.)

We shall not have space to assess the merits of these arguments for a government regulatory role. Our primary goal is to assure that future

112

arguments on the appropriateness of government regulation address the question to which the answer is often assumed: Given that intervention is necessary or desirable, why should the government be the intervenor? Let us assume that sufficient reason is provided. The next question on which we have focused our attention and marshaled empirical evidence is: Given that the government will intervene, should it rely predominantly on incentives or on command-and-control methods?

First Steps toward Incentives

Even if agreement is reached on (1) the failure of current regulatory approaches, (2) the comparative disadvantage of regulation versus incentives in medical care, and (3) the desirability of greater private-sector participation in policing medical care, it is not immediately clear where we should go now. We do not face a tabula rasa, but instead confront a complicated array of programs, legislation, interconnections among providers, state regulations, and pricing conventions that are not going to yield easily to new approaches. In fact, a large share of the industry may have a vested interest in the status quo.

As a first step we propose three guidelines:

• Take strong measures, but only a few at a time; much remains to be learned.

• Utilize the natural tendencies of free enterprise and the self-interest of private competition as much as possible; this effort would include providing inducements for new, for-profit providers to enter the marketplace.

• Focus on peaks of high-cost utilization, the "high-cost users of medical care," where precise policies supported by careful analysis can have a significant fiscal impact.

Let us focus on the third guideline. Regulation is relatively ineffective in dealing with the high-cost group of patients, for a variety of reasons, as we have seen—complexity, potential for detrimental adaptation to evade regulatory intent, poor information, many providers and categories of high-cost users, and poorly understood relationships between medical inputs and health outputs.

Two objectives seem particularly important in a new initiative. First, eliminate or substitute for costly hospital readmissions when ambulatory alternatives are available at similar quality. The high-cost users of medical care are more often predictable repeaters whose high costs were due to a series of hospitalizations rather than to a single, acute episode. There are at present few financial incentives for providers to strive to keep such patients out of the hospital, although timely application of follow-up care or ambulatory services clearly offers such potential. Care of repeaters represents an unexploited opportunity for greater cost efficiency in American medicine without reducing (and probably increasing) the quality of care.

Second, identify hospitals with a comparative advantage in a particular procedure or diagnostic category, and through reimbursement, encourage more efficient use of these facilities through patient redistribution (primarily applicable in densely populated metropolitan areas). Study of providers has shown large variations in skill levels and a strong relationship between accumulated experience and outcome. Other research has shown the important linkage of outcome (the absence of unexpected complications) to cost. Redistribution of patients (especially those predisposed to high-cost utilization) across hospitals in accordance with their comparative advantage and special competence might reduce system costs and improve quality of care.

Both of these objectives could be furthered under a financing system changed in the following three general ways:

1. Offer qualified providers prospectively set, long-term, actuarially determined annuities, possibly with a coinsurance or renegotiation provision in the event of extraordinary expense, to assume medical responsibility for continuing care of patients with particular chronic conditions. Examples would be spinal cord injury, cystic fibrosis, major stroke, alcoholism, or mental illness. Providers would then have a long-term financial stake in appropriate care of these potential high-cost users.

2. Require providers to report health outcomes and costs by diagnosis and procedure, and disseminate these data to prepaid HMOs and other providers.

3. Encourage new classes of entrants to the medical field by neutralizing tax provisions (at present favoring nonprofit institutions) and through new forms of public insurance reimbursement. New entrants might be providers who are especially skilled in certain chronic illnesses or more traditional forms of HMOs. Long-term financial rewards are needed for a provider who keeps his patient well and out of the hospital as opposed to the one who simply lowers the cost of each visit, with a possible increase in the frequency of visits or in the use of outside facilities. One way to begin might be to give enrollees of public insurance the opportunity to switch from traditional (and often high-cost) forms of insurance to new prospectively paid providers, with the cost difference shared by patient and insurer.

114

Conclusion

We have examined the rationale for and performance of regulation in the health care sector. Financial externalities and the inadequate flow of information provide the primary theoretical justification for government regulation of health care. Rarely, however, has government intervention been explicitly justified through an appeal to market failure arguments. Instead, the rapidly rising cost of health care (due to pecuniary externalities) in an inflationary economy is undoubtedly responsible for a substantial portion of government regulatory efforts.

The conceptual bases for intervention would be of limited practical concern if such intervention had been successful. But government performance in the regulation of the hospital sector has been disappointing. Why might this be? Quite simply, health care has few of the characteristics that suit it well to regulatory approaches. For example, products are heterogeneous, elasticities are substantial, and the problem is with the average performer in the system, not a few bad performers.

Yet the health care market cannot by any standard be said to be operating as a competitive market. Economists are accustomed to searching for market failures when seeking justifications for a government role. One logical error that may emerge in this search is to assume that the more severe the failure of the market, the more likely that regulation is the best approach to ameliorate matters. The error is that different conditions are relatively more favorable to regulatory performance, and that such conditions need not correlate with market performance. Other factors being equal, a market plagued with market imperfections will perform less well if it also has complex products. But complex and heterogeneous products tend to frustrate regulatory approaches to resource allocation much more than they do markets. If one had to regulate precisely one of two markets of equal size having, for example, equal concentration problems, the market with the simpler, more standardized product should be chosen for regulation. It is simply not true that the potential for regulation increases with the severity of the market failure.

The fundamental characteristics of the medical marketplace, combined with the performance of government regulation to date, suggest that the most widely employed command-and-control approaches to containing health care costs may never be successful. Improved performance might lie in one of four areas: (1) greater reliance on private payers as controllers of health care costs; (2) new modes of delivery or coverage, such as health maintenance organizations or prospective payment for certain conditions, which automatically impose incentives for cost containment; (3) modes of government regulation that are less invasive in their effects on detailed or patient-specific decisions; and (4) increased reliance on incentives, particularly in new roles, such as promoting healthful behavior or attacking special problems of the high-cost users of medical care.[49]

Both empirical evidence and economic logic suggest that the burden of proof for employing the traditional regulatory approach to health care, with its command-and-control methods, should now be shifted. To show that the market outcome is inadequate would be only a starting point in the argument. It must also be demonstrated that the government is the preferred intervenor, and that government-fostered incentive approaches would prove inferior to direct regulation. In the absence of such a demonstration, our nation should place greater reliance on incentive-based approaches to controlling the costs of health care.

---

[49] Health-promoting activities that eliminate deaths that utilize few health resources may increase discounted long-run health costs, since the individual will subsequently die in a substantially more expensive manner. Since our interest is in both health, for example, quality-adjusted life years, and resources, such expenditures are cost effective so long as the increment in health purchased is worth the increased expenditure of resources. For efficiency, the exchange rate between resources and health should be the marginal exchange rate found in other health programs.

Commentary

William D. White

Anyone reading these chapters can have little doubt that we face difficult policy choices in the health sector. There is a good deal of agreement between the authors about the reasons for these difficulties. Both adopt a comparative statics "market failure" approach in analyzing problems in the sector, and both agree that the industry is characterized by waste and inefficiency stemming from the problems of imperfect information, poorly functioning insurance markets, and nonprofit institutions.

As to what to do about these problems, or indeed whether much can be done, the authors differ. The thrust of Frech's paper is that the health sector has long been characterized by pervasive government regulation—much of which he suggests is of questionable value, such as occupational licensure—and that this regulation severely limits competition. Increasing the levels of competition by permitting advertising and reducing barriers to entry for organizations like HMOs could improve performance. Crandall draws on experience with insurance and regulation in a variety of industries outside the health sector to raise some sobering and thought-provoking questions, especially about the potential contribution of HMOs.

A number of points could be raised about the specific arguments in these papers. I would like to comment, however, on the authors' general approach to the problems of the industry. As both papers demonstrate, much can be learned from a "market failure" approach. Although valuable, this type of analysis tends to focus attention on conditions at a fixed point in time. Historical factors are likely to be ignored and with them some key policy issues.

Frech alludes to the long history of government involvement in the health sector. Some historical perspective is needed on this point, however; the government's role in the sector has changed significantly over time. In part, this change has been in response to the increasing cost and complexity of health care. At the same time, the changing role of

117

government in the sector reflects changes in our view of health care in our society.

Much of current concern about government involvement in health focuses on the fact that not only is the industry supposedly wasteful and inefficient, but it is growing. Growth is not normally a cardinal sin in our society. As Uwe Reinhardt aptly noted some time ago, if the auto industry grew at the same rate as the health industry, producers would receive a medal. The process of growth has been going on for a long time in the health sector, moreover, without previously provoking much government reaction. Why then is growth of such concern today?

Historically, government involvement in the sector was limited mainly to state occupational licensure laws during most of this century. Hospitals were not even licensed in most states until after the introduction of the Hill-Burton Act in 1946. The government indirectly subsidized some parts of the industry by granting tax-free status to nonprofit hospitals and, later, tax exemptions for health insurance. Government provision of services was limited, however, to local government hospitals. These public institutions served as vendors of last resort, providing direct care on the basis of need under rather spartan conditions.

This situation did not really change until the 1960s. The introduction of Medicare and Medicaid marked a key shift in policy from limited government provision of services in kind to a policy of government provision of equal financial access to care from private and public institutions for the target groups—the old and the poor—accompanied by a disavowal of any system of two-class medicine.

The effect of Medicare and Medicaid has been to shift a major share of the burden of paying for medical care to the federal government. This shift in the burden of costs, rather than rising costs per se, appears to be responsible for the key change in regulatory philosophy that has accompanied these programs. From regulating quality alone, the government has moved to a policy of also trying to regulate the cost and quantity of medical care.

The implementation of cost control efforts has been accompanied by considerable discussion about the declining marginal benefits of additional medical services. I think consumers remain largely unconvinced. The fact that efforts to limit utilization have been extended beyond the Medicare and Medicaid target groups seems to have more to do with the kind of second-order equity considerations discussed by Crandall in the context of insurance than with any broad public concern about efficiency. And while much has been said about waste and inefficiency in Medicare and Medicaid and in the industry in general, the issues clearly go beyond this. The underlying question that policy makers face in the sector is just how much access there should be to health care when scarce tax dollars are at stake. What makes policy choices so difficult in the industry is not only the problems generated by insurance and imperfect information and the complexity of services described in these two chapters, but also an absence of consensus on what is an acceptable level of care and the degree to which the concept of equal access should be expanded or abandoned.

Paul Starr

With many economists I share the conviction that the existing structure of incentives in the United States causes serious problems in medical care, that traditional forms of regulation are not the cure, and that different incentives are needed.* In this respect, I have no quarrel with the papers by Zeckhauser and Zook and by Pauly. But I disagree, mainly with the former, about (1) the origins of existing incentives; (2) the causes and effects of regulation and the role of other forms of government intervention; and (3) the criteria and strategy that ought to guide the introduction of new incentives and other changes in the organization of medical care. I want to show, moreover, that putting incentive systems and regulatory policies into a more adequate historical and political perspective leads to a different reading of the empirical evidence and the theoretical issues and points to an alternative view of what needs to be done.

How Incentives Became Distorted

Identifying the causes of the problem obviously shapes one's view of the remedy. Zeckhauser and Zook remark that the present pricing system with its "warped incentives" is "largely an outgrowth of government programs." This view neglects the overwhelming part played by cartels. As Blumberg has shown,[1] the incentives that physicians face in relative prices are, indeed, "warped"—particularly in favor of inhospital services. But the relative value scales were created by the medical profession, originally for use in Blue Shield plans, and reflect the power of certain specialties. Professional interests prevented adjustments to bring the scales into line with later changes in productivity. Similarly, cost-based reimbursement for hospitals was developed by Blue Cross at a time

---

* This commentary might have been entitled "On the Origin and Cure of Warped Incentives."—*Author's note.*

[1] Mark S. Blumberg, "Physician Fees as Incentives," in *Changing the Behavior of the Physician: A Management Perspective* (University of Chicago, Graduate Program in Hospital Administration, 1980), pp. 20–32.

when Blue Cross plans were directly controlled by hospitals.[2] To be sure, Medicare adopted cost-based reimbursement in its accommodation of the hospitals, but this is evidence more of governmental passivity in the face of private power than of an active role in warping incentives. The reimbursement formulas typically favor hospitals that are in affluent areas and that have relatively few bad debts over older hospitals in poorer neighborhoods; and as in the relative value scales, differences in influence may have been at work.

The basic incentives consumers face have been shaped by health insurance, but health insurance is itself the outcome of a long process of accommodating these same private interests.[3] It is an old story how medical societies succeeded in boycotting and blocking forms of prepaid group practice and other organizations that threatened to reduce their market power.[4] They also succeeded not only in defeating plans for compulsory health insurance but also in effacing any threat to their economic position from other reforms. The early reformers of the Progressive era were acutely aware of the dangers of fee-for-service reimbursement and wanted doctors paid on a capitation basis, but gave way in later proposals and programs as a result of intense professional opposition.[5]

Private health insurance had inflationary properties from its inception. At the time that Blue Cross began in the 1930s insurance experts warned, as they had before, that insurance was inappropriate for medical expenses, which violated some of the most fundamental principles of insurability.[6] Among these were that hazards insured against should be relatively rare events of high, but definite cost, and the insurance should not increase the hazard. The type of insurance that Blue Cross offered guaranteed coverage of hospital services of indefinite cost; furthermore, it was likely to encourage people to use hospitals, and encourage hos-

---

[2] Louis S. Reed, *Blue Cross and Medical Service Plans* (Washington, D.C.: Federal Security Agency, 1947), pp. 48–53.

[3] I give a more detailed account of the process of political and economic accommodation of professional interests in Book 2 of *The Social Transformation of American Medicine* (Basic Books, forthcoming).

[4] "The American Medical Association: Power, Purpose and Politics in Organized Medicine," *Yale Law Journal*, vol. 63 (1954), pp. 988–98; and Lawrence G. Goldberg and Warren Greenberg, "The Emergence of Physician-Sponsored Health Insurance: A Historical Perspective," in *Competition in the Health Care Sector: Past, Present, and Future* (Germantown, Md.: Aspen, 1978), pp. 231–54.

[5] I. M. Rubinow, *Social Insurance* (New York: Henry Holt & Co., 1916); and Ronald L. Numbers, *Almost Persuaded: American Physicians and Compulsory Health Insurance, 1912–1920* (Baltimore: Johns Hopkins University Press, 1978).

[6] Duncan M. MacIntyre, *Voluntary Health Insurance and Rate Making* (Ithaca, N.Y.: Cornell University Press, 1962), pp. 124–26.

pitals to increase their costs and charges. Originally, Blue Cross had some protection against this danger through the mechanism of hospital underwriting (which put member hospitals at risk for excessive claims), but this was soon effectively abandoned once reserves were accumulated. Blue Cross essentially represented not so much insurance in the traditional sense as a monopolistic system of prepayment.

In the 1940s commercial insurers who were anxious to secure part of the business set aside their traditional objections to insurance against medical expenses. By offering indemnity rather than service benefits, they were able to remedy only one of their original objections (regarding the definiteness of losses). But the problem of moral hazard remained and, indeed, became worse. Embroiled in competition with the service plans, the companies steadily abandoned traditional principles, providing coverage for many small medical expenses that they previously insisted should be budgeted rather than insured against.

Was this growth and liberalization of private insurance—once viewed as a triumph of voluntarism—primarily a result of the tax exemption for employers' contributions to benefit plans? No one who has studied the takeoff of private insurance in the late 1940s and 1950s would accept such an explanation. As historical accounts of the growth of negotiated health plans show, tax considerations were a relatively minor factor at the time.[7] These plans were a kind of private social security, which grew out of a new relation between industry and labor after World War II. The health plans strengthened the hold of the companies on the loyalties of their workers, and they helped the unions prove to their membership the value of collective bargaining and effective representation. The extent of the plans responded to the workers' demand for an inclusive system of prepayment, with certainty of coverage, rather than merely insurance against major risks.

Indirectly, government bears responsibility for the incentives of private health insurance, cost-based hospital reimbursement, and relative physician fees because of what it did *not* do: It did not pass national health insurance, vigorously enforce the antitrust laws, or aid the prepaid alternatives that might have provided cost control at a high standard of care. But the explanation for this withdrawal lies not with liberal government, but with the private interests that blocked alternatives and the conservative political forces that defended those interests. Conservatives, one might recall, used to be more interested in proving the virtues of voluntarism than in fostering competition and typically supported the

---

[7] Raymond Munts, *Bargaining for Health* (Madison: University of Wisconsin Press, 1967); and Joseph W. Garbarino, *Health Plans and Collective Bargaining* (Berkeley: University of California Press, 1960).

monopolistic arrangements of the American Medical Association and Blue Cross.[8] There is a certain forgetfulness today about who was on which side, and it would be an instructive act of penitence if some who once defended the genius of the medical cartels owned up to their share of the responsibility for the fix we are in now.

How Government Intervened

The expansion of state intervention in medical care after World War II did not involve governmental efforts to suppress an otherwise competitive market. On the contrary, the aim of state intervention was first to augment a market already restricted by private power, then to supplement it, and finally to save it from its own inflationary tendencies. The first postwar programs provided aid for hospital construction, medical research, and medical education. In these programs, incentives and regulations were inextricably joined; the incentives were for expansion, and the regulations that came with them were meant to ensure some minimal standard of quality and public accountability.

The second phase of government intervention—the redistributive programs of the 1960s—came at the climax of postwar prosperity. It is critical to see how these programs emerged from the dynamics of the market itself. By emphasizing group insurance linked primarily to employment, Blue Cross and the commercial insurers had limited the risks of adverse selection and greatly reduced acquisition and other administrative costs, which, in the old "industrial" forms of life and health insurance sold on an individual basis, had been as high as 50 percent of premium income.[9] But in solving these problems, Blue Cross and the commercial insurers had left out people who were unable to buy insurance on a group basis. Moreover, even with community rating, Blue Cross had a regressive impact on subscriber incomes because it substituted for the old sliding scale a uniform level of fees and did not charge wealthier families any more for coverage than it charged those with lower or middle incomes.[10] The higher charge that Blue Cross required for individual policies increased its regressive impact. Finally, when the commercial companies entered the health insurance business, they offered experience rating—a challenge that Blue Cross plans had to meet

[8] Senator Taft, for example. See Monty Poen, *Harry S. Truman versus the Medical Lobby* (Columbia, Mo.: University of Missouri Press, 1979).

[9] Marquis James, *The Metropolitan Life: A Study in Business Growth* (New York: Viking Press, 1947), pp. 73–93; and Rubinow, *Social Insurance*, p. 420.

[10] See the data presented in New York State Legislative Commission on Medical Care, *Medical Care for the People of New York State* (February 15, 1946), p. 81.

since it threatened to leave Blue Cross with the high-loss-cost groups. But experience rating, as the advocates of voluntary insurance understood at the time, made it impossible for Blue Cross ever to encompass the entire population, as its founders had hoped to do through the cross-subsidies of community rating. Once the move to experience rating began, government intervention to provide for the aged and others omitted from the private insurance system became unavoidable.

The third phase in government intervention—the increase in regulation and planning aimed at controlling costs—was also a response to the internal dynamics of the market. As a result primarily of the incentives of private health insurance, medical costs were already rising faster than the general price level in the late 1940s and 1950s. So long as the economy was growing happily, few were disturbed. The redistributive programs of the 1960s simply reinforced the tendencies toward growth and inflation, particularly because of their accommodating reimbursement provisions. In the 1970s, as costs mounted in a time of economic stagnation, the reaction was inevitable: First hesitantly, and then with increasing determination, all those organized interests that bore the costs of accommodation—the corporations and unions, insurance companies, and government—sought to control the appetite of the medical sector.

The support that the commercial insurance industry gave to regulation and planning ought particularly to be underlined. From its standpoint, the efforts of Blue Cross and the government to control costs by tightening reimbursement might result only in a shift in costs to the subscribers of commercial insurance, who pay regular charges. Only by securing some form of comprehensive cost containment could such a displacement of costs be avoided.[11] I mention their interest in regulation because somehow the insurance industry never enters into Pauly's model, which gives the impression that such interests either do not exist or have no political influence.

Although their methods are different, the papers by Zeckhauser and Zook and by Pauly both try to determine whether regulation as a general device of health policy tends to increase or contain expenditures. This seems to be a bit like asking whether screwdrivers have a general propensity to turn screws in or out. Under different conditions, regulation in its diverse forms can have varied and even opposite effects: It depends on who is turning the screws, which way and how hard they are turning them, and whom they are turning them on. Whether reg-

---

[11] For the industry view, see Louis A. Orsini, "Hospital Financing: Public Accountability—the Case for Rates Prospectivity Determined by State Agencies for All Patients," *Health Insurance Council Viewpoint*, January 1974.

123

ulation does control costs depends, in short, more on the configuration of political forces that acts upon the regulatory agencies than on any inherent characteristics of regulation itself.

In narrowly conceived empirical research, the political environment of regulation too often is ignored. Zeckhauser and Zook's paper accepts research of this sort—such as the Salkever-Bice study,[12] which uses data on certificate of need from 1968 to 1972—without taking into account the historical origins or the context of different types of regulation, nor even how long they had been allowed to work. Joskow's findings on the relative "success" of rate regulation in New York after 1975 bear out the point: The empirical results are contingent on historical conditions.[13] A fiscal crisis does wonders for the performance of cost control programs. We should be extremely cautious about premature diagnoses of regulatory failure that do not allow for the changing environment of regulation, nor even for the time it takes to establish administrative structures, learn methods of control, and adjust and correct for initial mistakes.

Zeckhauser and Zook's theoretical case against regulation is vitiated by gaps and ambiguities in their argument. The first difficulty occurs in moving between the general reasons for government intervention in private markets and the "conditions most favorable to 'traditional' modes of regulation." By showing that these latter conditions are not present in health care, Zeckhauser and Zook do not actually make out a case against government intervention since not all such intervention needs to be this sort of regulation, or even "regulation" at all. Yet they never address other possible forms of intervention (including government operation of health services, centrally coordinated planning or global budgeting, or changes in legal relations); nor do they rebut several possible reasons for intervention, such as distributive equity. Consequently, they leave suspended the basic questions about the desirability and appropriate form of intervention. I miss a clear argument why the planning of investment in the health sector (as is carried on in many countries other than the United States) or even hospital rate setting (as several states do here) cannot achieve significant—or perhaps, as Pauly suggests, overly restrictive—cost containment. The task may be difficult because of the complexity of health

---

[12] David S. Salkever and Thomas W. Bice, "The Impact of Certificate of Need Controls on Hospital Investment," *Milbank Memorial Fund Quarterly*, vol. 54 (1976), pp. 185–214.

[13] Paul Joskow, "Alternative Regulatory Mechanisms for Controlling Hospital Costs," in this volume; there is more bad news for advocates of competition in Joskow, "The Effects of Competition and Regulation on Hospital Bed Supply and the Reservation Quality of the Hospital," *Bell Journal of Economics*, vol. 11 (Autumn 1980), pp. 421–47.

services, but not impossible. If, as in other countries, planners can effectively control the total funds available for investment or total revenues available for operations, they need not evaluate every clinical or administrative decision. They are concerned not with the deviant cases, but with the bottom line, and they can be far less intrusive than in a system of detailed review.

Pauly's theoretical approach leads him to conclude that a government that is both payer and regulator will overconstrain health expenditures, and although this conclusion is certainly plausible, the way he arrives there is open to question. He so abstracts from the political world that interests such as insurance companies, employers, unions, and political parties fade from view. Any number of factors, such as organization among the poor, the relative power of left and right political parties, and alternative modes of taxation, could alter the result.[14] For this sort of problem we need the counterpart of what Schumpeter called "fiscal sociology"—a comprehensive analysis of the forces impinging upon the "regulatory budget."

The most serious problem in both these papers is that they fail to identify the links between the dynamics of the market and government intervention. By abstracting from the historical and political context, they lose sight of the basic forces that affect the nature and intensity of governmental activity. And this restricted vision limits their sense of our alternatives.

How Incentives May Be Improved

Zeckhauser and Zook argue that incentives, unlike regulation, have significant effects, and so they call for a variety of "specialized incentives" targeted to particular problems, such as unhealthy behavior and the high-cost users of medical care. I miss any evidence actually demonstrating the effectiveness of incentives in controlling the costs of unhealthy, high utilizers, but I do not deny that such incentives might hold down costs. The question is whether one wants to proceed in this way: taking one problem at a time, without changing the basic incentives or institutional structure of the system and without considering the distributive consequences of such policies. Their approach, which might be called "incentive tinkering," seems to be ironically similar to regulatory policies that attempt to alleviate particular problems here and there, also without changing basic incentives and institutional structure.

[14] Harold L. Wilensky, *The Welfare State and Equality* (Berkeley: University of California Press, 1975).

They seem to envision not a comprehensive reorganization of the market, such as Enthoven[15] and McClure[16] have proposed, but rather some marginal changes in the technical apparatus of government policy. And although they suggest that government need not always be the agent to oversee performance in the health sector, they have no design (as does Enthoven) for creating a nongovernmental system that would have autonomous incentives for controlling costs and for reflecting preferences.

While celebrating incentives, Zeckhauser and Zook do not make any clear, strategic choice among them. Not all incentives are of equal value, however, and the use of some incentives has a moral and psychological cost. In medical care, there is a critical choice to be made between the points of enrollment and utilization as the key moments when consumers will be asked to be cost conscious. On the one hand, some like Enthoven believe in using the prices of premiums rather than services as the key price mechanism, so that consumers may make choices while they are healthy, under no duress, and able to use information about their alternatives. Others, like Feldstein, want to make extensive use of service prices by requiring or encouraging deductibles and coinsurance.[17] The choice is not simply between two moments in time, but between two different "selves" of the consumer. As Schelling points out, at moments when people are more in command of themselves, they often try to make choices for those other times when they are not.[18] This may be why people have so often demanded health coverage without cost sharing. In times of distress, they do not want to deal with prices: They do not want to respond to incentives, and they buy policies that free them from that requirement. There is a message here that many economists seem professionally incapacitated from hearing. Any plan to shift costs to consumers at the point of treatment is likely to be resisted politically, or at least partly defeated by the purchase of supplementary coverage. Furthermore, shifting costs to consumers has the effect of removing costs from third parties and possibly reducing their interest in cost control. Finally, the interests of low-income people can be better protected if the point of cost consciousness is enrollment rather than utilization. At enrollment, the poor, subsidized through vouchers, may be given positive incentives to choose more efficient

[15] Alain C. Enthoven, *Health Plan* (Reading, Mass: Addison-Wesley, 1980).

[16] Walter McClure, *Comprehensive Market and Regulatory Strategies for Medical Care* (Minneapolis: Interstudy, 1979).

[17] Martin Feldstein, "Consequences of Hospital Controls," *Wall Street Journal*, April 12, 1979.

[18] Thomas Schelling, "The Intimate Contest for Self-command," *The Public Interest* (Summer 1980), pp. 94–118.

health plans, whereas the use of incentives at the point of utilization is almost necessarily negative, imposing upon the poor additional costs that they are ill-prepared to handle.

In general, the use of financial incentives affects low-income families more than any group, unless specific precautions are taken to protect their interests. The Enthoven plan does this not only by subsidizing their enrollment at a level that will enable them to buy into plans used by the middle class, but also by requiring that health plans transmit information to consumers through a government agency, as in the federal employee benefit system. After the Los Angeles experience with prepaid health plans, this seems to me a crucial means of preventing the exploitation of the sick poor. Equalizing the financial resources required for participation in the market is not enough; one needs also to reduce the chances for the manipulation of consumer ignorance.

Planning for Autonomy

In much recent work, including these papers, the universe of political alternatives is limited to "regulation" and the "market," or "regulation" and "incentives" (two dichotomies that are not strictly parallel since the government may employ incentives without allowing a market to function). I have already indicated that "regulation" ought not to be equated with all forms of government intervention; in particular, regulation seems to me distinct from planning. We have, for example, a multitude of regulations affecting the automobile industry, but we have no coordinated planning. Regulation is a typical expression of the American political system, with its fragmented responsibilities in Congress and among different branches of government, but one need only look to Japan, France, and the social democratic countries of Europe to find that more extensive planning, or coordination, not only is workable, but is working better than American-style regulation.

It is not my desire, however, to make a case for planning in the usual sense; I take as given the political incapacity of our system, except at wartime, for effective planning. Health care, moreover, involves moral choices that are best left decentralized. The sort of planning we need is what might be called "planning for autonomy"—that is, a transitional form of government intervention that reorganizes the incentives and institutional structure of medical care so that it becomes not only responsive to moral preferences and social needs, but also self-correcting. Two models exist for such autonomy. One is the model of the competitive market; the other is the model of democratic localism. In Hirschman's vocabulary, the first relies on opportunities for "exit," the second on opportunities for "voice," to control slack and unresponsiveness in organizations.[19]

In medical care, there is now a variety of "market" solutions, the best elaborated of which is the Enthoven plan, and a democratic localist proposal for a national health service. Supporters of one usually see no resemblance to the other, and the differences are enormous. But both have a similar intent and a similar difficulty. The intent is to subject medical care to more control by consumers; the difficulty is that this control may quickly be lost. The national health service proposal envisions what are, in effect, local monopolies, which could easily find ways to obstruct participation. The remedy to this problem seems to me the promotion of competition. But the market solution may also be evanescent: Competition could easily give way to concentration and, again, local monopoly. Moreover, because of the demands in health services for stability and continuity of care, it is not exactly clear that the public would like to see the "gale of creative destruction" (to borrow another phrase from Schumpeter) blow through the medical market. In addition, consumers have an interest in preserving the sense of moral responsibility that professionalism helps to cultivate, and there is a real danger that a corporate structure would remove the locus of control and responsibility to a distant tier of management. I think a takeover of medical care by national corporations is the antithesis of what either professionals or patients would like to see. Consequently, I would argue that while competition is desirable to make at least partial use of the "exit" or market mechanism, the service-providing organizations permitted to enter the competition ought to be restricted to nonprofit community enterprises, with substantial consumer representation in policy making.[20] The point here is primarily to preserve local control and professional responsibility while making use of competition and moving toward greater equality. I recognize this is not a position widely shared on either the left or right, but it is one around which I believe a new consensus might someday be built.

[19] Albert Hirschman, *Exit, Voice and Loyalty* (Cambridge, Mass.: Harvard University Press, 1970).

[20] For further arguments on the need to combine "voice" and "exit" mechanisms in medical care, see Paul Starr, "The Undelivered Health System," *The Public Interest* (Winter 1976), esp. pp. 81–84, and "Changing the Balance of Power in American Medicine," *Milbank Memorial Fund Quarterly*, vol. 58 (Winter 1980), 166–72.

Part Two

Experience Abroad: Is It So Different?

Alternative Systems of Health Care Provision: An Essay on Motes and Beams

A. J. Culyer, Alan Maynard, and Alan Williams

> *And why beholdest thou the mote in thy brother's eye but considerest not the beam that is in thine own eye?*
>
> *Matthew 7:3*

There are difficulties in both principle and practice in critically evaluating different ways of providing health care. It is worth reflecting on these difficulties before beginning the task.

The problems of *principle* concern the nature of the critique that is to be attempted. Suppose there are two significantly different ways of organizing the delivery of health care, which we will call system X and system Y. Suppose further that system X is designed faithfully to reflect one ideology (viewpoint A) and system Y another ideology (viewpoint B). One possibility would be to appraise system X with reference to viewpoint A, and Y with reference to B, and this method would be appropriate if we were trying to answer the question: How efficient is each system according to its own pretensions?

A second kind of critique would take each system in turn and appraise it with reference to one particular viewpoint. In such a comparison, it would be a devastating criticism of system X to show that it was worse than system Y when judged from viewpoint A, but it would not make much impact if one merely showed that X was worse than Y from viewpoint B, because the proponents of viewpoint A would regard that as irrelevant. The foregoing statements obviously also apply, mutatis mutandis, where the roles are reversed. This cross-cultural critique is therefore relevant if one wants to answer the question: Do "we" want "their" system here?

Yet a third kind of critique might be purely ideological and consist of an argument about the moral superiority of viewpoint A over view-

131

point B or vice versa. This method would be relevant if one were trying to convince one's fellow citizens that there is a better way of looking at health care systems, and if one were successful, this argument might change their views about the relative merits of systems X and Y by changing the criteria by which the systems are judged.

The main concern of this chapter is the first kind of critique—that is, we wish to examine each system according to its lights, to highlight the differences (and note the similarities) between them. We will also comment on how these differences are perceived from the opposite viewpoint, and in so doing take a limited excursion into the second type of critique.

The *practical* problems in making such comparisons concern two main features: the context within which the system works and the availability of relevant data on its performance.

The dominant contextual variable is the level of real income in the society, since it has been shown to play a dominant role in determining both the level of health in the community and the total amount of resources devoted to health care. Its effect on the level of health seems to work through levels of nutrition, sanitation, housing, education, and so forth. The evidence that health care itself is effective at the margin in improving either length or quality of life in most advanced countries is, to put it mildly, not strong.[1] But this evidence is by no means conclusive, because we lack comprehensive data on a comparable basis between systems, and even within a system one must generalize from rather scanty general surveys and rather piecemeal case studies.[2] This lack of information inevitably leads to differences in judgment about the significance of one item of evidence compared with another. Such differences seem to arise out of the questionable status of health care as a "luxury" item.[3]

[1] See, for example, T. McKeown, *The Modern Rise of Population* (London: Arnold, 1976); H. D. Walker, *Market Power and Price Levels in the Ethical Drug Industry* (Bloomington: Indiana University Press, 1971); F. Ederer, "The Randomized Clinical Trial," in C. I. Phillips and J. N. Wolfe, eds., *Clinical Practice and Economics* (London: Pitmans, 1977); J. Bunker, "Surgical Manpower: A Comparison of Operations and Surgeons in the United States and Wales," *New England Journal of Medicine,* vol. 282 (1970), pp. 135–44; E. Vayda, "A Comparison of Surgical Rates in Canada and England and Wales," *New England Journal of Medicine,* vol. 289 (1973), pp. 224–29; and A. L. Cochrane, *Effectiveness and Efficiency: Random Reflections on Health Services* (London: Nuffield Provincial Hospitals Trust, 1972).

[2] See, for example, R. Maxwell, *International Comparisons of Health Needs and Health Services* (London: McKinsey & Co., 1978); Organization of Economic Cooperation and Development, *Public Expenditure on Health,* 1977, table 1; and Great Britain, Royal Commission on the National Health Services, *Final Report,* 1979.

[3] J. P. Newhouse, "Development and Allocation of Medical Care Resources," in T. Takemi et al., eds., *Development and Allocation of Medical Resources* (Tokyo: Japanese Medical Association, 1975).

We are now faced with a dilemma. If we pursue the discussion with prototypes of systems and idealized viewpoints, we run the risk of formulating a vacuous essay in stylized history. If we open the discussion with a specific case study, we run the risk of being sidetracked in arguments about particular features of the selected cases to the detriment of the main theme. We have struck an uneasy compromise between these two extremes in that we have associated the United Kingdom and the National Health Service (NHS) explicitly with viewpoint B and system Y, but we have not associated viewpoint A and system X with any particular country. In thinking about the issues posed, however, we have had in mind countries such as the United States and West Germany. This procedure has caused us problems because of the disparities in wealth between the countries "in our minds' eye." In a more comprehensive analysis it might be better to adopt a comparative scheme more like the following one:

	System X	System Y
Rich	United States, West Germany	Scandinavia
Not-so-rich	France	United Kingdom

Since our special knowledge is with respect to the United Kingdom, however, and the conference for which this paper was written was largely about the United States, this tactical decision seems justified on this occasion. Our readers will, in the main, be able to apply their knowledge of the institutional features (especially for the United States) that we lack and thereby extend the comparisons that we make.

The chapter will first summarize viewpoints A and B, following Donabedian closely.[4] The prototypical systems X and Y will then be sketched out and some immediately obvious implications identified. Each will be scrutinized according to its own lights, and then according to the opposing ideology. Finally we shall speculate about the future of each system.

Idealized Viewpoints

It is possible to distinguish sharply between two rival ethical bases, on each of which a system of health care can be constructed and justified. The first considers access to health care to be essentially similar to access to all the other good things in society (food, shelter, leisure pursuits);

[4] A. Donabedian, "Social Responsibility for Personal Health Services: An Examination of Basic Values," *Inquiry,* vol. 8, no. 2 (1971), pp. 3–19.

that is, it is part of society's reward system. The second regards access to health care as a citizen's right, like access to the ballot box or to the courts of justice, which should not depend in any way on an individual's income and wealth. Economists' models of the efficiency of alternative systems have sometimes bridged these two views, especially when externalities have been introduced.[5] We shall not, however, develop that line of argument here. These two positions have been epitomized by Donabedian as viewpoint A and viewpoint B.[6] They are, he argues, each typically associated with a complex of other attitudes toward health care, as illustrated in table 1. These syndromes should be kept in mind when viewpoints A and B are referred to later in the text.

Prototypical Systems

System X has as its guiding principle consumer sovereignty in a decentralized market, in which access to health care is selective according to willingness and the ability to pay. It seeks to achieve this sovereignty by private insurance; it allows insured services to be available partially free at time of consumption; it allows private ownership of the means of production and has minimal state control over budgets and resource distribution; and it allows the rewards of suppliers to be determined in the market.

System Y has as its guiding principle the improvement of health for the population at large; it allows selective access according to the effectiveness of health care in improving health ("need"). It seeks to improve the health of the population at large through a tax-financed system free at the point of service. It allows public ownership of the means of production subject to central control of budgets; it allows some physical direction of resources; and it allows the use of countervailing monopsony power to influence the rewards of suppliers.

Both systems (in principle) offer choice of practitioner to patients, and clinical freedom of practitioners in the treatment of patients. Both systems ration access, but the excluded patients have predictably different characteristics and manifest themselves in different ways. Poor people and people in areas where it is not very rewarding to supply health care will be the excluded population in system X, except to the extent that an enclave of system Y is introduced alongside to take care of needy groups. The excluded population under system Y will be those for whom medical care is not cost effective in health terms, and they

---

[5] A. J. Culyer and H. Simpson, "Externality Models and Health: A Rückblick over the Last Twenty Years," *Economic Record*, vol. 56, no. 154 (1980), pp. 222–30.

[6] Donabedian, "Social Responsibility for Personal Health Services."

TABLE 1

ATTITUDES TYPICALLY ASSOCIATED WITH VIEWPOINTS A AND B

	Viewpoint A	*Viewpoint B*
Personal responsibility	Personal responsibility for achievement is very important, and this is weakened if people are offered unearned rewards. Moreover, such unearned rewards weaken the motive force that assures economic well-being, and in so doing they also undermine moral well-being, because of the intimate connection between moral well-being and the personal effort to achieve.	Personal incentives to achieve are desirable, but economic failure is not equated with moral depravity or social worthlessness.
Social concern	Social Darwinism dictates a seemingly cruel indifference to the fate of those who cannot make the grade. A less extreme position is that charity, expressed and effected preferably under private auspices, is the proper vehicle, but it needs to be exercised under carefully prescribed conditions, for example, such that the potential recipient must first mobilize all his own resources and, when helped, must not be in as favorable a position as those who are self-supporting (the principle of "lesser eligibility").	Private charitable action is not rejected but is seen as potentially dangerous morally (because it is often demeaning to the recipient and corrupting to the donor) and usually inequitable. It seems preferable to create social mechanisms that create and sustain self-sufficiency and that are accessible according to precise rules concerning entitlement that are applied equitably and explicitly sanctioned by society at large.
Freedom	Freedom is to be sought as a supreme good in itself. Compulsion attenuates	Freedom is seen as the presence of real opportunities of choice,

(*table continues on next page*)

TABLE 1 (continued)

	Viewpoint A	*Viewpoint B*
	both personal responsibility and individualistic and voluntary expressions of social concern. Centralized health planning and a large governmental role in health care financing are seen as an unwarranted abridgment of the freedom of clients as well as of health professionals, and private medicine is thereby viewed as a bulwark against totalitarianism.	and although economic constraints are less openly coercive than political constraints, they are nonetheless real, and often the effective limits on choice. Freedom is not indivisible but may be sacrificed in one respect in order to obtain greater freedom in some other. Government is not an external threat to individuals in the society but is the means by which individuals achieve greater scope for action (that is, greater real freedom).
Equality	Equality before the law is the key concept, with clear precedence being given to freedom over equality wherever the two conflict.	Since the only moral justification for using personal achievement as the basis for distributing rewards is that everyone has equal opportunities for such achievement, then the main emphasis is on equality of opportunity, and where this cannot be assured, the moral worth of achievement is thereby undermined. Equality is seen as an extension to the many of the freedom actually enjoyed by only the few.

will show themselves in waiting lists (if they are close to the margin established by the priority system), unless system Y allows an enclave of system X alongside to allow those with the requisite willingness and ability to pay to be taken care of outside the main system. Both systems incorporate an agency relationship between doctors and patients, and wherever market mechanisms impinge upon the workings of either system, they are invariably imperfect.[7]

Performance: System X

If system X is examined from viewpoint A, the first issue on which to focus is whether the insurance mechanism achieves the level and pattern of care that a well-informed free market would have generated.

The coverage of system X is characterized by duality: on one hand, a private health care sector made up of competing nonprofit insurers and nonprofit medical service institutions; on the other, a government health care sector offering subsidized care to especially deserving or needy groups that in practice are likely to include the poor, the old, the chronically sick, and war veterans. The degree of insurance coverage, and hence the effective demand for health care, depends on income, attitude toward risk, and the pooling of risks. It also depends on whether premiums are tax offsets and whether they are partly paid by employers. There is likely to be general overinsurance, as judged from viewpoint A,[8] as well as specific instances of underinsurance.[9]

The coverage of the government sector under system X will be imperfect because the state programs are not coordinated. That is, not all hardship groups will be covered. The typical hardship group is the poor. Generally a large proportion, at least 60 percent, of the poor are over sixty or under twenty years old. Furthermore, it is unlikely that such groups will consist predominantly of minority ethnic groups; they will generally be white, and a large percentage will be rural inhabitants. All epidemiological studies show these classes of people to be most in need of health care.

Typically, government intervention in system X will be aimed at assisting these groups but will be piecemeal and will adopt some of the characteristics of private insurance. A health care plan for the aged who

[7] See the following discussions by R. G. Evans: *Price Formation in the Market for Physician Services in Canada 1957–1969* (Ottawa: Queen's Printer, 1972); "Supplier Induced Demand: Some Empirical Evidence and Implications," in M. Perlman, ed., *The Economics of Health and Medical Care* (London: Macmillan, 1974); and "Modelling the Objectives of the Physician," in R. Fraser, ed., *Health Economics Symposium* (Kingston, Ontario: Queen's University Industrial Relations Centre, 1976).

[8] See M. V. Pauly, "A Measure of the Welfare Cost of Health Insurance," *Health Services Research* (Winter 1969), pp. 281–92; and M. S. Feldstein, "The Welfare Loss of Excess Health Insurance," *Journal of Political Economy,* vol. 81 (1973), pp. 251–79.

[9] See K. J. Arrow, "Uncertainty and the Welfare Economics of Medical Care," *American Economic Review,* vol. 53 (1963), pp. 941–73.

are in receipt of social security, for instance, would consist of two parts. The first part would provide relatively comprehensive hospital insurance, but would be subject to quite substantial deductible and coinsurance provisions. The second part of this program would consist of voluntary supplementary insurance for physicians' services, outpatient care, and supplies, financed by premiums matched by government contributions and also incorporating coinsurance and deductibles.

Another government program is likely to be directed at the nonaged poor and would be linked to eligibility for welfare. Given the decentralization and selectivity objectives lying behind system X, the associated income maintenance (social security) system will probably be complex and incomplete in its coverage. Thus provision of health care in this sector (the nonaged poor) will also be incomplete and characterized by complex sets of regulations about eligibility. Furthermore, eligibility and coverage will be made more complex by the fact that the benefits will be provided by state governments, but federal authorities will seek to equalize them.

Such programs will have predictable outcomes. Because many people are tied to the welfare program, they will not receive benefits although they are poor. If eligibility is restricted to the aged, the blind, the disabled, and one-parent families, for instance, then significant proportions of the rural and urban poor will get no benefits. Those in receipt of care will find large geographical differences in facilities. Payments for doctors' services will be higher in metropolitan areas than in nonmetropolitan areas, and higher in the high-income areas than in the low-income areas. Considerable interjurisdictional benefit differences will also exist, and there will be large differences in the services received by the different races: Average benefits for white recipients, for example, will be higher than for nonwhites.

Those in receipt of publicly financed health care and those eligible for privately financed health care will face deductibles and coinsurance. Most of the evidence from countries that, like the United States, have a system X pattern indicates that the effect of such price barriers will be that demand patterns will be changed; the less affluent, who are often those with the poorest health status, will reduce their demand for care the most. Prices will reduce demand for those who are ill and in need of care, as the California experiments have shown. With members of the population having unequal effective demand and facing price barriers, care will go to the more affluent (and the relatively more healthy) because of demand patterns.

To the extent that demands are reduced by deductibles and coinsurance, the patients' agents (doctors) may be able to compensate for the reduced demands for their services by changing their diagnoses and generating extra demand for their services. These effects will be more pronounced in affluent areas and will ensure that cost containment is difficult to achieve in system X. Relatively high health care spending will be reflected in higher physician incomes, higher-technology medicine, and a higher rate of intervention than is expected in the NHS. In Cochrane's epidemiological survey of seven countries, therefore, it is not surprising to find that the United States ranked first in terms of its health spending as a proportion of gross national product (GNP) (whereas England and Wales ranked seventh), while ranking sixth or seventh in perinatal, infant, and mature male and female mortality rates (compared with England and Wales, which ranked third or fourth on average). Similarly, the rate of introduction of new (and untested for effectiveness on clinical outcomes) technologies like the Computed Tomography Scanner is immeasurably faster in the United States than in the United Kingdom, where the technologies are centralized in regional neurological specialties.[10] It is well established from many cross-national epidemiological studies that the rate of surgical intervention is two or three times higher in the United States than in the United Kingdom.[11]

It therefore seems likely that the selective approach of system X will fail to provide an effectively guaranteed floor of health care provision, and that the inequalities in health care consumption and health status will be more marked in system X than in system Y. The price of tying health care to the reward system is great inequality in provision, access, consumption, and health status. Such outcomes can be seen in several X-type systems.[12]

The decentralized decision-making framework of system X is reflected in a multiplicity of private insurers, although usually there is a marked propensity for concentration in ownership, with the market being dominated by a few insurance carriers. The public sector is made up of overlapping agencies providing care for the poor, the aged, and special groups such as veterans, which make for a lack of integration in the delivery of health care and related services.

Although doctors will be prepared to transfer patients among themselves, they will be wary of referring patients out of the immediate health care system because to do so would result in a loss of fees. In some X-

---

[10] H. D. Banta, "The Diffusion of the Computed Tomography (CT) Scanner in the U.S.," *International Journal of Health Services,* vol. 10 (1980), pp. 251–69.

[11] One such study is Bunker's "Surgical Manpower."

[12] See, for example, K. Davis and C. Schoen, *Health and the War on Poverty,* Brookings Institution Studies in Social Economics (Washington, D.C., 1978); and U.S. Department of Health, Education, and Welfare, Public Health Service Office of Health Research, Statistics, and Technology, *Health—United States 1979,* Publication PHS 80–1232, 1980.

type health care systems (for example, West Germany) payment of a fee per item of service has led to the development of extensive diagnostic equipment in doctors' offices, where it is underused, and a lack of development in the numbers of hospital outpatients, because the primary-care doctors do not want to lose the income from the diagnostic fees that they could claim for patients, even though some standardization of provision would have been in the patients' interest.

The decentralization of health care ensures that coordination between financing and supplying agencies is limited and that doctor monopoly power is not confronted with a monopsony. Similarly, other provider agencies, including the pharmaceutical industry, are not countervailed by any concentrations of buying power. Such agencies are likely to be strong supporters of system X (especially vis-à-vis system Y).

The lack of coordination in organization and the unbalanced use of resources within system X also characterize its dealings with other social service agencies. Their federal-state nature makes coordination difficult and integration with the health care system well nigh impossible.

Thus system X provides an expensive choice for the majority having insurance, but a limited choice for the poor minority, and for decentralized agencies that do not cooperate extensively. The problems of this sector, expenditure inflation, and the failure to provide "minimum" health care for the whole population, tend to precipitate increased government intervention and the extension of government planning, that is, the grafting of system Y elements onto system X.

Performance: System Y

Since the overall objective of system Y is to improve the health of the community, it seems reasonable to start by asking whether it is more efficient in its effort than system X. Here we immediately run into considerable problems concerning the definition of health, but if we take three common indicators (perinatal mortality, life expectancy at age one, and maternal mortality) and if we compare these for a range of advanced economies, we obtain the data presented in table 2.

In commenting on this table the Royal Commission on the NHS observes:

> . . . the general trend is for countries with a high per capita expenditure on health to have a relatively low perinatal mortality rate, though Japan and the USA diverge from this pattern. . . . in 1974 West Germany and the USA had much larger national incomes and per capita health expenditure than England and Wales but were performing worse in terms of perinatal

TABLE 2
HEALTH SERVICE RESOURCES AND RESULTS: INTERNATIONAL COMPARISONS, 1974 OR NEAR DATE

Country	Per Capita Total Expenditure on Health (US$)[a]	Percent Trend GDP[b]	Doctors (per 10,000, 1974)	Nurses (per 10,000, 1974)	Life Expectancy[c] M	Life Expectancy[c] F	Perinatal Mortality (per 1,000 live births)	Maternal Mortality (per 100,000 births)
Australia	308	6.5	13.9	54.1	68.5	75.4	22.4	11.3
Canada	408	6.8	16.6	57.8	69.7	77.0	17.7	10.8
Finland	265	5.8	13.3	46.0	66.8	75.5	17.1	10.6
France	352	6.9	13.9	23.7	69.5	77.1	18.8	24.0
Italy	191	6.0	19.9	7.8	70.0	76.0	29.6	42.4
Japan	166	4.0	11.6	16.1	70.8	76.0	18.0	38.3
Netherlands	312	7.3	14.9	22.5	71.2	76.9	16.4	10.3
Norway	270	5.6	16.5	46.4	71.4	77.7	16.8	3.3
Sweden	416	7.3	16.2	58.6	72.0	77.4	14.1	2.7
United States	491	7.4	16.5	40.4	68.0	75.6	24.8	15.2
West Germany	336	6.7	19.4	27.6	68.6	74.9	23.2	45.9
England and Wales	} 212	} 5.2	13.1	33.7	69.5	75.6	21.3	13.0
Scotland			16.1	45.6	67.7	74.0	22.7	21.5
Northern Ireland			15.3	36.6	67.0	73.6	25.9	17.1

[a] The column is indicative rather than definitive: It has been derived by multiplying percentage of trend GDP (gross domestic product) spent on health care by actual GDP adjusted for purchasing power differences.

[b] Trend GDP is used to avoid the influence of cyclical business fluctuations on the level of output, which could distort the measured share of health expenditure in that output. See Organization for Economic Cooperation and Development (OECD). *Public Expenditure on Health*, 1977, p. 9.

[c] At age one.

SOURCES: There are a number of caveats concerning the figures in this table. Details are given in the following sources: OECD, *Public Expenditure on Health*, 1977, table 1; R. Maxwell, *International Comparisons of Health Needs and Health Services* (London: McKinsey & Co., 1978); Irving B. Kravis, Alan W. Heston, and Robert Summers, "Real GDP per Capita for More Than One Hundred Countries," *Economic Journal* (June 1978), table 4; table 3.8 of the Report of the Royal Commission on the NHS, Cmnd. 7615, Her Majesty's Stationery Office, London, 1979.

mortality and maternal mortality, and no better on life expectancy. . . .[13]

Although much more sophisticated analysis is called for if one is to pinpoint the precise *sources* of these differences, it seems clear that in terms of cost effectiveness (where effectiveness relates to health) system Y is the best buy.

Viewpoint B also sets great store on equality of opportunity and the use of health care as a compensatory mechanism where the absence of such equality generates casualties in health terms.

At the level of formal entitlement, system Y offers universal access to a wide range of services, so in that respect there is no problem. But a more severe test of its performance is the extent to which those who would benefit most from health care are the ones who utilize it. In the United Kingdom this discussion has centered on two distinct but related issues, first, the unequal geographical dispersion of health and health care and, second, the social class gradient in health and health care utilization.

The early days of the NHS were characterized by the surprising degree to which medical discretion was given free play to dispose of available resources, while the availability of resources was for many years what had been inherited from the past. This complacency is, perhaps, less surprising when one realizes that systematic empirical epidemiology is still largely in its infancy. On the other hand, it is remarkable that the first study of the territorial distribution of resources occurred in 1970, twenty-two years after the inception of the NHS, and that it was a study sponsored by the British Medical Association and not an official one.[14]

At the aggregate level of resource allocation, only recently have resources been allocated in a way that is consistent with the achievement of the goal of universality. The ability of each district to provide services was, in part, determined by the stock of facilities (including personnel) they inherited in 1948, and in part by the extent of subsequent redistribution to reduce pre-1948 inequalities.[15] Resource flows—and capital

---

[13] Great Britain, Royal Commission, *Final Report.*

[14] M. H. Cooper and A. J. Culyer, "An Economic Assessment of Some Aspects of the Operation of the National Health Service," *Health Services Financing* (London: British Medical Association, 1970), appendix A.

[15] See details in Ibid. and in two other studies by M. H. Cooper and A. J. Culyer: "An Economic Survey of the Nature and Intent of the British National Health Service," *Social Science and Medicine,* vol. 5 (1971), pp. 1–13; and "Equality in the National Health Service: Intention, Performance and Problem in Evaluation," in M. M. Hauser, ed., *The Economics of Medical Care* (London: Allen and Unwin, 1972). See also A. Maynard, "Inequalities in Psychiatric Care in England and Wales," *Social Science and Medicine,* vol. 6 (1972), pp. 221–27.

flows in particular—have been affected by the requirements of economic stabilization policies and by the reluctance of the government to adopt policies of positive discrimination in favor of the relatively deprived areas (especially the English regions outside the London area).

There have been some direct controls on resource deployment by the central government, particularly in attempting to shift the regional distribution of resources. Thus because of policies such as "negative direction" some geographical areas have been declared to be provided adequately with general practitioners and new practices are not allowed. Central government has also controlled the creation of new hospital specialist (consultant) posts to shift resources into particular specialties and geographical areas, as perceived needs suggest is desirable.

Until 1970, budgets were allocated on the basis of a crude incremental formula: what was received last year $+ x$ percent for inflation and growth $+ y$ percent to rectify any "scandals" revealed by the media. Since 1970 a series of specific resource allocation formulas have evolved, the objective of which is to reduce the disparities in the allocation of budgets within each of the four parts of the United Kingdom. These policies were initiated by a Conservative government, elaborated by a Labour government, and are being retained by the present Conservative government. If prosecuted with vigor, they will reduce inequalities in resource endowments among the four parts of the United Kingdom and among the English regions (especially inequalities between London and the rest of the country).

The present formulas, which allocate resources on the basis of population weighted, inter alia, by mortality (as a proxy for morbidity), are applied only within England, Scotland, and Wales, and so do not tackle the problem of differences among the component parts of Britain. If the Resource Allocation Working Party (RAWP) formula[16] were applied to the whole country as if it were a single unit, the health care budgets of Scotland and Ulster would be reduced by 14.9 and 13.7 percent, respectively.[17]

As for the social class gradient, it seems that the participants in the political debate in the 1940s thought that the removal of the price barrier to consumption would eradicate the major obstacle to equal access.[18] This attitude proved naïve. Whether the consequence of the abolition

---

[16] As in Great Britain, Department of Health and Social Security, *Sharing Resources in England*, 1976.

[17] See A. Maynard and A. Ludbrook, "Applying the Resource Allocation Formulae to the Constituent Parts of the U.K.," *Lancet*, vol. 1 (1980), pp. 85–87; and their "Budget Allocation in the National Health Service," *Journal of Social Policy*, vol. 9, no. 3 (1980), pp. 289–312.

[18] See M. Foot, *Aneurin Bevan 1945–60: A Biography*, vol. 2 (London: Poynter, 1973).

of the so-called price-barrier is greater or lesser, "inequality" depends on the rationing system that becomes effective. At the doctor-patient level, the doctor, as the patient's agent, is in a position to ration access using nonpecuniary criteria such as clinical condition, age, sex, color, religion, socioeconomic class, actual or potential nuisance values, and so on. In other words, the effective demand for health care depends partly on the decisions of patients to initiate a spell of care and partly on professional judgments by the doctor about the marginal product of health care in terms of its effect on the health status of patients. Demand for care must also be partly related to what generates job satisfaction for the physician. Thus it is related both to the supplier's concept of productivity and to the patient's view of expected marginal benefit. The doctor-patient relationship is not distorted by artificial incentives to supply unproductive, but remunerative, services, although there are, in the absence of close monitoring mechanisms, greater incentives under the NHS to maximize a "quiet life" (for example, to refer patients unnecessarily to specialists in the hospitals). While these effects at the level of the general practitioner do not adversely affect the universality principle, it is clear that progress has not gone as far as might have been expected in the direction of devising incentive structures to bring actual practice more closely in line with what is believed to be "best practice." On the other hand, the financial anxieties that would otherwise accompany ill-health in the form of uncertainty as to what one's insurance actually covered or concern that one might not, without considerable sacrifice, be able to afford copayments, are completely removed.

There is still a long way to go, however, if the objective is to eliminate differences in health (and health care utilization) between social classes.[19] It is increasingly argued that this task may require not so much improved health services for the poor, as coordinated improvement in a whole package of services, of which health care would be only one. From the beginning of the NHS it has been recognized that although health *care* (an input) and good *health* (an output) are linked, the nature of the health production function is more comprehensive than this. Good health[20]

---

[19] See evidence in Great Britain, Department of Health and Social Security, *Inequalities in Health: Report of a Committee under the Chairmanship of Sir Douglas Black,* 1980. See also, J. LeGrand, "The Distribution of Public Expenditure: Health," *Economica,* vol. 45 (1978), pp. 125–42.

[20] See Alan Williams, "Measuring the Effectiveness of Health Care Systems," in M. Perlman, ed., *The Economics of Health and Medical Care* (London: Macmillan, 1974); and his " 'Need'—An Economic Exegesis," in A. J. Culyer and K. G. Wright, eds., *Economic Aspects of Health Services* (London: Martin Robertson, 1978). See also, A. J. Culyer, "Need Values and Health Status Measurement," in Culyer and Wright, *Economic Aspects of Health Services.*

or healthy days in Grossman's terms[21] is the flow of services from a stock of health capital whose level is influenced by inputs such as income, education, housing, social security programs, and family time, as well as health care. Some of these other determining variables are the responsibility of other bodies, mainly local authorities and the central government. Beveridge analyzed the problems of the welfare state in terms of the eradication of the five "giants" of Want, Disease, Ignorance, Squalor, and Idleness, emphasizing the interaction of these facets of social policy and the consequent need for integration of the policies to deal with them.[22] Under the NHS, government health departments sought to integrate policy in a variety of areas.

The NHS Act nationalized the hospital system and brought together the previously separate voluntary (nonprofit) sector with the local government sector. Problems of coordination with local government social services and other government agencies remain, however. In 1976 funds were made available for the NHS to finance local government projects that would enable the NHS to discharge patients more rapidly and to use resources more efficiently.

These problems of integration are compounded by the nature of resource allocation at the microlevel in the NHS. The principal decision maker is the doctor, and he typically has neither the training, the inclination, nor the incentives to practice efficient (that is, cost-effective) medicine. The NHS does not provide sufficient information about the costs and benefits of alternative therapies and medical practice. It, and the universities, trains doctors to act decisively rather than to appraise scientifically the attributes of alternative procedures. Even if the efficient NHS doctor does evaluate his practice, the results of his work are not likely to be applied by his colleagues because they have few incentives to minimize costs and maximize output. The NHS budgeting system generates little useful information routinely[23] and often presents perverse incentives to decision makers.[24] The NHS structure can be best interpreted as *enabling:* It *removes* some of the main incentives for

---

[21] M. Grossman, "On the Concept of Health Capital and the Demand for Health," *Journal of Political Economy,* vol. 80 (1972), pp. 223–55; and M. Grossman, *The Demand for Health: A Theoretical and Empirical Investigation,* National Bureau of Economic Research Occasional Paper no. 119 (New York, 1972).

[22] W. Beveridge, *Report on Social Insurance and Allied Services* (London: Her Majesty's Stationery Office, 1942).

[23] Alan Williams, "The Budget as a (mis)-Information System," in A. J. Culyer and K. G. Wright, *Economic Aspects of Health Services* (London: Martin Robertson, 1978).

[24] J. Perrin et al., *Management of Financial Resources in the National Health Service,* Royal Commission on the National Health Service, Research paper no. 2 (London: Her Majesty's Stationery Office, 1978).

ineffective care and opens the way for the unprejudiced application of professional judgments. It does not, as yet, provide incentives aimed directly at the production of the most cost-effective care.

There are signs that these problems are being recognized by the profession and that the NHS is becoming more aware of the need to evaluate and the need to provide more incentives (monetary and non-monetary) for doctors to be efficient in their resource allocation. The tight overall financial control (through predetermined cash limits) is reinforcing the necessity to evaluate: In a no-growth world new developments can be adopted only if old programs are dropped. These pressures are sharpening the debate about choices and are forcing doctors to take more seriously economic appraisals of their activities.

The existence of private practice also introduces distortions. In particular, the principal nonprice rationing mechanism for non-urgent hospital admission is waiting time.[25] Patients waiting for admission are almost entirely surgical cases whose conditions—for example, squints, hernias, varicose veins, hemorrhoids, and hip replacements—offer no threat to life. Elective surgery cases admitted from the waiting list constituted about a quarter of all admissions in 1977 (the rest being direct admissions or transfers from other hospitals), and they were on the waiting list an average of sixteen weeks. Control of the waiting lists by consultants who also have private practice is a means of diverting NHS patients into private practice and, for the unscrupulous, offers little incentive to use NHS beds as efficiently as possible.

The existence of private practice extends, of course, the scope of choice for both doctor and patient and enables patients to avoid waiting. Although private medicine in the United Kingdom is not comprehensive (for example, cervical smears are not routinely taken in cases of termination of pregnancy in the private sector, with the result that some cases have had catastrophic consequences among this high-risk class of women), it typically offers better hospital hotel-type facilities. It also provides patients with a choice they do *not* have under the NHS, that is, the choice of surgeon who performs the operation. Under the NHS one chooses (in consultation with the general practitioner) one's consultant, but that choice assures only that a member of *his team* will perform the operation. In the private hospital sector, since only consultants may practice privately, one can be sure that the senior man of the team himself will perform the operation. Epidemiological evidence suggests, however, that this situation brings no clinical advantage and may, for the routine operations that form the stock-in-trade of private

[25] A. J. Culyer and J. Cullis, "Hospital Waiting Lists and the Demand and Supply of Inpatient Care," *Social and Economic Administration*, vol. 9, no. 1 (1975).

surgery, even be a disadvantage, since the senior man will tend to take only the more complex cases and be less practiced at routine ones. Thus in the United Kingdom the private sector represents a grafting of a system X offshoot onto a predominantly Y-type system.

Although neither the Beveridge report nor the coalition government's White Paper advocated the nationalization of the hospital system, the medical profession and other interest groups accepted it with little resistance.[26] Experience with the Emergency Medical Service during World War II had taught physicians that government intervention and money did not necessarily restrict their freedom to practice.

The Department of Health has, of course, been more active as the chief representative of the NHS against monopolistic suppliers. Government power has been used to influence the quality and prices of pharmaceutical products. The 1968 Medicines Act and the Medicines Commission, which regulate the quality of drugs, are similar to the Food and Drug Administration of the United States. The prices of pharmaceutical products have been regulated by the government of the United Kingdom since 1957. The current pharmaceutical price regulation scheme is a product of the last Labour government. Cooper has argued that price regulation has reduced the prices of pharmaceutical products in the United Kingdom, but even if his conclusions are correct, the industry continues to prosper.[27] Its important contribution to exports from the United Kindgom undoubtedly gives it considerable political clout.

Hospital doctors are salaried, and general practitioners are paid largely on a capitation basis. Additional remuneration depends on the age of the doctor (seniority payments), and his participation in the provision of certain services such as vaccinations, family planning, and out-of-hour home visits in order to encourage comprehensive health care. Salary negotiations take place through a review body made up of the "great and the good," who recommend pay awards relative to changes in the remuneration of other professions. While denying NHS doctors the opportunity to acquire substantial wealth, this system maintains the medical profession in a high place on the scale of remuneration of professional people.

The arguments over the terms and conditions of employment are intense, but the principles on which they are based retain the ideas of 1948: If he so wishes, the physician can elect to be a wholly private, a

[26] For details of the coalition government's White Paper, see Great Britain, Ministry of Health, "A National Health Service," Command 6502, 1944.

[27] M. H. Cooper and A. J. Cooper, *International Price Comparisons* (London: National Economic Development Office, 1972); and M. H. Cooper, *European Pharmaceutical Prices 1964–1974* (London: Croom Helm, 1975).

wholly public, or a private-and-public worker. Very few are wholly private, as the system not only provides modern and effective care but does so while ensuring that the professionals remain in high social standing and are paid at rates not inferior to those of their professional peers in other walks of life.

Doctors' salaries are low by European standards,[28] as are most salaries of professionals in the United Kingdom, and a familiar and fallacious conclusion to draw is that emigration is high.[29] Although the output of medical schools in the United Kingdom has risen from around 2,800 in 1968 to about 4,000 in 1979, the outflow of doctors has remained fairly constant at around 300 per year (less than the annual output of the medical schools). Certainly if the fluctuations in the emigration rate are taken as indicators of doctors' morale, they imply no impending doom for the NHS. Surveys conducted to ascertain more about the morale of doctors in the United Kingdom indicate that the morale of the profession is high and that the level of professional complaints about the NHS is small: 86 percent of NHS doctors would choose a career in medicine in the United Kingdom if they lived their lives again.[30]

Although it is difficult to evaluate in a scientific fashion whether choice has been exercised by those patients and doctors wishing to do so, the available evidence suggests that both parties are, in general, content with the NHS. Compared with assertions derived from the casual analysis of some NHS critics, the practice of the NHS is not far removed from its principles in respect of freedom of choice. Whether systems of control devised to serve better the other objectives of the NHS would seriously impede clinical freedom remains to be seen.

Summary and Conclusions

Our broad characterization of the two systems is summarized in table 3, and our general assessment of their respective achievements to date is presented in table 4.

In both cases we noted the incursion of "alien" viewpoints (hardly surprising in pluralistic democratic systems) that have led to the grafting of small offshoots of the other system onto the rootstock of the indig-

---

[28] See, for example, A. Maynard, *Health Care in the European Community* (London and Pittsburgh: Croom Helm and Pittsburgh University Press, 1975); and B. Abel-Smith and A. Maynard, *The Organisation, Financing and Cost of Health Care in the European Community*, Social Policy Series no. 36 (Brussels: Commission of the European Communities, 1979).

[29] See, for example, C. M. Lindsay, *National Health Issues: The British Experience* (New York: Hoffmann–La Roche, 1980).

[30] Consumer's Association, "How Do You Rate Your Job?" *Which* (September 1977).

TABLE 3

Comparative Features of Two Systems of Health Care

System X	System Y
Seeks to satisfy consumers in a market situation in which access to health care is part of the reward system of the society, hence determined by willingness and ability to pay.	Seeks to promote the general level of health in a community in which access to health care is the right of every citizen who stands to benefit therefrom.
Consumers insure and gain access to insured services (when required) at a reduced price at the point of consumption.	Consumers pay through the general tax system and pay nothing (or a nominal fee) at the point of consumption.
Private ownership of the means of production mainly by non-profit-making organizations.	Public ownership of the means of production.
Minimal governmental control over budgets and resource distribution.	Central control over budgets and some physical direction of resources.
Inputs to the service rewarded according to market forces.	Use of countervailing monopsony power to moderate the impact of other market forces.

enous system. This phenomenon leads us to ask whether the two systems will hybridize and become indistinguishable through convergence, or does the one have greater (Darwinian) power to survive sociopolitical changes in the environment.

Notwithstanding the difficulty of predicting ideological changes, at least one argument suggests that viewpoint B is more likely to gain ground in democratic countries over viewpoint A; that is the crude evolutionary argument that the countries now having Y-type health care systems did previously have X-type systems and chose to get rid of them, whereas we know of only one country (Australia) that has moved in the other direction. (This argument might be especially attractive to economists schooled in "revealed preference" theory.)

A different approach, which comes closer to being a direct ideological challenge, would be to ask whether one is more comfortable with a system in which the discontented minority are the poor and needy, or one in which the discontented minority are the more well-to-do members of society. Ultimately, of course, you just have to stand up and be counted. We wish to register as subscribing to viewpoint B, and our quotation from St. Matthew is to be read in that light.

TABLE 4

ACHIEVEMENTS OF TWO SYSTEMS OF HEALTH CARE

System X	*System Y*

Consumer sovereignty:
  Good for some, but vulnerable to
  exploitation in the context of the
  agency relationship.
	Health status:
	  Good in relation to resources
	  used.

Selectivity:
  Patchwork a bit threadbare in
  places.
	Universality:
	  Late developer; could do better.

Integration and coordination:
  Not efficacious owing to very
  imperfect markets.
	Integration and coordination:
	  Working at it.

Our prime concern, then, is to make system Y in the United Kingdom perform better according to its own lights. If, in the process, we can be of practical assistance to holders of viewpoint B elsewhere by offering a working model of system Y that is more attractive to them than any working model of system X, so much the better. Whether such a system will ever be attractive to holders of viewpoint A, or will convert them to viewpoint B, is another matter.

Health Insurance and Cost Containment Policies: The Experience Abroad

Uwe E. Reinhardt

Many health economists in the United States have recently dedicated themselves to the task of resurrecting "the market" in health care. The first phase of this campaign has been a hard-fought battle to demonstrate that, properly viewed, health care is just an ordinary consumer good that ought to be treated as such. Supported by theoretical armament and empirical ordnance, economists have carried their skirmishes to almost every corner of the health care sector. At the time of this writing, the smell of victory is in the air. Even die-hard public healthniks now grudgingly admit that the demand curve for health care slopes downward to the right, that its supply curve slopes upward to the right, and that in the absence of government meddling there would emerge a market-clearing price for the stuff. In short, the market seems to "work" here as elsewhere.[1]

Remarkably, while American economists were toiling in the trenches, scoring impressive victories in the realm of thought, their fellow citizens yawned and went right on socializing[2] this well-behaved commodity. The notion continued to spread that health care is one of those commodities to which every citizen in a civilized society is entitled regardless of ability to pay. To be sure, in their mellower moments even economists allow that a society might guarantee the individual access to certain basic health services, just as it might guarantee access to minimum amounts of food, clothing, and shelter. What vexes a guardian of efficiency is that this sentiment now threatens to engulf *all* technically

---

[1] It is, of course, never quite clear what economists mean when they say the "market works." They may mean simply that markets work in predictable fashion. Alternatively, they may mean that markets work to produce socially desirable, or at least acceptable outcomes. Sometimes the first is, thoughtlessly, assumed to imply the second.

[2] By "socializing" a commodity a society makes it available to the individual regardless of his or her ability to pay for it.

151

available health care, regardless of its cost.[3] Equally vexatious is the folklore, highly popular among the laity and widely reflected in public policy, that individual consumers are technically incompetent to influence the quality and the cost of their care, so that cost sharing by patients cannot be defended on resource-allocative grounds. Economists see in these strange notions a threat to our nation's economic welfare.

Although the urge to socialize the distribution of health care has eaten itself deeply into the fabric of American society, important bridgeheads have survived the collectivist siege. About 30 percent of all personal health care expenditures in the United States, for example, are still borne directly by patients at point of service. Of the remaining 70 percent, only slightly more than half are financed with public funds; the balance is covered by nongovernmental third parties, predominantly under insurance policies that have been sold in private markets at prices patterned more or less closely on actuarial principles.[4] Even the aged, whose health care was socialized in 1966 under the government's Medicare program, still cover an average of about a third of the cost of their health care out of their own financial resources,[5] either directly in the form of copayments or indirectly through insurance premiums. While none of these bridgeheads is secure, and many of them are far from the ideal, they nevertheless represent terrain from which one could foray into the now occupied territories of the health care sector, to liberate them for governance by market forces.

Other nations have fared much worse. In neighboring Canada, for example, and in the Western European nations, the antimarket forces have by now completely overrun the entire health care sector.[6] Table 1 conveys a bird's-eye view of the devastation in its summary of the main features of the health insurance systems in Canada, France, and West Germany.

In each of the three countries, comprehensive first-dollar health insurance coverage has befallen almost the entire population—a total of about 140 million people. Only France retains some vestige of cost sharing by patients, but the degree is trivial. No attempt is made in these nations to price health insurance to the individual household on

---

[3] Implicit in this egalitarian sentiment is the notion that unless a society can make a given medical intervention available to *all* persons who might benefit from it, the intervention ought not be available to anyone.

[4] See U.S. Department of Health, Education, and Welfare, *Health—United States 1978*, Publication no. PHS 78–1232, December 1978.

[5] See U. E. Reinhardt, "Medicare: Its Financing and Future," *American Economic Review*, vol. 69, no. 2 (May 1979), pp. 279–83.

[6] In Canada, only dental care and pharmaceuticals have escaped socialization in health care. In Europe, these two items are typically socialized as well.

anything approximating actuarial principles. On the contrary, policy makers in these countries pride themselves on the fact that they finance health care on the *principle of solidarity*. In practice this means that the household's contribution to the insurance pool is governed solely by its financial ability to contribute to the pool and is completely unrelated to its size, its age-sex composition, and the health status of its members.

The following section considers the development and modus operandi of these three health insurance systems in greater detail.[7] The reasons for the extensive socialization of health care in these countries will then be taken up. The chapter concludes with some thoughts on the virtues and vices of market forces in health care.

Health Insurance in Canada, France, and West Germany

Development and Structure. National health insurance in Canada is an agglomerate of independent provincial insurance plans. In each of the ten provinces, coverage for hospital care is administered by a plan distinct from that for physician services. The hospital plans were established in 1958 under the federal Hospital Insurance Diagnostic Services Act. Comprehensive coverage for physician services was introduced during 1968–1971 under the federal Medical Care Act of 1966, although the province of Saskatchewan had such a program as early as 1962.

Under the two acts, the federal government agreed to share roughly half the costs of any provincial insurance plan that met a set of stringent federal guidelines. According to the Medical Care Act, for example, the provincial plans must be publicly administered; they must be universally accessible on equal terms to all residents, and they must remove all financial barriers to covered services. Substantial cost sharing on the part of patients is inconsistent with the spirit of federal legislation.

Because responsibility for health care falls within the domain of the provinces, this peculiar federal-provincial arrangement is the closest politically feasible approximation to a bona fide *national* health insurance scheme in Canada. The cost-sharing mechanism is also the main vehicle through which the federal government can exert control over aggregate health expenditures. In 1977, for example, the federal government began to limit the growth of its contribution to the growth of gross national product, leaving the provinces to absorb a greater share where aggregate outlays grew at a faster rate. More recently the federal government has decided to make its contribution not solely in cash but

---

[7] The section "Health Insurance in Canada, France, and West Germany" is drawn from U. E. Reinhardt, "Health Insurance and Cost-Containment Policies: The Experience Abroad," *American Economic Review*, vol. 70, no. 2 (May 1980), pp. 149–56.

TABLE 1

Overview of National Health Insurance Systems

Parameter	Canada	France	West Germany
Administration	Ten independent provincial medical and hospital plans operating within federal guidelines and with federal cost sharing.	A national system of sickness funds organized on a geographic basis and supervised by the Ministry of Health and Social Security.	A mosaic of over 1,500 sickness funds organized in state and national associations and operating within federal statutes.
Role of private insurance	Confined to provision of supplemental coverage.	Confined to provision of supplemental coverage.	Covers some 7% of the population for basic benefits.
Population coverage	Public system provides universal coverage on equal terms.	The national system now covers 99% of the population.	Statutory system covers 93% of the population. Some 7% have private coverage; 1% have no coverage.
Benefits	Medical services, hospital services, for special groups: dental care, drugs.	Medical services, hospital services, prescription drugs, medical appliances, cash benefits.	Medical services, hospital services, dental care, prescription drugs, medical appliances, cash benefits.
Predominant mode of reimbursing providers	Hospitals: global budgets Physician: fee-for-service reimbursement under	Hospitals: per diems plus fee-for-service for physician services	Hospitals: per diems Hospital physician: salary Private physician: fee-for-

	province-wide, negotiated fee schedules	Hospital physician: salary Private physician: fee-for-service	service
Financing	A combination of taxes and direct premiums. Combination varies from province to province. Federal government bears about 50% of costs.	Basically a payroll tax; about 3.5% of income paid by employee; about 12.5% paid by employer.	A payroll tax of about 11% of earnings shared equally by employer and employee.
Cost sharing by patients	Originally rare. Increasing somewhat in provinces that permit physicians to opt out of the system.	Coinsurance rate of between 30% to zero, depending on severity of illness. Average rate is about 10%.	There is no cost sharing except for a modest copayment per prescription.
Percentage growth in health expenditures (average annual increase for period indicated)	1971–74: 12.1 1974–75: 18.0 1975–77: 13.0[a]	1970–75: 16.8[b] 1975–78: 15.9 1978–79: 16.8[a]	1970–75: 20.1[c] 1975–76: 9.8[c] 1976–77: 4.8 1977–78: 7.1[a]
Health care as a percentage of gross national product	1975: 7.1 1976: 7.2 1977: 7.1[a]	1975: 6.8[b] 1978: 7.1 1979: 7.3[a]	1976: 9 to 10[d]

[a] Preliminary estimates.
[b] The French figures are akin to the U.S. "personal health care" series.
[c] Outlays under the statutory health insurance system only.
[d] Rough estimate. A figure comparable to the U.S. "national health expenditures."

SOURCE: Uwe E. Reinhardt, "Health Insurance and Cost-Containment Policies: The Experience Abroad," *American Economic Review*, vol. 70, no. 2 (May 1980), pp. 149–56.

substantially in the form of tax points that vacate a share of the federal tax base in favor of the provinces. More direct forms of cost control are thus fully in the hands of the provinces.

The West German health insurance system is a network of about 1,500 fiscally and administratively independent "sickness funds" (*Krankenkassen*) whose common element is, as in Canada, that they operate within a framework of strict federal statutes. The sickness funds trace their origin to the friendly (cooperative) societies established during the late nineteenth century by unions or other associations of workers. They were forged into a national system in 1883 when membership in a sickness fund was made compulsory for certain groups of blue-collar workers.

The main thrust of the early sickness funds was to provide their members with cash benefits during episodes of illness and with a limited range of medical services. In the ensuing century, this system has gradually evolved in two directions: (1) Emphasis has shifted from cash benefits toward comprehensive medical benefits in kind, and (2) an ever larger proportion of the population has come under compulsory membership or has been granted the right to join the statutory system.

The premiums for insurance coverage under the statutory system are based on the insured's ability to pay rather than on actuarial principles. As of August 1979, the premium covering an employed person (along with dependent family members) ranged from 7 to 13.8 percent of the employee's gross income, with half that premium being paid by the employee and the other half by his or her employer.[8] Coverage for retired persons is paid by their pension funds, although at rates below actuarial costs. At this time only about 7 percent of the population (mainly civil servants entitled to generous federal cash indemnities and the self-employed) are covered by truly private commercial insurance.[9]

Although West Germany's sickness funds are controlled by strict federal statutes, they are nevertheless private, not-for-profit organizations that are expected to ensure their own fiscal stability. It may be thought that the very number of them—about 1,500—must introduce stiff competition for members. Actually, that number is deceptive. West Germans typically have only limited freedom in the choice of their sickness fund, because membership tends to be dictated by the insured's occupation and/or geographic location. Furthermore, the federal statutes impose on all funds a common benefit package that is so extraor-

---

[8] *Die Ortskrankenkasse,* vol. 61 (November 1, 1979), p. 821.

[9] Ulrich Geissler, "Health Care Cost Containment in the Federal Republic of Germany," mimeographed (November 1978).

dinarily broad as to leave only modest room for competition through benefits.

Some occupational groups, notably white-collar workers, do have the option of joining a "substitute fund" (*Ersatzkasse*) instead of the fund their employment would otherwise dictate. Persons who join the statutory system voluntarily also may elect one of the substitute funds that form an integral part of the statutory system. The substitute funds may offer voluntary members cash indemnities rather than service benefits—a right denied the other funds. The substitute funds also have tended to pay physicians higher fees and are therefore thought by the insured to provide superior physician services. Finally, the substitute funds were instrumental in forcing the conversion of the erstwhile capitation reimbursement of physicians (predominant until the late 1960s) to the current fee-for-service method. Such limited competition as there has been among West German sickness funds has therefore tended to favor the economic position of physicians. Since the substitute funds are chosen voluntarily and have registered a growing membership, their impact seems to have been favored by at least some proportion of the insured. Depending upon a statutory system's prevailing position, then, competition among insurers may increase or decrease the cost of health services.

Like the West German system—and like so many other systems on the European continent—the French system is composed of a network of sickness funds that trace their origin to cooperative societies of industrial workers. Over time, however, the system has come to be dominated by the "general scheme" (*Régime Générale*), a regionally organized but centrally directed network of some 120 local, primary sickness funds (*caisses primaires d'assurance maladie*) that covers most of the country's industrial work force and their dependents (thus, altogether, some three quarters of the French population).The primary sickness funds of the general scheme are supervised by sixteen regional funds (*caisses regionales d'assurance maladie*) that, in turn, are coordinated and supervised at the national level by the National Sickness Fund Association (*Caisse National d'Assurance Maladie*). The latter is a public corporation whose task it is to assure the fiscal viability of the entire network of funds through the setting of premiums, the definition of benefit packages, and the extension of grants and loans from a central fund to individual local sickness funds. At the apex of this system stands the Ministry of Health of the central government, which now has considerable statutory authority over the system, including the approval of negotiated fee schedules. The thrust of recent legislation has been to fold the remaining distinct groupings of sickness funds (for example, funds covering agricultural or railroad workers) into the general scheme and thus to convert the French system into a truly uniform, centrally directed national health insurance system.

Control over Costs and Expenditures. Table 1 indicates that the rapid secular growth in aggregate health care expenditures during the 1970s is not unique to the United States. The experience has been shared by most other industrialized nations—certainly by Canada, France, and West Germany. Indeed, an enduring conclusion from the numerous recent international conferences on the "health care cost explosion" has been that the phenomenon has so far been rather insensitive to the particular financial scheme grafted onto the health care delivery system. This point is brought out even more clearly in table 2, in which data from the United States are compared with data from Canada, after adjustments for differentials in inflation rates and population growth. It is striking how similar the growth in real per capita expenditures has been, in spite of the great differences in the health insurance systems of these two nations. Incidentally, it has become customary in the United States to cite the rising cost of health care in Canada as evidence of the inflationary tendencies inherent in national health insurance. One might

TABLE 2

AVERAGE ANNUAL GROWTH IN NATIONAL HEALTH CARE
EXPENDITURES, CANADA AND THE UNITED STATES, 1970–1975

	Year	Canada	United States
National health care expenditures,	1975	Can$11,372	US$122,231
billions of current dollars	1970	6,081	69,201
Average annual growth in national			
health care expenditures		13.3%	12.1%
National health care expenditures per	1975	Can$ 350	US$ 407
capita, constant (1970) dollars	1970	286	334
Average annual growth in constant-			
dollar health care expenditures per			
capita		4.1%	4.0%
Average annual growth in the price			
index of:			
Medical care (United States)			6.9%
Health and personal care			
(Canada)		6.3%	

SOURCE: U. E. Reinhardt, "Can the United States Learn from Foreign Medical Systems?" *Hospital Progress* (November 1978), p. 61.

adopt a different posture, however, and ask how Canada managed to offer its citizens as much health care and financial security as it did and still keep costs per capita somewhat below those registered in the United States.

During the first part of the 1970s, the growth of health care expenditures everywhere tended merely to be observed with some concern. Concern gave way to alarm sometime during the mid-1970s. At about that time, most nations began attempts to curb the growth in expenditures through overt public intervention. The form of this intervention has varied from country to country, in line with the institutional framework through which such intervention must work. The explicit or implicit goal of these policies, however, has been identical: to peg the growth of national health care expenditures to the growth of gross national product, at least over the long run. That goal is, of course, rather arbitrary, for there is no empirical support for the proposition that a society either should or would prefer to allocate a constant proportion of its resource budget to a commodity such as health care.

Policies to reduce aggregate expenditures on health care have been aimed at various combinations of the potential targets listed in table 3. The targets could be impacted indirectly through the provision of suitable financial incentives. A preferred approach seems to have been more direct regulation.

A widely accepted hypothesis among American economists is that an appropriate degree of expenditure containment could be achieved simply by assuring competition in the market for health services and by confronting the actors in these markets—consumers, producers, and third-party payers—with appropriate financial incentives. On this hypothesis public policy need not be targeted directly on any of the variables in table 3 at all but merely needs to ensure a framework for the appropriate determination of targets A and B, thus obviating the need for policies such as certificates of need for hospital facilities (target B.4). The sine qua non of such a framework is thought to be competitive markets for health services—the ostensible goal of current endeavors by the Federal Trade Commission—and substantial cost sharing on the part of patients. A more indirect approach to the development of the framework would be the establishment of truly competitive health insurance markets, an approach best exemplified in the Consumer-Choice Health Plan proposed by Enthoven.[10]

Health care providers in the United States—and elsewhere, for that matter—typically profess support for the concept of the competitive

[10] A. C. Enthoven, "Consumer-Choice Health Plan," *New England Journal of Medicine* (March 1978), pp. 650–709.

TABLE 3

POTENTIAL TARGETS OF POLICIES ON COST AND EXPENDITURE
CONTAINMENT IN HEALTH CARE

A. The utilization of health services
- A.1 Direct control of the behavior of patients and providers (e.g., through production profiles on individual physicians)
- A.2 Indirect control through financial incentives (e.g., rationing via money prices through cost sharing by patients or through competitively marketed health care alliances)
- A.3 Indirect control through limits on the capacity of providers (i.e., rationing via time prices or on the basis of the providers' medical judgement)

B. The prices of health services
- B.1 Direct control over prices (e.g., through negotiated fee schedules or limits on the per diem charges of inpatient facilities)
- B.2 Caps on the revenues of particular providers
- B.3 Indirect control over output prices through direct control over the prices of inputs (e.g., control over the salaries of health workers or over the prices of drugs, supplies, and equipment)
- B.4 Indirect control over output prices through direct control over the organization of health care production (e.g., prescribed staffing ratios for facilities or limits on capital expenditures).

market approach, if only because that approach draws fire away from targets closer to home (for example, B.1 to B.4). Unfortunately, the providers' enthusiasm for the model tends to wane once the meaning of "competition" is explained to them more concretely within the context of their own markets. Physicians, for example, generally show little enthusiasm for competition from self-employed paramedical manpower, for an expanded supply of medical manpower, or for policies to inform consumers better with regard to both the price and the quality of medical treatments.

As suggested in the introduction to this chapter, American policy makers seem even less impressed by the potential of competitive markets for health services and insurance. Although this set of decision makers cannot be said to represent one view, actual health policy in this country does betray a penchant for more direct forms of intervention—be it direct constraints on physical inputs (target A.3) under the Health Planning and Resources Development Act (1975), constraints on health care utilization (target A.1) through professional standards review organizations (PSROs), unilaterally imposed limits on fees and per diems (target B.1) under the Medicare and Medicaid programs, or the repeatedly proposed caps on hospital revenues (target B.2).

This skepticism toward the market model is shared by policy makers in other countries as well. Canada, France, and West Germany, for example, do not rely at all on the notion of competitive markets in their approach to cost and expenditure containment. Broadly speaking, the main thrust of their policies has been to constrain expenditures on physician services through negotiated or imposed fee schedules, and expenditures on inpatient services through controlled per diems or global budgets, on the one hand, and controls on physical capacity on the other. Table 4 presents a highly condensed summary of the main cost control instruments used in the three countries.

Of the three countries, only West Germany has introduced a formal cost containment law—the federal Health Care Cost Containment Act of 1977. The overall thrust of this legislation is to constrain the growth of expenditures through annually negotiated predetermined budgets at the aggregate level. The act mandates the establishment of a National Health Conference (*Konzertierte Aktion*) embracing all major groups active in the health care sector, including the sickness funds, the associations of sickness fund physicians, hospitals, the pharmaceutical industry, unions (representing consumers), associations of employers, the state (*land*) governments and the federal government.[11] This conference of interest groups is to develop annually a consensus on guidelines for the economic development of the statutory health insurance system, including, of course, the growth of total expenditures and increases in fees and prices. Although these guidelines are nonbinding, they are nevertheless apt to influence the negotiations on these points, and even more so the compulsory arbitration that is triggered when negotiations break down. The law represents an attempt to replace the vacuum left by the secular erosion of market forces with a new type of market—one in which interest groups bargain collectively toward a national consensus.

It is too early to assess the effectiveness of this new "market." As table 1 shows, the growth of expenditures under West Germany's statutory health insurance system has abated markedly in recent years, although the sharpest decline in the growth rate actually precedes the introduction of the Cost Containment Act of 1977. The explanation generally given for this early decline is that health care providers agreed to a stringent voluntary cost containment effort in anticipation of federal legislation, to demonstrate its redundancy.

---

[11] See Geissler, "Health Care Cost Containment in the Federal Republic of Germany."

TABLE 4
DOMINANT ELEMENTS IN THE CONTROL OF HEALTH CARE EXPENDITURES

Target	Canada	France	West Germany
Expenditures on Physician Services			
Fees	Fairly effective provincial control through negotiated schedules.	Fairly effective control through negotiated schedules that require central government approval.	Negotiated fee schedules with compulsory arbitration, but without requirement of explicit government approval.
Utilization of services	Controlled to some extent through monitoring of physician profiles.	Controlled to some extent through monitoring of physician profiles.	Controlled to some extent through monitoring of physician profiles.
Supply of physicians	No formal policy to limit supply strictly, although immigration of MDs is discouraged.	No formal policy to limit supply for purposes of cost control.	No formal policy to limit supply for purposes of cost control.
Cost sharing by patients	No intention as yet to introduce it formally, although opting out by physicians introduces an element of cost sharing.	There is a modest degree of cost sharing, but it is not viewed as a workhorse of cost containment.	No intention as yet to introduce it.

Global caps on aggregate outlays	None.	None.	It has been attempted in recent years to agree on a total outlay for physician services and prescription drugs ex ante.
Expenditures on Hospital Care			
Revenues	The individual hospital's revenues are predetermined through budgets that must be approved by the provincial government.	Control is attempted through negotiated per diems that require the approval of the department's prefect.	Control is attempted through negotiated per diems that require the approval of the state government, which can, in principle, set the per diems.
Utilization	No direct control.	No direct control.	No direct control.
Capacity of hospitals	Controlled through regional planning by the provincial governments which finance roughly two thirds of capital outlays.	Controlled through regional planning supervised by the central government.	Because capital expenditures are financed by a combination of state and federal funds, there is authority at the state level to limit capacity through regional planning.
Prices of hospital inputs	No direct control.	No direct control.	No direct control.
Cost sharing by patients	None.	Virtually none.	None.

SOURCE: U. E. Reinhardt, "Health Insurance and Cost-Containment Policies: The Experience Abroad," *American Economic Review*, vol. 70, no. 2 (1980), pp. 149–56.

None of the three countries assigns a significant role to patients in the cost control process. As already noted, there remains a modest degree of coinsurance in France (table 1), but its average impact has declined over time and is likely to do so in the future. Canada and West Germany have adopted first-dollar coverage as a matter of principle. Although physicians in both nations have called for cost sharing on the part of patients, neither consumers nor their legislative representatives have so far shown any inclination to move in that direction.

Physicians typically make the case for cost sharing on the ground that it would elicit more responsible conduct on the part of patients, would free medical practice from trivial cases, and would contribute toward expenditure containment. There may be some merit to the first argument, and possibly also to the second. One doubts, however, that physicians seriously believe the third. Organized medicine is not known to favor policies that reduce the aggregate flow of funds to physicians. As Barer et al. have argued, a more plausible explanation for the profession's posture is that cost sharing, coupled with third-party coverage, is believed by physicians to draw more fiscal nourishment to the physician sector than could otherwise be had from third-party payers under universal first-dollar coverage.[12] They may well be right.

Why patients and policy makers in other nations are so reluctant to embrace the notion of cost sharing is an even more intriguing question. Indeed, reverting to the theme struck in the introduction to this chapter, one may broaden the question to ask why some 140 million people have permitted their health care systems to come under the thumb of insurance systems believed—at least by American economists—to detract seriously from the economic welfare of these people. This question will be considered in the following section.

Why Socialized Health Care?

To be completely fair and exhaustive in thinking about the question just raised, one ought to entertain at least three rival hypotheses:

- Economists are very smart, but almost everybody else is less so.
- The obverse is more nearly the case.
- Most people are about as smart as economists, but the political process in a Western democracy perverts even the most sensible intentions.

Among economists hypothesis A has enormous intuitive appeal.

---

[12] M. L. Barer, R. G. Evans, and G. L. Stoddart, *Controlling Health Care Costs by Direct Charges to Patients: Snare or Delusion?* Ontario Economic Council Occasional Paper no. 10 (Toronto, Canada, 1979).

Unfortunately, as Fuchs has impudently reminded us, we shall find it awkward to maintain that hypothesis and, at the same time, to market our cherished neoclassical paradigm that depends so heavily on the assumption that most individuals are well informed and rational.[13]

For reasons that may, in fact, corroborate the first hypothesis, the second appears to have wide currency today, especially among the media. Ironically, Fuchs may inadvertently have lent respectability to this disrespectful view, for he suggests that American economists simply do not understand the typical consumer's motivation. Fuchs argues that consumers may desire first-dollar health insurance coverage not only to reduce uncertainty (as is assumed by economists), but also to obviate the need for troublesome moral choices between money and medical treatment during episodes of illness. If the sole purpose of insurance coverage were reduction of uncertainty, the optimal (utility-maximizing) coinsurance rate would not generally be zero. Preference for a zero coinsurance rate is more readily explained by what Fuchs calls a penchant for "precommitment"—a conscious decision to avoid the necessity of weighing money prices when making choices about the use of health care.[14]

A penchant for precommitment, as Fuchs points out, could also explain a preference for the simple and compulsory insurance schemes that seem to be preferred in Canada and Europe. Such schemes may be preferred not only because choosing among alternative insurance schemes—each with a different benefit package and cost—is time consuming and thus costly. There is also the probability of regret over choice of an option that has turned out, ex post, to have been inappropriate. Although it is not clear why this probability should increase monotonically with the number of options available, neither is it clear that consumers will invariably favor free choice among several options to one easily understood compulsory scheme.

For present purposes, however, let us focus on the third hypothesis, the notion that the political process tends to pervert the individual's best intentions. As Usher has demonstrated, one can construct a theory according to which enlightened self-interest on the part of the individual will lead to the socialization of a certain commodity if public policy in these matters is governed by majority rule, even if that decision ultimately leads to an overall loss in economic efficiency.[15]

---

[13] V. R. Fuchs, "Economics, Health and Post-industrial Society," *Health and Society,* vol. 57 (Spring 1979), pp. 153–82.

[14] Ibid., p. 170.

[15] D. Usher, "The Welfare Economics of the Socialization of Commodities," *Journal of Public Economics,* vol. 8 (1978), pp. 151–68.

Usher defines socialization as the acquisition of the total output of a commodity by a public entity and its redistribution among consumers according to some nonpecuniary criterion.[16] In his analysis Usher abstracts completely from certain commonly assumed reasons for the socialization of commodities: externalities, economies of scale in production or distribution, insurance, or altruism. Instead, Usher sees as the driving force behind socialization what he calls the "income inequality motive":

> Under a regime of proportional or progressive income taxation, socialization can be beneficial to the poorer half of the community which pays less in tax than the per capita cost of the output of the socialized industry. The rich, of course, have a comparable motive for voting against socialization, but the distribution of income is almost always skewed in such a way that the gainers can outvote the losers as long as the tax structure is not drastically regressive.[17]

The reason why not all commodities are socialized under these conditions lies in the diversity of tastes for particular commodities. Using a simple model "incorporating diversity of tastes and a conflict of interest between rich and poor" Usher demonstrates that, given any degree of income inequality, the more homogeneous people's tastes are for a particular commodity, the more likely it is that a majority will favor the socialization of that commodity. Similarly, he shows that, given a distribution of tastes, the greater the skewness of a society's income distribution, the greater is the likelihood that particular commodities will be socialized under majority rule.

Finally, Usher demonstrates that as an alternative to the socialization of a commodity one ought, in principle, to be able to find a redistribution simply of income that can make every individual as well or better off than he or she would be under socialization, that is, that socialization appears to be Pareto inferior. He goes on to note, however, that in spite of the apparent Pareto superiority of income redistribution—for example, through a negative income tax—the socialization of commodities such as health care or education seems to be preferred universally.

An explanation for which there is no room in Usher's model, but which is pertinent in the real world, is that altruism does play a role in decisions on socialization after all, albeit altruism of a specific variety. Economists all too frequently assume that a proper social objective

[16] Ibid., p. 152.
[17] Ibid.

function is to maximize the utility of the poor for any given tax burden their support imposes on the rich. One may view this as altruism in its purest form. A plausible alternative hypothesis is that the rich derive more utility from seeing the poor consume minimal target rates of particular commodities (such as education and health care) than they would from the knowledge that the poor maximized their utility for given tax expenditures even if the target-consumption approach occasioned higher tax burdens than would a redistribution of income. If so, the socialization of a commodity may well be Pareto superior to a simple redistribution of the tax proceeds required by the socialization.

Yet another explanation for the manifest preference to socialize, one explicitly treated by Usher, is that the producers of socialized commodities may derive added income from socialization and, therefore, favor it. One suspects that educators typically favor the socialization of their services for precisely this reason. A reversion to market forces in American higher education, for example, would decimate that industry. Physicians also would be expected to favor at least partial socialization of their services should they find themselves in surplus relative to a private market's willingness to pay for physician care. One may wonder, for example, whether orthopedic surgeons in the United States, heavily dependent as they are on business from the aged population, would genuinely favor the abolition of the Medicare program.

Socialization will, of course, not invariably bestow pecuniary blessings on the providers of the socialized commodity. While socialization of a commodity does tend to increase the demand for it, the financing mechanism used for this purpose may, under certain circumstances, be used by nonproviders to extract economic rents enjoyed by providers prior to socialization. In such instances, providers can be expected to oppose socialization.

It is natural to inquire which of the two motivating forces has dominated the development of national health insurance in the countries under consideration: the "income inequality motive" (that is, consumers' preferences) or the desire of health care providers to expand the demand for their services.

By and large, the impetus to socialize health care in these countries does not appear to have come predominantly from health care providers. To the extent that pressure for socialization came from providers at all, it has probably been confined to the hospital sector. Hospitals in almost any industrialized nation have found it difficult to maintain their plant and to keep up with modern technology without an assured source of financing. If they did not actively push for socialized financing of their services, they usually welcomed it.

In contrast, physicians in the three countries have tended to view comprehensive *national* health insurance as a threat to their economic position. Physicians in Canada, for example, stood in overt opposition to the introduction of the Medical Care Act of 1966, as had Saskatchewan physicians to the introduction of compulsory and universal health insurance in that Canadian province in 1962. In Germany and France, too, physicians tend to favor a less comprehensive and more pluralistic insurance system, presumably on the theory that such a system would enhance both their professional and economic position.

To make physicians acquiesce to complete socialization of health care, countries embarking upon that strategy appear to grant physicians a considerable degree of market power in return for their cooperation.

In West Germany, for example, physicians practicing under the statutory insurance system enjoy a state-granted, airtight monopoly over the provision of ambulatory care. This monopoly precludes the establishment of outpatient departments by hospitals and even the performance of ambulatory preadmission diagnostics by hospitals. It would certainly not permit experimentation with physician assistants on the U.S. model. In France, too, physicians enjoy a well-protected monopoly over the provision of ambulatory care. Indeed, so strong are the profession's prerogatives that physicians are not even required to identify a diagnosis when billing the insurance pools for health services rendered.[18] In either country, it would be unthinkable to subject physicians to government-sponsored survey research of the sort regularly performed in the United States. And in both countries physicians have been able to negotiate fee schedules that place them at the very top of the nation's income distribution.

The position of physicians in the Canadian scheme has remained less clearly established. By and large, physicians in that country enjoy about the same degree of market protection as do physicians in the United States. But while the immediate effect of the introduction of national health insurance on physicians' incomes was strongly positive, Canadian physicians have suffered a subsequent decline in real income almost throughout the 1970s. An attempt appears to have been made by the rest of society to extract through control over fee schedules whatever economic rents physicians had once enjoyed. Just how far this policy can be pushed in Canada remains yet to be seen. Thus far Canada appears to have furnished the clearest example of the introduction of socialized health care financing at the behest of and to the economic advantage of the consumer.

---

[18] A physician, for example, may bill for treatment of Mme. X a sum equal to K30, which means thirty times the base value associated with fee schedule K (for surgery).

Concluding Remarks

The health insurance systems in Canada, France, and West Germany clearly reflect the belief that the allocation of health care resources cannot be entrusted to the play of market forces. Although it is not pretended in these countries that the socialization of health care proceeds without problems, thus far they have not proposed to address these problems with a resurrection of the marketplace in health care. The thrust of policy in West Germany has been to develop arbitration mechanisms that fall somewhere between classical, atomistic markets and the centralized administration favored in France.[19] The ideal decision-making units in these quasi markets are freestanding associations of the individual professions and institutions that are active in health care (for example, associations of providers, of insurers, of the insured, and so on), and the atomistic *tatonnement* of classical markets gives way to open collective bargaining among the freestanding associations, all within a statutory framework that guards the rights of weaker parties and that provides for compulsory arbitration of inconclusive negotiations.

As already noted, economists in the United States have little faith in the administrative systems or quasi markets favored elsewhere. It is thought that freely competitive market forces could work toward socially desirable ends if only they were given a chance, even if the play of these forces need to be reigned in somewhat by the distinct ethical precepts modern society may wish to impose on the distribution of health care. There is a good chance that economists may have taken themselves entirely too seriously on this issue and, indeed, that they may have allowed themselves to be used.

In their decade-old battle in favor of "markets" over "regulation," economists found themselves cheered on by health care providers who saw in the economists' toil a potent weapon against unwanted public interference in the medical market. There is, on the surface, something unnatural in an alliance between true believers in the virtue of competition and health care providers. After all, competition as conceived by economists is an arrangement designed in the main to benefit consumers by making life hard for providers. One can only wonder why health care providers would cheer on a philosophy whose implementation would greatly unsettle their economic existence. Indeed, one can only wonder whether in our current political context the development of a truly competitive health care market stands a reasonable chance of success.

---

[19] In this connection, see, for example, Philipp Herder-Dornreich, *Strukturwandel und Soziale Ordnungspolitik* (Cologne: 1977).

FIGURE 1
LITMUS TEST FOR MARKETEERS

Do you favor independently practicing

—Dental hygienists who provide prophylaxes?

| Yes | |
| No | |

—Dental nurses on the New Zealand/Saskatchewan model?

| Yes | |
| No | |

—Denturists?

| Yes | |
| No | |

—Pediatric nurse practitioners delivering well-child care?

| Yes | |
| No | |

NOTE: Independent practitioners are persons who sell their services on a fee-for-service basis in competition with dentists or physicians.

To identify his or her own attitude toward competition in, say, the primary medical or dental care market, the reader may wish to complete the "litmus test for marketeers" presented in figure 1. As is well known, the organized medical and dental professions have so far answered all questions in this test in the negative, and they have never hesitated to engage the coercive powers of the government—in the form of licensure laws—in imposing their view on this matter on the rest of society. These providers, then, do not oppose government intervention in principle. Rather, their opposition to such intervention has always been judiciously selective and has certainly not extended to interventions, such as mandatory licensure, that serve to enhance the market power of these professions.

It is often argued by health care providers that the government regulations they favor serve primarily to protect consumers from low-quality care and that any economic benefits such interventions bestow on the professions are purely coincidental. Two critical comments can be registered on this point. First, to quote Paul Feldstein:

It would appear . . . that the concern of the medical profession (as well as of other health professions) with quality is selective. Quality measures that might adversely affect the incomes of their members are opposed, such as reexamination, relicensing, continuing education, and any measures that attempt to monitor the quality of care. The hypothesis that quality measures [such as licensure laws] are instituted to raise the return of

170

practicing physicians appears to be consistent with the position on quality taken by the medical profession.[20]

Second, even if it could be demonstrated that independently practicing dental hygienists or pediatric nurses render care of a relatively lower quality than do physicians who render similar services, a market approach to health care would certainly permit consumers to choose between high-priced–high-quality care and relatively lower-priced–lower-quality care. If one is unwilling to trust consumers with this particular trade-off, on what foundation, other than self-interest, does one rest one's case for the "market"?

In thinking about the relative merits of systems of health care, say, in Europe and the United States, then, one ought not to compare the actual modus operandi of the former with the economists' *conception* of a truly competitive market system. It remains to be seen whether our health care providers can live with effective competition, or how long. Quite possibly economists, like good soldiers everywhere, may learn that they have been had by the folks on the home front.

[20] P. Feldstein, *Health Care Economics* (New York: John Wiley, 1979), p. 327.

Can Equality and Efficiency Be Combined? The Experience of the Planned Swedish Health Care System

Ingemar Ståhl

American economists seem to have the impression that health care in Sweden is provided through a planned and integrated system, giving citizens equal access to health care regardless of their economic and social position. The egalitarian health planner looks upon this system as an ideal arrangement and dismisses some of its disadvantages (for example, no choice of doctor or hospital and the difficulties in acquiring certain special treatments even if an individual is willing to pay the full cost) as a small price for buying the equality. This chapter challenges some of these widespread impressions by showing that the central planning process is almost nonexistent and that the Swedish system actually consists of twenty-six different health delivery corporations having a regional monopoly and taxation power. Central government is rather weak, whereas government on the county council level is strong and trade unions are increasing their power. The individual consumer is the weakest part of the overall system.

The discussion also shows that in this rather small and ethnically homogeneous nation of 8.3 million inhabitants there are still large differences in the regional supply of health services and that these differences are largely related to the general income level in each county. There are also differences in treatment practices that obviously do not reflect the operation of some central master plan. The recent cost explosion in Sweden has been exceptional, but few measures have been taken to contain costs successfully.

The chapter also develops an argument of "market failures" in the health sector that may seem rather obvious but that nonetheless has received limited attention in the standard literature. In 1976 about 15 percent of the population was above sixty-five years of age, but this group consumed more than 65 percent of all hospital days in somatic care—including long-term care. If health care had been financed by age-related insurance premiums—instead of a proportional tax on incomes—the premium would have approached 2,000 SKr (US\$1 = 4.2 SKr at September 1980 exchange rates) for individuals between the ages of thirty-five and forty-four, but would probably have been in the range of 10,000 to 15,000 SKr for individuals above the age of seventy. At present the basic annual pension in the social insurance system is 18,000 SKr. A market approach would thus imply that the pension level should be increased considerably—for the very old it should be almost doubled.

One way of looking at the transfers taking place in the Swedish health care system is to suggest that the main redistribution of incomes takes place between generations and not between the healthy and the sick.[1] This view of the health care system is pursued in the last part of the chapter, which summarizes some proposals by Swedish health economists for a "voucher" system combining the present redistribution of income with increased competition and greater scope for individual choices.

The Swedish Health Care System—Some General Outlines

The Swedish health care system is typical of the health care systems common in Scandinavian countries and the United Kingdom, which rely heavily on tax financing and attempt to substitute planning and administrative coordination for the market mechanism. It would be tempting to associate this development with the long periods in power of social-democratic labor parties, but the general structure of the Swedish system has never been a major issue of political controversy.

One crucial feature of the Swedish system—in which it differs from the U.K. National Health Service (NHS)—is the strong role played by the twenty-six county councils (including some independent major cities), which have independent power to tax. The Swedish county is an administrative unit of about 200,000–700,000 inhabitants (Stockholm with 1.5 million is an exception). Health care is now the main concern of the counties, which have their own politically elected councils. Most of the cost of the health care system is financed by a proportional income

---

[1] Sweden has a larger proportion of the population in age groups above sixty-five years than does the United States. There is, however, no difference in health consumption per capita. Thus it is probable that the Swedish health care system allocates a larger share to the old-age groups and a smaller share to the active part of the population. Is there a bias in favor of care rather than cure in a tax-financed system?

, TABLE 1

EXPENDITURES FOR HEALTH CARE IN SWEDEN, 1977
(millions of SKr, current prices)

Type of Expenditure	County councils	National government	Consumer expenditures	Social security insurance expenditures	Total Expenditures
			Sources of Expenditures		
Public hospitals and public physicians[a]	23,413	300	822	1,951	26,486
Private physicians	—	—	382	211	593
Private dental care	—	—	482	1,000	1,482
Pharmaceutical drugs[b]	—	—	746	1,694	2,440
Sundries	—	—	610	—	610
Total consumption	23,413	300	3,042	4,856	31,611

NOTE: Amounts exclude research and construction costs.
[a] Includes public dental care.
[b] Drugs taken outside of the hospital.
SOURCE: National Accounts, National Bureau of Statistics, Sweden.

tax set by the county councils. On an average the tax level is about 12 percent of taxable income. In addition to the county income tax, the counties receive substantial lump-sum transfers from the central government.

The social insurance system (a national system that includes, for example, the general old-age pension system and maternity leave benefits) provides two types of coverage in the health field—a general sickness benefit and some types of outpatient care. The health care component of the social insurance system is financed by means of a proportional payroll tax. A general outline of expenditures for health care in 1977 is indicated in table 1.

Out of total expenditures of 31, 611 million SKr, the consumer paid less than 10 percent in out-of-pocket costs. Besides sundry items such as eyeglasses and some dental care, these out-of-pocket costs were paid mainly as coinsurance or deductibles in outpatient care and included drugs.

Compared with many other European countries—for example, Germany—Sweden was rather late in establishing a comprehensive and compulsory health insurance scheme. Not until 1955 was the step taken from voluntary, government-subsidized schemes and employer-financed schemes to a national compulsory health insurance. Since 1964 inpatient care has been supplied by hospitals managed and financed by the county councils (and larger cities). Private hospitals or nonprofit organizations have never played a significant role in this system. For outpatient care the traditional structure has been a combination of a state system of district physicians (mainly for rural areas) and private doctors, both groups working on a fee-for-service basis. Up to 1963 mental hospitals were excluded from the county council system and were managed and financed by the central government.

Development since the 1950s has been mainly toward expanding the role of the county councils.[2] Mental hospitals were transferred from the central government to county councils in 1963, and about the same time the system of district physicians was taken over by the county councils. A further important change took place in 1970 when all outpatient care was reorganized through the seven-crowns reform. This reform provided a uniform flat-rate fee for outpatient care, removed physicians employed by county councils from direct money transactions with patients, and abolished fee-for-service outpatient care and physicians' care of private patients at county council facilities. Physicians employed by the county councils have since been paid salaries that are in accordance with the scales for civil servants. Promotion and higher salaries are to a large degree dependent on seniority and scientific and administrative abilities. The reform also introduced an important change in the conditions of practice for the still remaining private physicians, who would charge the patient a small nominal fee (somewhat higher than it would be in a county council outpatient clinic), while the social insurance system would pay the additional fee, determined in central negotiations between the central government agency responsible for the social insurance system and the Swedish Medical Association. One side effect of the change was improved tax control of the incomes of private physicians. The final reform in 1974 extended health insurance to cover dental care, with rules very similar to those for outpatient care.

These changes have led to a system in which the major part of medical services are provided by the county councils. Although the function of the social insurance system is mainly to provide sickness benefits, the system also pays most of the fees going to private physicians and private dentists. In addition, there is a transfer of funds to the county councils for each visit and hospital day produced. For outpatient care this transfer covers a considerable share of the costs of the county councils; for hospitals the transfer is a token.

---

[2] For a general description of the development, see A. J. Heidenheimer and N. Elvander, eds., *The Shaping of the Swedish Health System* (London: Croom Helm, 1980).

175

Private physicians are declining in number and the number of new recruits is low, but private dentists still dominate the market for dental care. The drug industry, as another supplier of health care, is private with the exception of one major Swedish firm—Kabi—that was nationalized in the late 1960s. It is important to remember, however, that more than 50 percent of all pharmaceutical drugs are imported. This reliance on imports has been used to argue against nationalization of the drug industry, which is favored by a large fraction of the Labor party. The pharmacies were previously organized as a regulated cartel of privately owned pharmacies but were nationalized and organized as a nonprofit corporation in the early 1970s. In addition, it should be mentioned that medical schools and nurses' training colleges are wholly financed and administered by the government.

Social services for old people—for example, housing arrangements, home services, supplementary financial assistance, and special homes for those who need nonmedical care—are the responsibility of the municipalities, an administrative level below county level. Each municipality has the authority to levy taxes and the municipality tax is a proportional tax on incomes. County and municipality taxes added together now average 29 percent of taxable income. The strong political and financial independence of local government has great bearing on the failure by and large of central government to control health care costs. The border between the domain of county councils and that of municipalities is thus dependent on the health status of the individual: If he is ill and needs considerable medical care, he will be a case for the county councils, otherwise for the municipalities. Obviously, cases of this type cannot be defined rigorously, and there are great differences in how the borderline has been drawn throughout the country.

If You Get Sick in Sweden—Some Basic Rules

Because there are so many differences between the Swedish system and the health care most Americans are used to, it would be helpful to describe in concrete terms the way a Swede would behave—and pay—if he became ill. The first, most important step is to contact the social insurance administration and to report the incidence of sickness in order to receive the sickness benefit from the social security system covering roughly 90 percent of the wage income forgone, up to a limit equal to an annual income of about 120,000 SKr (US$28,000). For the part of the income above this level all publicly employed and almost all privately employed individuals are covered by additional insurance or sickness salary paid by the employer. There is generally one waiting day, which can be avoided if the report is made the night before. After seven days the social insurance administration will request a physician's certificate. In order to prevent misuse, the administration can carry out home visits or request certificates after less than seven days. Short-term absence and misuse have been a growing concern during the last few years, but the trade unions in particular seem strongly opposed to increased controls or to an increase in the number of waiting days. The number of short-term absences related to sickness has also increased with the higher rate of participation by women in the labor market, a fact that complicates the political issue.

If a person can manage with self-medication, he can obtain several off-the-counter drugs at a nonsubsidized price. The rules governing nonprescribed versus prescribed drugs seem to be somewhat stricter than similar rules in the United States or United Kingdom.

If there is a need to see a doctor, the choice is generally limited. Of about 18,000 doctors (for a population of 8.3 million) only 700 are full-time private physicians and 1,100 work part-time (the latter group comprising retired physicians and county council physicians working extra hours in the private sector). Most private physicians are located in the three largest cities. Thus, an individual living in one of these cities may have a chance of seeing his "own" physician; otherwise he will have to turn up at a county council health center or at the outpatient clinic of a county council hospital, where the possibility of choosing a physician is limited. The out-of-pocket cost will be 20 SKr (less than US$5), but somewhat more if one goes to a private physician.

During recent years there has been considerable political concern regarding stable or continuous doctor-patient relationships, but bills to establish a system of general practitioners (or a "family doctor" system) have been turned down in parliament. The support for these bills has come mainly from liberals and conservatives, whereas the Labor party, the county councils, and the medical profession have shown varying degrees of resistance.

Waiting lists and queues are common in the health centers and clinics, especially in the larger cities, and thus many sick persons tend to turn up at the acute wards, where they cannot be refused, but only discouraged by queuing. As we have noted, the county council receives a standard payment—regardless of the type of treatment—from the social insurance system for each visit to outpatient care facilities. Physicians in the county council health center or clinic work entirely on a salary basis while private physicians receive a treatment-related fee from the social insurance system. The present level of fees for private physicians is such that a physician generally will do better being employed by the county councils, especially when it comes to career options and research facilities.

Contraceptive advice, including examination and prescription, has no out-of-pocket fee. Some counties have also adopted a system in which the total sum of out-of-pocket costs for one individual during one year has an upper limit, for example 100 SKr, meaning that the sixth visit will be free.[3]

For prescriptions that may include any number of drugs and off-the-counter drugs, the general rule is that the patient pays 100 percent of the costs below 10 SKr, 50 percent between 10 and 40 SKr, and nothing above 40 SKr. This means that the maximum out-of-pocket cost is 25 SKr. In addition, some drugs for long-term treatment are financed entirely by the social insurance system.

The cost sharing for dental care has some different features. There are no out-of-pocket costs for children who use county council dentists. For adults the general rule is that half of the total fee—regulated by the social insurance administration—is paid by the social insurance. For more expensive treatments, the patient's share decreases. Such treatments have to be approved by the insurance administration, however. Dentists employed by the county councils are salaried whereas private dentists work on a fee-for-service basis.

For private dentists, as well as for private physicians, there is a control for establishing a practice if it is connected with the social insurance system. The general aim of this control—executed by the social insurance administration—is not to allow new practices in areas where the county councils have vacancies on their staffs.

If a patient needs hospital care, his only option will be the county hospital in the area. In general a patient will find it extremely difficult to choose a hospital or clinic according to his own preferences, especially one outside his own county, and he may even run the risk of having to pay the whole bill himself. To cover the cost of care at specialized clinics there are agreements between counties to charge each other according to standardized day costs. The overall system consists of three levels of hospitals: local hospitals with undifferentiated clinics; county hospitals covering most specialties; and seven regional hospitals connected with the medical schools.

The regional hospital is financed mainly by the county council where it is situated, although part of the income derives from fees from other county councils and from the central government, which pays the extra costs of education and research—an arrangement that required considerable negotiation between the county councils and the central government.

---

[3] Some of the fees will be revised in 1981, mainly in order to adapt to general inflation.

Inpatient care has no out-of-pocket fees. A person entitled to a cash sickness benefit, however, will have the benefit reduced by at most 30 SKr, depending on income. (The argument behind this rule seems to be that meals are free in the hospital.) County councils are allowed to charge a small nominal fee for persons staying in a hospital more than one year, according to the patient's income or financial status. This charge is generally less than the fee that the patient would otherwise have to pay for services in a retirement home or for home assistance supplied and financed by the municipalities.

The Growth of the Health Care Sector in a Period of Stagflation

The conventional wisdom about the growth of health care expenditures is that there is a rather stable relationship between the level of per capita income and the level of expenditures for health care. A simple analysis of cross-country data from nineteen countries of the Organization for Economic Cooperation and Development (OECD) in 1974 indicates an elasticity of 1.2 for gross domestic product (GDP) per capita, which means that health expenditure grows at a rate of 1.2 percent for every 1 percent of growth in GDP. Time series data indicate somewhat higher figures—for Sweden during the period 1963–1975 they indicate an elasticity of about 1.5.[4] International comparisons also show that differences in GDP per capita account for a large percentage—about 85 percent—of the differences in total health care expenditures. The age factor, measured as the share of population above sixty-five years, plays an insignificant role.

This simple income hypothesis does not lead to any significant "political" explanations for the level of health care expenditures. The lower share of GDP spent on health care and the slower growth in health care expenditures in the United Kingdom compared with Sweden or the United States is thus more a matter of lower income level and a slower general growth than a matter of "better" planning in the highly centralized NHS compared with the regionalized Swedish system or the "unplanned" pluralism of systems in the United States.

More recent data on health care expenditures indicate, however, the presence of some other phenomena that may be contrary to the

---

[4] I. Ståhl, "Health Costs and Expenditures in Sweden—The Problems of a Private Good in the Public Sector," in *International Health Costs and Expenditures,* DHEW Publication no. (NIH) 76–1067 (1975); I. Ståhl, *Health Care and Drug Development—Production and Productivity Development in the Health Sector* (Lund, Sweden: Department of Economics, Lund University, 1979); and B. Jönsson, "Sjukvårdssektorns expansion—hot eller hopp?" in *Hälsooch sjukvårdsforskning* (Universitetet i Linköping, 1979).

TABLE 2

THE GROSS DOMESTIC PRODUCT AND HEALTH CARE CONSUMPTION IN SWEDEN, 1968–1977

(millions of SKr, 1975 prices)

Year	Gross Domestic Product	Growth from Previous Year (%)	Private and Public Health Care Consumption	Growth from Previous Year (%)	Health Care Consumption as % of GDP
1968	237,675	—	17,188	—	7.2
1969	248,588	4.6	18,041	5.0	7.3
1970	261,108	5.0	18,726	3.7	7.2
1971	260,290	−0.3	19,985	6.7	7.7
1972	264,835	1.7	20,183	1.0	7.6
1973	273,694	3.3	20,438	1.2	7.5
1974	285,075	4.1	21,344	4.4	7.5
1975	287,524	0.8	22,570	5.7	7.7
1976	291,336	1.3	23,644	4.8	8.2
1977	284,004	−2.5	24,688	4.4	8.7

SOURCE: National Accounts, Statistical reports N 1979:7.4, National Bureau of Statistics, Sweden.

simple income hypothesis. During the 1960s growth of GDP in Sweden was at an annual average rate of 4.5 percent. Since 1970 the growth rate has not only slowed down considerably—to a level of 1–2 percent—but it has also shown greater variations. Table 2 contains data on real growth of GDP and total health care costs for the period 1968–1977. For the period after 1970 it is tempting to formulate a hypothesis of counter-cyclical behavior for the growth of health care costs. (The reader will also be surprised to find that the Swedish trade cycle is out of phase with regard to the international trade cycle, since a peak occurred in 1974 and an exceptionally deep recession in 1977.) Data on the development are given in current prices in table 3.

Disregarding a sociomedical hypothesis that bad economic conditions create illness, we can easily find more attractive economic explanations. The first is that health care systems expand more readily in a slack labor market. It is not necessary to assume a deliberate policy of expanding health care employment during slack periods, since the health care system always has vacancies that are easier to fill when the private sector reaches the bottom of a recession. A second hypothesis arises from some specific rules of the Swedish tax system, according to which

TABLE 3

HEALTH CARE CONSUMPTION IN SWEDEN, 1968–1977
(millions of SKr, current prices)

Year	Health Care Consumption			Total Health Care Consumption as Share of GDP	
	Private[a]	Public[a]	Total	Market prices	Factor prices
1968	1,679	6,842	8,521	6.0	6.8
1969	1,809	7,556	9,365	6.1	6.9
1970	1,826	8,996	10,822	6.3	7.2
1971	1,988	10,705	12,693	7.0	8.0
1972	2,086	12,000	14,086	7.1	8.2
1973	2,218	13,223	15,441	7.0	8.2
1974	1,985	16,423	18,408	7.4	8.4
1975	2,095	20,291	22,386	7.8	8.9
1976	2,589	23,511	26,100	8.1	9.2
1977	3,042	29,033	32,075	9.1	10.4

[a] "Private" consumption includes all out-of-pocket costs. Social insurance payments to private doctors or dentists are included in "public" consumption.
SOURCE: See table 2.

the county councils obtain their tax income with a delay of almost two years. Tax rates are determined by the county councils, but taxes are collected by the central government and handed over to the county councils, hence a time lag.

But the result looks staggering: From 1970 to 1977 the total real growth of the economy in Sweden was 8.7 percent. During the same period total real costs for health care rose by 31.7 percent, whereas the share paid directly by the consumers decreased from 16.9 percent to 9.5 percent. Between 1969 and 1970—the year of the seven-crowns reform—the share paid by consumers had dropped from 19.3 percent to 16.9 percent.

The main conclusion is obvious: During a period of exceptionally low growth in the economy, the health care sector continued to grow at a rapid pace.

As is common in measuring costs among public service sectors, all estimates of the real costs have been made from the input side. But what happened to outputs during the same period? Table 4 contains some of the most important (intermediary) outputs in health care in Sweden for the years 1970 and 1977. In acute somatic care the number of beds decreased by 5.7 percent, but during the same period the number

TABLE 4

OUTPUT INDICATORS FOR SWEDISH HEALTH CARE, 1970 AND 1977

Kind of Care	1970	1977	Change (%)
Acute somatic care			
Number of beds	49,078	46,308	− 5.6
Number of admissions	1,181,815	1,316,451	+11.4
Number of hospital days	13,340,000	12,330,000	− 7.6
Long-term care			
Number of beds	33,558	40,913	+21.9
Number of admissions	53,658	57,354	+ 6.9
Number of hospital days	10,702,000	14,009,000	+30.9
Psychiatric care			
Number of beds	37,038	34,437	− 7.0
Number of admissions	102,757	133,778	+30.2
Number of hospital days	12,340,000	10,804,000	−12.4
Outpatient visits			
Hospitals	8,822,000	10,472,000	+18.7
District physicians	5,586,000	6,961,000	+24.6

NOTE: Standard costs used for calculating the volume index are as follows: somatic care: 1,000 SKr/admission, 500 SKr/hospital day; long-term care: 150 SKr/hospital day; psychiatric care: 300 SKr/hospital day; outpatient visits: 150 SKr/visit.
SOURCE: *Allmän hälso-och sjukvåvd* (Stockholm: Socialstyrelsen, 1977).

of admissions increased by 11.3 percent and the number of hospital days decreased by 7.6 percent. Average length of stay decreased from 11.2 days to 9.4 days.

In the long-term facilities the number of beds increased by 21.9 percent, the number of admissions by 6.8 percent, and the number of hospital days by 30.9 percent, indicating both a higher utilization rate of beds available and longer average stays. The average in 1977 was more than 240 days. In psychiatric care there was an 8.0 percent reduction in beds available, a drastic increase in the number of admissions (up 30.2 percent), and a reduction in the number of hospital days (down 12.5 percent).

Outpatient visits increased by 18.7 percent in hospitals and 24.6 percent in health centers and at offices of district physicians. During this period there was an unexplained reduction in the visits to private physicians. (Private physicians probably account for about 3 million visits compared with 17.5 million visits in the public sector.) In international comparisons the number of visits per capita is extremely low in Sweden—

about 2.5 visits per inhabitant annually, compared with more than 6 visits per year in Belgium and Austria (where doctors work on a fee-for-service basis).

How to interpret the data is not altogether clear. With an increasing number of beds for long-term care we would expect that cases were brought over from acute somatic care to long-term hospitals. Such a transfer would diminish, ceteris paribus, the number of hospital days in acute somatic care and would decrease the average length of stay for the remaining cases, assuming that transferred cases had lengths of stay above the average. The number of admissions in acute somatic care has increased, however. If a "new," marginal case had less serious ailments, this would also tend to reduce the length of stay in acute somatic care. Technological changes might, however, work in both directions; for some treatments there have been drastic decreases in treatment time, often with more intensive care. For other treatments, particularly involving older patients, there are longer stays, and some new treatments such as renal dialysis and open-heart surgery may have treatment times above the average.

Why has average length of stay increased for long-term care? One possible explanation is that patients who are expected to live longer have been transferred from retirement homes and other institutions. The transfer of an increasing number of cases of senile dementia and similar diseases from psychiatric hospitals may be another reason; this transfer would also explain in part the 12.5 percent reduction in hospital days for psychiatric care despite a 30 percent increase in admissions. The fact that most new cases are alcoholics and drug addicts is an indication of the medicalization of social problems.

By constructing a measure of the total output on the basis of the data in table 4 and using standardized costs for different outputs in "guesstimated" 1975 prices, we find that the total volume of health services increased by less than 1 percent during the period. The weights used here are somewhat arbitrary, since it is difficult to divide the costs for acute treatments into one part covering costs of surgery, examinations, and so on, which are independent of length of stay, and another part covering costs of "hotel" services provided. The calculation does not take into account the quality changes that may have occurred during the period. As we have said, these changes work in both directions.

Even after a reduction for quality improvements, it seems obvious that a substantial decrease in productivity has occurred. We can observe an increase in input costs (in 1975 prices) of more than 30 percent and an almost constant total production. Even if the output weight for long-term care—the most expansive sector—is doubled, the output volume increases by only 3.5 percent.

Nor can we attribute the rise in costs to the introduction of new, expensive technologies; scanners are few and the procurement of a handful cannot explain annual cost increases of 1 billion SEK per year. Open-heart surgery is less common in Sweden than in the United Kingdom or the United States. There is an obvious contradiction between the stable elasticities that have been calculated both from cross-country data and from time series data for Sweden for earlier periods and the explosion of health care costs during recent years. Although a stable relationship was expected, with a moderate elasticity above 1, in recent years it was found to be closer to 3. Although we cannot be certain without further analysis, the contradiction may lie in the low or negative productivity development in Swedish health care during recent years. The almost constant output—measured as intermediary products— means that the relative price of health care has risen close to 30 percent. The output measure used in this chapter is as yet crude, but the difference between health care consumption deflated in the traditional way by the use of input prices and consumption deflated by output prices may give a hint of a possible explanation of the contradiction.

But why should there have been a drastic decrease in productivity during the last decade? At this early stage of research we can only speculate about the possible causes. Some important institutional reforms and changes have affected incentives. A previous fee-for-service system has been abandoned, and all medical staff are now on fixed salaries. New work legislation and increasing marginal taxes have increased part-time work, decreased overtime work, and led to a general decrease in working hours. Between 1972 and 1976 employment in the health care sector rose by 38 percent while hours worked rose only by 25 percent. The average number of working hours decreased from 1,470 hours per year to 1,335 hours (all staff categories). An increasing number of inexperienced new employees are substituting for the decrease in working hours of the experienced personnel.

Health Care and Age

It is well known that consumption of health services increases with age. Data in table 5 on the number of hospital days per inhabitant in different age groups show that consumption increases rapidly for the very old. Another striking feature is that between 1964 and 1976 the average number of hospital days decreased for all age groups except for persons above seventy-five years of age.

A preliminary conclusion may be that productivity increases in health care resulting from improved technology and from a tendency

TABLE 5

HOSPITAL DAYS PER INHABITANT, BY AGE GROUP, IN SWEDEN, 1964 AND 1976

Age (years)	Somatic Care		Psychiatric Care	
	1964	1976	1964	1976
0–4	1.2	0.9	0	0
5–14	0.5	0.3	0	0
15–24	1.1	0.6	0.4	0.3
25–34	1.2	0.6	0.9	0.7
35–44	1.3	0.9	1.3	0.9
45–54	1.9	1.4	1.8	1.1
55–64	2.8	2.4	2.5	1.6
65–69	4.8	4.0	—	—
70 or older	10.9	14.2	—	—
65–74	—	5.2	3.1	3.0
75 or older	—	19.6	4.8	8.2

SOURCE: Patientstatistik (Uppsalaregionen).

to produce more "intensive" care during a shorter hospital stay are the main causes of the decrease for the groups below seventy-five years. An improved general state of health can also be part of the explanation. Increasing costs per hospital day are thus partly offset by shorter stays.

For the group of very old persons there is a considerable increase in the length of stay, which is probably related to a combination of factors—technological changes, for example, have made it possible to perform surgery or complicated treatments at higher ages. An increased amount of resources available also facilitates treatment of patients who previously were regarded as marginal. In addition there has probably been a considerable shifting of care from homes and other institutions to the health care system. Changing economic incentives and an increased participation of women in the labor force may be important contributory factors. For a very large number of these old patients—for example, those with senile dementia—it is a matter of care and not cure. From mortality statistics we find that there are no changes in life expectancy accompanying the increasing hospitalization of the old-age population.

A Lorenz diagram (figure 1) illustrates the distribution of hospital care, outpatient care, and consumption of pharmaceutical drugs in Sweden. The older age groups are to the right in the diagram. The distribution of outpatient visits is remarkably even, whereas the distribution

FIGURE 1
Lorenz Curves for the Distribution of Hospital Care, Outpatient Care, and Drug Consumption, Sweden, 1976

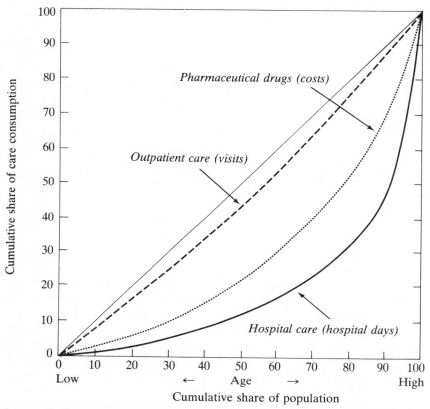

SOURCE: B. Jönsson, "Den ändrade ålders fördelningens effekter på sjukvårdskonsumtionen Institutet för häldo och sjukrårels ekonomi" (1980), p. 3.

of hospital services is very uneven. Drug consumption takes an intermediary position.

From further statistical analysis of the Swedish data it is evident that the increasing share of the population reaching old age plays a rather small role in the growth of the health care sector. In a study by Dahlberg[5] on the growth of the health care expenditures, the shift to-

[5] L. Dahlberg, "Why Does the Swedish Consumption of Medical Care Grow—Outline of an Answer," in "Empirical Studies in Public Planning" (Ph.D. diss., Gothenburg University, 1976).

186

wards an older population could explain only 10 percent of the total growth for the period 1963–1973. Multivariate analysis of data from different counties in Sweden for 1973–1977 shows no correlation between the share of population over seventy years and the health care cost per capita.[6]

This is not the place to raise the crucial ethical question whether the quality of life improves when there is an increase in institutional care over long periods of time for very old citizens. On the other hand, increasing health care consumption by these groups will raise some important economic questions. With the present pension system it would be almost impossible to have a market for health insurance for these groups, as the annual premiums would be the same size as the annual pension. If individuals had entered into a combined pension and health insurance contract decades ago, the contracting partners probably would never have expected the present high level of care consumption of the very old. What we observe is partly the result of a technological change, before which many lives were terminated by sudden death or pneumonia after a rather short spell in bed. Today, however, even severe cases of brain stroke or senile dementia will live a miserable life possibly for years in an institution and will require the attention of one to three full-time working persons.

A systematic bias favoring increased demand for long-term care in institutions is built into the incentive structure of the Swedish financing system. A family that takes care of its own old people will in most cases bear all or almost all of the costs. On the other hand, institutional care is highly subsidized. In many cases a person in long-term care will be able to save a large part of his pension and the family may expect to inherit a considerable sum. Individuals in retirement homes managed by the municipalities pay fees based on their income and wealth and will thus find long-term care financed by the county councils a more attractive alternative from an economic point of view.

Regional Differences

It seems obvious that individual income in Sweden will have little effect on access to health care. Out-of-pocket costs are negligible and the sickness insurance system covering the whole population plus a system of supplementary individual welfare benefits guarantee that illness or expensive treatments will not create economic distress. Almost no studies have been carried out on the relationship between income level and

---

[6] B. Jönsson, "Sjukvårdssektorns expansion—hot eller hopp?"; and R. Granquist, "Studier i sjukvårdsekonomi" (Ph.D. diss., Stockholm University, 1978).

health care consumption in Sweden—no doubt because the question has not been regarded as a problem.

One other question concerning individual need is worth a short comment. In principle, resources in Sweden are allocated according to some never explicitly stated principle of "need," such as some kind of medical judgment. We may ask, however, whether all people are equal in bargaining and negotiating situations that arise in a system based on rationing health care according to need. Thus far, there have been no systematic investigations of this question, but casual observations indicate that education, income, and social status may play a role. Before the seven-crowns reform, single rooms in hospitals were allocated according to both need and the willingness to pay for the extra cost. Even in a public hospital it was possible to pay a physician for extra services or for special surgery (or earlier surgery in the case of elective surgery with long waiting lists). These options are no longer available: Equal access has turned into a principle of "equal treatment."

Without doubt, socioeconomic variables are important in the allocation process. Knowledge, which means bargaining power, and social status may improve the position on waiting lists; an "old school-boys' network" will work as an additional ingredient in the allocation process.

A more tangible problem is the regional differences that still persist. Table 6 illustrates some of these regional differences in health care supply and some simple health status indicators. The data are taken from an official study by the national health authorities in which the investigators compared five counties with the highest number of hospital beds per capita (the "max-group") with five counties having the lowest number of beds per capita (the "min-group"). The conclusion was that the differences in supply did not seem to have any effect on the health-oriented indicators.

More sophisticated analyses by Jönsson[7] and Granquist[8] show that the differences in health care costs between counties are related to average per capita income. Age, as an indicator of need, cannot explain the differences.

The county-financed health expenditures for different counties ranged in 1977 from 2,600 SKr to 3,800 SKr per capita, with an average of 3,000 SKr.[9] The number of doctors per 1,000 inhabitants ranged from 1.1 to 3.2, with an average around 1.8 (including private doctors).

If the analysis of regional differences is brought down to a level of

---

[7] B. Jönsson, "Sjukvårdssektorns expansion—hot eller hopp?"

[8] Granquist, "Studier i sjukvårdsekonomi."

[9] Patients from one county treated in another county are included in the average for the county of their origin.

TABLE 6

COUNTIES WITH MANY HOSPITAL BEDS (MAX-GROUP) COMPARED WITH COUNTIES WITH FEW HOSPITAL BEDS (MIN-GROUP)

Health Factors Compared	Max-Group	Min-Group
Number of beds in somatic acute care per 1,000		
inhabitants	5.9	4.7
Population:		
Percentage of inhabitants over 65 years old	15.8	16.9
over 75 years old	6.1	6.4
Resources:		
Number of beds in somatic long-term care per		
1,000	6.2	5.8
Home assistance	6.7	4.2
Number of physicians per 1,000 inhabitants	1.20	1.23
Hospital costs per inhabitant (SKr)	2,698	2,443
Consumption:		
Hospital days in somatic acute care per 1,000		
inhabitants	1,528	1,393
Hospital days in long-term care	2,077	1,893
Outpatient visits per 1,000 inhabitants	2,088	2,078
Health indicators:		
Death rate	11.6	11.6
Number of days with sickness benefits per		
inhabitant	22.5	20.8
Early retirement per 1,000	34	28
Newly detected tumors per 1,000	3.6	3.4

SOURCE: *Sjukvårdsresurser och vårdutnyttjande* (Stockholm: Socialstyrelven, 1980).

different specialties or diagnostic groups, the differences between counties become even greater. As a typical example, the number of hospital days in gynecological clinics per 1,000 women above the age of fifteen ranged from 100 in some counties to 350 in other counties. The extreme values were held by counties dominated by farming and forestry, while the major cities were close to the average. In the case of performed laparoscopies, the number ranged from below 1 to more than 5 operations per 1,000 over fifteen years.[10] The conclusion is that attempts to attain uniform levels of health services throughout the country have not been successful. Substantial regional differences remain in supply, and it appears that an otherwise highly rigid system gives considerable scope

[10] National Board for Health and Social Welfare, *Sjukvårdsresurser och vårdutnyttjande*, (Stockholm: Socialstyrelsen, 1980).

189

for clinical freedom—or perhaps scope for rather arbitrary decisions by the local physicians in accordance with tradition and previous training.

Some Conclusions Regarding the Planning System

The main conclusion of this chapter is that any attempt at the macrolevel to keep health care costs down in Sweden during the last decade has failed.[11] This conclusion is perhaps obvious from the limited control that the central government exercises over twenty-six independent county councils, which have a constitutional right to determine the rate of the county tax. The main effort of the central government during this time has been to reach voluntary agreements with the Federation of County Councils concerning a recommended growth rate. For most years in which there has been an agreement, the ex post facto growth has been considerably above the recommended level. Suggestions that the central government might be allowed to determine the county tax rate have been opposed as infringements on the constitutional rights of the county councils.

The other "planning" instruments available to the central government are the allocation of new positions for physicians and internships and an approval procedure for new hospital construction. The objective of the centralized allocation of positions has been to bring about a more even distribution of physicians throughout the country. This allocation process has, however, been counteracted by market forces: In principle, salaries are uniform over the whole country and the result has been vacant positions in less attractive counties or districts.

With increasing marginal tax rates—a physician working full-time will have a marginal tax rate around 85 percent (which occurs above an income of 120,000 SKr [US $28,000]—the main interest of the Swedish Medical Association seems to be to negotiate for better working conditions, including shorter working hours, rather than for higher salaries. It is difficult today to convince a physician to work overtime, and most prefer compensation in the form of extended leisure time. Although there has been a record output from medical schools for a number of years, new physicians seem to have been absorbed readily into the market because of a general tendency toward shorter working hours.

Similar tendencies are evident for other staff categories. Owing to a complicated system of income-related subsidies for housing, day care

---

[11] In the discussion of the planning system, I will for obvious reasons exclude all "planning" at the microlevel, as most of this planning is routine administrative work in running an organization.

centers, and so on, it is possible to reach high marginal tax rates far down on the income ladder. The sickness insurance system gives generous benefits to parents staying at home when children are sick. Part-time work and long leaves are more often the rule rather than the exception. As a far from unique example, at present there are more than two persons employed for every "position" at the Lund University hospital.

During the 1970s Sweden experienced a disorganization of the health care labor market, which offset an attempt at central planning, and which probably accounts for some of the decrease in productivity that seems to have occurred. An increasing tendency to involve all staff categories in decision making after the introduction of new labor relations legislation has obviously led to time-consuming conferences and has made efficient management more difficult. The main reasons for decreased productivity, however, are probably new legislation regarding working time and the increased possibilities for part-time work, for leaves for adult education, or for maternal (and paternal) leaves paid by the social insurance system.

The substantial regional differences also seem to contradict the system when it comes to planning; the standard is supposed to be a uniform number of beds per 1,000 inhabitants for each type of clinical specialty. Many planning procedures have probably been mere formalities having limited effect on the local level, except in the case of major decisions regarding localization, number, and size of hospitals. Decisions concerning the treatments provided and the methods used are outside the province of planners and have been left to the medical profession.

What we find in Sweden, then, is a system that offers low out-of-pocket costs to the consumers and that has to resort to rationing and queues. The consumers have almost no choice of doctor or hospital and are almost completely unaware of the real costs involved. Recent studies also show that consumers tend to underestimate the costs of producing a visit or a hospital day. Because no financial transactions are involved, hospitals never keep track of costs for individual patients or for specific medical treatments. Hospitals and clinics are given fixed budgets within a budgetary process of the county council. The system will create almost no economic incentives for increasing production or efficiency. Long queues and waiting lists might even create a pressure in the political budgetary process to increase capacity—queues and waiting lists being the most obvious signs of "need" in the political decision process.

Local politicians have a chief interest in the job opportunities county councils offer. It has been observed more frequently that members of county councils (the politically elected assemblies) are also employees of the county councils.[12] The situation resembles a classical public choice case of government failure where benefits are concentrated among a few and costs are spread out among all taxpayers.

In a situation where county council health care production has almost gained a position of monopoly, it is extremely difficult to make meaningful cost comparisons. Attempts at budget cutting will be vigorously resisted by an administration that also has an information monopoly and that will always compare marginal budget cuts with intramarginal cuts in production.

Are There Alternatives?

There is no doubt that the Swedish system has achieved a high degree of equality in the sense of equal access to health care regardless of economic position.[13] On the other side, there are efficiency problems. We are at present spending 10 percent of our total resources to consume, on average, 4.5 hospital days per year and 2.5 visits to a physician per year. There are strong indications of a substantial decrease in productivity during the last decade. The public sector (public consumption, investments, and transfers) has grown to about 65 percent of GDP; and the central government deficit stands at 10 percent of GDP (the current accounts deficit is 4–5 percent of GDP). Further growth of the health care sector and a corresponding increase in tax rates may have serious

---

[12] A recent study of the professional background of Swedish politicians showed a clear overrepresentation for the public sector. The following table gives the background of candidates in the 1979 election in the Stockholm county (percent):

Party	Public sector	Self-employed	Blue-Collar Workers	White-Collar Workers	Trade Union Officials and Full-Time Politicians	House-wives	Other
Conservatives	35	10	—	24	13	8	10
Liberals	46	7	—	19	17	4	7
Center party	33	15	3	14	18	9	8
Labor party	45	1	15	7	25	2	5
Population over 16 years	24	3	38		—	19	16

SOURCE: Alf Sjöström: *Politikers yrkesbakgrund* [Professional background of politicians], (Stockholm, 1979).

[13] O. W. Anderson, *Health Care: Can There Be Equity? The United States, Sweden and England* (New York: John Wiley and Sons, 1972); O. W. Anderson and J. W. Björkman, "Equity and Health Care: Sweden, Britain and the United States," in A. J. Heidenheimer and N. Elvander, eds., *The Shaping of the Swedish Health System* (London: Croom Helm, 1980).

effects on the working of the economy, mainly on work incentives. There are no incentives within the system to control or curb costs—the development is rather in the direction of a monopoly managed by the employees, but with taxation power.

A final question to raise is whether the inefficiencies are the price we have to pay for the equality of access. Lack of competition, lack of consumer choice, inadequate cost consciousness, and a decision process dominated by professional groups, trade unions, and employment-minded local politicians—are these qualities necessarily characteristic of a tax-financed and comprehensive health care system?

The current attempts to control health care costs in Sweden follow mainly two different lines of approach. The first is to increase out-of-pocket costs. Next year's budget will contain proposals to increase fees for outpatient care and for pharmaceutical drugs. Possibly, waiting days will be reintroduced in the sickness benefit insurance. Measures of this type will have little effect on the basic incentive mechanisms, and any positive effects on the finance minister's purse will be limited.

The second approach is to introduce more control and restrictions. One proposal would put a ceiling on the county council tax rate. With three different levels of government, each having independent taxation power, it seems almost necessary that the central government should have the final responsibility for the *total* tax level. This alternative would raise some crucial constitutional issues regarding the independence of the county councils. More planning in the sense of increased central regulation will probably not work, as instruments such as the allocation of internships and approval of new positions can be evaded easily at the local level. Health care is probably too complicated and demands too much information to lend itself to management by central planning.

Disregarding the strong professional interests in the system of today, there are, at least theoretically, wide scopes for changes that would preserve the present income redistribution and at the same time introduce greater competition. A plan based on a voucher scheme has been presented in a number of recent articles.[14] The basic idea is simple; all real resources and the tax-financing system already exist. Instead of obtaining the right of "free" access to a specific county hospital or health center, the individual will receive a voucher, with a value determined by age and possibly sex, and calculated on an actuarial basis. This voucher would allow the individual to enter into an insurance contract with a combined provider of health care and health insurance, say, a

---

[14] I. Ståhl, "Sjukvården—problem och losningar," *Ekonomisk Debatt*, vol. 7, no. 7 (1979), pp. 476–82; Å. Blomquist, "Konsumentönskemål och effewtivitet i sjukvården," *Ekonomisk Debatt*, vol. 8, no. 1 (1980).

health maintenance organization (HMO).[15] The main idea is to introduce a market relationship while preserving some of the virtues of the present system and getting rid of the vices. Much of the discussion in the United States regarding the pros and cons of HMOs is relevant to a system of the proposed type.

A "chop and shop" plan would mean that the present monolithic structure of health care provision would have to be abandoned and replaced by a competitive system featuring new combinations of health centers, hospitals, and private physicians. County councils could still operate different facilities but would have to rely on the consumers and vouchers they could attract. Providers would become more conscious about costs and effects in a competitive setting in which revenue is determined not by taxation power but by competitiveness. Consumers would, in a similar way, develop stronger incentives to search the marketplace for good and efficient providers.

A voucher plan could easily be combined with coinsurance and deductibles but would operate on a voluntary contractual basis.

The financing of health care by a proportional income tax means a redistribution of income between generations from the young to the old and within generations from high-income earners to low-income earners. A voucher scheme would make the present redistributions obvious to the taxpayers, who would be able to compare the value of their vouchers with what they pay as county council tax. For persons under sixty-five years, the value of a voucher (or a corresponding health insurance premium) would be of the size that almost everybody could afford in order to pay the premium directly. As a possible long-term solution, it would thus make sense to separate at least the intergenerational redistribution and to include this part in the pension system. One possibility is some type of contingency contract in which the value of the pension is a function of the health status of the individual. This approach also would offer a way of solving the difficult borderline problem existing between different institutions in the care of the old and would create incentives for an economic selection between institutional care and home care.

The main point of the proposal is that, at least theoretically, it can be shown that equity and economic efficiency could be combined. Most of the problems of adverse risk selection, with healthy individuals running away from sick individuals, can probably be avoided if vouchers are tax-financed and based only on age and sex and on an additional

---

[15] A. C. Enthoven, *Health Plan—the Only Practical Solution to the Soaring Costs of Medical Care* (Reading, Mass.: Addison-Wesley Publishing Co., 1980).

rule that health service providers should not refuse an individual as long as he transfers his voucher. Any arguments against introducing a more competitive market can hardly be defended on egalitarian grounds. At least the discussion of the voucher plan has revealed that different vested interests are present in the bureaucratic system in Sweden, interests that no longer can seek shelter behind egalitarian arguments.

Commentary

J. Rogers Hollingsworth

All of the medical delivery systems in Western Europe and North America have gradually evolved from a market-type system toward one that is increasingly centralized and coordinated by the state. Of course, there is variation in the rate with which these national systems have moved in this direction. My comments focus on how the historical evolution of several national medical systems has influenced some of the current variations in performance, particularly in terms of access to medical care, distribution of medical resources in spatial terms, and level of spending.

My first observation is that as medical technology becomes more efficacious and as the costs for medical technology mount, there will be more pressure on the state to increase its responsibility for providing medical services. And once the provision of medical services shifts from the private to the public sector, the medical delivery system, by definition, becomes more centralized and departs from a market-type system. As the system becomes more centralized, it becomes more state coordinated and introduces more equalization in the spatial distribution of resources, and in the access to care. But equalization of access and equalization in the spatial distribution of resources do not necessarily lead to equalization in levels of health (see figure 1).

Unfortunately, the three papers in this part do not emphasize adequately the variation in state coordination and equality of the various systems. Although Culyer, Maynard, and Williams do discuss the difference in the degree of state coordination between the British system and the American system, they emphasize the amount of inequality in the distribution of medical resources that still exists in the British National Health Service (NHS). Since much of the British literature cited in their paper is concerned with inequality at one point in time, Culyer, Maynard, and Williams are able to conclude that the British system is still quite inegalitarian. Of course, there is inequity in the British system, but it would be desirable to present a comparative perspective of ine-

FIGURE 1
THEORETICAL FRAMEWORK FOR HEALTH AND OTHER CONSUMPTION POLICY AREAS

Delivery System Changes

Rising levels of effectiveness, complexity, and costs of technology $\xrightarrow{+}$ Increased demands for equal rights $\xrightarrow{+}$ Public funding $\xrightarrow{+}$ Centralization $\xrightarrow{+}$ Equitable resources $\xrightarrow{+}$ Equitable access $\xrightarrow{?}$ More equitable outcomes for individuals

SOURCE: J. Rogers Hollingsworth, *Inequality in Levels of Health in England and Wales, 1891–1971*, Discussion Paper DP581-79 (Madison, Wis.: Institute for Research on Poverty, 1979), p. 4.

197

quality in one system relative to another, along with the long-term trend in a particular system toward equality of access and equality in the spatial distribution of resources, and the variables that move a system toward greater equality. My own investigation of these topics suggests that increasing centralization has been responsible for the greater access to medical services and the narrower regional distribution of medical resources that have developed in Great Britain over time in comparison with the relatively decentralized system that has evolved in the United States. Ståhl's paper correctly points out that there is considerable variability in the spatial distribution of Swedish medical resources. For many types of resources this variability is greater than it is in Great Britain, probably because Sweden's system is much more decentralized.

In their discussion of inequality, Culyer, Maynard, and Williams point out that cross-sectional data demonstrate that under the British National Health Service lower-income groups use fewer medical resources than do upper-income groups per illness. Although this is true, a great deal of evidence demonstrates that the NHS substantially narrowed the differential in use rates per illness that had existed prior to 1948. No system will ever be completely egalitarian on any measure. Despite the shortcomings identified by Culyer, Maynard, and Williams, the British system is the most egalitarian system in any highly industrialized country.

This point leads to my second observation. The more the medical delivery system departs from a market-type system and becomes more coordinated by the state, the lower the level of medical expenditures. To test this generalization, Jerald Hage and I, in a forthcoming study, attempted to explain the level of medical expenditures in France, Great Britain, Sweden, and the United States for the period 1890–1970. Two variables in our equation measure the degree of departure from a market-type system: (1) the degree of control by the state over the source of revenue for medical care; and (2) the degree of control exercised by the state over prices of medical services and the appointment of personnel. Controlling for exogenous and other medical delivery system variables, our study demonstrates that the greater the percentage of all expenditures for medical care provided by the state, the higher the level of medical expenditures. This finding is consistent with the widely accepted view that once the U.S. government began to fund Medicare and Medicaid, the level of medical care expenditures increased substantially. On the other hand, the greater the control the state exercises over the price of medical goods and services and over the appointment of personnel, the lower the level of medical expenditures. Not surprisingly, our results also reveal a higher level of medical expenditures when there are more doctors and medical specialists. Perhaps one reason that Hage and I find that political explanations do shape the level of medical expenditures, while the studies cited by Ståhl do not, is that we disaggregated the different ways by which governments interact with the medical delivery system.

But we have not yet explained why there is cross-national variation in some of the key variables of the medical delivery systems of Western Europe and North America, and why some medical delivery systems are more market oriented whereas others are more state coordinated. (We might also ask why there is cross-national variation in the level of medical specialization.) The explanation is a historical one and requires us to assess the relative power of various interest groups at the time that the issues involving medical delivery became salient. Some brief and very broad generalizations about the British and U.S. systems will serve to illustrate my point.

At the turn of the twentieth century, several obvious contrasts in the two systems stand out. First, among the medical providers of Great Britain, there were sharp differences between general practitioners and the hospital-based doctors: In Great Britain medical providers were much more rigidly stratified than they were in the United States, where historically the profession had been more egalitarian and therefore was politically less fragmented. For this reason, the profession in the United States was more successful in dictating the conditions under which medical services would be provided than was the case in Great Britain. But the more important contrast lies in the nature of the consuming public in the two countries. In Great Britain at the turn of the century, approximately 4.5 million working-class members of friendly societies had entered into contractual relations with general practitioners. The friendly societies determined the conditions under which medical services were provided to their members. As a result, consumers played a relatively important role in this system. In the United States—where there was considerable ethnic and racial cleavage and a lower level of industrialization—workingmen's organizations were slower to develop and thus had little influence on the provision of medical services. Because the medical profession was more fragmented and because consumers of medical care were much better organized in Great Britain than in the United States, the British medical profession has historically been much less successful in shaping the conditions under which medical care is provided.

This differential in power between consumers and providers was responsible for the emergence of the British National Health Insurance System (NHI) in 1911. Many of the British friendly societies had to pay out more in medical and sickness benefits than they received from their members so that early in the twentieth century they found themselves on the verge of bankruptcy. Because the friendly societies had difficulty in funding their medical services, the conditions under which doctors worked with friendly societies became increasingly objectionable to much of the medical profession. Because of these financial problems, both the general practitioners and the friendly societies favored a National Health Insurance system in which the government would make certain that there was funding for the type of services that the friendly societies had previously provided. Since professionals prefer not to depart from a system with which they are familiar, the NHI kept most of the previous arrangements under which doctors had worked. The NHI did not apply to hospital-based doctors, however, and those to whom it did apply continued to be paid by a capitation system.

From today's perspective, what has been the significance of this process? Britain was one of the first countries to introduce national health insurance and did so at a time when hospital-based technology was relatively unimportant. Similarly, in other countries that introduced national health insurance before the existence of a complex hospital technology, the administrative and financial structure established by the state encouraged large numbers of practitioners to engage in general practice. Significantly, the adoption of a national health insurance system at an early date helped these countries to resist the trend toward specialization. As a result, by the time that the British National Health Service came into existence in 1948 a large proportion of Britain's medical profession was still engaged in general practice. And by limiting the number of specialists' posts that are available in hospitals, the National Health Service has been able to keep the percentage of doctors who specialize in a minority. This helps to explain why Britain in the 1970s had approximately 70 percent of its medical profession in general practice and 30 percent in specialty practice. As Reinhardt points out here, even though the proportion of all doctors who were specialists was somewhat higher in Germany than in Great Britain, the proportion of specialists in Germany was closer to the British pattern than that in the United States.

In countries that developed national health insurance later (such as Sweden and Canada) or not at all (for example, the United States), there was no financial and administrative structure to provide the incentive for the medical profession to engage primarily in non-hospital-based general practice. Instead, as medical technology shifted toward the hospital, there developed considerable incentives for doctors in those countries to specialize. As a result, the ratio of specialists to general practitioners in the United States and Sweden has been almost the reverse of that in Great Britain. (During the 1970s, almost 80 percent of all doctors in the United States were specialists, and approximately 20 percent were general practitioners.)

The difference in the timing of a national health insurance system in these countries helps us to understand the variation in the specialist–general practitioner ratio. And when we compare the relative strength of consumers vis-à-vis providers, we are better able to understand the emergence of the National Health Insurance System in Great Britain in 1911. Because Britain turned to a centralized and state-coordinated system relatively early, it introduced more equality of access and equality in the spatial distribution of resources earlier than did the United States; and overall it has spent a lower percentage of its gross national product on medical care.

The intriguing question is why Germany, which had a national health insurance system even earlier than Great Britain, now has much less state coordination and regulation of the medical delivery system. One reason, of course, is that Germany never had the same level of consumer strength vis-à-vis providers that existed in Great Britain. Furthermore, it was Bismarck, not the consuming public, who for strategic political reasons introduced the German national health insurance system. And in contrast to Great Britain, historically providers have been more powerful than consumers in Germany. As a result, doctors in Germany have resisted efforts of the state to implement effective cost containment. Moreover, the decentralized and fragmented structure of the German political system has made it difficult for the public to mobilize sufficient power to override the economic interests of physicians.

In Sweden, the consumers have been mobilized to demand egalitarian access to medical care, although it was later in coming because industrialization came relatively late. State coordination of the medical delivery system is more decentralized in Sweden than in Britain, however, and thus Sweden has been less successful in containing medical expenditures.

In conclusion, a centralized medical delivery system that is not under the domination of the medical providers is best able to control the escalation of medical costs. The differences in medical delivery systems—in the degree to which they have centralized coordinated mechanisms and in the degree to which they are dominated by providers—can be explained in large part by differences in their historical evolution.

Joseph P. Newhouse

We might begin a discussion about the rationing of medical services by asking what determines the volume of resources that a country devotes to medical care—that, after all, will fundamentally determine the severity of the rationing that its residents face.[1] It turns out that the answer is surprisingly simple. Per capita gross domestic product (GDP) can explain an extremely high percentage of the variance in per capita spending on medical care across countries. Ståhl estimates this to be 85 percent; using a somewhat different sample, I estimated it to be even higher.[2] Irrespective of the exact number, when one considers the amount of measurement error in expenditure figures because of noncomparable definitions across countries, such a high R^2 is indeed impressive. It is hard to imagine that anything other than income could be of much importance. The other interesting finding from these studies is that the income elasticity exceeds 1.0; hence, one might expect disproportionately less severe rationing as income grows. One might also expect that exercises designed to keep the growth of health expenditures at the same level as GDP may not be well advised, as Reinhardt notes.

As for the rationing of resources among regions within a country, Ståhl suggests that in Sweden income is also an important determinant of the quantity of resources across regions. A similar relation appears to hold in the United Kingdom, given the greater endowments of London, and would also hold, when computed in the same fashion as in these papers, in the United States.

When we consider regional differences, however, border crossing for medical care can confound the interpretation of the extent to which income determines the severity of rationing. Large cities will tend to have higher nominal income and will also be the location of specialized services; hence, regions with large cities will have somewhat better endowments than other regions.

Border crossing for the purpose of using specialized services can appreciably narrow apparent discrepancies in physician endowments. For example, the number of board-certified surgeons per person in metropolitan areas of the United States is approximately double that of nonmetropolitan areas, but that does not imply that rationing is almost twice as severe in nonmetropolitan areas. Approximately 30 percent of

---

[1] Rationing, as used here, includes the entire structure of relations that determines the volume and distribution of medical care resources. It does not refer to a particular method of distribution, for example, centralized allocation of physical quantities.

[2] Joseph P. Newhouse, "Medical Care Expenditure: A Cross National Survey," *Journal of Human Resources,* vol. 12, no. 1 (Winter 1977), pp. 115–25.

operations on nonmetropolitan residents are performed in metropolitan hospitals presumably by metropolitan surgeons.[3] Adjusting for this border crossing closes about 60 percent of the gap between metropolitan and nonmetropolitan areas in surgeons per person. Another 20 percent is closed by the reduced working hours of surgeons in metropolitan areas. Thus, it is not as difficult for a nonmetropolitan resident to have surgery performed by a board-certified surgeon as the discrepancy in surgeons per person suggests.

It might be argued, however, that nonmetropolitan residents should not have to travel to metropolitan areas; such travel does, after all, impose a cost that metropolitan residents do not have to bear. But it has also been argued that the technical quality of medical care would be higher if surgery were still more regionalized—which in this context probably implies even more border crossing.[4] Thus, travel may be quite appropriate.

To sum up, residents of poorer countries almost certainly face more severe rationing of medical services, whereas residents of poorer regions face such constraints to a lesser degree because a number of them travel to wealthier regions to receive care (and because physicians in metropolitan areas work fewer hours). This situation makes it difficult to determine the severity of rationing among residents of different regions.

Below the level of the nation and the region lies the individual patient. What determines who receives what kind of care for what kind of problem within a region or market area? At this microlevel professional ethics, government regulation, and markets all exert effects on the distribution and nature of services.

In the case of government regulation, much has been written about its effects, but in the United States regulation of the certificate-of-need variety has not yet greatly influenced how different individuals are treated (see, for example, the paper by Joskow in this volume). At the same time, actions of the government that are not usually classified as regulatory clearly have had substantial effects on the nature of rationing. One such action has been the policy of the past two decades to increase the output of medical schools. That increase should profoundly affect who receives what kind of service for what kind of problem over the next two decades. The enactment of Medicare and Medicaid has also clearly affected the distribution of services; for example, hospital days

[3] Victor R. Fuchs, "The Supply of Surgeons and the Demand for Operations," *Journal of Human Resources,* vol. 13, supplement (1978), pp. 35–56.

[4] Harold S. Luft, John P. Bunker, and Alain C. Enthoven, "Should Operations Be Regionalized? The Empirical Relation between Surgical Volume and Mortality," *New England Journal of Medicine,* vol. 301 (December 20, 1979), pp. 1364–69.

were distributed away from the age group under sixty-five to the group over sixty-five after the passage of Medicare.[5] Moreover, physician visits by income class now resemble a shallow U for both adults and children, whereas before Medicaid was enacted visits rose steadily with income.[6]

In the United States the market also clearly plays a role in the rationing of services. The questions usually raised in this context are whether it should play a greater or smaller role. Many of those favoring a greater role for the market argue that the current lack of competition has been responsible for a loss of efficiency, especially in the hospital sector. Ståhl makes this argument in his paper. This field has been well plowed, and I do not propose to till it again. Suffice it to say that a potential drawback to increasing competition is the possibility that an equilibrium would not exist and that poor risks would be discriminated against. Healthy individuals have, in effect, an incentive to run away from sick individuals, and the sick individuals to chase after them.[7] We know little about the extent to which such problems arise under competitive arrangements.[8]

Those favoring a smaller role for the market generally base their arguments on equity, the typical one being that reduction of consumer payments will reduce the inequality in use of services across income classes. All three papers here discuss this issue.

Contrary to the popular view, economic theory does not give an unambiguous prediction about how a reduction in out-of-pocket price will affect different income groups. Culyer, Maynard, and Williams cite the Montreal experience in support of the proposition that inequality will fall as out-of-pocket costs fall; another example from Canada, the Saskatchewan experience, also supports this view.[9] But other evidence is less clear. LeGrande, for example, in a study cited by Culyer, Maynard, and Williams, estimates that expenditures in the National Health

[5] U.S. National Center for Health Statistics, Vital and Health Statistics, Data from the National Health Survey, "Utilization of Short-Stay Hospitals, United States, 1965," series 13, no. 2, 1967; and the National Health Survey, "Utilization of Short-Stay Hospitals, United States, 1970," series 13, no. 14, 1973 (DHEW no. HRA74–1765).

[6] U.S. National Center for Health Statistics, Vital and Health Statistics, Data from the National Health Survey, "Volume of Physician Visits, United States, July 1963–June 1964," series 10, no. 18, 1965; and the National Health Survey, "Physician Visits, United States, 1975," series 10, no. 128, 1979 (DHEW no. PHS79–1556).

[7] Michael Rothschild and Joseph Stiglitz, "Equilibrium in Competitive Insurance Markets: An Essay on the Economics of Imperfect Information," *Quarterly Journal of Economics*, vol. 90, no. 4 (November 1976), pp. 629–49.

[8] Harold S. Luft, *Health Maintenance Organizations: Dimensions of Performance* (New York: John Wiley and Sons-Interscience, 1981).

[9] R. G. Beck, "The Effects of Co-payment on the Poor," *Journal of Human Resources*, vol. 9, no. 1 (Winter 1974), pp. 129–42.

TABLE 1

RATE OF TONSILLECTOMY, WITH OR WITHOUT ADENOIDECTOMY, IN
THE UNITED STATES, 1965–1975

(operations per 1,000 persons, 15 years or under)

Year	Male	Female
1965	16.3	16.5
1968	14.3	13.7
1973	11.1	12.1
1975	8.5	9.1

SOURCE: National Center for Health Statistics, *Vital and Health Statistics, Data from the National Health Survey*, Series 13, Nos. 7, 11, 24, 34 (Washington, D.C., various years).

Service of the United Kingdom for Social Classes I and II (professional and managerial) are around 40 percent higher than for Classes V and VI (semiskilled and unskilled labor).[10] (The calculation roughly controls for health status.) The United States does not have an exactly comparable statistic, but use of hospital days and physician visits across income classes, also roughly controlling for health status, suggests near equality.[11] There are certainly issues of equity in the U.S. system, as Culyer, Maynard, and Williams point out, but the LeGrande figures, if correct, make it difficult to argue that less reliance on the market will unambiguously reduce the role of income in allocating medical resources.

What might cause the LeGrande results? Culyer, Maynard, and Williams, as well as Ståhl, suggest that professional preferences for patients, which might also be called professional ethics, are a contributing factor. Clearly physician preferences or ethics do play an important role in all systems, although that role is not well understood. For example, there has been a marked decline in the tonsillectomy and adenoidectomy rate in the United States over the past several years (table 1). It is certainly difficult to account for this decline in terms of regulatory forces. If market forces account for the decline, they are stronger than is commonly believed. The decline may be related to a changed medical view of the efficacy of this procedure. Such an explanation, centered on professional ethics, fits uncomfortably with many models of how the fee-for-service physician behaves.

[10] Julian LeGrande, "The Distribution of Public Expenditure: The Case of Health Care," *Economica*, vol. 45 (May 1978), pp. 125–42.

[11] LuAnn Aday, Ronald Andersen, and Gretchen V. Fleming, *Health Care in the U.S.: Equitable for Whom?* (Beverly Hills, Calif.: Sage Publications, 1980).

To date both positive economics and normative economics have had relatively little to say about the role of professional ethics. Reinhardt points out that several Western European nations espouse a principle of solidarity through the normative criterion that all technically available care should be equally available to all: "Everyone should be in the same boat." The Culyer, Maynard, and Williams paper also alludes to universal access to care as a criterion. Reinhardt contrasts such a criterion with one that makes certain minimums available to all and at the same time permits inequalities, apparently the criterion in the United States.

Although the solidarity criterion may seem sensible to some, I do not find it a practical one, for reasons that fall in the area of professional ethics. (The second or "minimums" criterion is less vulnerable on this score.) How is one to judge whether the solidarity criterion has been satisfied? That is, we must ask how one might implement such a criterion. How, for example, could a report card on this score be constructed for the U.S. or the U.K. systems, as Culyer, Maynard, and Williams seek to do? To implement this criterion seems to presuppose that there is a unidimensional, readily observable, measure of health status with negligible heterogeneity among individuals in their valuations of health. (Or, if there is more than one dimension of health status, marginal rates of substitution are well defined.) I doubt that any of these conditions obtain. The difficulties are readily illustrated by some examples.

Individual A is a child with asthma; individual B is a child that needs orthodontia. Who should receive treatment if treatment is equally costly and resources suffice to treat only one of these individuals? Individual C is a teenager with acne; individual D is a teenager with hay fever. Who is to be treated? Individual E is an adult who needs psychotherapy; individual F is an adult who needs physical therapy to recover from a stroke. Who is to be attended? Clearly no one, including the physician, has a sufficiently good measure of health status to determine that treatment would give child A three units of health status, but child B only two units, and hence that child A should be given the resources. Nor do we know anything about how the individuals concerned value remediation of these problems. Acne may cause serious interpersonal problems for one teenager, but not for another.

One response to this problem is that such decisions must be left in the hands of the physician, to be determined, presumably, by professional ethics. Clearly that answer begs the question. We have no way to measure how well the physician resolves such issues, but it is clear that all individuals will not necessarily have equal access to all available care—that is, they will not necessarily be in the same boat. If individual

E who needs psychotherapy is perceived as a hypochondriac, while individual F who needs physical therapy is perceived to have more "legitimate" needs, the system may not give the two individuals equal access. Put another way, potential inequalities across persons with different medical problems may well exceed those across persons of different income or education, yet attention seems devoted almost exclusively to the latter cases.

To complicate matters, we cannot pretend that a single practicing physician is resolving these problems. Many, if not most, medical problems are not treated by a single physician, but rather treated by specialists with specialized resources: psychiatrists, orthodontists, dermatologists, physical therapists, allergists, and so forth. Thus, exactly which specialists and specialized resources are available will help to determine who is seen for what type of problem. To what degree can the objective of equal access be considered when policy makers make decisions affecting the availability of resources?

One more example may be needed because the point seems quite important. I am told that the National Health Service in the United Kingdom rarely dialyzes any patient with end-stage renal disease over the age of forty-five and that it does few coronary bypass surgeries. Both services seem rationed more severely than in the United States, but that is not the point of interest here. (Almost certainly one could find some services that are rationed less severely in the United Kingdom.) How can one say that this distribution is more equitable than performing dialysis on people up to age fifty and even fewer bypass surgeries? Or dialysis to age forty and more bypass surgeries? Which of these allocations best satisfies the principle of solidarity? Or which is fairest? Are they all equally fair? Are people with renal failure and people with coronary artery problems really being treated equally?

In short, individuals have different kinds of medical problems, and even those with similar problems may value remediation differently. It does not seem likely that equity will be achieved merely by making money prices zero. That viewpoint requires a rather large leap of faith, namely that individuals situated differently with respect to medical problems are treated equitably when we have no ready method to measure equity. To rest the case for equity solely on the distribution across income classes appears to assume that if the distribution among income classes is equitable, only minor inequities are left. But what if income inequities are only one inequity amidst many?

I cannot enter here into a further discussion of this issue, but merely call attention to it. Investigation of how differently situated individuals are treated, especially as the overall volume of resources varies, would no doubt be fruitful.

Unfortunately we do not live in the type of world chronicled by St. Matthew: "Everyone that asketh receiveth, and he that seeketh findeth." Medical resources are rationed in every society, and everyone that asks does not receive. As this volume has brought out, we really know rather little about who does and does not receive. If the volume succeeds in promoting additional research into these issues, it will have served its purpose well.

Part Three

Regulation: Can It Improve Incentives?

Regulation: Incentives Rather Than Command and Control

Graham Atkinson and Jack Cook

The general conception of government regulation is that the regulator provides by means of the regulation precise and detailed direction as to how the regulatee is to behave. In many instances, probably most instances, in fact, this is an accurate perception. Consider, for example, the fire and safety codes. These specify in detail architectural features of a plant or facility which are required for compliance with the codes. The purpose of this paper is to demonstrate that there is an alternative view of regulation, which is that regulation can provide economic incentives to the regulatee which in many cases can be substitutes for market forces. We will attempt to show that this view of regulation can explain why many regulations have been unsuccessful and can aid the regulator in designing regulations that are likely to achieve their goals. The examples will be drawn from the hospital regulation field, since this is the field in which the authors have had the greatest experience. Similar examples could be found in many other fields, however.

We will examine several different attempts at regulation of hospital costs. The analysis will consider in what ways the regulation was successful and in what ways it failed. We will then describe a regulatory system that incorporates the ideas, and we will evaluate its successes and failures.

An underlying theme of this paper is that the regulatee generally knows much more about how to manage his organization than does the regulator. Unfortunately, the effect of regulation is to direct the regulatee in too detailed a manner. In regard to hospital costs, as with airline fares and public utility rates, regulation has been deemed to be necessary because of the failure of the market. We argue that the appropriate role for the regulator is to attempt to introduce incentives that replace the missing market forces. The role of the regulator should not be to provide

211

detailed direction as to how the institution should be run, since in almost every instance the bureaucrat doing the regulating is less competent to determine how the institution should be managed than the managers currently running the institution.

Some Examples of Hospital Cost Regulation and Their Impact

In this section we shall discuss two examples of government regulation of hospital costs: (1) regulations regarding payments for Medicare beneficiaries; and (2) hospital rate regulation in Maryland. In each of these examples, we will describe briefly the form and purpose of the regulation and will discuss the incentives embodied in the regulatory system, both the desirable incentives and the undesirable ones. We will then examine the effect of the incentives. This is often not the effect that was sought by the individuals who drafted the regulation.

Medicare Regulations. Medicare legislation sought to ensure access to hospital care for people having particular need for such care, namely, the elderly, the disabled, and sufferers of chronic renal disease. The intention of the legislation was not to affect the ways in which health care was provided or hospitals were managed. The federal government, under Medicare, accepted the responsibility of paying for the care of beneficiaries. The problem was defining the cost of that care. The federal government was unwilling to simply pay the standard hospital charge for the service. Instead it decided to pay what it considered to be its share of the hospital's costs. The definition of the elements of cost for Medicare is, for the most part, prescribed by generally accepted accounting practices. It will suffice for our purposes to note that charity and bad debts are not costs under the Medicare definition of the term, but depreciation is a cost. The second question that has to be addressed is how to define the Medicare share of costs. This is done in two parts: (1) for routine service centers the Medicare share is defined to be the ratio of the number of days of care provided to Medicare beneficiaries to the total number of days of care provided, and (2) for ancillary service centers the Medicare share is defined to be the ratio of the charges for services to Medicare beneficiaries to the total charges for all patients.

The intention of this reimbursement system was to pay the hospitals fairly and to ensure that the federal government was not overcharged for the services provided Medicare beneficiaries. As mentioned earlier, it was not intended to affect the way in which hospitals were managed.

Let us consider the incentives in this system and the problems that they create for a hospital in which a large proportion of patients are paid for by means of this cost-based reimbursement system. An immediate effect is that hospitals with a large bad-debt rate and low depreciation allowance are placed in difficult financial circumstances. It is possible in states in which Blue Cross also pays hospitals according to a cost formula that 80 percent of the hospital's patients are covered by cost-based payers. If we assume that bad debt and charity care amounts to 5 percent of total revenue (a realistic estimate for many states), in order to recover this 5 percent from the 15 percent of patients who actually pay charges, a hospital would have to set charges 33 percent above costs. For many hospitals it has not been practicable to charge at this high level, and so they have lost money. On the other hand, new hospitals in affluent areas would have low bad debts and a high depreciation allowance, and so would be in good financial condition under this reimbursement system.

The next undesirable effect is that the hospital manager loses much of the incentive to control the costs of the hospital, since, within certain limits, no matter how much is spent, the cost-based payers will pay their share. On the other hand, not spending money could alienate the medical staff or other hospital employees. The probable impact of this system should now be obvious.

The last undesirable incentive concerns the impact on the financial management of hospitals. The way to maximize revenue under a system of this type is to manipulate the charges so that services heavily used by patients who are covered by cost-based payers are overpriced relative to the other services. This approach will artificially inflate the payer's share of charges and thus of costs.

Having described the incentives embodied in the cost-based reimbursement system, let us now examine what has happened to the hospital industry in the years since Medicare and Medicaid were enacted. One conspicuous feature is that many inner-city hospitals are having severe financial problems, while suburban hospitals are in excellent financial condition, as we would have anticipated. The second noticeable feature is that hospital cost inflation has become considerably worse. It is almost impossible to determine the impact of the use of cost-based reimbursement by Medicare and Medicaid because of numerous other confounding factors and the fact that there is no control group to use for comparison purposes. Experts generally agree, however, that cost-based reimbursement has been a major factor in the rapid rise of health care costs. As Caspar Weinberger, former secretary of the Department of Health, Education, and Welfare, has noted:

> I . . . firmly believe that the faulty design of Medicare and Medicaid is the principal culprit responsible for this super inflation in health care costs. The guaranteed government pay-

ment of health care costs in virtually any amount submitted by the provider, and with normal market forces absent in the health care area, inflation was bound to happen, and it did.[1]

Routine Daily Patient Care Cost Limitations

Another extremely perverse aspect of the design of the Medicare payment system is the limitation on payments for routine service costs. The cost limitations on routine patient care place an upper limit on the costs per day that Medicare will pay for routine daily patient care. (The dollar limitation varies by geographic region, metropolitan or nonmetropolitan location, and size of hospital, but these details are not pertinent to our present discussion.) The perversity of this limitation is that it was specifically aimed at constraining costs, but in practice it attacks the wrong problem and probably increases costs. The reason that hospital costs have become a major issue is that the rate of inflation in total hospital costs has been considerably higher than the rate of inflation in the economy as a whole (at least until the latest surge in inflation, mainly driven by oil prices). This difference is directly related to the increasing number of services that hospitals are providing to their patients, mainly ancillary services and procedures. To illustrate the magnitude of this problem, between the calendar years 1970 and 1978, the average annual increase in adjusted expense per inpatient day was 12.9 percent. The net service intensity increase was 4.5 percent.[2] In that same period the average increase in the Consumer Price Index (CPI) was 6.6 percent. Thus, most of the difference between the CPI increase and the increase in adjusted expense per inpatient day is due to the intensity increase.

The routine cost limitation ignores this problem in that no limit is placed on ancillary services, which are the driving force behind hospital cost inflation. Instead, the limits are on routine costs, which are much less inflationary. It would be bad enough if the limitations simply ignored the problem of increasing intensity, but they actually make matters worse by encouraging hospitals to increase costs. To illustrate why this is the case, an example would be helpful.

Example. Consider a hospital running at relatively low occupancy. Suppose that the limitation on routine costs per day for that hospital is $100, that the hospital is budgeting 10,000 patient-days at a cost of $110 per

[1] Testimony to the Subcommittee on Health of the House Ways and Means Committee, June 12, 1975.

[2] Mark S. Freeland, Gerard Anderson, and Carol Ellen Schendler, "National Hospital Input Price Index," *Health Care Financing Review,* vol. 1 (Summer 1979).

day, and that the marginal cost of an extra patient-day is 50 percent of the average cost. At the budgeted volume, then, the hospital would suffer a cost penalty of $10,000 × (110 − 100) = $100,000. If the hospital increases its patient-days by 25 percent to 12,500, however, its total cost will be $(10,000 × 110) + (2,500 × 110 × 0.5) = $1,237,500, which is an average cost of $99. Since this amount is under the $100 limit, the hospital would not be subject to any penalty.

This example shows that if a hospital is in danger of exceeding the routine cost limitations, it has a strong incentive to drive up the number of days of care provided, either by increasing admissions or by allowing the length of stay to increase, or both. These strategies increase the total cost of health care even though they assist the hospital in beating the routine cost limitations. In addition to increasing the number of inpatient-days, a hospital facing the Medicare routine daily patient care limitation can make a number of accounting and billing changes—for example, charging for all drugs, including aspirin. These changes increase total costs but decrease or eliminate Medicare penalties.

Thus, routine cost limitations, designed to control Medicare's payments to hospitals not only fail to address the major cause of inflation in hospital costs, but actually encourage hospitals to provide excessive days of care.

Hospital Rate Regulation in Maryland

The example we will focus on is the hospital cost experience under rate regulation in Maryland, where one system of regulations operated for two to three years and then was replaced by a new system in several hospitals. Since that time, there have been two regulatory systems with substantially different incentives operating in parallel on different sets of hospitals.

Under the first rate-setting system applied in Maryland by the Health Services Cost Review Commission, the factor being regulated was the charge per unit of service, by department. For example, the commission established the average charge per day in the medical/surgical unit, the average charge per minute in the operating room, and the average charge per relative value unit (established by the American College of Radiologists) for radiology. These rates were adjusted annually for the reasonable increase in factor costs and for changes in the volume of service provided. The purpose of the adjustment for volume change was to ensure that a hospital did not realize profits or incur losses simply because the actual volumes were greater than or less than those originally budgeted. The incentive under such a system is to produce units of service at a lower cost per unit, since the hospital keeps any savings resulting from efficiencies that cause its costs to increase more slowly than the inflation factor allowed by the commission. There is no incentive, however, to control the amount of services provided to patients.

Given the original rate review system, which focused on costs per unit, there was an incentive to increase the volume of service, and thereby to reduce the average cost per unit by spreading the fixed costs of the hospital over more units. The response to the incentive to become more efficient can be seen by the fact that the financial condition of the hospitals improved, although the rates were originally set so that the hospitals would break even. The response to the lack of (that is, negative) incentive to control volume of service is seen from the fact that while charges rose approximately 7 percent per annum, the cost per equivalent inpatient-day rose 11 percent per annum.

Incentive-Based Rate-Setting System

Our observation of the 7 and 11 percent rates of increase just mentioned prompted us to develop and implement a payment system that would give hospitals an incentive to control the resource use per admission. The system has been in operation in six hospitals since 1976 and now applies to fifteen hospitals. It is unnecessary to go into the details of this Guaranteed Inpatient Revenue System (GIR) here, except to say that a hospital is guaranteed a certain amount of inpatient revenue. This amount is adjusted annually for reasonable inflation in factor costs, change in the case-mix of the hospital, and changes in the number of admissions. It is not adjusted for changes in the amount of resources used per admission not justified by case-mix changes. Under the GIR system, if a hospital increases length of stay or performs more ancillary tests per admission, it will incur additional costs but not receive additional revenue. Conversely, if the hospital reduces its average length of stay or performs fewer ancillary tests per admission, it will have lower costs, but there will not be a corresponding reduction in revenue. Thus the incentive is clearly to reduce length of stay and ancillary services.

Table 1 shows the rate of increase in cost per equivalent admission[3]

[3] Equivalent admissions are calculated as follows:

$$\begin{pmatrix} \text{number of equiva-} \\ \text{lent admissions} \end{pmatrix} = \begin{pmatrix} \text{number of} \\ \text{admissions} \end{pmatrix}$$

$$+ \left[\begin{pmatrix} \text{number of} \\ \text{outpatient} \\ \text{visits} \end{pmatrix} \times \frac{\text{(revenue per outpatient visit)}}{\text{(revenue per admission)}} \right]$$

TABLE 1

INCREASE IN COST PER EQUIVALENT ADMISSION, FY 1977–FY 1979
(percent)

Kind of Hospital	Increase from FY 1977 to FY 1978	Increase from FY 1978 to FY 1979
GIR	6.9	9.9
Non-GIR	8.1	12.8

SOURCE: Data submitted by hospitals to the Maryland Health Services Cost Review Commission.

for GIR and non-GIR hospitals from fiscal year 1977 to fiscal year 1978 and from fiscal year 1978 to fiscal year 1979. Six hospitals were on the GIR for more than half of 1978; thirteen hospitals were on the GIR for more than half of 1979. The rate of increase in cost per equivalent admission was substantially lower in the GIR hospitals than in the non-GIR hospitals. These data demonstrate that hospitals can, and do, respond to incentives in the payment system.

Management Flexibility

The two hospital regulatory systems currently operating in Maryland have one important feature in common. Neither specifies how a hospital is to spend its money. Both set the revenue that the hospital is permitted to generate, and how a hospital uses that revenue is up to its management. Furthermore, the manner in which hospitals respond to the incentives in the system is up to the internal management. In this way, hospitals in Maryland can adjust their response according to the areas in which they know they can make changes. Some hospitals have reduced length of stay, others have concentrated on using ancillary services, but all have been successful in their goal of reducing resource use per admission.

It is noteworthy that Maryland's system is a clear instance of the regulator trying to correct for the missing market forces, and that the pressures being placed on hospital management are, at least in part, the pressures that would exist if there were a functioning marketplace for health care services. If consumers of health care were concerned about the cost of their care, they would be shopping around and putting pressure on hospital management to control the charges. Then, as in the payment system just described, it would be up to hospital management to determine just how that control would be accomplished.

217

Conclusion

Rate regulation becomes necessary in an industry when there is a breakdown in the normal market forces that would otherwise exert pressure to control prices and numbers of services provided. In many instances, the rate design is poor, and insufficient thought is given to the question of what factor should be controlled. Also, most regulators will try to direct the application of the available resources even though they generally have less competence to do this than the managers employed in the regulated industry. This chapter has suggested that the most important step in the regulatory process is the design of the rate structure, which should be based on an analysis of desired incentives in the structure. The structure should be designed to embody these incentives, and then it should be examined to determine whether any perverse incentives have been inadvertently incorporated in it. Once corrective incentives are introduced, the job of the regulator is simply to ensure correct application of the rate-setting system, and to let industry managers respond to the incentives in the systems and allocate resources internally in the manner they consider most effective.

The analysis of the Medicare routine patient care cost limitation demonstrated the problems that arise when the incentives in the system are inappropriate, and the discussion of the GIR showed the level of success that can be expected from a good system design.

Alternative Regulatory Mechanisms for Controlling Hospital Costs

Paul L. Joskow

Until the late 1960s most government intervention in the hospital sector was oriented toward improving the quality and distribution of hospital services. During this period of time, the hospital sector was not normally among the set of industries studied by students of economic regulation. During the 1970s, however, a complex system of economic planning and regulation evolved having as one of its primary goals the control of the costs of hospital care. Thus the federal government has come to play an increasingly important role in promoting the economic regulation of hospitals. Many of its efforts have been predicated on the assumption that enormous "waste and inefficiency" exist in the hospital system and that the same quality of care can be delivered at a substantially lower cost.

This chapter explores the prospects and problems associated with various regulatory interventions that have been implemented or proposed and that are supposedly aimed at increasing the efficiency with which hospital care is provided in the United States. The focus here on regulatory alternatives for controlling hospital costs is *not* based on a conclusion that "regulatory" solutions are necessarily superior to "market-oriented" solutions. Rather it is based on the observation that the current direction of public policy is to seek solutions to perceived problems of resource allocation in this sector by creating regulatory institutions to deal with them. We should therefore have some understanding

This chapter is a short version of several chapters of my book, *Controlling Hospital Costs: The Role of Government Regulation,* to be published by MIT Press. Research support from the National Science Foundation is gratefully acknowledged. I want to to thank Jeffrey Harris, Richard Schmalensee, Christopher DeMuth, Joseph Newhouse, Charles Phelps, and Mancur Olson for helpful comments. I am especially grateful to Dr. William Schwartz, who first interested me in this subject and from whom I have learned so much.

of the strengths and weaknesses of the regulatory initiatives that have been proposed or that are already in place.

A complete analysis of the rationale for government regulation and the effects of alternative regulatory instruments should attempt to answer the following questions:

1. What market imperfections or market distortions suggest that the performance of prevailing institutions in allocating resources to and within the hospital sector is unsatisfactory? What kinds of market failures and associated inefficiencies exist?

2. Since all markets are "imperfect" compared with some abstract ideal—as are all regulatory systems—how important empirically are the inefficiencies that have been identified? Are the costs engendered by imperfect markets large enough to warrant efforts to ameliorate them with imperfect government regulation?

3. How well matched, as a theoretical matter, are alternative instruments for dealing with the problems that are of concern? Which regulatory systems appear to be most desirable?

4. How well have alternative policy instruments performed in practice in this sector or in others like it?

Market Distortions, Market Imperfections, and Resource Allocation in the Hospital Sector

Research by economists and other social scientists has generated a long list of potential market distortions, potential market imperfections, and behavioral characteristics indicating that too many resources flow into the hospital sector. Let us briefly examine some important structural and behavioral problems that have been identified.

Resource allocation problems in the hospital sector and in the overall health care system have been widely attributed to the characteristics of insurance contracts. Since the need for health care and the costs of that care are uncertain and since consumers are thought to be risk averse,[1] the availability of at least some insurance will increase welfare by reducing uncertainty. Once illness has occurred, however, the patient has the opportunity to choose among different levels of hospital care, each one carrying a different amount of resource utilization as well as potentially different expected benefits. The patient with some insurance has an ex post subsidy to the consumption of hospital care that leads to an efficiency loss due to "moral hazard." The size of

[1] M. J. Bailey, M. Olson, and P. Wonnacott, "The Marginal Utility of Income Does Not Increase: Borrowing, Lending, and Friedman-Savage Gambles," *American Economic Review*, vol. 70, no. 3 (June 1979), pp. 372–79.

this ex post efficiency loss depends on demand and supply conditions (including technological change) in the hospital sector and on the ability of insurance contracts to be structured so as to deter inefficient consumption behavior by insured individuals when they become ill.

The optimal insurance contract, characterized in many theoretical models by an aggregate coinsurance rate, is determined by trading off the risk-spreading benefits of a lower coinsurance rate against the efficiency losses associated with the ex post subsidy on the consumption care.[2] The more inelastic are demand and supply, the lower the optimal coinsurance rate will be, and vice versa. In the presence of moral hazard, the optimal insurance contract will be incomplete, so that patients will have some incentive to restrict consumption. This insurance contract is optimal *given* assumptions about demand and supply responses. It is, however, inferior to some "ideal" contract that might restrict patient responses after illness occurs. With reference to some "perfect" insurance policy, the presence of moral hazard problems means that there is an inherent inefficiency in the hospital market. In characterizing the present system as being inefficient on account of moral hazard problems, we must be careful to note that it is inefficient only in relation to an abstract ideal that is unlikely to be economically achievable in the real world. From a useful policy perspective, we can characterize the resulting allocation of resources as being inefficient only if we can identify institutional changes or government interventions that reduce the inefficiencies associated with moral hazard problems without incurring greater risk-bearing costs and transactions costs.

The assumption that insurance markets are competitive and that as such they will yield insurance contracts that are optimal, given moral hazard, is the starting point for the literature that examines the effects on resource allocation of tax subsidies to health insurance premiums. The most extensive work in this area, conducted by Feldstein,[3] observes that the U.S. tax system provides a major subsidy to the purchase of health insurance, since employers' contributions for their employees' health insurance plans are tax-deductible business expenses but are not taxable income to the employees and are not included in the base on which social security taxes are levied. Feldstein and Freidman estimate that on the margin the subsidy amounts to about 35 percent of the

[2] For example, K. Arrow, "Welfare Analysis of Changes in Health Coinsurance Rates," in R. Rosett, ed., *The Role of Health Insurance in the Health Services Sector* (New York: National Bureau of Economic Research, 1976).

[3] See M. S. Feldstein, "The Welfare Loss of Excess Health Insurance," *Journal of Political Economy,* vol. 81 (1973), pp. 251–80; "Hospital Cost Inflation: A Study of Non-Profit Price Dynamics," *American Economic Review,* vol. 6 (1971), pp. 835–72; "Quality Change and the Demand for Hospital Care," *Econometrica,* vol. 45 (1977), pp. 1681–1702.

premium.[4] The subsidy encourages individuals (presumably through their group plans) to purchase "too much" insurance in the sense that coinsurance payments and deductibles will be lower than they would otherwise have been. By encouraging the purchase of more complete insurance, ex post inefficiencies are increased, social welfare is reduced, and hospital expenditures rise. Feldstein imputes large welfare losses to these subsidies and argues that the prevalence of too much insurance is the major cause of the rapid rate of growth in the quantity, quality, and resource costs of hospital care.

The view that there is too much insurance and the computations that underlie estimates of the welfare losses and increases in hospital expenditures associated with this distortion cannot, however, turn entirely on tax subsidies, since less than half of the expenditures in acute hospitals are attributable to patients with private insurance plans. The majority of health care expenditures are paid for by government plans (primarily Medicare and Medicaid) or by uninsured individuals. In order to expand the notion that health insurance plans are generally "too complete," there must be a presumption that as well, the federal government and state governments are providing too much insurance through the Medicare and Medicaid plans. The argument here would be that the coinsurance rates and deductibles of the Medicare program, for example, are too low.

Other structural and behavioral characteristics of the hospital sector have led some to believe that resources will not be allocated efficiently even absent the tax subsidy problem. One issue raised is the extent of competition in the health insurance market. Most theoretical and empirical considerations of "optimal" insurance assume that private hospital insurance is available in a competitive market. This assumption is at the very least a candidate for careful scrutiny. Private hospital insurance is provided by Blue Cross plans and by private insurance companies. Although, in some states, private insurance companies together have a larger share of the market than does Blue Cross, individual companies generally have a much smaller share than does Blue Cross.[5] Blue Cross is generally the dominant insurance carrier.

Blue Cross plans were originally created by state hospital societies during the depression to help assure that they would be paid for services

---

[4] M. S. Feldstein and B. Friedman, "Tax Subsidies, the Rational Demand for Insurance, and the Health Care Crises," *Journal of Public Economics,* vol. 7 (1977), pp. 155–78.

[5] See statement of Morton D. Miller in U.S. Congress, Senate, Subcommittee on Health of the Committee on Finance, *Hearings, Health Care Cost Containment,* 96th Congress, 1st session, March 13, 1979.

provided.[6] Although the close linkages between the hospitals and the Blue Cross plans have eroded, they have not disappeared. Blue Cross plans often reimburse hospitals at lower rates than do commercial insurers and in a number of states have a variety of tax and regulatory advantages. To the extent that Blue Cross has power—through its cost advantages, through its linkages with hospitals, or through its size—to define the basic form for hospital insurance contracts, it could be in a position to affect the kinds of insurance contracts available to consumers in the market as well as the contractual relationships between insurers and providers. Given its size, Blue Cross should be in an excellent position to exploit all available instruments to reduce moral hazard problems through its contractual relationships with consumers, their surrogate groups, and health care providers. The question is whether Blue Cross is exploiting the opportunities to the fullest or whether it is pursuing other objectives as a result of limited constraints from competing insurance firms. These issues have not been investigated extensively in the literature and are worthy of much more attention.[7]

A related set of potential problems involves public and private restrictions on institutional arrangements for the delivery of health care and the relationships between third-party payers and providers. Over the years the formation of group practices has sometimes been restricted by state medical societies as has the development of health maintenance organizations. Health insurers may find it difficult to restrict coverage to particular sets of providers (whether they be physicians or hospitals) even if economic efficiency considerations indicate that such restrictions are desirable. Innovative health insurance policies are unlikely to be successful in the market if collective boycotts against individual insurance carriers by physicians or hospitals make providers reluctant to propose changes that will adversely affect them.

Although the literature has focused primarily on the contractual relationship between individuals and insurance firms, the relationship between hospitals and insurance firms is also of considerable importance. Third-party payers reimburse hospitals according to the individual hospital's posted "charges" or contractual "costs" accumulated by the patient, up to the limits of the insurance contract less the deductible and coinsurance payments. If one hospital has higher charges than another,

---

[6] See O. Anderson, *Blue Cross since 1929: Accountability and the Public Trust* (Cambridge, Mass.: Ballinger, 1975).

[7] See H. E. Frech and P. G. Ginsburg, "Competition among Health Insurers," in *Competition in the Health Care Sector: Past, Present and Future* (Federal Trade Commission, March 1978); and D. Kass and P. Pautler, *Staff Report on Physician Control of Blue Shield Plans* (Federal Trade Commission, November 1979).

the individual hospital's charges are reimbursed even if the patient could have obtained the same care more cheaply elsewhere.[8]

The combination of extensive, nearly complete insurance coverage and a reimbursement system that essentially pays whatever resource expenditures are incurred by the hospitals leads to another potential source of inefficiency in that almost no price competition exists between hospitals serving a particular area and no natural selection mechanism exists to constrain hospitals that produce inefficiently. The contractual relationships between patient and insurer and between patient and provider do not provide any independent cost-minimizing incentives.[9]

The combination of complete insurance and full cost reimbursement to individual nonprofit hospitals restricts the normal market forces that stimulate cost-minimizing behavior, given current technology and input prices, as well as process innovations that might reduce the costs of providing various diagnostic and therapeutic techniques over time. Nonetheless, hospitals are still in competition with one another. Whatever particular model of hospital objectives is employed, it will imply that hospitals would like to increase the number of patients they handle and the quality and range of diagnostic and therapeutic services they offer.[10] If a hospital cannot attract patients (through their physicians) by reducing the cost of care, then it will try other methods. The most effective way to attract patients and physicians would be to increase the *scope* and *intensity* of services that are available. Thus in competing for patients, hospitals are likely to resort to "quality" competition as characterized by the availability of a full range of diagnostic and therapeutic services, more intensive care of patients, and amenities.[11] As insurance contracts become more complete in the context of traditional reimbursement arrangements between insurers and hospitals, incentives for

[8] Why this type of reimbursement system has emerged and how it could change are discussed in more detail in a longer version of this study.

[9] This does not mean that we cannot conceptualize incentive contracts. See, for example, J. Newhouse and V. Taylor, "How Shall We Pay for Hospital Care?" *The Public Interest*, vol. 23 (Spring 1971), pp. 78–92. The problem is that these types of contracts are not being made available by the market—whether because of transactions costs or the effects of tax subsidies on the demand for insurance is unknown.

[10] There is considerable literature on hospital objective functions and associated hospital behavior. See, for example, J. P. Newhouse, "Toward a Theory of Non-profit Institutions: An Economic Model of a Hospital," *American Economic Review*, vol. 60 (1970), pp. 145–55.

[11] For example, if one hospital has a CT Scanner, other hospitals in the area will want to have CT scanners in order to attract patients and physicians, even if economies of scale dictate that only one hospital in a particular area should have this service. Facility duplication resulting from this type of service rivalry will be amplified by independent objectives of nonprofit hospitals to increase the scope and intensity of care.

cost-minimizing behavior decrease and incentives for service rivalry and other forms of nonprice competition increase.[12] These supply-side responses are likely to lead to the provision of hospital care at other than minimum cost. The inefficiency of such a system will probably be coupled with dynamic responses—in terms of a rate-of-product innovation that is too high and a rate-of-process innovation that is too low—that are even more costly.

Little has been said about the physician up until now, but clearly the physician cannot be ignored, since he is the primary intermediary between the patient and the hospital and is largely responsible for the kinds of services a patient receives. The physician is normally thought of as the *patient's* agent in this system. Ideally, the physician possesses the training and knowledge to apply medical technology in the best interest of the patient. The reimbursement system now operating in the United States conforms with the objectives that the "ideal" physician is taught to have: Do whatever is possible to resolve your patient's medical problem. If patients had only incomplete insurance, physicians would have to trade off beneficial health care against the patient's ability and willingness to pay for it. The prevalance of low deductible insurance among most of the population relieves the physician of participating in such "tragic choices." One could, of course, conceptualize a physician who provided care only up to the point that expected benefits and costs were equal on the margin. But the physician is not trained to do this, he faces no incentives to do this under traditional institutional arrangements, and his insured patient would not want him to do this unless insurance institutions enabled the patient to obtain insurance at a lower price commensurate with the reduction in moral hazard associated with choosing a more restrictive physician.[13] We therefore should not expect the physician to act independently in order to reduce the inherent "inefficiencies" in the system. To the extent that he acts on the interests of the individual insured patients, he provides the knowledge that guarantees that these inefficiencies will be realized.

[12] See P. L. Joskow, "The Effects of Competition and Regulation on Hospital Bed Supply and the Reservation Quality of the Hospital," *Bell Journal of Economics,* vol. 11 (Autumn 1980), pp. 421–47.

[13] When patients choose to insure themselves by enrolling in a health maintenance organization (HMO), they may be making this type of implicit contract. HMOs are organized to give physicians incentives to contain costs. The effects of these incentives may be revealed in various ways reflecting both the elimination of care that provides no benefits and the elimination of care that provides benefits that are below the associated resource costs. A great deal of the savings attributed to HMOs appears to be the result of much lower hospital admission rates. See H. Luft, "How Do Health Maintenance Organizations Achieve Their Savings: Rhetoric and Evidence," *New England Journal of Medicine,* vol. 298 (1978), pp. 1336–43.

Under traditional insurance and reimbursement institutions, however, we should recognize that the physician is in a position to *increase* the inefficiencies of the system. That is, physicians may not always act in the best interests of their patients. In particular, they may have personal financial incentives to prescribe *more* care than is beneficial to the patient. The fact that the insured patient pays little or nothing on the margin may encourage such behavior. To the extent that this "agency problem" is important, more resources in general will be expended than they would be otherwise without any additional patient benefits and perhaps causing harm. Malpractice laws, and internal hospital review committees, for example, may help to deter the most serious departures from good medical practice that actually harm the patient, but along that portion of the benefit curve where marginal benefits are very small we can expect personal financial interests to lead the physician to push the quantity and quality of care as far out as possible.

These structural and behavioral characteristics of the hospital sector have led many economists to conclude that it is marked by excessive demands for hospital services and a variety of distortions on the supply side. The major source of distortion on both the supply and demand sides is an insurance and reimbursement system that has almost eliminated fiscal constraints on insured patients and hospital care providers. The principal agents in the system—patient, physician, and hospital—have little if any incentive to consider the cost of care when making decisions about consumption and production. Price competition between hospitals is all but eliminated and is supplanted by vigorous quality competition much like that experienced in price-constrained airline markets.[14] The resulting inefficiencies include: (1) overutilization of hospital services, (2) duplication of hospital facilities engendered by nonprice competition and resulting failure to fully exploit economies of scale, (3) an excessive rate of technological change biased toward product rather than process innovations, and (4) organizational slack. Note carefully, however, that these are the *symptoms* not the fundamental *causes* of the problem.

Historical Patterns of Hospital Expenditures and Hospital Utilization

It is convenient to think of increases in hospital expenditures as being composed of three basic components:

- increases in the cost of inputs (labor, capital, materials)

[14] See, for example, G. Douglas and J. Miller, *Economic Regulation of Domestic Air Transport* (Washington, D.C.: Brookings Institution, 1974).

TABLE 1

HOSPITAL EXPENDITURES AND HOSPITAL UTILIZATION,
NONFEDERAL SHORT-TERM HOSPITALS, 1960–1979
(compound rates of growth; percent)

	1960–1979	1960–1966	1966–1970	1970–1975	1975–1979
Expenditures	13.9	10.7	17.5	14.8	14.1
Hospitals	0.5	1.2	0.2	0.4	− 0.2
Beds	2.3	3.1	2.5	2.2	1.1
Admissions	2.3	2.7	2.1	2.8	1.2
Adjusted patient-days	NA	NA	3.0	2.1	1.1
Average cost/stay	NA	NA	15.1	11.1	12.3
CPI	5.0	1.5	4.6	6.7	8.5
GNP deflator	4.8	1.9	4.4	6.8	7.1
Hospital input price index	NA	NA	NA	7.8	8.8
Hospital input price index (AHA)	NA	NA	NA	7.1	9.0

NA = not available.
SOURCE: Derived from American Hospital Association (AHA) and federal government data (various years).

- increases in the scope and intensity of hospital services resulting from technological change and from increases in demand
- increases in the quantity of services reflecting population growth and changes in demographic characteristics, and increases in individual demands for care

Although it is impossible to separate these components completely, the trichotomy provides a useful conceptual basis for determining the underlying sources of increased hospital costs. Table 1 presents aggregate U.S. data from the period 1960–1979 on a variety of indicators of hospital expenditures and hospital utilization. Although real hospital expenditures increased at a compound annual rate of about 9.4 percent per year[15] during this time, the real rate of growth in expenditures fluctuated considerably. It was highest from 1966 to 1970 following the introduction of Medicare and Medicaid, declined from 1970 to 1975, and since then has continued to decline.

[15] This depends on which input price index one uses.

TABLE 2

HOSPITAL INPUT COST INDEXES AND HOSPITAL INTENSITY INDEX,
1970–1979

(annual rates of change; percent)

Year	HCI (AHA)	HIPI (HCFA)	HII (AHA)
1970	8.7	7.5	9.6
1971	6.3	6.4	5.3
1972	3.4	5.8	3.2
1973	4.9	6.0	1.8
1974	9.2	10.1	4.0
1975	11.9	10.6	4.6
1976	10.3	8.8	5.8
1977	9.1	8.1	4.4
1978	7.2	8.4	4.8
1979	9.3	10.1	2.8

NOTE: HCI and HIPI are input prices indexes; HII is a real resource index.
SOURCE: Derived from American Hospital Association (AHA) and Health Care Financing Administration (HCFA) data.

The components of changing hospital expenditures are further demonstrated in table 2, which presents two indexes for hospital input prices and a third index measuring the change in real resource inputs per inpatient-day (HCI and HIPI are input price indexes and HII is a real resource index).[16] Together with the data in table 1, these data show that about 60 percent of the increase in expenditures has resulted from increases in input prices, about 10 percent from additional admissions and outpatient visits, and about 30 percent from an increase in the "intensity" of care. (It should be noted, however, that input price changes are not likely to be completely independent of the demand for factor inputs.) The increase in the "intensity" of care appears to be the result of a high rate of technological change.

An important characteristic of the hospital sector is, of course, that the opportunity set of diagnostic and therapeutic techniques is not fixed, but that it constantly changes as new knowledge is accumulated. In short, the hospital sector is characterized by rapid technological change, which generally occurs in two dimensions: new ways of providing existing diagnostic and therapeutic services may reduce the cost of providing

---

[16] Derived from data obtained from the American Hospital Association and from the Department of Health, Education, and Welfare, Health Care Financing Administration. Rates of change indicated are compound growth rates.

these services (process innovations);[17] and new diagnostic and thera-peutic services may improve health care outcomes (product innova-tions). Product innovations may supplement or replace existing services, and they may be more or less expensive than the services they replace.

Since 1960 the direction of technological change seems to have been most heavily weighted toward product rather than process innovations, toward innovations that supplement rather than replace existing mo-dalities, and toward more expensive rather than less expensive tech-niques.[18] As a result, many policy makers have come to view techno-logical change as a major cause of our "cost problem." Unlike any other industry in the economy, technological change in the hospital sector is commonly referred to as a "bad" rather than a "good" phenomenon. This view is both simplistic and misleading.[19]

How much of the increase in hospital expenditures since 1960 can we associate with one or more of the inefficiencies noted in the preceding section? It is fair to say that we just do not know with any precision. Merely comparing changes in expenditures with changes in aggregate economic activity or comparing changes in the cost per patient-day with the consumer price index is not particularly meaningful. Over this period of time, the population and per capita income have grown and demo-graphic characteristics have changed, insurance coverage has increased greatly, real wages for hospital employees have increased, and, most

[17] The automation of various clinical laboratory procedures would fall into this category. Open-heart surgery would fall into the second. CT scanning has characteristics of both a product and a process innovation, since it can provide new diagnostic services and is a substitute for certain existing diagnostic services.

[18] National Academy of Sciences, *Medical Technology and the Health Care System: A Study of the Diffusion of Equipment Embodied Technology,* Committee on Technology and Health Care of the National Research Council and the Institute of Medicine, 1979; S. H. Altman and R. J. Blendon, eds., *Medical Technology: The Culprit behind Health Care Costs?* Proceedings of the 1977 Sun Valley Conference on Health Care, Department of Health, Education, and Welfare, 1979; M. T. Rabkin and C. N. Melin, "The Impact of Technology upon the Cost and Quality of Hospital Care and a Proposal for Control of New Expensive Technology," in R. Egdahl and P. Gertman, eds., *Technology and the Quality of Health Care* (Germantown, Md.: Aspen Systems Corporation, 1978).

[19] It is misleading in a number of ways. As with other industries in the economy, tech-nological innovation can improve the well-being of society. The problem in this sector is that there is too little process innovation and the utilization of product innovations does not reflect the true resource costs of providing the associated services. To the extent that technological change is a problem, it is a symptom of the broader underlying incentives in the system that lead to departures from cost-minimizing behavior and overconsumption. Even with optimal (as opposed to ideal) insurance contracts, we can expect these types of inefficiencies to arise as a result of moral hazard. Other market distortions and market imperfections may make the problem worse. In fashioning schemes to reduce these inef-ficiencies economically, we must be careful not to throw the baby out with the bath water. By focusing on the symptoms of the problem rather than on the causes, we are more likely to do just that.

important, the "product" that hospitals deliver has changed profoundly. Comparing the "price" of a day in the hospital today with the "price" twenty years ago is like comparing the price of a 1980 Ford with the price of a Model T. Thinking about the issues of resource misallocation only in the context of "price inflation" is completely misleading. To identify the types and magnitudes of these inefficiencies and to separate increases in expenditures that are in some sense "optimal" from expenditures that represent waste and inefficiency requires that we engage in a much deeper inquiry.

To date, only Feldstein has obtained comprehensive quantitative results.[20] His work has focused on the effects of increased insurance coverage on hospital expenditures and the effects of tax subsidies to insurance—and associated reductions in the average coinsurance rate—on hospital expenditures and consumer welfare. As we have seen, Feldstein found that a large fraction of the increase in hospital expenditures is related to reductions in the aggregate coinsurance rate and, owing to tax incentives, the aggregate coinsurance rate is below the optimal level. Thus, by comparing the actual coinsurance rate with the "optimal" coinsurance rate, values for the welfare losses and increased expenditures associated with excessive insurance coverage can be developed.[21] Feldstein's estimates of the welfare losses and increased expenditures on hospital care reflect increases in the quantity and quality of hospital care amounting to several billion dollars per year. This work is subject to a number of theoretical and empirical criticisms, however, some of which have been discussed by Harris,[22] so that the numerical results must be considered to be uncertain. The results depend on particular assumptions about consumer preferences as well as uncertain empirical relationships between the average coinsurance rate and the demand and supply of hospital services. Notwithstanding the legitimate criticisms of this work, it represents the only comprehensive empirical effort to assess the effects of increased insurance coverage and the welfare losses induced by tax subsidies.

Those who argue that large inefficiencies exist in the hospital system generally rely on other types of evidence. Wide cross-sectional disparities in surgical rates, hospital beds per capita, average length of hospital stay, physicians per capita, cost per admission, etc., without detectable

---

[20] Feldstein, "The Welfare Loss of Excess Health Insurance."

[21] Ibid.

[22] See J. Harris, "The Aggregate Coinsurance Rate and the Supply of Innovations in the Hospital Sector" (Mimeographed), 1979. Note also that Feldstein's results do not cover the post-1973 period when government regulation of hospital costs expanded in both scope and intensity.

commensurate differences in health status are often pointed to as evidence that additional resource expenditures on hospital care yield at best marginal health benefits.[23] Inherent difficulties in measuring health status and differences in the demographic and health characteristics of the population, for example, make it difficult to draw strong implications from such observations. The general thrust of these observations is consistent with Feldstein's studies, however, and with the general observation that as insurance coverage becomes more complete, we should observe an increasing disparity between benefits and costs on the margin. On the other hand, it is difficult to make welfare judgments from such observations without some assessment of the appropriate trade-off between the risk-spreading benefits of insurance, the efficiency losses associated with moral hazard, and the efficiency with which current institutions constrain the behavior that leads to a moral hazard problem. To use these observations in a policy context as a motivation for institutional change, one must either believe, as Feldstein does, that the system generates excessive insurance coverage or that other institutional arrangements can constrain demand-and-supply behavior—reduce the efficiency losses associated with moral hazard—without incurring more than commensurate increases in risk-bearing and transaction costs.

These general observations of cross-sectional disparities can be supplemented by specific studies of particular diagnostic or treatment techniques. Several reviews of surgical procedures indicate that a significant fraction of surgical patients are operated on without appropriate indications.[24] The figures obtained for particular procedures vary widely, however, and a deep controversy has arisen concerning this approach to surgical procedures.[25] Similarly, some have suggested that high non-

---

[23] See J. Bunker, "Surgical Manpower: A Comparison of Operations and Surgeons in the United States and England and Wales," *New England Journal of Medicine,* vol. 289 (1970), pp. 135–44; P. Lembke, "Measuring the Quality of Medical Care through Vital Statistics Based on Hospital Service Areas I: Comparative Study of Appendectomy Rates," *American Journal of Public Health,* vol. 42 (1952), pp. 276–86; Testimony of J. Wennberg in U.S. Congress, House of Representatives, *Hearings before the Subcommittee on Oversight and Investigations of the Committee on Interstate and Foreign Commerce,* 94th Congress, 1st session (no. 94–37), July 15, 1975.

[24] See, for example, J. Doyle, "Unnecessary Hysterectomies," *Journal of the American Medical Association,* vol. 151 (1953), p. 360; R. E. Trussell et al., "The Quantity, Quality and Costs of Medical and Hospital Care Secured by a Sample of Teamster Families in the New York Area" (New York: Columbia University School of Public Health and Administrative Medicine, 1962).

[25] R. Emerson, "Unjustified Surgery, Fact or Myth?" *New York State Journal of Medicine,* vol. 76 (1976), p. 454; F. Moore, "What to Do When Physicians Disagree: A Second Look at Second Opinions," *Archives of Surgery,* vol. 113 (1978), pp. 1379–1400; New York Medical Society, *Report of the Cholecystectomy Subcommittee of the Quality of Care Committee* (New York, 1970); I. M. Rutkow and G. D. Zuidema, " 'Unnecessary' Surgery: An Update," *Surgery,* vol. 63 (1978), pp. 671–78.

confirmation rates in surgical second-opinion programs indicate that a significant fraction of the surgery performed in the United States is "unnecessary."[26] These results, too, may be open to serious misinterpretation.

Similar studies of diagnostic procedures have also been made. Studies of the routine use of chest X-rays, for example, indicate that for some classes of patients X-rays produce no useful diagnostic information; similar findings are reported in studies of laboratory tests.[27] Studies of CT scanning have yielded conflicting results regarding both benefits and costs. Despite widespread controversy, the weight of the evidence seems to be that CT scanning is beneficial for many patients and may actually save money for some classes of patients.[28]

These studies suggest that on the margin diagnostic and therapeutic techniques are used up to a point at which benefits expected are very small. The would-be regulator must decide, then, whether there are ways to control effectively what is essentially a moral hazard problem, or a moral hazard problem compounded by excessive insurance, without changing the coinsurance rate faced by insured patients. In the first case, we must determine whether there are better ways to control patient or provider behavior so that ex post consumption and production decisions are more efficient without sacrificing the risk-spreading benefits of insurance. To the extent that this problem is reinforced by excessive insurance coverage, we must be willing to change the incentives to purchase too much insurance or we must devise mechanisms that can improve welfare, carefully accounting for both the ex ante and ex post efficiency considerations.

Finally, a few studies of the supply side of the system have tried to determine whether current patterns of care can be provided more efficiently. McClure, for example, has examined the cost of excess beds.[29] Finkler has examined the savings that might be achieved by eliminating duplication in open-heart surgery and cardiac catheterization

---

[26] This approach was used in the much cited congressional study, *Surgical Performance: Necessity and Quality,* U.S. Congress, House Committee on Interstate and Foreign Commerce, Subcommittee on Oversight and Investigations, 95th Congress, 2d session, 1978.

[27] H. Abrams, "The 'Overutilization' of X-Rays," *New England Journal of Medicine,* vol. 300 (1979), pp. 1213–16; J. M. Eisenberg, "Computer Based Audit to Detect and Correct Overutilization of Laboratory Tests," *Medical Care,* vol. 15 (1977), pp. 915–21.

[28] See, for example, H. Fineberg, R. Bauman, and M. Sosman, "Computerized Cranial Tomography: Effect on Diagnostic and Therapeutic Plans," *Journal of the American Medical Association,* vol. 238 (1977), pp. 224–27; G. Wortzman, "Cranial Computed Tomography: An Evaluation of Cost Effectiveness," *Radiology,* vol. 117 (1975), pp. 75–77.

[29] W. McClure, "Reducing Excess Hospital Capacity" (Excelsior, Minn.: InterStudy, October 15, 1976).

facilities.[30] When Schwartz and Joskow examined theoretical savings that might be achieved through facility consolidation indicated by the federal guidelines for CT scanners, open-heart surgery facilities, therapeutic radiology facilities, and general hospital beds, they found that the savings were surprisingly small.[31] Unlike other evidence, however, data on facility duplication and other inefficiencies in the supply side require less difficult welfare judgments. If current patterns of care are provided at other than minimum cost, any changes that economically reduce the costs of providing this care are pure welfare gains and do not involve a sacrifice of either ex ante or ex post benefits.

Overall, empirical observations on the performance of the hospital sector are generally consistent with what one would expect to find given the theoretical concepts we have discussed up to this point.[32] There appear to be many possibilities for reducing expenditures without making equivalent sacrifices in health care benefits. The literature indicates that if we group potential efficiency losses into two categories, one reflecting distortions that lead hospitals to provide particular levels and patterns of care at other than minimum cost and the other reflecting distortions associated wtih excessive quantities and intensities of care, the losses from "non-cost-minimizing behavior" are small relative to the losses associated with consumption distortions and associated supply-side responses to satisfy excessive demands for care.

Alternative Regulatory Approaches

Regulatory solutions to perceived imperfections in the allocation of resources in the hospital sector may be viewed in terms of a search for institutional arrangements that allow us to come closer to simulating a set of "ideal" insurance contracts. If it were not for moral hazard problems (demand responses by insured patients and associated supply responses by providers), supply-side distortions induced by low coinsurance rates, and agency problems, the ideal insurance policy would involve complete insurance. From a regulatory perspective, the issue is

---

[30] S. Finkler, "Cost Effectiveness of Regionalization: The Heart Surgery Example," *Inquiry,* vol. 16 (1979), pp. 264–70.

[31] William B. Schwartz and Paul L. Joskow, "Duplicated Hospital Facilities," *New England Journal of Medicine,* vol. 202, no. 25 (December 18, 1980), pp. 1449–57.

[32] Note carefully that this does not say that there will be no sacrifice in benefits, only that the benefits appear to be less than the costs. Although many critics of the health care system in the United States argue that many diagnostic and therapeutic techniques are used extensively in situations in which they provide no benefits, the evidence to support this proposition is meager. In light of the previous discussion, we do expect that *on the margin* benefits will be very small.

whether or not we can create regulatory institutions that effectively reduce moral hazard problems, eliminate supply-side distortions, and reduce agency problems without incurring additional costs that offset the gains.

In evaluating alternative regulatory instruments, let us assume that prevailing contractual relationships between individuals and their insurers remain as they are now. The system is assumed to provide almost complete insurance coverage in the sense that the out-of-pocket expenses to the patient for all care received represents a tiny fraction of the cost of that care. In other words, the direct consumption incentives that individual consumers face as a result of prevailing insurance contracts remain unchanged and patient demands for care associated with this incentive are unchanged. Regulatory initiatives can affect the *supply side* of the system directly, however, by constraining the ability of hospitals to provide particular services at the quantities that would otherwise be demanded (through certificate-of-need type regulations), or indirectly by affecting the ways in which providers are reimbursed for supplying care (reimbursement regulation).

The following evaluation of the alternative supply-side regulations is conducted in the context of a set of performance characteristics reflecting the inefficiencies that motivate an interest in regulatory intervention and the costs associated with the regulatory instruments themselves.

Direct Controls on Facility Construction through Certificate-of-Need Regulation. Let us first consider, on a conceptual level, regulatory interventions on the supply side of the hospital sector that directly constrain the ability of hospitals to add new facilities and to expand or renovate existing facilities. The process through which such constraints are applied requires individual hospitals to obtain a permit to add, expand, or renovate capital facilities when the associated investment expenditures exceed some threshold value. That is, hospitals must satisfy some set of "need" criteria to obtain permission to make the desired capital expenditures. This type of regulatory constraint on capital investment is embodied in the "certificate-of-need" process. At present forty-eight states have certificate-of-need programs in place (see table 3). The investment threshold is normally $100,000 or $150,000.[33] These programs have been supplemented by voluntary agreements between the states and the federal government under Section 1122 of the Social Security Act whereby the federal government can deny reimbursement

[33] To meet minimum standards a CON program must have a threshold of no more than $150,000. Many states have established lower thresholds.

TABLE 3

STATUS OF STATE CERTIFICATE-OF-NEED AND SECTION 1122
PROGRAMS IN THE UNITED STATES, 1980

State	Year CON Enacted	Section 1122 Agreement
Alabama	1977	yes/modified
Alaska	1976	yes
Arizona	1971	no
Arkansas	1975	yes
California	1969	no
Colorado	1973	terminated
Connecticut	1969	no
Delaware	1978	yes
Florida	1972	terminated
Georgia	1974	yes
Hawaii	1974	terminated
Idaho	—	yes
Illinois	1974	yes
Indiana	—	yes
Iowa	1977	yes
Kansas	1972	yes
Kentucky	1972	yes
Louisiana	—	yes
Maine	1978	yes
Maryland	1968	terminated
Massachusetts	1971	no
Michigan	1972	yes
Minnesota	1971	yes
Missouri	1979	yes
Mississippi	1979	yes
Montana	1975	yes
Nebraska	1979	yes
Nevada	1971	yes
New Hampshire	1979	terminated
New Jersey	1971	yes
New Mexico	1978	yes
New York	1964	terminated
North Carolina	1978	yes
North Dakota	1971	yes
Ohio	1975	terminated

(*table continues on next page*)

TABLE 3 (continued)

State	Year CON Enacted	Section 1122 Agreement
Oklahoma	1971	yes
Oregon	1971	terminated
Pennsylvania	1979	terminated
Rhode Island	1968	no
South Carolina	1971	yes
South Dakota	1972	no
Tennessee	1973	no
Texas	1975	no
Utah	1979	terminated
Vermont	1979	terminated
Virginia	1973	terminated
Washington	1971	yes
West Virginia	1977	yes
Wisconsin	1977	terminated
Wyoming	1977	terminated

SOURCE: U.S. Department of Health and Human Services.

to hospitals under federal programs if facilities have not been approved by a Health Systems Agency (HSA) established under Public Law 93–641.[34] In addition, in some states Blue Cross plans will not reimburse for facilities that have not been approved by HSAs.[35]

The concept of "need" is necessarily ambiguous. This discussion will develop two alternative conceptualizations of the objectives that certificate-of-need programs might be thought to have. The first model of the certificate-of-need process (CON1) focuses primarily on facility duplication. The notion is that the hospital system supplies any particular level of demand at other than minimum cost because (for the reasons we have discussed) more hospitals offer specific services in any health service area than would be economically efficient. The efficiency loss is the result of the system's failure to fully exploit economies of scale. Since a major source of facility duplication is nonprice competition among hospitals, CON1 may be said to represent objectives similar to those of a hospital cartel wishing to restrict quality competition. Independent hospital objectives to offer a wide range of services however,

[34] The National Health Planning and Resource Development Act of 1974, January 4, 1975, 88 Stat. 2225.
[35] Lewin and Associates, Inc., "Nationwide Survey of State Health Regulations" (Washington, D.C.: September 1974).

FIGURE 1
VARIATION OF UNIT COST WITH VOLUME FOR A HYPOTHETICAL FACILITY

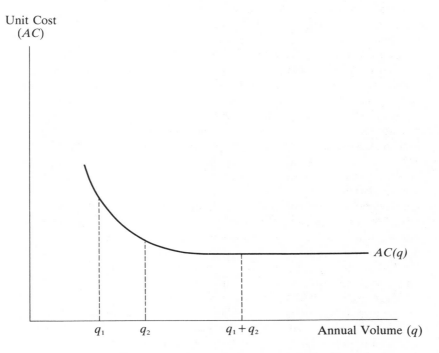

imply that the objectives implicit in CON1 and the interests of the hospitals do not completely coincide.[36]

This situation is depicted graphically in figure 1. Let us assume that we are focusing on open-heart surgery facilities and that over some range of utilization these facilities are characterized by increasing returns. Let us say that two hospitals in proximity offer this service with annual utilization rates of q_1 and q_2, respectively. If all the patients were treated in a single facility ($q_1 + q_2$), scale economies would be more fully exploited and the total cost of providing these services would decline. Note that we are taking demand as given; if only one hospital offered the service, the total volume of open-heart procedures in this area would not change. In this conceptualization of certificate-of-need regulation only one facility would be able to obtain a permit unless it

[36] This requires that hospitals would not be joint profit maximizers even if they could collude effectively because they value the scope and intensity of care that each can deliver individually.

could be shown that the areawide demand is high enough to allow a second facility to exploit scale economies fully as well. To the extent that facility duplication of this type can be constrained, we have a clear welfare gain. Demand is unaffected, but the costs of delivering care are reduced. There may be additional benefits associated with establishing minimum annual volumes for particular facilities related to medical efficacy rather than production.[37]

This simple conceptualization of CON regulation requires that the regulatory agency establish utilization criteria to guide its decisions regarding particular applications for the addition or renovation of facilities. To establish such criteria, the agency requires information on facility cost functions and on current and expected demand patterns in terms of aggregate volumes and patient locations. Not only must the regulatory agency examine "technical" economies of scale, but consideration must also be given to travel costs associated with requiring patients to travel longer distances when a smaller number of facilities are available. Even if a particular facility is not fully exploiting "technical" scale economies, the costs of transporting patients over longer distances will at some point outweigh the savings in unit production costs that may be achieved by consolidating care into a smaller number of facilities. These costs involve "ordinary" travel costs as well as sacrifices in the quality of care associated with imposing longer treatment delays on trauma patients. These additional costs are of special concern in evaluating facilities in areas of low population density where area demands are unlikely to be large enough to exploit all available scale economies. The federal government has promulgated facility guidelines for several different categories of facilities.[38] Individual state commissions have sometimes promulgated their own guidelines.[39] Until fairly recently the major focus has been on the supply of general hospital beds.[40]

For a number of reasons, the overall effects of this type of certificate-of-need process on potential inefficiences in the hospital sector and on total hospital expenditures are likely to be minimal. First, CON1 focuses directly on only one of the many potential performance failures of the hospital sector—facility duplication. Since demand is taken as

---

[37] See H. Luft et al., "Should Operations Be Regionalized? The Empirical Relation between Surgical Volume and Mortality," *New England Journal of Medicine*, vol. 301 (1979), pp. 1364–69.

[38] National Guidelines for Health Planning, 42CFR 121.1–121.6, 121.201–121.211.

[39] For example, the Commonwealth of Massachusetts has developed its own standards for facilities such as CT scanners, intensive and coronary care units, and general acute care beds.

[40] See, for example, W. J. Bicknell and D. C. Walsh, "Certificate-of-Need: The Massachusetts Experience," *New England Journal of Medicine*, vol. 292 (1975), pp. 1054–61.

given, this type of regulation endeavors to reorganize the system so that available scale economies are better exploited. The basic quantities and intensities of care do not change. In evaluating theoretical savings that might be achieved via consolidations consistent with federal guidelines in four areas that have attracted considerable attention, Schwartz and Joskow[41] concluded that the anticipated savings—ignoring administrative costs and implementation difficulties—represent a small fraction of total hospital expenditures and that such consolidations can accomplish only a small fraction of the national cost containment goals. Also, since CON regulation operates on the margin, it may take a long time to achieve even these savings.

Some indirect effects of certificate-of-need regulation, however, may be worth considering. By reducing the number of facilities that the hospital system can build, the market for new diagnostic and therapeutic techniques becomes smaller. To the extent that efforts to develop new products are related to the anticipated size of the market, this effect might conceivably reduce the rate of product innovation. This indirect effect is difficult to quantify, and the disincentives associated with a smaller U.S. market are attenuated by the fact that many of these techniques are made available internationally.

Second, although the CON agency may have only formal authority to consider applications for new facilities or for facility renovations whose associated capital expenditures exceed some threshold value, this authority may provide leverage for a CON agency to extend its authority beyond the boundaries of the statute. A hospital applying for authority to build a new ten-bed intensive care unit, for example, may be told (informally) that the application will be approved only if it closes its obstetrical unit or agrees to provide expanded outpatient facilities that would reduce inpatient utilization. How far a CON agency can legally go in creating what amounts to an informal regulatory process based on informal bargaining between the regulatory staff and the applicant is unclear. These types of informal regulatory processes have evolved in other regulated industries,[42] however, and there is some evidence that it has become an important component of the certificate-of-need process in some states.[43]

Third, the "reach" of this type of regulation, which depends on

[41] CT scanners, open-heart surgery and cardiac catheterization, therapeutic radiology, and general hospital beds.

[42] P. L. Joskow, "Pricing Decisions of Regulated Firms: A Behavioral Approach," *Bell Journal of Economics and Management Science,* vol. 4 (1973), pp. 118–40.

[43] Policy Analysis, Inc., *Evaluation of the Effects of Certificate-of-Need Programs,* Draft Final Report, vol. 3 (Brookline, Mass.: January 1980).

establishing general utilization criteria for particular types of facilities, is limited by the complexity of hospital supply characteristics and by the diversity of the "product" provided by hospitals. As a result, the number of services for which this type of regulation can be applied effectively without incurring enormous information costs is probably quite limited.

Fourth, by establishing high threshold capital expenditures to trigger CON review, the CON process covers only a fraction of the facility and equipment decisions that a hospital makes every year. Furthermore, by focusing regulation on a particular input—capital—the process may ignore some of the most costly supply decisions that hospitals make. Hospitals are not particularly capital intensive. Interest and depreciation expenses account for only about 10 percent of total hospital expenditures, and there is no simple relationship between the capital expenditures associated with making a particular service available and the total costs of that service.[44] Where substitution between capital and other inputs is possible, CON regulation may encourage the introduction of less capital-intensive but more expensive ways of making particular services available.

Fifth, the establishment of utilization criteria may create perverse incentives for hospitals and physicians to increase the utilization of particular services beyond what would otherwise be desirable in order to satisfy the guidelines.[45] If one believes in the "supply creates demand" theory (which I do not), this kind of distortion must also be considered.

Finally, Havighurst[46] and others have suggested that this process may be easy to "capture" by existing hospitals with substantial political power. Thus, new hospitals or free-standing facilities may find it difficult to enter the market when it means that these new facilities will make it difficult for existing hospitals to expand their own facilities or that the effects of increased competition will be undesirable from the perspective of existing providers. To the extent that new entrants such as HMOs or free-standing clinics can provide services more efficiently, this entry restriction represents another potential distortion in the system. A re-

[44] Applied Management Sciences, *A Feasibility Study of the Influence of Capital Expenditures on Hospital Operating Costs,* Final Report, Health Care Financing Agency, Research and Demonstration Series #6, 1978; R. Evans and R. Jost, "Economic Analysis of Body Computed Tomography Units Including Data on Utilization," *Radiology,* vol. 127 (1978), p. 151; K. E. Warner, "The Cost of Embodied Medical Technology," in National Academy of Sciences, *Medical Technology and the Health Care System,* 1979.

[45] For example, hospitals could satisfy the average occupancy rate guideline by delaying discharges and increasing the average length of stay.

[46] C. C. Havighurst, "Regulation of Health Facilities and Services by 'Certificate-of-Need,' " *Virginia Law Review,* vol. 59 (1973), pp. 1143–1232; R. Posner, "Certificate-of-Need for Health Care Facilities: A Dissenting View," in C. C. Havighurst, ed., *Regulating Health Facilities Construction* (Washington, D.C.: American Enterprise Institute, 1974).

lated problem is the prospect that large powerful teaching hospitals located in urban areas will be able to exploit this process at the expense of smaller and less powerful rural and suburban hospitals.

Overall, we can expect this form of CON regulation to be successful in reducing the most egregious departures from minimum cost production associated with facility duplication. The opportunities for cost saving here are relatively small, however, and are reduced further by the administrative costs of such regulations as well as by potential distortions that the system might generate. It would not be surprising to find, for example, that in states with vigorous CON programs we can identify significant effects of these regulations on the supply of beds and the number of specific diagnostic and therapeutic facilities without being able to identify a substantial effect on total hospital expenditures.[47]

The second conceptualization of the CON process (CON2) allows the certificate-of-need agency to expand its notion of "need." Here, the agency recognizes not only that inefficiencies are associated with facility duplication, but also that the quantity and quality of care generated by the system are, in some ideal sense, "too high." CON regulation is viewed here as an effort to do more than merely reorganize the system so that prevailing demand levels can be supplied more efficiently, but also as an effort to place a binding supply constraint on the system by controlling hospital investments. The "capital constraint" strategy tries to restrict the ability of hospitals to expand their capacity sufficiently to meet all demand that is generated by the market, *even if* facility expansion is accomplished at minimum efficiency scale. The idea is to constrain the system from expanding in order to satisfy fully the demands for care generated by a system with complete insurance in the hope that "low valued" uses will somehow be rationed out of the system. The CON process becomes a "technology" for inducing hospitals to ration care and hopes to be successful in ameliorating moral hazard problems.[48]

This model of certificate-of-need agency objectives reflects a concern about overconsumption associated with moral hazard problems as

---

[47] Schwartz and Joskow, "Duplicated Hospital Facilities."

[48] Early versions of the Carter administration's cost containment proposals included provisions for a national ceiling on annual capital expenditures that would be allocated among the states according to a variety of state characteristics, in the first-year population. Effectively, the capital constraint would have given state CON agencies a "budget constraint" limiting the total amount of capital expenditures they could approve. See proposed Hospital Cost Containment Act of 1977 (H.R. 6575), *Congressional Record* (April 25, 1977), page H3527. A revised bill introduced in 1979 did not have a capital investment ceiling (S. 570, 96th Congress, 1st session). The capital expenditure ceiling was subsequently included in the Carter administration's national health insurance proposals (proposed National Health Insurance Act, H.R. 5400, 96th Congress, 1st session).

well as supply inefficiencies associated with facility duplication.[49] The idea is not just that there are too many CT scanners to satisfy demand efficiently, but that too many patients are being provided with CT scans. Thus, the CON process can be viewed as trying to force the system to generate appropriate levels of care by constraining supply. Supply is constrained in turn by restricting the amount of one input—capital— that can be used to produce hospital services. At least in theory, this conceptualization has greater opportunities to reduce resource expenditures because it affects both the unit costs of care and the capacity of the system to deliver care.

In practice, this type of regulatory objective places greater burdens on both the regulatory agencies and the hospitals than does the CON1 model. To implement a capital constraint scheme such as this one, the CON agency needs the same kinds of information that it needs to implement the less restrictive objectives embodied in CON1. In addition, the agency must be willing and able to make decisions about the availability of capacity to perform a wide range of diagnostic and therapeutic techniques relative to the anticipated demand for that capacity. To do so efficiently, it must make determinations about costs and benefits on the margin for many different types of facilities located in many different communities. Assuming that it could put the "right" amount of capacity in place, it then must rely on hospitals to allocate the available resources to their highest valued uses. As we have noted, hospitals are not now organized to make such trade-offs,[50] and this regulatory strategy provides no independent incentives for patients or physicians to accommodate reduced supply with concomitant reductions in the demand for care with the lowest expected benefits. Furthermore, by biasing the supply constraint to certain types of facilities that the CON agency can control rather than providing a general resource constraint, hospital responses may also be distorted in undefinable ways. Ideally, hospitals would have to develop some internal rationing mechanism that allocates available resources to their highest valued uses. By placing constraints on a single input satisfying some lower-bound threshold, CON regulation limits the ability of hospitals to ration efficiently.

The information requirements for implementing CON2 effectively are enormous. Thus the CON agency will have to reduce the moral

---

[49] We can also think of it as reflecting concern about the so-called Roemer Effect and related agency problems.

[50] See J. R. Harris, "The Internal Organization of Hospitals: Some Economic Implications," *Bell Journal of Economics,* vol. 8 (1977), pp. 467–82, and "Regulation and Internal Control in Hospitals," *Bulletin of the New York Academy of Medicine,* vol. 55 (1979), pp. 88–103.

hazard problem by restricting the amount of care available by approving supply for what it estimates is a more "appropriate" aggregate level of care and hope that the hospitals can ration the excess demand efficiently. Furthermore, the CON agency must try to do this by controlling only one input—capital—rather than total expenditures. The coverage over the capital input will be incomplete because of the limited "reach" of administrative decisions over the complex nature of hospital supply. The process may also be subject to considerable political maneuvering and extensive litigation by hospitals and individual communities. With the broader constraints implicit in the CON2 mode, the stakes increase beyond narrow issues such as the number of specific facilities needed to satisfy demand efficiently to the question of the aggregate amount and quality of care that will be available in an individual state or community.[51] As a result, therefore, it is difficult to be optimistic that this model of the certificate-of-need process is a viable, long-run regulatory strategy.

Government Control of Reimbursement Rates and Aggregate Hospital Expenditures. Supply-side constraints by administrative agencies need not be in the form of certificates of need. We can think of an alternative regulatory system that alters the incentives for hospitals to supply various types and quantities of services. To affect hospital incentives while leaving patient incentives unaltered,[52] we must intervene in the system by which hospitals are reimbursed for providing care. Ideally, such regulatory initiatives should strive to alter the incentives that hospitals have to supply care, to depart from cost-minimizing behavior, and to engage in service rivalry and quality competition.

Several states have established agencies to regulate hospital charges, reimbursement rates, or total hospital expenditures[53] (see table 4). In addition, Blue Cross plans in several states have turned to detailed cost and reimbursement review programs that reimburse hospitals prospectively on the basis of estimates of future costs and utilization patterns rather than retrospectively on the basis of actual costs incurred by in-

---

[51] Such issues helped to defeat the Carter administration's cost containment proposals by generating opposition from congressmen representing communities with relatively less sophisticated hospitals.

[52] That is, the explicit terms of the insurance contract as represented by the coinsurance provisions do not change. The implicit terms of the contract do change, of course, if supply constraints make it impossible for the system to satisfy all demands that would ordinarily be made given the explicit terms of the contract.

[53] These programs are discussed in detail in P. L. Joskow, *Controlling Hospital Costs: The Role of Government Regulation* (Cambridge, Mass.: MIT Press, 1981).

TABLE 4

STATES WITH MANDATORY HOSPITAL RATE REGULATION
PROGRAMS

State	Inception Date
Colorado	1977
Connecticut	1974
Maryland	1973
Massachusetts	1971
New Jersey	1971
New York	1969
Rhode Island	1971
Washington	1973
Wisconsin	1975

NOTE: HEW normally lists Rhode Island with the mandatory states even though the cooperative program between the state government, Blue Cross and hospital association is not mandated by statute. Hospitals must participate to get Blue Cross and Medicaid reimbursement, and coverage is 100 percent of hospitals. The AHA lists this as a voluntary program. The Colorado program was terminated in 1980.
SOURCE: Department of Health, Education, and Welfare, American Hospital Association, and private communications. Inception dates vary by source reflecting in part changing statutory authorities.

dividual hospitals.[54] Recently New Jersey launched an experiment in which hospitals are reimbursed a flat fee for particular medical problems.[55]

Early conceptualizations of rate or reimbursement regulation seem to have been based on the public utility model of rate regulation for individual franchised monopolies such as electric utilities and telephone companies rather than on reimbursement regulation as a means of altering suppliers' incentives in particular ways. The application of the public utility model to hospitals is problematic for a number of reasons.

First, the problem is not primarily one of monopoly pricing—in which regulatory efforts must be directed toward ensuring that prices

---

[54] See Lewin and Associates, Inc., "Nationwide Survey of State Health Regulations"; and American Hospital Association, "Report on Budget and Rate Review Programs," 1978 (Mimeographed). It appears that many Blue Cross plans have become more active in trying to constrain hospital expenditures and utilization. This change may reflect increasing difficulties in obtaining approvals for increases in health insurance premiums. See Harry Schwartz, "Health Insurance: A Fight for Survival," *New York Times,* October 20, 1977, p. 3; "New Blue Shield Policies Stir Protests from Michigan MD's," *American Medical News,* September 19, 1977.

[55] "Jersey Hospitals Go from Time Clock to Piece Work," *New York Times,* April 27, 1980, p. 6.

and costs are equal (at least in the aggregate) so that excess profits are eliminated and deadweight losses due to monopoly minimized. On the contrary, the basic problem is that expenditures keep increasing because of expanding utilization and increasing intensity of care. The insurance system and its interaction with demographic and technological changes cause increases in demand. Hospitals have strong incentives to satisfy this demand, perhaps inefficiently, as long as they are assured that they will be reimbursed for the full costs of providing the additional care. Just passing on costs, without some normative criterion to determine the terms of reimbursement, is not likely to be productive because it does not alter the basic incentive mechanisms that lead to the perceived problems. In addition, nonprice competition and the independent "rent absorption" incentives of nonprofit hospitals will probably ensure that any potential monopoly profits are dissipated by resource expenditures.[56]

Second, traditionally, monopoly prices distort consumer behavior because prices are greater than marginal cost. Unregulated monopolies are generally thought to have strong incentives to minimize costs, although efforts to control prices may distort production decisions.[57] In the hospital setting, the overwhelming majority of patients do not see the posted charges anyway, since they have almost complete insurance coverage. Thus, adjusting rate structures is not likely to affect the behavior of insured patients.[58]

Third, there are over 5,000 short-term hospitals in the United States. Superimposing a regulatory scheme such as that used to regulate public utilities in place of the current process of reimbursement negotiation between providers and insurers will probably entail great increases in transaction costs.

For rate regulation to have a significant effect on this system we

---

[56] Let me add one caveat to this view. If we think of the hospital as offering a range of services characterized by some economies of scale and engaged in noncooperative service rivalry, price discrimination may be said to enable a hospital to subsidize some services that would not otherwise be sustainable on their own. By requiring the hospital to set charges for individual services that are pegged to the average total cost of providing each service, hospitals may be forced to drop some services. It appears that services like emergency rooms and outpatient clinics would be the most adversely affected by the elimination of cross-subsidization.

[57] See H. Averch and L. Johnson, "Behavior of the Firm under Regulatory Constraint," *American Economic Review*, vol. 52 (1962), pp. 1053–69.

[58] J. Harris, "Pricing Rules for Hospitals," *Bell Journal of Economics*, vol. 10 (Spring 1979), pp. 224–43, suggests otherwise. The idea in this paper is to develop a rate structure which departs from marginal costs so as to achieve a second best optimum in the face of low coinsurance rates. The problem is that patients with cost-based insurance policies never really see the posted charges.

must clearly go beyond the traditional public utility model, which tries to match revenues with costs. Nonprofit hospitals probably do this on their own. We must focus on the interaction between alternative reimbursement criteria and the incentives that different reimbursement formulas give to hospitals to supply care. We need normative criteria that focus on the "reasonableness" of the costs themselves rather than complicated accounting that matches posted prices (which are largely irrelevant here) with "actual" costs incurred.[59] The responses from the system will depend largely on the criteria used to determine what expenditures are reimbursable and what are not.

Alternative Reimbursement Criteria. A number of approaches have been suggested for determining the costs that should be reimbursed. This discussion will consider three "prototypes." Although they are discussed independently, variations of each or combinations of the three are possible.

The comparable hospital approach. This approach assembles data on sets of "comparable" hospitals in order to distinguish efficient from inefficient hospitals and to reimburse only for "efficient costs."[60] Within each set, we compute the average expenditures per day, or per service, for example, and then reimburse for no more than the mean (whether it is the mean or the median or the 80th percentile is not important for this discussion) for the group. Hospitals with costs above the mean must either reduce their unit costs or run a loss. Hospitals having costs below the mean receive a little extra revenue that they can spend as they see fit.

This procedure may also be viewed in terms of running a regression of unit costs (let us say per diem costs) against all relevant characteristics of hospitals for a large sample of hospitals.[61] Such characteristics might be size, occupancy rate, patient mix, service offerings, teaching status, average length of stay, etc. We can then compare the actual costs for a particular hospital with certain characteristics with the "predicted" costs from the regression. The residuals distinguish the efficient from the inefficient. We might allow only for reimbursement of "predicted" costs or predicted costs plus something. Hospitals above the regression

---

[59] This is what Medicare and other cost-based reimbursement plans are doing already.

[60] See J. Lave and L. Lave, "Hospital Cost Function Analysis: Implications for Cost Controls," in M. Zubkoff, et al., eds. , *Hosptial Cost Containment: Selected Notes for Future Policy* (New York: Prodist 1978). The comparable hospital approach was incorporated in the last version of the Carter administration's cost containment bill (S. 570, 1979).

[61] Ibid.

line will be forced to respond by reducing costs so that they approach the reimbursement standard or else they will incur losses.[62]

Unfortunately, this procedure makes the most sense in a static world in which the major problem is that similar hospitals produce the same services with different levels of efficiency. It may be an effective way to deal with organizational slack and perhaps to encourage process innovations. The problem in the hospital sector, however, is that expenditures increase as utilization and the intensity of care increase. There is no static production set or simple per diem or per illness cost function on which to anchor such a reimbursement process. Characteristics that are used to group hospitals are precisely the factors that lead to increased expenditures. As a result, this approach is unlikely to affect the major dynamic elements of increasing hospital expenditures or the sources of inefficiency in the system.[63]

Specific criterion formulas. A second way of determining what expenditures should be reimbursed is to apply specific normative criteria to utilization rates for entire hospitals or for specific services within hospitals. A regulatory agency may determine, for example, that general hospitals should have occupancy rates of at least 80 percent, obstetrical units occupancy rates of at least 65 percent, pediatric units occupancy rates of at least 70 percent, and so forth. If the utilization rate of a particular hospital is higher than the criterion, then the costs are fully reimbursed. If its utilization level is below the criterion, then its unit costs are recomputed to reflect what they would be if the criterion had been satisfied. The hospitals are subsequently reimbursed as if they had satisfied the criterion.

As with the comparable hospital approach, hospitals finding that their costs are not fully reimbursed because they fail to meet the normative criterion specified must either respond so as to achieve the criterion or find some way to subsidize the service. Assuming that cross-subsidization is not permitted, hospitals can respond in one of two ways: by reducing supply, reducing either the hospital's capacity to supply a particular service or eliminating that service completely; or by increasing utilization. Doctors may be encouraged to increase the average length of stay for inpatients or to treat more patients on an inpatient basis, or the hospital may engage in a variety of activities to attract patients from

[62] Hospitals falling below the regression line may be allowed to keep some of the difference as an "incentive." We can anticipate, however, that nonprofit hospitals will find some way to spend the surplus.

[63] Of course, "fixing" the production set at a point in time could provide a rather stringent constraint. It makes more sense to think of this in the context of the "formula approach" discussed later.

neighboring facilities. The first response will probably lead to a reduction in expenditures from a more complete exploitation of economies of scale. The second response could lead to increases in expenditures.

Many aspects of this regulatory approach are similar to the first view of the certificate-of-need process. Specific utilization criteria for general hospital beds and specific services must be developed. In the CON process such criteria can be used in evaluating new capital expenditures over some specific size. In this case, the criteria are used simply to determine the extent to which the cost incurred will be reimbursed. Both approaches have essentially the same performance characteristics, including the same relatively small prospects for expenditure savings. The use of reimbursement incentives, however, rather than utilization or quantity criteria for new facilities, in the context of a permit process, has a number of potential advantages:

1. The CON process normally applies the criteria to new projects that must seek approvals rather than to the existing stock (although informal negotiations may expand the de facto reach of certificate of need). Symmetrical reimbursement formulas can affect the entire stock of facilities and yield whatever additional economies of scale are to be had more quickly.

2. General reimbursement criteria will not discriminate against "new entrants," which may be able to produce specific services more efficiently than existing hospitals. It may also be more difficult for politically strong institutions to manipulate the system.

3. The combination of criterion reimbursement with comparable hospital data can provide incentives to eliminate organizational slack and to create better incentives for process innovations.

As with certificate-of-need regulations the major savings to be expected from this approach arise from the elimination of facility duplication so that scale economies can be better exploited. Additional savings accrue from eliminating biases against new facilities relative to existing facilities. Combining utilization criteria with a comparable cost formula may in addition help to eliminate organizational slack and may create incentives for process innovations. The number of dimensions over which useful normative criteria can be specified (primarily regarding utilization rates) remains limited, however, and hospitals could respond perversely to these criteria by expanding utilization in various ways.[64] This regulatory approach deals primarily with static efficiency

[64] Needless to say, there is also considerable controversy over the appropriate normative criteria for cost considerations and efficiency considerations. I am always amazed at how quickly policy makers accept particular clinical judgments that support a particular policy when a fair reading of the clinical literature clearly indicates considerable uncertainty and profound disagreements.

gains resulting from reductions in the unit costs of particular levels of care. It has little if any effect on the major causes of increases in hosptial expenditures associated with demands for the quantity and intensity of care that are too high. Demand is not rationed; it is only reallocated so that it can be satisfied more efficiently.

General budget constraints. A third approach is to take the bull by the horns, to recognize that as a general matter hospital expenditures are too high and growing too rapidly, and simply to give hospitals a binding expenditure constraint that is below what they would otherwise incur if unconstrained. This is essentially the approach that the Carter administration urged Congress to take (without success).[65] We might assume, for example, that unconstrained, real hospital expenditures will grow at 5 percent per year. The regulatory authorities will determine that this rate of growth is too high and will decide that a 1 percent real growth rate is "right." All hospitals will then be told that they will be reimbursed in year t only for expenditures calculated according to the following formula:

$$E_t = E_{t-1} (1 + I + 0.01)$$

where E_t are current year expenditures, E_{t-1} are last year's expenditures, and I is an index of general inflation (percentage change in input prices $\div$ 100).

Although in theory this approach has a number of advantages over alternative efforts to control expenditures by administrative regulation, it also has a number of theoretical and practical problems. Let us first discuss the advantages:

1. We avoid hospital-by-hospital and service-by-service cost and reimbursement regulation by applying a general budget constraint to all hospitals; the result is a regulatory process that is on the surface less complex, arbitrary, and discriminatory.

2. We allow individual hospitals to allocate their limited resources rather than rely on regulators to specify utilization criteria or a laundry list of specific services. Since the "reach" of regulatory criteria is necessarily limited by the vast array and complexity of services provided, the general budget constrains expenditures over the full range of services offered by the hospitals and places the burden of normative criteria and internal resource allocation on those who best know the opportunity set.

---

[65] The Carter administration's cost containment proposal has changed over time in response to congressional opposition. The simple original proposal has been replaced by a more complicated scheme involving much more regulation by the secretary of human resources.

3. We provide incentives to eliminate organizational slack and to introduce process innovations.

4. We not only encourage static efficiency and process innovations, but we constrain the hospital from expending resources on new product innovations and on more intensive use of existing diagnostic and therapeutic techniques. By placing a binding budgetary constraint on hospitals, we do not allow them to provide all additional services demanded, which are the major source of increasing expenditures, without cutting back somewhere else.

5. We encourage changes in the internal organization of hospitals by forcing hospitals to develop internal mechanisms for allocating what are now scarce resources. If done properly, consumption inefficiencies or moral hazard problems can be reduced.

These theoretical advantages are accompanied by several practical disadvantages, some of which weaken the chances of sustaining this type of regulatory system when it is superimposed on the prevailing insurance system.

1. A severe constraint on real increases in expenditures of the type favored by the Carter administration will almost inevitably lead to an excess demand situation. This regulatory strategy does not affect the economic incentives to demand more and better services; it merely constrains the ability of hospitals to supply them. Neither the patient nor his physician has any additional incentives to conserve resources. The hospital simply will not be in a position to supply what is demanded. No matter how well the hospitals can allocate the available resources and thereby ameliorate moral hazard problems, patients are not likely to be satisfied with an insurance entitlement that promises "free" care but does not have the capability to supply it. Since the choice of any particular number for the "right" growth rate in real expenditures is largely arbitrary, consumers are unlikely to perceive the benefits of such constraints in lower insurance premiums; and consumers are not free to choose among insurance plans with different implicit restrictions on benefits.

2. The general and uniform budgetary constraint that treats all hospitals equally is predicated on the assumption that all hospitals should be treated equally. There is no reason to believe this. Hospitals differ as to the kinds of patients they serve, changes over time in population served, the "base" level of services offered (less sophisticated southern or rural hospitals may argue that they should be allowed to catch up to the more sophisticated northern or urban hospitals), and a wide variety of teaching responsibilities. A large proportion of hospitals will inevit-

ably find plausible reasons for obtaining exceptions to the general formula.[66]

3. Since hospitals are not now organized so as to allocate scarce resources to their best uses, the rapid introduction of a severe budget constraint could easily lead to chaotic and arbitrary allocational rules that may be neither efficient nor fair. This transitional problem can probably be avoided if the budget constraint is tightened gradually in order to give hospitals sufficient time to adapt their internal processes for resources allocation to a binding budget constraint. In the long run, however, one must be skeptical about the willingness of different groups in society to accept the criteria established by the hospital. As with any supply-constrained system, some individuals will learn to use it to their advantage, while others may be discriminated against. Excess demand, combined with real or imagined inequities in the decisions about who gets served will inevitably lead to pressures to have the budget constraints relaxed.

In light of problems with stringent budget constraints, it is not surprising that Congress was reluctant to pass the cost containment legislation proposed by the Carter administration. Even if such legislation were to be passed, it would probably be emasculated by exceptions, administrative complexity, and political pressures to relax the constraints. Hospitals are perceived to be spending too much money, so we pass a law requiring that they spend less. In the process, we do give hospitals fiscal incentives to conserve resources, but similar incentives are still not given to the patient or to his physician. On balance, however, this approach may be the most productive of the various alternatives.

The Effects of Certificate-of-Need and State Regulation of Hospital Reimbursement Rates

This discussion leads to a number of tentative hypotheses. First, CON regulation is most likely to reflect the "weak" considerations inherent in the first model of CON agency objectives rather than the "strong" considerations involving binding capacity constraints inherent in CON2. Second, most CON behavior has focused on acute hospital bed supplies and only to a lesser extent on ancillary facilities. Third, for these reasons and a variety of other restrictions on the "reach" of CON regulation, we would expect to find some effect on bed supplies, but small effects on total hospital expenditures. Fourth, state regulation of hospital reim-

---

[66] The evolution of the Carter administration's proposals is itself evidence of this tendency to create an increasingly complicated formula.

bursement rates has the prospect of achieving much larger responses from the hospital sector, but these regulations are likely to be most effective when formal normative criteria for reviewing hospital budgets and hospital reimbursement rates have been translated into binding budgetary constraints.

Let us now briefly summarize the available empirical results regarding the effects of certificate-of-need regulation and reimbursement regulation by the states. We cannot expect "instantaneous" effects in any of these regulatory programs, for regulatory agencies may take many years to become "mature" in terms of their analytical capabilities to affect hospital behavior or the fraction of hospital facilities and expenditures that can be controlled either by statute or regulation. In Massachusetts, for example, a CON statute was first enacted in 1971 and made permanent in 1972. Initially the agency operated without funding or staff. Its early focus was on reviewing applications for expansions in the supply of general hospital beds, but formal bed criteria were not adopted until 1976. Formal criteria for a small set of ancillary services were not adopted until 1978. Similarly, a rate-setting commission was originally established in 1968, but its authority, organization, and regulatory methodology evolved gradually over the entire decade of the 1970s.[67] Prospective criteria for establishing Medicaid rates were not initiated until 1974 and more general regulation of hospital charges was not in operation until 1975.[68] Similar lags characterize the other state programs.[69] By the mid-1970s, however, several regulatory programs should have had sufficient time to mature, that any potential effects that they might have should have begun to reveal themselves in the expediture data.

Several studies of the effects of certificate-of-need and reimbursement regulation have appeared in the literature, all of them based primarily on pre-1975 data. In a much cited study, Salkever and Bice examined state data on changes in total plant assets, total beds, plant assets per bed and per capita hospital costs for the period 1968–1972 to determine the effects of certificate-of-need regulation.[70] They found that

---

[67] Commonwealth of Massachusetts, "Proposal in Response to Request for Proposal No. SSA-76-0127 for Type II Development Contract," Rate Setting Commission, January 15, 1976.

[68] Ibid. In May 1980, new regulations were proposed by the Massachusetts Rate Setting Commission that would increase regulatory scrutiny considerably. The proposed regulations would impede cross-subsidization and would restrict hospitals from passing on to other payers underpayments attributable to care provided to certain Medicaid and Medicare patients.

[69] For more detail, see Joskow, *Controlling Hospital Costs.*

[70] D. C. Salkever and T. W. Bice, "The Impact of Certificate-of-Needs Controls on Hospital Investment," *Milbank Memorial Fund Quarterly,* vol. 185 (Spring 1976), pp. 185–213.

CON regulation reduced the growth rate in beds but increased the growth rate in assets per bed. Salkever and Bice conclude that while CON regulation constrained bed supplies, it led to the substitution of other forms of capital investment for bed investments. They also found that states with CON programs had slightly higher growth rates in costs per capita.

While these results are not theoretically implausible, the CON programs "measured" in the study by Salkever and Bice were in place for too short a period of time to expect any significant effects, and the perverse effects associated with the CON variable are probably due to other factors. In particular, it is not unreasonable to assume that CON regulations were first introduced in states with higher than average per capita hospital costs and perhaps in response to rapid growth in sophisticated ancillary services. Salkever and Bice's arguments about "preemptive" investment appear implausible given the relatively long lead times for observing changes in investment plans in capital stocks and the reasonable assumption that during this period of time it would take several years before CON regulations became a serious constraint on hospital behavior.

Hellinger[71] used cross-sectional state data for the period 1971–1973 to examine the effects of CON regulation on total plant assets and total investment. Hellinger found that CON regulation had an insignificant effect on total plant assets in 1973 and that the passage of CON regulation in 1971 and 1972 had a significant *positive* effect on the rate of investment in those years. He concluded that the second set of results imply the existence of "preemptive" investments. For the same reasons that we may question the robustness of Salkever and Bice's results we may be skeptical about Hellinger's results as well.

Sloan and Steinwald[72] used cross-sectional data on a large sample of community hospitals to examine the effects of a wide range of regulatory variables on hospital costs and input use for the period 1970–1975. Five variables designed to capture differences in CON programs were used; two variables to measure the presence of Section 1122 agreements and Blue Cross approval requirements were included; and two variables were used to indicate the existence of some form of prospective reimbursement program. Over all, the authors concluded that during this period of time state regulatory variables showed little if any constraining effect on hospital costs.

The effects of hospital regulation and interhospital competition on

[71] F. J. Hellinger, "The Effect of Certificate-of-Need Legislation on Hospital Investment," *Inquiry*, vol. 13 (June 1976), pp. 187–93.
[72] F. A. Sloan and B. Steinwald, "Effects of Regulation on Hospital Costs and Input Use," *Journal of Law and Economics*, vol. 23 (April 1980), pp. 81–110.

hospital bed supply decisions were recently examined in the context of a simple queuing model that focuses on the reservation quality of hospitals given a stochastic demand for services.[73] That study found that CON regulation and prospective reimbursement programs have consistently negative effects on hospital reserve margins. The effects of CON regulation are insignificantly different from zero when a dummy variable indicating the presence or absence of such programs is used. When the number of years that a program has been in effect is used (linearly and nonlinearly), however, the effects of CON regulation on hospital reserve margins are negative and highly significant. This result is interpreted as reflecting both agency learning and the fact that since CON regulation only affects the flow of beds directly, significant effects will be observed on bed stocks only over a period of years. The results for the prospective reimbursement variable are more variable but are uniformly negative.

A draft report prepared by Policy Analysis, Inc.,[74] under contract from HEW provides perhaps the most comprehensive descriptive and statistical analysis of CON programs and their effects on the level and rate of change in hospital costs. The empirical work was based largely on the data used by Sloan and Steinwald but was "augmented" in various ways and extended to cover 1976. Overall, the study found that CON programs alone have little if any independent effects on the level or rate of growth in hospital costs. Rate reimbursement constraints, however, appear to have a significant effect on hospital costs. There is also some evidence presented (which is of some importance in light of previous studies) that many states that instituted CON programs earliest had higher costs prior to the establishment of regulatory authority than did other states. The report correctly does not attribute this effect to "preemptive" behavior.

The evidence for the period up to 1975 suggests that CON regulation may have had some effect on the supply of hospital beds but little apparent effect on the level or growth rate of total hospital costs. Some studies have concluded that higher costs or higher investment levels in states that first instituted CON programs reflect "perverse" responses. It is probably more likely, given the time frame in which these analyses were done, that the causality goes the other way. There is also some evidence that the presence of reimbursement regulation and active Blue Cross constraint programs have had some dampening effect on the

[73] P. Joskow, "The Effects of Competition and Regulation on Hospital Bed Supply and the Reservation Quality of the Hospital," *Bell Journal of Economics*, vol. 11 (Fall 1980).

[74] Policy Analysis, Inc., and Urban Systems Research and Engineering, Inc., *Evaluation of the Effects of Certificate-of-Need Programs*, Draft Report, vol. 3 (January 1980).

growth in hospital expenditures. At least up to 1976, the effects of economic regulation on hospital behavior and performance are not particularly impressive.

In a forthcoming monograph on hospital cost regulation[75] I make an effort to extend the analysis of the effects of hospital regulation through 1979. It is essential that we analyze more recent data because it is only in the last few years that state regulatory agencies have begun to take their cost control mandates seriously and have had the authority and capability to implement cost containment objectives seriously. This additional analysis examines recent hospital cost and utilization experience in four rather simple ways which I believe are illuminating. First I compare behavior between Pennsylvania and New York pre- and post-1975. These are two comparable states except that Pennsylvania has imposed few if any regulatory constraints while New York has imposed just about all of them. I have divided the data into two periods: a "pre-constraint" period (1971–1975) and a "constraint" period (1975–1978) reflecting hypothesized budgetary constraints imposed in New York, but not in Pennsylvania.

Second, I examined aggregate experience on costs for all states with mature state reimbursement regulation programs and mature certificate-of-need programs in comparison with states lacking such programs. Third, I performed a more comprehensive statistical analysis of the effects of CON regulation and state reimbursement regulation programs on the growth rate in hospital costs from 1973 to 1979. Finally, I examined the diffusion of CT scanners among the states to see if facility regulation or reimbursement regulation has had constraining effects on a specific ancillary service that has attracted considerable attention.

The general conclusions that emerge from these analyses are broadly consistent with earlier work. There is no evidence that certificate-of-need regulation alone affects either the level or rate of growth of expenditures. There is substantial evidence that mandatory state reimbursement regulation is associated with a significant reduction in the rate of growth of hospital expenditures. States that have introduced mandatory reimbursement regulation were high-cost states to begin with, however, and despite a reduced rate of growth for their expenditures they remain relatively high-cost states. Reimbursement regulation also appears to have constrained the diffusion in CT scanning equipment. This constraint appears to have "pushed" a larger proportion of CT scanners out of hospitals and into physicians' offices, where they can escape regulation. The effects of CON regulation on the diffusion of CT scanners is insignificant. Other evidence indicates that indirect forms of

[75] Joskow, *Controlling Hospital Costs.*

reimbursement rules have also reduced the rate of growth of hospital expenditures. Among the states, New York appears to have the most severe regulatory constraints and has achieved the largest reductions in hospital expenditure growth. However, the reductions in facilities and the deterioration in the availability of hospital care, especially in certain parts of New York City, have resulted in considerable controversy. Once New York went beyond "squeezing out the fat," the attendant excess demand problems led to dissatisfaction among the various groups that have been affected the most.

Conclusions

Both the theoretical and empirical evidence is consistent with the view that excessive resources are being devoted to hospital care in the United States. Allocational inefficiencies arise as a result of a complex set of market distortions and market imperfections that interact with inherent moral hazard problems of markets in which at least some insurance is desirable. Ideally, we would like to remove any market distortions or market imperfections that exist. Clearly, inefficiencies associated with monopolistic or oligopolistic health insurance markets point to a need for public policies that promote full and fair competition among insurers. Related restrictions on the availability of a full range of insurance contracts and health delivery organizations should also be eliminated. Inefficiencies associated with tax subsidies to the purchase of insurance are more problematical. For better or worse, the federal government has decided to subsidize the purchase of health insurance *in a way that provides that the size of the subsidy vary directly with the cost of the insurance.* As long as subsidies *of this type* are in place, the distortions that have been associated with them will continue. And as long as Congress and the executive believe that the costs of these subsidies are worth the distributional and political benefits of having them, the subsidies will not be removed. Similarly, there is little prospect that the terms of public insurance programs will be drastically altered. Finally, even if all market distortions and market imperfections can be removed, we will still have to deal with the moral hazard problem. We must still ask whether various regulatory schemes represent "technologies" for controlling moral hazard problems that are superior to the contractual and noncontractual constraints that would be forthcoming from the market.

Government regulation of hospital costs and of hospital utilization is certainly not the only possibility. The regulatory instruments are blunt and imperfect instruments that focus on the symptoms of the problem rather than on its causes. Some forms of government regulation are likely to yield improvements on the status quo, however, and if government constraints on hospital performance represent the only game that is politically feasible to play, it makes good sense to distinguish between productive and unproductive regulatory efforts and to focus on those that can best improve on the status quo. It also makes good sense to understand the limitations of even the most desirable regulatory schemes.

Our analysis points to a number of conclusions regarding the choice among regulatory instruments and the limitations of the best of them. First, both in theory and in practice, certificate-of-need regulation offers limited prospects for improving the allocation of resources. This process involves millions of dollars a year in public and private expenditures and has yielded few if any estimable benefits. Even in areas in which CON regulation can have or has had desirable effects, it is generally dominated by alternative regulatory instruments. All the evidence indicates that the massive planning and certificate-of-need apparatus that has been created should be scrapped.

In addition, reimbursement constraints can have significant effects on the rate of growth in hospital expenditures in theory and they have had in practice. They certainly dominate regulation based on any certificate-of-need model. Among the alternative reimbursement regulation systems that have been conceptualized or put into practice, a system that directly or indirectly gives hospitals general budgetary constraints appears to have the most desirable properties. Although the evidence available to date is not sufficient to indicate ultimate effectiveness, it is encouraging enough to allow us to move forward cautiously with such regulatory instruments, especially if the primary sources of distortions remain intact. In moving forward with this mode of regulation, however, we must constantly be aware of its fundamental limitations and we must work to correct the market failures that lie at the heart of the problem.

A Design for Resolving the Conflicts Resulting from Separate Regulation of Hospital Rates and Hospital Capacity

Harold A. Cohen and Carl J. Schramm

This chapter distinguishes between the reasons for regulating the nation's hospitals and the reasons for regulating traditional public utilities such as telephones and electricity. It then explores the problems of one existing design for regulating the hospital industry: In Maryland, Massachusetts, and Washington the services to be provided by individual hospitals, their capacity, and their capital costs are subject to the approval of the health planning process—a federally sponsored program.[1] The operating costs of these hospitals and the rates they can charge are subject to the approval of state-created rate-setting agencies. The weaknesses of this bifurcated regulatory design are examined, and suggestions are made for improving the two-agency model by imposing ceilings on the total social expenditures for hospital care that they can approve collectively.

The Market for Hospital Services

The universally recognized problem in the American hospital industry is that at no point in the hospital transaction do the participants have to recognize the opportunity cost of their decisions. Patients are encouraged to treat opportunity costs as personal gains from insurance; because of the separation of payment for hospital care and physician service under the traditional fee-for-service system, physicians are encouraged to have hospital costs increase as long as some increase occurs in physician productivity; and hospitals are encouraged to capture opportunity costs through cost-based reimbursement. Insurance companies

---

[1] Three other states, New Jersey, New York, and Connecticut, have placed rate setting and planning within the same agency.

258

are often treated as conduits by state insurance commissions, and all are allowed to pass on the higher hospital costs.[2] And, of course, the tax laws stimulate continuous growth of the entire hospital-medical complex. Given the absence of direct trade-offs that would accompany a fully working market, it is not surprising to find general concern about the results of decisions that have been forced on those who cannot "pass on" the costs. Thus, employers faced with elastic demand curves must trade off higher insurance premiums for higher salaries. And politicians faced with a limited willingness to supply tax dollars must curtail other expenditures.[3] Indeed, the pressure to control Medicaid expenditures is a major reason for state-level activity in rate review where it exists, and the pressure to control Medicare dollars is a major reason for capital expenditure review.

These background comments are important because much of the literature that evaluates the prospects for regulatory success in the hospital sector on the basis of the failure of public utility regulation overlooks an entirely different rationale underlying the "perceived need" for hospital regulation. The rationale for public utility regulation is based on supply-side problems such as the existence of a natural monopoly or some technical limitation on the number of entrants (for example, radio frequencies). Economists have suggested that society use various auction techniques to capture monopoly rents, or they point to the possibility of "interindustry" competition. The supply-side problems, however, are not the cause of the disproportionate share of society's resources being claimed by hospital care. The failure of the hospital market rests largely with demand-side factors.[4] And it is the demand side of the market that must be the focus of both regulatory and market solutions.

We must emphasize that by comparing two regulatory models we are not endorsing a regulatory solution. Rather, we endorse structural change that will bring opportunity cost considerations to the hospital marketplace—either by making patients directly aware of the economic consequences of their decisions, or by establishing competition among insurers and/or providers. We support competitive bidding and/or voucher experiments.[5] This chapter examines one aspect of the current

[2] Maryland Blue Cross appealed a decision by the Maryland Comprehensive Health Planning Agency to approve a capital project of approximately $20,000,000 at a Baltimore hospital. Their challenge was dismissed by the courts on the ground that they were a conduit for subscriber funds and, as such, did not have standing.

[3] Pressure on the Medicare budget has engendered utilization review as well.

[4] Joseph P. Newhouse, "Inflation and Health Insurance," in Michael Zubkoff, ed., *Health: A Victim or Cause of Inflation* (New York: Milbank Memorial Fund, 1976).

[5] Maryland's Health Services Cost Review Commission has called for a voucher experiment for Maryland's veterans rather than construction of the federally approved new 300-bed hospital in Baltimore, Maryland.

hospital regulatory framework that must be changed if system outcomes are to improve.

The Standard Regulatory Design

The typical public utility regulation rests on an assumption that natural monopoly results in the need to provide subsidies if marginal cost pricing is selected. The provision of subsidies is often considered politically undesirable, and full cost pricing is used instead.[6] The utility agency's deliberations involve applying the following formula:

$$Rate \ of \ return \ = \ \frac{revenue \ - \ expenses}{rate \ base}$$

Much of the utility literature is devoted to determining the proper rate of return. The theoretical rate of return is the opportunity cost of capital that will lead utility companies to want to invest the proper number of dollars. Since captial expenditures appear in the denominator as well as the numerator of the equation, an incentive exists for over-investment at any given level of output (the Averch/Johnson effect).[7] Since the rate of return is often set higher than the opportunity cost of capital (the captured regulator effect?), the utility company has an incentive to design a rate structure that will encourage more consumption and thus support more investment. In a decreasing-cost industry, this incentive is reflected in rate structures such as decreasing block charges that have rates at the margin for many consumers near the firm's marginal cost. (This increased output may be a move toward allocative efficiency; but one must be mindful of the question of the monopolist's discount rate versus the society's discount rate.) The important point is that consumers are not insured against the unit price on the margin so that neither suppliers nor demanders are inclined to allow price to be less than opportunity costs borne by the firm.

The public utility regulator who approves the marginal rate also approves the investment that makes up the rate base. Obviously, the interests of the regulator and regulatee converge under this system. The regulator generally wants to approve the lowest rates possible. The regulated firm wants to maintain a large investment. These interests converge because of the economies of scale that cause the natural mo-

[6] Martin Loeb and Wesley A. Magat, "A Decentralized Method for Utility Regulation," *Journal of Law and Economics*, vol. 22, no. 2 (October 1979). See also W. W. Sharkey's *Comment* in the same issue.

[7] Harvey Averch and Leland L. Johnson, "Behavior of the Firm under Regulatory Constraint," *American Economic Review*, vol. 52, no. 6 (December 1962).

nopoly. Recent concerns about long-run opportunity costs seem to have increased the conflict between regulated utilities and utility commissions.[8] To the extent that increased capacity leads to lower unit prices, the utility commission often can lower rates when expansion is approved. Commissioners may want to assure themselves, however, that sufficient demand will develop so that they will not have to raise rates or force the sole supplier of some key service out of the market. The commission, too, has an interest in holding down the cost of capital to the utility company, since higher capital costs lead to higher rates. The regulatory response to this latter need has often been a "comfort order."[9]

A Hospital Regulatory Design

Few aspects of the utility model are applicable to the hospital industry. The not-for-profit nature of this industry reduces the public utility regulator's equation to revenues = expenses. A "comfort order" really amounts to nothing more than incorporating sufficient cash flow in revenues to meet the debt service obligations made to creditors, not to shareholders.

The dominant regulatory model used in our nation's hospital industry is fundamentally different from that typical of public utility regulation. Hospital regulation is dominated by federally sponsored planning agencies that approve capital projects and payers (where rate-setting agencies do not exist), that recognize the costs of approved projects in rates. This chapter focuses, however, on a particular regulatory framework that exists in half the states with hospital rate-setting commissions. That structure is one in which the planning agency approves services, capacities, and capital costs, while the rate-setting agency approves operating costs and rates. The outcome of this bifurcated regulatory structure is an environment in which inherent conflict exists within government to the detriment of both the industry and the consumers. Let us now examine this phenomenon.

Planning. As Stigler has pointed out, the demand for regulation gen-

---

[8] Paul L. Joskow, "Inflation and Environmental Concern: Structural Changes in the Process of Public Utility Price Regulation," *Journal of Law and Economics*, vol. 17, no. 2 (October 1974). This article is particularly insightful and is strongly recommended.

[9] A "comfort order" is a statement in the utility's prospectus saying the investment for which the capital is being raised will be recognized in the rate base. The regulatory agency may go so far as to indicate that a fair return will be allowed even if the projected volume does not materialize. While such a decision might seem appropriate to the regulator in a given case, it clearly gives a distortion to the capital market.

erally comes from an industry that wants protection from competition.[10] Individual consumers do not spend a large enough proportion of their wealth on the services provided by any public utility to make it worth their while to learn about the industry or to spend their time trying to influence the way it is regulated.[11] The industry itself, however, is instrumental in designing the way it is regulated. Both physicians and hospitals, for example, have powerful incentives to design a regulatory structure that allows them to continue to capture social opportunity costs for their personal or institutional gain. Health planning legislation (which has a de facto focus on the hospital industry) largely accommodates vested interests by concentrating on "financial feasibility" and "need," and by leaving a key role in decision making to local health systems agencies (HSAs).

In an industry dominated by cost-based reimbursement, almost any approved cost is "financially feasible," except for the cost allocated to people who do not pay their bills. If a hospital has more of these bad debts than the net revenues it generates from charge-paying patients, insolvency may follow. Both philanthropy and government bail-outs (as in New York) are still available to make even these costs "financially feasible." (Since hospitals are often forced to provide services—especially emergency services—regardless of the customer's ability to pay, it is conceivable, but hardly likely, that the health systems agency might deny an application on the ground that the service will benefit a large number of poor people who cannot afford to pay.)

The initial decision to approve a proposed capital expenditure or new service is made by the local HSA. These agencies, as Shapiro and Russell have observed,[12] are inherently weak and are likely to compromise the consumer's interest in having a local hospital industry of rational size. Their weakness is due both to the traditional public utility problems leading to provider dominance (for example, in the control of data, or incentives to become involved)[13] and to the fact that the local providers receive the benefit of the service or capital expenditure under consideration while the payment for the proposed expenditure is borne in large part by national and statewide insurance mechanisms. Applying a "need" criteria to new services, HSA governing bodies—which have a

[10] George J. Stigler, "The Theory of Economic Regulation," *The Bell Journal of Economics and Management Science,* vol. 2, no. 1 (Spring 1971).

[11] Mancur Olson, *The Logic of Collective Action* (Cambridge, Mass.: Harvard University Press, 1965).

[12] J. R. Shapiro and E. L. Russell, "P.L. 93–641: Fundamental Problems," *New England Journal of Medicine,* vol. 295, no. 13 (September 23, 1976), p. 726.

[13] Roger G. Noll, "The Consequences of Public Utility Regulation of Hospitals," *Regulation in the Health Care Industry,* National Academy of Sciences, Institute of Medicine, 1974.

significant portion of seats preserved by law for provider representatives—approve the vast majority of capital applications both because medical evidence of need, however suspect, invariably "convinces" lay representatives and because it provides a socially acceptable and quantitatively unlimiting rationale with which to tap the insurance pools.

Let us examine in more detail one type of decision that planning agencies must make regarding hospital applications. Faced with an application, local agencies apply national and state "guidelines" to determine whether a new service is subject to their review and, if so, to determine whether it is appropriate. From the planner's perspective, however, this is not a simple inquiry. Is ultrasound, for example, a new service? Is CT scanning a new service? Is an intensive-care unit a new service? Are more X-rays per patient for patients with a given diagnosis a new service? Are more nurses in the psychiatric ward a new service? Is the fourth blood count each day for patients who formerly had only three blood tests a new service? Although none of these examples need be associated with any change in the types of patients treated, they all describe changes in the way patients are treated. Each HSA, in reviewing the need for the above types of new services decides for itself whether the new ways of treating patients are "appropriate." As a result, the decision regarding the appropriateness, and the eventual approval, of a proposed new service will be made differently from agency to agency, and from time to time within the same agency.

One reason for an acute problem of inefficiency in the planning process is that the decisions planning agencies make regarding the day-to-day operations of a facility are precisely the type of decisions that regulatory history says cannot be made well by bureaucrats. The professional judgment brought to both sides of the contested case varies widely. The possibility for stifling innovation is great. The regulatory agency cannot win, nor can it move the system toward improved operating efficiency.

Rate Setting. Because planning approval essentially makes capital projects financially feasible, except for bad debts, what happens when state rate-setting agencies are directed, as typically they are either by statute or by judicial decree, to (1) pass through all costs of planning approved projects, and (2) recognize bad debts as an element of cost? Clearly, all perceived capital needs become financially feasible. Since local planning agencies, representing the community that will receive the benefit of new services, have no cause to let cost play a limiting role in financing perceived "needs," we have succeeded in preserving for the hospital industry the ability to avoid opportunity cost considerations relative to capital projects.

The difficulties of having regulatory authority divided between planning and rate-setting agencies are compounded when the rate-setting agency must sanction planning decisions by making rates reflect the cost of new capital expenditures. The following examples point out some undesirable outcomes of such a situation:

1. The Joint Commission on Accreditation of Hospitals calls for corridors eight feet wide because there is a nonnegative probability that two beds with I.V. poles and attendants will pass on emergencies. Result: Planning agencies approve the expenditure of millions of dollars in replacing hospitals with seven-foot corridors in neighborhoods where six people sleep in a bedroom six feet wide.

2. Local physicians claim that quality is enhanced by giving patients private rooms. Result: Planners approve the expenditure of millions of dollars turning two-patient rooms into single rooms in communities having forty students in grade school classes.

3. The fire marshal decides that hospitals should meet the newest life safety code. Result: Planning agencies approve tens of millions of dollars to raise hospitals from 95 percent to 98 percent compliance with the life safety code in communities where public housing is meeting less than 30 percent compliance with appropriate life safety codes.[14]

Such incidents occur principally because planning agencies are concerned only with questions of appropriateness in an environment where each successive technical advance looks necessary at the moment, and where financial feasibility is automatically determined on the basis of a declaration of need. Thus, planning agencies grant approval for capital expenditures—and necessarily for the expenses of operating the facility throughout its life—without regard to the financial resources that might be expended to build and support the facility. Planning decisions such as those illustrated above reflect the total absence of concern for opportunity costs. The planning model proceeds on the assumption that decisions on hospital construction can be made from some absolute determination of "need" based upon demographic and epidemiologic considerations and that financial resources are not a constraint.

Problems of Regulating with the Two-Agency Model

One alternative is for rate-setting agencies to first decide reasonable rates. For example, if rate setters independently set rates for the above

---

[14] R. Feeley, D. C. Walsh, and J. E. Fielding, "Structural Codes and Patient Safety: Does Strict Compliance Make Sense?" *American Journal of Law and Medicine*, vol. 3, no. 4 (1979).

types of "new services," these rates, along with volume projections and nonpatient revenue sources, would tell the planning agency in advance whether a particular service was "financially feasible" or not. Of course, the hospital industry has continually and successfully argued against determining financial feasibility in this manner. Its battle cry is that determinations should first be made solely on the basis of "need" and "quality of care" and that resources should follow those determinations. But these concepts do not recognize the notion of society-wide trade-offs, the absence of which is at the heart of the industry's market failure.

Howell has described graphically the interaction of planning and rate setting in Massachusetts, which typifies the relationship we are describing.[15] Her diagram is reproduced here as figure 1. The analysis performed by the rate-setting commission is referred to as advice on financial feasibility. While the planning agency is not bound by the commission's advice, the commission is bound by the planning agency's decisions, so that advice on financial feasibility is really advice on reasonability. Whatever that advice, planning approval makes a project financially feasible. (This process is at least as circular as having utility commissions set rates on the basis of capitalized value.) Howell concludes:

> At present, as long as an institution can demonstrate "need," CON (the Certificate of Need granting planning agency) must approve the project. . . . In the health care arena the number of legitimate "needs" is virtually limitless. . . . Yet, as a country, we are increasingly being brought to the realization that the resources available to address these needs are definitely finite. The major failing of the Certificate of Need process at present then is that it is based on standards of absolute need and does not provide a means for allocating limited resources. Under present procedures, trade-offs are not required, either among the worthy projects of a single institution or among those of the various hospitals serving a particular population. Hence, Certificate of Need does not now constrain capital investment in total and can, therefore, make only a limited contribution to the ultimate objective of restraining further increases in the consumption of real resources by the hospital sector.[16]

In addition to the arbitrary definition of a "new service," the planning law establishes an arbitrary threshold for reviewing capital projects. Capital projects not involving new services or additional beds are subject

---

[15] Julianne Howell, "Regulating Hospital Capital Investment: The Experience in Massachusetts" (Ph.D. diss., Harvard University, 1980).

[16] Ibid., pp. 349–50.

266

FIGURE 1
THE MASSACHUSETTS DETERMINATION OF NEED PROCESS AND KEY PARTICIPANTS

Application   *Review*   *Decision*   *Appeal*

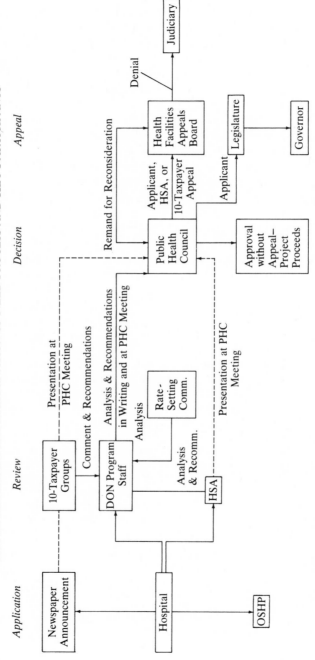

NOTE: OSHP = Office of State Health Planning
        HSA = Health Systems Agency
        PHC = Public Health Council
        DON = Determination of Need

SOURCE: Julianne Howell, "Regulating Hospital Capital Investment:The Experience in Massachusetts" (Ph.D. diss., Harvard University, 1980,

to planning only if they exceed $150,000. Howell found that in Massachusetts 84 percent of capital expenditures on plant during 1967–1976 were or would have been subject to CON review, but only 37 percent of expenditures on major movable equipment would have been subject to review.[17] Perhaps this situation explains why CT scanners have become a type of cause célèbre within health planning circles and why the national guidelines for health planning address CT scanners and dialysis but not laboratories or diagnostic X-ray services other than CT scanning.

The planning process is far from costless. In 1979 the Central Maryland Health Systems Agency approved all thirty-four projects it reviewed. Those reviews went through many levels and took a great deal of each applicant's time. They also established certain conditions of approval, for example, the supplying of long-term data on project use, the sharing of new facilities with other health providers in the community (but never to the extent of opening up physician privileges), and the promise that an applicant institution would not seek higher rates to support a particular project.

The national guidelines for health planning as well as the Health Planning and Development Act itself are both responses to the industry's reactions to the misincentives in the health care marketplace. A key element of that marketplace is Medicare and Medicaid's cost-based reimbursement system. Hospital expenditures are automatically passed on to the government payers subject to very minimal restraints. Interest and depreciation are allowable cost elements but only amount to 5–10 percent of hospital costs. Presumably the planning law reflects some belief that more capacity will lead to more use and that the way to control operating costs is to stop the hospital from offering new services—a regulatory schema with virtually no hope of success.

One aspect of the relationship between separate rate-setting agencies and health planning agencies is that the health planning agencies continue to follow the priorities and policies established as reactions to cost-based reimbursement even though cost-based reimbursement may be nonexistent in their state or area. This phenomenon is shown most clearly in Maryland.

Some Maryland Experiences. Maryland's Health Services Cost Review Commission originally conducted reviews of hospital budgets. All hospitals had their budgets reviewed once. The review had easy screens (80th percentile by department) and established cost-related revenues after the initial review. All the traditional regulatory problems arose in

[17] Ibid., p. 271.

the attempt to do zero-based budgets—for example, control of data and relative expertise. The commission decided that budget review was an inefficient way to regulate. Today, while the commission can initiate reviews of hospitals, the vast bulk of the revenues for Maryland's hospitals are adjusted automatically each year under one of two systems. The first system—which was in effect for all hospitals after their initial rate setting—is referred to as the inflation adjustment system. Under this system the hospital's approved revenue is adjusted every year for changes that are considered beyond the hospital's control and for variables (such as percentage of Medicaid patients) that the commission does not want the hospital to try to control.

It is instructive to explain how the original review established a base equipment allowance.[18] The equipment budget was determined in two parts. The first part, the general equipment allowance, covers all parts of the hospital except for equipment-intense patient care areas (as specified by regulation). The general equipment allowance is included in every hospital's rates as an industry-wide average in expenditures per bed. Thus, individual hospitals received a per bed equipment allowance based upon an audit of cash needs prior to the commission's rate-setting activity. For capital-intensive areas, the hospitals were required to submit an equipment balance sheet that included the replacement value of all equipment in those capital-intensive departments—including equipment fully depreciated (in the accounting sense). The commission's rate-approval level included replacement cost depreciation for such equipment.

The inflation adjustment system adjusts this part of the hospital's base rates by annually inflating the per bed equipment allowance and by inflating the replacement cost depreciation figure for the particular hospital. The inflation indices used are not hospital equipment specific but general equipment inflation indices. This aspect of the commission's annual rate adjustment program is common to all hospitals in Maryland. Thus, Maryland hospitals never have their rates adjusted to reflect actual equipment purchases for existing services. The commission does not review or receive detailed equipment budgets from hospitals. Thus, the rate-setting agency is not pitted against physicians and other hospital experts in arguing whether a hospital "needs" a particular piece of equipment. The hospital decides within its overall budget (of which the equipment amount is a part but no line-item review exists) what to spend on equipment and what equipment to purchase. No "wish list" budgets are submitted. Hospitals have no clear incentive to overpurchase equip-

---

[18] Base revenue elements are inflated, but no controls or review constrains how aggregate approved revenues are used.

ment, except to the extent that it helps in the competition for physicians.[19]

Further, since replacement cost depreciation is provided, the commission does not adjust rates to reflect financing costs of replacement equipment. In short, hospital decisions as to what capital/labor ratio to adopt in providing currently approved services and hospital decisions as to the replacement policy and the type of financing they desire in their capital management plans are matters left entirely to the discretion of hospital management and have no effect upon charges to the public. Yet, Maryland's planning community still reviews such applications as if hospital revenue were affected.

As we have noted, base-approved revenues are adjusted. Rates would never be increased as a result of the addition of labor-saving equipment. Yet, under the bifurcated regulatory framework, hospitals are required to receive planning approval before they can purchase labor-saving equipment. Hospitals are required to receive planning approval, for example, before they purchase computer hardware to automate their management information systems. A recent case in Maryland involved a hospital that wished to automate its laboratory. The commission's recommendation to the planning agency was that such projects should not require planning approval but that if they did, then the planning agency should not condition its approval on the requirement that the hospital seek lower rates as a result of the savings identified in the application. To do otherwise would be to resurrect the old cost reimbursement incentives—or lack of them—which resulted in few hospitals' applying for labor-saving capital projects.

The rate-setting agency in Maryland, as we have said, has two basic rate structures. These structures vary in how they measure the quantity of inpatient service. Under the basic inflation adjustment system (IAS), a hospital's base period departmental revenues are adjusted to provide subsequent departmental revenues. Final departmental revenues are adjusted so as to be neutral with regard to actual inflation in factor costs (measured by nonhospital-based index numbers, or, where necessary, for example, blood plasma and malpractice insurance, by industry-wide performance). Thus, the next period's rates include an adjustment to correct for over- or underprojection of inflation and for over- or undercollection of fixed costs associated with volume changes as measured

---

[19] Cost-based reimbursers pay hospitals their cash expenditures for labor and historical book depreciation for equipment. This has the property of better maintaining the hospital's equity base when it has a low capital/labor ratio—a type of reverse Averch-Johnson effect. The industry may be collectively overcapitalized (because there are too many hospitals) but individually may be undercapitalized at least insofar as labor-saving equipment is concerned.

by departmental volumes—for example, patient-days in areas with patient beds and relative value units in ancillary service areas.

Maryland's hospitals have succeeded in controlling unit costs where positive incentives exist but have performed at the national average in controlling intensity increases. (If our marginal cost estimates are correct, the above system pays for increased intensity in much the same way that cost-based reimbursement does.) In order to alter this behavior, the commission adopted a second system known as the guaranteed inpatient revenue system (GIR) and applied it to all the large hospitals in Maryland—and it has been extending this system to smaller hospitals. The GIR, which was first applied in late 1977, differs from the inflation adjustment system in that inpatient volume is measured by the case-mix adjusted number of admissions.[20] It has been pointed out that:

> The key to this rate system is that it puts hospitals at risk for the style of medical practice used in the hospital once a patient is admitted. Hospital management has the incentive to see that the patient's treatment is efficient both from the standpoint of cost per unit of input and from the standpoint of the number and type of inputs.[21]

Elsewhere in this volume Atkinson and Cook[22] discuss the effect of these incentives on hospital management, but we want to relate them to the bifurcation between rate-setting and planning agencies that denies the state of Maryland some important benefits of these improved incentives.

As a result of adhering to the priorities in the national guidelines for health planning, Maryland's planning agency does not act any differently toward hospitals on the original inflation adjustment system where departmental volumes determine inpatient revenue than it does toward those on the guaranteed inpatient revenue system where inpatient admissions determine inpatient revenue.[23] An example is the recent denial by the state Health Planning and Development Agency of requests for CT scanners from four GIR hospitals (in which they reversed HSA approval). At an appeals hearing before the deputy secretary, the

---

[20] Harold A. Cohen and John S. Cook, "Hospital Reimbursement and Utilization Incentives: A Maryland Experiment," in John C. Gaffney, ed., *Profile of Medical Practice* (Monroe, Wis.: American Medical Association, 1978).

[21] Harold A. Cohen, "Rate Setting and Competition: Are They Compatible?" paper presented at conference sponsored by Project Hope, May 22–25, 1980.

[22] J. Graham Atkinson and John S. Cook, "Regulation Incentives Rather Than Command and Control."

[23] Professional standards review organizations (PSROs) also treat both sets the same. Clearly the second set should be reviewed for diagnosis reporting but need not be reviewed for length of stay.

TABLE 1

PROJECTS REVIEWED BY MARYLAND'S PLANNING AGENCY, LAST
HALF OF JULY 1980

Hospital	Project Description	Estimated Cost
Baltimore City Hospital, Baltimore	Proposal to license an additional 27 skilled-nursing beds	$38,561
Provident Hospital, Baltimore	Proposed transfer of 9 beds from pediatrics to medicine, 8 beds from surgery to medicine, and 17 beds from medicine to psychiatry	NO COST
Fallston General, Fallston	Proposed addition of 24 acute medical surgical beds	NO COST
University of Maryland, Baltimore	Proposed continuous ambulatory peritoneal dialysis	NO COST

SOURCE: Maryland Health Planning and Development Agency Newsletter, August 1, 1980.

commission's executive director testified that while each hospital would receive a rate for its new CT scanner service, the charges per case-mix-adjusted admission would not change. Nevertheless, the planning agency wanted to tell hospitals how they could treat their patients even if the new service the hospital wanted would not raise charges.

A second reaction to the bifurcated system, most prevalent among IAS hospitals, has been for hospitals to seek planning approval for services that have very little, if any, capital cost and major operating cost implications. This trend reached a peak just recently, as indicated in table 1. The four new services that would require only $38,561 in new capital would lead to additional charges to the public of almost $4 million in the first year. This outcome further illustrates the problem of making financial feasibility a criterion on which planners must judge new projects. Quite obviously, all the projects listed in table 1 appear financially feasible from a capital perspective.

A United Approach

Since it is unlikely that the utopion notion of a fully working marketplace will emerge to ration health care in the near future, we propose a means of increasing the effectiveness of planning and rate-setting agencies in

271

controlling total social expenditures on health care. Of course, federal and state statutes could be revised to bring about a single agency. But short of this, significant improvement can be made in the response of the bifurcated regulatory system to the question of social trade-offs between health care and all other competing needs.

The first requirement of the new model is that the state legislature or the governor determines annually what the total expenditure for hospital care within the jurisdiction will be each year. Only with the a priori establishment of a limit on the size of the hospital economy can regulators concerned with entry, new services, and the elimination of excess capacity proceed with their task of priority setting under a politically meaningful mandate. Once this issue is settled, the next task is to redefine the affirmative duties of the agencies.

Under our modified plan the planning agency would set boundaries for service needs. It would identify services in excess capacity, minimum access criteria, and inappropriate services. The rate-setting agency would set boundaries for the availability of revenues to the hospitals, that is, budgets, on the basis of the hospital's case-mix adjusted revenue per admission, unit rates, and gross revenues. The rates should be such that hospitals have incentives to have low charges and to be efficient in providing care. Moreover, as a hospital becomes more efficient, its profit should continue to grow without regulatory attempts to reduce marginal returns.

Faced with a clearer expression of its regulatory constraints than exists at present, the hospital would have complete freedom to decide how to serve its patients. With regard to existing services, hospitals could change the way they provide existing services and replace existing equipment without planning approval provided that inappropriate services are not involved, that there is no increase in charge per admission, and that there is no increase in the hospital's gross or net revenue.

Hospitals wishing to develop new services could do so at will provided that their adjusted charges are no more, say, than 110 percent of the average in their region, that their quality of care meets minimum standards, and that there will be no increase in gross or net revenue.[24] Any hospital could eliminate services if such an elimination would not impair some minimal standard of community access. Hospitals could develop new services that would require increased revenue by offsetting savings from eliminated services without planning review.

[24] Hospitals could be grouped by health service area or professional standards review organization jurisdictions. Charges would be adjusted not only for case-mix differences, but also to recognize different labor markets, whether hospital-based physicians were included in hospital charges or in billing patients directly, and other adjustments required to make the comparisons more valid.

A hospital contemplating a change of service would have to notify the planning agency, which would block the change only if community access were threatened.[25] The rate-setting agency, which would also have to be notified, would merely advise the hospital if the proposed steps might, from the agency's perspective, threaten the institution's solvency.

This scheme helps to shift managerial discretion back to the hospital and goes a long way toward reducing the regulatory burden. The hospital is put at risk for its own decisions, but it has an incentive to engage in risk-taking behavior. Any profits made, except those linked to increased volume or overcharging approved rates, would accrue to the institution. Thus, savings resulting from improved productivity, efficient investment of profits and endowment funds, improvements in revenue collections, and success in raising endowment capital, would stay with the hospital, making it increasingly stable financially if it is well managed. Poorly managed institutions would be at risk of eventual closure if numerous mistakes were made.

Conclusion

Only by recognizing that hospitals are at least as well qualified to participate in the management of their futures as regulating agencies, can we begin to move toward a more responsive market system. The goal of a unified regulatory system should be to make hospitals take responsibility for their decisions by rewarding good management and penalizing bad management by putting institutions at risk for their own management decisions. Within an articulated industry-wide budget, all institutions will have strong incentives to behave more efficiently.

In considering our proposal, which is basically ameliorative, we are concerned that the coordinated regulatory model we envision might constrain the growth in health care expenditures sufficiently to reduce the pressures for market reform. We remind the reader that the political process is such that this regulatory approach can lead to a reduced rate of growth, but that only significant market change is likely to produce shrinkage if—as we suspect—shrinkage of the acute-care sector represents allocative efficiency.

[25] We are hesitant to propose mandating continuation of service given the problems regulators caused the railroad industry by overruling the marketplace. We could be easily persuaded to forgo this suggestion, which is more a concession than a recommendation.

Regulatory Approaches to Hospital Cost Containment: A Synthesis of the Empirical Evidence

Bruce Steinwald and Frank A. Sloan

Expenditures on health services consumed approximately 6 percent of gross national product (GNP) in the United States in 1960; by 1978 this share had grown to more than 9 percent. Most of the increase was due to escalation in expenditures for hospital services, which constituted more than 45 percent of personal health care expenditures in 1978. In 1960, a relatively modest $8.5 billion was spent on hospital services in the United States. By 1970 this expenditure had risen to $27.8 billion, and by 1978 to $76.0 billion.[1] Costs per unit of hospital service have been rising much more rapidly than the general level of inflation in the economy for several years. In the hospital industry, the measures most commonly used to gauge trends in unit costs are hospital admissions and patient-days. Between 1965 and 1978, inflation-adjusted unit expenditures on these outputs rose at annual rates of 6.2 and 6.5 percent, respectively.[2] A recent government study projects further sharp in-

Preparation of this manuscript was supported in part by Grant No. 18–P–97090/4 from the Department of Health and Human Services, Health Care Financing Administration, to Vanderbilt University and by Grant No. 95–P–97176/3 from the Health Care Financing Administration to the Urban Institute, with a subgrant to Vanderbilt University. We thank Mancur Olson for helpful comments on an earlier draft.

[1] U.S. Bureau of Census, *Statistical Abstract of the United States—1979,* 100th ed., 1979, table 145.

[2] These estimates were calculated from data provided in American Hospital Association, *Hospital Statistics, 1979 Edition: Data from the American Hospital Association 1978 Annual Survey* (Chicago, 1979), table 1. Admission and patient-day figures are adjusted to incorporate trends in outpatient visits. The percentages refer to nonfederal hospitals with a mean length of stay less than thirty days.

creases in hospital expenditures between 1978 and 1990 at rates that exceed those of expenditures for other types of personal health care.[3]

These trends plus structural characteristics of the hospital industry were used to justify extensive regulation of hospitals during the 1970s. The notion that virtually complete third-party reimbursement is largely responsible for inflation in hospital expenditures is now accepted by even the staunchest advocates of health insurance.[4] Although most recently implemented controls on hospitals are designed to counteract this inflationary influence, there is growing realization even among proponents of hospital regulation that success is not automatic, for programs appearing meritorious on paper may fail to achieve their objectives and/ or may generate serious unintended side effects when implemented.[5] Our aim is to evaluate the success or failure of regulation in controlling hospital costs and expenditures by examining recent empirical evidence on this topic.

This chapter synthesizes several studies of hospitals conducted during the 1970s. It does not discuss theoretical work in this area, as such exercises are not very helpful except to inspire caution about judging the remedial effects of regulatory programs without reference to empirical evidence, and they are available elsewhere.[6] We confine our attention to research on major regulatory initiatives (including some "self-regulation" within the private sector) and exclude most internal evaluations produced by regulatory agencies. A few references to the general literature on regulation are made where experiences in other industries appear germane to the evidence on hospitals.[7]

---

[3] See M. Freeland, G. Cabat, and C. Schendler, "Projections of National Health Expenditures, 1980, 1985 and 1990," *Health Care Financing Review,* vol. 1, no. 3 (Winter 1980), pp. 1–28. Other personal health expenditures include physicians' services, dental services, eyeglasses, nursing home care, and so forth.

[4] At present, approximately 90 percent of expenditures for hospital services is covered by health insurance. Trends in the percentage of hospital service expenditures covered by third parties are presented in J. P. Newhouse, *The Erosion of the Medical Care Marketplace,* No. R–2141–1–HEW (Santa Monica, Calif.: Rand Corporation, December 1978). For most recent data see R. M. Gibson, "National Health Expenditures, 1978," *Health Care Financing Review,* vol. 1, no. 1 (Summer 1979), pp. 1–36.

[5] For general discussions of this point, see, for example, S. Breyer, "Analyzing Regulatory Failure: Mismatches, Less Restrictive Alternatives, and Reform," *Harvard Law Review,* vol. 92, no. 3 (January 1979), pp. 549–609; P. H. Schuck, "Regulation: Asking the Right Questions," *National Journal,* vol. 11, no. 17 (April 28, 1979), pp. 711–17; and C. Wolf, "A Theory of Nonmarket Failure: Framework for Implementation Analysis," *Journal of Law and Economics,* vol. 22 (April 1979), pp. 107–39.

[6] See F. A. Sloan and B. Steinwald, *Insurance, Regulation, and Hospital Costs* (Lexington, Mass.: D. C. Heath, 1980), chap. 2, for a theoretical analysis of the effects of regulation on hospitals.

[7] In view of the size of the hospital industry and the significance of recent regulatory trends, it is perplexing that the general literature on regulation in the United States

Specific regulatory programs are briefly described in the next section. The effects of hospital controls are discussed in a third section summarizing research on regulation and hospital costs. The concluding section examines the relative successes and failures of hospital regulatory programs and discusses implications of current trends in public policy toward the hospital industry.

Current Regulatory Programs

Most contemporary hospital regulations originated after the enactment of Medicare and Medicaid, which made the federal government a major purchaser of health services. When inflation strained federal health care budgets and pushed expenditures far beyond projections, the political foundations for federal control of hospital costs were laid. Federal initiatives have been paralleled to some extent by cost containment efforts of state governments and private-sector organizations.

The hospital regulatory movement of the late 1960s and 1970s has proceeded on three fronts: controls on expansion of hospital capital,[8] regulation of hospital rates (prices) and allowable revenues, and controls on utilization, which are generally accompanied by quality assurance programs. Under capital controls are included state certificate-of-need laws mandated by Public Law 93–641, federal reviews of capital and service expansion authorized by Public Law 92–603, Section 1122, and Blue Cross requirements for planning agency approval of capital expansion programs. Under hospital rate and revenue controls are included prospective reimbursement (PR) programs governing third-party payments to hospitals; the Nixon administration's Economic Stabilization Program (ESP); and the hospital industry's Voluntary Effort (VE) to control hospital service expenditures. Under utilization controls are included the professional standards review organization (PSRO) program established by Public Law 92–603 and mandatory external review of appropriateness and necessity of hospital services required by some

---

virtually ignores hospitals. Most industry case study compendiums on regulation—for example, Paul W. MacAvoy, *The Regulated Industries and the Economy* (New York: W. W. Norton, 1979)—give considerable attention to airlines, motor vehicles, and public utilities, but seldom include a chapter on the hospital industry. A recent book, Murray L. Weidenbaum, *Business, Government, and the Public* (Englewood Cliffs, N.J.: Prentice-Hall, 1979), contains a detailed table reporting major expansions in federal regulatory activities from 1962 to 1974 without mentioning the omnibus Public Laws 92–603 (1972) or 93–641 (1974), which mandated extensive hospital regulation. We suspect that the primary reason for lack of attention to the hospital industry is unfamiliarity with its structural and regulatory institutions.

[8] Most controls on hospital capital expansion also include controls on facility and service expansion, but reducing growth of hospital capital is the primary focus of this type of regulation.

Medicaid and Blue Cross programs. By no means do these programs constitute all controls currently placed on hospitals, nor do they cover all hospitals. Data on the effects of these programs, however, provide a reasonably clear picture of the cost consequences of hospital regulation.

Capital Expansion Regulation. Current controls on expansion of hospital capital originated in the voluntary health planning movement in the United States. The federal role in health planning was initiated by the Hill-Burton Act of 1946 (which provides federal funds for hospital construction and renovation) and was augmented considerably in the 1960s by the Regional Medical Program and the Comprehensive Health Planning Act. Expansion of hospitals in the wake of Medicare and Medicaid has contributed to the discredit of the "planning without teeth" concept embodied in these two programs, but health planning per se has continued to have many strong supporters in government. Consequently, voluntarism has been discarded as the chief cause of the ineffectiveness of health planning and compulsory programs have been substituted.[9]

Regulation of capital expansion emphasizes control of the number and distribution of hospital beds. This type of regulation finds its rationale in "Roemer's Law," which asserts that the supply of hospital beds creates its own demand.[10] Capital controls reflect concerns that insulation of hospitals from competitive pressures leads to costly excess capacity, duplication of services, and poorly distributed facilities with regard to the public's "needs." In principle, not only do such controls reduce capital expenditures, but they also reduce employment of labor and nonlabor inputs and associated expenditures.

Certificate of need. At the state level, compulsory hospital capital expansion regulation was initiated with enactment in 1964 of New York's Metcalf-McCloskey Act. Similar regulations were subsequently adopted by Maryland, Rhode Island, California, and Connecticut. All certificate-of-need laws require that state agencies review and approve changes in hospital bed capacity and major equipment purchases. State laws vary primarily in the level of dollar thresholds for equipment purchases above which certificate-of-need approval is required and in the extent to which changes in services irrespective of capital expansion must also be re-

---

[9] For an evaluation of the efficacy of voluntary planning efforts, see J. J. May, "The Planning and Licensing Agencies," in Clark C. Havighurst, ed., *Regulating Health Facilities Construction* (Washington, D.C.: American Enterprise Institute, 1974), pp. 47–68.

[10] M. I. Roemer and M. Shain, *Hospital Utilization under Insurance* (Chicago: American Hospital Association, 1959); M. I. Roemer, "Hospital Utilization and the Supply of Physicians," *Journal of the American Medical Association,* vol. 178 (December 1961), pp. 933–89.

viewed and approved.[11] The American Hospital Association endorsed this approach to hospital regulation in 1968.[12]

Federal support for certificate-of-need controls was provided by Public Law 93–641, the National Health Planning and Resource Development Act of 1974, which created a network of health systems agencies (HSAs) to guide allocation of health resources within the states. HSAs determine local health capital and service needs and recommend approval or denial to state agencies regarding certificate-of-need awards. Public Law 93–641 mandated the development of certificate-of-need controls in all states by 1980. As of February 1980, all but three states had enacted such laws.[13] Certificate-of-need laws exclude coverage of physicians' offices, inviting a shift in some forms of capital rather than a reduction. Also, such laws lack decertification power in the vast majority of states, suggesting that potential entrants would be hampered much more than established firms.[14]

Section 1122 controls. Compulsory health planning was initially given federal support by Section 1122 of Public Law 92–603 (1972 Social Security Amendments). This section authorizes state-designated planning agencies to review hospital plans for facility or service expansion. Hospital expenditures (primarily interest and depreciation) related to unapproved capital projects are not reimbursed by Medicare, Medicaid, or Maternal and Child Health programs; the hospital may secure funds to recover these lost revenues from other sources, including other third-party payers. Designated planning agencies contract with the federal government and receive funding to perform this function. The review criteria of Section 1122 are standardized nationally—approval of hospital capital expenditures exceeding $100,000, of changes in bed capacity, and of changes in services offered is required as a precondition for full

[11] Further details on particular state programs are provided in Policy Analysis Incorporated–Urban Systems Engineering, Incorporated, "Evaluation of the Effects of Certificate-of-Need Programs," report to Department of Health, Education, and Welfare under Contract no. HRA–230–7F–0165 (Washington, D.C., 1980).

[12] W. J. Curran, "A National Survey and Analysis of State Certificate-of-Need Laws for Health Facilities," in Clark C. Havighurst, ed., *Regulating Health Facilities Construction* (Washington, D.C.: American Enterprise Institute, 1974), pp. 85–112.

[13] Bureau of Health Planning, U.S. Department of Health, Education, and Welfare, "Dates of Certificate-of-Need Enactment and 1122 Agreement" (mimeograph), February 1980. The three states are Idaho, Indiana, and Louisiana. Implications of Public Law 93–641 for health planning and certificate-of-need are discussed in detail by J. F. Blumstein and F. A. Sloan, "Health Planning and Regulation through Certificate of Need: An Overview," *Utah Law Review,* vol. 3, no. 1 (1978), pp. 3–38.

[14] Blumstein and Sloan, "Health Planning and Regulation through Certificate of Need"; R. Bovbjerg, "Problems and Prospects for Health Planning: The Importance of Incentives, Standards, and Procedures," *Utah Law Review,* vol. 3, no. 1 (1978), pp. 83–122; and W. G. Kopit, E. J. Krill, and K. F. Bonnie, "Hospital Decertification: Legitimate Regulation or a Taking of Private Property?" *Utah Law Review,* vol. 3, no. 1 (1978), pp. 179–210.

reimbursement. Most states began participating in the 1122 program in 1973 or 1974, but several withdrew in the late 1970s, probably to avoid competing with certificate-of-need agencies. As of February 1980, twenty-seven states were participating in the Section 1122 program.[15]

Blue Cross planning agency approval requirements. In the private sector, some Blue Cross plans—using an approach analogous to the Section 1122 process—make full reimbursement for hospital services rendered to their subscribers dependent on approval of capital expansion by health planning agencies. Available sanctions include denial of reimbursement for capital costs related to unapproved capital investment projects or denial of the Blue Cross participatory status to nonconforming hospitals. Usually the Blue Cross plan accepts the review determinations of agencies acting under the authority of certificate-of-need and Section 1122 programs.[16] As of July 1979, slightly less than half of the seventy-two Blue Cross plans had hospital contracts with planning agency approval requirements.[17]

Rate and Revenue Regulation. Rate and revenue controls are broadly analogous to price controls in other industries. This area of regulation is slightly more complex in the hospital industry because direct purchases of hospital services by consumers are uncommon. Instead, public and private insurers, which pay almost all hospital expenditures, have established several criteria to determine what hospital costs or charges are "reasonable," and various sanctions are imposed when these criteria are not met.[18] Rates may be prices, but they may also be payments per

[15] In February 1980, fifteen states had terminated or were terminating their 1122 programs. See Bureau of Health Planning, "Dates of Certificate-of-Need Enactment and 1122 Agreement."

[16] Lewin and Associates, Inc., *An Analysis of State and Regional Health Regulation,* final report to the Health Resources Administration under Contract no. HEW–05–73–212, February 1975.

[17] M. Hoover and R. P. Mullen, "Blue Cross Contract Provisions" (mimeograph) (Chicago: American Hospital Association, December 1979).

[18] An "old" controversy in the hospital industry is the debate over the relative merits of cost versus charge-based systems for determining third-party payments for hospital services. Federal insistence on using cost-based systems under Medicare and Medicaid intensified criticism that hospitals are motivated to increase costs in order to maximize reimbursements. We do not review this debate here except to note that research has not consistently shown that cost-based reimbursement is more inflationary than charge-based systems. See Mark V. Pauly and D. F. Drake, "Effect of Third-Party Methods of Reimbursement on Hospital Performance," in H. E. Klarman, ed., *Empirical Studies in Health Economics* (Baltimore, Md.: Johns Hopkins University Press, 1970), pp. 297–314; K. Davis, "Theories of Hospital Inflation: Some Empirical Evidence," *Journal of Human Resources,* vol. 8, no. 2 (Spring 1973), pp. 181–201; and Sloan and Steinwald, *Insurance, Regulation, and Hospital Costs.* In recent years, emphasis has shifted to the retrospective nature of most hospital reimbursement (as opposed to whether it is cost or charge based) as an important source of hospital cost inflation.

unit of service privately negotiated between a third party and a hospital. The concept of revenue regulation has become popular among governmental agencies because it relates to aggregate expenditures more directly than does regulation of prices. In addition to amounts of payment, this type of regulation often controls methods of determining payment.

State and private-sector prospective reimbursement programs. The most significant contemporary development in the area of hospital rate and revenue control is the adoption of prospective reimbursement (PR) systems in place of retrospective cost-based and charge-based systems. Dowling[19] has suggested that the establishment of rates in advance and payment of these rates regardless of costs actually incurred are the fundamental characteristics of all PR systems. Because PR shifts part of the risk of cost increases from insurers to hospitals, its proponents assert that hospitals reimbursed through PR have an incentive to be more cost conscious than they would be under retrospective systems, since third-party payers do not routinely cover "overruns." If prospective rates are exceeded, the hospital suffers financial losses; if unit costs are below the prospective rate, it keeps at least part of the savings.[20]

Some PR programs have been developed entirely within the private sector, principally by Blue Cross plans, but others are run by state governments. Important program variations include payers covered, units of payment, type of rate-setting methodology, and the degree to which hospitals must adhere to rate-setting decisions.[21] Only a few programs currently cover all payers. Medicaid and Blue Cross are the most common participants. As of July 1979, eight states had PR programs mandated by state law requiring hospitals to participate; four had legally mandated programs without a requirement that hospitals abide by agency determination; and another fifteen had private-sector programs operated by a Blue Cross plan, a hospital association, or a combination thereof.[22] The compulsory state-mandated programs represent the most stringent form of prospective reimbursement and for this reason merit the attention of the policy analyst.[23]

---

[19] W. L. Dowling, "Prospective Reimbursement of Hospitals," *Inquiry*, vol. 11, no. 3 (September 1974), pp. 163–80.

[20] In fact, the relative effects of retrospective and prospective reimbursement are difficult to deduce theoretically. See Sloan and Steinwald, *Insurance, Regulation, and Hospital Costs*, chap. 2.

[21] Variations in prospective reimbursement programs are described by J. M. Boeh, "Report on Budget/Rate Review Programs," mimeographed (Chicago: American Hospital Association, 1979); and D. Hamilton, ed., *Rate Regulation—Topics in Health Care Financing*, vol. 6, no. 1 (Fall 1979).

[22] Boeh, "Report on Budget/Rate Review Programs."

[23] The eight states referred to in the text are Colorado, Connecticut, Maryland, Massachusetts, New Jersey, New York, Washington, and Wisconsin; Boeh, "Report on Budget/

State regulation, which may be seen as an alternative to federal hospital rate regulation, has been actively encouraged and supported by the federal government. Most state-mandated PR programs have received federal grant support, whereas only a few of the others have received federal funds.[24] The Carter administration's Hospital Cost Containment Act of 1979, which died in Congress, had provisions for the exemption of hospitals subject to state-imposed rate controls and for federal funding of some administrative costs of state rate setting.[25]

Economic Stabilization Program. The Nixon administration's Economic Stabilization Program (ESP) had special provisions for the hospital industry. ESP was implemented in August 1971 and regulations specific to institutional health care providers were issued in December 1972. These regulations limited the growth in annual hospital revenue resulting from price increases to 6 percent, and all price increases had to be cost justified. Limitations on increases in specific costs included 5.5 percent for wages, 2.5 percent for nonlabor costs, and 1.7 percent for new technology. Eventually, wages of low-income employees were exempted from the 5.5 percent limitation. Patterned after the general ESP program, the hospital variant of ESP emphasized limitations on price increases. Many health care experts would have preferred emphasis to be placed on controlling expenditure increases. Numerous administrative problems had developed by the time of the program's demise in early 1974.

The Voluntary Effort. Initiated in December 1977 as a private-sector alternative to government regulation, the hospital industry's Voluntary Effort (VE) consists of joint activities at the state level by the American Hospital Association, the American Medical Association, and the Federation of American Hospitals (the for-profit hospitals' trade organization) to control the rate of growth of hospital costs. An elaborate system for industry self-regulation, including fifty state-level cost-containment committees, was organized with the short-term objective of reducing the rate of increase in hospital expenditures in 1978 and 1979

Rate Review Programs." For reasons identified by B. W. Singleton, "Hospital Budget and Rate Regulation: Why Colorado Failed," *Hospitals*, vol. 54, no. 5 (March 1, 1980), pp. 63–66, Colorado's program went out of existence in February 1980. Rhode Island's system is listed as a private-sector program by the American Hospital Association (Boeh, "Report on Budget/Rate Review Programs"), but research conducted by the Congressional Budget Office, *Controlling Rising Hospital Costs*, September 1979, and by F. A. Sloan, "Regulation and the Rising Cost of Hospital Care," *Review of Economics and Statistics* (forthcoming), regards Rhode Island's program as mandatory.

[24] Boeh, "Report on Budget/Rate Review Programs."

[25] Congressional Budget Office, *Controlling Rising Hospital Costs*.

each by two percentage points.[26] We include the VE in our discussion of regulatory programs because it provides a useful barometer of the influence of the "threat effect" of regulation on hospital performance.

Utilization and Quality Regulation. Prior to the 1970s, most regulation in the hospital industry was oriented toward "quality assurance." Even though occupational and institutional licensure and certification, for example, have existed for decades, they are not accorded much attention in the current regulatory debate. Institutional utilization review (UR) was developed as a self-policing mechanism for hospitals to evaluate both the technical quality and necessity of services prescribed and delivered by their medical staff members, and maintenance of UR programs has long been an important factor in the hospital certification process.[27] The notion of mandatory utilization and quality control imposed by an external authority with sanctions levied for deficiencies, however, is relatively recent.

The principal difference between utilization and quality controls and other hospital controls is that the former directly involve physicians in the regulatory process. Consequently, organized medicine and individual physicians have participated to a far greater extent in shaping utilization and quality review programs than they have in shaping other forms of hospital regulation. Some observers believe that physician involvement in program development tends to emasculate the cost-reducing potential of utilization controls because they consider physician emphasis on preserving quality to be self-serving. The efficacy of self-policing is clearly open to question, irrespective of whether one accepts the notion of physician-induced demand or more standard economic assumptions about physician behavior.[28] Because UR decisions are typically made on the grounds of medical necessity, however, some degree of physician participation is an absolute requirement.

Mandated utilization review. Since the mid-1960s criteria structured to meet utilization review requirements have been mandatory for hospitals receiving reimbursement for treatment of Medicare and Medicaid

---

[26] For more detailed descriptions of the VE program, see Congressional Budget Office, *Controlling Rising Hospital Costs; Hospitals,* vol. 52, no. 13 (July 1, 1978), pp. 55–74; and C. L. Rosenberg, "What Is Hospital Cost-Cutting Doing to Doctors?" *Medical Economics* (May 26, 1980), pp. 165–78.

[27] Periodic onsite reviews by the Joint Commission on Accreditation of Hospitals (JCAH) are the mainstay of the hospital certification process in the United States. Hospitals must demonstrate the ongoing existence of utilization review activities to acquire and maintain JCAH accreditation. Joint Commission on Accreditation of Hospitals, *Accreditation Manual for Hospitals 1979* (Chicago, 1978).

[28] This issue is explored by F. A. Sloan and R. D. Feldman, "Competition among Physicians," in Warren Greenberg, ed., *Competition in the Health Care Sector: Past, Present, and Future* (Germantown, Md.: Aspen Systems, 1978), pp. 45–102.

patients. These requirements include review of necessity for admission, length of stay, and services delivered. Patients with extended stays must be recertified at periodic intervals to establish ongoing necessity for hospital care. Emphasis has been placed on extended stay recertification in the belief that this is the area of greatest abuse and greatest potential savings.[29]

In addition to federally mandated institutional UR, several state Medicaid programs and Blue Cross plans require utilization review to be conducted by reviewers outside the hospital.[30] Blue Cross and other private and public insurers also conduct claims review activities to determine whether and to what extent patients are entitled to reimbursement. Although it would appear to be in the best interest of insurers to screen claims carefully for necessity of service, the possibility of conflicts with hospitals, doctors, and patients-subscribers, all of whom may become responsible for payment of a denied claim, has caused insurers to pursue utilization-reduction activities with limited aggressiveness.

Professional Standards Review Organizations. Motives of cost and quality regulation underlie the establishment of Professional Standards Review Organizations (PSROs) which, like the Section 1122 review program, were mandated by Public Law 92–603.[31] The PSRO program hopes to achieve cost containment by reducing unnecessary utilization, but the law also identifies assurance of "proper quality of care" as a primary objective. Since utilization reduction and quality enhancement are potentially conflicting objectives, they are unequally stressed by different parties and vested interests, with organized medicine being the chief exponent of the quality orientation.[32]

The PSRO program calls for local reviews of quality and appropriateness of hospital services.[33] This responsibility is vested in organizations that cover as much as an entire state or as little as a few ZIP code areas within a single city. Implementation of the PSRO program

---

[29] J. D. Blum, P. M. Gertman, and J. Rabinow, *PSROs and the Law* (Germantown, Md.: Aspen Systems, 1977).

[30] Sloan and Steinwald, *Insurance, Regulation, and Hospital Costs.*

[31] Another aspect of Public Law 92–603, the Section 223 limits on hospital revenue increases, is not discussed in this article, principally because of late implementation and lack of empirical evidence on the effects of this program.

[32] Clark C. Havighurst and J. F. Blumstein, "Coping with Quality/Cost Trade-offs in Medical Care: The Role of PSROs," *Northwestern Law Review,* vol. 70 (March/April 1975), pp. 6–68; Health Care Financing Administration, *Professional Standards Review Organization Program Evaluation,* 1980.

[33] For details on PSRO program characteristics, see B. Decker and P. Bonner, *PSROs: Organization for Regional Peer Review* (Cambridge, Mass.: Ballinger, 1973); and Blum, Gertman, and Rabinow, *PSROs and the Law.*

was slow but steady through the 1970s. By July 1979, the United States had been divided into 195 designated PSRO areas of which 186 had "conditional" status PSROs operating. By that time, however, no PSROs had been established as fully implemented programs satisfying all requirements of the law.[34]

Evidence on Effects of Regulation on Hospital Costs

This section reviews results of most of the major empirical studies of hospital regulation undertaken in the past five years. Anecdotal evidence and case studies have been excluded in order to conserve space; such evidence, while sometimes informative, does not easily lend itself to generalization. Most studies cited present original empirical research findings and are available in the public domain. We also include a few summary reviews of case studies and minor research projects, and we cite some previously unpublished findings from the Reimbursement Survey of U.S. hospitals conducted by the American Hospital Association (AHA) in 1979.[35] The discussion does not consider potential effects of regulation on access to and quality of hospital services—very little empirical research has been conducted on these topics.[36]

Research findings are summarized in table 1, which identifies studies by author and date and briefly describes data, methodology, and principal findings. Some studies are cited more than once as they cover more than one regulatory program or more than one empirical effort. To conserve space, results are presented in capsule form. As in any field, studies vary in quality. Rather than stress methodological deficiencies in particular studies, we stress results that in our view merit confidence. Inevitably, some qualifiers and caveats of authors have been lost. Nevertheless, we believe we have captured the overall thrust of the findings. The discussion of table 1 follows the three classes of regulatory programs set forth in the previous section.

[34] Health Care Financing Administration, *Professional Standards Review Organization Program Evaluation.*

[35] Mail questionnaires were sent to 3,411 nonfederal, short-term general hospitals; all such hospitals with 100 beds or more were surveyed, as were 500 such hospitals with fewer than 100 beds. The overall response rate was 65.5 percent. Observations have been weighted to achieve a representative sample of U.S. community hospitals. American Hospital Association, *Reimbursement Survey* (Chicago, October 1979).

[36] One of the most comprehensive evaluations of regulatory effects on quality of care is a study of New Mexico's EMCRO program (Medicaid utilization review) by K. Lohr, R. Brook, and M. Kaufman, "Quality of Care in the New Mexico Medicaid Program (1971–75): The Effect of the New Mexico Experimental Medical Care Review Organization on the Use of Antibiotics for Common Infectious Diseases," *Medical Care,* vol. 18, no. 1 (January 1980) supplement. In addition, several case studies of prospective reimbursement programs, reviewed in D. S. Salkever, *Hospital-Sector Inflation* (Lexington, Mass.: D. C. Heath, 1979), and in Sloan and Steinwald, *Insurance, Regulation, and Hospital Costs,* have indicated no appreciable effects of PR on hospital quality of care.

Capital Expansion Regulation. The most important policy instruments possessed by health planning agencies in the United States are state certificate-of-need laws. Research on this form of hospital regulation has produced remarkably consistent results. The empirical evidence indicates that certificate-of-need laws have not been successful in restraining per diem, per case, or per capita hospital costs. Particularly disturbing is the evidence on compensatory and anticipatory effects reported in a number of studies.

In their seminal work, Salkever and Bice[37] found that certificate-of-need controls have caused some hospitals to swap other forms of capital for beds, with no net effect on total assets. Sloan and Steinwald[38] found compensatory responses on the labor side but did not detect the type of transfer between bed and nonbed plant assets suggested by Salkever and Bice; overall, however, both studies found no effect on hospital costs. Studies by Coelen and Sullivan[39] and Policy Analysis–Urban Systems[40] also found no effect of certificate-of-need laws on costs per unit of hospital output. In addition, the latter study assessed certificate-of-need influences on aggregate county investment, on distribution of hospital capital within counties, and on hospital response by ownership type without obtaining significant evidence of an effect.

Both Hellinger[41] and Sloan and Steinwald[42] found a slight anticipatory response to certificate-of-need controls; that is, hospitals in states where certificate-of-need legislation was imminent tended to step up their timetables for facility expansion before these controls became effective.[43] Proponents of certificate of need advanced the view that early studies did not allow for a "breaking-in" period for responsible agencies

---

[37] D. S. Salkever and T. W. Bice, "The Impact of Certificate-of-Need Controls on Hospital Investment," *Milbank Memorial Fund Quarterly*, vol. 54 (Spring 1976), pp. 185–214; and D. S. Salkever and T. W. Bice, *Hospital Certificate-of-Need Controls: Impact on Investment, Costs, and Use* (Washington, D.C.: American Enterprise Institute, 1979).

[38] Sloan and Steinwald, *Insurance, Regulation, and Hospital Costs;* F. A. Sloan and B. Steinwald, "Effects of Regulation on Hospital Costs and Input Use," *Journal of Law and Economics*, vol. 23 (April 1980), pp. 81–109.

[39] C. Coelen and D. Sullivan, "An Analysis of the Effects of Prospective Reimbursement Programs on Hospital Cost," mimeographed (Cambridge, Mass.: Abt Associates, Inc., August 1980).

[40] Policy Analysis, Inc.–Urban Systems Engineering, Inc., "Evaluation of the Effects of Certificate-of-Need Programs."

[41] F. J. Hellinger, "The Effect of Certificate-of-Need Legislation on Hospital Investment," *Inquiry*, vol. 13, no. 2 (June 1976), pp. 187–93.

[42] Sloan and Steinwald, *Insurance, Regulation, and Hospital Costs;* Sloan and Steinwald, "Effects of Regulation on Hospital Costs and Input Use."

[43] One dramatic example of the effect of a phased-in certificate-of-need program is Florida's experience, where it is estimated that 2,150 "grandfather" certificates were issued before the effective date of the statute. This example is especially striking when one considers that in the year after the program took effect, only 123 certificates of need were issued. See Lewin and Associates, Inc., *An Analysis of State and Regional Health Regulation.*

TABLE 1

SUMMARY OF EMPIRICAL RESEARCH FINDINGS ON THE EFFECTS OF REGULATION ON HOSPITAL COSTS

Regulatory Program	Study	Data and Approach	Findings
Certificate of need (CON)	Salkever and Bice (1976, 1979)	Regression analysis of state aggregate data on short-term hospitals for 1968 through 1972.	Evidence indicated that CON had retarded bed supply expansion but had increased assets per bed. No net effect on total asset expansion.
Certificate of need	Sloan and Steinwald (1980a, 1980b)	Regression analysis of a time series of data on 1,228 short-term hospitals for 1969 through 1975. Dependent variables included both cost and input measures.	Comprehensive CON programs (those that review service expansion and relatively inexpensive equipment purchases) were found to have no effect on costs while noncomprehensive CON programs (those that focus primarily on bed expansion) had a positive effect on costs. No appreciable effect of the age of the CON program was detected. Evidence of a slight (but statistically significant) positive anticipatory effect of CON on cost per adjusted patient-day and on bed expansion.
Certificate of need	Wendling and Werner (1980)	Logit regression analysis of state adoption, no action, or defeat of CON legislation for 1968 through 1973.	Adoption of CON was found to be related positively to decreases in average occupancy rates and to hospital concentration, but no effect of trends in hospital expenditures per patient-day was detected. Results are generally consistent with the view that

			adoption of CON is dependent on costs and benefits to existing firms in the industry.
Certificate of need	American Hospital Association (1979)	Tabulations of survey responses from a representative sample of hospitals in late 1979.	Fifty-three percent of hospitals that had discontinued capital expansion plans in 1978–79 indicated that this decision was influenced by failure to obtain, or costs of obtaining, a certificate of need.
Certificate of need	Sloan (1980)	Regression analysis of a time series of state aggregate data on private nonprofit hospitals for 1963 through 1978.	CON parameter estimates in various regression specifications were unstable and most were statistically insignificant; the overall conclusion was that CON had no effect on hospital costs. No effect of age of the CON program was detected.
Certificate of need	Policy Analysis, Inc. –Urban Systems (1980)	Regression analysis of state and county aggregate data and individual hospital data over differing time periods ending in 1976 or 1977.	No consistent negative effects of CON on aggregate hospital investment, costs per unit of output, distribution of hospital capital, or hospital industry structure were detected. No evidence that mature programs perform better than new programs.
Certificate of need	Coelen and Sullivan (1980)	Regression analysis of a time series of cross-sectional data on 2,693 nonfederal short-term general hospitals for 1969–1978.	No negative effect of CON on costs per adjusted patient-day or per admission was detected.
Certificate of need, Section 1122 review	Hellinger (1976)	Regression analysis of state aggregate mean plant assets of	Negative but statistically insignificant estimates of effects of CON and 1122 reviews

(table continues on next page)

TABLE 1 (continued)

Regulatory Program	Study	Data and Approach	Findings
		short-term hospitals in 1972 and 1973.	on mean assets were obtained. Tentative evidence of anticipatory increases in assets.
Section 1122 review	Sloan and Steinwald (1980a, 1980b)	See above under CON	No consistent effect of Section 1122 review on hospital costs was detected.
Section 1122 review	Sloan (1980)	See above under CON	Mixed results indicating negative and no effect on hospital costs were obtained in alternative specifications. Overall, evidence indicated that Section 1122 is more effective than CON in controlling hospital costs, but instability of parameter estimates led the author to doubt that Section 1122 has a reliable cost-reducing impact.
Section 1122 review	Policy Analysis, Inc. –Urban Systems (1980)	See above under CON	Evidence that Section 1122 review had reduced county average hospital costs per admission and patient-day but not the corresponding individual hospital costs.
Section 1122 review	American Hospital Association (1979)	See above under CON	Three percent of hospitals located in 1122 review states indicated they had experienced disallowances or reductions in payment by third parties owing to 1122 review in 1978–79. Forty-one percent of hospitals in such areas that had discontinued capital

Policy/Program	Study	Data/Method	Findings
			expansion plans in 1978–79 indicated that this decision was influenced by Section 1122 programs.
Blue Cross planning agency approval requirements	Sloan and Steinwald (1980a, 1980b)	See above under CON	Evidence of small negative effects on average cost per admission and on bed expansion. No effect on average cost per adjusted patient-day.
Blue Cross planning agency approval requirements	American Hospital Association (1979)	See above under CON	Two percent of hospitals located in areas with Blue Cross planning agency approval requirements indicated they had experienced disallowances or reductions in payment by Blue Cross due to disapproval of capital expansion. Twenty-two percent of hospitals in such areas that had discontinued capital expansion plans in 1978–79 indicated that this decision was influenced by Blue Cross planning agency approval requirements.
Economic Stabilization Program (ESP)	Altman and Eichenholz (1976)	Tabular national data on average annual increases in hospital costs and revenues from 1950 to 1975.	Rates of increase in hospital room-and-board rates declined by 50 percent during ESP. Rates of increases in costs per patient-day and per admission declined by about 25 percent.
Economic Stabilization Program	Ginsburg (1978)	Regression analysis of quarterly national hospital data for 1963 through 1973.	No effect of ESP on hospital costs was detected. Data on post-ESP period were not included.

(table continues on next page)

TABLE 1 (continued)

Regulatory Program	Study	Data and Approach	Findings
Economic Stabilization Program	Sloan and Steinwald (1980a, 1980b)	See above under CON. Also includes descriptive evidence on hopital trends from 1970 through 1975.	Descriptive evidence indicates substantial negative effects of ESP on hospital costs and input intensity. Multivariate evidence indicates slight (less than 1 percent), but statistically significant, negative effects on hospital costs.
Economic Stabilization Program	Sloan (1980)	See above under CON	Statistically significant results showing a negative effect of ESP on hospital costs from 2 to 3 percent were obtained.
Prospective reimbursement (PR)	Salkever (1979)	Evaluation of empirically based state case studies of PR	Summary estimate of weak evidence of slight negative effects of PR on hospital rates offset by weak evidence of slight positive effects on volume of services in some states.
Prospective reimbursement	Sloan and Steinwald (1980a, 1980b)	See above under CON	Mixed results in alternative specifications produced overall uncertainty regarding PR effects on hospital costs. Evidence suggests that budget-based PR performs better than formula-based PR.
Prospective reimbursement	Policy Analysis, Inc. –Urban Systems (1980)	See above under CON	Evidence that both formula and budget PR had reduced county and individual average costs per hospital admission and patient-

			day. PR effects were stronger the longer such programs were in existence.
Propective reimbursement (private sector/nonmandated systems)	Congressional Budget Office (1979)	Regression analysis of state aggregate data on hospital expenditures per capita for 1976, 1977, and 1978.	Evidence of slight, statistically insignificant, negative effect on hospital expenditures per capita.
Prospective reimbursement (mandated state rate setting)	Congressional Budget Office (1979)	See above	Statistically significant evidence of substantial (more than 3 percent) reductions in rates of increase in expenditures per capita was obtained.
Prospective reimbursement (mandated state rate setting)	Health Care Financing Administration (1980a)	Tabular data on state average increase in hospital expenditures for 1977 to 1978.	Evidence of substantially lower rates of increase in expense per admission, expense per patient-day, and total expenditures in mandatory rate-setting states, compared with other states, was obtained.
Prospective reimbursement (mandated state rate setting)	Sloan (1980)	See above under CON	Statistically significant evidence of substantial (7 to 20 percent in equilibrium) negative effect of "mature" (three years or more old) programs on costs per admission and per patient-day. No effect of newer programs and no effect on hospital profits were detected.
Prospective reimbursement (mandated state rate setting)	American Hospital Association (1979)	See above under CON	The ratio of total hospital reimbursements to total charges was 3.4 percentage points lower, on average (a statistically significant

(table continues on next page)

291

TABLE 1 (continued)

Regulatory Program	Study	Data and Approach	Findings
			difference), in states with mandatory rate setting compared with states with no PR.
Prospective reimbursement (mandated state rate setting)	Biles, Schramm, and Atkinson (1980)	Tabular state data on hospital costs 1970–78	Comparisons of increases in state average cost per adjusted admission show an average increase for 1976–78 of 11.2 percent per year in six states with mandatory rate-setting versus 14.3 percent per year in all other states.
Prospective reimbursement (mandated state rate setting)	Coelen and Sullivan (1980)	See above under CON	Evidence was obtained that mandated rate setting had reduced hospital costs per admission and per patient-day by more than 2 percent for 1976–78.
AHA Voluntary Effort (VE)	Congressional Budget Office (1979)	Regression analysis of quarterly national data on community hospitals for 1964 through 1978.	Statistically insignificant evidence of slight reductions in hospital expenditures and expenditure growth rates due to VE. VE was in effect for too little of the study period to obtain precise estimates.
AHA Voluntary Effort	Sloan (1980)	See above under CON	Statistically significant estimates of negative effects of VE on cost per admission (2.8 to 4.6 percent) and on cost per patient-day (4.2 to 4.9 percent) and positive effects on profits (6.4 percent) were obtained.

Utilization review (UR)	Sloan and Steinwald (1980a)	Review of several minor studies, confined mainly to single localities or hospitals, on effects of UR on hospital costs and utilization.	Mixed results of studies led to a summary judgment that early (pre-PRSO) forms of UR had no appreciable cost-reducing effects on hospitals.
Utilization review	Sloan and Steinwald (1980a, 1980b)	See above under CON	Mixed results in alternative specifications led to uncertainty regarding effects of external UR conducted by some Medicaid and Blue Cross plans.
Utilization review, PSRO	Gertman et al. (1979)	Regression analysis of data from a national survey of U.S. hospitals conducted from late 1976 to early 1977.	No effect on changes or levels of utilization of Medicare beneficiaries from binding UR or from having a conditional PSRO in the hospital's area was detected. Mean cost per extended stay termination or admission denial was estimated to be more than $4,000 in 1976–77 dollars.
PSRO	Health Care Financing Administration (1980b)	Regression analysis of Medicare beneficiary data for 1978 comparing utilization in 108 areas of the United States with active PSROs with 81 areas without active PSROs.	A statistically insignificant estimate of a reduction in days of care per Medicare beneficiary of 1.7 percent due to PSROs was obtained. Evidence of wide interregional variations in PSRO impact, including a positive impact on utilization in southern United States.
PSRO	Health Care Financing Administration (1980b)	Regression analysis of Medicare hospital discharge data for	In four out of five diagnoses and procedures that had been identified by medical

(table continues on next page)

TABLE 1 (continued)

Regulatory Program	Study	Data and Approach	Findings
		1973 through 1977 comparing PSRO impact on utilization for selected diagnoses and procedures.	experts to be amenable to PSRO review, a significant negative effect of PSRO was detected. In four out of four diagnoses and procedures identified as not amenable to PSRO review, no significant impact was detected.
PSRO	Health Care Financing Administration (1980b)	Descriptive analysis of PSRO discharge data on average length of stay and case-mix in 12 PSROs for 1977–78.	Evidence was obtained indicating that virtually all 12 PSROs experienced shifts in case mix in direction of cases with typically longer hospital stays. Findings also suggested declines in case-mix-adjusted average lengths of stay of Medicare and Medicaid beneficiaries.
PSRO	American Hospital Association (1979)	See above under CON	Twenty-eight percent of hospitals located in areas with active PSROs indicated that they had experienced disallowances or reductions in payment owing to UR/PSRO reviews of services delivered under Medicare, Medicaid, and Blue Cross. Twenty-one percent of hospitals not located in areas with active PSROs indicated they had experienced such disallowances or reductions—a statistically significant difference.

| PSRO | Coelen and Sullivan (1980) | See above under CON | No evidence of an effect of binding PSRO review on hospital costs per patient-day or per admission was obtained. |

SOURCES: S. J. Altman and J. Eichenholz, "Inflation in the Health Industry—Causes and Cures," in M. Zubkoff, ed., *Health: A Victim or Cause of Inflation?* (New York: Prodist, 1976), pp. 7–30; American Hospital Association, *Reimbursement Survey* (Chicago: The Association, October 1979); B. Biles, C. J. Schramm, and J. G. Atkinson, "Hospital Cost Inflation under State Rate-Setting Programs," *New England Journal of Medicine*, vol. 303, no. 12 (September 18, 1980), pp. 665–68; C. Coelen and D. Sullivan, "An Analysis of the Effects of Prospective Reimbursement Programs on Hospital Cost" (mimeograph) (Cambridge, Mass.: Abt Associates, Inc., August 1980); Congressional Budget Office, *Controlling Rising Hospital Costs* (Washington, D.C.: Government Printing Office, September 1979); P. M. Gertman, A. C. Monheit, J. J. Anderson, J. B. Engle, and D. K. Levenson, "Utilization Review in the United States: Results from a 1976–77 National Survey of Hospitals," *Medical Care*, vol. 17, no. 8 (August 1979) supplement; P. B. Ginsburg, "Impact of the Economic Stabilization Program on Hospitals: An Analysis with Aggregate Data," in M. Zubkoff, I. Raskin, and R. S. Hanft, eds., *Hospital Cost Containment* (New York: Prodist, 1978), pp. 293–323; Health Care Financing Administration, *Research and Demonstrations in Health Care Financing* (Washington, D.C.: Government Printing Office, 1980a); Health Care Financing Administration, *Professional Standards Review Organization Program Evaluation* (Washington, D.C.: Government Printing Office, 1980b); F. J. Hellinger, "The Effect of Certificate-of-Need Legislation on Hospital Investment," *Inquiry*, vol. 13, no. 2 (June 1976), pp. 187–193; Policy Analysis, Inc. and Urban Systems Engineering, Inc., "Evaluation of the Effects of Certificate-of-Need Programs," Report to DHEW under Contract No. HRA–230–7F–0165 (Washington, D.C., 1980); D. S. Salkever, *Hospital-Sector Inflation* (Lexington, Mass.: D. C. Heath, 1979); D. S. Salkever and T. W. Bice, "The Impact of Certificate-of-Need Controls on Hospital Investment," *Milbank Memorial Fund Quarterly*, vol. 54 (Spring 1976), pp. 185–214; D. S. Salkever and T. W. Bice, *Hospital Certificate-of-Need Controls: Impact on Investment, Costs, and Use* (Washington, D.C.: American Enterprise Institute, 1979); F. A. Sloan, "Regulation and the Rising Cost of Hospital Care," *Review of Economics and Statistics* (forthcoming); F. A. Sloan and B. Steinwald, *Insurance, Regulation, and Hospital Costs* (Lexington, Mass.: D. C. Heath, 1980a); F. A. Sloan and B. Steinwald, "Effects of Regulation on Hospital Costs and Input Use," *Journal of Law and Economics*, vol. 23 (April 1980), pp. 81–109; W. Wendling and J. Werner, "Nonprofit Firms and the Economic Theory of Regulation," *Quarterly Review of Economics and Business*, vol. 20, no. 3 (Fall 1980), pp. 6–18.

to become effective by learning how to implement certificate-of-need controls. Studies by Sloan and Steinwald,[44] Policy Analysis–Urban Systems,[45] and Sloan,[46] however, included terms representing the age of certificate-of-need programs and detected no effects of program vintage on hospital cost dependent variables. The Sloan[47] data base extends through 1978; by that time programs in several states had been in place for years.

Responses to the AHA's 1979 Reimbursement Survey indicate that an appreciable number of hospitals curtailed their plans for expansion because of certificate-of-need controls, but this type of evidence is unreliable as a barometer of program effectiveness.[48] Even the most comprehensive certificate-of-need laws do not cover all possible avenues of capital expansion. In addition, the possibility that certificate of need might enhance some hospitals' expansion capabilities should not be disregarded. Evidence of Wendling and Werner,[49] that adoption of certificate-of-need controls has been insensitive to trends in hospital expenditures per patient-day but positively related to hospital concentration and declines in occupancy rates, supports the view that certificate-of-need agencies are subject to capture by existing firms in the hospital industry.

Skepticism about entry and expansion controls has been founded on research on performance of other regulated industries and in the hospital industry has been based on early evidence of the failure of health planning to control hospital capital expansion.[50] Moreover, "war stories" about the certificate-of-need process have indicated considerable politicization. The current evidence cited previously suggests that certificate-of-need controls, initiated by the states and mandated by PL 93–641, may be regarded as a classic example of regulatory failure.[51]

Information on other forms of capital expansion regulation, Section

[44] Sloan and Steinwald, *Insurance, Regulation, and Hospital Costs;* Sloan and Steinwald, "Effects of Regulation on Hospital Costs and Input Use."

[45] Policy Analysis, Inc.–Urban Systems Engineering, Inc., *Evaluation of the Effects of Certificate-of-Need Programs.*

[46] Sloan, "Regulation and the Rising Cost of Hospital Care."

[47] Ibid.

[48] This type of evidence is often cited by proponents of capital expansion regulation to demonstrate success in cost containment. For additional discussion of why such evidence is unreliable, see Salkever and Bice, "The Impact of Certificate-of-Need Controls on Hospital Investment."

[49] W. Wendling and J. Werner, "Nonprofit Firms and the Economic Theory of Regulation," *Quarterly Review of Economics and Business,* vol. 20, no. 3 (Fall 1980), pp. 6–18.

[50] See J. J. May, "The Planning and Licensing Agencies."

[51] See Breyer, "Analyzing Regulatory Failure," and Wolf, "A Theory of Nonmarket Failure," for general discussions of regulatory failure which are relevant to the evidence on certificate-of-need.

1122 controls and Blue Cross requirements for planning agency compliance, does not dispel the negative conclusions based on studies of certificate of need. Much less evidence is available on these programs, however, and not all of it shows them to be ineffective. Hellinger,[52] Sloan and Steinwald,[53] Policy Analysis–Urban Systems,[54] and Sloan[55] included Section 1122 review program variables in their analyses of hospital costs.[56] Generally, results were mixed, but some specifications produced findings of a negative effect. Similarly, Sloan and Steinwald[57] found small negative effects of Blue Cross compliance programs on average cost per admission (but not on cost per patient-day) and on bed expansion. The AHA Reimbursement Survey suggests that few hospitals have had expenses disallowed owing to unapproved capital investment; however, a significant proportion of hospitals claim to have discontinued expansion plans because of these programs, particularly the Section 1122 program.

Although the Section 1122 and Blue Cross compliance programs appear more favorable than certificate of need, we do not wish to emphasize this difference unduly. First, compared with research findings on certificate of need, information on their results is scant and in any case these programs do not consistently show negative effects on hospital costs. Second, at least on paper, certificate of need is the more stringent form of capital control.

Rate and Revenue Regulation. Rate and revenue controls represent a potpourri of federal, state, and private-sector efforts to contain hospital costs. These programs all respond to the evils of cost-based reimbursement—they seek to counteract the unrestrained nature of hospital reimbursement by superimposing constraints that the market cannot provide, but they do so in different ways.

As in other industries, wage-price controls embodied in the Economic Stabilization Program represent an extreme method of controlling inflation in the hospital industry. Few analysts or policy makers endorse this method as a general, ongoing regulatory strategy, but it always has

---

[52] Hellinger, "The Effect of Certificate-of-Need Legislation on Hospital Investment."

[53] Sloan and Steinwald, *Insurance, Regulation, and Hospital Costs;* Sloan and Steinwald, "Effects of Regulation on Hospital Costs and Input Use."

[54] Policy Analysis, Inc.–Urban Systems Engineering, Inc., *Evaluation of the Effects of Certificate-of-Need Programs.*

[55] Sloan, "Regulation and the Rising Cost of Hospital Care."

[56] Hellinger, "The Effect of Certificate-of-Need Legislation on Hospital Investment," assessed joint effects of Section 1122 review and certificate-of-need laws.

[57] Sloan and Steinwald, *Insurance, Regulation, and Hospital Costs;* Sloan and Steinwald, "Effects of Regulation on Hospital Costs and Input Use."

numerous proponents during periods of prolonged and intractable inflation. Descriptive studies of ESP, such as that of Altman and Eichenholz[58] and the descriptive sections of Sloan and Steinwald,[59] show a reduction of several percentage points in hospital cost increases during the ESP period. Multivariate analyses by Ginsburg[60] and by Sloan and Steinwald[61] show little or no effect of ESP on hospital costs. Somewhat larger cost-inhibiting impacts, more consistent with the descriptive evidence, are reported by Sloan.[62] Our summary assessment, based on both descriptive and multivariate evidence, is that ESP did have a moderating effect on hospital cost inflation, but we are cautious about extending this conclusion to project possible consequences of a long-standing program of this sort. Numerous administrative problems requiring specific piecemeal solutions emerged during ESP's three-year history.

The eight mandatory state rate-setting programs represent the most stringent group of prospective reimbursement programs operating at the state or substate level. The state rate-setting agencies operate in a fashion similar to public utility commissions in their review of cost justifications for price increases—the foremost regulatory function of such commissions.[63] Descriptive evidence suggests that increases in expense per admission, expense per patient-day, and total expenses were considerably lower in 1977 and 1978 in states with mandated rate setting than elsewhere in the United States. Rates of increase in total hospital expenses in the eight mandatory states were 9.7 and 8.6 percent for 1976–1977 and 1977–1978, respectively, versus 15.8 and 14.0 percent for the other states and the District of Columbia.[64] Although descriptive evidence may be an unreliable indicator of true program effects, regulatory skeptics should not expect such evidence to be ignored simply because it violates ceteris paribus.

Several recent multivariate hospital cost studies based on time series

---

[58] S. J. Altman and J. Eichenholz, "Inflation in the Health Industry—Causes and Cures," in M. Zubkoff, ed., *Health: A Victim or Cause of Inflation?* (New York: Prodist, 1976), pp. 7–30.

[59] Sloan and Steinwald, *Insurance, Regulation, and Hospital Costs.*

[60] P. B. Ginsburg, "Impact of the Economic Stabilization Program on Hospitals: An Analysis with Aggregate Data," in M. Zubkoff, I. Raskin, and R. F. Hanft, eds., *Hospital Cost Containment* (New York: Prodist, 1978), pp. 293–323.

[61] Sloan and Steinwald, *Insurance, Regulation, and Hospital Costs;* and Sloan and Steinwald, "Effects of Regulation on Hospital Costs and Input Use."

[62] Sloan, "Regulation and the Rising Cost of Hospital Care."

[63] A. E. Kahn, *The Economics of Regulation: Principles and Institutions* (New York: John Wiley, 1970).

[64] Health Care Financing Administration, *Research and Demonstrations in Health Care Financing,* 1980. See also B. Biles, C. J. Schramm, and J. G. Atkinson, "Hospital Cost Inflation under State Rate-Setting Programs," *New England Journal of Medicine,* vol. 303, no. 12 (September 18, 1980), pp. 664–68.

of state aggregates of hospital data incorporate measures of mandatory rate setting. The Congressional Budget Office[65] found that state rate setting reduced hospital expenditures per capita in states with these programs by about three percentage points over 1976–1978. Sloan[66] distinguished between new state programs (less than three years old) and mature ones (three or more years old). He found no effect of new state rate-setting programs on hospital costs, but he found that mature programs reduce both levels and growth rates of hospital costs per adjusted admission and per adjusted patient-day. Sloan's estimates imply that if all payers were subject to mature state rate setting, equilibrium cost reductions would range from 7 to 20 percent. Somewhat smaller statistically significant negative effects on individual hospital costs were obtained by Coelen and Sullivan.[67] This study, like most other recent analyses of hospital rate setting, found that the negative effects on hospital costs have materialized in the latter half of the 1970s.

Descriptive evidence from the AHA's Reimbursement Survey supports the multivariate results indicating that mandated state rate setting reduces hospital expenditures. In states having such programs, the average ratio of total hospital revenues to total charges was 3.4 percentage points less than in states without prospective rate setting. That voluntary PR programs are less effective in controlling costs than mandatory programs is confirmed by multivariate evidence presented by the Congressional Budget Office,[68] which found that voluntary rate setting reduced annual hospital expenditure growth slightly over 1976 to 1978, on average, compared with areas without rate-setting programs.

Other evaluations of the effects of prospective reimbursement on hospital costs are based on data from an earlier period and cover both mandatory and nonmandatory programs. Results from these studies are far less favorable to PR. The Social Security Administration funded several case studies of PR programs in the early 1970s, and from his review of five such case studies, Salkever[69] concluded that two of the studies indicated that PR reduced average unit cost, but this evidence was offset by (weak) evidence of slight positive effects on volume of services in some states.[70] Regression analysis of a time series of cross-

[65] Congressional Budget Office, *Controlling Rising Hospital Costs.*

[66] Sloan, "Regulation and the Rising Cost of Hospital Care."

[67] C. Coelen and D. Sullivan, "An Analysis of the Effects of Prospective Reimbursement Programs on Hospital Cost."

[68] Congressional Budget Office, *Controlling Rising Hospital Costs.*

[69] D. S. Salkever, *Hospital-Sector Inflation* (Lexington, Mass.: D.C. Heath, 1979).

[70] The five case studies were of Indiana, New Jersey, upstate New York, downstate New York (New York City area), and Rhode Island. Four of the five PR programs studied were among those currently designated as state mandated, but the case studies were performed during the early 1970s.

sectional data on individual hospitals covering 1970–1975 by Sloan and Steinwald[71] yielded mixed results concerning PR effects on hospital costs. Their study distinguished between formula and budget-based methods of prospective rate determination. The regressions indicated that budget-based systems tend to perform slightly better than formula-based systems, but for technical reasons the authors expressed little confidence in this result. The distinction between formula and budget-review systems is becoming blurred as many PR programs have adopted elements of both. Research conducted by Policy Analysis–Urban Systems[72] found that both budget and formula PR systems tend to improve in cost-reducing performance the longer they are in existence.

The major self-regulatory program considered in this review is the hospital industry's Voluntary Effort to control hospital costs, which has been analyzed in two multivariate studies. The Congressional Budget Office[73] estimated that in 1978 the VE had a small negative impact of 0.9 percent on hospital expenditure increases, but the coefficient underlying this finding was not statistically significant at conventional levels. Sloan,[74] however, obtained statistically significant estimates of a negative effect of the VE on costs per adjusted admission and per adjusted patient-day on the order of 3 to 5 percent, but a positive effect on profits (total hospital revenue minus expenses). Sloan's assessment of the relative effects of VE on hospital costs and profits may inspire cynicism regarding the consequences of self-regulation, since his results indicate that cost savings are not passed on to consumers. More important, however, is the realization that the incentives that generate self-regulation are likely to depend upon the threat of more stringent government-sponsored controls.

In contrast to analyses of capital controls, studies of rate and revenue regulation have reported evidence of cost reductions. Particularly important in terms of implementing a long-term strategy for controlling inflation in hospital costs and expenditures is the finding that when PR is instituted as a state-mandated program with authority to set hospital reimbursement rates and when such programs have operated for sufficient time to become institutionalized, savings in hospital costs and expenditures may materialize. Although many would argue that the

---

[71] Sloan and Steinwald, *Insurance, Regulation, and Hospital Costs;* and Sloan and Steinwald, "Effects of Regulation on Hospital Costs and Input Use."

[72] Policy Analysis, Inc.–Urban Systems Engineering, Inc., *Evaluation of the Effects of Certificate-of-Need Programs.*

[73] Congressional Budget Office, *Controlling Rising Hospital Costs.*

[74] Sloan, "Regulation and the Rising Cost of Hospital Care." The Sloan sample is composed of state aggregates of voluntary hospital data; government and proprietary hospital data are excluded.

passage of time provides greater opportunity for capture by self-interested parties, potential positive benefits of learning-by-doing should not be ruled out in advance.[75] The implications of this evidence are discussed further in our concluding section.

Utilization and Quality Controls. Unfortunately, less information is available on current forms of utilization and quality controls than on other types of hospital regulation. Although utilization review has existed for decades, few large-scale studies have investigated its effects on hospital expenditures. In reviewing a number of small-scale, localized studies of UR, Sloan and Steinwald[76] observed that the results of these studies were so inconsistent that no overall systematic effect of UR on hospital expenditures could be detected. The multivariate analysis of Sloan and Steinwald[77] included terms representing UR in the early 1970s by reviewers external to hospitals mandated by some Blue Cross plans and Medicaid programs. The mixed results of this analysis indicated some cost-reducing potential of this type of UR, but inadequate data on UR programs and instability of the statistical estimates caused the authors to have little confidence in their results.

Brook et al.[78] evaluated the Experimental Medical Care Review Organization (EMCRO) program in New Mexico during 1971–1975 and considered it to be a PSRO prototype, although applicable only to Medicaid. Their study yielded no significant evidence of a negative effect of EMCRO utilization review activities on rates on hospital admission, length of stay, or hospital days of care for the Medicaid population in New Mexico. In an analysis of nationwide effects of UR and PSRO activities on Medicare patient utilization rates during 1974–1976, Gertman et al.[79] found no effect of binding utilization review or (more generally) of having a conditional PSRO in a hospital's area on levels of, or changes in, Medicare utilization rates. Similarly, on the basis of regression analysis of a time series of data on individual hospitals from

---

[75] Regulators with field experience maintain that hospital budgets are frequently in such disarray as to preclude meaningful budgetary review in the early phases of PR program implementation. This may be one reason why PR programs become more effective over time.

[76] Sloan and Steinwald, *Insurance, Regulation, and Hospital Costs.*

[77] Ibid.; Sloan and Steinwald, "Effects of Regulation on Hospital Costs and Input Use."

[78] R. H. Brook, K. N. Williams, and J. E. Rolf, "Controlling the Use and Cost of Medical Services: The New Mexico Experimental Medical Care Review Organization—A Four-Year Case Study," *Medical Care,* vol. 16, no. 9 (September 1978), supplement. This study is not included in table 1 because it is confined to a single state.

[79] P. M. Gertman et al., "Utilization Review in the United States: Results from a 1976–77 National Survey of Hospitals," *Medical Care,* vol. 17, no. 8 (August 1979), supplement.

1970 to 1978, Coelen and Sullivan[80] found no effect of binding PSRO review on hospital costs per admission or per adjusted patient-day.

The most comprehensive evaluation of the PSRO program was conducted by the Health Care Financing Administration,[81] and it is cited several times in table 1 because of its scope and the paucity of other information on this topic. The most important aspect of this study was its multivariate comparison of Medicare beneficiary utilization during 1978 in 108 areas of the United States having active PSROs with that in 81 areas not having active PSROs. On the basis of a statistically insignificant coefficient, PSROs were estimated in the aggregate to have reduced hospitalized days of Medicare beneficiaries by 1.7 percent. The results also indicate, inexplicably, that PSRO effects differ markedly in some parts of the United States. In the South, PSRO effects on Medicare hospital utilization were positive and relatively large, whereas in the West no effect was detected. Although the analysis may have suffered to an unknown degree from omission of several variables that may also have affected hospital utilization of Medicare beneficiaries, it is also possible that regulatory effectiveness is region specific. If so, it would be important to know why.

The Health Care Financing Administration study included other analyses, perhaps the most interesting of which was an attempt to assess diagnosis-specific differences in PSRO effectiveness. On the basis of expert medical opinion, several procedures and diagnoses were identified ex ante as being either likely or unlikely to be influenced by PSRO review. In four out of five diagnoses and procedures identified as amenable to influence by PSRO review, a significant negative impact of PSRO was detected. In all four diagnoses and procedures hypothesized not to be influenceable by PSRO review, there was indeed no PSRO influence. Recognizing several methodological problems with this analysis, the authors nonetheless concluded from their results that the effectiveness of PSRO review relates systematically to the nature of disease and/or treatment procedures.

The AHA's 1979 Reimbursement Survey requested information from hospitals on the effects of several regulatory programs. In response to a question asking whether the hospital had experienced any disallowances or reduction of payments under Medicare, Medicaid, or Blue Cross due to utilization review or PSRO review procedures from fall 1978 to fall 1979, 26.4 percent of hospitals indicated that they had ex-

[80] Coelen and Sullivan, "An Analysis of the Effects of Prospective Reimbursement Programs on Hospital Cost."

[81] Health Care Financing Administration, *Professional Standards Review Organization Program Evaluation, 1980.* An earlier PSRO evaluation by the Health Care Financing Administration is not reviewed here since the more recent study appears to supersede it.

perienced such reductions. When hospitals were divided into two groups representing those located in areas with and without active PSROs during half or more of the questionnaire's reference period, 28 percent of hospitals located in PSRO areas and 21 percent of those in non-PSRO areas said they experienced reductions.

Although data on utilization controls are mixed, there is a slight indication of increased effectiveness over time. Studies of early (pre-PRSO) forms of UR have produced no evidence of systematic reductions in hospital utilization or expenditures, but recent evidence suggests the possibility of cost and expenditure reductions arising from PSRO utilization review activities.[82] We hasten to add, however, that this evidence is scant. The most comprehensive analysis conducted to date is that of the Health Care Financing Administration. We are somewhat uneasy about this study's findings because of regional differences in estimated PSRO effectiveness and the strong possibility that omitted area effects may have caused bias in the estimated parameters. Considering all the evidence available, we are inclined to suspend judgment on the cost-reducing effectiveness of the PSRO program.

Conclusions

Every industry has its anomalous features, but the hospital industry is regarded as more anomalous than most. Factors such as consumer ignorance, insulation of providers and consumers from the price mechanism because of insurance coverage, and the "merit want" nature of medical care are often used to set health services apart from the mainstream of the U.S. economy and to justify replacing an inadequate marketplace with the machinery of planning and regulation. This approach to the hospital industry stems from the traditional emphasis of hospital regulation on social issues—maintenance of a high standard of quality and enhancement of access to health services by disadvantaged groups have long been goals of government intervention in this industry. Despite the apparent differences between hospitals and other industries, however, many tools of hospital regulation, particularly those that control entry and capital expansion and that set limits on rate increases, have been widely used in other sectors of the economy.

---

[82] Our focus on hospital costs leads to emphasis of the utilization component of utilization-quality controls. Our approach to the quality component has been simply to be sensitive to any evidence of quality changes arising from utilization controls. We have not detected any such evidence, although admittedly quality is a difficult concept to assess empirically and little quality-related evidence is available. The inference that utilization reductions result in expenditure decreases requires several assumptions about provider and consumer behavior. For further discussion of this point see Health Care Financing Administration, *Professional Standards Review Organization Program Evaluation*, June 1979.

There is now a vast literature, both theoretical and empirical, on regulatory effects in a variety of industries. Much of this work suggests that regulation often produces unintended and undesirable side effects and that under the best of circumstances regulatory objectives are difficult to achieve. Analogies between regulatory effects on hospitals and those on other industries can be carried too far. Uncritical acceptance of lessons from the airlines or telecommunications industries, for example, would be rejected by experts in the health field and, to some extent, rightly so. Furthermore, there is little evidence to suggest that hospitals have been the beneficiaries of regulatory protectionism to the same degree as the trucking industry.[83] One lesson from the general literature on regulation, however, is clearly relevant to hospitals: To identify a problem is one matter; to develop and implement an effective regulatory strategy to deal with the problem is quite another.[84] Available evidence on the effects of regulation on hospital costs indicates that this principle holds true for the hospital industry.

The Evidence in Perspective. Certificate-of-need laws and other forms of control on hospital capital expansion are the successors to voluntary health planning, a system that is widely recognized to be ineffectual in constraining health service expenditures. Adding the "teeth" of regulatory sanctions to the concept of health planning apparently has not been an effective means of containing costs. Moreover, overall experience with health planning is broadly consistent with the generally negative effects of entry regulation on other industries, which include favoritism toward enfranchised firms, stifling of innovation, unfavorable side effects, and overall susceptibility to cooption or "capture" by the regulated industry.[85]

Planning is the antithesis of competition; it attempts to displace market forces rather than enhance them, and it creates vast bureaucracies to administer such regulations that may further impede the implementation of competitive solutions to hospital cost inflation.[86] Al-

[83] For a summary of theories of regulation emphasizing benefits to existing firms see B. M. Owen and R. Braeutigam, *The Regulation Game* (Cambridge, Mass.: Ballinger, 1978). For a view of regulation from the hospital industry's perspective see D. M. Kinzer, *Health Controls Out of Control: Warnings to the Nation from Massachusetts* (Chicago: Teach'em, 1977).

[84] This point is emphasized in recent articles by Breyer, "Analyzing Regulatory Failure," Schuck, "Regulation," and Wolf, "A Theory of Nonmarket Failure."

[85] See Clark C. Havighurst, ed., *Regulating Health Facilities Construction* (Washington, D.C.: American Enterprise Institute, 1974).

[86] For further discussion of this point see Clark C. Havighurst and Glenn M. Hackbarth, "Competition and Health Care: Planning for Deregulation," *Regulation,* vol. 4, no. 3 (May/June 1980), pp. 39–48.

though some have proposed a role for planning in promoting competition (for example, encouraging entry of alternative delivery systems to fee-for-service),[87] we have no faith that this approach would ever work, given the ideology of planning.

The results of rate and revenue regulation have been more encouraging, particularly in state-mandated, compulsory prospective reimbursement programs. We hasten to add some caveats, however. First, at present only a few states, principally those clustered in the Northeast, have mandatory rate-setting programs, and one must question whether this method is as politically feasible and otherwise workable in Montana and Tennessee, for example, as it is in New York and Maryland. Second, the favorable results of the mandatory programs pertain mainly to the mature programs three or more years old, since to date most of them have had a substantial startup period. Third, rate regulation is widely believed to create market distortions in the long run. Similar problems occurred during the latter stages of the Economic Stabilization Program. Finally, an overriding issue is whether policy makers can tolerate the results of effective controls on hospital rates and revenues. In New York, for example, compulsory prospective reimbursement has now existed for a decade and political pressure arising from financial distress of three public hospitals has led to the use of Medicaid demonstration funds to prevent closure.[88] The potential effectiveness of this regulatory strategy may be seriously undermined if firms are not allowed to exit from the industry.[89]

The price-regulation activities of state hospital rate-setting agencies closely resemble the primary regulatory function of public utility commissions. Although hospitals do not meet many of the economic criteria of utility industries summarized by Phillips[90] and others, the issue of whether or not hospitals should be regarded as public utilities for regulatory purposes has been debated for several years—both pro[91]

---

[87] See, for example, National Chamber Foundation, *How Business Can Improve Health Planning and Regulation* (Excelsior, Minn.: InterStudy, 1978).

[88] *Washington Report on Medicine and Health,* vol. 34, no. 26 (June 30, 1980).

[89] One effect of regulation may be to confer on regulated firms legal rights to continued existence. See Owen and Brauetigam, *The Regulation Game,* for a discussion on this point. In the hospital industry, the prospect of hospital closure often generates local political pressure to keep institutions in business, even when purely economic criteria would suggest that closure was indicated. See A. R. Somers and H. M. Somers, *Health and Health Care: Policies in Perspective* (Germantown, Md.: Aspen Systems, 1977).

[90] A. Phillips, ed., *Promoting Competition in Regulated Markets* (Washington, D.C.: Brookings Institution, 1975).

[91] A. R. Somers, *Hospital Regulation: The Dilemma of Public Policy* (Princeton, N.J.: Princeton University Press, 1969); A.J.G. Priest, "Possible Adaptation of Public Utility Concepts in the Health Care Field," *Law and Contemporary Problems,* vol. 34, no. 839 (Fall 1970), pp. 839–48; W. McClure, "Reducing Excess Hospital Capacity," prepared

and con.[92] This issue is beyond the scope of our evaluation. We do expect, however, that the relative success of the state rate-setting agencies will generate renewed debate of the hospitals-as-utilities issue in policy circles.

There are relatively few analogues between regulation of utilization and quality of hospital services and regulation in other industries. Quality regulation in other industries has been shown in some cases to lead to too much quality, as in the airline industry,[93] but in the health field quality is a highly complex subject. On the conceptual level it pertains to production of health benefits; on the practical level it is often equated with "service intensity" (that is, the number of services performed for a patient, holding diagnosis and other patient-related factors constant). The complexity of quality review has led to serious difficulties in establishing quality standards and the process orientation of most review activities forces utilization review to incorporate assessments of quality. In other industries, regulations have been developed to increase the availability of services,[94] but this activity is more akin to promoting access to health services than to controlling utilization.

The results of utilization review, particularly as embodied in the PSRO program, are less clear than the outcomes of other forms of hospital regulation. Considerable evidence that UR per se has not been particularly successful is being challenged by recent studies of the structured utilization controls of the PSRO program, which emphasize prospective limitations on use of services and "educational" feedback to physicians who tend to overuse hospital services; these studies have produced some evidence of cost reductions, but the data are too inadequate to indicate whether or not this form of hospital regulation is effective in controlling costs or expenditures.

Inherent in the PSRO program is a constant tension between quality enhancement and cost control. On one hand, it might be argued that

---

for the Bureau of Health Planning and Resources Development, Department of Health, Education and Welfare, under Contract no. HRA–230–76–0086 (Excelsior, Minn.: InterStudy, October 15, 1976).

[92] D. Drake, "The Hospital as a Public Utility," in *Regulating the Hospital: A Report of the 1972 National Forum on Hospital and Health Affairs* (Durham, N.C.: Duke University, Graduate Program in Hospital Administration, 1973); Clark C. Havighurst, "Regulation of Health Facilities and Services by 'Certificate of Need,' " *Virginia Law Review,* vol. 59, no. 7 (October 1973), pp. 1142–1225; R. G. Noll, "The Consequences of Public Utility Regulation of Hospitals," in *Controls on Health Care* (Washington, D.C.: National Academy of Sciences, 1975), pp. 25–48.

[93] G. W. Douglas and J. C. Miller, "Quality Competition, Industry Equilibrium, and Efficiency in the Price-Constrained Airline Market," *American Economic Review,* vol. 64, no. 4 (September 1974), pp. 657–69.

[94] Breyer, "Analyzing Regulatory Failure."

the present circumstances, with intense political and public sentiment favoring cost control, are ideal for effecting cost reductions through utilization review. The corollary view is that reductions in cost-control pressures may lead to increased emphasis on the quality-enhancement aspect of the program. The importance of physicians in the PSRO program should not be discounted, for physicians have had a key role in program development and make most of the decisions about necessity and appropriateness of services. The view that physician incentives would seem to favor high quality and high levels of utilization has caused many analysts, including some who are not opposed to hospital regulation generally,[95] to be pessimistic about the cost-inhibiting potential of the PSRO program.

Regulatory versus Competitive Strategies for the 1980s. The notion that political rewards accrue to the enactment of regulations rather than their successful implementation[96] is very apparent in the hospital industry. The proliferation of regulatory controls on hospitals during the 1970s, based on faith rather than empirical evidence, is almost as alarming as increases in hospital expenditures over this period. That we have understated the scope of hospital regulation in this chapter becomes evident from Kinzer's[97] list of forty types of hospital regulation in force in Massachusetts. Kinzer, while representing an industry perspective, argues convincingly that these regulations often work at cross-purposes and have little effect in inhibiting costs.

Despite the current antiregulatory mood of Congress, substantial deregulation of hospitals is unlikely[98]—in the words of MacAvoy, "real regulatory change is impolitic."[99] Yet we may at least hope for some consolidation of regulatory activities and greater attentiveness to indications of regulatory effectiveness (or lack thereof) as both new and old regulatory approaches are advanced in the 1980s.

Most regulatory reform in the health field at present is oriented toward creating or enhancing competitive incentives. In a somewhat

[95] See, for example, Somers and Somers, *Health and Health Care.*

[96] See Schuck, "Regulation," and Wolf, "A Theory of Nonmarket Failure," for relevant discussion.

[97] Kinzer, *Health Controls Out of Control: Warnings to the Nation from Massachusetts.* Many industry positions could be referenced, but we have chosen to cite Kinzer because of his wealth of detail and articulate expression. Kinzer also provides some back-of-the-envelope estimates that regulation has cost Massachusetts hospitals $40–60 million annually since 1966, mainly in clerical, administrative, and legal expenses. Because of scope and space limitations, we have not examined administrative and compliance costs of hospital regulation. Since compliance costs find their way onto hospital budgets and balance sheets, however, they are indirectly reflected in the empirical evidence.

[98] Havighurst and Hackbarth, "Competition and Health Care."

[99] MacAvoy, *The Regulated Industries and the Economy,* p. 125.

ironic move, for example, the 1979 amendments to the National Health Planning and Resources Development Act of 1974 (P.L. 93–641) direct health planning agencies to allow competition to allocate health resources in their catchment areas under certain circumstances.[100] Elsewhere, proposals for reform of income tax laws have been advanced to increase consumer cost consciousness in health service and insurance purchases.[101] In addition, antitrust statutes are increasingly being used to reduce anticompetitive practices in the health field, such as those restricting dissemination of information to consumers,[102] while several procompetition health insurance proposals such as that of Enthoven[103] are acquiring many converts.

We applaud these reform proposals and hope that they will be given serious consideration by policy makers. Although many of these proposals make a great deal of sense to us, we must admit that most antiregulatory reform measures are based primarily on knowledge of how markets function but have little empirical underpinning. Of course, the empirical approach to evaluating competitive solutions to hospital cost inflation can be applied only if such solutions are implemented. At present, very few competition-based programs have advanced beyond the proposal stage. Nevertheless, we hope to have the opportunity, sometime in the 1980s, to evaluate evidence on the effects of competition on hospital costs.

[100] Havighurst and Hackbarth, "Competition and Health Care."

[101] N. T. Greenspan and R. J. Vogel, "Taxation and Its Effect upon Public and Private Health Insurance and Medical Demand," *Health Care Financing Review*, vol. 1, no. 4 (Spring 1980), pp. 39–46; Congressional Budget Office, *Tax Subsidies for Medical Care: Current Policies and Possible Alternatives,* January 1980.

[102] Clark C. Havighurst, "Antitrust Enforcement in the Medical Services Industry: What Does It All Mean?" *Milbank Memorial Fund Quarterly,* vol. 58, no. 1 (Winter 1980), pp. 89–124.

[103] A. Enthoven, *Health Plan* (Reading, Mass.: Addison-Wesley, 1980).

Commentary

Thomas R. McCarthy

There are two commonalities in the papers in this part, both of which reflect the scope of the analysis contained in this session.

First, all the papers review or discuss the hospital regulatory experience strictly from a supply-side perspective; that is, the emphasis is on controlling which hospital services are produced and how efficiently they are produced. Although Cohen and Schramm and particularly Joskow state their appreciation that the fundamental sources of our health care problems are found on the demand side, no demand-side reforms are presented in any of the papers. The weight of this observation is simply to suggest at the outset that any strictly supply-side strategy is doomed to failure, since it attacks the symptoms of a market breakdown rather than the causes, as Joskow carefully observes.

Second, all the papers ignore any review of or attempt at the theoretical modeling of hospital decision making (although Joskow comes closest). The papers implicitly assume that hospitals are net revenue maximizers and thus are sensitive to constraints imposed on unit costs, total expenditures, or rates. Although the major focus of hospital behavior may properly be net revenue maximization, the hospital objective function literature indicates the strong possibility of multiple objectives. Trade-offs that may exist between revenue and quality (or any other dimension of hospital performance), for example, could produce the unintended incentives that regulators constantly fight to constrain (see the Atkinson and Cook paper). Cohen and Schramm implicitly recognize the need for a fully developed theory of hospital behavior in proposing their "unified regulatory approach," which requires that the planning agency identify "appropriate" services, excess capacity services, and minimum access criteria. The important point here is that hospitals should be given a set of constraints, at least one for each dimension of hospital performance, not just a single constraint targeted at unit cost as reflected in a reimbursement formula. Consider now specific observations on each of the papers.

The Cohen and Schramm paper is nearly anecdotal in its insightful description of the structural conflicts between facilities-planning bureaucracies and rate setters. The planners provide certificate-of-need (CON) approvals based on "medical need" (which presumably requires only that the marginal benefits of the project exceed zero). The rate setters are then forced to guarantee financial feasibility, since the costs of the newly approved project must be factored into the hospital's prospective reimbursement budget. Thus, the opportunity costs of the project may never be fully considered. This scenario not only helps to explain the general failure of CON programs referred to by all the authors but lends support to Olson's "vested interest" perspective (see his introductory comments), which is that the regulatory process is structured so as never to impinge upon any established group. In this instance, the medical community dictates its own "needs."

To reinforce their claim that economically infeasible projects are forced upon the rate setter, Cohen and Schramm could insert some evidence of the project approval rates under CON programs according to project type and planning-board composition (that is, the extent of medical community participation), as well as a comparison of CON approval rates based on state regulatory structures. Such evidence would help to show whether the regulatory failures are related to regulatory conflict arising from bureaucratic structure or to other factors, such as the adjudication of medical need by vested interests or perhaps distortions created on the demand side.

Cohen and Schramm clearly demonstrate the evolution of hospital regulation by documenting the Maryland Commission's growth from early naiveté to more mature and successful control over hospital costs. The thought that we may be iterating our way along the learning curve toward a more effective regulatory scheme is one of the few encouraging aspects of the overall hospital regulatory experience.

Closely linked to Cohen and Schramm's analysis is the work by Atkinson and Cook. Somewhat narrow in focus, their paper argues basically that the best regulation is by broad incentive structures that at least allow the regulatee to make expert and unharassed day-to-day decisions. I have no argument with this point. I am skeptical, however, that any single, simple incentive structure can satisfy the multiple goals of efficiency, access, quality, and appropriate innovation rates that health planners desire for the hospital sector.

Atkinson and Cook demonstrate that older regulatory programs produced unintended side effects that required revision, whereas the newest regulatory approach by the Maryland Commission, Guaranteed Inpatient Revenue System (GIR), has produced encouraging results in terms of a reduced rate of growth in costs per adjusted patient admission.

This is clearly a measure of improved hospital performance, but it is an improvement along only one dimension of hospital performance. Can we be sure that quality or access or innovation is not being unreasonably constrained by unintended side effects similar to those that were so carefully documented in the early sections of the paper? One would suspect that under GIR hospitals are unintentionally encouraged to take on the less sick patients who require less costly daily services and who can be discharged earlier.

To aid future planning decisions, the Maryland Commission would have a clearer picture of hospital behavior if its planners were able to identify the sources of the savings realized by hospitals under the GIR scheme. If serious reductions in access, innovation, or quality are found, secondary constraints may be necessary. Similarly, a clear picture of the hospital's goals at the margin might be developed by monitoring what hospitals are doing with any surplus gained under GIR.

In the case of Steinwald and Sloan's paper, their review of the empirical literature is a remarkably useful, cautious, and clear evaluation of the major studies in the field of hospital cost regulation. I would offer two minor suggestions for extending this already commendable paper. First, the success or failure of any given regulatory strategy relative to alternative strategies cannot be explained without an understanding of the hospital's objectives. Although the authors state explicitly that their purpose is to review empirical studies, the addition of a review of the theoretical literature would have provided the strongest foundation both for interpreting our recent regulatory experience and for planning future research. The empirical literature, for example, clearly suggests that CON programs are ineffective in controlling costs, but the review offers little indication of the source of the failure. Perhaps the behavioral model upon which CON programs were predicated is inappropriate for gauging hospital responses. More complete conceptual models of hospital response might imply more successful policy prescriptions.

A second suggestion is to recommend that future research investigate the effects of the various recent regulatory programs on the quality, access, and innovation measures of hospital performance.

Of all the papers, the excellent and carefully reasoned paper by Joskow perhaps best identifies the true nature of the regulatory problem. The introduction is clear and correct in establishing that the supply-side problems usually targeted by regulatory agencies (overutilization, duplication, organizational slack, and excessive rates of technological innovation) are symptoms rather than sources of inefficiency in the hospital sector. As Joskow suggests, "the major source of distortion . . . is an insurance and reimbursement system that has virtually eliminated all fiscal constraints on insured patients and hospital care providers."

This observation not only helps to explain current regulatory shortcomings but also suggests that successful regulation of providers will require increasingly detailed analysis of demand formation in the health care sector if an optimal (supply-side) crimping of the resource pipeline to the hospital sector is to be achieved.

To date, the regulatory approach has been relatively straightforward. Because we are able to observe problems such as overutilization and excess capacity, which are said to result from excessively loose reimbursements (for example, cost-plus), we attempt to constrain utilization mainly from the supply side through prospective reimbursement formulas and capital budget limitations. With less revenue (based on tightly defined reimbursable costs and fewer inputs), hospitals are then forced to prioritize the provision of their services and ration care accordingly. It is hoped that regulation will constrain utilization to a point at which the marginal costs (MC) of particular services will be brought into line with their expected marginal benefits ($E[MB]$).

Even if we assume that in their rationing decisions hospitals respond in some socially acceptable manner (and there is no reason to believe that they necessarily would), Joskow points out that consumer and physician incentives remain untouched. We might elaborate on the importance of Joskow's observation by identifying a preference aggregation problem that remains when only hospitals are manipulated by regulation.

Rather than employing society's expected-value criterion, the individual risk-averse consumer (who, for a given type of health loss, is not likely to face the repeated trials that provide the logic behind the socially valid expected-value decision rule) purchases almost complete insurance coverage and thus services at the time of illness with $E(MB)$s much less than their MC. The physician, acting appropriately as agent (as well as on his own behalf), encourages this socially "excessive" consumption. Thus, an inevitably frustrating problem of preference aggregation develops. Whereas society prefers services to be provided up to the point that $E(MB) = MC$, patients, using an alternative but fully rational decision rule (expected utility maximization), prefer more. Even if regulatory bodies could determine the point at which the socially defined measures of benefits and costs are exactly matched, this tension on the demand side would continue. By not altering the incentives of patients and physicians, supply-side regulation that could possibly be efficient in a social sense would no doubt crumble under the pressure of dissatisfied patients and physicians. The proper focus of health care regulation, then, is optimally to alter the demand-side decisions, not only the supply-side responses to these distortive demand-side pressures.

(I leave the discussion of the particular strategies to the contributors on consumer incentive policies and to Joskow as an additional alternative regulatory strategy to be considered in his broader manuscript.) In the end, except for reducing gross productive inefficiencies, the few effective regulatory constraints on hospitals may serve mainly as an incentive for hospitals eventually to pressure public policy makers into developing programs that put patients and physicians more at risk for their utilization decisions, so that the hospital may be relieved of the total responsibility for rationing care. As Joskow appropriately concludes, over the longer run these supply-side programs are not likely to offer economically efficient control in such a dynamic market.

Christopher Clague

The combination of fee-for-service medicine and third-party reimbursement to the provider is at the heart of much of the criticism of medical care in the United States today. The physician is led by his concern for the patient's welfare to order medical treatments that may be of greater cost to society than they are of benefit to the patient. Meanwhile the patient, who tends to defer to the superior knowledge of the physician even when he has to pay the entire bill, under third-party reimbursement encourages or presses the physician to prescribe additional treatments. The financial interest of the physician reinforces his concern for the patient's welfare and leads him to order the excessive treatment. To be sure, the physician is also influenced by professional ethics, which do not condone fraud but which under present circumstances lead him to focus on what is best for the patient rather than on the efficient allocation of scarce resources. Professional ethics call for providing at least the customary standard of treatment, which at present tends to entail excessive social costs.

Third-party reimbursement via private health insurance has arisen in part from the combination of risk aversion of the population and the increasing costs of medical treatments. Private health insurance has additionally been encouraged by its favorable tax treatment. Third-party payment has also been used by the government to provide medical care to the poor and the elderly. Since there is political pressure to extend publicly supported provision to other segments of the population, the difficulties arising from third-party reimbursement under our present system may well increase in severity.

Two fundamentally different approaches to improving allocation in the health sector are market-based strategies and regulation. Market-based strategies on one hand rely on coinsurance and other devices to make the patient pay for part of the costs of treatment, and on the other hand encourage health maintenance organizations (HMOs) to compete successfully with fee-for-service medicine. Market-based strategies—these strategies are discussed elsewhere in this volume—for various reasons attract the attention of economists.

Probably the vast majority of economists concerned with the health sector would favor increased reliance on market mechanisms of one sort or another. The papers in this part, however, are concerned primarily with regulation. It makes sense to look at regulatory strategies carefully, for in the first place economists may not prevail (not only because we have to contend with powerful vested interests but also because we seem to be unable to persuade disinterested noneconomist observers that we are right), and in the second place economists may be insufficiently cognizant of shortcomings of the market.

In any discussion of regulation, I would include the possibility of direct public provision of hospital and physician services. Although this provision would not normally be called regulation, it is a natural extension of detailed regulation of hospitals and physicians and it may offer some advantages over regulation. The system of public provision that might be a good alternative to regulation is basically that of the National Health Service in Great Britain. The key features of the system for present purposes are payment of general practitioners on a capitation basis, the allocation of hospital services on the basis of medical need as perceived by health professionals, and the existence of the private market as a safety valve for those who are dissatisfied with the quality or the availability of publicly provided care.

It is obvious that under public provision of care there is no automatic mechanism to ensure that resources are allocated efficiently. The question is whether the inefficiencies and inequities under such a system would be greater than under any alternative system, which in this case is regulation. The major advantages of public provision of care would seem to be that coverage of serious illness would be nearly universal, and that costs would be easier to contain. These points can be amplified in terms of incentives facing the individual physician. Consider first a physician working on salary versus one working on a fee-for-service basis under third-party reimbursement; the physician might be working in either a clinic or a hospital. (The physician working under a capitation system will be discussed later.) The two types of remuneration—salary or fee for service—could be characterized as hourly compensation and piecework. Or the first type could be considered transactions within an organization and the second transactions across a market. Williamson has written insightfully on the characteristics of transactions that make them better suited to markets or internal organizations.[1]

The difference between the two types of compensation does not lie primarily in the relationship between the physician and the patient, but rather in the relationship between the physician and the payer—or, the physician's supervisor and the reimburser. As Williamson has argued, in dealing across a market with a stranger or a casual acquaintance, the seller has an incentive to maximize short-run advantages from the exchange. If product quality is a variable and is hard to measure, the seller has an incentive to overstate the quality of his product and to adulterate it. On the other hand, the employee dealing with an employer may have some incentive to exaggerate his personal contribution, but that incentive will be relatively weak, since there are repeated transactions with the same individual, and the employer has means to assess the employee's truthfulness.[2]

The application of these ideas to the remuneration of physicians is rather obvious. One does not have to argue that physicians are dishonest to make the point that they would be less candid in dealing with the reimbursing bureaucracy's directives than with the directives of their supervisors. The supervisor can explain that since the clinic or the hospital has a limited budget, care must be allocated to the patients who are judged to have the greatest medical need. A similar message coming from the reimbursing bureaucracy, however, is likely to have much less effect.

As Joskow points out in his discussion of New York State, cost containment can occur under conditions of severe budgetary stringency in our present fee-for-service system, but the way in which the cutbacks in spending are carried out is likely to impair the universality of coverage to a greater extent than would occur under public provision. The essential point is that the physician acquires detailed knowledge of the patient's condition, which he may or may not share with his supervisor or his reimburser. Under conditions of budgetary stringency, the reimburser will issue rules restricting coverage to the most serious illnesses, but since physicians will vary enormously in their interpretation of the rules, the allocation of resources will become highly inequitable as well as inefficient.

Another significant aspect of the relationship between the physician

---

[1] Oliver Williamson, *Markets and Hierarchies: Analysis and Antitrust Implications* (New York: Free Press, 1975).

[2] See ibid.; and Oliver Williamson, Michael Wachter, and Jeffrey Harris, "Understanding the Employment Relation: The Analysis of Idiosyncratic Exchange," *Bell Journal of Economics*, vol. 6, no. 1 (Spring 1975), pp. 250–78.

and his payer is whether the physician adopts a calculating or a non-calculating mode of behavior.[3] In general it is perfectly acceptable to adopt a calculating mode of behavior in market transactions, especially with strangers. One may explore all the angles, be openly mistrustful of the other person's motives, and try to obtain the best possible deal for oneself—consider how most people behave when they buy or sell a car or a house, or consider their relationship with the Internal Revenue Service. In an employer-employee relationship, on the other hand, intensive calculation of self-interest is often met with social disapproval.

A physician dealing with a reimbursing bureaucracy would be likely to adopt a calculating mode of behavior, while a physician dealing with his supervisor would tend to do so to a lesser degree. Part of the calculating mode of behavior would be to withhold information about a patient's condition when that behavior would enable the physician to serve his patients better and to earn more money at the same time.

We have been considering the incentives facing the salaried physician who is in a position to allocate or to influence the allocation of hospital resources. Under public provision of health care, the primary-access physicians would be operating under a capitation system. These physicians would not have an incentive to order excessive treatment, and professional ethics as well as personal inclination would probably lead them to allocate their time and other resources according to their perceptions of medical need.

My specific comments on the papers presented here will be brief, mainly because I lack the expertise in the health area to make detailed criticisms. The basic message of the paper by Cohen and Schramm is that constraints on capital expansion and restrictions on current expenditures for a given case load should be integrated into an overall limitation on annual expenditures. This point seems sound, and although it could have been stated with greater clarity and succinctness, the paper contains some useful examples of the inefficiencies of bifurcated regulation. The paper by Atkinson and Cook also describes vividly the pitfalls of regulation; the Guaranteed Inpatient Revenue System is a sensible response to the situation in which the Health Service Cost Review Commission found itself, but given a little time the hospitals will probably find ways of circumventing the regulations. The incentive facing the hospital administrator is to overstate the degree of severity of illness of the patients who are admitted.

Steinwald and Sloan provide an excellent review of the empirical literature on hospital cost containment. Their negative findings on cer-

---

[3] My ideas on this point are based on Harvey Leibenstein, *Beyond Economic Man: A New Foundation for Microeconomics* (Cambridge, Mass.: Harvard University Press, 1976).

tificate of need (CON) dovetail with Paul Joskow's arguments that CON regulation is unable to solve the problem of excessive use of hospital services. Joskow's paper is extremely interesting and well balanced. His pessimism about the success of hospital regulation seems amply justified. In his concluding section he says that the difficulties of regulation should lead us toward examination of market-oriented alternatives. We might also take a look at public provision as an alternative. Public provision of health care would handle rather well two of the problems dealt with in the papers here: (1) the coordination of expensive equipment in different hospitals, and (2) the balancing of capital expenditures and current expenditures in the production of health care.

Part
Four

The Health Professions: "The Dog That
Didn't Bark?"

Physician and Medical Society Influence on Blue Shield Plans: Effects on Physician Reimbursement

David I. Kass and Paul A. Pautler

The rapid rise in the cost of health care has motivated health policy makers to search for ways to reduce health care expenditures without sacrificing the quality of care. In light of this search, the hypothesis has been advanced that physician or medical society influence on the boards of directors of health insurers results in higher physician fees. This chapter tests that hypothesis.

Initially, one might suppose that physician control of a health insurer would not affect physician fees, since competition would constrain firms to make efficient decisions.[1] Nonprofit Blue Shield plans may not be as tightly constrained as are other insurers, however, owing to their reduced state tax obligations relative to commercial insurers. In addition, they observe territorial restrictions that by and large eliminate interplan competition. Finally, where a physician-controlled Blue Shield plan is merged with the local Blue Cross plan and that Blue Cross plan has a competitive advantage over its rival insurers because of discounts received from hospitals, physician directors may be able to transfer part of that advantage to physicians in the form of higher fees. Consequently, the substantial physician involvement now existing on Blue Shield boards could result in higher reimbursement rates.

Much of the previous literature examining physician fees places

The views expressed in this paper are those of the authors and should not be taken to represent the views of any other member of the Federal Trade Commission staff or individual commissioners. We would like to thank John Peterman, Keith Anderson, Robert Brogan, William Comanor, Michael Klass, William Lynk, Donald Sant, Andrew Stone, and Lester Taylor for their comments during the time this paper was prepared.
[1] See G. Becker, "Irrational Behavior and Economic Theory," *Journal of Political Economy*, vol. 70 (February 1962), pp. 1–13.

little or no emphasis on the issue of "physician control."[2] Despite considerable analysis of the effect of medical insurance on physician fees, little attention has been given to the incentives driving the decisions of health insurers. Some recent research, however, attempts to shed light on this issue by examining the relationship between physician fees and physician involvement on the boards of nonprofit insurers.[3] Theories presented by Arnould and Eisenstadt and by Sloan are somewhat similar in that they both posit a dominant status for the Blue Shield plans as purchasers of physician services. In addition, both assume that medical societies act as dominant sellers of these services. The resulting bilateral monopoly models predict that medical society control can lead to higher equilibrium physician fees if such control makes the Blue Shield plan a passive actor in the fee negotiation process.[4] Although the models are similar in this respect, the analyses differ in that Arnould and Eisenstadt emphasize the competitive advantage that Blue Shield plans may have in the form of tax advantages.[5] This potential competitive advantage is

[2] See M. S. Feldstein, "The Rising Price of Physician Services," *Review of Economics and Statistics*, vol. 52 (May 1970), pp. 121–33; J. Newhouse, "A Model of Physician Pricing," *Southern Economic Journal*, vol. 37 (October 1970), pp. 174–83; Mark V. Pauly and Mark A. Satterthwaite, "The Effect of Provider Supply on Price" (Unpublished paper, Northwestern University, June 1978); V. Fuchs and M. Kramer, *Determinants of Expenditures for Physicians' Services in the United States 1948–1968* (New York: National Bureau of Economic Research, 1972); B. Steinwald and F. Sloan, "Determinants of Physicians' Fees," *Journal of Business*, vol. 47 (October 1974), pp. 493–511; F. Sloan, "Physician Fee Inflation: Evidence from the Late 1960's," in R. Rosett, ed., *The Role of Health Insurance in the Health Services Sector* (New York: National Bureau of Economic Research, 1976), pp. 321–61.

[3] D. I. Kass and P. A. Pautler, *Physician Control of Blue Shield Plans*, Staff Report to the Federal Trade Commission, November 1979; R. Arnould and D. Eisenstadt, "The Effects of Blue Shield Monopoly Power on Surgical Fees: A Theoretical and Empirical Analysis" (Unpublished paper, University of Illinois, February 1980); W. Lynk, "Regulatory Control of the Members of Blue Shield Boards of Directors" (Paper presented at the Western Economic Association meeting, March 1980); F. Sloan, "Physicians and Blue Shield: A Study of Effects of Physician Control" (Paper presented at Department of Health, Education, and Welfare conference, Washington, D.C., February 27, 1980).

[4] We note that if Blue Shield is a monopsonist purchaser of physician services, the advent of physician control may offset this original distortion and lead to either competitive or supracompetitive fee levels. In either case we would observe higher physician fees where control existed.

[5] The significance (or lack thereof) of the tax advantages accruing to some Blue Cross and/or Blue Shield plans has been discussed and analyzed by several authors. For examples see R. Vogel, "The Effects of Taxation on the Differential Efficiency of Non-profit Health Insurance," *Economic Inquiry*, vol. 15 (October 1977), pp. 605–9; H. E. Frech III and P. B. Ginsburg, "Competition among Health Insurers," in Warren Greenberg, ed., *Competition in the Health Care Sector*, proceedings of a conference sponsored by the Bureau of Economics, Federal Trade Commission, Washington, D.C., June 1–2, 1977 (Germantown, Md.: Aspen Systems, 1978); D. Eisenstadt and T. Kennedy, "Control and Behavior of Non-profit Firms: The Case of Blue Shield" (Unpublished paper, Northern Illinois University, March 1980); F. W. McElroy, "Comments," in response to a request for Comment and Advance Notice of Proposed Rulemaking, Federal Trade Commission File 761–0036, May 1980.

then built into their empirical work, whereas it is omitted from Sloan's analysis. Using different data sets and model specifications, each study concludes that medical societies influence the behavior of Blue Shield plans. Specifically, Sloan finds that greater medical society involvement in board selection tends to increase payments for certain types of physician services. Arnould and Eisenstadt, reaching a more limited conclusion from their empirical results, find that medical society control of a plan is related to higher fees (commercial insurer conversion factors) only if the plan enjoys a tax advantage over its commercial insurance rivals.[6]

This chapter supplements previous literature by examining the relationship between medical society or physician control of Blue Shield plans and Blue Shield payment limits in terms of a competitive advantage that has been ignored: that is, the advantage that a Blue Shield plan may obtain from its Blue Cross counterpart in the form of a transfer of the Blue Cross discount. Although some Blue Shield plans receive competitive advantages in the form of lower tax rates, in many areas these advantages are small relative to the transfer that can occur from Blue Cross plans that are merged with the local Blue Shield plan. Where such a merger exists, a medical-society-controlled board might be able to transfer a Blue Cross hospital discount to physicians in the form of higher fees.[7] Such a possibility appears to require three elements: the merger, medical society or physician control, and a Blue Cross hospital discount. We will examine whether, on average, plans having these

---

[6] The conclusions of Sloan, Arnould and Eisenstadt, and those presented here based on our research to date, have been challenged by McElroy, "Comments," and the Blue Shield Association, "Comment," in response to a request for Comment and Advance Notice of Proposed Rulemaking, Federal Trade Commission File 761–0036, May 1980. A different model with contradictory conclusions is presented by Lynk, "Regulatory Control of the Members of Blue Shield Boards of Directors." He posits a median voter model of medical society behavior that assumes symmetric costs and benefits to physicians affected by a change in Blue Shield's fee limits. In Lynk's model, the majority of physicians would desire reduced fee limits to make their higher-priced competitors less viable substitutes. As a result, medical societies would desire lower fee limits, and one might expect that control of a Blue Shield plan would have such an effect. The empirical results obtained by Lynk confirm this expectation, but they are derived from a model that ignores the possible competitive advantages accruing to Blue Shield plans. In addition, the data aggregation techniques can lead to heteroskedasticity problems. Finally, Lynk does not examine a variable that indicates the presence or absence of medical society influence on a board of directors.

[7] Apparently Blue Cross's competitors consider a hospital discount to be an important advantage. See "Commercial Insurers Renew Drive to End Blue's Discount," *Business Insurance*, vol. 10 (December 13, 1976), p. 11; and W. J. Brown, "Comments on the Federal Trade Commission's Blue Shield Investigation," in response to a request for Comment and Advance Notice of Proposed Rulemaking, Federal Trade Commission File 761–0036, May 1980. Such an effect might be possible even where the Blue Shield plan has no market power in the traditional sense. The transfer revenue would be generated by the Blue Cross plan's ability to obtain a discount.

characteristics tend to have higher maximum payment limits than do other Blue Shield plans.

It is also possible that control could affect fee levels more directly if physicians or medical society involvement facilitated an increase in the general level of fees apart from the transfer. To examine this aspect, we allow for both a direct and an indirect effect of control in the empirical specification. We will not, however, discuss the precise mechanisms through which this involvement actually operates to affect fees.[8]

The Physician Fee Data

The maximum reimbursement rates paid by Blue Shield to physicians vary across plans, as indicated in table 1, which lists the mean, standard deviation, coefficient of variation, and minimum and maximum "ceiling" reimbursement rates for five common medical procedures covered by sixty Blue Shield plans in 1977. These rates are the dollar amount of the maximum allowance under the "customary" criterion of each plan's "usual, customary, and reasonable" (UCR) fee reimbursement policy. Under a UCR system, a plan maintains a fee profile for each physician in which the physician's "usual" charge per procedure is typically defined as his modal fee. A distribution of all physicians' modal fees is then compiled for each procedure. Separate fee distributions may also be assembled for physician specialties and geographic subareas. The customary limit in any geographic area (or for a specialty) is then defined as a particular point—for example, the ninetieth percentile— on each distribution. Typically, the physician will be reimbursed the lower of his usual charge or the customary limit. A plan will occasionally pay a physician's charge that exceeds the customary limit if a peer review committee decides that the charge is reasonable in light of unusual circumstances surrounding a particular procedure. Each plan determines its own frequency of UCR updating, and most plans compute new ceilings at least once a year.[9]

In the following analysis, we examine whether the ceiling reim-

---

[8] For example, it is possible that physician involvement on Blue Shield boards facilitates collusion among physicians or causes the gains from lower costs to result in higher fees. The exact mechanisms by which this could come about are not clear. It is also possible that control could influence utilization rates as well as fees. The data required for such an investigation do not appear to be available, however.

[9] In this study, if a plan had different payments for the same procedure performed by a specialist or a general practitioner, data relating to the specialists were used. If different payments were made to different specialists, the specialty corresponding to the procedure's "Type of Service Code" was used.

TABLE 1

MAXIMUM REIMBURSEMENT RATES ACROSS SIXTY BLUE SHIELD
PLANS, FIVE COMMON PROCEDURES, 1977

Procedures	Mean (dollars)	Standard Deviation (dollars)	Minimum Value (dollars)	Maximum Value (dollars)	Coefficient of Variation
Total hysterectomy	699.88	172.18	428.00	1,500.00	0.25
Total obstetrical care	466.35	98.39	300.00	950.00	0.21
Appendectomy	410.32	95.02	257.00	810.00	0.23
Cholecystectomy	629.63	151.31	420.00	1,500.00	0.24
Radical mastectomy	791.87	193.85	400.00	1,775.00	0.24

SOURCE: Blue Shield Association survey data.

bursement rates are related to physician or medical society involvement on Blue Shield boards. The rates are derived from actual fee distributions and are assumed to be proxies for average fees.[10]

The Model

The Control Variables. Individual physicians as well as physician organizations might have incentives to control Blue Shield plans. This possibility, in itself, tells us little about the point at which physician control exists, or the extent of its influence. It is possible, for example, that the majority of the board must be physicians before control occurs. Alternatively, a smaller proportion of the board made up of physicians might carry substantial weight in the decision-making process if they represented the views of a large proportion of all physicians. Furthermore, physicians might have a disproportionate effect on board policy if they had extraordinary expertise on Blue Shield matters. In fact, there

---

[10] Our analysis of fees relies on ceiling reimbursement limits since they constitute the most complete data set available to us. For those procedures where both median and ceiling price data were reported, a simple correlation between these charges was calculated and equals 0.98. Furthermore, for those observations, a ratio of median charge to ceiling charge was computed. This ratio was then correlated with variables (later defined) measuring the degree of physician involvement on Blue Shield boards. The correlation coefficient in each case is positive, indicating that median charges more closely approximate ceiling rates in physician-controlled plans than they do in the other plans. Thus, our statistical tests, which measure the difference in reimbursement ceilings between plans as a function of physician control and other explanatory variables, may understate the difference between average prices in the physician- and nonphysician-controlled plans.

is no single measure that might capture all potential effects of physician influence.[11] As a result, we rely on several alternative measures indicating the extent to which physicians compose or select the members of the boards of directors of Blue Shield plans.

The alternative measures of physician control are as follows:

$MDSOC$ = a dummy variable equal to 1 if the local medical society (or formally organized group of physicians) nominates, elects, or approves any number of board members. The members may be physicians or nonphysicians.

$PMDSOC$ = percentage of a board that a medical society nominates, elects, or approves.

$PHYS$ = percentage of a board that is made up of physicians (this includes both medical doctors and doctors of osteopathy).[12]

$PCTPAR$ = percentage of a board that is nominated or elected by participating physicians.[13]

Each control measure was chosen to capture the specific effects of various types of physician control. The variables $MDSOC$ and $PMDSOC$ measure the impact of medical societies, through their influence on the selection of board members, on fee limits. The variable $PCTPAR$ measures the effect of percentage increases in the selection of board members by participating physicians. Although participating physicians are not formally organized, their influence on policy concerning fees could be substantial. The variable $PHYS$ is used to determine whether higher

[11] For a discussion of the role of boards of directors see L. Solomon, "Restructuring the Corporate Board of Directors: Fond Hope—Faint Promise," *Michigan Law Review*, vol. 76 (March 1978), pp. 581–610; M. N. Zald, "The Power and Functions of Boards of Directors: A Theoretical Synthesis," *American Journal of Sociology*, vol. 75 (July 1969), pp. 79–111; and "End of the Directors' Rubber Stamp," *Business Week*, no. 2602 (September 10, 1979), pp. 72–83. Although we focus on the influence of physicians on the boards of directors, there are a multitude of methods through which physicians or medical societies might possibly affect fee levels (such as threatened or actual physician boycotts). To the extent that these alternative methods are used, our measures of board influence might fail to yield strong support for the proposition that physician influence matters. See A. Stone et al., *Medical Participation in Control of Blue Shield and Certain Other Open-Panel Medical Prepayment Plans*, Bureau of Competition Staff Report to the Federal Trade Commission, April 1979, especially pp. 87–124.

[12] Every plan has at least one physician on its board of directors. To the extent that this physician influence has the effect of raising fees everywhere, it reduces the likelihood that we would observe a positive relationship between our measures of medical society or physician control and Blue Shield reimbursement rates.

[13] Participating physicians generally accept Blue Shield reimbursement as payment in full. The vast majority of Blue Shield plans have participation agreements with at least 50 percent of all physicians in their area.

reimbursement rates are associated with increases in direct physician representation on boards.[14]

In addition to these direct measures of control, we include variables indicative of the ability of controlled plans to transfer income internally to physicians in the form of higher fee payments. Each variable— *MERDMDS, MERDPMD, MERDPHYS,* or *MERDPP* (depending on which of the four control measures is used)—consists of the product of a dummy variable indicating whether the Blue Shield plan is merged with a Blue Cross plan, a dummy variable indicating whether the Blue Cross plan has a hospital discount, and the physician control variable chosen. Thus, the four income transfer variables are equal to the control measure if both the merged status and discount requirements exist. If the plan can transfer the competitive advantage of the discount to physicians in the form of higher fee limits, we should observe a positive coefficient on these triple-interaction terms.

Model Specification. Reduced form models for five medical/surgical procedures were formulated using, in addition to the control variables, several demand and supply determinants of physician fees. The equation estimated is:

$$LUCR = a_1 CONTROL + a_2 MERDCON + a_3 MALP$$
$$+ a_4 PCYBGT + a_5 PFEM + a_6 UNION$$
$$+ a_7 URBAN + a_8 SOUTH + a_9 WEST$$
$$+ \sum_{i=1}^{4} a_{(i+9)} P_i + \text{constant} + \varepsilon$$

where

$LUCR$ = the logarithm of UCR reimbursement limits for the five procedures by plan.[15]

$CONTROL$ = a generic term indicating either of the previously defined control measures.

---

[14] Medical societies or physicians might have a greater incentive to gain influence on Blue Shield boards where fee limits are particularly low. This possibility implies that initially one could observe a negative relationship between fee limits and control. To the extent that this incentive structure is a problem, it works against finding our hypothesized positive relationship.

[15] We also ran regressions that used an index to convert nominal price data to relative values. The index is formed by the ratio of the local intermediate family budget to the U.S. average intermediate family budget. In relatively high (low) family budget areas, the variable is adjusted downward (upward) by the index. This index is an imperfect adjustment for cost-of-living differences across plans. The results indicated that use of the cost-of-living adjustment was not crucial to the findings.

MERDCON = a generic triple-interaction term for any of the four control measures. *MERDCON* is the product of three conditions: (1) a dummy variable indicating whether the Blue Shield plan is merged with a Blue Cross plan, (2) a dummy variable indicating whether the Blue Cross plan has a hospital discount, and (3) the dummy or continuous control variable.[16]

MALP = annual malpractice premiums ($\div$ 100) paid by the physician specialty most likely to perform the individual procedure.

PCYBGT = per capita income ($\div$ 100), adjusted to allow for cost-of-living differences.

PFEM = percentage of area population who are females.

UNION = percentage of state nonagricultural employees that are unionized.

URBAN = percentage of population living in urban areas.

SOUTH = a dummy variable equal to 1 if the plan is located in the South.

WEST = a dummy variable equal to 1 if the plan is located in the West.

P_i = a dummy variable equal to 1 if the observation applies to the *i*th procedure.[17]

The procedures examined are: (1) total hysterectomy, (2) total obstetrical care, (3) appendectomy, (4) cholecystectomy, and (5) radical mastectomy.[18]

The cost of malpractice insurance, *MALP*, is included in the equations, since it is expected to have a positive effect on fees stemming from its impact on physician costs. *PCYBGT* (or adjusted per capita income) is hypothesized to be related positively to fees because of its effect on demand. Similarly, the percentage of women in the population,

---

[16] Discount data were available only in binary form from the Blue Shield Association. Of the plans used in the sample only eleven fulfill both the initial criteria of merged status and hospital discount. Further, for the *MDSOC* and *PMDSOC* control measures only two plans meet all three requirements, and for *PCTPAR* only one plan fulfills all three. Thus, the results of the triple interaction are dependent on comparisons among a very small number of plans.

[17] Data on the physician control measures, Blue Cross discount, and UCR fee limits in 111 reimbursement areas for sixty plans were supplied by the Blue Shield Association. The remaining data for the independent variables were obtained from the Department of Health, Education, and Welfare; the *Statistical Abstract of the United States*; the *Blue Cross/Blue Shield Factbook*; and the Institute of Medicine. A more detailed list of data sources may be found in D. Kass and P. Pautler, *Physician Control of Blue Shield Plans*.

[18] Procedure 5 is used as the base procedure in regressions using pooled procedure data. While more procedure data exist in the Blue Shield survey, they were not used for a variety of reasons, including suspected inaccuracy and inappropriateness of pooling.

PFEM, is expected to have a positive effect on fees.[19] The a priori relationship between *UNION* and fees is ambiguous. It is possible that increases in the percentage of the unionized work force could result in a higher demand for services and therefore higher fees, since union labor contracts typically contain generous health care coverages. But unions may also be expected to exert pressure on insurers to keep fees down so that money saved might be distributed to their members through more complete coverage or in some other manner.

URBAN is included because differences between urban and rural areas may influence physician fees, for example, differences in physician density and costs as well as in attitudes toward medical care. The regional variables *SOUTH* and *WEST* are included to correct for geographical differences on the part of Blue Shield plans, physicians, or patients.[20] Finally, the procedure dummies *P1–P4* are included to account for the separate relative effects of each procedure on total fees.

Data Aggregation. The Blue Shield survey data on five common surgical procedures pose a problem in the method of aggregation. The data were collected on the basis of reimbursement area, and since the plans have different numbers of these areas, it is not clear whether reimbursement areas or plan areas should be used as the unit of observation. A plan area approach (which averages the fee area data to obtain one observation per plan for each procedure) allows for equal weighting of each plan in the regression analysis. In some instances it also allows the observational area of the independent variables to match more closely the observational area of the dependent variables. A reimbursement area approach, on the other hand, equally weights each area in which fees are set and allows for the use of the added information contained in the disaggregated reimbursement area data. We therefore present estimates using both aggregation methods.

The Results

Plan Area Data Results. Table 2 presents the results for the models using pooled plan area data for five procedures. We obtain the plan area data by averaging the data for each procedure across reimbursement areas.

---

[19] J. Sindelar, "Why Women Use More Medical Care" (Paper presented to Bureau of Economics Staff, Federal Trade Commission, February 16, 1979), has argued that women demand more medical care than men after adjusting for the incidence of female-related health care services.

[20] In early work we found that variables designating regions other than the South and West were insignificant and that their deletion did not affect the control measures. As a result, other regional dummies were not included in this model.

329

TABLE 2

PHYSICIAN CONTROL AND FEES: REGRESSION ANALYSIS OF FEE
LIMITS FOR FIVE COMMON PROCEDURES, PLAN AREA DATA, 1977

Independent Variable	Alternative Physician Control Models			
	Med. society dummy model (1)	Med. society percentage model (2)	Physician percentage model (3)	Participating physician model (4)
MDSOC	0.0500			
	(3.21)			
MERDMDS	0.2949			
	(9.74)			
PMDSOC		0.0002		
		(1.01)		
MERDPMD		0.0142		
		(8.95)		
PHYS			−0.0008	
			(1.22)	
MERDPHYS			0.0034	
			(3.11)	
PCTPAR				0.00003
				(0.10)
MERDPP				−0.0004
				(0.09)
MALP	0.0017	0.0021	0.0022	0.0021
	(4.28)	(4.82)	(4.54)	(4.19)
PCYBGT	0.0056	0.0037	0.0008	0.0001
	(3.92)	(2.46)	(0.48)	(0.04)
PFEM	0.0351	0.0342	0.0396	0.0550
	(4.93)	(4.48)	(4.51)	(5.94)
UNION	−0.0058	−0.0053	−0.0052	−0.0053
	(5.66)	(4.78)	(4.16)	(3.95)
URBAN	0.0036	0.0043	0.0048	0.0051
	(5.28)	(5.87)	(5.89)	(5.96)
SOUTH	0.0176	0.0190	0.0407	0.0656
	(0.88)	(0.87)	(1.72)	(2.65)
WEST	0.0209	−0.0051	0.0317	0.0239
	(0.61)	(0.13)	(0.72)	(0.56)
HCORR	4.3040	4.4110	4.2950	3.5110
	(12.05)	(11.54)	(9.45)	(7.59)
R^2	.9997	.9996	.9995	.9995

NOTES: Values for the procedure dummy variables are not reported, but all were significant at the 0.01 level. HCORR is a variable equal to the square root of the number of reimbursement areas within the plan and replaces the constant in regressions in which a heteroscedasticity adjustment is made. The number of observations for each regression is 271. The regression analysis uses the ordinary least squares method with a correction for heteroscedasticity in the residuals. The t-statistics are in parentheses.

Since this averaging technique leads to heteroscedasticity problems, we have weighted each observation by the square root of the number of reimbursement areas within each plan.[21] For the first model, where *MDSOC* is the physician control variable, each explanatory variable, other than the two regional dummies, is significant at the 0.05 level. The variables of greatest interest, *MDSOC* and *MERDMDS*, are both significant at the 0.01 level. These coefficients indicate that medical society selection of board members is associated with an average UCR fee limit (and therefore with an expected price of the average medical procedure) that is 5 percent higher than the average for plans in which medical society selection is absent regardless of merged status of the plan. The coefficient of the triple-interaction term indicates that if all three conditions hold—that is, merger, discount, and medical society influence—the average procedure fee limit is approximately 29 percent higher. Thus, for these plans, the presence of medical society influence is associated with a 34 percent increase in average fee limits. These results are consistent with the hypotheses that physician control has a direct positive relationship with respect to fee limits and that physicians might be able to transfer funds internally from the Blue Cross segment of the merged plans.

The coefficients associated with the continuous medical society control measure reveal a similar sign pattern. The positive but insignificant coefficient of *PMDSOC* (column 2) implies that each additional 10 percent of a board's members selected by a medical society is associated with a 0.2 percent increase in the average procedure price. The coefficient of the interaction term is highly significant and indicates that each additional 10 percent of a board's members selected by a medical society is associated with an increase of 14 percent in the average procedure fee limit for plans meeting these three conditions.

The coefficients of the remaining control measures present a mixed picture. The coefficient of *PHYS* shown in column 3 implies that each additional 10 percent of a board's membership made up of physicians is associated with an insignificant but lower average procedure price,

[21] If one assumes that homoscedastic disturbances existed in the reimbursement area data, then an averaging procedure using unequal numbers of observations across plans necessarily introduces heteroscedasticity problems. In essence, the variance associated with the reimbursement area data is compressed in yielding the average, and thus the remaining variance associated with those observations is reduced. This reduction in variance could lead to a negative relationship between the number of reimbursement areas and the observed variance, as we found when applying the Goldfeld-Quandt test for homoscedasticity to the residuals of the unadjusted plan area data. To correct this potential problem we weighted each observation used in the averaged data regressions by the square root of the number of reimbursement areas. This adjustment more heavily weights those plans with a large number of reimbursement areas and can return the error term to a desired homoscedastic structure. Results of plan area data regressions weighted in this manner are presented along with the results of the reimbursement area data regressions.

while the coefficient of the interaction term, *MERDPHYS*, indicates a positive and significant 3.4 percent influence. The coefficients of the measures of participating physician involvement, *PCTPAR* and *MERDPP*, indicate no significant relationship between participating physician influence on Blue Shield and fee limits. The results in table 2 suggest that both medical society influence in the selection of board members and physician presence on these boards may be associated with higher reimbursement rates, with the most powerful effect occurring when organized groups of physicians are involved in the selection of board members.[22]

The coefficients of the remaining explanatory variables are usually consistent (at least in sign) across the various models. We will therefore examine only the results of the *MDSOC* model. The coefficient of *MALP* is positive and significant. It indicates that prices increase by 1.7 percent for each $1,000 increase in malpractice premiums. An increase of $1,000 in indexed per capita income, *PCYBGT*, is associated with a 5.6 pecent average price increase,[23] while a 1 percent increase in female population, *PFEM*, is associated with a 3.5 percent rise in fees. The coefficient of *UNION* is negative and significant, indicating that a 10 percent increase in unionization is associated with an average price decrease of about 5.8 percent. It appears that the cost containment pressures exerted by unions dominate the higher demand for health services resulting from increased unionization. A 10 percent increase in an area's urbanization, *URBAN*, is associated with a 3.6 percent increase in the average fee.

The insignificant but positive coefficients of both *SOUTH* and *WEST* indicate that plans located in these areas might have slightly higher relative fee limits. In the *SOUTH* and *WEST*, average fees were about 2 percent above those of other areas.[24]

---

[22] We also estimated the model using the plan area data without the heteroscedasticity correction. In those models the results followed a pattern somewhat similar to those shown in table 2. The direct coefficient of *MDSOC* is positive but significant only at the 0.06 level. The interaction terms associated with MDSOC, *PMDSOC*, and *PHYS* are all positive and significant. The remaining control variable coefficients are insignificant, although the coefficient of *PHYS* is negative and significant at the 0.10 level.

[23] The relationship between *PCYBGT* and physician fees is not significant across all models, however.

[24] L. Huang and O. Koropecky, *The Effects of the Medicare Method of Reimbursement on Physicians' Fees and on Beneficiaries' Utilization*, vol. 2, part 1 (Washington, D.C.: Robert Nathan Associates, 1973); and I. Burney et al., "Geographic Variation in Physicians' Fees," *Journal of the American Medical Association*, vol. 240 (September 22, 1978), pp. 1368–71, have previously noted that regional variables are important in explaining variations in physician fees. The significance of the regional dummies in table 3 (reimbursement area data) denotes systematic differences in southern and western states that would preferably be explained by other factors.

Reimbursement Area Data Results. Given the potential problems involved in using a plan area unit of observation, we have also estimated the model using reimbursement area data. These results, presented in table 3, indicate a pattern that is slightly different from that found in the plan area data in that all the medical society control variables and interactions have positive and significant coefficients. The other control measures, which emphasize the role of individual physicians, are insignificant, with the exception of *MERDPHYS*, which is positive and significant.

Other Specifications. The original Blue Shield reimbursement survey included information on twenty different medical procedures. The five most expensive procedures were emphasized here because reporting errors exist for some procedures and because the model is capable of passing an *F*- test for the equality of the coefficients as a group for these five procedures, but not for the twenty procedures. In addition, pooling only the five most expensive surgical procedures allows us to pool procedures that have relatively equal variances in individual procedure regressions. Despite these apparent problems, we also estimated the models with the entire twenty-procedure sample in order to examine the sensitivity of the control coefficients. Where the plan area data (corrected for heteroscedasticity) were used, the pattern is close to that found in table 2.[25] Only in the case of *PCTPAR* was there a discernible change. In that case the control coefficients retained the same signs but became considerably larger. They remained insignificant, however. For the reimbursement area data the results of the control variables followed the general pattern observed in table 3, except that the coefficients of the interaction terms for both *MDSOC* and *PMDSOC* were smaller but still highly significant. In addition, the direct positive effect of *PHYS* and *PCTPAR* were larger and the coefficient on *PHYS* was highly significant.

The model presented in tables 2 and 3 allows for the transfer of a competitive advantage from Blue Cross to the Blue Shield segment of a merged plan only when some form of physician control exists. Of course, such a transfer could occur without the existence of such influence.[26] To allow for this possibility, we included in the model a double-interaction term, *MERDIS*, which is the product of the merged status

---

[25] If the model is estimated with plan area data that are not corrected, the results are very close to those discussed previously for that particular aggregation method.

[26] The incentive for such a transfer of funds is less clear in the absence of physician or medical society control, however. One could argue that any organized group with a stake in the distribution of revenues from Blue Shield could influence the decision. Given such

indicator and the discount indicator variables. In general, the coefficient of this added term, although smaller than that of the triple-interaction variable, was positive and significant, and its inclusion did not alter the qualitative results significantly in the bulk of the five-procedure pooled regressions. In the case of *PHYS*, however, the coefficient of the triple-interaction term, *MERDPHYS*, became negative and significant, as opposed to its previous positive and significant sign. In addition, the coefficients of *PMDSOC* and *PCTPAR* increased in size and became significant.

Since the effect of control appears to flow largely from the competitive advantage available to some plans, we wished to examine the relationships when both the tax and discount advantages are considered in one model. To do this, we added another term to the model which was the product of the control measure and a dummy variable indicating the existence of a Blue Shield tax advantage. Given the work of Arnould and Eisenstadt,[27] one might expect the coefficient of this term to be positive and significant. However, this coefficient was always found to be negative and insignificant for procedure plan area data, and negative and usually significant for reimbursement area data.[28] When this alternative specification was used, the coefficients of the direct effect and triple interactions were always positive and significant for the medical society measures, and were sometimes positive and significant for the variables indicating physician representation on plan boards. The measures of participating physician influence, however, were never significant.

We also examined the effects of some variables measuring the percentage of the area population over the age of sixty-five; the area educational level; the per capita level of private, Medicare, and Medicaid insurance; and the percentage of the population employed in manufac-

---

an interpretation, a positive coefficient on the double interaction would be consistent with an effort by physicians (or any other group) to transfer revenues into higher fee limits. It may also be that the mere existence of the competitive advantage allows the plans to reduce cost containment efforts so that fee limits may rise regardless of the control status.

[27] R. Arnould and D. Eisenstadt, "The Effects of Blue Shield Monopoly Power on Surgical Fees."

[28] Our results do not agree with those of Arnould and Eisenstadt partly because of differences in the model specification (Arnould and Eisenstadt use measures of insurance coverage, the percentage of the population over sixty-five, the surgeon-population ratio, and a wage index as independent variables, in addition to their control measures), and partly because of differences in the dependent variables (Arnould and Eisenstadt use a measure of commercial insurer reimbursement limits). In addition, our Blue Shield tax rate data are derived from actual premium tax payments made by these plans, while Arnould and Eisenstadt's data come from another source.

TABLE 3

PHYSICIAN CONTROL AND FEES: REGRESSION ANALYSIS OF FEE
LIMITS FOR FIVE COMMON PROCEDURES, REIMBURSEMENT AREA
DATA, 1977

	Alternative Physician Control Models			
Independent Variable	Med. society dummy model (1)	Med. society percentage model (2)	Physician percentage model (3)	Participating physician model (4)
MDSOC	0.0541			
	(3.85)			
MERDMDS	0.2304			
	(8.32)			
·PMDSOC		0.0005		
		(2.45)		
MERDPMD		0.0120		
PHYS			0.0003	
			(0.51)	
MERDPHYS			0.0025	
			(2.92)	
PCTPAR				0.0002
				(0.075)
MERDPP				−0.0009
				(0.22)
MALP	0.0017	0.0019	0.0021	0.0020
	(4.67)	(5.24)	(5.23)	(4.98)
PCYBGT	0.0069	0.0054	0.0026	0.0022
	(5.37)	(4.18)	(1.93)	(1.67)
PFEM	0.0560	0.0535	0.0648	0.0727
	(8.66)	(8.11)	(8.83)	(9.92)
UNION	−0.0077	−0.0072	−0.0073	−0.0073
	(8.26)	(7.47)	(7.11)	(6.89)
URBAN	0.0029	0.0035	0.0043	0.0041
	(4.64)	(5.42)	(6.24)	(5.96)
SOUTH	0.1182	0.1199	0.1400	0.1513
	(6.53)	(6.38)	(7.15)	(7.61)
WEST	0.0730	0.0450	0.0696	0.0811
	(2.33)	(1.36)	(1.90)	(2.36)
Constant	3.2190	3.3894	2.917	2.5666
	(9.90)	(10.25)	(7.67)	(6.98)
R^2	.8118	.8007	.7735	.7692

NOTES: Values for the procedure dummy variables are not reported, but all were significant at the 0.01 level. The number of observations for each regression is 519. The regression analysis uses the ordinary least squares method. The t-statistics are in parentheses.

turing.[29] These measures were added to the basic model shown in table 2 but with the double-interaction term, *MERDIS,* already included. Although the qualitative results of the control variables and associated interactions are not affected by the inclusion of these variables, the direct-effect coefficient of *PMDSOC* becomes positive and significant. Focusing on the added variable results, the coefficients of the population over the age of sixty-five, education, and percentage in manufacturing were negative, but only percentage in manufacturing was generally significant. The insurance variable obtained a significant positive coefficient, as would be expected if insurance increased demand for physician services.[30]

Some Final Considerations. Some measures of physician control, especially those relating to medical society influence in the selection of board members, appear to be associated with substantially higher Blue Shield reimbursement rates in various model specifications. These results lead one to wonder why some plans are not physician controlled, and why this control has in fact declined.[31] If control is a means to gain higher

[29] Other variables measuring Blue Shield's market share, the physician-population ratio, and the percentage of the population covered by health maintenance organizations (HMOs) were also examined. Since these variables would seem to be endogenous, they were not included in the original model. Adding these variables as a group did not appear to affect the general pattern of results—that is, for the five-procedure regressions, the coefficient of *MDSOC* and its interaction were positive and significant, as was the coefficient of the *PMDSOC* interaction term. Including these variables in the twenty-procedure regressions can lead to positive but insignificant *MDSOC* and *PMDSOC* coefficients. However, the associated triple interactions remain significant and positive. In the case of the five-procedure regressions, the market share proxy obtains a significant negative coefficient and the physician-population ratio coefficient is generally positive. The latter result may be nonintuitive, but it is certainly a common empirical finding in the health economics literature. The coefficient of the *HMO* variable was negative and significant. If it is included in the model by itself (without the other two measures), however, its coefficient is generally insignificant. Thus, these results are ambiguous with regard to the proposition that HMOs cause lower physician fees through competitive pressure. L. Goldberg and Warren Greenberg, *The Health Maintenance Organization and Its Effects on Competition,* Staff Report to the Federal Trade Commission, July 1977; and H. Luft, "HMOs, Competition, Cost Containment, and NHI," in Mark Pauly, ed., *National Health Insurance: What Now, What Later, What Never?* (Washington, D.C.: American Enterprise Institute, 1980), pp. 283–306.

[30] These significant variables were not included in the basic model, since they were insignificant when added individually. We also estimated models containing *MDSOC* and its triple-interaction term along with other control measures (for example, *MDSOC, MERDMDS, PCTPAR,* and *MERDPP*) in one equation. The results do not differ substantially from those shown in table 2.

[31] Physician influence on Blue Shield boards of directors has been declining recently, partly because of the efforts of the Blue Shield Association. In 1977, however, approximately 43 percent of all Blue Shield enrollees were covered by plans having physician majorities on the board. In addition, thirty-five of the seventy plans had board members selected by local medical societies.

fees, there would presumably exist strong pressures to secure and retain control. It is possible that legal limitations, unexamined regulatory restraints, or the local political climate are reasons for the lack of physician control in some areas. A systematic examination of these factors on a plan-by-plan basis has not been attempted. We did examine the extent of state insurance regulation, since such regulation could be stringent enough to keep gains to physicians to a minimum by reducing their incentive to gain control. We reviewed data on the state insurance departments' control of Blue Shield's rates and on the time spent by department staff on Blue Cross and Blue Shield regulation. No systematic differences appear to exist in this regard between plans that are physician controlled and those that are not.[32] Furthermore, physicians might be expected to migrate toward areas in which fees are relatively high, so that fees would fall to the long-run equilibrium level. While Benham et al. and Kehrer[33] found some weak indications of this migration, it does not seem to have reduced the fee differential to an insignificant level.[34]

It is also possible that physician quality may be systematically higher in the physician-controlled plan areas, perhaps because higher fees in these areas attract higher-quality doctors. If so, our physician control variables may be picking up an effect of quality differences on fees as well as any effect of physician control. We were unable to obtain a reliable physician quality measure for the period studied,[35] however,

[32] For a discussion of state regulation of Blue Shield plans, see Lewin and Associates, Inc., *Nationwide Survey of State Health Regulations* (Washington, D.C.: Health Resources Administration, 1974).

[33] L. Benham, A. Maurizi, and M. Reder, "Migration, Location, and Remuneration of Medical Personnel: Physicians and Dentists," *Review of Economics and Statistics,* vol. 50 (August 1968), pp. 332–47; B. H. Kehrer, "Health Policy and Physician Behavior," *The Mathematica Policy Research Newsletter,* vol. 1 (Spring 1979), pp. 6–10.

[34] This could be taken as an indication of the imperfection of medical service markets. Poor information by doctors and/or patients would be consistent with large persistent fee differentials. Alternatively, in the short run, if fees are fixed in some form of stable cartel arrangement in the physician-controlled areas, we might not observe the reduction in fees as migration occurred. In that case, migration might only serve to increase physician density. The persistence of fee differentials across plans may also be due to migration restrictions accompanying physician licensure. In any event, the migration of physicians might not necessarily lead to lower fees due to information problems. See Pauly and Satterthwaite, "The Effect of Provider Supply on Price."

[35] In a study of physician licensure restriction, K. Leffler, "Physician Licensure: Competition and Monopoly in American Medicine," *Journal of Law and Economics,* vol. 21 (April 1978), pp. 165–86, attempted to form a physician quality measure for the period 1963–1967. He defined states as having high-quality physicians if 35 percent or more of a state's physician candidates passed a relatively difficult national examination. Low-quality states were defined as those in which 25 percent or less of the candidates passed this examination. A careful analysis of this potential quality measure led to the conclusion that it should not be applied to 1977 owing to its initial imprecision as well as to the increased licensure reciprocity between the states that has occurred since 1968.

and thus could make no adjustment for differences in physician quality across plans.

Finally, we have examined only one of the several corporate relationships between the Blue Cross and Blue Shield plans—that is, the merged status with one board of directors for both entities. Alternative relationships exist in which otherwise separate Blue Cross and Blue Shield plans share staff and a chief executive, or share only some staff. Since our data on control apply only to the Blue Shield boards or to the single board of a merged plan, we cannot reliably examine these other plan relationships. In addition, the existence of two separate boards would considerably complicate the problem of determining how plan policy is actually set. The transfer of revenue to physicians might be less likely to occur if the Blue Cross plan was separately governed by its own board.

Conclusion

We have attempted to verify empirically whether any relationship exists between alternative definitions of physician control and Blue Shield reimbursement rates. Theories based on bilateral monopoly models imply that such a relationship might exist if medical society (or physician) influence caused the Blue Shield plan to become a passive actor in the negotiation of physician fee limits. In addition, potential competitive advantages enjoyed by the plans might allow such behavior to continue even in the absence of traditional market power on the part of the Blue Shield plans in the insurance market.

The empirical results for many model specifications indicate that reimbursement rates are significantly higher where a local medical society or other organized group of physicians selects board members. This result is consistent with the theories discussed above and can be direct or indirect through the transfer of funds from the Blue Cross portion of the merged plan.[36] The evidence of a systematic relationship between individual physician or participating physician control and higher rates is considerably weaker.

The market for medical services is complex, and substantial interaction undoubtedly exists among physicians' fees, utilization rates, insurance premiums, hospital costs, and regulation. We have not attempted to construct a model capable of disentangling all these complexities. Our research does indicate, however, that there may be some adverse effects of medical society influence on Blue Shield plans.

---

[36] The evidence on the indirect transfer is based on a small sample of plans, however.

338

The Effects of Provider-Controlled Blue Shield Plans: Regulatory Options

Richard Arnould and David Eisenstadt

Research amassed within the past five years on Blue Cross–Blue Shield suggests that the nation's largest network of private health insurance plans reduces consumer welfare.[1] Frech[2] in a recent paper states that the basic conclusion of previous studies "is that the Blues, largely as a result of their special position in medicine, hold some market or monopoly power and that they use this power to benefit the providers of care and those operating the Blue Cross and Blue Shield plans, but at

NOTE: The views expressed in the paper are not necessarily those of the Antitrust Division of the U.S. Department of Justice. The authors wish to express their appreciation to Clark Havighurst for his invaluable assistance in the research that led to this manuscript and to R. McGuckin, Ted Frech, and Bill Lynk for valuable comments on an earlier draft.

[1] Richard J. Arnould and David Eisenstadt, "Blue Shield Fee Setting in the Physicians' Market: A Theoretical and Empirical Analysis" (report submitted for research conducted under National Center for Health Services Research Grant No. HSO 1539, Clark C. Havighurst, principal investigator); David Eisenstadt and Richard J. Arnould, "The Effects of Medical Society Control of Blue Shield on Fees in the Physician Service Market: Some Preliminary Evidence" (Paper presented at the Eastern Economic Association, Boston, May 1979); David Eisenstadt and Thomas E. Kennedy, "Control and Behavior of Nonprofit Firms: The Case of Blue Shield," *Southern Economic Journal* (forthcoming July 1981); H. E. Frech III, "Blue Cross, Blue Shield, and Health Care Costs: A Review of Economic Evidence," in Mark Pauly, ed., *National Health Insurance: What Now, What Later, What Never?* (Washington, D.C.: American Enterprise Institute, 1980), pp. 250–63; H. E. Frech III, "The Property Rights Theory of the Firm: Empirical Results from a Natural Experiment," *Journal of Political Economy*, vol. 84, no. 1 (February 1976), pp. 143–52; H. E. Frech III, *The Regulation of Health Insurance* (Ph.D. diss., University of California, Los Angeles, 1979); H. E. Frech III and Paul B. Ginsburg, "Competition among Health Insurers," in Warren Greenberg, ed., *Competition in the Health Care Sector: Past, Present, and Future* (Germantown, Md.: Aspen Systems Corporation, 1978), pp. 210–37; Clark C. Havighurst, "Professional Restraints in Innovation in Health Care Financing," *Duke Law Journal*, vol. 1978, no. 2 (1978), pp. 303–87; Ronald J. Vogel, "The Effects of Taxation on the Differential Efficiency of Nonprofit Health Insurers," *Economic Inquiry*, vol. 15, no. 4 (June 1977), pp. 605–9.

[2] Frech, "Blue Cross, Blue Shield, and Health Care Costs."

the expense of consumers in general."[3] While Frech admits there are serious disagreements on many points, he finds "the overall picture painted by the critics of the Blues' power convincing."[4]

There is little disagreement that Blue Cross or Blue Shield, because of regulatory advantages and/or close links with organized provider groups, possess potential market power that could result in supracompetitive hospital charges or physicians' fees. Empirical research on the "Blues" has not determined, however, whether regulatory advantages, provider-plan links, or some mix thereof, serve as the basis for Blue Cross–Blue Shield market power.

Blue Cross and Blue Shield plans contain two basic distinguishing features: regulatory tax and other advantages; and provider control over the level of plan reimbursement made to hospitals and doctors. It is therefore not surprising that recommendations to change the nature of Blue Shield plans have focused on eliminating or augmenting these characteristics. Previous research has, however, provided a basis for implementing policy based on a change in one characteristic without simultaneously considering or evaluating the effect of the other. For instance, Frech and Ginsburg conclude that:

> there is evidence that regulatory advantages of Blue Cross plans are used to raise market share and also to allow administrative costs to rise. The first seems related to the fact that more complete insurance raises demand for hospital care, while the latter would be expected for any nonprofit firm.[5]

Conversely, a recent report of the Federal Trade Commission (FTC) pertaining to physician control of Blue Shield plans considers the effect on fees of physician domination of Blue Shield and empirically ignores the interaction between organized medical control over the plan and the regulatory environment within which the plans operate.[6] The FTC report finds evidence of a positive relationship between maximum Blue Shield plan payments and various measures of physician/medical society control over the plan. The possibility that these plans might also possess regulatory advantages partly responsible for higher plan payments is not explicitly considered in the empirical work. One might reason, however, that organized medical or physician control over Blue Shield would have little long-run impact on fees if all other aspects of the health insurance market were competitive. A competitive insurance market would pro-

[3] Ibid., p. 250.

[4] Ibid.

[5] Frech and Ginsburg, "Competition among Health Insurers," p. 234.

[6] David I. Kass and Paul A. Pautler, "Physician Control of Blue Shield Plans," Staff Report of the Bureau of Economics to the Federal Trade Commission, November 1979.

duce the optimal mix of insurance coverage and administrative costs; any deviation from that combination by a Blue Shield plan would place the plan at a competitive disadvantage vis-à-vis another insurer, or might induce the entry of aggressive, cost-cutting health underwriters. Hence, one might hypothesize that antitrust policy that curbed physician control over Blue Shield (or policy that rescinded regulatory advantages) would be necessary only in those plans possessing some regulatory advantage over commercial health insurers.[7]

Alternatively, eliminating the regulatory advantages would be ineffective if medical control over the plan was the primary determinant of higher medical costs, regardless of a regulatory climate. A doctor-controlled plan without a regulatory advantage could wield substantial monopoly power by explicitly or implicitly advocating the boycott of non-medical-society-approved health insurers. In this case, barriers preventing the entry of aggressive health insurers would exist simply because new insurers could not attract policy holders. However, medical society control of a Blue Shield plan is not necessary to carry out such a boycott. There are a number of other economic and political mechanisms that medical societies could use to force capitulation of other third parties. In either case, the plan could increase insurance coverage, and hence physicians' fees, without risking successful competitive retaliation by other third parties.

Clearly, joint consideration of plan regulatory advantage via tax exemptions and the nature of physician involvement with the plan is important to examining the market effects of Blue Shield plans. This chapter empirically assesses the conditions under which regulatory treatment of Blue Shield, and medical society control over the plan, leads to higher physicians' fees.

The chapter is organized into three sections. First, the origins of Blue Shield monopoly power are considered. Next, a model of the health insurance market is presented depicting the effects of Blue Shield monopoly power. The subsequent section empirically ascertains which, if any, of these sources of market power are responsible for affecting surgical charges. The paper concludes with a discussion of the econometric results as they pertain to future efforts by antitrust enforcement (and other) agencies to diffuse medical society control over Blue Shield plans.

---

[7] Even here, however, use of antitrust policy may be based on equity grounds. Any regulatory advantage, like a tax exemption, will give the plan a cost advantage over other health insurers. This cost advantage could be caputured by a physician-controlled plan in the form of higher plan payments, or other plan inputs in the form of rents or slack. Antitrust policy that limited physician control could result in the transfer of rents to other inputs.

The Sources and Nature of Blue Shield Monopoly Power

Most Blue Shield plans were formed during the 1940s and 1950s by county and state medical societies. Plans typically secured passage of enabling legislation from respective states, which sometimes stipulated organized medical or physician control over the plan and usually exempted plans (or subjected them to reduced rates) from payment of state income and premium taxes. In addition, almost all Blue Shield plans are exempt from payment of state and federal income taxes and, in certain states, incur decreased local and/or state property tax liability. State premium taxes, which we treat as the primary form of Blue Shield regulatory advantage, generally are assessed on an ad valorem basis, the rate ranging from 2 to 4 percent of premium income, depending upon the state.

The early Blue Shield plans obtained much of their support from the American Medical Association, which encouraged the formation of medical-society-sponsored, nonprofit health insurance plans. As a result, speculation has flourished that medical society control of Blue Shield could result in supracompetitive fees in the physicians' services market.[8] The potential for parental medical societies to exert monopolistic influence over filial plans has been mitigated, however.

As plans grew in size, the interaction between the sponsoring providers and plan subscribers became less harmonious. Subscribers of physician- or medical-society-controlled plans were alienated by high premiums they felt resulted from elevated doctor fees. Stringent reimbursement methods, on the other hand, disaffected the providers and led to a loss of support from organized medicine. This conflict led to increased public participation in plan decision making. Alternatively, growth in plan size led to demands for larger and more specialized administrative units. These administrators performed the support activities critical to plan survival such as claims administration, actuarial services, public relations, and so forth. The precipitous growth in plan size meant that administrators could perceive themselves as decision makers largely independent from the original organized medical community that formed the plan. The result of greater administrator autonomy has been a decrease in the influence over plan policies by or-

---

[8] The first significant documentation of Blue Shield comes from Reed, who hypothesizes that physicians could use Blue Shield plans as vehicles for raising their incomes. Louis Reed, *Blue Cross and the Medical Service Plans* (Washington, D.C., 1947). Avedis Donebedian, *Benefits in Medical Care Programs* (Cambridge, Mass.: Harvard University Press, 1976), contemplates the possibility that "when implementation of the payment system is left in the hands of an agency such as Blue Shield that is controlled by physicians and responsible to their wants, policy and regulations will be interpreted in a manner most likely to aid physicians in the quest for higher prices."

ganized medicine and an increase in the role of administrators and subscribers, each of whom has differing objectives.

Current evidence suggests considerable variation in the extent of medical society control over individual plans. In 1977, eleven plans operated without the sanction of the jurisdictional medical society(ies), and in twenty-three of the fifty-eight plans comprising the data base used in this study, medical societies played no formal role in the selection of members to the plan's board of directors.[9]

The growth in plan membership and consequent rise in administrator responsibility/status create an interesting property rights conflict between administrators and sponsoring medical societies. There is no direct transfer of wealth to each of these groups via stock dividends, or other forms of profit sharing, since plans are nonprofit organizations. Therefore, the only way each group can financially benefit from controlling plan decision making is by competing for and absorbing plan premiums (revenues).

Medical societies acting on behalf of various physicians who receive reimbursement from the plan would attempt to capture plan revenues by elevating and expanding plan fee schedules. The most common strategy employed to assure this result is preserving medical society control of the plan board of directors. Control of plan boards could be achieved by stipulating that board members be approved by the jurisdictional medical society. Those plan boards should be more responsive to medical society demands for more liberal plan reimbursement by: (1) stipulating more frequent updating of plan fee schedules; (2) adopting lenient rules for the determination of usual, customary, and reasonable (UCR) fees; and (3) broadening the range of covered services typically delivered by physicians. In other words, the immediate impact of medical society control over plan decision making is on the rules used to determine the level of plan reimbursement and the scope of benefits provided by the plan.

A variety of intraplan mechanisms exist for medical-society-controlled boards to dictate plan reimbursement. Each Blue Shield plan features various committees that maintain jurisdiction over elements of the reimbursement process. For instance, peer review committees determine whether physician charges meet the "reasonable" criteria for (UCR) reimbursement. In addition, the fee schedule committee recommends changes in relative value scales or conversion factors. A utilization review committee monitors physician treatment patterns to prevent or judge excessive utilization. It is important to recognize, however,

---

[9] Data referring to medical society control or affiliation with the plan come from the *Blue Shield Renewal of Membership Applications*.

that medical society control over the plan board of directors determines the existence of and physician domination of these various committees. In the empirical work that follows, medical society control over the board selection process rather than interplan differences in physician representation on the various committees is considered to be the primary dimension of medical society control.

We do not have accurate data reflecting the various reimbursement features of every plan. It is reasonable to argue, however, that the separate criteria used by the plans to determine payment levels is less important than the existence of medical society control, since such control will result in the adoption of a set of reimbursement policies and criteria that maximizes payment to physicians. Obviously, strategies that increase plan reimbursements raise the demand for and price of physicians' services.

Alternatively, plan administrators could absorb revenues through administrative slack—opting for more staff, higher salaries, and more comfortable surroundings. Discretionary behavior by administrators reduces the amount of potential insurance coverage offered by the plan.

If the health insurance market were competitive, administrators or medical societies (acting as the bargaining agent for member physicians) could not succeed in capturing rents. Hence, the property rights conflict between administrators and medical societies has economic significance only when the health insurance market contains noncompetitive elements. Regulatory tax advantages given to Blue Shield plans and medical society efforts to force other insurers to duplicate a Blue Shield plan's higher level of coverage or reimbursement level, or otherwise to deter competition from other health insurers represent some of the noncompetitive aspects of the health insurance market.[10]

The premium tax exemption gives Blue Shield plans a competitive advantage over for-profit commercial health insurers not exempt from payment of those taxes. For instance, in 1976, the mean administrative expense (net of premium taxes) as a percentage of premium income for Blue Shield plans not merged with Blue Cross was 11.6 percent.[11] Given a mean Blue Shield tax advantage over foreign commercial underwriters (those with home offices outside the taxing jurisdiction) of 1.76 percent, a typical nonmerged plan has a 13 percent cost advantage over for-profit

---

[10] The commercial segment of the health insurance market is largely unconcentrated, and conditions of free entry are assumed by most researchers. In 1976, approximately 800 for-profit or mutual companies operated nationwide, while 70 Blue Cross and 69 Blue Shield plans were situated in the continental United States and Hawaii. For data on individual commercial health insurers see *Argus Chart of Health Insurance* (Cincinnati, Ohio: National Underwriter Co., 1976).

[11] Eisenstadt and Kennedy, "Control and Behavior of Nonprofit Firms," p. 19.

insurers. In general, the premium tax advantage held by Blue Shield over foreign commercial underwriters exceeds the advantage maintained over domestic companies (those with home offices in the taxing state).

The premium tax advantage creates a subsidy that could be used by plans in several ways. If the subsidy were efficiently used, the plan would increase insurance coverage and force the for-profit companies to exit from the health insurance market. The observation that commercial firms continue to enter and operate in most states has prompted researchers, however, to question whether the Blues are using the tax advantage efficiently. The property rights issue suggests that either administrator- or medical-society-controlled plans could exhaust the subsidy through administrative slack or overinsurance. The presence of administrator or medical society control over a plan should, in theory, dictate how the subsidy is used to the pecuniary gain of either party. If the component of the premium constituting the subsidy were internalized by either group, commercial companies could remain in the market.

A medical-society-controlled Blue Shield plan could produce rents for area physicians if it possessed market power independent of the tax advantage.[12] For instance, a plan could force the commercial insurers to duplicate its coverage levels by sanctioning a physician boycott of commercially insured patients. This situation transpired in Oregon in the early 1940s.[13] Commercial insurers were forced to follow Oregon Blue Shield's reimbursement policies after the Oregon State Medical Association sanctioned a physician boycott of commercially insured policy holders. While boycott may be an effective tactic for tempering practices of aggressive commercial underwriters, it constitutes a per se violation of federal (and state) antitrust laws. Implicit threats of boycott as well as commercial company recognition of Blue Shield as the "market leader" could achieve the same desired result.

Let us now illustrate the possible effects of plans with/without tax advantages and with/without medical society control on the quantity of health insurance coverage, and hence on the demand for and price of physicians' services. The foundation for the model comes from Ehrlich

---

[12] We have dismissed the possibility that administrators in plans without tax advantages possess market power. It is assumed that market forces constrain discretionary behavior among administrators in these plans.

[13] For a chronology and analysis of the Oregon situation see Lawrence G. Goldberg and Warren Greenberg, "The Emergence of Physician-Sponsored Health Insurance: A Historical Perspective," in Warren Greenberg, ed., *Competition in the Health Care Sector: Past, Present, and Future*, proceedings of a conference sponsored by the Bureau of Economics, Federal Trade Commission, Washington, D.C., June 1–2, 1977 (Germantown, Md.: Aspen Systems, 1978), pp. 231–54. For a broader statement of this situation see Clark C. Havighurst, "Professional Restraints on Innovation in Health Care Financing," pp. 303–87.

and Becker.[14] It is separated into three parts. First, the competitive equilibrium position of a representative consumer in an insurance market without Blue Shield regulatory tax advantages is described. Next, the effect of the premium tax exemptions is incorporated into the model, and the change in the industry competitive equilibrium is analyzed. Finally, the effects of medical society efforts to increase insurance coverage in plans with and without a tax advantage are discussed.

The model assumes that individuals maximize expected utility of income over two states of nature, health and sickness. Income in the sick state (I_S) can be augmented by the purchase of health insurance. Purchases of health insurance require payment of a positive premium that reduces the level of income in the health state (I_H). Individuals face probabilities of health and sickness of p and $1-p$, respectively.[15] In addition, they exhibit global risk aversion (utility functions are strictly concave) while insurers are assumed to be risk neutral. Consumer preferences are represented by a Von Neumann–Morgenstern expected utility function.

Prior to the purchase of insurance, individuals are endowed with a particular level of wealth in each state. In figure 1, this is shown as point E, with coordinates I_H^e and I_S^e. Endowment point E lies on expected utility indifference curve U_0. The locus of all points denoting equal incomes in states H and S is given by the 45° line. The vertical distance between E and the 45° line gives the level of medical expenditures if state S occurs. Any purchase of insurance is assumed to move individuals "northwest" toward the 45° line.

Now, let the utility-maximizing consumer be provided the option of buying insurance from an underwriter at odds p and $1-p$. Further, assume a competitive insurance market with expected economic profits

[14] Issac Ehrlich and Gary S. Becker, "Market Insurance, Self-insurance, and Self-protection," *Journal of Political Economy*, vol. 80, no. 4 (July/August 1972), pp. 623–48.

[15] The assumption eliminates the possibility of moral hazard in the health insurance market. Conditions of moral hazard exist if the probabilities of S and H depend on the quantity of insurance purchased. Moral hazard is not a necessary condition for medical society control of Blue Shield to result in higher payments to physicians. Higher fee schedules or other types of plan reimbursement, holding utilization of insured services (the probability of S) constant, can increase physicians' fees. However, the probability of S, and hence the price of insured services are also increased if physicians induce moral hazard by prescribing greater quantities of the insured service at the old or new fee schedule. While exclusion of moral hazard from the model does not affect the basis for the empirical work, our results cannot distinguish moral hazard–induced fee increases from higher prices attributable to greater plan reimbursement schedules. For models of insurance markets with moral hazard, see H. E. Frech III, "The Regulation of Health Insurance and the Medical Market: A Theoretical and Empirical Study" (Working Paper in Economics no. 37, University of California, Santa Barbara, August 1975); Richard Kihlstrom and Mark V. Pauly, "The Role of Insurance in the Allocation of Risk," *American Economic Review*, vol. 61 (May 1971), pp. 371–79.

set equal to zero. Then consumer utility is maximized by the well-known solution:[16]

$$\frac{pU'(I_H)}{(1-p)U'(I_S)} = \frac{p}{\alpha(1-p)} \tag{1}$$

where α is the loading charge, such that $1 < \alpha < \infty$.[17]

The equilibrium condition states that consumers will maximize expected utility where the ratio of the expected marginal utilities of income in states H and S equals the reciprocal of the market price of insurance. Since α must be greater than one (a positive markup), the marginal utility of income in state S will exceed the marginal utility of income in state H, implying that less than complete coverage will be purchased. The optimal policy in a competitive insurance market is depicted as point L in figure 1.[18] The horizontal distance between E and L measures premiums paid, and the vertical distance captures benefits (to the policy holder) or reimbursement (by the underwriter).

Blue Shield Tax Advantages. The first part of the model assumed that all underwriters offered insurance at identical prices. Enabling legislation in most states, however, excludes Blue Shield (and Blue Cross)

---

[16] Expected underwriting profit, $E(\pi_u)$, for the insurer is given by:

$$E(\pi_u) = p(I_H^c - I_H) + (1-p)(I_S^c - I_S)\alpha \tag{2}$$

where $I_H^c - I_H$ represents premiums paid, $I_S^c - I_S$ denotes reimbursements, and α is the loading charge. In a competitive insurance market with economic profits set equal to zero, the rate at which income in the healthy state can be exchanged for income in the sick state is derived from equation (2) and is given by:

$$-\frac{1}{P\alpha} \tag{3}$$

where $P = (1-p)/p$, and $1/P\alpha$ gives the market price of insurance. Maximizing expected utility subject to the zero profit constraint (3) gives the following Lagrangian:

$$L = pU(I_H) + (1-p)U(I_S) + \lambda\{I_H^c - I_H + P(I_S^c - I_S)\alpha\} \tag{4}$$

with first-order conditions

$$L_{I_H} = pU'(I_H) - \lambda = 0 \tag{5}$$

$$L_{I_S} = (1-p)U'(I_S) - \lambda\alpha P = 0 \tag{6}$$

$$L_\lambda = I_H^c - I_H + P(I_S^c - I_S)\alpha = 0 \tag{7}$$

Dividing (5) by (6) provides equilibrium condition (1).

[17] The loading charge in this model consists of all costs in excess of the actuarial portion of the premium. An α equal to 1.2 indicates a 20 percent markup over the actual premium. An α equal to one requires that insurance be sold at actuarially fair odds. Since insurers incur costs aside from claims expenses, α is assumed to be greater than one.

[18] Policy L is analogous to the policy which would be offered by a no tax advantage, non-medical-society-controlled Blue Shield plan.

FIGURE 1
A Graphical Analysis of the Health Insurance Market

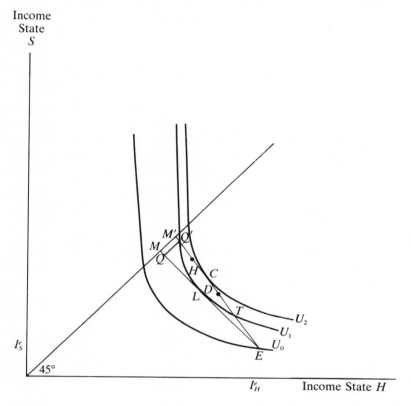

from payment of state and local premium taxes. In theory, the exemptions will permit Blue Shield to realize a cost advantage in the sale of health insurance and will force the commercial companies to exit from the industry.

Functionally, the effect of the tax advantage is to lower α for Blue Shield relative to the commercial underwriters. Graphically, the tax advantage rotates (clockwise) the zero profit constraint for Blue Shield around point E in figure 1. The extent of the rotation depends on the size of Blue Shield's tax advantage. Iso-profit line EM' denotes the set of break-even policies for Blue Shield given a certain level of tax advantage. Blue Shield can offer policy D, identical in coverage to policy L, for a lower premium. Alternatively, higher-coverage policy H can be sold for the same premium as L. Any policy offered to the left of T along EM' makes consumers better off than policy L. Since T provides a lower level of coverage than L, expected utility will necessarily increase

348

if the tax advantage—that is, a lower α—is used by Blue Shield to raise coverage.[19]

Hence, a lower α results in the purchase of more insurance.[20] Blue Shield's policy, given the tax advantage, is shown as point C along EM'. Policy C places consumers on a higher expected utility indifference curve than policy L. By efficiently utilizing its tax advantage to raise insurance coverage, Blue Shield can force the exit of the commercial health underwriters.

As we have noted, the commercial companies may remain in the market if administrators or physicians who control Blue Shield plans use the subsidy in a manner that does not maximize consumer welfare, that is, point C.[21] To see how this could happen, return to figure 1. If the subsidy is captured by administrators, Blue Shield's cost advantage dissipates and zero profit constraint EM' would shift down to EM; the tax advantage would produce no change in insurance coverage as the subsidy is absorbed by administrative slack (higher α). Alternatively, medical-society-controlled plans could exhaust the subsidy by oversupplying insurance. For instance, policy Q, along EM', provides such relatively

---

[19] This can be determined by looking at the change in reimbursements $I_S - I_S^\varepsilon$ relative to a change in α. That is written as

$$\frac{\partial(I_S - I_S^\varepsilon)}{\partial\alpha} = \frac{\partial I_S}{\partial\alpha} - \frac{\partial I_S^\varepsilon}{\partial\alpha} \tag{8}$$

Since $\partial I_S^\varepsilon/\partial\alpha$ is assumed to be equal to zero, the only term for which a sign must be determined is $dI_S/d\alpha$, which equals:

$$\frac{dI_S}{d\alpha} = \frac{-\lambda P - pU'(I_H)p(I_S^\varepsilon - I_S)\alpha P}{-(1-p)U''(I_S) - pU''(I_H)(\alpha P)^2} \tag{9}$$

and is shown in appendix 1 to be unambiguously negative.

[20] Since endowment income is fixed in state S, income in that state can increase only if insurance coverage increases.

[21] Numerous other explanations can be offered for the continued presence of firms in the commercial segment of the health insurance market. First, commercial companies generally sell health insurance as part of a package to employers. Krizay and Wilson have suggested that these firms use health coverage as a "loss leader" to induce the purchase of more profitable lines like life insurance. John Krizay and Andrew Wilson, *The Patient as a Consumer: Health Care Financing in the United States* (Lexington, Mass.: D. C. Heath and Company, 1974). In addition, incomplete Blue Shield (or Blue Cross) market dominance may be attributable to the historical failure of the Blues to underwrite national accounts. At one time this was a serious problem for both Blue Cross and Blue Shield because benefit packages and underwriting practices were not coordinated across plans. Although agencies were established by the Blues to facilitate the enrollment of national organizations, subscriber growth of these groups was retarded in the 1960s. For a discussion of commercial health insurance as a loss leader see Robert Eilers, "The Changing Environment for Blue Shield," *Medical Care*, vol. 6, no. 2 (January/February 1968), p. 62; Robert Eilers, *Regulation of Blue Cross–Blue Shield Plans* (Homewood, Ill.: S. S. Huebner Insurance Foundation, 1963); Krizay and Wilson, *The Patient as a Consumer*; Duncan M. MacIntyre, *Voluntary Health Insurance and Rate Making* (Ithaca, N.Y.: Cornell University, 1962).

complete insurance that individuals are indifferent between it and policy *L*, offered by the for-profit companies. Hence, medical-society-controlled plans with a tax advantage induce the sale of too much insurance (relative to policy *C*).

Medical-society-controlled plans without a tax advantage could attempt to offer policy *Q'*, identical in benefit to *Q*. In a competitive insurance market, however, with perfect information consumers would choose to purchase policy *L*, offered by the commercial companies. A medical-society-dominated plan offering *Q'* would be placed at a competitive disadvantage unless it possessed market power that could be exercised against the commercial insurers.

As in the previous discussion, the model describes four possible settings in which Blue Shield plans operate. In three of those settings, it is conceivable that Blue Shield could raise the demand for and price of physicians' services.[22] Those settings are: medical-society-controlled plans with a tax advantage; medical-society-controlled plans without a tax advantage; and noncontrolled tax advantage plans that use the subsidy efficiently. The statistical work in the ensuing section tests whether, ceteris paribus, higher surgical fees exist in these markets.

Estimation and Results

A surgical fee equation utilizing pooled cross section–time series data was used to estimate the effect of Blue Shield monopoly power on unit fees (conversion factors) for surgical procedures across Blue Shield market areas.[23] The dependent variable *RCF* is the mean deflated con-

[22] Another scenario can be developed to show that medical society control of Blue Shield would result in greater insurance coverage. Suppose that an administrator-controlled plan used the tax advantage efficiently and offered policy *T*, thereby providing too little health insurance. If a medical-society-controlled plan with the same tax advantage provided policy C, more coverage would result, and consumers would be better off. There are conflicting arguments for and against this result, which we feel weigh against the likelihood of this occurring. First, a plan that offered policy C would succeed in driving the commercial health insurers from the health insurance market. Institutional phenomena may be sufficient, however, to allow the commercials to persist (see footnote 21). Alternatively, it is not clear what incentives administrators have to provide policy *T*. It seems unlikely to us that administrator utility will be maximized by using the tax advantage in this manner.

[23] One might wonder why differences in physicians' fees or economic rents are not equalized by physicians migrating from low-fee (rent) to high-fee (rent) plan areas. First, physicians currently practicing in one area may react slowly to observed price differences due to nonpecuniary motives. For instance, physicians tend to locate medical practices in areas where they attend medical school. Benham et al. found that the state-specific location decision of physicians was positively related to the capacity of medical school classes in the particular state. The latter variable can be viewed as proxy for the number of medical school graduates in the state. L. Benham, A. Maurizi, and M. Reder, "Migration, Location, and Renumeration of Medical Personnel: Physicians and Dentists," *Review of Economics and Statistics*, vol. 50 (August 1968), pp. 332–47. Second, a variety

version factor for surgical services in a Blue Shield market area. Nominal mean conversion factors used to compute *RCF* come from the Health Insurance Association of America (HIAA), *Prevailing Health Care Charges System* (PHCS). The conversion factors are derived by the HIAA using the 1964 California Relative Value Study. Three PHCS series representing 1974, 1975, and 1976 were used in the econometric work.

Each PHCS contains surgical charges submitted by practitioners treating commercially insured policy holders with major medical coverage. Fees are collected for approximately 250 three-digit ZIP code areas around the country. The ZIP code areas are aggregated (where appropriate) by the HIAA to determine prevailing charge areas and physicians' customary fees. These fees are assumed to be representative of market prices for physicians' services. If price discrimination on the basis of insurance coverage were still a widespread pricing phenomenon, use of HIAA conversion factors as proxies for market fees would not be justified. Sloan and Feldman[24] remarked in 1978, however, that point-of-delivery price discrimination is no longer a widespread pricing strategy among doctors.[25]

Fees submitted for individual procedures were not used as the dependent variable because the model developed in the previous section provides no insight into which surgical fees should be affected by Blue Shield monopoly power. Mean conversion factors were calculated for each Blue Shield market area and were deflated by an area price index, using the method described by Sloan.[26]

The regressors used in the surgical fee equation are divided into

---

of institutional barriers may impede geographic mobility among doctors; recent medical school graduates may have difficulty passing state boards in states where medical societies earn rents (through control of Blue Shield) for member physicians, and staff privileges at hospitals in such areas may be more difficult to obtain.

[24] Frank Sloan and Roger Feldman, "Monopolistic Elements in the Market for Physicians' Services," in Greenberg, *Competition in the Health Care Sector,* pp. 57–131.

[25] Ibid.

[26] Frank Sloan, "Physician Fee Inflation: Evidence from the Late 1960's," in R. Rosett, ed., *The Role of Health Insurance in the Health Services Sector* (New York: NBER, 1976), pp. 321–54. Sloan calculates a weighted average of the cost-of-living values in each cross-sectional area. Cities in the Blue Shield market areas with a corresponding cost-of-living value were treated as representative of all urban areas within a Blue Shield plan jurisdiction. When no city within a Blue Shield plan area had an associated cost-of-living value reported by the BLS, the BLS city of nearest proximity was used. The cost-of-living figure was weighted by the percentage of the Blue Shield market area population residing in urban areas. Nonmetropolitan cost-of-living figures were used for nonurban areas within each Blue Shield jurisdiction. Each cost-of-living figure was divided by the average cost-of-living figure for each year. To obtain temporally deflated cost-of-living values the cross-sectionally deflated values were deflated by a national cost-of-living index for the respective years, 1975 = 100. Nominal conversion factors were divided by this cost-of-living index to obtain real conversion factors.

two sets. The first group of independent variables reflect Blue Shield tax advantages and medical society control. The second set is included to improve the efficiency of the estimation, since regressors in this set account for conditions in the physicians' services market external to the existence of Blue Shield market power. A priori, they are expected to exhibit little or no relationship to the "monopoly power" variables. Exclusion of these regressors, however, would have raised the error variance on the coefficient estimates of the Blue Shield variables, causing the null hypothesis of no linear relationship between the Blue Shield monopoly power variables and *RCF* to be accepted with greater frequency.[27]

Three Blue Shield–related variables were used in the surgical fee equation. The first two measure the extent of medical society control over the Blue Shield plan. Medical societies can dictate plan reimbursement policies by controlling the selection of the plan's decision-making body—the board of directors. Bylaws in each plan generally specify how board representatives are chosen. Typically, they are composed of doctors, lay representatives or subscribers, and hospital officials from the plan area. In most plans, any change in the method and level of physician reimbursement must be legislated or approved by the board. *TOTMS-CON* is a binary variable, equaling one if the jurisdictional medical society(ies) either (1) elects, nominates, or approves physician and public members to the plan board of directors or (2) has veto power over any board-approved change in the level of physician reimbursement. *MSCONDRB* is also a dummy variable assigned a value of one when the medical society controls the appointment of only the physicians on the board. Because it is impossible to know a priori which of these measures reflects the true or relevant extent of medical society control over reimbursement decisions, each of these regressors was used in the estimation.

DIFTXF, DIFTXD, DUMTXF, and *DUMTXD,* are all included to measure Blue Shield's premium tax advantage over commercial health insurers. *DIFTXF* and *DIFTXD* are continuous, while *DUMTXF* and *DUMTXD* are binary variables. *DIFTXF* is the difference between the premium tax rate assessed foreign commercial insurers and the rate applied to Blue Shield. *DIFTXD* is the difference between the domestic commercial health underwriter premium tax rate and the statutory rate levied on Blue Shield plans. *DUMTXF* and *DUMTXD* are dummy variables equaling one when the local Blue Shield plan maintains a tax advantage over foreign commercial and domestic for-profit underwrit-

---

[27] For a discussion of the effects of specification bias, see Jan Kmenta, *Elements of Econometrics* (New York: The Macmillan Company, 1971).

ers, respectively. Each tax advantage variable appears separately as a regressor, and is interacted with the relevant measure of medical society control over the plan.

Four standardizing variables are used to account for differences in surgical fees across plans not attributable to differences in Blue Shield market power. *INS* is the percentage of the Blue Shield market area population under age sixty-five with medical-surgical or major medical coverage. Positive increases in *INS* should raise the demand for and price of surgical services. *POP65* gives the percentage of the population in the plan area over age sixty-five. This variable reflects the higher demand by the elderly for surgical services, and also the level of Medicare Part B coverage in a Blue Shield area. While the aged have greater demands for physicians' services because of a higher incidence of illness, the level of coverage under Medicare Part B is generally inferior to private underwriter medical-surgical policies such as *UCR* insurance. The higher incidence of illness would be expected to increase surgical fees while the Medicare Part B coverage effect would reduce *RCF*, ceteris paribus. A priori, it is impossible to predict the directional relationship between *POP65* and *RCF*. *SURPOP* gives the surgeon-population ratio in each Blue Shield market area. In previous studies, the physician-population ratio has been used as a proxy for the relative supply of doctors, as a "shift" parameter in the physicians' demand curve, and as a measure of consumer ignorance in the physicians' services market. Without reviewing the rationale for including this variable as a regressor in earlier research, *SURPOP* is utilized in this study to pick up any or all of the above "market" effects. *SECT* is defined as wages paid to clerical help in each Blue Shield market area. This variable accounts for differences in surgeons' costs of maintaining office practices in Blue Shield market areas. Predicted values for *SECT* are generated from a regression using Bureau of Labor Statistics Area Wage Surveys.[28] Values for each *SECT* observation are deflated by the area price index described above.

The fee equation can be written as:

$$RCF = B_0 + B_1 DIFTXF + B_2 DIFTXF \cdot MSCONDRB$$
$$+ B_3 MSCONDRB + B_4 INS + B_5 POP65 \qquad (10)$$
$$+ B_6 SURPOP + B_7 SECT + E_i$$

[28] U.S. Bureau of Labor Statistics Area Wage Surveys were used for 1974, 1975, and 1976. Each survey contains wages of secretarial or clerical help for approximately seventy-five SMSAs. Hourly earnings for clerical secretaries were regressed on median city family income, dummy variables corresponding to the four major census regions, and dummy variables for the years 1974 and 1975. Approximately half of the variation in clerical wages was explained by these regressors. Predicted nominal values for *SECT* were subsequently deflated by the cost-of-living index described above.

where B_0 is the intercept and E_i is the population disturbance term. The coefficient of $DIFTXF$ (or the relevant tax advantage measure) measures the effect on deflated conversion factors of the tax advantage in plans without medical society control. B_3 reflects the effect on fees of no-tax-advantage plans with medical society control. B_2 measures the marginal impact on fees attributable to medical-society-controlled plans with a tax advantage. The sum of B_2 and B_3 indicates the overall effect of medical society control over Blue Shield in plans with a tax advantage.[29]

Equation (10) was estimated using three years of pooled data. A covariance model as well as an ordinary least squares (OLS) estimation were used initially to determine whether the intercept term varied across temporal and spatial observations. For the different tax advantage measures and the two proxies of medical society control over the plan, the F-statistic calculated to determine whether pooling and OLS were appropriate was significant at the 1 percent level or better. Hence, OLS could not be used. The error components estimation technique specified by Fuller and Battese was utilized.[30] The Fuller-Battese method requires the estimation of four least squares equations. The first three are used to obtain weights to reflect the temporal, spatial, and random components of the error variance. The weights are subsequently used in the fourth equation to obtain generalized least squares (GLS) estimates of the coefficients. Since R^2 and F-statistics are of dubious value in GLS estimation, they are not reported.[31] Mean square error, another measure of goodness of fit, is reported for each equation.

Table 1 shows that the effect of the tax advantage on fees in non-medical-society-controlled plans is positive in only two of the eight reported equations. In four of these (10b, 10d, 10f, 10h) non-medical-society-controlled tax advantage plans have a negative but insignificant

---

[29] The t-statistic used to determine whether $B_2 + B_3$ is significantly different from zero is:

$$t = \frac{\hat{B}_2 \, \overline{DIFTXF} + \hat{B}_3}{\sqrt{S^2_{\hat{e}_{\hat{B}_2}} \cdot \overline{DIFTXF}^2 + S^2_{\hat{e}_{\hat{B}_3}} + 2\overline{DIFTXF} \cdot COV(\hat{B}_2, \hat{B}_3)}} \quad (11)$$

where $\overline{DIFTXF}$ is the mean tax advantage held over foreign commercial companies, $S^2_{\hat{e}_{\hat{B}_2}}$ and $S^2_{\hat{e}_{\hat{B}_3}}$ are the coefficient variances of $\hat{B}_2$ and $\hat{B}_3$, and $COV(\hat{B}_2, \hat{B}_3)$ is the covariance between $\hat{B}_2$ and $\hat{B}_3$. If $DUMTXD$ and $DUMTXF$ are used instead of a continuous tax advantage variable, $\overline{DIFTXF}$ would equal 1.

[30] W. A. Fuller and G. E. Battese, "Estimation of Linear Models with Crosses-Error Structure," *Journal of Econometrics*, vol. 2 (May 1974), pp. 67–78.

[31] Buse, "Goodness of Fit in Generalized Least Squares Estimation," pp. 106–8; Walter Haessel, "Measuring Goodness of Fit in Linear and Nonlinear Models," *Southern Economic Journal*, vol. 44 (January 1978), pp. 648–52. When an R^2 of the type used in OLS estimation is used to specify goodness of fit, the values are exaggerated and, therefore, not useful.

impact on fees. In estimated equation 10b, a plan with a mean premium tax advantage (0.998 percent) over domestic for-profit insurers lowers unit conversion factors by approximately \$0.20 (0.998 × −0.197). The insignificant effect of the tax advantage on fees in these plans suggests administrative slack or inefficiency. Administrators in these plans absorb the tax subsidy through inefficiency, reducing the potential amount of coverage the plan can offer.

The result is not inconsistent with the possibility that administrator-controlled plans use the tax advantage efficiently to provide insufficient coverage. For instance, in figure 1, T reflects a level of coverage consistent with such a policy. Indeed, the negative coefficient on the tax variable in equations 10b–10d and 10f–10h are consistent with administrators' using the tax advantage efficiently to lower coverage. At a minimum, however, the coefficients of tax variables imply that administrators do not use the tax advantage to increase insurance coverage that would result in an increase in physicians' fees.

The total effect of medical-society-controlled plans given a Blue Shield premium tax advantage is represented by the sum of B_2 and B_3 ($B_2 + B_3\overline{TAX}$ in plans where the tax advantage is measured continuously). Table 2 reports these coefficient sums and t-statistics for each of the eight reported equations. The impact of medical-society-controlled plans with positive tax advantage on RCF ranges from \$0.32 to \$0.42. Given a mean real conversion factor of \$8.27 in these plans, medical society control over Blue Shield raises unit fees, on average, between 4 and 5 percent. For all the equations, this positive impact on fees is significant at the 10 percent level or better.[32]

An interesting result, in contrast to the findings of the FTC and Eisenstadt and Arnould,[33] is that medical society control of Blue Shield plans, independent of the tax advantage, has a positive but not statistically significant effect (at the 10 percent level) on RCF. The two equations where the interaction coefficient is negative measure the tax advantage as the difference between the premium tax rate levied on foreign commercial underwriters and the local Blue Shield plan. The negative sign on the interaction coefficient in these equations is not surprising, since plans maintaining a tax advantage over foreign companies are not necessarily given preferential treatment over domestic insurers. The converse is always true, however. Thus, a positive tax advantage over foreign commercial insurers is less comprehensive and provides a smaller

---

[32] The theory does not provide for the possibility of doctor control resulting in lower doctor fees. Therefore, a one-tailed test is the appropriate test.

[33] Kass and Paulter, "Physician Control of Blue Shield Plans," and Eisenstadt and Arnould, "The Effects of Medical Society Control of Blue Shield on Fees in the Physician Service Market."

TABLE 1

SUMMARY OF RESULTS OF SURGICAL FEE EQUATIONS
(dependent variable is real conversion factor)

Independent Variable	Equations							
	10a	10b	10c	10d	10e	10f	10g	10h
Intercept	4.673 (4.133)	5.048 (4.633)	4.951 (3.740)	5.041 (4.667)	4.808 (4.876)	5.153 (5.441)	5.082 (4.304)	5.131 (5.442)
DIFTXF	.075 (.439)				.073 (.444)			
DIFTXD		-.197 (-1.373)				-.197 (-1.475)		
DUMTXF			-.135 (-.172)				-.144 (-.192)	
DUMTXD				-.269 (-1.413)				-.257 (-1.480)
TOTMSCON*DIFTXF	-.118 (-.571)							
TOTMSCON*DIFTXD		.153 (.889)						
TOTMSCON*DUMTXF			.130 (.158)					
TOTMSCON*DUMTXD				.166 (.553)				

	(1)	(2)	(3)	(4)	(5)	(6)	(7)	(8)
MSCONDRB*DIFTXF					−.115 (−.611)			
MSCONDRB*DIFTXD						.158 (1.028)		
MSCONDRB*DUMTXF							.144 (.187)	
MSCONDRB*DUMTXD								.203 (.860)
TOTMSCON	.537 (1.237)	.204 (.718)	.203 (.250)	.231 (.819)				
MSCONDRB					.535 (1.379)	.200 (1.029)	.194 (1.039)	.218 (.908)
INS	.219 (.973)	.209 (.947)	.217 (.946)	.204 (.925)	.183 (1.023)	.180 (1.029)	.187 (1.039)	.181 (1.03)
POP65	−.076 (−1.290)	−.075 (−1.30)	−.077 (−1.29)	−.079 (−1.386)	−.074 (−1.616)	−.072 (−1.591)	−.074 (−1.612)	−.075 (−1.67)
SURPOP	−.001 (−1.233)	−.001 (−1.239)	−.001 (−1.265)	−.001 (−1.251)	−.001 (−1.299)	−.001 (−1.307)	−.001 (−1.328)	−.001 (−1.33)
SECT	.963 (5.240)	.948 (5.194)	.962 (5.221)	.956 (5.254)	.934 (5.826)	.921 (5.767)	.933 (5.805)	.926 (5.803)
Mean square error	.07	.07	.07	.07	.06	.06	.06	.06
Degrees of freedom	118	118	118	118	163	163	163	163

*Significant at the 0.10 level.
SOURCE: The authors.

TABLE 2

THE EFFECT OF MEDICAL-SOCIETY-CONTROLLED BLUE SHIELD
PLANS ON RCF IN PLANS MAINTAINING A TAX ADVANTAGE OVER
COMMERCIAL HEALTH INSURERS

	Equation							
Value	10a[a]	10b[b]	10c	10d	10e[c]	10f[d]	10g	10h
$\hat{B}_2 + \hat{B}_3$	.32	.35	.33	.39	.33	.36	.33	.42
t-statistic	1.84**	1.75**	1.47*	1.90**	1.90**	1.80**	1.65**	2.10***
Standard error	.173	.200	.224	.265	.173	.200	.200	.200

[a] The mean tax advantage maintained over foreign commercial insurers is 1.782 percent.
[b] The mean tax advantage maintained over domestic commercial insurers is 0.998 percent.
[c] The mean tax advantage maintained over foreign commercial insurers is 1.769 percent.
[d] The mean tax advantage maintained over domestic commercial insurers is 0.998 percent.
  * Significant at the 0.10 level (one-tailed test).
 ** Significant at the 0.05 level (one-tailed test).
*** Significant at the 0.025 level (one-tailed test).
SOURCE: The authors.

possible subsidy to be absorbed by physicians or administrators. As a result, the coefficients of B_1 and B_2 are less likely to be significantly different from zero in equations where a tax advantage exists over foreign underwriters. Therefore, the effect of medical-society-controlled plans is positive and statistically significant only in conjunction with the existence of a positive tax advantage. This result, when taken in light of the lack of positive and significant B_1's, suggests that a policy aimed solely at the elimination of "doctor control" might have little effect on the efficiency of the insurance market. Rather, it could result in a shift in the benefits from the tax advantage from doctors to administrators.

Turning to the standardizing variables, the coefficient of *INS* is, as expected, positive. However, it is never statistically significant. A rise of 1 percent in the percentage of a Blue Shield market area's population with either medical-surgical or major medical coverage raises *RCF* by approximately $0.02, ceteris paribus.

*POP*65 generally impacts negatively on *RCF*. A rise of 1 percent in the percentage of the market area's population over age sixty-five lowers real conversion factors from between $0.07 and $0.08, depending on the equation.

A rise in the surgeon-population ratio of 10 percent lowers *RCF* by only $0.00001. The coefficient of *SURPOP* is never statistically different from zero at conventional significance levels. *SECT* shows a strong positive relationship with *RCF*. A $1.00 increase in real wages paid to physicians' clerical assistants raises *RCF* by $0.90 or more in all the estimated equations. The effect is always significant at the .001 level, or better.

Conclusion

Our results provide an interesting rationale for adopting certain public policies in the health insurance industry. The insignificant effect on fees of medical-society-controlled plans without tax advantages suggests that the deleterious effects of physician (and administrator) control over Blue Shield could be eliminated if the tax advantage were abolished. Absent Blue Shield tax advantages, the results imply that medical society control over individual plans does not lead to statistically significant higher physician fees. These results, however, do not lessen the possibility that noncompetitive prices exist in markets where Blue Shield plans have no tax advantage. These prices could result from boycotts or threatened boycotts, neither of which requires medical society control. Similarly, noncompetitive prices could result from other Blue Shield advantages such as property tax benefits or advantages over commercial insurers in the design of policies. Clearly, if the no-tax advantage, noncontrolled price is supracompetitive, total medical society influence on fees is underestimated. This caveat aside, the empirical results support the theory developed earlier; medical-society-controlled plans without a tax advantage are unlikely to monopolize insurance markets successfully unless they can restrict entry by or competition among the for-profit insurance companies. Since boycott and other conspicuous forms of behavior are not common, more subtle means of inducing the capitulation of commercial underwriters are likely to be observed. The empirical results suggest that these strategies are, on average, innocuous; medical-society-controlled plans without a tax advantage do not successfully monopolize insurance markets to raise coverage and fees.

The lack of systematic effect which medical-society-controlled plans with no tax advantages have on fees indicates that removal of the tax advantage is, as other researchers have noted, the best policy option. However, the probability of states rescinding, en masse, Blue Shield tax advantages is not promising. The cost of executing such policy on a state-by-state basis appears to be quite high. Barring revision of state-enabling statutes to eliminate the tax advantage, a second best policy for reform must be adopted.

Our results suggest that concern by antitrust enforcement agencies over the extent of medical society control or affiliation with filial Blue Shield plans may be justified only when the plans maintain a positive tax advantage over commercial health insurers. Even when the plan has a tax advantage and is controlled by the medical society, antitrust policy may do little to improve consumer welfare. Divesting medical control from plans may cause the tax advantage to be shifted from doctors to plan administrators. Hence, using public policy to promulgate a rule limiting medical society control over Blue Shield is necessary in that subset of controlled plans without a tax advantage. For the moment, implementation of this rule in the nine plans without an advantage over domestic health underwriters or the six plans without an advantage over foreign health insurance carriers may be premature, and certainly is not justifiable on purely theoretical grounds.

Postscript

On April 23, 1981, the FTC announced its intention to review the legality of physician groups' control of medical prepayment plans on a case-by-case basis. The decision to pursue a more disaggregated enforcement strategy, as opposed to earlier FTC rule-making efforts, seems appropriate. Empirical studies pertaining to Blue Shield and physician fee setting depict only average effects on fees from medical representation. The results from those studies cannot serve as the basis for rejecting the claim that an individual plan's performance may deviate from the average. Clearly, there may be instances where medical representation in a plan without a tax advantage has adverse consequences, as well as situations where such representation in a tax-advantaged plan has little fee-elevating effect. The policy recommendation discussed in this chapter assumed that intended public policy was the formulation of a rule that applied to a set of Blue Shield plans. That policy recommendation is relevant only if a rule making is the stipulated form for public policy.

Appendix: The Effect of a Change in the Loading Factor on Insurance Purchases

To determine the sign of $dI_S/d\alpha$, the first-order conditions (5–8) are totally differentiated with respect to I_H, I_S, λ, and α, to yield the following system of differentials:

$$\begin{vmatrix} pU''(I_H) & 0 & -1 \\ 0 & (1-p)U''(I_S) & -\alpha P \\ -1 & -\alpha P & 0 \end{vmatrix} \begin{vmatrix} dI_H \\ dI_S \\ d\lambda \end{vmatrix} = \begin{vmatrix} 0 \\ \lambda P d\alpha \\ -P(I_S^e - I_S)d\alpha \end{vmatrix}$$

Using Cramer's Rule to solve for dI_S and dividing by $d\alpha$ yields:

$$\frac{dI_S}{d\alpha} = \frac{-\lambda P + -pU''(I_H)p(I_S^e - I_S)\alpha P}{-(1-p)U''(I_S) - pU''(I_H)(\alpha P)^2} < 0$$

The denominator is positive if conditions for a maximum are satisfied. The numerator is negative if λ is positive and marginal utility of income is decreasing.

Provider-Influenced Insurance Plans and Their Impact on Competition: Lessons from Dentistry

Warren Greenberg

A number of recent studies have examined the relationship between physician influence on the boards of directors of Blue Shield medical insurance plans and fees paid by Blue Shield to physicians.[1] In addition, the U.S. Federal Trade Commission has been investigating such a relationship since 1975.[2] The primary objective of this chapter is to examine the behavior of third parties in dentistry, in which Blue Shield without dental providers on its board competes with Delta Dental Plan, begun and staffed by dentists, and the commercial insurers.[3] Similarities between the practice of dentistry and medicine may provide insight into the nature of Blue Shield behavior in medicine.

First, however, we will review briefly empirical studies that test the relationship between the membership on the Blue Shield boards of

I would like to thank James Bonk, Robert Caffrey, Charles Weller, and Dr. Selvin Sonken for helpful discussions prior to the writing of this chapter. I am especially grateful to Ross H. Arnett III, Department of Health and Human Services, for generously furnishing most of the data used here and for the comments of Jack Meyer and Mancur Olson. The author is, of course, solely responsible for the paper's content.

[1] David I. Kass and Paul A. Pautler, *Physician Control of Blue Shield Plans: Staff Report of the Bureau of Economics to the Federal Trade Commission* (Washington, D.C.: 1980); William J. Lynk, "Regulatory Control of the Membership of Blue Shield Boards of Directors" (Unpublished manuscript, March 1980); Frank A. Sloan, "Physicians and Blue Shield: A Study of the Effect of Physician Control of Blue Shield Reimbursements" (Paper presented at Studies of Microsurvey Data on Physician Practice, Costs, and Income, Department of Health, Education, and Welfare, February 27, 1980); and Richard Arnould and David Eisenstadt, "The Effects of Provider Control of Blue Shield Plans: Regulatory Options" (Working Paper, University of Illinois at Urbana-Champaign, February 1980).

[2] See Bureau of Competition, Federal Trade Commission, *Medical Participation in Control of Blue Shield and Certain Other Open-Panel Medical Prepayment Plans*, April 1979.

[3] As in medical care, Blue Shield also actively competes against Blue Cross in portions of Pennsylvania, Wisconsin, Oregon, Washington, and California. (Conversation with James Bonk, Delta Dental Plans Association, November 25, 1980.)

directors and fees paid to physicians. Second, we will examine the origin of several provider-influenced insurance plans in order to assess the potential competitive efficiencies or distortions of the reimbursement policies of Blue Shield plans that are alleged to be under physician control. The chapter concludes by suggesting that substantial competition among third-party insurers may account for some differences in Blue Shield behavior in the dental and medical insurer markets.

Empirical Studies of the Blue Shield–Physician Fee Relationship

Kass and Pautler, using various measures of physician influence, generally found a positive relationship between such influence and fees paid to physicians for selected procedures in more than sixty Blue Shield plans in 1977.[4] Using a data set similar to that of Kass and Pautler, Lynk found, in contrast, that increased physician influence on Blue Shield boards resulted in a lower average level of physician fees for covered procedures.[5] In a less comprehensive study based on a survey of twenty-seven Blue Shield plans and six medical procedures, Sloan obtained results similar to those of Kass and Pautler.[6] Finally, Arnould and Eisenstadt have used a "commercial insurer conversion factor" in lieu of Blue Shield data[7] to show a positive relationship between physician influence on Blue Shield boards and unit fees paid to physicians for those plans with premium tax advantages.

Apart from any weaknesses in the data collected and the econometrics applied, these studies can be criticized on a broader level. First, missing from each is a precise theory of the behavior of Blue Shield. It has not been established, for example, why physician influence on Blue Shield boards would result in greater or lesser payments to physicians in a supposedly competitive insurance market, or how physician influence is defined. Further, does physician influence consist of a single physician, a majority of physicians, or complete physician domination of Blue Shield boards?

Second, each study uses fees paid to physicians for a selected number of procedures as the dependent variable. Data may be difficult to secure on the *number* of *procedures* performed, but the only datum of public policy interest is the total amount paid to physicians, that is, physician fees multiplied by the number of procedures. With insurance coverage, an increased number of procedures may be performed by the

[4] Kass and Pautler, *Physician Control of Blue Shield Plans.*
[5] Lynk, "Regulatory Control of the Membership of Blue Shield Boards of Directors."
[6] Sloan, "Physicians and Blue Shield."
[7] Arnould and Eisenstadt, "The Effects of Provider Control of Blue Shield Plans."

physician in order to compensate for an alteration in physician fees.[8] Thus, studies that consider only the relationship between physician membership on the boards of directors of Blue Shield plans and fees paid to physicians ignore pertinent relationships between board membership and total amount paid to physicians.

Finally, the remainder of this chapter focuses on the following criticism: Each Blue Shield plan has at least one physician on its board of directors in addition to a number of cost advantages over the other insurers. An examination of the relationship between physician influence and physician fees among Blue Shield plans overlooks the possibility that *all* Blue Shield plans in health care are paying physicians higher fees than other insurers and that they are allowing a larger number of services relative to an insurance market (such as dental care) in which Blue Shield does not have on its board any providers who are reimbursed and in which Blue Shield has reduced cost advantages.[9]

The Creation of Physician-Influenced Health Insurance

The creation of physician-influenced health insurance in the early 1940s in the state of Oregon has been previously documented in a study[10] showing that the Oregon Physicians Service—the present-day Blue Shield—was founded by physicians in order to curtail cost control by the for-profit commercial insurance firms. The physicians in Oregon desired a plan of their own by which the presence of insurance might increase demand for their services without insurer surveillance of fees or procedures. Similarly in the state of Washington, the King County Medical–Blue Shield plan was formed in 1933 by physicians who were uneasy over the growth of closed-panel HMO-like group plans.[11] Physicians in Washington were losing patients and income to group practices in the Great Depression. The alleged purpose of the Blue Shield plan, whose board was composed solely of medical society members, was to contract for the treatment of low-salaried wage earners.[12] Membership

---

[8] See Robert G. Evans, "Supplier-Induced Demand: Some Empirical Evidence and Implications," in Mark Perlman, ed., *The Economics of Health and Medical Care* (London: Wiley, 1974), pp. 162–73.

[9] For an accounting of the number of physicians on individual Blue Shield boards, see Bureau of Competition, Federal Trade Commission, *Medical Participation in Control of Blue Shield and Certain Other Open-Panel Medical Prepayment Plans,* appendix B.

[10] Lawrence G. Goldberg and Warren Greenberg, "The Effect of Physician-Controlled Health Insurance: U.S. v. Oregon State Medical Society," *Journal of Health Politics, Policy and Law* (Spring 1977), pp. 48–78.

[11] See Steven D. Helgerson, "The Founding of a Medical Service Bureau in King County, Washington—1933," *The Western Journal of Medicine* (January 1976), pp. 67–69.

[12] Steven D. Helgerson, "Control Practice and the Medical Services Bureaus of King and Pierce Counties 1900–1933" (M.A. thesis, University of Washington, 1971), p. 61.

in the plan was "denied" to any physician who was employed in any competing industrial contract practice.[13] In November 1949, the Group Health Cooperative of Puget Sound, a prepaid group practice, brought suit against the King County Medical Society for attempting "to eliminate competition . . . restraining trade . . . and bringing about a boycott of any person or organization furnishing care who are not members of the Medical Society."[14]

Still other Blue Shield plans were created by the medical profession throughout the United States, so that by January 1, 1980, there were sixty-nine active plans with a total enrollment of 70,096,426.[15]

Each of these physician-sponsored plans appears to have three objectives. First, the physician-sponsored plan would help to eliminate cost containment behavior by insurers. Physicians with a plan of their own might dissuade patients from selecting a health insurance plan that controlled physician behavior by questioning the quality of such plans, while, at the same time,[16] encouraging patients to join the physician-sponsored plan.

Second, a physician-sponsored plan would offer an alternative to closed-panel prepaid plans. Closed-panel, prepaid plans can compete with fee-for-service physicians by enlisting only a limited number of physicians and hospitals to serve the patient.

Finally, the formation and promotion of any medical insurance plan can increase the demand for physicians' services from potential patients by reducing the net price of care.

Formation of Additional Professional Insurance Plans

In the state of Ohio, the Ohio Optometric Association (OOA) in 1966 established the Ohio Vision Service (OVS) to enroll groups in vision care insurance.[17] According to the Ohio Attorney General's Office, at least two-thirds of the board of trustees of the OVS had been OOA member optometrists.[18] By 1978, OVS provided vision care coverage

---

[13] *Group Health Cooperative* v. *King County Medical Society,* 237 P.2d, 737, p. 745.

[14] Ibid., pp. 741–42. The Court ruled in favor of Group Health Cooperative enjoining the medical society from "following any course of conduct . . . preventing or discouraging members from . . . rendering professional services in association with appellant physicians, or for the latters' patients or at any hospital, on the sole ground that such physicians or such hospitals are practicing, or providing facilities for the practice of, contract medicine in substantially the manner followed by appellants, as herein described."

[15] *Blue Cross/Blue Shield Factbook, 1980* (Chicago: 1980), p. 3.

[16] See Goldberg and Greenberg, "The Effect of Physician-Controlled Health Insurance."

[17] *State of Ohio* v. *Ohio Vision Service and Ohio Optometric Association,* Civil Action No. C–2–80–388, filed May 12, 1980, p. 3.

[18] Ibid., p. 3.

to approximately 250,000 insureds in Ohio, with vision care benefits paid equaling approximately $2.9 million.[19]

Like the physician service plans, OVS was organized as a nonprofit corporation[20] and became the dominant plan for vision care in the state of Ohio.[21]

On May 12, 1980, the state of Ohio filed an antitrust complaint against the Ohio Vision Service and the Ohio Optometric Association for "engaging in an unlawful combination and conspiracy to maintain and raise the price of vision care services and materials and to restrict the manner in which vision care providers practice in violation of Section 1 of the Sherman Act. . . ."[22] Chief among the remedies of the attorney general of Ohio was to enjoin any person employed or associated with OOA from exerting "any control over the determination of prices paid to OVS for vision care services and materials or any other OVS policy directly or indirectly affecting competition in the vision care industry."[23]

There are additional examples of other professional groups beginning insurance plans staffed by professionals. In California, in 1974, the California Lawyers Service, a nonprofit organization sponsored by the State Bar of California, submitted a prepaid legal services proposal to the Department of Justice for review.[24] The board of directors of the California Lawyers Service would initially be composed of lawyers, but after a period of three years the nine-member board was to be composed of at least four attorneys.[25] In a business review letter issued by the Department of Justice, the department would not give assurance that it would not bring legal action against the plan, because, among other reasons, "[R]etention of control over the program for even a three-year period by those competitors directly involved in providing the proposed services would create serious competition risks."[26]

Origins of Dental Insurance

Unlike the beginnings of physician-controlled health insurance, dental insurance benefits seemed to have originated not with provider groups

[19] Ibid., p. 2.

[20] Ibid., p. 4.

[21] Ibid.

[22] Ibid.

[23] Ibid., p. 5.

[24] U.S. Department of Justice news release, August 13, 1974, p. 1.

[25] Letter from Peter F. Sloss, counsel, California Lawyers' Service, to Thomas E. Kauper, assistant attorney general, March 5, 1974.

[26] Letter from Thomas E. Kauper, assistant attorney general, Antitrust Division, to Peter F. Sloss, August 5, 1974, p. 2.

but with the International Longshoremen's and Warehousemen's Union-Pacific Maritime Association (ILWU-PMA), seeking additional benefits from the West Coast shipping industry in 1954.[27] Under this program, dental care benefits were organized and financed by Delta Dental Plan, a not-for-profit plan sponsored by the dental profession.[28] Additional state dental societies also began forming in the mid-1950s, in part, to "project the voice of organized dentistry into the rapidly growing marketplace for prepaid dental programs, and thus assure the application of professional judgments in such critical matters as benefit design, scope of services provided, method of provider compensation, and cost and quality control mechanisms."[29] Today, there are forty-three Delta dental plans or dental service corporations in forty-seven states (Connecticut, Indiana, and Texas do not have dental service corporations.)[30]

In 1979, an antitrust suit was brought against the Delta Dental Plan of Ohio by the Ohio attorney general.[31] The settlement specified that the Ohio Dental Association and Ohio dentists may not elect, nominate, approve, or appoint any of Delta Dental's fifteen board members. Prior to the settlement all fifteen board members were selected by dentists.[32]

Economic Effects of Provider-Influenced Insurance Plans

There are a number of economic effects associated with nonprofit insurance plans with provider influence on the board of directors.

It may be possible that merely the formation of such plans may inhibit the growth of competing closed-panel or fee-for-service plans. The formation of the Oregon Physicians Service by physicians lends support to this view. If provider-influenced insurance plans do not enjoy cost advantages in the insurance industry, however, inefficiencies may not be associated with such plans in the long run. If, for example, Blue Shield pays physicians higher than a competitive fee or reimburses physicians for a greater number of services than other insurance firms, it may lose enrollees either to a prepaid or less expensive health insurance firms. Although a majority of enrollees have their choice of insurance

---

[27] American Dental Association, *Dental Prepayment,* April 1980, p. 1. See also, Delta Dental Plans Association (n.d.).

[28] Delta Dental Plans Association (n.d.).

[29] See "The Delta Dental Plan," *Delta and the Dentist: Questions That Dentists Ask about Dental Service Corporations* (n.d.).

[30] American Dental Association, "Delta Dental Plans Association," *Supplement to Annual Reports and Resolutions* (1976), pp. 52–55.

[31] See Charles D. Weller, "Summary of Antitrust Settlement," January 1980. The date of the suit and settlement was November 15, 1979, in Cleveland, Ohio.

[32] Ibid., p. 3.

plan distorted by the nation's tax laws, on the margin the price of the plan must be considered.[33] Inefficiencies in professional participation and control of insurance plans would occur only if these plans enjoyed cost advantages relative to other firms.

A number of potential cost advantages that professional participation and control of nonprofit insurers might enjoy over commercial insurers have already been discussed in the literature. Some researchers have suggested, for example, that the nonprofit Blue Cross/Blue Shield firms are exempt from insurance premium taxes and property taxes. Required reserves for insurance purposes may be lower than the reserves for commercial firms in most states.[34] Others have cited the hospital price differential that Blue Cross has secured from hospitals that may subsidize Blue Shield plans in the twenty-three areas in which Blue Cross and Blue Shield are merged.[35] Still others have suggested that the Blue Shield trademark may provide Blue Shield with market power over the commercial insurers.[36]

Supporters of Blue Shield have maintained, in contrast, that Blue Shield could bear higher costs by enrolling individuals on a community rating, open-enrollment basis, or by being more closely regulated.[37] Additional research is needed to ascertain the extent to which the cost advantages of Blue Shield have offset potential adverse risk selection in enrollment.

Third-Party Behavior in Dental Care

Dental insurance has grown enormously in the past decade. In 1965, only 2 million people were enrolled in prepaid dental plans offered by

---

[33] For a review of the current tax subsidies for medical care, see Congressional Budget Office, *Tax Subsidies for Medical Care; Current Policies and Possible Alternatives,* January 1980.

[34] See H. E. Frech III and Paul B. Ginsburg, "Competition among Health Insurers," in Warren Greenberg, ed., *Competition in the Health Care Sector: Past, Present, and Future* Proceedings of a conference sponsored by the Bureau of Economics, Federal Trade Commission, Washington, D.C., June 1–2, 1977 (Germantown, Md.: Aspen Systems, 1978), pp. 167–87.

[35] See, for example, David Robbins, "Comment on 'Competition in the Health among Health Insurers,' " in Greenberg, *Competition in the Health Care Sector,* pp. 207–11. See *Blue Cross/Blue Shield Factbook 1979* (Chicago: 1972), pp. 7–9.

[36] See Bureau of Competition, *Medical Participation in Control of Blue Shield,* p. 186. In a recent antitrust case it was found that Borden, Inc.'s Realemon trademark was responsible for the firm's excessive earnings, which were three times higher than the average for all manufacturing corporations. See Federal Trade Commission, *Borden, Inc.,* FTC Docket 8978, November 7, 1978; and Jack Meyer, "Competition in Health Care: Tax Incentives Are Not Enough," this volume.

[37] See, for example, Howard Berman, "Comment on 'Competition among Health Insurers,' " in Greenberg, *Competition in the Health Care Sector,* pp. 189–206.

fewer than 100 employers. By 1976, however, 30 million people had dental coverage with more than 11,000 employer groups.[38] By the end of 1978 nearly 68 million Americans were covered by various dental care plans.[39]

How do third parties, including Blue Shield and Delta Dental Plan, control dental costs while at the same time assuring quality care? Unlike most third parties in medical care, dental insurers appear to be containing costs rather than, by their presence, solely stimulating increases in costs. Dental insurers, with dental assistants and dentists on their staffs, attempt to control costs and assess the quality of care by eliminating the asymmetry of information on dental procedures and dental fees that exists between the knowledgeable provider and the uninformed patient. (Dental insurers may have information on an array of dental procedures and dental fees, whereas the patient generally is ignorant of many procedures and fees.) In addition, third parties with a number of enrollees have greater bargaining power than do individual patients in negotiating fees and procedures with dentists.[40]

All dental plans, including Blue Shield and Delta Dental, review dental claims in two stages.[41] During the first stage—also known as pretreatment review, precertification, prior authorization, or predetermination of benefits—the insurance carrier will review a proposed treatment that is expected to cost in excess of a certain dollar value for "necessity and appropriateness."[42] This review attempts to eliminate misunderstandings among the patient, the dentist, and the insurance firm before work is performed. Second, under the Alternative Course of Treatment (ACT) program, dental consultants on the insurer's staff suggest alternatives to the work plan of the patient's dentist, if necessary.

Under a United Automobile Workers' contract, one of the largest prepaid dental contracts in the United States, Aetna Life and Casualty,

---

[38] See American Dental Association, *Prepaid Dental Care* (Chicago: n.d.), p. 1.

[39] The American Dental Association's projection for 1985 is 95 million enrollees. See American Dental Association, Council on Dental Care Programs, *Fact Sheet: Dental Insurance* (February 1980). The Health Insurance Association of America reports that in 1977, the latest year for which data were available, 178 million people had some form of health insurance. See *Source Book of Health Insurance Data, 1978–79* (Washington, D.C.: Health Insurance Institute, n.d.), table 1–1, p. 9.

[40] Unified opposition among dentists to third-party behavior has sometimes arisen. See "Texas Dentists' Group Conspired to Impede Cost-Cutting Measures by Insurers, FTC Complaint Says," *F.T.C. News Summary,* June 22, 1980, p. 2.

[41] For a complete history and organization of the pretreatment review program, see S. T. Reisine and H. L. Bailit, "History and Organization of Pretreatment Review, a Dental Utilization Review System," *Public Health Reports* (May–June 1980), pp. 282–90.

[42] See Executive Office of the President, Council on Wage and Price Stability, *The Complex Puzzle of Rising Health Care Costs: Can the Private Sector Fit It Together?* December 1976, p. 116.

for example, questions not only whether various procedures are covered but also questions ". . . claims where the charges are for services and supplies which appear not to be necessary for treatment, or where the charges appear to be above the prevailing charge level."[43] In addition, Aetna's investigation of questionable claims might utilize investigatory procedures such as:

- discussion with the attending dentist
- examination of dental X-rays, study models, etc.
- case review by Aetna's dental consultant when professional judgment is required
- oral examination of the patient by Aetna's dental consultant
- referral to the local Dental Society Review Committee[44]

In a study of three dental service plans, three Blue Shield plans, and three commercial carriers, Nash, Garfinkel, and Bryan found that the Delta plans and Blue Shield plans and two of the commercial carriers requested some type of pretreatment review.[45] For each of these eight carriers, automatic pretreatment review is specified for certain dental procedures such as gold or bridgework.[46] It is interesting to note that in the first stage of pretreatment review, one Blue Shield plan is willing to employ "unlicensed, foreign-trained dentists as pretreatment review clerks while another Blue Shield plan provides on-the-job training (OJT) by a part-time dental consultant."[47]

In their description of the workings of one Blue Shield plan, Nash and colleagues illustrate the carrier's relationship with dentists.

> The consulting dentist reviews all claims submitted to him based on a submitted treatment plan, X-rays, and/or accompanying explanations and information. In many cases, claims are submitted to a dental consultant for review when only a subset of all procedures on an entire claim form is questionable. In any case the dental consultant provides a recommendation regarding the extent of coverage under the contract and examines fees for excessiveness. The extent to which a given claim will be reviewed by a consultant depends upon the particular claim in question. There appears to be no predetermined

---

[43] *Summary of United Auto Workers Dental Benefits, Claim Cost Control* (Detroit: n.d.), item 3.

[44] Ibid.

[45] The identity of the plans was not disclosed in the study. See Kent D. Nash, Steven A. Garfinkel, and Fred A. Bryan, *Identify and Describe the Quality Assurance Methodologies Employed by Selected Third Party Carriers of Prepaid Dental Plans, Final Report*, vol. 1 (November 1975), p. 26.

[46] Ibid., p. 36.

[47] Ibid., pp. 36–37.

set of instructions to guide the dental consultant in his review. Differing aspects of a claim may be noted and reviewed by the dental consultant. Even though an examiner may refer a claim for dental consultant review, based on a question about a given procedure, the dental consultant may review the claim in greater detail covering other prodecures on the claim, the recommended treatment plan in the case of predetermination of benefits, the assessment of alternative treatment possibilities and other questions relating to the particular claim. He may identify other problems (through the examination of X-rays) not related to the problems raised by the examiner or other problems that are related to the reason for referral but not indicated on the claims form.[48]

Their description appears to be consistent with a recent brochure of Blue Shield of Maryland, Inc., which states, "When there are optimal techniques of treating a condition (that is, varying techniques, substances and appliances) carrying different fees, payment shall not exceed the lesser fee, unless the treatment carrying the greater fee is the only adequate treatment as determined under Maryland Dental Plan."[49]

In addition to pretreatment review, substantial copayments and deductibles appear to be used by the carriers. In a recent survey of third-party behavior, 73.2 percent of the commercial programs used copayments, deductibles, annual maximums, and employee contributions. Blue Cross and Blue Shield used three cost-sharing mechanisms in 48 percent of their programs, while Delta used a combination of three and four of the mechanisms in 33 percent and 38 percent of their programs, respectively.[50]

What has been the effect of third-party activity on dental fees and services? Without a great deal of evidence it is difficult to determine the precise influence of active third parties, since other factors such as changes in technology, changes in the age distribution of the population, and the presence of insurance itself are not held constant. A few glimpses are possible, however. Despite an increasing proportion of dental expenditures paid by third parties (see table 1), the consumer price index

---

[48] Ibid., p. 54.

[49] Blue Shield Dental Department, "Basic Service, Levels I and II," brochure, June 1979, p. 2.

[50] Israel L. Praiss et al., "Changing Patterns and Implication for Cost and Quality of Dental Care," *Inquiry* (Summer 1979), p. 135. For a further review of cost containment mechanisms in dentistry, see Israel L. Praiss, Kenneth A. Tannenbaum, and Cheryl A. Gelder-Kogan, "Quality of Dental Care—The Role of Third Party Payers: A Literature Review," *Medical Care Review* (December 1978), pp. 1211–33.

TABLE 1

OUT-OF-POCKET AND THIRD-PARTY PAYMENTS FOR DENTISTS'
SERVICES, 1965–1977
(millions of dollars)

Year	Out-of-Pocket Expenditures	Third-Party Public Expenditures	Third-Party Private Expenditures (benefits incurred)	Total Expenditures	Third-Party Expenditures (as percent of total)
1965	2,716.8	48.5	N.A.	—	—
1966	2,824.0	83.7	N.A.	—	—
1967	3,118.8	161.6	N.A.	—	—
1968	3,325.5	240.7	99.1	3,665.3	9.3
1969	3,809.5	233.1	140.8	4,183.4	8.9
1970	4,286.4	223.1	217.0	4,726.5	9.3
1971	4,502.9	265.1	268.6	5,036.6	10.6
1972	4,945.0	298.6	343.7	5,587.3	11.5
1973	5,640.7	330.0	437.6	6,408.3	12.0
1974	6,074.7	378.8	623.0	7,076.5	14.2
1975	6,412.3	467.1	1,100.8	7,980.2	19.6
1976	7,046.6	481.8	1,960.4	9,488.8	25.7
1977	7,745.1	492.9	2,371.6	10,609.6	27.0

NOTE: N.A. indicates not available.
SOURCE: Marjorie Smith Carroll and Ross H. Arnett III (unpublished data), Health Care
Financing Administration, Department of Health and Human Services.

for "dentists' fees" increased from 92.2 in 1965 to 185.1 in 1977.[51] This
increase compares favorably with the consumer price index for "physicians' fees," which increased from 88.3 in 1965 to 206.0 in 1977 (although the portion of the physician expenditures paid by third parties
also increased during this same time period[52]) and the "all item" consumer price index, which increased from 94.5 to 181.5 in 1977.[53] Never-

[51] See U.S. Department of Labor, Bureau of Labor Statistics, "Consumer Price Index for
Urban Wage Earners and Clerical Workers," U.S. City Average, Dentists' Fees (Mimeographed, n.d.).

[52] Third-party payments as a percentage of total expenditures for physicians' services
increased from 38.7 percent to 65.1 percent between 1965 and 1977. See Robert M.
Gibson, "National Health Expenditures, 1979," Health Care Financing Review (Summer
1980), table 6, p. 32; and Robert M. Gibson, "National Health Expenditures, 1978,"
Health Care Financing Review (Summer 1979), table 5, p. 27.

[53] U.S. Department of Labor, "Physicians' Fees," and "All Items—Series A" (n.d.).

theless, the number of services performed increased as per capita expenditures for dentists' services rose nearly fourfold from $14.20 in 1965 to $52.69 in 1977.[54] During this same period per capita expenditures on physicians' services increased from $42.86 to $141.29.[55]

Further analysis might examine, on a case study basis, the *potential* increase in procedures and fees that were curtailed by active third-party behavior. Thus far, only Pennsylvania Blue Shield has reported preliminary evidence. In 1970, Pennsylvania Blue Shield reviewed and visited 152 dental offices specializing in oral surgical services. Of these, 101 reported services "which ranged from honest mistakes and differences of opinion to possible fraud."[56]

Possible Explanations for Differences in Activity between Medical and Dental Insurers

Intrinsic differences between medicine and dentistry account for some of the differences in behavior between medical and dental insurers. Greater uncertainty of outcome, greater risk of certain procedures, and more emergency or quasi-emergency treatments may force health insurers to behave differently in degree from dental insurers. Certain aspects of medicine and dentistry are similar, however, such as state licensing, emphasis on autonomy and self-policing of the professions, specialized areas of professional care, technical expertise, and professional emphasis on best possible care without regard to price.

This chapter contends, nevertheless, that the substantial competition existing among the Dental Service Corporation (Delta), Blue Cross, Blue Shield, and the commercial carriers may explain some of the differences in behavior between medical and dental insurers. Unlike Blue Shield, Delta—which was begun by state dental societies[57]—must compete with the nonprofit Blue Cross and Blue Shield plans that may have transactions economies because of their health and medical insurance

---

[54] Department of Health and Human Services, Health Care Financing Administration, *Health Care Financing Review* (Summer 1979), pp. 23–24.

[55] Ibid.

[56] Donald S. Mayes, D.D.S., "Blue Shield's Quality Assurance Program," *Journal of Public Health Dentistry* (Fall 1974), p.215. It is unknown if the results of Blue Shield's program were typical. Dr. Mayes writes, "I think that this percentage does not represent the total number of dentists who will intentionally misreport services. It does show, however, the extent of abuse or overcharging that may occur in a program where the provider feels that no one is likely to check what he is reporting. I should point out that the records reviewed were for services performed during a period when no one expected Blue Shield to see if the service reported actually had been performed," p. 215.

[57] "The Delta Dental Plan," *Delta and the Dentist*, p. 3.

TABLE 2

TOTAL BENEFITS INCURRED AND MARKET SHARES OF DENTAL
THIRD-PARTY PAYERS, 1968–1977

Year	Total Benefits Incurred (millions of dollars)	Market Shares of Dental Third-Party Payers (percent)				
		Delta	Commercial carriers	Blue Cross	Blue Shield	Independents[a]
1968	99.1	24.7	59.5	3.5	2.6	9.6
1969	140.8	26.2	58.9	0.6	1.1	13.1
1970	217.0	18.4	67.7	0.8	0.9	12.0
1971	268.6	15.3	70.7	2.2	1.2	10.6
1972	343.7	24.1	60.3	2.4	1.5	11.8
1973	437.6	24.2	57.1	3.1	2.2	13.4
1974	623.0	20.6	57.5	5.1	3.5	13.3
1975	1,100.8	14.4	61:6	5.4	6.5	12.1
1976	1,960.4	9.7	69.5	4.0	5.0	11.8
1977	2,371.6	9.6	64.6	4.1	5.9	15.8

NOTE: Public programs are excluded. Percentages may not add to 100 because of rounding.
[a] "Independents" consist of prepaid and self-insured health plans.
SOURCE: Marjorie Smith Carroll and Ross H. Arnett III (unpublished data), Health Care Financing Administration, Department of Health and Human Services.

options. Also, Delta does not receive any subsidies from discounts on hospital charges that Blue Shield may potentially receive from Blue Cross in medical care. Finally, it should be noted that Delta dental plans do not appear to have the same well-known trademarks of Blue Cross and Blue Shield.

Some evidence indicates that there may be competition in the dental insurance market. Between 1968 and 1977 (1977 is the latest year for which data are available), Delta's market share declined from 24.7 percent to 9.6 percent in terms of benefits incurred and from 23.1 percent to 11.7 percent in terms of gross enrollment (see tables 2 and 3). In addition, Delta's market share has shown considerable variation in this period, which may also indicate a certain degree of competition among insurers.

In contrast to the dental insurance market, Blue Shield is a monopoly in nonprofit medical insurance having all of the attendant, potential advantages. These advantages may explain the relative size of Blue Shield's market share, which has increased from 34 to 36 percent between 1968 and 1977 (table 4). Furthermore, the Blue Shield market

TABLE 3

Total Gross Enrollment and Market Shares of Dental Third-Party Payers, 1968–1977

Year	Total Gross Enrollment (thousands of enrollees)	Market Shares of Dental Third-Party Payers (percent)			
		Delta	Commercial carriers	Blue Cross Blue Shield[a]	Independents[b]
1968	5,435	23.1	57.5	0.6	18.8
1969	7,764	17.4	62.0	1.8	18.8
1970	10,796	20.3	61.9	2.5	15.2
1971	13,293	17.8	59.5	8.3	14.4
1972	16,915	17.7	53.7	6.6	22.1
1973	20,499	18.2	55.3	8.5	18.1
1974	27,941	14.9	60.3	13.6	11.2
1975	30,332	15.4	62.7	10.9	10.9
1976	41,659	12.6	64.0	10.5	12.9
1977	50,300	11.7	64.0	10.5	13.7

NOTE: Gross enrollment includes enrollment where, for example, two partners in a single family have dental coverage. Public programs are excluded. Percentages may not add to 100 because of rounding.
[a] Data were not available for Blue Cross and Blue Shield separately.
[b] "Independents" consist of prepaid and self-insured health plans.
SOURCE: Marjorie Smith Carroll and Ross H. Arnett III (unpublished data), Health Care Financing Administration, Department of Health and Human Services.

share has remained remarkably stable during this interval.[58] Finally, it is interesting to note Blue Shield's market share in the dental insurance market. It reached its peak (on a benefits-incurred basis) in 1977, with 5.9 percent of dental insurance (table 2), which may be compared with Blue Shield's dominance in medical insurance. Absence of provider control as well as little or no cost advantages over the commercial insurers and Delta Dental may account for this reduced market share. In dentistry, for example, it is not clear that Blue Shield receives any subsidies from Blue Cross on discounts on hospital charges. Furthermore, Blue Shield's trademark advantages may not be transferred to dentistry.

Conclusions

This chapter has emphasized some differences in cost containment behavior between Blue Shield in dentistry and Blue Shield in medicine.

[58] Frech and Ginsburg initially made this point with regard to both Blue Shield and Blue Cross. See Frech and Ginsburg, "Competition among Health Insurers," pp. 167–87.

TABLE 4

BLUE SHIELD AND TOTAL PRIVATE THIRD-PARTY BENEFIT EXPENDITURES FOR PHYSICIANS' SERVICES, 1968–1977

Year	Blue Shield Benefit Expenditures ($ millions)	Total Private Third-Party Benefit Expenditures ($ millions)	Blue Shield Benefit Expenditures as a % of Total Private Third-Party Benefit Expenditures
1968	1,185.6	3,477	34.1
1069	1,458.7	4,029	36.2
1970	1,840.8	4,908	37.5
1971	2,026.0	5,430	37.3
1972	2,215.5	6,068	36.5
1973	2,498.7	6,824	36.6
1974	2,981.8	8,100	36.8
1975	3,553.3	9,639	36.9
1976	3,824.1	11,066	34.6
1977	4,383.3	12,124	36.2

SOURCES: For years 1968–1971, Marjorie Smith Carroll, "Private Health Insurance," *Social Security Bulletin;* for years 1972–1977, Marjorie Smith Carroll and Ross H. Arnett III (unpublished data), Health Care Financing Administration, Department of Health and Human Services.

Aside from the intrinsic differences between dentistry and medicine, it has been suggested that the cost advantages of the provider-influenced Blue Shield plans in medicine may account for relatively greater Blue Shild cost containment activity in dentistry relative to medicine. In dentistry, Blue Shield is not provider influenced and must compete with Delta Dental Plan, with similar cost advantages, as well as with the commercial insurers. Apparently the mere existence of provider-influenced Blue Shield without cost advantages would not be sufficient to exert anticompetitive influences in the long run, since employers have the option of offering competing plans to their employees. The declining market share of the provider-influenced Delta Dental Plan in dentistry appears to lend support to this argument.

A more general theme is expressed here, however. Previous economic literature found that the presence of health insurance (any kind or form of health insurance) exerts upward pressures on the prices of health care.[59] Although insurance undoubtedly can and does have this

[59] Martin S. Feldstein has done much of the valuable work in this area. See "The Welfare Loss of Excess Health Insurance," *Journal of Political Economy* (March/April 1973), pp. 251–80, and *The Rising Cost of Hospital Care* (Washington, D.C.: Information Resources Press, 1971).

effect, this chapter has attempted to show that it may be an error to treat all insurers alike, and that insurers in some markets may, at least, act to dampen cost increases.[60] Imperfections in competition among insurers can impede this process and can raise prices to consumers. It should be emphasized that the complexities of medicine are such that even with substantial competition among insurers, cost containment will continue to be a public policy issue.[61]

As usual, a good deal of research remains to be done. First, rather than emphasize research on the configurations of provider influence on Blue Shield boards, we ought to examine closely some advantages that Blue Shield may enjoy. Second, additional research should be conducted on the differences in third-party performance between medicine and dentistry as well as on differences between medicine and dentistry in general. If public policy is to consider seriously the implications of third-party competition in health care, it would be well to eliminate any impediments to that type of competition.

[60] This appears to be consistent with other recent literature and options for public policy. See Goldberg and Greenberg, "The Effect of Physician-Controlled Health Insurance," pp. 48–78. See also Alain C. Enthoven, "Consumer-Choice Health Plan," *The New England Journal of Medicine* (March 23 and March 30, 1978), pp. 650–58 and 709–20.

[61] See Warren Greenberg, "A Perspective on Market Initiatives in Health Care" (manuscript in preparation).

Enforcing the Rules of Free Enterprise in an Imperfect Market: The Case of Individual Practice Associations

Clark C. Havighurst and Glenn M. Hackbarth

The advocates of a market-oriented national health policy have been gratified by the spate of "procompetitive" health bills recently introduced in Congress. Not very long ago, after all, Washington regarded anyone who saw work for the free market's invisible hand in the health care marketplace as an offbeat ideologue out of step with the times. In the 96th Congress, however, this conventional view of the market strategy and its adherents began to give way to deregulatory impulses, with the result that market reform now numbers among its sponsors some of the brightest, most astute members of Congress. Even dyed-in-the-wool regulators are acknowledging that the market advocates have seized the intellectual initiative.

Although the new bills embodying the market strategy have been useful in making the idea of competition credible, too great a fixation on the legislative package needed to implement that strategy can distract attention from what can and should be done right now, without new legislation, to rejuvenate the markets for health services and health insurance. This chapter examines a dimension of the market strategy that is not addressed in the market reform bills—namely, the antitrust enforcement effort. Our thesis is that giving full effect to the antitrust laws makes good sense, here and now, without regard to progress in implementing the grand design. We hope to show why it is not essential or desirable to wait for all the conditions that contribute to a working market to be satisfied before pushing ahead on the antitrust front.

In focusing attention away from new legislative measures on behalf

Work on this paper was supported by Grant No. HS01539 from the National Center for Health Services Research, Department of Health and Human Services. Although Professor Havighurst has served as a consultant to the Federal Trade Commission, the views expressed herein do not necessarily coincide with those of the commission or its staff.

of competition, we do not mean to indicate any doubt about the value of most of the steps proposed in the market reform bills. On the contrary, we believe that Congress would do well to require employers to offer their employees a multiple choice of health plans,[1] to change the tax treatment of employer contributions to such plans,[2] and to allow Medicare and Medicaid beneficiaries to enroll in competing health plans with public assistance.[3] These steps would encourage consumers to make economizing choices when they buy health care coverage—exactly what is needed to induce cost-containment efforts in the competitive private sector. Despite Congress's new receptivity to these procompetitive ideas, however, the nation may not yet be ready to undertake such far-reaching changes. Thus, it is useful to consider precisely what the new procompetitive thrust can mean in view of the current, less than satisfactory state of the market and private incentives.

If one assumes that the immediate prospects for incentive-altering legislation are not good—a fact we do not concede—serious questions can be raised about the wisdom of even tolerating competition, to say nothing of energetically enforcing the antitrust laws to increase its vigor. Many argue, for example, that if incentives are not right, competition actually drives the market away from optimal performance. And, indeed, to the extent that price and cost do not have to be weighed by consumers, competition in health services does focus to an inordinate degree on small increments of quality and on amenities and thus induces the provision and consumption of more, and more costly, care than consumers would normally choose. Although this argument against permitting competition under current incentives has some validity, it is an even more powerful argument in favor of enacting incentive-oriented market reform legislation. Frankly, we find it unacceptable to argue that enforcement of the antitrust laws (which are themselves an expression of congressional will) should be withheld or distorted in order to avoid the natural outcome of competition under prevailing incentives. Because Congress can readily alter those incentives, any decision not to do so should, we think, be deemed a legislative acceptance of the equilibrium produced by competition under them. Of course, Congress may choose to impose regulation to alter that equilibrium, perhaps by curbing non-price competition as has been done in the health planning legislation. But we would reject the argument that the executive and judicial branches of government should be given free reign to attenuate competition beyond the extent expressly provided for by Congress.

---

[1] See, for example, H.R. 5740, S. 1485, and S. 1590, 96th Congress, 1st session (1979).

[2] Ibid.

[3] See, for example, H.R. 4000 and S. 1530, 96th Congress, 1st session (1979).

The philosophical disposition to leave fundamental policy choices to Congress underlies this entire chapter. Since health policy debates are rarely won with grand(iose) assertions of principle, however, we will attempt to flesh out our philosophical position with more specific and pragmatic legal and policy arguments for strictly enforcing the antitrust laws against collusive market practices in this industry. In particular, we will examine the argument that "cost containment," of whatever kind, is so important that the antitrust laws should not be enforced against concerted actions of health care providers that may in the short run actually reduce health care costs. As it turns out, such arguments against giving the antitrust laws their due effect are subject to challenge not only on the foregoing philosophical ground but also on firm legal grounds. Perhaps most important, they are vulnerable on their own pragmatic ground as well.

The Antitrust Threat to Industry Good Works

The antitrust laws threaten to penalize certain collective actions of competing providers of health services that, on their face at least, are having a beneficial effect from the standpoint of the public at large. The so-called Voluntary Effort (VE), through which physicians and hospitals have worked together to contain hospital costs, is one example; although the antitrust status of the VE has not been challenged, the Justice Department refused to give a favorable opinion of it,[4] and its operation has undoubtedly been inhibited by the need to obey antitrust rules. Another example is "peer-review" programs sponsored by the medical profession that monitor spending and the quality of care; although professional standards review organizations (PSROs) performing these functions for the Medicare and Medicaid programs need not fear antitrust liability unless they abuse their power,[5] PSROs or other profession-sponsored peer-review mechanisms (including foundations for medical care, discussed below) run serious risks when they set out to check excessive fees and utilization under *private* financing programs.[6] Agreements among competing hospitals to cut back arguably unneeded services are a third example of purportedly constructive competitor collab-

[4] "Justice Declines to Take Antitrust Position on Hospital Cost Containment," *Antitrust and Trade Regulation Report* (June 22, 1978), p. A–17.
[5] Silver v. New York Stock Exchange, 373 U.S. 341 (1963), the leading precedent on the scope of antitrust liability for a statutory self-regulatory agency, would seem to impose on PSROs certain procedural requirements designed to assure fairness to private parties, such as HMOs. *Silver* also suggests a "breathing space" for self-regulation so that not every mistake by a PSRO would result in an antitrust judgment. But see 373 U.S. at 360.
[6] See this chapter's discussion of peer review in the section "Assessing Competitive Effects."

oration that has aroused the interest of antitrust enforcers; the Justice Department recently declined to promise tolerance of such multihospital arrangements, even those brokered by a local health systems agency charged by law with reducing duplication.[7]

This chapter will focus on yet another industry-initiated reform that has encountered an antitrust challenge despite its possible benefits: "individual practice associations" (IPAs), which are local physician organizations that contract directly or indirectly with consumers to provide services in return for a fixed monthly premium. IPAs are thus a species of health maintenance organization (HMO), and they are recognized as such in the federal Health Maintenance Organization Act of 1973, as amended. Although IPAs can be organized by anyone, we will focus on IPAs created by local medical societies. Such IPAs are quite similar to "foundations for medical care" (FMCs). Although FMCs differ from IPAs in not putting the participating physicians at financial risk, they too provide peer review of fees and utilization and thus allow local professionals to offer an alternative type of health care coverage, the costs of which are managed by the FMC and are underwritten by health insurers. IPAs also closely resemble the Pacific Northwest's "medical service bureaus," county-level, profession-sponsored plans similar to Blue Shield plans. In short, IPAs, FMCs, and service bureaus permit local representatives of organized medicine to bind community physicians together in a single economic unit and thus to control health care costs—both unnecessary utilization and fee escalation. (Our references hereinafter to IPAs will ordinarily encompass FMCs and service bureaus.)

Both within and without the medical profession, IPAs and FMCs have generally been viewed as significant and desirable reforms. The widespread belief in the fitness and propriety of these collective endeavors stems from public acceptance of the medical profession as an arbiter of the public interest and a legitimate guardian of the quality of care against alleged threats associated with "commercialism." The antitrust laws also enjoy a reasonable measure of public support, however, and thus a confrontation between antitrust principles and well-meaning professional responses to the problem of rising health care costs would pit two of society's semisacred cows against each other. Although application of the antitrust laws to the health care industry has caused only mild controversy to date, the law is only beginning to be invoked formally in areas where the motives of the challenged professional groups are not obviously open to question. The stage is thus set for enforcement

---

[7] "The Hospital Industry's New Vulnerability to Antitrust," *Regulation*, vol. 4 (September/October 1980), pp. 12–13.

agencies and courts to consider whether the antitrust laws do, or should, bar professional actions that are generally consistent with a long tradition of deference to the organized professions and that appear to have demonstrable short-term benefits.

This chapter is largely a discussion of the Federal Trade Commission's prospective antitrust challenge to the medical profession's control of certain Blue Shield plans and IPAs. The discussion first seeks to demonstrate that the antitrust laws, as they have been interpreted, do not permit the courts even to consider the essentially legislative question of whether competition is or is not desirable in particular market circumstances. The final section of this chapter then considers whether the enforcement agencies can or should exercise their prosecutorial discretion to look the other way when confronted with an anticompetitive (and illegal) practice that has some possible short-term benefits. Here the problem is, in part, to assess correctly the actual, long-run benefits and harms of the practice in question—that is, to look beyond their face value. Attention is also given to the problems of smoothing the transition to competition, of convincing others to assume decision-making responsibilities that the medical profession has long arrogated, and of changing the market's overall tone to encourage innovation and challenges to professional authority.

The Antitrust Laws and Profession-Controlled IPAs

In an April 1979 report entitled *Medical Participation in Control of Blue Shield and Certain Other Open-Panel Medical Prepayment Plans,* the Federal Trade Commission's (FTC) Bureau of Competition recommended to the commission that it propose a trade-regulation rule divesting organized medicine of control over various health care financing plans.[8] The main focus of that report was the profession's domination of Blue Shield plans, but the staff also wrote a chapter dealing with the profession's control of financing plans of other kinds, including IPAs.[9] The staff could see no material respect in which IPAs and other controlled plans were different from Blue Shield plans and raised the possibility that most of its legal conclusions with respect to Blue Shield might apply equally to IPAs. The FTC has yet to act definitively on the staff's recommendations, but there is no question that they are being taken seriously.

---

[8] Federal Trade Commission, Bureau of Competition, *Staff Report on Medical Participation in Control of Blue Shield and Certain Other Open-Panel Medical Prepayment Plans,* April 1979, pp. 308–72.

[9] Ibid., pp. 283–307.

In November 1979, the Bureau of Economics of the FTC issued another report on the same general subject. Entitled *Physician Control of Blue Shield Plans,* this economic analysis purported to discover some price-raising effects associated with the medical profession's domination of Blue Shield.[10] Although this finding of harmful impact has been widely regarded as an essential item of proof needed to support the Bureau of Competition's legal theory, we shall argue that the legal questions do not turn on the validity of this economic study's conclusions. This is a crucially important point because if the legality of profession-controlled financing plans did depend on a showing that those plans raised physician fees, the Bureau of Competition probably could not make a case against the many IPAs that have had an apparent restraining effect on fee escalation and on the utilization of medical services. Our discussion should help to isolate the true legal issues and should show why concerns about actual price and cost impacts are not the proper business of the courts and are best left to legislative, or possibly prosecutorial, discretion. We have elected to concentrate on the IPA issue because it nicely poises the competing values that we wish to consider.

The Law: Competition Required, for Better or for Worse. Antitrust law does not permit the possible benefits of an anticompetitive practice to be weighed against the harm to competition. Perhaps the clearest statement of that principle appeared in the 1978 case of *National Society of Professional Engineers* v. *United States.*[11] In that case, the engineers claimed that their ethical prohibition against competitive bidding did not violate the antitrust laws because the limitation on competition was socially advantageous. Competitive bidding for engineering contracts would result, they argued, in poor engineering work and in threats to public safety. The Supreme Court made it clear, however, that such arguments are not cognizable in view of Congress's decision, embodied in the antitrust laws, that competition should not be impaired by private agreements.[12] In short, the Court held that Congress alone may carve out exceptions to the antitrust laws, a ruling that seems clearly right, since one could hardly wish to have federal judges making the essentially legislative choice of whether competition would or would not be a good thing in a given industry setting.

In *Professional Engineers,* the Court was reiterating a long-standing, but sometimes ignored, principle. Perhaps the most eloquent state-

---

[10] Federal Trade Commission, Bureau of Economics, *Staff Report on Physician Control of Blue Shield Plans,* November 1979, p. 58.

[11] 435 U.S. 679 (1978).

[12] 435 U.S. at 689–90, 692–96.

ment of that principle appeared in an 1899 opinion by then Circuit Judge (later Chief Justice) William Howard Taft. Judge Taft criticized judges who "have set sail on a sea of doubt, and have assumed the power to say . . . how much restraint of competition is in the public interest, and how much is not."[13] In such cases, he said, "there is no measure of what is necessary . . . except the vague and varying opinion of judges as to how much, on principles of political economy, men ought to be allowed to restrain competition."[14] Unfortunately, however, courts have not always heeded Judge Taft's warning. Thus, some courts have interpreted antitrust law's "rule of reason" to permit judgments about whether a restraint was more beneficial than harmful. In these decisions, which must now be viewed as aberrational, the restraint's effect on competition was but one consideration; other "social values" were also considered.[15] Although courts will probably continue to misapply the rule of reason in occasional future cases, the only issue that *should* concern them in applying that rule is whether competitor collaboration has in fact impaired competition.

The *Professional Engineers* decision restores clarity to the law by reestablishing that the law requires competition, for better or for worse, leaving to Congress the creation of exceptions to this rule. On the other hand, competitor collaboration will be permitted if it does not impair competition in the larger marketplace,[16] an exception that Judge Taft defined by identifying certain restraints as being merely "ancillary"[17] and thus distinguishable from what have since been called "naked" restraints. Ancillary restraints are lawful because, even though they may eliminate competition among the agreeing parties, they are incidental to carrying out a legitimate and overriding business purpose the achievement of which does not reduce the market's overall competitive vigor. In the new formulation of Judge Taft's rule set out in *Professional Engineers,* the test is whether the competitor collaboration *promotes* competition. This test would usually be satisfied if the result of the collaboration was to produce a new service or a new competitive entrant in the larger market. Competitors can also legally join together to generate and disseminate information; even though information may disadvantage some competitors, its availability promotes competition as

---

[13] United States v. Addyston Pipe & Steel Co., 85 Fed. 271, 284 (6th Cir. 1898).

[14] 85 Fed. at 283.

[15] For example, Chicago Board of Trade v. United States, 246 U.S. 231 (1918); see also Robert H. Bork, *The Antitrust Paradox* (New York: Basic Books, 1978), pp. 21–47.

[16] National Society of Professional Engineers v. United States, 435 U.S. 679, 691, 696 (1978).

[17] United States v. Addyston Pipe & Steel Co., 85 Fed. 271, 280–83 (6th Cir. 1898).

long as decisions concerning its value and use are made by others in a decentralized market in which consumer preferences are effectively registered.[18]

These formulations are helpful in analyzing the legal status of IPAs. Clearly, a limited number of physicians who in combination do not wield market power would be free to participate in a joint venture to offer their services to consumers. On the other hand, if the joint venture involved all or nearly all physicians in the community, we believe (for reasons discussed later) that the effect would not be to "promote" competition in the larger market. Instead, competition would likely be suppressed by bringing all competitors under the same marketing scheme.

The FTC staff's view of IPAs is basically in keeping with this formulation of the issues. The Bureau of Competition charges that Blue Shield and other prepayment plans controlled by physician organizations entail agreements among competing physicians to "fix prices" and to engage in "boycotts" of competitors, two types of joint action that are normally regarded as per se violations of the law—that is, practices that have been judged under the rule of reason to be so dangerously anticompetitive that no further inquiry into their effect on competition in specific cases is necessary. Aside from the boycott characterization, which we think is inaccurate,[19] we believe that the staff has formulated the issues in a helpful and constructive way. The ensuing discussion will attempt, however, to put the matter in a somewhat broader substantive and procedural perspective, while focusing strongly on the law's exclusive concern with the effect of IPAs on competition.

The Appropriateness of the Rule-making Process. Although the Bureau of Competition focused its attention on two specific incidents of the control of Blue Shield and other prepayment plans by physician orga-

---

[18] Certification of medical specialists by physician groups is an example of acceptable competitor collaboration that generates information for the consumer. Nevertheless, specialty boards must deal fairly with their members and aspirants for certification, and they may not use their position coercively (for example, to organize boycotts). Clark Havighurst, "Professional Restraints on Innovation in Health Care Financing," *Duke Law Journal,* vol. 1978 (May), p. 366.

[19] In our view, the per se rule against boycotts was meant to apply only to concerted refusals (plural) to deal by competitors and thus is not applicable to a refusal (singular) to deal by a single entity, even one controlled by a combination of competitors. Although a recent leading case appeared to attach the boycott label to a profession-controlled plan's refusal to deal with certain health care providers, the court did not treat the refusal to deal as a per se violation. Virginia Academy of Clinical Psychologists v. Blue Shield of Virginia, Docket No. 79–1345 (4th Cir., decided June 16, 1980). Instead the court held the plan's refusal to deal unlawful only after finding that the medical profession's plan was "a dominant source" of health insurance coverage in Virginia. In our view, the court's analysis and result were sound even though it misapplied the boycott label.

nizations, the real concerns in the proceeding transcend the technical issues thus raised. Neither the price-fixing theory nor the boycott theory advanced by the staff in their legal analysis captures or conveys the full import of the conflict-of-interests problem that exists when providers control the prepayment mechanism by which they are paid for rendering specific services. At each step in the design of benefits, assessment of premiums, enlistment of providers, adoption of payment policies, and administration of claims, a plan under the medical profession's influence faces choices that affect the profession's economic interests. Thus, such an arrangement may well conflict with the antitrust premise that competitors acting in concert should not be permitted to shape the economic environment in which they do business. The challenged arrangements therefore appear to raise issues that go to the heart of antitrust law's concern for maintaining competitive conditions in the face of concerted actions by competitors collaborating in powerful groups.

Although the "price fixing" label attached by the FTC staff is an oversimplification, it is an appropriate starting place for the necessary analysis. Because professional control of a prepayment plan necessarily implies some influence over the prices paid for professional services and the form and conditions of payment, the proposed rule making can be viewed as determining whether the well-founded and salutary rule against competitors' tampering with prices should be extended to these facts. This should not be a mechanistic inquiry or labeling effort but a sincere attempt to appraise the conduct in question in the light of antitrust policy and experience. So long as that analysis is properly conducted, it is of no great consequence whether the commission ends up attaching the price-fixing label, with the result that a per se violation is established, or writing a new per se rule in the light of a new assessment of power, purpose, and effect under the rule of reason. Either way, a violation would not exist unless the commission found that the prohibited conduct imposed a restraint on competition that henceforth might be conclusively deemed inherently unreasonable.

It may be that there are enough differences between the "price fixing" implicit in a professional organization's control of a prepayment plan and the forms that have already been held to be per se violations that any rule developed by the FTC would be seen as an extension of the existing precedents. In particular, the commission must reckon with the argument that whatever price agreement physician control might entail is "ancillary" to a procompetitive joint venture—that is, the establishment of a service-benefit prepayment plan. Two recent decisions, *Broadcast Music, Inc.* v. *Columbia Broadcasting System, Inc.*,[20] and

[20] 441 U.S. 1 (1979).

Arizona v. *Maricopa County Medical Society*,[21] suggest that the courts are receptive to this line of argument and are thus reluctant to extend per se rules to business arrangements that can plausibly claim to be procompetitive. As the Supreme Court said in *Broadcast Music,* "It is only after considerable experience with business relationships that courts classify them as per se violations. . . ."[22] Moreover, the *Professional Engineers* opinion observed that "by their nature, professional services may differ significantly from other business services, and, accordingly, the nature of the competition in such services may vary."[23] This latter consideration, which may be read to imply the need for at least a "truncated" rule of reason inquiry[24] where professional services paid for by third parties are involved, apparently weighed heavily in the court's refusal to apply a per se rule in the *Maricopa County* case, where an FMC comprising more than 80 percent of the local doctors was setting maximum fees.

Although lawyerlike caution is warranted when deciding whether to extend per se rules to conduct that differs from conduct previously held unlawful, there should be no doubt that once a sufficient inquiry has been made, new per se rules can be established either by extension of or by analogy to established rules. Since per se rules in antitrust are merely rules of precedent that reflect earlier applications of the rule of reason, they can be extended by a rule-of-reason analysis. The extent of the required analysis will, of course, vary according to the degree of similarity between the new restraint and those held previously to be per se violations. If the new restraint is quite different, an extensive analysis of its competitive effect is required. If, on the other hand, the analogy to an existing per se violation is strong, the competitive analysis can be done without extensive new hearings.

---

[21] 1980–1 Trade Cases (CCH) ¶ 63,239 (9th Cir. 1980).

[22] Broadcast Music, Inc. v. Columbia Broadcasting System, Inc., 441 U.S. 1, 9 (1979), *quoting* United States v. Topco Associates, Inc., 405 U.S. 596, 607–8 (1972).

[23] National Society of Professional Engineers v. United States, 435 U.S. 679, 696 (1978).

[24] Several recent cases can be read to suggest that a "truncated" rule-of-reason analysis is to be undertaken when a restraint that is ordinarily per se illegal—for example, an agreement on price involving competing firms or individuals—can be plausibly argued to be ancillary to a legitimate, procompetitive business venture. In such cases, the dividing line between a per se approach and a classic rule-of-reason approach becomes less distinct. Although the courts should not hastily attach the per se label in these cases, the scrutiny required "must not merely subsume the burdensome analysis required under the rule of reason or else we would apply the rule of reason from the start." Broadcast Music, Inc. v. Columbia Broadcasting System, Inc., 441 U.S. 1, 19 n.33 (1979). For a discussion of the "truncated" rule-of-reason analysis, see Lawrence Sullivan and John Wiley, "Recent Antitrust Developments: Defining the Scope of Exemptions, Expanding Coverage, and Refining the Rule of Reason," *U.C.L.A. Law Review*, vol. 27 (December 1979), pp. 330–36 and 341–42.

A further point is that the FTC or a court faced with a similar legal issue should not worry unduly about making a per se rule that may inhibit some conduct that is in fact innocuous or even marginally pro-competitive. Per se rules in antitrust law are based in large measure on the *net* value of having clear rules and of avoiding costly and frequently inconclusive case-by-case inquiries into the power and purposes of the challenged parties and into the effect of their business arrangement.[25] Once it is concluded that the conduct in question substantially endangers competition and is of a type seldom likely to be procompetitive in practice, sound antitrust principles permit the establishment of a firm prohibition. On the other hand, a per se rule does not necessarily authorize all practices that it does not condemn. In the instant situation, for example, any relationship between physician organizations and prepayment plans that the FTC or a court might choose not to prohibit as a per se violation would remain open to case-by-case scrutiny to determine competitive effects.

The rule-making proceeding proposed by the FTC staff is perhaps best conceived as telescoping the case-by-case establishment of a new per se rule prohibiting control of prepayment plans by physician organizations. The commission is, after all, in an excellent position to accumulate, in one proceeding, "considerable experience with [these] business relationships" and thus to decide whether (and to what extent) they can be classified by an express rule as per se violations of the antitrust laws. By acting through a rule-making proceeding that examines a variety of profession-sponsored prepayment plans in many different markets, the commission could bring order, openness, expertise, and perspective to the development of the new rule that could not be duplicated through haphazard, case-by-case development. The proposed rule making should thus be viewed as an extension of, and improvement upon, antitrust law's time-honored adjudicative tradition.

With this conceptualization of the rule-making proceeding in mind, the Bureau of Competition's report can be read as asking the commission to initiate a proceeding that is likely to lead to the conclusion that, on the basis of reason, experience, and such evidence as is adduced, certain concerted activities of physicians are irredeemably anticompetitive and can be condemned without further specific inquiry into their purpose or effect. Admittedly, the bureau does not expressly adopt this characterization of the proceeding, and the organization of its report, in putting the per se argument first and then rejecting all arguments against it, may make the staff's analysis seem an unduly simplistic insistence on

---

[25] Northern Pacific Railway Co. v. United States, 356 U.S. 1 (1958).

the per se principle. Nevertheless, the report's examination of the ancillarity defense and its rule-of-reason analysis raise most of the relevant factual issues and address them in appropriate terms.

The Key Issues in the Proposed Rule Making. Having concluded that the proposed rule making would be an appropriate forum for analyzing the issues raised by the medical profession's control of prepayment plans, we will now discuss the key substantive issues in such a proceeding. Emphasis will be given to issues that have proved especially troublesome for the FTC staff and others.

The need to establish an effect on competition, not necessarily on prices. The object in a rule-of-reason inquiry is, as noted, to determine the effect of the alleged restraint on competition. Although proof of a price-increasing effect would indicate a violation, it is not the same thing, and an adverse effect on competition can be established in other ways. In this proceeding, the FTC must not be drawn into the trap of having the legality of a medical group's control of a prepayment plan turn on the establishment or direction of price effects (as happened to Judge Sneed in the *Maricopa County* case). The validity of the study by the Bureau of Economics and of other similar studies finding a statistical relationship between professional control of a prepayment plan and higher fees[26] is not the crucial issue in the FTC proceeding, although those studies, if found to be valid, would help to establish that competition was indeed impaired.

Even if physician-controlled Blue Shield plans could produce persuasive empirical analysis showing that physician control correlates with lower fees, such a correlation would not be decisive in their favor. Such studies merely compare prices among Blue Shield plans that are and are not controlled, and they ignore several possibilities. One possible explanation of any correlation between control and lower prices is that controlled plans invite stiffer regulation by insurance regulators. Another explanation might be that competition is inoperative, or restrained in other ways, in markets where the Blue Shield plan is not controlled by physicians. If, for example, boycotts of and collective bargaining with insurers were effectively employed by physicians in markets where their control of Blue Shield was attenuated, prices in those areas might also be above competitive levels. Empirical analysis of physician control

---

[26] Arnould and Eisenstadt have found that professional control of a Blue Shield plan is associated with significantly higher physician fees only when the state government grants the Blue Shield plan certain tax advantages—for example, an exemption from income, premium, and property taxes. Richard Arnould and David Eisenstadt, "The Effects of Provider-Controlled Blue Shield Plans: Regulatory Options," this volume.

would then be measuring only the relative efficacy of particular restraints, not the full effect of physician control of prepayment plans. In short, a market in which Blue Shield is independent of the medical profession is not necessarily a model of competition, and it is therefore of little value for comparative purposes.

The insight that the effect on competition, not prices, is the crucial issue will be particularly relevant in deciding whether to adopt a rule governing profession-sponsored IPAs. Although it now seems possible that some IPAs do reduce some physician fees and hospitalization,[27] a demonstration of these benefits does not establish that the profession's control of IPAs is consistent with competition. Before deferring to the appearance of altruism on the part of the profession, the FTC should recognize the possibility that any cost containment benefits apparently yielded by IPAs may simply represent limit-entry pricing by a cartel or an organized response to political pressures. Moreover, the greatest IPA savings may result from reduced hospitalization,[28] so that hospitals, more than the physicians themselves, are being pinched in the name of cost containment. To accept an IPA's arguable cost containment benefits without question would be tantamount to accepting a "reasonable price" defense for price fixing and the notion of a benign cartel.

Under antitrust law's rule of reason, the inquiry as to effect on prices is undertaken to determine whether collaborating competitors have the power to affect the market's performance, not to determine whether the effect achieved is desirable or undesirable[29]—Judge Sneed's unfortunate confusion in the *Maricopa County* case notwithstanding. It is thus important that the FTC's case against profession control of financing plans not be seen to turn on evidence of price effects. Other evidence is more likely to be probative of the requisite adverse effects on competition.

---

[27] See, for example, R. H. Egdahl, C. H. Taft, J. Friedland, and K. Linde, "The Potential of Organizations of Fee-for-Service Physicians for Achieving Significant Decreases in Hospitalization," *Annals of Surgery,* vol. 186 (September 1977), pp. 388–99; see also Harold Luft, "HMO's and Medical Costs: The Rhetoric and the Evidence," *New England Journal of Medicine,* vol. 298 (June 15, 1978), pp. 1336–43.

[28] In his review of the literature on the utilization patterns of HMOs, Luft found that IPA enrollees have 20 percent fewer hospital days than fee-for-service patients. Luft, "HMO's and Medical Costs," p. 1339. On the other hand, IPA patients have more ambulatory visits than either fee-for-service patients or enrollees in prepaid group practice HMOs. Ibid., p. 1338. Moreover, Luft concluded from his review of the literature that "there is no documented evidence that costs for enrollees in individual practice associations are lower than those for people with conventional insurance." Ibid., p. 1337. Overall, Luft's findings are consistent with (but certainly do not prove) the hypothesis that the primary effect of IPAs is to redistribute income away from hospitals and toward physicians.

[29] United States v. Addyston Pipe & Steel Co., 85 Fed. 271, 282–83 (6th Cir. 1898); United States v. Trans-Missouri Freight Assn., 166 U.S. 290, 340–42 (1897).

Assessing competitive effects. In examining effects on competition (as opposed to prices), the FTC must envision the forms that price competition could be expected to take in a market characterized by heavy insurance coverage. The essential ingredient of such competition must be the existence of vigorous arm's-length bargaining—including bargaining over utilization practices and administrative controls, as well as negotiation of fees—between competing health plans on the one hand and competing professionals on the other. The absence of competitive bargaining at the crucial interface between plans and professionals is the ultimate problem in this industry, and antitrust enforcement must focus on remedying this problem above all others.[30] Control by the profession of its own financing plan obviously eliminates arm's-length bargaining between individual physicians and the controlled plan. While this makes the profession's control vulnerable to antitrust attack, it should not be taken as conclusive evidence of a violation without further examination of its effect on competition in the larger market.

The medical profession argues that its control of a prepayment plan can make no difference if the controlled plan faces effective competition from other plans that are independent of professional control. Thus, the profession maintains that the antitrust agencies need not concern themselves with professional control if the larger marketplace is competitive. Although such an argument has never been accepted as a defense for truly anticompetitive acts, the point does direct attention to the appropriate level of inquiry—that is, whether profession-controlled plans may have adverse effects on competitition in the larger marketplace. Although most evidence on this score is impressionistic, there seems to be good reason to fear that a controlled plan might serve the medical profession as a "fighting ship," discouraging competition at the interface between physicians and independent plans in any or all of the following ways:

- by increasing doctors' solidarity and sense of interdependence and thus the risk of boycotts, explicit or tacit, against innovative insurers and others addressing consumers' cost concerns
- by threatening a potential competitor or innovator with temporary entry-discouraging or disciplinary price cutting, facilitated by the plan's ability to shift much of the burden to hospitals and to distribute the remaining losses equitably among the physicians whose long-term interests it is defending

[30] Clark Havighurst and Glenn Hackbarth, "Private Cost Containment," *New England Journal of Medicine,* vol. 300 (June 7, 1979), pp. 1298–1305; Havighurst, "Professional Restraints," pp. 303–87.

- by giving the profession a sanction to employ against its members who engage in competitive behavior[31]
- by setting self-enforcing norms of acceptable insurer and physician behavior
- by providing a vehicle for price signaling among physicians
- by keeping the processes of change under the profession's control
- by reinforcing the profession's perceived legitimacy as the dominant decision maker in the industry, thereby reducing the likelihood of competitive developments

While all of the foregoing hazards are speculative and difficult to document, they need not be proved definitively before they can appropriately influence a rule-of-reason analysis of a scheme that eliminates price competition among physicians and that is subject to condemnation under basic price-fixing principles unless some procompetitive benefit can be found. The hazards mentioned enter into the analysis only as considerations helpful in rejecting the arguments for distinguishing this kind of price fixing from more ordinary kinds. The rule-of-reason calculus allows speculative hazards based on a dynamic analysis to be weighed and to be used to offset claims that the challenged anticompetitive practices are either innocuous—not a defense in any case—or procompetitive in their net effect.[32] Certainly the alleged procompetitive benefits of the challenged arrangements are no less speculative than the enumerated anticompetitive hazards.

To appreciate fully how allowing the medical profession to control its own financing plan can affect the vigor of competition at the plan-physician interface in the market as a whole, the FTC should take into account the profession's pivotal role in erecting other barriers both to competition among physicians and to competition-stimulating innovation by prepayment plans. Although each particular restraint may seem innocuous when viewed alone, their interrelatedness and cumulative power are striking. Fortunately, the expertise acquired by the FTC from its other enforcement activities in this industry make it particularly well suited for judging how physician control fits into the broader picture. The courts would take substantial time and effort to develop comparable insight.

The following paragraphs sketch the various ways, besides direct control of financing mechanisms, in which physicians, through collective

[31] See, for example, Medical Service Corporation of Spokane County, 88 F.T.C. 906 (1976).
[32] Cf. Phillip Areeda, *Antitrust Analysis: Problems, Text, Cases* (Boston, Mass.: Little, Brown and Company, 1974), p. 348.

action, have kept competition in the market for health services from focusing on the crucial elements of price and output:

1. *Boycotts and related restraints.* Concerted refusals by physicians to deal with third parties have been employed from time to time as disciplinary weapons.[33] Concerted refusals to cooperate with third-party cost containment efforts are a related type of restraint.[34] That such classic boycotts violate the antitrust laws is firmly established.[35] Remedying these problems may be difficult, however, because effective restraints may sometimes be organized without explicit calls to collective action. Given doctors' strong sense of solidarity and interdependence, expressions of collective opinion may be enough.

2. *Collective bargaining.* Because of the sanctions that organized medicine can bring to bear, insurers often feel compelled to secure the medical society's blessing for any change they wish to introduce.[36] The society's "seal of approval" will be issued only after the profession's concerns are accommodated.[37] The argument that "getting doctors to cooperate" is a desirable feature of such negotiations is specious, since it implies the legitimacy of collective professional action. The logic of competition requires that doctors decide whether to cooperate on an individual basis and without advice from a professional organization.[38] That principle should apply even if the collective bargaining is initiated by an insurer. Obviously, distinctions must be drawn between collective negotiations and the provision of information and opinion without implicit threats of boycott or other sanction. Among the indicia of a bargaining or negotiating relationship would be the existence of negotiating committees, actual agreements, actual or implied threats, inflammatory publicity concerning disputes, and official endorsement or disapproval. It will be particularly difficult to decide what significance to attach to

---

[33] See, for example, Michigan State Medical Society, Docket No. 9129 (FTC, filed July 27, 1979); see also Lawrence Goldberg and Warren Greenberg, "The Effect of Physician-Controlled Health Insurance: United States v. Oregon State Medical Society," *Journal of Health Politics, Policy and Law*, vol. 2 (Spring 1977), pp. 48–78.

[34] See, for example, Indiana Federation of Dentists, Docket No. 9118 (FTC, decided March 25, 1980).

[35] Klor's Inc. v. Broadway-Hale Corp., 359 U.S. 207 (1959).

[36] See, for example, Metropolitan Life Insurance Company, "Cost Containment at Metropolitan," p. 8: "When engaged in implementing and monitoring of a cost containment program, the [Metropolitan] Claim Consultant suggests programs to meet a particular Policyholder's needs. Arrangements are also made with the appropriate professional societies or organizations to obtain their approval of the program and to assure their cooperative participation."

[37] See, for example, Michigan State Medical Society, Docket No. 9129 (FTC, filed July 27, 1979).

[38] Columbia River Packers Assn. v. Hinton, 315 U.S. 143 (1942).

limited participation in control of a prepayment plan by physicians who represent professional interests; a flat prohibition might well be warranted in view of the problem of monitoring the relationship to assure that collective bargaining or a conspiracy between the plan and organized providers is not involved.

3. *Restrictions on how physicians may sell their services.* The FTC has ruled that the profession's ethical restrictions on "contract practice" violate the FTC Act.[39] Even so, opposition to such arrangements is deeply ingrained in the profession. As a result, participation agreements with insurers not under professional control may continue to be uncommon. Professional disapproval of such participation agreements reflects a recognition that such agreements would split the profession into competing provider groups, each marketed by a competing insurer or other health plan.

4. *Prescription of payment methods by the profession.* Relative value studies sponsored by the profession, collective efforts to establish or liberalize UCR payment systems, and insistence that commercial insurers indemnify patients rather than enter into participation agreements with providers all represent attempts by the profession to structure the payment system in the physician's interest and to head off competition among insurance plans in finding new ways of enlisting and paying doctors.[40] Although the only existing case on relative value studies held that they do not violate the antitrust laws,[41] their effect on competition among insurers—which would in turn trigger competition among physicians—seemed to escape the attention of the court.

5. *Peer review.* The medical profession's readiness to mediate fee disputes and to undertake utilization review likewise forecloses competitive innovation in the procurement of professional services by competing health plans. Even though a beneficent cartel would be preferable to a malevolent cartel, the law prohibits both kinds. Tampering with prices and substituting centralized decisions for the competitive process are unlawful, whatever the motives of the collaborators.[42] The seeming reluctance of some, including Judge Sneed in the *Maricopa County* case,

---

[39] American Medical Assn., Docket No. 9064 (FTC, October 12, 1979), *affirmed* American Medical Assn. v. Federal Trade Commission, Docket No. 79–4214 (2d Cir., decided October 7, 1980).

[40] This thesis is further developed in Clark Havighurst and Philip Kissam, "The Antitrust Implications of Relative Value Studies in Medicine," *Journal of Health Politics, Policy and Law*, vol. 4 (Spring 1979), pp. 48–86.

[41] United States v. American Society of Anesthesiologists, 473 F. Supp. 147 (1979).

[42] But cf. Pireno v. New York State Chiropractic Assn., 1979–2 Trade Cases (CCH) ¶ 62,758 (S.D.N.Y. 1979); Bartholomew v. Virginia Chiropractors Assn., 612 F.2d 812 (1979), *cert. denied* 100 S.Ct. 2158 (1980).

to accept this principle in the health services field seems to result at least in part from an inability to picture how financing entities in a truly competitive market could and would limit prices and control inappropriate utilization.

The FTC Bureau of Competition report is somewhat deficient in that it treats professional control of prepayment plans in a vacuum, without the benefit of a full picture of how this particular restraint relates to the others catalogued above. As a result, the remarkable success of the medical profession in controlling its economic environment is not immediately apparent. In following up on its staff's initiative, the FTC must use its processes and expertise to reveal the full implications of the medical profession's assorted activities. Although a broader rule-making proceeding would be more difficult to manage, a full assessment of the probable benefits and harms to competition that flow from professional control of prepayment plans requires that this particular restraint not be viewed in isolation.

The preeminent question of the collaborators' power. Only where collaborating competitors possess market power can their collaboration have anticompetitive effects in the market as a whole. Indeed, power alone can raise a hazard that justifies condemning a practice even where its ostensible purposes are defensible and its effects on competition cannot be proved adverse. It should be clear, therefore, that wherever a questionable purpose and some indication of adverse effects appear (anecdotal evidence may serve), power can be the clincher in establishing an antitrust violation.

In the case of physician control of prepayment plans, power seems the crucial element. The best indicia of power in this context may be the percentage of the market's physicians involved in the organization participating in control of a plan and the percentage of the market's physicians being paid through the physician-controlled plan. If a low percentage of the market's physicians is involved, the anticompetitive threat would probably be small, and the plan would appear to be pro-competitive in its impact. If a high percentage is involved, there would be greater probability that the plan would be used to limit, rather than promote, competition.

In their analysis of power, many critics of the Bureau of Competition's report have focused on the power and market share of the physician-controlled plans themselves, rather than on the power of the sponsoring or participating physician groups. This line of argument seems to go to the *effect* of the combination on competition, which one might expect to be less where the controlled plan's market share was low. A powerful organization of physicians should not, however, be permitted to use even an arguably weak anticompetitive tool—particularly when, as suggested above, it is only one of many anticompetitive tools at the profession's disposal. Of course, if the alleged check on the power of the physician-controlled plan was the existence of other competing organizations of physicians, then the power of the sponsoring physician group and the power of their plan would be the same thing. But such competition is rare.

Certainly the power of a large sponsoring physician organization is not limited by the existence of many competing insurers if those insurers do not—and perhaps cannot—buy physician services on a competitive basis and as a result compete only by achieving administrative economies and by carefully selecting the risks they insure. In such cases, focusing on the limited market share of the physician-sponsored plan can only mislead an analysis of power. Indeed, Arnould and Eisenstadt found at one stage of their studies that when markets with physician-controlled Blue Shield plans were compared, those featuring controlled plans with smaller market shares had higher fees.[43] More intense regulation of larger Blue Shield plans could account for this result, but so could other factors, including the medical profession's ability to use any controlled plan, large or small, to keep insurers passive. The key, then, to the analysis of the power element in a rule-of-reason assessment is the power of the controlling organization, taking into consideration not only the percentage of the market's physicians involved in the organization but also the other anticompetitive tools at the organization's disposal.

The Bureau of Competition's original proposed rule[44] did not attempt to make distinctions on the basis of the power of the controlling physician organization or the power of the group of physicians eligible to be paid under a plan. The bureau simply proposed that a group of competing physicians be prohibited from controlling an "open-panel plan"—that is, a plan paying physicians who compete with one another to provide services under the plan. As a result, the proposed rule caused great consternation among some procompetitive HMOs who are not controlled by the medical profession and who lack market power but who provide services through effectively competing physicians.

The *Federal Register* notice requesting comments on the Bureau of

---

[43] David Eisenstadt and Richard Arnould, "Blue Shield Fee Setting in the Physicians' Service Market: A Theoretical and Empirical Analysis" (Unpublished paper, April 1978), pp. 69–82. It should be noted, however, that when Eisenstadt and Arnould used another method of calculating market share in another statistical equation, market share was found not to have a statistically significant effect on fees.

[44] Federal Trade Commission, Bureau of Competition, *Staff Report on Medical Participation*, pp. 308–72.

Competition's report indicated that the bureau is now prepared to narrow its definition of "open-panel."[45] Under the new definition, only plans that will pay more than some percentage—say, 50 percent—of the physicians in the market would be considered open-panel plans and subjected to limitations on physician participation in ownership and control. This is a step in the right direction, but any rule should also impose a similar limit on the size of a physician organization controlling even a closed-panel plan.

Exercising Prosecutorial Discretion: Weighing the Public Interest

Even if it is stipulated that organized medicine's control of a medical prepayment plan violates the letter of the antitrust laws, many observers would question the wisdom of investing public resources to prosecute such violations. Although the antitrust enforcement agencies are bound in a general sense to enforce the law, they possess, as a practical matter, considerable discretion in choosing their targets. More than ordinary prosecutors, the antitrust agencies are recognized as having a substantial policy-making function. In deciding whether to file a complaint, they are therefore free to weigh some public-interest factors that a court could not consider in deciding the cases, once initiated. As a result, it is legitimate to suggest that antitrust enforcers should tolerate profession-controlled health plans, even if those plans are technically unlawful.

Prosecutors who choose to press the antitrust case against IPAs and FMCs must be prepared to justify their actions in the face of evidence that IPAs and FMCs lower costs and thus advance the high-priority objective of health care cost containment. Studies confirm that at least some profession-dominated plans have in fact lowered hospital utilization,[46] and the plans could probably show that they have reduced some professional fees. Because of this evidence, the path of least resistance for the antitrust agencies would probably be to accept tacitly the argument that in an inflationary time the public's need for some kind of cost containment—any kind—is great enough that the profession's cost-containment activities should not be subject to antitrust challenge. This acceptance would simply mean not challenging physician conduct that, on the face of it, seems the opposite of antisocial. Even though private suits would still be possible, the only parties with enough provable damages to warrant a suit would probably be physicians whose excessive

---

[45] *Federal Register*, vol. 45 (March 17, 1980), pp. 17019–20.

[46] See, for example, Egdahl, Taft, Friedland, and Linde, "Organizations of Fee-for-Service Physicians," pp. 388–97.

fees were being restrained, and such unappealing plaintiffs would likely find it impossible to establish liability.

The antitrust enforcers who challenge IPAs and FMCs must also contend with the perception that IPAs and FMCs are part of a sincere effort by the more progressive and conscientious members of the medical profession to improve the profession's performance. To adherents of this view, the antitrust challenge appears to frustrate the very efforts that the public at large seems to be demanding and to threaten the very physicians who have demonstrated the greatest sense of public responsibility. The easy answer to these objections is that the antitrust laws are concerned with more than motives and that there is no desire to punish individuals. Even though criminal penalties would not be invoked and only prospective relief would be sought, the agencies' critics would not be satisfied with this answer. Moreover, in an era when governmental infringement on businessmen's freedom has become a potent political issue—witness the FTC's recent difficulties in Congress[47]—the predictable complaints about unnecessary harassment would receive a sympathetic hearing from the antitrust agencies' congressional overseers. The prospect of such political pressures unavoidably influences prosecutorial decisions. For this reason, the agencies' answers to the questions posed may need to be more than intellectually satisfying.

The challenge confronting the FTC and other antitrust agencies is summed up in the following question: Why must we sacrifice the bird in the hand—profession-sponsored cost containment—for the bird in the bush of competition? The answer to this question has two principal aspects. First, it is necessary to consider how valuable in fact the bird in the hand is. Second, the question implies that the bird in the bush is (to mix the metaphor) either a will-o'-the-wisp or a chimera, and the answer must therefore address whether competition is a fanciful or a real and immediate prospect. Our answer will thus be organized under headings corresponding to these issues. It should become apparent why society cannot hope to enjoy both the short-run benefits of profession-sponsored reforms and the long-run benefits of competition.

Valuing the Bird in the Hand. The bird in the hand, profession-sponsored reform, is probably too meager to justify a departure from the generally well-founded premise that competition will ultimately yield better performance than a cartel or a professional monopoly. Although a profession-sponsored IPA or FMC may have the administrative tools (participation agreements and utilization review) necessary to control costs, its incentives will determine how vigorously these tools are used. Al-

---

[47] James Singer, "Out Like a Lamb," *National Journal*, vol. 12 (May 24, 1980), p. 867.

though the profession's good will and its opposition to what it considers price gouging and utilization abuses might alone be enough to yield some economic benefits for consumers, the deeper motivation for strengthening efforts in these areas may be nothing more than a fear that the profession's traditional prerogatives will be progressively expropriated by government unless a better showing is made. Thus, the value of the bird in the hand probably depends in part on the public's maintaining the political pressure that the profession now feels.

An antitrust rule against profession-sponsored IPAs would not necessarily mean the loss of those plans already in existence. Many such plans have contractual commitments that would make it difficult to dismantle them. Thus, existing plans might well continue under new and less questionable auspices, just as Ohio Medical Indemnity, Inc., previously a medical-society-controlled Blue Shield plan, was reorganized under an antitrust decree as a mutual insurance company.[48] Already possessing the tools needed to contain costs, these plans might become aggressive purchasers of professional services.

As to the IPAs and FMCs that would not be established because of the proposed antitrust rule, one can ask whether we might not be better off without them. The evidence suggests that most IPAs and FMCs have been started to head off or respond to competition. For example, the original FMC, the San Joaquin Foundation for Medical Care, was created explicitly to discourage the Kaiser Foundation Health Plan from entering the participating doctors' territory.[49] In other communities, IPAs have been started because local doctors feared, or were actually confronted with, the development of a closed-panel HMO and saw the IPA as a method of self-defense. In such circumstances, the very existence of the profession-controlled plan may succeed in deterring or defeating the development of independent, truly competitive plans. Independent plans may be harmed by a profession-sponsored plan because the controlled plan reinforces the profession's sense of solidarity in resisting change, and thereby leads individual physicians to refuse to participate in the competitive plan, to grant its doctors hospital privileges, or to accept referrals from it. Also, the IPA may engage in limit-entry pricing to deter threatened entry, or in predatory pricing to eliminate or discipline any entrant that might appear. Thus the price of the apparent bird in the hand may often be the sacrifice of a competitive bird in the bush, rather than the other way around. Prohibiting profes-

---

[48] Settlement Agreement, Ohio v. Ohio Medical Indemnity, Inc., Civ. No. C–2–75–473 (S.D. Ohio, filed March 22, 1979).

[49] Richard Egdahl, "Foundations for Medical Care," *New England Journal of Medicine*, vol. 288 (March 8, 1973), p. 491.

sion-controlled plans may therefore facilitate the appearance of plans with immediate competitive value, more than offsetting the apparent loss.

In organizing IPAs and similar mechanisms, then, the medical profession functions precisely as a monopoly would function in responding to threats to its power. The IPA is simply a way of reorganizing the profession's internal operations so that it can better protect itself against both government intrusion and competition. The organized profession is more willing to tolerate changes in its economic environment if it can control the nature, and limit the extent, of such change. Where an independent entity controls the process of change, the profession may regard any concession as too dangerous a precedent. A controlled plan, on the other hand, is a valuable instrument that permits the profession to retreat in measured decrements to new lines of defense.

In the absence of recognizable external threats, IPAs are unlikely to make anything more than token cost-containment efforts. Indeed, efforts not needed for purposes of self-defense would precipitate a crisis within the sponsoring physician group, which, because it encompasses most of the market's physicians, must be responsive to the recalcitrant as well as the progressive members of the physician community. Such an intracartel squabble appears to have caused the breakup of the ChoiceCare IPA in Fort Collins, Colorado.[50] Other instances of conflict within professional cartels have surfaced in the courts, where disaffected practitioners have sought to register their objections to the fee-restraining actions of profession-controlled plans.[51] It is ironic that these lawsuits have been brought under the antitrust laws, with the plaintiff professionals claiming that their fees have been "fixed"; adding to the irony is that these plaintiffs have studiously avoided reference to the fact that the plans being attacked are under their own cartel's control. IPA proponents cite these cases as evidence of the plan's effectiveness in containing costs, but it should come as no surprise that within a cartel differences of opinion exist concerning the correct strategy and profit-maximizing price. It seems clear, then, that the bird in the hand that many people seem to value is but a feature of professional monopoly.

In markets where profession-sponsored IPAs already face vigorous competition, their value may seem greater because they are more cost conscious in such markets than they are where the professional monop-

---

[50] See Kenneth Olds, "How Our Model IPA Went Bankrupt," *Medical Economics*, vol. 57 (March 17, 1980), p. 158; see also "It Wasn't Just a Matter of Bad Management," *Medical Economics*, vol. 57 (March 17, 1980), p. 158.

[51] See, for example, Manasen v. California Dental Service, Docket No. C-75-0329 WHO (N.D. Cal. 1980); Pireno v. New York State Chiropractic Assn., 1979-2 Trade Cases (CCH) ¶ 62,758 (S.D.N.Y. 1979).

oly remains intact. Here, however, the bird in the bush of competition is already in hand, and it seems clear that the achievements of IPAs in the more dynamic markets should be credited to competition, not to the IPAs. In already competitive markets, the IPA is merely the vehicle by which the more traditional elements of the profession fight their rearguard action against competition, and, as such, it is not worth preserving. Even if the cost savings achieved by the IPA in competitive markets are greater than IPAs achieve when the external threat is less palpable, those savings are likely to be less than the savings of competing independent plans. The higher costs of IPAs are the almost inevitable result of their failing to seek out those physicians who practice in a cost-conscious manner and of opening their doors instead to virtually any member of the local medical society. That, at least, may be one lesson of the experience of the profession-controlled Physicians' Health Plan (PHP) in the comparatively competitive Twin Cities market. In the Twin Cities, there are six other HMOs, and the PHP, far from being in the vanguard of cost containment, has found itself scrambling to keep pace with the others. Whatever success the PHP has had in controlling costs is directly attributable to the pressure exerted by the other independent plans.[52]

In a competitive market like the Twin Cities, disbanding the profession-sponsored plan would not be a serious setback for cost containment. Indeed, it would likely provide an additional stimulus to the strengthening of competition and cost containment. Many physicians who to that point had contracted only with the profession's plan could be expected, in its absence, to contract with other independent plans, and thus would contribute to the division of the market's physicians into competing panels. Physicians who object to the style of medicine promoted by the existing independent plans could create their own plans and market them competitively. Physicians, as well as consumers, would then be guaranteed variety in their choice of plans. If demand existed (as it probably would) for an open-panel, service-benefit plan offering no-questions-asked coverage and free choice of provider, an insurer independent of the profession's control could establish such a plan.

Admittedly, the medical profession's sense of solidarity may cause some initial reluctance among traditionalist physicians to align themselves with competing plans, even after the profession's plan has disbanded. If the profession cannot have its own plan, some physicians will

---

[52] Jon Christianson and Walter McClure, "Competition in the Delivery of Medical Care," *New England Journal of Medicine*, vol. 301 (October 11, 1979), p. 812; John Iglehart, "HMOs Are Alive and Well in the Twin Cities Region," *National Journal*, vol. 10 (July 22, 1978), pp. 1164–65.

prefer to contract with no plan at all because they abhor the idea that the profession would be divided into competing panels. That, after all, was a primary reason why, until the FTC intervened, the profession's ethical code prohibited "contract practice" under the auspices of a lay-controlled insurer.[53] Nevertheless, most physicians should soon recognize the advantages of consolidating their market position early, before competition and the increasing supply of physicians have had their full impact. Indeed, physicians who cling too long to traditional financing mechanisms will probably find that they are increasingly dependent on government programs and that the more attractive market opportunities have already been seized by others.

From this discussion, it may be concluded that IPAs, standing alone, are not impressive birds in the hand and that they may readily be sacrificed in the interest of enhancing competition. As a result, antitrust enforcers should not hesitate to attack these arrangements whenever they appear to be significant obstacles to competition. Perhaps a market like the Twin Cities has become competitive enough so that the IPA no longer possesses enough power to justify investing public resources in a legal attack. But there should be no hesitation in embracing the legal principle that all physician-sponsored prepayment plans are unlawful if the controlling physicians have substantial market power.

The Prospects for Competition. The premise underlying the widely held belief that profession-controlled prepayment plans are the best available instrument for changing physician behavior is that competition is unworkable in health care financing. The best reasons for holding this view, however, do not amount to a persuasive case for prosecutors' tolerating profession-dominated reforms such as IPAs.

The single most important cause of the market's weakness is the tax subsidy for employer-purchased health benefits, which induces people to overinsure against health care expenses.[54] This distorting factor should not affect the antitrust analysis because, as we have noted, Congress must be deemed to have intended the effect of its tax policies. Whatever one thinks of that somewhat conceptual argument, antitrust

---

[53] See American Medical Assn., Docket No. 9064 (FTC, October 12, 1979), *affirmed* American Medical Assn. v. Federal Trade Comm'n, Docket No. 79–4214 (2d Cir., decided October 7, 1980).

[54] See, for example, Martin Feldstein and Bernard Friedman, "Tax Subsidies, the Rational Demand for Insurance and the Health Care Crisis," *Journal of Public Economics*, vol. 7 (April 1977), pp. 155–78; Ronald Vogel, "The Tax Treatment of Health Insurance Premiums as a Cause of Overinsurance," in Mark Pauly, ed., *National Health Insurance: What Now, What Later, What Never?* (Washington, D.C.: American Enterprise Institute, 1980), pp. 220–49.

prosecutors should be encouraged for other reasons to challenge even good-faith professional efforts to contain costs and thus to offset the tax law's distortions. A dominant consideration might be that the profession has a powerful motive to preserve those public policies that artificially inflate the demand for medical services. Thus, even if antitrust enforcement should set back the profession's efforts and actually raise the cost of medical care (a result that we are persuaded would not occur), that result should be deemed tolerable because it allows the public and the Congress to see more clearly the destructive consequences of the prevailing tax policy. A political solution to the underlying problem of distorted private incentives—whether a change in the tax law or a new regulatory initiative—must be deemed preferable to whatever the organized medical profession sees fit to volunteer.

The other market distortion that helps to account for the lack of cost-conscious competition and for the failure of independent health plans to deal more aggressively with physicians is the strength of the organized medical profession itself, which is precisely the target of the antitrust enforcement effort.[55] It is unlikely that antitrust enforcers would conclude that the medical profession must be left in its powerful position because it can show that it has occasionally thrown crumbs to the public. Similarly, antitrust enforcers should not respect profession-controlled financing plans on the ground that they facilitate the throwing of such crumbs.

The idea that competition is unattainable or is so speculative a prospect that short-term cost containment should not be sacrificed in its name is clearly belied by the evidence that the successes of IPAs themselves in cost containment are usually attributable to the stimulus of actual or potential competition. Far from being a chimera, competition is materializing, in fact. Indeed, the profession's establishment of an IPA is usually a sign that a palpable competitive threat to professional power is developing. Thus, a legal rule against such sponsorship of an IPA is likely to bite precisely where the competitive potential is most real.

Antitrust enforcers need to have a clear sense of competition's potential, of the many forms it can usefully take, and of the various and sundry threats to it that the medical profession can mount. In proposing its "Blue Shield" rule and raising the issue of the rule's applicability to IPAs, the FTC staff has revealed a rather clear perception of the problems that competition has encountered in the past and a good strategic sense of how the market can be made more efficient. With this and its

---

[55] See Havighurst, "Professional Restraints."

other enforcement initiatives,[56] the Bureau of Competition has launched a coherent, well-conceived, and highly realistic campaign to free third parties of all kinds from profession-imposed restraints that have heretofore prevented competing health insurers and service-benefit plans from acting in the consumer's interest. With a good appreciation of the market's past problems and future potential, antitrust enforcers should have the self-confidence necessary to confront criticism of and political resistance to their challenges to professional power—even if the profession's anticompetitive intent is not manifest.

Antitrust enforcers should also gain confidence from a recognition of their place in the larger policy framework. The antitrust agencies have frequently raised questions concerning anticompetitive practices in other industries that were being tolerated or actively fostered either by regulatory agencies closely allied with industry interests or by Congress itself. In many instances, the antitrust agencies have succeeded in getting policies and practices changed, with the result that competition was restored to a prominent place.[57] In other cases, policy reappraisals triggered by the agencies' efforts have resulted in a tightening of regulatory control over areas where competition was deemed inappropriate but regulatory abuses had been discovered. In both situations, policy problems that otherwise would have been ignored were identified and corrected. Thus, by advocating competition and not deferring to conventional views or to agencies supposedly endowed with special expertise, the antitrust agencies have helped to keep the policy-making process attuned to fundamental issues that Congress, the regulators, and the regulated industry were inclined to avoid or ignore.

The antitrust agencies should continue to perform this watchdog role in the health services industry. The FTC was the first advocate of health sector competition within the federal establishment, and its efforts gave the idea credibility that it had otherwise been unable to achieve. In fact, recent congressional reexamination of the role of competition

---

[56] These enforcement initiatives are discussed in Clark Havighurst, "Antitrust Enforcement in the Medical Services Industry: What Does It All Mean?" *Milbank Memorial Fund Quarterly*, vol. 58 (Winter 1980), pp. 89–124.

[57] See, for example, Gordon v. New York Stock Exchange, 422 U.S. 659 (1975). The U.S. Department of Justice had long opposed the system of fixed commission rates for transactions on the New York and American Stock Exchanges that was challenged in *Gordon*. As a result, the department filed an *amicus curiae* brief supporting the plaintiff's claim that the fixed rates violated the antitrust laws. The department was not moved by the defendants' argument that the fixed-rate system was exempt from the antitrust laws because it was subject to the overriding supervision of the Securities and Exchange Commission (SEC). Shortly before the Supreme Court ruled that the fixed-rate system was indeed exempt from antitrust scrutiny, the SEC itself eliminated fixed commission rates effective May 1, 1975.

under the health planning legislation[58] owes much to the FTC and the Justice Department's keeping the flag of competition flying. Precisely because competition has so long been ignored in this industry, those who have become most expert in health policy are at least naive about competition and may even be hostile to it either for ideological reasons or because their expertise is threatened with devaluation by the adoption of new premises. In these circumstances, the antitrust agencies may be seen as valuable counterweights to the policy assumptions of the past. Moreover, their insistence on competition is subject to congressional review. If Congress wants to reject the competitive premise of antitrust, it can do so explicitly.

The performance of the HMO program of the Department of Health and Human Services (DHHS) illustrates why an active advocate of competition is needed within the government itself. Charged with promoting and subsidizing HMOs, DHHS failed to discriminate between procompetitive and anticompetitive HMOs. It therefore welcomed medical-society initiatives for their supposed contribution to cost containment and was shocked to learn that the FTC believed DHHS had certified and subsidized violations of the Sherman Act. DHHS may have altered its policy toward IPAs somewhat in light of the FTC's identification of the problem. In any event, the FTC's efforts probably assure that the antitrust issues discussed in this chapter will be debated when Congress decides whether to renew the HMO program in 1981.

To sum up, the antitrust agencies should not refrain from giving effect to the letter of the antitrust laws in this industry. Such efforts to hold the industry to the implications of the national policy of competition establish a badly needed benchmark from which further policy discussions can proceed. Even if some short-run costs are incurred as a result of the antitrust effort, there is great benefit in forcing policy makers to face rather than avoid fundamental choices among competition, regulation, and continued cartelization as mechanisms of social control. The invocation of antitrust principles brings to light abuses and problems that Congress and DHHS, as political organs capable of contemplating only incremental change, are inclined to neglect. Whether enforcement of antitrust principles against profession-sponsored IPAs would in fact immediately benefit or harm consumers is therefore not the most important issue. What is important is the need to call attention to a major violation of the fundamental policy of competition. Even though Con-

---

[58] See the Health Planning and Resources Development Amendments of 1979, Public Law No. 96–79, 96th Congress, 1st session (1979). For a description and analysis of these amendments, see Clark Havighurst and Glenn Hackbarth, "Competition and Health Care: Planning for Deregulation," *Regulation*, vol. 4 (May/June 1980), pp. 39–48.

gress might decide that IPAs are on balance a good thing and that IPAs should be exempted from antitrust scrutiny, at least it would do so with some recognition of the implications and consequences of that choice. That result would be greatly preferable from the standpoint of good government to perpetuating the medical monopoly by default. The best result of all would, of course, be to give the antitrust laws their due effect by eliminating one of organized medicine's most potent remaining tools for shaping the economic environment of medical practice.

Postscript

On April 23, 1981, the FTC announced its decision on how to approach the question of the antitrust status of physician participation in the control of Blue Shield and other medical prepayment plans.[59] Accepting a staff recommendation that differed from earlier staff advice, the commission has elected to pursue the issue on a case-by-case basis rather than through a rule-making proceeding. Acting Chairman David A. Clanton issued a statement giving some reasons for rejecting the rule-making approach, including the complexity of such factual issues as market definition and the degree of physician participation in the plan's decisions. He also cited a new Bureau of Economics study indicating that higher fees were prevalent only where control was exercised by formally organized doctors' groups. An official statement of enforcement policy, lacking the conclusiveness of a trade regulation rule and the formal status of an industry "guide," is expected to be issued at a later date.

Whether the FTC's action reflects a change of position on the legal issues was not clear. The apparent acceptance of a rule-of-reason approach is not necessarily inconsistent with the staff's original position as explained previously. On the other hand, the commission's press release and Clanton's statement indicated possible acceptance of the view, vigorously disputed above, that an actual fee-increasing effect might have to be proved before a violation could be found. This legal question may be authoritatively resolved, however, as the result of another recent development—the Supreme Court's acceptance of an appeal in the *Maricopa County* case.[60] It seems likely that the commission's future actions will be determined to a large degree by the Court's decision in this case.

Because the commission's recent action reducing the immediacy

---

[59] *Federal Register*, vol. 46 (May 21, 1981), p. 27768.

[60] Arizona v. Maricopa County Medical Society, 1980–81 Trade Cases (CCH), ¶63, 239 (9th Circuit 1980), *certiorari granted* 49 *U.S.L.W.* 3663 (1981).

and scope of the threat to established physician-plan relationships occurred in the midst of intense political pressure on the agency, it is possible to view it as a retreat from vigorous enforcement. It remains possible, however, that the forthcoming statement of enforcement intentions may reveal a firm commitment to attack arrangements that are destructive of competition's prospects.

Commentary

Alvin K. Klevorick

The papers by Warren Greenberg and by Clark Havighurst and Glenn Hackbarth investigate questions of competition in the health services delivery system when those who provide the service and those who provide the means to pay for the service (with insurance or other types of premiums) are closely interrelated. In his paper, Greenberg examines the behavior of third parties in the dental care insurance market, a market in which, he argues, there is substantial competition among insurers. He seeks answers to two sets of questions. First, how does Blue Shield's behavior—particularly its efforts at cost containment—as a dental insurer, which faces competition, has no providers on its board, and enjoys reduced cost advantages, compare with its behavior in the medical insurance market, where it has "a monopoly in non-profit medical insurance" and does have providers on its board? Second, because the Delta Dental Plan was begun by dentists and is staffed by dentists, will an examination of the market for dental insurance yield some insight into how differences in market conditions—as those between medical insurance and dental insurance—affect the performance of provider-influenced insurance plans? As part of his presentation, Greenberg traces the origins of a number of Blue Shield physician-sponsored health insurance plans and compares them with insurance plans that were begun by several other professional groups. This discussion contains interesting bits of history and draws, in particular, upon the discussion of the origin of physician-influenced health insurance in Oregon, which appeared in an earlier article by Greenberg and Goldberg (1977).

Greenberg concludes that Blue Shield does behave differently as a dental insurer than as a medical insurer and that provider influence alone does not suffice to ensure long-run market dominance. More generally, from his examination of dental insurers, the author concludes that it may be an error to treat all insurers alike and to focus particularly on the upward pressure that health insurance exerts on the prices of health care. Insurers in some markets, he concludes, may act to dampen cost increases, and he offers dental insurers as one example.

Inquiries into the role that third-party payers do play, and the part that they can play, in containing health care costs are interesting and important. Moreover, I am quite confident that insurers in some health care markets do act to dampen cost increases; and perhaps dental care insurers comprise one such set of third-party payers. But I have a number of difficulties with Greenberg's analysis and, in particular, with the contrasts he draws between insurers of medical care and insurers of dental care.

Let me begin by noting that a more appropriate title for the paper would be "The Impact of Competition on Provider-Influenced Insurance Plans: Lessons from Dentistry." The theme in much of the paper's examination of third-party behavior in the dental insurance market is about how the provider-influenced Delta Dental Plan—begun and staffed by dentists—fares in comparison with how provider-influenced Blue Shield fares in the market for medical insurance. My point is not simply semantic, for the questions suggested by the two titles are different. Indeed, one would ideally like to have an examination of a health insurance market, whether it be for medical insurance or dental insurance, that focuses prominently on the simultaneous interdependence between market structure and company behavior.

A principal point in Greenberg's discussion is that there is substantial competition among insurers in dental care. The basic evidence of competition that is offered concerns market shares and changes in those shares over time. The evidence, however, is not strong. From the data in the paper, one can most reasonably characterize the dental insurers' market as an oligopoly with a "fringe" of independents. But no information is given about the nature of the oligopolistic interrelationships in the market. Greenberg notes that Delta Dental Plan's market share has declined over the period 1968–1977, but no explanation of the decline is provided. In addition, the data presented indicate the large role played by commercial carriers, with their share of total benefits incurred ranging from 57.1 percent to 70.7 percent during the period; but the information about how this share itself divides and how many carriers there are is not presented. In short, without a closer and more careful examination of the dental insurers' market structure, the reader cannot assess how much competition exists or what effects more competition would bring.

To support his conclusion that dental insurers have acted to dampen cost increases, Greenberg compares the consumer price index (CPI) for dentists' fees with the index for physicians' fees and with the "all item" CPI. Unfortunately, as he does recognize, this comparison does not tell us anything about either the counterfactual question (How much would the index have risen in the absence of these insurers?) or the normative issue (How much would the index have increased if the delivery of dental care had been optimal?).

In addition, Greenberg cites evidence on per capita expenditures for dentists' services and for physicians' services and the respective increases in each set of expenditures. The evidence is presumably consistent with a criticism he makes of various studies of the relationship between physicians' fees and physician membership on Blue Shield boards of directors—namely, that those studies focused only on fees paid to physicians for a selected number of procedures. Greenberg argues that "the only datum of public policy interest is the total amount paid to physicians, i.e., physician fees multiplied by the number of procedures." It is, of course, correct to note that we should take account of the elasticity of demand (or supply or supplier-created demand), but it is not clear why we must focus only on the total amount paid. Again, this information cannot shed much light on either the relevant counterfactual issue or the relevant normative concern. With regard to the latter, we must ask why public policy is no longer concerned with comparisons of costs and benefits.

Greenberg also describes specific ways in which third parties in the dental care market act to control costs and improve quality. This discussion raises several questions. First, in assessing whether dental insurers do a better job of cost/quality control than medical care insurers do, it is important, as Greenberg notes, to compare medicine and dentistry themselves. The comparison seems critical with respect to one of the principal cost-control elements he discusses, namely, "pretreatment review," in which an insurance carrier reviews the "necessity and appropriateness" of proposed treatments that are expected to cost more than a specified amount. To evaluate this policy and its potential for insurers of medical care, one must have information about how the distribution of costs of proposed treatments in dentistry compares with that in medicine. In particular, does the cost distribution for treatment in dentistry make pretreatment reviews, with an expenditure threshold, more feasible in dental care? One must also recognize, as Greenberg also does, that emergency and quasi-emergency treatment situations, in which pretreatment review is not feasible, occur more frequently in medical care than in dental care.

Second, Greenberg mentions the dental insurers' Alternative Course of Treatment program as part of the claims review process, which helps to control costs. One would like to know how often the alternatives suggested by dental consultants on the insurer's staff are adopted.

Third, the author's discussion of third-parties' claims review raises an interesting question about what we might call "organizational cog-

409

nitive dissonance." Greenberg portrays Blue Shield and other commercial carriers as undertaking systematic programs to control the costs of dental care but as making no similar efforts with regard to medical care. One can only speculate about how this critical difference in orientation is reconciled with a unified view of the organization's mission or objective.

Finally, in describing the ways in which dental insurers attempt to control costs and improve the quality of care, Greenberg emphasizes the role of dentists and dental assistants on the insurers' staffs. This discussion raises the question of why the presence of doctors on the boards and staffs of medical insurers does not have a similar beneficial effect. It also raises the more general issue of the nature and effects of professional self-regulation. In this regard, one must recognize the distinction between the reasons a physician-sponsored plan might originate (Greenberg cites the desire to eliminate the insurer's monitoring of physicians' behavior, to curb the loss of patients to closed-panel prepaid plans, and to increase demand for physicians' services) and how such a plan might function. The theory of origination is not necessarily informative about theoretical or actual practice. A researcher concerned with the way professionals in an insurance setting monitor their peers' behavior might profitably consider, as well, the effectiveness of professional self-regulation in other health care settings: for example, licensing boards, disciplinary committees (in malpractice cases), and hospital issue committees (with regard to the lifting of admitting privileges). Professional self-regulation is an important feature of the health care market, and we would do well to further our understanding of how well it functions.

•　　•　　•

Clark Havighurst and Glenn Hackbarth have given us an interesting, thoughtful discussion of the role of antitrust enforcement in the health services market. Their chapter focuses, in particular, on the Federal Trade Commission's (FTC) prospective antitrust challange to individual practice associations (IPAs) created by local medical societies. These organizations "contract directly or indirectly with consumers to provide services in return for a fixed monthly premium," and they "are mechanisms permitting local representatives of organized medicine to bind community physicians together in a single economic unit and thus to control health care costs—both unnecessary utilization and fee escalation." Havighurst and Hackbarth discuss two different, though interrelated, roles for antitrust enforcement vis-à-vis IPAs. The first is to fulfill the legislative mandate of bringing about competition in all markets except those for which Congress itself has "carved out" explicit exceptions. The second function is to focus the attention of Congress on the need to confront squarely the fundamental choices between competition and regulation—whether governmental or professional—as modes of social control in the health care market.

With regard to the first role, "giving effect to the letter of the antitrust laws," Havighurst and Hackbarth discuss why IPAs should be found in violation of the statutes. They discuss the explicit price-fixing charge leveled by the staff of the FTC's Bureau of Competition but argue that it fails to capture the full set of conflict-of-interest problems engendered by provider-controlled prepaid health care plans. Hence the authors expand the purview of the analysis beyond the price-fixing charge to a rule-of-reason approach or at least to the "truncated" rule-of-reason inquiry that may be required when professional services are under scrutiny.

They explicitly reject the view that the legal merits of the FTC's antitrust case against IPAs depend in any crucial way on economic evidence that such associations result in higher prices or higher costs. Havighurst and Hackbarth recognize that studies, such as the one undertaken by the FTC's Bureau of Economics demonstrating such undesirable effects of physician-controlled plans, would help to establish that competition was impaired. But they also point out some of the difficulties inherent in the interpretation of the results of such empirical investigations. The authors' consideration of the antitrust challenge encompasses an examination of other ways in which they argue the medical profession has restrained competition among providers and created barriers to competition-stimulating innovation by prepayment plans. Considering the interrelatedness and cumulative power of these actions, Havighurst and Hackbarth argue that there is, almost without question, an antitrust violation.

The question one must ask, and each reader must answer for himself or herself, is whether the authors have met the one argument with which they said "the commission must reckon," namely "the argument that whatever price agreement physician control might entail is 'ancillary' to a procompetitive joint venture—that is, the establishment of a service-benefit prepayment plan." This part of their analysis may be open to differences of opinion because, as Havighurst and Hackbarth say, the evidence to support the concern "that a controlled plan might serve the medical profession as a kind of 'fighting ship,' discouraging competition at the interface between physicians and independent plans" is "mostly impressionistic," "speculative and difficult to document."

Having argued that once an enforcement measure is brought against concerted actions of health care providers, like IPAs, it is improper for a court to go beyond the letter of the law and ask whether the concerted action is, overall, socially beneficial, Havighurst and Hackbarth then discuss the role for prosecutorial discretion in deciding whether to file a complaint. They recognize the substantial policy-making function of the antitrust enforcement agencies and the fact that in deciding whether to bring an action, those agencies are free to take account of public-interest factors that a court should not weigh in deciding a case. As they say, "it is legitimate to suggest that antitrust enforcers should tolerate profession-controlled health plans, even if those plans are technically unlawful." They go on to present their assessment that the "bird in the hand," professional cost containment, should be sacrificed for the "bird in the bush," competition in the health care market. Consequently, they argue, the prosecutor who performs correctly the social benefit/cost analysis will decide to go forward with the complaint against physician-sponsored health care plans.

Of particular interest in Havighurst and Hackbarth's view of how antitrust enforcers should evaluate the relative merits of physician-sponsored plans and competition is the second role they describe for such enforcement agencies. Though they characterize it as a "watchdog" function as an advocate of competition, it is perhaps better characterized as an agenda-setting function. They argue that by raising questions, in the form of an antitrust complaint, about what are perceived to be anticompetitive practices, the antitrust enforcement agencies can keep the policy-making process—in particular, the legislative process—focused on fundamental issues of health care policy. This suggestion, which typifies the authors' sensitive treatment of issues of institutional competence, is interesting and merits consideration.

When the fundamental choices between competition and regulation are faced, two issues deserve somewhat more consideration than Havighurst and Hackbarth were able to give them in this particular chapter. First, careful attention must be given to the nature of the competition that one can expect in the market for health care services and health care insurance. The continuing antitrust scrutiny that such a market would be likely to require ought to be recognized. As Havighurst and Hackbarth themselves say, in their discussion of the problems with evaluating the effects of physician-controlled plans, "a market in which Blue Shield is independent of the medical profession is not necessarily a model of competition," and I assume they are referring to the economist's notion of competitive markets. Antitrust enforcement must be prepared to be vigilant about the monopolistic competition aspects and oligopolistic interactions that are likely to appear in the deregulated market Havighurst and Hackbarth envision.

Second, the authors raise the issue of the transition to competition, but they do not discuss it in any detail. This seems to be a very important concern. They recognize the second-best nature of the problem they are considering—the "argument against permitting competition under current incentives has some validity"—but they regard it "as an even more powerful argument in favor of enacting incentive-oriented market reform legislation." No matter what inference one draws from prevailing incentives in the health care market for the direction of reform in that market or for the intensity of the antitrust enforcement effort, one must consider how the desired new market structure is to be attained. Transitions from one way of organizing a market to another structure invariably involve disruptions, and sound policy making will plan for the transition as well as the endpoint. In terms of the antitrust efforts Havighurst and Hackbarth discuss, the desirability of effecting a smooth transition may well have more implications for the nature of the relief sought than for the enforcement agency's decision to bring an action.

Wallace E. Oates

People of the same trade seldom meet together, even for merriment and diversion, but the conversation ends in a conspiracy against the public, or in some contrivance to raise prices.

As this familiar remark of Adam Smith reminds us, economists have long been suspicious of circumstances that permit suppliers of goods and services to exercise control over the economic environments in which they operate. The papers in this session are in the Smithian tradition. In particular, their point of departure is the suspicion that physician or medical society influence on the boards of directors of health insurers results in a manipulation of the fee structure to the gain of physicians at the expense of the public.

The underlying hypothesis in the papers by Arnould and Eisenstadt, Kass and Pautler, and Greenberg is that physicians (or dentists) will try to raise fees *wherever* they have the capacity to do so. In fact, as Greenberg points out, there is some compelling historical evidence of specific instances of precisely this form of behavior in certain states in the United States. More generally, the potential for establishing relatively high prices for physician services depends on two conditions: (1) physicians must be in a position of influence with regard to the determination of the level of physician fees; and (2) market circumstances (in this case, the position of Blue Shield insurers) must provide some monopoly power for the supplier to exploit.

The extent to which these two conditions are met varies considerably across reimbursement areas in the United States. First, the extent of physician participation and influence in the determination of fees seems to exhibit substantial diversity; in some areas physicians may nominate or elect some locally specified fraction of the board of directors of the Blue Shield program, while in others they may actually make up a certain proportion of the board itself. Second, Blue Shield plans in some areas possess certain cost advantages over competing commercial health insurers. These advantages again vary somewhat across areas depending, in particular, on the extent of state and local tax exemptions and on the availability of hospital discounts made possible when a Blue Shield plan is merged with the local Blue Cross plan. In short, there appears to exist considerable variation across reimbursement areas in both the extent of physician influence on their fees and on the degree of market power afforded the local Blue Shield organization by its relatively advantageous cost position.

Arnould and Eisenstadt and Kass and Pautler test their hypotheses by exploring this variation econometrically across Blue Shield areas. In particular, they regress a measure of the level of fees on various measures of physician influence or control, on measures of the cost advantage of the local Blue Shield plan, and on certain control variables that reflect local demand and cost conditions. The specifications of the reduced-form equations also include certain interaction terms reflecting the presumed interdependence between physician control and market power in the determination of fee levels.

The econometric work in both papers reflects a careful and sophisticated effort to test statistically the hypotheses of a positive influence of physician control and market power on the level of fees. The authors have experimented widely with different definitions of the key variables and various functional forms, and they have also introduced the appropriate econometric techniques to deal with certain complications such as heteroscedasticity and the use of pooled data. I find no major fault with the econometric procedures in either paper.

The findings provide some support for the hypothesized effects of physician influence and market power on physicians' fees. Kass and Pautler, for example, find that the estimated coefficient for a dummy variable (*MDSOC*)—equal to 1 if the local medical society nominates, elects, or approves any number of board members and zero otherwise— is generally positive and statistically significant. Likewise, the Kass and Pautler interaction terms reflecting both physician control and the Blue Shield cost advantage possess the expected sign and are generally significantly different from zero. Using a different body of data and definitions of the key variables, Arnould and Eisenstadt provide further evidence that physician influence *in conjunction with* a cost advantage for the Blue Shield plan is positively and significantly associated with the level of physicians' fees.

The results, however, are not entirely convincing. The studies use various measures of physician control: Some of them "work" and others do not. Moreover, since the *t*-statistics are often not very large, we should regard certain of the estimated coefficients as only "marginally" significant. It seems clear in this regard, as the authors are quite ready to admit, that many of the results are fairly sensitive to the particular specification of the estimated equation. All this, incidentally, is not really a criticism of the studies; it is rather a matter of acknowledging that, as in many empirical studies, the results are not too robust and are probably best taken as providing only "modest" or "tentative" support for the hypothesis rather than a strong confirmation.

It is also noteworthy that the findings of Kass and Pautler and Arnould and Eisenstadt are not entirely consistent. The former find that one of their measures of physician control (*MDSOC*) is significantly associated with fee levels; Arnould and Eisenstadt can find *no* significant effect of physician control *in the absence of a Blue Shield cost advantage*. This is not a trifling matter, for it has some important policy implications. If Arnould and Eisenstadt are correct, then the undesired effects of physician control on fees can be dealt with simply by eliminating the cost advantages available to Blue Shield plans so that there will effectively be no market power to exploit. If Kass and Pautler are right, however, physician influence in its own right affects fees, and therefore some limitations on the role of physicians may be in order.

These results become all the more difficult to assess because we can evaluate them only in terms of alternative reduced-form equations. There is no real theory or explicit "model" of the behavior of boards of directors that underlies the econometric analyses. This is the major weak link in both papers. In the absence of a model of board behavior, the authors are forced to proceed in a relatively ad hoc fashion: they try different measures of physician influence and market power to see which of them "work." There is no theory to suggest the appropriate measure; hence, we are forced to choose among the alternatives solely on the basis of statistical tests. This difficulty is admittedly easier to point up than to resolve; the formulation of an explicit model of fee determination incorporating the role of physicians and health insurers is a formidable assignment.

The issues are further clouded by another study in which William Lynk constructs a model of physician behavior that predicts that greater physician influence is likely to have a *negative* influence on fees; Lynk finds, moreover, that this prediction is borne out by a large econometric study of reimbursement and other data for Blue Shield plans.[1] In brief, Lynk posits a kind of "median-voter" model in which physician influence on boards of directors works in the direction of the median of desired reimbursement levels among physicians.

The basic argument is that physicians charging above the reimbursement level—above the "maximum customary allowance" (MCA)—would favor a higher MCA, since this would reduce the out-of-pocket costs to a subscriber of patronizing these physicians; in contrast, physicians whose fees are below the MCA would seek a reduction in the reimbursable fee, since it would have no effect on their price to subscribers but would raise the out-of-pocket costs of using certain of their competitors, namely, the higher-priced physicians. In a model in which physician representatives on Blue Shield boards seek to maximize their support among the local community of their peers, the median level of preferred fees represents the equilibrium outcome.[2] Since observed MCAs are almost always well above the median of the observed charge distribution, Lynk concludes that greater physician influence on reimbursable fees should operate to reduce the MCA toward the median level of physician charges. Lynk then undertakes a large econometric study in which he regresses average payment levels to physicians on two alternative measures of physician influence (percentage of physicians on the board and percentage of the board selected by the local medical society) and on a number of control variables. Regardless of the definition of physician influence, the estimated coefficient of the influence variable is negative and significantly different from zero at a 0.99 level of confidence.

The Lynk analysis is subject to certain reservations. The model is simplistic; one might argue, for example, that the entire schedule of desired physician fees is a function of physician control and market power so that the median of the distribution of desired reimbursement fees is itself positively related to physician influence on Blue Shield boards and any Blue Shield cost advantages. The econometric analysis is also open to certain questions: The use of Blue Shield market share as a regressor may be a source of bias in the results, since it is presumably an endogenous variable. Nevertheless, the Lynk study stands as one having a plausible (if not wholly *persuasive*) conceptual foundation and

---

[1] William J. Lynk, "Regulatory Control of the Membership of Blue Shield Boards of Directors," unpublished paper (March 1980).

[2] The median of the preferred levels is the "equilibrium" outcome in the sense that the median level (and only the median) would obtain majority support when paired against *any* alternative level. See Duncan Black, "On the Rationale of Group Decision Making," *Journal of Political Economy*, vol. 56 (1948), pp. 23–34.

supporting empirical results. In this context, the Lynk results (using Lynk's data) have apparently been replicated by the Federal Trade Commission. The Lynk data base, incidentally, is not identical with either that of Kass and Pautler or Arnould and Eisenstadt, but it appears to be roughly comparable.

This leaves us with a puzzle. The studies of Kass and Pautler and Arnould and Eisenstadt provide some tentative, but not entirely consistent, results that suggest that greater physician influence on Blue Shield boards is associated with a higher level of physician fees. The Lynk study, in contrast, generates the opposite finding.

How can we explain this seeming contradiction? There are two lines of work that offer some potential for clarifying the issues. The first is an effort to understand the decision-making processes of the Blue Shield boards. What is needed is a model of these processes that makes explicit the objectives of each of the participants and that describes how the participants interact in board decisions; such a model might generate predictions of the effects on fees of increasing the extent of physician influence on the board and of Blue Shield cost advantages. This is not an easy task, but perhaps there are sources of information (for example, board minutes or information from actual board members) that could facilitate the formulation of such a model.

Second, it would be useful to make a detailed comparison of the results of Kass and Pautler and Arnould and Eisenstadt on the one side, and the Lynk findings on the other. It is hard to believe that different data account for the divergent results, particularly since the data bases for all the studies not only appear comparable, but are quite large. My conjecture is that there are certain crucial differences in the specifications of the equations that are responsible for the contrasting outcomes. One obvious and suspect difference in specifications is the earlier mentioned inclusion of the Blue Shield market share as an independent variable in the Lynk equation, a variable that possesses a very large explanatory power. In brief, it would be instructive to explore the comparative econometrics in these studies to obtain a clearer idea of the sources of the divergent findings.

In conclusion, while the existing econometric work may not, at this juncture, be conclusive on the issue of physician influence and fees, we obviously cannot infer that no such effect exists. In fact, there are clear historical instances of the use of medical society influence for the purpose of increasing physician fees. Moreover, it may be that the effects sought in this econometric work are hard to find because the crucial variation does not exist across reimbursement areas. As Greenberg notes, each Blue Shield plan has at least one physician on its board of directors; if the crucial distinction is between no physicians and some physicians, then econometric studies of the differences among *existing* boards will obviously not find the major effect. Nevertheless, the econometric work we are discussing is of real interest; it is of high quality and is surely worth pursuing somewhat further if at least to clarify the remaining inconsistencies in the findings. The Smithian kind of suspicion concerning the effects of physician influence on Blue Shield boards may yet prove correct.

Part Five

One Step toward the New Approach

A Brief Outline of the Competition Strategy for Health Services Delivery System Reform

Alain C. Enthoven

Competition strategy for health services delivery system reform refers to the proposed application of four principles of health care finance not generally applied today. These principles are

1. Multiple choice: Once a year, consumers would be offered the opportunity to enroll for the coming year in any of the qualified health plans operating in their areas.

2. Fixed-dollar subsidy: The amount of financial help each consumer would receive toward the purchase of health plan membership would be in a fixed-dollar amount independent of the plan chosen. Thus, the person who chose a more costly health plan would pay the extra cost and therefore would be cost conscious.

3. Same rules for all competitors: Rules would govern premium-setting practices, minimum-benefit packages, catastrophic-expense protection, et cetera, in order to prevent preferred-risk selection, excessive costs for high-risk persons, and deceptive or inadequate coverage. The same rules would apply to all qualified health plans.

4. Physicians in competing economic units: The market would include limited-provider, preferred-provider, or closed-panel plans in which the health care financing plan is associated with a limited set of physicians. The premium each health care financing plan charged would then reflect the ability of its associated physicians to control costs. (This arrangement can be contrasted to one in which all health care financing plans offer a free choice of doctor.)

The Consumer Choice Health Plan (CCHP) refers to a proposal I made in September 1977 to Joseph Califano, then secretary of the Department of Health, Education, and Welfare.[1] CCHP is a system of universal health insurance based on fair economic competition in the private sector. In CCHP, every eligible person would receive a subsidy toward the premium of a qualified health care plan. The subsidy would be related to predicted medical need (that is, the population would be stratified into actuarial categories, with premiums and subsidies related to expected medical need in each category) and to income. Qualified plans would meet the following conditions:

1. participation in an annual open enrollment in which all applicants would be accepted regardless of medical need

2. community rating by actuarial category

3. catastrophic expense protection (that is, a limit on each family's out-of-pocket expenses)

4. coverage of at least a standard package of basic health care services (which could be subject to consumer cost-sharing up to the prescribed limit)

The nearest existing legislative approximation to CCHP is the National Health Care Reform Act of 1980 introduced by Representatives Richard Gephardt and David Stockman.[2] This bill and CCHP differ, however, on the permissible amount of consumer cost-sharing, an issue discussed in the following papers.

The principles of the competition strategy are also reflected in incremental proposals that would work within the context of today's health insurance system based on employee groups, Medicare, and Medicaid. The main bills embodying these proposals are Senator David Durenberger's Health Incentives Reform Act of 1979[3] and Representative Al Ullman's Health Cost Restraint Act of 1979.[4] The main elements of these bills are

1. to require all employers above a certain size to offer employees a choice of health plans and to make fixed-dollar contributions (as opposed to the current open-ended commitments of employers)

2. to limit the exclusion of employers' contributions to employee health benefits from the employee's taxable income to about $120–125 (in 1980 dollars) per family per month

[1] Alain C. Enthoven, Memorandum for Secretary of HEW Joseph Califano on National Health Insurance, Washington, D.C., September 22, 1977. See also "Consumer-Choice Health Plan," *New England Journal of Medicine*, vol. 298 (1978), pp. 650–58, 709–20.

[2] H.R. 7527, The National Health Care Reform Act, introduced by Representatives Richard Gephardt (D.-Mo.) and David Stockman (R.-Mich.) on June 9, 1980.

[3] S. 1485, Health Incentives Reform Act of 1979, introduced by Senator David Durenberger (R.-Minn.) on July 12, 1979; and S. 1968 introduced on November 9, 1979.

[4] H.R. 5740, The Health Cost Restraint Act of 1979, introduced by Representative Al Ullman (D.-Oreg.) on October 30, 1979.

3. to impose uniform minimum standards, such as catastrophic expense protection, for all tax-favored health insurance plans

4. to allow Medicare beneficiaries to direct that their "adjusted average per capita cost" to Medicare be paid to the health maintenance organization (HMO) or to a similar qualified health care plan of their choice as a premium fixed in advance

5. (in Ullman's bill) to direct a state-wide Medicaid demonstration based on Project Health of Multnomah County, Oregon, a county-sponsored health care financing system in which low-income persons are given a subsidized choice of competing comprehensive private health care plans

Representatives James Jones and Sam Gibbons and Senator Richard Schweiker also introduced bills containing some of these provisions.[5] Another bill, President Carter's National Health Plan, requires expanded choices, equal employer contributions with respect to the choice of a health plan, and an HMO option for Medicare beneficiaries.[6]

All of these provisions are explained in greater detail in my new book, *Health Plan.*[7]

[5] H.R. 7528, Consumer Health Expense Control Act, introduced by Representatives James Jones (D.-Okla.) and Sam Gibbons (D.-Fla.) on June 9, 1980; S. 1590, The Comprehensive Health Care Reform Act, introduced by Senator Richard Schweiker (R.-Penn.) on July 26, 1979.

[6] S. 1812, The National Health Plan Act, introduced by Senator Abraham Ribicoff (D.-Conn.) on September 25, 1979.

[7] Alain C. Enthoven, *Health Plan: The Only Practical Solution to the Soaring Cost of Medical Care* (Reading, Mass.: Addison-Wesley, 1980).

Health Care Competition: Are Tax Incentives Enough?

Jack A. Meyer

In trying to explain the sharp increase in health care spending that has occurred in the United States over the past three decades, many observers have pointed to the enormous growth in insurance coverage as the culprit. Insurance, it is claimed, has led consumers to demand a quantity and a quality of health care services that exceed the level at which the benefits derived from these services would be commensurate with the costs.[1]

Although the expansion of insurance coverage has led consumers to purchase more health care services than they might otherwise choose, rising health insurance costs are not merely the result of increments in the *proportion* of costs covered by insurance, but are inextricably linked to the *nature* of insurance reimbursement plans. Most health insurance plans reimburse patients on the same basis, whether the patients choose efficient or inefficient providers. Under prevalent practices today, consumers may patronize any accredited providers in a medical market area, and consumers who deal with extravagant providers will be reimbursed on a similar basis as those who search out economical providers.[2]

Doctors who are careful not to hospitalize patients when ambulatory care is an effective substitute, who avoid overtesting their patients, who are careful about prescribing too many drugs, and who would be reluctant to put their patients in a hospital on Friday for procedures that are

[1] See Martin Feldstein, *The Rapid Rise of Hospital Costs* (Washington, D.C.: U.S. Council on Wage and Price Stability, January 1977); Feldstein, "Quality Changes and the Demand for Hospital Care," *Econometrica*, vol. 45, no. 7 (October 1977); and Mark Pauly, "Is Medical Care Different?" in Warren Greenberg, ed., *Competition in the Health Care Sector: Past, Present, and Future* (Washington, D.C.: Federal Trade Commission, March 1978), pp. 19–48.

[2] Alain Enthoven, "The Politics of NHI," in Cotton M. Lindsay, ed., *New Directions in Public Health Care: A Prescription for the 1980s* (San Francisco, Calif.: Institute for Contemporary Studies, February 1980), p. 228.

424

not scheduled to begin until Monday are not rewarded under this prevailing health care reimbursement system in ways that efficient providers
who conserve resources are normally rewarded in other markets. Until
this aspect of the health care system is reformed, both in public and
private reimbursement policies, we will not make meaningful progress
against the sharp escalation of health care costs. As Enthoven has observed, the normal rules rewarding buyers and sellers for economy in
the use of resources are violated by institutional arrangements that reward hospitals for generating costs under Medicare, Medicaid, and many
Blue Cross plans and that reward doctors for providing more services
in higher-cost settings.[3]

This chapter examines one of two general approaches to cost containment—a market incentives approach keyed to changes in the federal
tax treatment of health care expenditures—in an effort to suggest some
potential pitfalls lying between modifications in tax laws designed to
encourage people to *economize* on the use of health services and the
actual achievement of moderation in health care cost increases. To what
extent would a better set of incentives discourage the predominant practice of no-questions-asked cost reimbursement that lies at the heart of
escalating expenditures? While this chapter attempts to show that "there
is many a slip between the cup and the lip" with regard to the actual
realization of cost savings elicited by structural modifications in tax laws
or reimbursement mechanisms, it also argues that the incentives approach—unlike its chief rival, a regulatory approach—is at least raising
the right glass.

Alternative Approaches to Cost Control

Two fundamentally different approaches to cost containment distinguish
one group of proposals from another. One approach emphasizes the
need to control providers—doctors and hospitals—and its various advocates propose controls on physician fees, limitations on hospital revenues, and restrictions on hospital capital expenditures. The other strategy focuses on changes in the tax incentives related to the purchase of
insurance and on the need for increasing competition among different
types of insurance arrangements and delivery mechanisms. Advocates
of this approach argue that their proposed reforms will reduce the
"waste" component of demand and encourage more competition among
providers and insurers.

The first approach diagnoses the problem in terms of excess capacity
(for example, unneeded hospital beds), alleged to be caused by the

[3] Enthoven, "The Politics of NHI," p. 228.

power of providers to increase supply even if demand is lacking; its sponsors believe that as excess capacity is utilized, controls on providers will allow demand to increase without raising costs. The second approach suggests that through incentives to economize on resources rather than to waste them, we can accommodate an increase in coverage—and spending—by the underserved through cutbacks in spending across the general population.

These two approaches—one geared to controls and the other to incentives—reflect a basic division of opinion among health care economists regarding the nature of the market for medical care. Those favoring more regulation of providers stress the inherent "market failure" in medical markets and believe that supply creates its own demand; the answer, then, is to control supply. Those who favor tax reform and incentives for consumers to shop for health insurance stress the importance of "regulatory failures" in health care markets and argue that the alleged excess spending for health could be corrected through altering the system of signals and incentives to which providers, patients, and insurers respond.

The problems with the regulatory approach to containing health care costs are well known and will be mentioned here only briefly.[4] A system of rigid controls on spending confuses budgeting and economizing. Economizing makes it possible to obtain the same quantity and quality of services for lower total outlays. Budgeting simply makes it possible to achieve lower outlays, but not without some sacrifice in quantity and quality. As a society, we can arbitrarily set any budget for health care spending, and we can even make it stick if we have the political will to keep rigid controls in place for a long time period. But we would not necessarily be better off with lower dollar outlays and inferior services than with higher outlays and better services. Imposing a system of controls that allows for only a specified growth in health care spending papers over inefficiencies in the current system and as Enthoven has argued, "rewards the fat and punishes the lean."[5]

A different approach is incorporated in the tax incentive bills offered by former Representative Al Ullman (H.R. 5740), Representative James G. Martin (R-N.C.) (H.R. 6405), Senator David Durenberger (R-Minn.) (S. 1968), former Senator Richard Schweiker (S. 1590), for-

---

[4] For further discussion, see Alain C. Enthoven and Roger Noll, "Regulatory and Nonregulatory Strategies for Controlling Health Care Costs" (Paper prepared for the Sun Valley Forum on National Health, August 1977); and Clark C. Havighurst, "Federal Regulation of the Health Care Delivery System," *University of Toledo Law Review,* vol. 6, no. 3 (Spring 1975).

[5] Alain C. Enthoven, "Consumer-Centered versus Job-Centered Health Insurance," *Harvard Business Review,* vol. 57, no. 1 (January/February 1979), p. 143.

mer Representative David Stockman and Representative Richard Gephardt (D-Mo.) (H.R. 850), and Representative James Jones (D-Okla.)
(H.R. 7528). Shunning the regulatory approach, they would attempt,
instead, to improve incentives to economize on health spending by (1)
imposing a limit on the tax-free premium that an employer could contribute to a health plan, (2) requiring employers to offer a range of
options, and (3) allowing employees who selected a low-cost plan to
reap the savings (or requiring those who selected a high-cost plan to pay
the excess premium over a fixed employer contribution). Under prevalent circumstances today, insurance is job centered, and employers
either offer no choice of health plans or pay more on behalf of workers
who select high-cost plans than on behalf of those choosing efficient
plans. Since insurers often reimburse fully in both situations, providers
have little incentive to be efficient.

In addition to changing the open-ended nature of federal tax subsidies for health insurance, the Stockman-Gephardt bill would sharply
scale back government regulation of charges, utilization, and capital
investment and incorporate the principle of fixed-dollar contributions
to the plans of the beneficiaries' choice into the Medicare and Medicaid
programs.

The tax incentive bills do have a realistic chance of slowing the
increase in health care costs. At least, this approach recognizes that a
major cause of the increase in costs is the combination of broader insurance coverage *and* the lack of incentives to select a low-cost insurance
plan. Moreover, these bills would economize not merely by fostering
consumer cost sharing, but primarily by stimulating competition among
alternative health care plans—and delivery systems—so as to *hold down
the cost level itself,* irrespective of how that cost is shared between workers and firms. Finally, with the tax incentives approach, it would be *in
the interest of providers* to hold down costs (for example, by avoiding
unnecessary testing and unnecessary hospitalization of patients) because
people who chose efficient providers would ultimately reap the benefit.
The incentives approach is preferable to one that tries to wring the waste
out of the system through controlling providers' fees and charges, but
that leaves the forces driving costs upward largely intact.

It should be noted at the outset that all the proposed health care
bills—whether they follow a regulatory or an incentives approach—are
designed not only to hold down cost increases, but also to assure all
Americans a minimum degree of protection against health care expenses. This chapter focuses on the factors that will influence the actual
cost savings flowing from an incentives plan. But even if the cost saving
potential of a particular plan turns out to be limited, that plan should
not necessarily be brushed aside. There is merit in giving people a fair

choice among alternative health plans even if the subsequent pattern of their selection does not produce significant cost reductions.

Limitations of the Tax Incentives Approach

Enthoven's analysis of the underlying causes of rapid escalation of health care costs is sound, and his criticism of the command and control regulatory approach is on the mark. In this section, it is argued that Enthoven's Consumer Choice Health Plan (CCHP)—and its legislative modifications—have limitations of their own that need to be taken into account in assessing the impact of the tax incentives approach to cost containment. Unlike the regulatory approach, the tax incentives approach does seem geared to the heart of the problem, and Enthoven deserves credit for carefully devising a comprehensive blueprint of the competitive model. The limitations of the tax incentives approach involve not the conceptual framework underpinning it, but rather the multiple levels of uncertainty or skepticism concerning the actual savings it could generate in practice.

Three levels of skepticism will be discussed here. The first concerns how much could actually be saved under the Enthoven plan or its various legislative offshoots, in view of the constraints imposed by the authors of these plans. The second level of skepticism focuses on the extent to which apparent cost savings associated with alternative delivery plans such as HMOs reflect real efficiencies, as opposed to either selection biases or differences in quality of service between "conventional" and "innovative" plans. In other words, if modifications in the tax laws along the lines recommended by Enthoven will result in a larger market share for alternative health plans such as health maintenance organizations (HMOs), health care alliances, or independent practice associations (IPAs), and if this spread of innovative plans is to be responsible for anticipated cost savings, it is important to ascertain the extent to which the cost savings are "real." To the extent that lower costs emerge from differences in the type or quality of services delivered or in the characteristics, tastes, and preferences of consumers enrolled in "conventional" and "innovative" health plans, the "incentives" strategy for achieving cost containment could be built on a shaky foundation.

A third level of skepticism questions the extent to which cost savings—even assuming they are real savings—will actually stimulate consumers to select the lower-cost plans. Let us turn to some of the impediments—legal, economic, and attitudinal—that might stand in the way of actualizing the potential cost savings resulting from the alleged greater efficiency of alternative delivery plans.

428

Regulatory Aspects of the Competitive Plans. One of the major pitfalls for an incentives-based strategy is the possibility that cost savings which appear significant in theory may shrink as a "minimum benefit requirement" is expanded. Although tax incentives might induce consumers to shop for the mix of premiums, copayments, and risk that suits their preferences, the more comprehensive the accompanying universal "floor" on covered benefits, the less meaningful the consumers' actual choice. The initial benefit package might indeed represent minimum coverage that no one should be without; once the principle of a minimum was established, however, it would be easy to enrich the package regularly. Indeed, including a mandatory basic benefits provision in a legislative package designed primarily to stimulate more competition among insurers could, ironically, turn out to be an inadvertent, backdoor approach to a "regulation style" comprehensive national health insurance program. Congressman Ullman's Health Cost Restraint Act of 1979 (H.R. 5740) illustrates this problem. It lists eight types of services that all plans would have to include in order to qualify for favorable tax treatment. Some of these are indeed basic (for example, hospital and physician services), but others are less clearly examples of coverage that no one should be without (for example, rental or purchase of durable medical equipment, ambulance service). And, it would not be surprising if this list of eight categories were expanded to ten or fifteen categories during the course of legislative deliberation. Special-interest groups could be expected to come forth with convincing arguments in favor of just one more service—say chiropractic services—in the standard package. In piecemeal fashion, the basic benefits package would be upgraded. In final form, such a bill—intended to be an alternative to a comprehensive national health insurance plan—could *turn into* the equivalent of such a plan.

Enthoven has stipulated that under CCHP all health benefit plans should be required to quote premiums for at least one standard package of covered services because he is concerned with consumer protection and facilitating rational consumer choices.

> One important part of such a program would be standardization of the list of covered services so that consumers can compare health plans without having to master many pages of fine print or to make actuarial comparisons of one complex package with another. To make price comparisons easy, we must require all health plans to quote premiums for at least one standard package of covered services.[6]

---

[6] Alain C. Enthoven, *Health Plan* (Reading: Mass.: Addison-Wesley, 1980), p. 81.

Enthoven's concern with protecting consumers from policies with gaping holes is understandable. It is worth emphasizing, however, that an exclusion from coverage that is deemed unconscionable by some observers may be depicted as justifiable by others. In other words, the line distinguishing exclusions that foster sensible cost sharing from those that leave consumers with "unacceptable" risks may become blurred; such a line is apt to be somewhat subjective and arbitrary.

Suppose that current laws forced everyone to buy a Cadillac or no car at all. Imagine a change in the law permitting consumers to choose their favorite models, but only from a set including Cadillac Sevilles, Lincoln Continentals, and Chrysler Imperials. Other cars would be deemed unacceptable because they would be beneath the government's minimum standard for consumers' well-being.

Suppose that another advocate of change suggests a standard package of acceptable features with a little more leeway—enough to make the Chevrolet Impala and the Oldsmobile Cutlass "acceptable." This package gives consumers a little more selection. Buy why truncate the spectrum of choices at all? Who are we to rule out Pintos, Chevettes, or Toyotas? Allowing consumers to choose among several high-priced cars—or several "high option" health insurance policies— is better than no choice at all. But, it is not good enough.

The point is that selecting an "appropriate" standard for minimum benefits is subjective—a car that is a rattletrap to you may be satisfactory to me, particularly if that is all that I can afford. Perhaps I would like a "lower option" car and a "higher option" house.

Leaving luxuries aside, food, housing, and education needs all compete with health care for the consumers' dollar. By setting a floor under the amount of health insurance all families or individuals must possess, we foreclose the choice of a lower-option insurance package (with the concomitant risk of higher direct outlays) that would release dollars for the consumer to spend on food, housing, or education.

Providing consumers with total flexibility in their selection of "low option" packages may not generate significant savings initially, as most consumers opt for rather comprehensive coverage. But it would permit those with higher risk preferences to exercise freedom of choice, and it might avoid the erosion of whatever cost savings could emerge from a tax incentives plan by eliminating the possibility of an upward-creeping floor. It should be noted that the flexibility favored here refers to each choice of insurance, not to total freedom to switch packages at any time. I concur with Enthoven's concern about the "free rider" problem and endorse his suggestion of a charge for the option of switching to a more comprehensive plan. The "free rider" problem calls for some limitations on, or charges for, switching among insurance packages, but it does not justify limitation on the choice among packages at a given point in time. Advocates of a minimum benefit requirement contend that it would avoid useless detailed "product differentiation" among insurance packages. Certainly a degree of differentiation is desirable and sought by consumers. "Excesses" in this area—for example, fraudulent claims, misleading information, or mind-boggling detail—could be handled more appropriately through consumer protection legislation.

The establishment of common basic benefits is not the only limitation that Enthoven would place on the free play of market forces. Several other provisions, each designed to protect consumers, are included in the CCHP.

> To summarize, for a workable competitive private-market system that makes affordable health insurance available to everybody, we need some form of mandatory premium contributions or what amounts to the same thing, substantial tax subsidy; some limits on the range of choices so that people cannot take advantage of the system in ways that undermine it; periodic open enrollment; community rating; common basic benefits in all plans; subsidies of health plan membership purchases by low-income people; standardization of benefit packages and other aspects of policies; and information disclosure.[7]

Each of these provisions can be linked to an understandable desire to protect consumers from discrimination or confusion. And Enthoven has taken considerable care to limit restrictions to those he believes are absolutely necessary to prevent such occurrences as the development of prohibitive premium rates for people deemed to be poor risks. Thus he would limit community rating to a market area rather than a broader region in order to reduce the possibility of inefficient and inequitable cross-subsidies between areas that have different health cost levels.

This line of reasoning could be extended one step further to allow experience rating even within market areas and demographic categories. Enthoven's justification for community rating is his concern about the unfairness of adverse selection. I share this concern, but community rating will not stop adverse selection, although it might change the pattern by which it is practiced. Even in the case of HMOs practicing community rating today, we can observe cream skimming occurring through selective marketing techniques and the location of clinics. Since community rating probably will not solve the adverse selection problem, it becomes important to ask whether community rating generates unwanted inefficiencies or side effects. Without doubt it does, in the form of inefficient cross-subsidies (largely obscured from view) that can be

[7] Ibid., p. 82.

reduced but not eliminated by restricting the size of the area over which community rating applies.

If we are concerned about adverse selection, it is not enough to make the case against community rating. An alternative approach is needed. It is important to distinguish between members of employee units covered by group health plans, Medicare, and Medicaid enrollees, and those who fall between the cracks of public and private group insurance. In the case of group plans for employees, firms and workers could probably develop their own solutions to the problem; further, the problem itself may not be too serious for this population, which accounts for the majority of U.S. residents. It is unlikely that differences in health status or health care needs would vary significantly from, say, U.S. Steel to Bethlehem Steel, or from General Motors to Ford, so that allowing experience rating across firms (or across plants in a market area) probably would not result in major differences in premiums.

Thus, for proposals such as the Ullman or Gephardt bills, under which insurance for most working people would still be provided on an employee-group basis, community rating would not be a necessary adjunct to the proposed tax changes designed to improve incentives for workers to select an efficient plan. Indeed, community rating is not called for in these bills. In the case of CCHP—which would provide insurance on an individual or family basis—since Enthoven's tax credits are (properly) scaled to demographic characteristics such as age, much of the discrimination against high-risk people would be compensated for without community rating. The issue is whether the scaled subsidies would go far enough in correcting for premium variation, and if they would not, whether community rating is the appropriate tool for dealing with the remaining within-group premium variations. Enthoven's scaled subsidies—without community rating—would probably be a sufficient buffer against controllable forms of risk selection practices.

Adverse selection *is* a real threat, however, for individuals not attached to employee groups; here, the law of large numbers does not obtain, and a high-risk individual could face an enormous premium; this possibility should clearly be avoided. "Compensating" for demographic characteristics here would not be sufficient. Alleviating this problem, however, does not require that we mandate community rating on a universal basis. Rather, it calls for a plan tailored primarily to the needs of nonworking people who are ineligible for federal assistance.

One approach with merit is contained in former Senator Schweiker's health care proposal (S.1590). States would be encouraged to establish a program of risk pooling that assigns to insurance companies, in proportion to the companies' business in the state, employees of small firms

432

(fewer than fifty workers), uninsurable risks, and the self-employed.[8] To assure continued involvement in federal programs, insurance companies must enroll these assigned individuals in catastrophic insurance programs. Premiums for such people could not exceed 125 percent of comparable large-group rates for similar protection in that region. A voucher system is another way to underwrite the needs of people requiring help. This plan would place minimal constraints on private-sector decision making, and would be less tied to conventional fee-for-service care than a pooled-risk approach.

In sum, the market-oriented reforms discussed here are promising because incentives for providers to economize are substituted for government regulation of *providers*. It would be unfortunate if this important thrust were to be offset by excessive government regulation of *insurers*.

Questioning the Evidence on Cost Savings. The favorable incentives associated with competitive national health insurance proposals are expected to generate cost savings by stimulating the development and greater utilization of various lower-cost delivery forms such as HMOs, IPAs, and Health Care Alliances. It is argued that in a more competitive environment for the purchase of health insurance, the deck would be less stacked against such innovative insurance plans. The anticipated expansion in the market shares of such arrangements is expected to lead to cost savings in two ways. First, there would be some direct savings as the share of the market going to lower-cost approaches expands. Second, some *indirect* savings would arise from the expected imitation effects in which conventional providers would adopt some of the more efficient measures of the others in order to remain competitive.

There is ample evidence supporting the contention that HMO enrollees have lower medical care expenditures than people with conventional insurance coverage. One estimate of the magnitude of such savings, based primarily on California comparisons between those enrolled in Kaiser plans and those with conventional coverage, indicates that total health costs for the former were 10 to 40 percent below those for the latter.[9]

It is important not to jump from evidence of relatively lower health expenditures for current HMO enrollees to the conclusion that an ex-

---

[8] For a discussion of Connecticut's Health Reinsurance Association through which persons, otherwise unable to obtain insurance, can secure coverage, see *State Health Legislation Report* (Chicago: American Medical Association, Public Affairs Group, 1980).

[9] Harold S. Luft, "How Do Health Maintenance Organizations Achieve Their 'Savings'?" *New England Journal of Medicine,* vol. 298, no. 24 (June 15, 1978), p. 1337.

pansion of the market share of HMOs would generate proportionate savings. First, it is necessary to ascertain the extent to which HMOs produce genuine savings by delivering a comparable quality of service to a comparable population at a lower price. Before we can be sanguine about the *potential* for HMO growth to general cost savings, we must be able to assert that HMOs save money through real efficiencies—the same services at lower costs—rather than through (1) providing a lower level of quality or (2) serving a group of enrollees healthier or less inclined to utilize medical services. Consumers may be concerned with the pace of rising health care costs, but they are also concerned with the availability of health care services that meet their standards.

In order to assess the performance of HMOs appropriately, it is useful to summarize briefly the *nature* or *source* of the observed cost savings. Luft has found that HMO cost savings arise not from more efficient production of a given set of services, but from changes in the number and mix of services provided.[10] In other words, the observed differences in health care expenditures between HMOs and fee-for-service systems reflect differences in practice patterns rather than a finding that HMOs can deliver a day of hospital care or a visit to a doctor at a lower cost. Reviewing evidence from various studies, Luft has further concluded that HMOs do not save money by reducing ambulatory visits, but rather by reducing hospital days. Moreover, the savings in the hospitalization category emerge primarily from lower *rates* of hospitalization among HMO enrollees, as opposed to shorter lengths of stay.[11] Finally, Luft finds that while HMOs have lower cost levels, there is no clear evidence that these cost levels grow more slowly over time than cost levels in conventional plans. Therefore HMOs may generate one-time savings, but they have not uncovered the key to ongoing cost control.

Luft argues that if HMO desirability is to be confirmed both on cost and quality grounds, HMO cost savings must occur largely in so-called discretionary or unnecessary cases—so that HMOs are identifying and screening out cases that do not require hospitalization. While Luft finds that people in HMOs do have lower surgical rates and very low rates of hospitalization for some specific "discretionary" procedures, he also finds that nonsurgical admissions tend to be equally low and that both long-stay and short-stay admissions are comparably reduced by HMOs. He concludes that "the data do not support the expectation that HMOs differentially reduce discretionary procedures."[12]

Luft offers four possible explanations for lower hospital admissions in HMOs: (1) HMOs avoid discretionary admissions; (2) HMOs un-

[10] Ibid.
[11] Ibid., pp. 1338–40.
[12] Ibid., p. 1341.

dertreat (or traditional providers overtreat) nondiscretionary cases; (3) HMOs provide preventive care that reduces the incidence of some health problems requiring hospitalization; (4) lower HMO hospitalization rates result from self-selection among HMO enrollees.

Luft's survey of the available evidence on these questions indicates that (1) HMOs have lower rates of admission across the board; (2) the average HMO offers care comparable or somewhat superior to the "average" fee-for-service practitioner; (3) while HMOs typically provide more widespread coverage of preventive services than conventional plans, the comparisons in which both settings cover preventive services yield ambiguous results concerning actual care provided (and preventive services do not explain the lower hospitalization rates of HMOs); and (4) direct tests[13] indicate that self-selection can be an important factor (people joining prepaid group plans tended to be relatively low utilizers).[14]

Luft finds that:

> There is substantial evidence that the people most likely to join a PGP [prepaid group plan] are those who have no longstanding relationship with a physician. Such people are also lower users of medical care before joining the PGP than are people of the same age, sex, and employment status who choose to remain in a conventional reimbursement plan.[15]

He cautions, however, that self-selection per se is unlikely to explain the performance of mature HMOs, as HMO enrollees' utilization may be lower in their first year or so of membership than in subsequent periods.

Luft maintains that we do not have enough reliable evidence to choose between an explanation of the HMO cost savings that involves HMOs' attracting and providing the right incentives to cost-conscious physicians and one centered on self-selection, and he cautions that

> If this second scenario is close to reality, then the apparent HMO savings are illusory and merely result from isolating the low-cost people in HMOs. A major increase in HMO enrollment would have little direct effect on overall costs. The true situation probably lies somewhere between these two scenarios, but our ignorance of the real potential for HMO cost

---

[13] Direct tests examine a group of consumers before and after an HMO option is available and compare the utilization of those selecting an HMO—relative to their earlier utilization—with the corresponding patterns for those remaining in conventional plans.

[14] Luft, "Health Maintenance Organizations, Competition, Cost Containment, and National Health Insurance," in Mark Pauly, ed., *National Health Insurance: What Now, What Later, What Never?* (Washington, D.C.: American Enterprise Institute, 1980), pp. 283–306.

[15] Ibid., p. 299.

containment should give us pause in designing NHI [National Health Insurance].[16]

Impact of HMOs on conventional providers. In addition to the anticipated direct cost savings from a greater market share for lower cost prepaid group plans, a "copying" effect—in which conventional providers adopt prepaid group plan (PGP) cost containment policies— is counted on to generate more widespread savings. According to this notion, HMOs may cut health care expenditures not only by what they do, but also by what they encourage others to do for competitive reasons. Evidence suggests that a greater HMO presence is associated with lower hospital utilization of enrollees in conventional plans.[17] There is certainly historical evidence of a competitive response to Kaiser in California as conventional providers attempted to arrest the erosion of their market share. As in the case with the more direct cost savings, however, observed patterns of provider and insurer practices have alternative explanations: "Although this evidence supports the notion of a competitive response, it could also be attributable to a wide variety of other factors, such as a rapidly growing and a young population, or pressures on available medical resources."[18]

Enthoven highlights the experience in Hawaii as evidence of a competitive response to a prepaid plan. He maintains that Kaiser's entry into the market pressured the Hawaii Medical Service Association (HMSA) to improve coverage and to strengthen cost controls. Enthoven reports that even after an adjustment for age, Hawaii's hospital use is about 75 percent of the national average.[19]

Luft, however, cautions that the HMSA, nominally a Blue Shield plan, really acts more like an IPA or other alternative delivery forms and suggests that "The HMSA behavior actually reflects its special history rather than competition with Kaiser."[20] Luft also contends that the increased overall utilization in the Minneapolis–St. Paul metropolitan area in recent years in the face of a doubling of HMO enrollment and much lower hospital utilization among HMOs is consistent with either the lack of a competitive response or the selective enrollment of low utilizers in HMOs, although other factors could be involved.[21]

---

[16] Ibid.

[17] See, for example, Lawrence C. Goldberg and Warren Greenberg, *The HMO and Its Effects on Competition* (Washington, D.C.: Federal Trade Commission, Bureau of Economics, 1977).

[18] Luft, "Health Maintenance Organizations," p. 301.

[19] Enthoven, *Health Plan*, pp. 84–85.

[20] Luft, "Health Maintenance Organizations," p. 302.

[21] Ibid., p. 303.

Summing up the evidence on both the direct and indirect effects of HMOs on health care costs, Luft states that:

There are several implications in all this for the role of HMOs in promoting cost containment under NHI, but they must all be qualified by a single phrase—proceed with caution. Caution is warranted because we do not yet know enough about the effects of HMOs, either on their members or the conventional system, to predict accurately their performance under any but the most trivial NHI proposals.[22]

It is worth noting that Enthoven's Consumer Choice Health Plan does not explicitly endorse or foster HMOs and would contribute to a more pluralistic insurance environment in which various "hybrid" plans could compete with both HMOs and traditional fee-for-service arrangements. But optimism about the cost-reducing potential of HMOs has been at the heart of the anticipated cost reductions from a more competitive market, highlighting the importance of reexamining the evidence regarding HMO cost savings.

Impediments to Realizing Cost Savings. Assuming that cost savings associated with the spread of alternative health plans reflect real efficiencies, there is still doubt about the extent to which the market share of such plans would swell in response to altered tax incentives. Impediments to the actual realization of savings include: (1) observing the growth of PGPs in a few regions of the country may be a misleading guide to a potential nationwide spread of PGPs, as factors indigenous to those regions may be largely responsible for the substantial PGP presence; (2) changes in incentives may not be able to overcome the predominant position of Blue Cross, Blue Shield in certain market areas; (3) there may be legal or regulatory barriers to the spread of PGPs; and (4) some purchasers of health insurance may not believe that the potential savings from a more competitive environment are commensurate with the costs.

The danger of extrapolation. We know that PGPs seem to generate cost savings *in certain areas of the country;* how portable is this experience to other regions of the country? To what extent do observed cost savings in California or Hawaii reflect the deeply entrenched position of Kaiser in these areas? Does the Minneapolis experience result to a significant degree from the special efforts made there to interest local employers in a more competitive environment for health insurance? How typical an insurer is SAFECO likely to be in the next few years?

---

[22] Ibid., p. 305.

The Kaiser-Permanente Medical Care Program per se covered an estimated 55 percent of all enrollees in prepaid group practices in 1978 (3.5 million of 6.4 million). Indeed, most of the PGPs with significant enrollment, such as Ross-Loos in California, have been in operation for more than thirty years.[23] Many new PGPs have sprung up in recent years in areas other than the west coast, but they have generally not captured a substantial share of the market. While HMOs might begin to "catch on" with restructured tax incentives, it would be unrealistic to expect such a development to alter dramatically (or rapidly) the market share for HMOs. Indeed, even the Department of Health and Human Services, which is officially supportive of HMO growth, has modest expectations regarding the expansion of HMOs.

> The most optimistic projection of the Department of Health and Human Services is that not more than 10 percent of the population will be enrolled in an HMO by 1988. The fact is that, even with federal grant support and tax incentives, it would take considerable time to establish functioning HMOs in areas where they do not now exist.[24]

A recent study by the Federal Trade Commission (FTC) found that entry of HMOs into market areas was responsible for lower hospital utilization of people in conventional plans.[25] Enthoven notes, however, that when the four states with high market shares and low utilization patterns are omitted from the FTC study's data base, the negative relationship between hospital utilization by Blue Cross members and HMO market share is no longer statistically significant.[26]

Enthoven also cautions against overly sanguine expectations for the immediate impact of his Consumer Choice Health Plan:

> All of these factors should help us to recognize that bringing the benefits of competition to most people won't be easy. It won't come as the automatic consequence of a few simple actions. Employers and government will have to make a sustained effort to make it happen. The creation of competition will require that most people in each community be offered fair multiple choice and that physicians, business, and other

---

[23] Enthoven, *Health Plan*, pp. 51–58.

[24] John L. Palmer, Assistant Secretary for Planning and Evaluation, HHS, Letter to the Editor, *Regulation* (July/August 1980), pp. 2, 51.

[25] See Goldberg and Greenberg, *The HMO and Its Effects on Competition*.

[26] Alain C. Enthoven, "Competition of Alternative Delivery Systems," in Warren Greenberg, ed., *Competition in the Health Care Sector: Past, Present, and Future*, Proceedings of a conference sponsored by the Bureau of Economics, Federal Trade Commission, Washington, D.C., June 1–2, 1977 (Germantown, Md.: Aspen Systems, 1978), pp. 335–36. Enthoven suggests that ". . . the possibility remains too strong that other factors account for the generally lower utilization on the west coast" (p. 336).

institutions take the lead in establishing alternative delivery systems.

Even if fair multiple choice is offered to most people and alternative delivery systems are established, the benefits will not come overnight. It takes time to develop alternative delivery systems.[27]

In addition to the evidence of cost savings from HMOs, advocates of a CCHP approach to cost containment have pointed to the federal government's experience with multiple choice of health plans for its employees as an illustration of the workability and efficiency of CCHP on a nationwide basis. The Federal Employees' Health Benefits Program (FEHBP) offers about 10 million people a choice among service benefit plans, indemnity plans, "employee organization plans," IPAs, and PGPs. The government contributes a fixed amount for each employee equal to 60 percent of the average premium of six of the largest plans. Although the FEHBP approach is similar to the CCHP, it is not a pure model of it. For example, the government contribution cannot exceed 75 percent of any particular premium, so that it pays somewhat less on behalf of employees selecting some of the low-option plans.

Enthoven cites the Hsaio study as evidence of a reduced cost of claims administration under FEHBP. Hsaio found that such administrative costs were 26 percent higher in Medicare than in FEHBP.[28] But Enthoven presents no evidence regarding *nonadministrative* costs in the two settings. And he has forcefully argued elsewhere that it is misleading to think of competition largely in terms of administrative costs and profit margins—which account for only about 10 percent of total costs. Indeed, he argues that there *is* competition among insurers over administrative cost reduction even in the current "stacked deck" environment.[29] When service costs rather than administrative costs are examined, it will be important to compare the families of federal employees and retirees to a broader group than the Medicare population and to control for differences among the two populations in demographic characteristics and utilization patterns. Finally, it is worth noting that 88 percent of federal employees select high-option health benefit coverage, and that most federal workers who have the option of choosing prepaid plans do not take this option. But, the proportion of federal employees selecting prepaid plans appears higher than the corresponding proportion of the overall population. For example, in the Washington, D.C., area, about

[27] Enthoven, *Health Plan*, p. 132.

[28] William Hsaio, "Public versus Private Administration of Health Insurance: A Study in Relative Economic Efficiency," *Inquiry*, vol. 15, no. 4 (December 1978), pp. 379–87.

[29] Enthoven, "The Politics of NHI," pp. 228–29.

20 percent of federal workers belong to a prepaid group plan.[30] Thus, the federal model suggests that while a multiple fair choice environment might not generate tremendous savings—as the majority of consumers still opt for comprehensive fee-for-service coverage—it might move prepaid plans from the perimeter or fringe of the health insurance market into a viable option with a significant market share.

Overcoming the blues. The share of the health insurance market accounted for by Blue Cross, Blue Shield insurers varies greatly across states. Some states have almost no Blue presence while in others the Blues hold more than 80 percent of the market. The national average market share of the Blues is estimated to be 43 percent.[31] Furthermore, there is wide variation from state to state in the tax and regulatory treatment of Blues vis-à-vis commercial insurers.

Most Blue plans pay no premium tax; commercial insurers typically pay a premium tax of about 2 percent. To place this advantage in perspective, it is necessary to understand that only a small proportion of Blue Cross premiums is kept to pay expenses. Thus Frech argues that the 2 percentage point premium tax differential effectively confers a cost advantage of more than 30 percent on Blue Cross plans and more than 20 percent on Blue Shield plans.[32] Moreover, many states exempt Blues from other taxes such as the property tax and regulate the ratio of benefits to premiums for commercial carriers, but not for Blues. Other areas of state insurance regulation, such as financial rescue requirements or mandatory free choice of provider rules, may also favor Blues over their new challengers, although some aspects of state regulation may disadvantage the Blues.

Blue Cross, Blue Shield enrollees are also alleged to receive hospital price discounts, and these price differentials are reported to be particularly large in the northeastern industrial states. One estimate of the Blue Cross hospital price differential in these states, where the Blue Cross market share is generally large, is a range of 14–30 percent.[33] Discounts for Blues (and Medicare, Medicaid) will tend to raise the prices for patients insured by commercial companies or for those who self-pay hospital bills. If self-insurance by firms becomes more widespread, the hospital price discount practice will become more important

---

[30] U.S. Government, Office of Personnel Management.

[31] H. E. Frech III, "Blue Cross, Blue Shield, and Health Care Costs: A Review of the Economic Evidence," paper presented for conference on National Health Insurance, American Enterprise Institute, October 4–5, 1979, pp. 3–4, 7.

[32] Ibid., pp. 3–4.

[33] David Robbins, "Comment," in Greenberg, ed., *Competition in the Health Care Sector,* p. 263.

relative to premium tax waivers as a source of the Blue Cross, Blue Shield competitive advantage.

As a result of these advantages, the market share of Blues may not readily give way to innovative health plans. Unless the latter cut costs by more than the cost advantages conferred upon the Blues (other factors held constant), the innovators may be unable to attract enough business to remain viable. As a result, making cost savings from innovative plans a reality might require changes in state and local tax (and regulatory) treatment of third-party payers *in addition* to Enthoven's proposed changes in *federal* tax rules.

The competitive advantage enjoyed by the Blues contributes to a "market leadership" role in which Blues may set the standards of behavior for the insurance market. Moreover, market dominance need not occur through such blatant practices as price fixing or boycotts that can elicit legal challenges. It may manifest itself in more subtle ways, such as through the market-wide entrenchment of open-panel arrangements and through the notion that insurer cost containment measures involving second-guessing of provider decision making are "unprofessional" or an unwarranted adventure in "corporate medicine." A recent FTC investigation focused on provider influence on Blue Shield boards as a factor inhibiting competition in health insurance.

There are other areas, however, in which Blue policies do not seem automatically to spill over to commercial insurers (indeed, in some instances causation may be from a reverse direction). In the past, for example, community rating in Blue plans did not preclude the use of experience rating by commercial insurers, and there has been a gradual abandonment of community rating by Blue plans. In addition, the shallow coverage prevalent in Blue plans has coexisted with a greater degree of cost sharing in commercial plans.

In assessing the prospects for the development or extension of innovative health plans, we should be cognizant of the influence of organized medicine on third-party payers. There is a long history of provider resistance to innovative mechanisms[34] and of strong provider support for the "free choice of doctor" insurance arrangement. Havighurst suggests that HMOs slipped through the net of this opposition, but only through successful litigation.

> patterns violating the principle of "free choice of physician" have survived professional counterattacks in only a few places. The most notable success, of course, was the survival of prepaid group practice HMOs in the United States as a direct result

[34] See Elton Rayack, *Professional Power and American Medicine* (Cleveland: World Publishing Co., 1967).

of the invocation of the antitrust laws in the AMA case. Unfortunately, health insurance plans with cost containment and panel-medicine features failed in the Oregon State Medical Society case.[35]

It is possible that HMOs—initially resisted by organized medicine, have now become the "token" concession to cost containment and are tolerated in the belief that the HMO market share is unlikely to expand significantly. Indeed, the Blues themselves have become a dominant force in HMOs, as they now sponsor an estimated sixty-six HMOs, or about a third of the total number throughout the country.

What is tolerated by physicians or encouraged (some would say coopted) by the Blues in the current climate in which HMOs account for about 4 percent of the market might be contested in a more truly competitive environment. The growth of innovative plans could be stymied either by medical society pressure on providers experimenting with lower-cost practices or by "predatory" pricing on the part of individual Blue Cross, Blue Shield organizations. In other words, the competitive threat from an innovative set of providers could be thwarted either by efforts to raise the innovators' costs or by efforts to underprice innovators temporarily. The latter would require a degree of market power that some, but not all Blue plans possess.

Legal impediments to competition—can antitrust be trusted? Another barrier to the realization of anticipated savings from an incentives strategy to cost containment may arise if only weak legal remedies are available to innovators under attack by their opponents or if more traditional providers use legal remedies *against* innovators. The first question concerns the effectiveness of legal remedies against boycotts. If new types of insurance plans are successfully boycotted, or if they never appear in the first place out of fear of such retaliation, the stimulus to innovation provided by consumer incentives may end in frustration.

Havighurst suggests that although the likelihood of successful antitrust actions against professional groups has increased following recent Supreme Court decisions, there are still numerous obstacles to using antitrust law effectively to protect innovators. Unlike price fixing, professional restraints against organizational innovations do not require unanimous action in order to be effective; sporadic and incomplete boycotts may deter competitive challenges. Furthermore, according to Havighurst, the difficulty of proving the existence of a contract or conspiracy to boycott is a major impediment to the use of antitrust laws against professionals seeking to drive innovators from the market.[36]

---

[35] Clark C. Havighurst, "Professional Restraints on Innovation in Health Care Financing," *Duke Law Journal*, vol. 1978, no. 2 (May 1978), pp. 327–28.

[36] Ibid., p. 344–45

Havighurst contends that medical society pressure on innovative providers may be extremely subtle, working through code words, signals, letter writing, or newsletters. Moreover, legal challenges to such practices could be constrained by (1) the use of "professionalism" as a defense for boycotts; (2) the Noerr-Pennington doctrine, which sets First Amendment limits on the use of antitrust rules to control concerted action by competitors when political rights would be infringed; and (3) a "seal-of-approval" justification for activities, perceived as conveying information to consumers, that involve standard setting or disapproval of particular structures of third-party payment plans.[37]

Havighurst argues that an effective antitrust policy is an essential adjunct to a market-oriented health plan:

> The Enthoven plan or any other market-oriented health policy would require an effective antitrust enforcement strategy to maintain not just the appearance of choice in a pluralistic environment but the reality of a marketplace in which private financing and delivery mechanisms of all kinds could compete for consumers' dollars.[38]

Nor will devising such an effective strategy be easy:

> physicians have a considerable capacity to frustrate change at the local level and they could well succeed in many instances despite the best efforts of antitrust enforcers and the courts. Moreover, recognition of potential obstacles could deter all innovations except those acceptable to the profession, thus occasioning no overt behavior to which antitrust penalties could attach. Finally, even if an innovative plan were in fact the victim of egregiously predatory practices, it might be reluctant to sue, to threaten suit or to invoke the public prosecutor for fear of hardening the opposition still further, with only an uncertain prospect of ultimate relief. The better part of valor might be for the plan to accommodate itself to the profession's demands, dropping its more threatening features. The deal struck would be directly proportionate to the profession's de facto power, perhaps reduced, but not eliminated, by the antitrust threat.[39]

The second question concerns legal challenges to closed-panel arrangements by providers excluded from participation. Although such challenges could be deflected by a practice of penalizing but not excluding from plan participation certain providers who fail to adopt insurer cost containment requirements, it would be surprising if challenges

---

[37] Ibid., pp. 349–62.
[38] Ibid., p. 385.
[39] Ibid., p. 373.

did not occur. The practice of the closed panel of providers, like the practice of the closed shop in industrial relations, is likely to be a source of controversy that may lead to various judicial or legislative limitations.

The impact of regulatory requirements. Regulatory requirements and legislation may also stand in the way of the spread of HMOs and "hybrids" that combine various features of conventional plans and HMOs. One limitation on the expansion of innovative plans emerges, ironically, from the HMO legislative authority. The Health Maintenance Organization Act of 1973[40] was intended to foster the development of HMOs, but some observers believe that the legislation was drawn too narrowly.[41] Frech and Ginsburg suggested that the legislation has been ineffective, if not counterproductive.

> The immediate problem with regard to HMOs is to reverse current policies that discourage them. There is a long history of state laws hostile to the development of HMOs, and while federal policy became officially favorable with the passage in 1973 of the Health Maintenance Organization Act, one may suspect that the law was written by interests hostile to HMOs. Little help has actually been rendered and some provisions of the law are, indeed, harmful to the continued existence of HMOs.[42]

The chief barrier to HMO development emerging from the legislation may be related to the very high minimum standards of comprehensiveness of insured services, which in some cases exceed those typical in private health insurance policies. The HMO act, however, has been amended to relax these standards, and this legislation has helped to stimulate competition among delivery systems by requiring that employers offer qualified HMOs, where available, to their employees.

A further step in the direction of relaxing constraints on HMO development was incorporated in the 1979 Health Planning Amendments. Indeed, concern over the adverse impact of regulation on HMO growth led Congress to exempt HMOs almost entirely from regulatory requirements (which continue to cover conventional plans) on the grounds that HMOs are sufficiently disciplined by competition that the "market failure" rationale for regulation does not hold.[43] It is not clear,

---

[40] Public Law 93–222, 87 Stat. 914 (1973).

[41] See Walter McClure, "On Broadening the Definition of and Removing Regulatory Barriers to a Competitive Health Care System," *Journal of Health, Politics, and Law,* vol. 3, no. 3 (Fall 1978), p. 303.

[42] H. E. Frech III and Paul B. Ginsburg, *Public Insurance in Private Medical Markets: Some Problems with National Health Insurance* (Washington, D.C.: American Enterprise Institute, 1978), p. 67.

[43] Clark C. Havighurst and Glenn M. Hackbarth, "Competition and Health Care: Planning for Deregulation," *Regulation* (May/June 1980), p. 48.

however, whether this special treatment for HMOs will be helpful to other types of unconventional delivery systems. In addition, bills are under consideration in Congress that would enable Medicare beneficiaries to direct the Medicare program to pay 95 percent of the average cost of serving their actuarial category to an HMO as a prospective payment. Such proposed legislation would help to expand the business of HMOs, but, in current form, only HMOs.

Regulatory requirements may combine with other factors to generate a "threshold" effect that inhibits the development of meaningful competition in the market for health insurance. Until some threshold level of penetration by innovative plans is achieved, the competitive impact of such plans on market-wide performance may be quite limited. Thus we may need to remove impediments to the formation of such a critical mass.

One set of impediments includes various limitations on the supply of different types of medical staff. Restrictions against the use of paramedical personnel and discouragement of physician advertising, for example, could contribute to bottlenecks that would inhibit the growth of innovative delivery systems.

McClure contends that although meaningful competition becomes a realistic vision once several "alternative" plans are under way in an area, the hostile climate toward such plans makes it difficult to launch the first few plans. The first few plans, he suggests, will encounter physician resistance and will be unfamiliar to most consumers and employers. McClure stresses the need for educational efforts and pressure on skeptics from business, labor, government, and concerned providers.[44]

McClure argues that even though traditional plans and providers may try to frustrate a competitive challenge by such means as predatory pricing, these tactics are not unique, and modern market economies have effective means of minimizing such occurrences. But, he concedes that:

> the skeptics indeed have a case before the basic market is established. The worst realistic scenario occurs if the first few health care plans in an area become content with their market share after they have acquired 20–30,000 enrollees or so to assure stability. Then, relatively few consumers, unions and employers understand or demand fair market choice. There is not enough pluralism for more economic styles of practice to gain professional acceptance, and traditional physicians can ostracize colleagues thinking of participating in new plans.

[44] Walter McClure, *Comprehensive and Regulatory Strategies for Medical Care* (Excelsior, Minn.: InterStudy, 1980), pp. 135–45.

Growth and competitive forces grind to a halt or never get off the ground.[45]

In addition to the possibility that a critical number of HMOs or other alternative plans may be needed to effectuate meaningful competition, the savings emerging from individual HMOs may be a function of HMO size. New HMOs may not immediately generate efficiencies that are associated with larger enrollment. There is some reported evidence of scale economies for HMOs.[46]

Breaking old habits. It might be misleading to think of open-ended tax subsidies for health care as a system that has been thrust upon the population, frustrating or distorting people's desire to economize on the use of resources for health care. This notion implies that if we converted to fixed tax subsidies, consumers would pressure insurers (who in turn would pressure providers) to hold costs in line with expected benefits.

Consumers, however, may confound this premise by continuing to divert resources to health care up to the point at which expected benefits approach zero, and thus may purchase individual treatments that are not "worth" their cost. Some people view such use of the health care system beyond the point at which benefits are estimated to be commensurate with costs as a clearly undesirable event. As Louise Russell has observed, however, a medical care system that treats resources almost as free might be considered a manifestation of rational consumer preferences.[47] According to this viewpoint, the basic "cause" of health cost increases is consumer preferences for a system in which almost any treatment with a reasonable chance of producing some benefit to the patient can be received irrespective of cost. These values, or preferences, lead to a system of signals, incentives, regulations, and subsidies that encourage consumers to purchase an increasingly expensive product. Russell, however, points out that:

> This point of view may be correct. But it rests on the questionable assumption that people fully understand the consequences of the current system, in terms of money and in terms of medical risk, and that they understand these to be the consequences of the system and neither accidental nor short term.[48]

I question the extent to which consumers would really respond

---

[45] Ibid., p. 142.

[46] See General Accounting Office, *Health Maintenance Organizations Can Help Control Health Care Costs,* May 1980, p. 29.

[47] Louise B. Russell, "Medical Care Costs," in Joseph P. Pechman, ed., *Setting National Priorities: The 1978 Budget* (Washington, D.C.: Brookings Institution, 1977), p. 187.

[48] Ibid.

differently to an altered set of financial incentives for the purchase of health insurance. Other factors being equal, consumers clearly prefer to pay less for the same package of benefits than more, or to receive more for the same outlays. Other factors, however, are rarely constant. Many HMOs, for example, offer more comprehensive coverage than conventional plans, and, if coverage differences are taken into account, lower costs. Also, many HMOs feature shorter waiting times for doctors after an appointment is made. Luft reports, on the other hand, that consumers have expressed dissatisfaction with the length of time an HMO enrollee must wait for an appointment in the first place. Members were also unable to see their usual physician for urgent visits and complained of limited communication and warmth in their physician-patient relationships.[49]

For some, the favorable features of HMOs will clearly outweigh the negative factors. Indeed, many consumers who discount the importance of such drawbacks to HMOs—or do not view them as a problem at all—are already enrolled in HMOs. Others, spurred by the savings passed through to consumers, will join the HMO ranks. Nonetheless, a significant proportion of consumers might still reject innovative plans even after a change that improves the payoff from selecting a lower-cost approach. For this group, the cost saving will not be enough to eclipse the perceived disadvantages, which may reflect nonfinancial, but real costs.

We must recognize also the deep skepticism, or at least caution, of business and labor toward the altered treatment of federal tax breaks for health care. Although much of this concern may stem from misconceptions about a plan like CCHP, it would be inadvisable to push these concerns aside. Enthoven has correctly observed that while the principles of CCHP are not incompatible with organized labor's long-standing commitment to universal comprehensive health insurance, the emphasis on diversity and choice in CCHP suggests to some that it conflicts with the notion of a single standard of care.[50] Furthermore, since many major unions have won health benefit packages that currently cost their employers between $200 and $300 per month, it would not be surprising to find them opposed to a plan like the Ullman bill, which would limit employer contributions to $120 per month in 1981 dollars and which would thereby convert at least half of the existing employer payments into taxable income to the workers.

Enthoven also presents several reasons why many business firms (with notable exceptions) have been cool to the idea of applying com-

---

[49] See Luft, "Health Maintenance Organizations,"pp. 296–97.
[50] Enthoven, "The Politics of NHI," pp. 238–39.

petitive principles to the purchase of health insurance. These reasons include (probably overblown) concern with the administrative cost of multiple choice, the tendency to offer the "best" health plan in order to attract skilled workers or as a bargaining pawn in labor negotiations.[51]

Conclusion

This chapter appears to praise the Enthoven plan with faint criticism, and that praise is not entirely unintentional, for Enthoven's approach is essentially sound and represents a proposed solution that is targeted to the problem. His plan contrasts sharply with elaborate new regulatory schemes that would attack the symptoms of the problem, while glossing over the problem itself.

Nonetheless, it is important to sound a cautionary note about the potential pitfalls that lie between an incentives-based proposal and the achievement of its intended results. The practice of reimbursing, if not rewarding inefficiency, is deeply entrenched in the health care system and will not easily be dislodged. It is embodied both in government policy and in private-sector behavior. There are, to be sure, encouraging signs in both the public and private arenas that advocates of market incentives are winning recruits; but old habits change slowly, and we should not confuse intimations of interest in a few quarters with broad public acceptance.

This chapter discusses three questionable aspects of the transformation of an incentives-based blueprint for health care cost containment into a working plan with demonstrable results: Will accompanying regulatory requirements, however well intentioned, undermine the potential cost savings? Do cost savings achieved in innovative plans to date reflect real economic efficiency? Will potential savings from lower-cost plans actually stimulate consumers to keep the pressure on insurers and providers to practice cost-conscious medicine?

The last question is particularly troublesome. It brings us face to face with the dominant position of the Blues in many market areas, with the long-standing reluctance of organized medicine to practice meaningful cost containment, with the apparent preferences of many consumers for individual practice fee-for-service medical care, and with the persistent penchant of the government for cost lids and regulatory policies. The fundamental question, however, is whether the public is willing to break out of the "cost-pass-through" mentality with which it appears rather comfortable.

The bottom line is this—Do consumers want lower health care costs

[51] Ibid., pp. 241–43.

enough to break with firmly established habits and institutions? Are they as concerned about "cost control" as the federal government is, and are they willing to "pay" for it through a gradual abandonment of patterns and practices with which they are familiar? The answer to these questions will be crucial to the ultimate cost-saving potential of market-oriented cost containment strategies. We should lay this choice before consumers (move toward a fair-choice environment) and be prepared to live with the results. In a fair-choice environment, if health care expenditures continue to grow relative to other categories of spending, such an increase should be taken not as a signal for corrective government action, but as a manifestation of rational consumer preferences for more health care, for which consumers are willing to sacrifice other goods and services.

Consumer Choice Health Plan and the Patient Cost-Sharing Strategy: Can They Be Reconciled?

Laurence S. Seidman

Advocates of a market-oriented approach to health insurance policy have emphasized two distinct strategies that may at first glance appear to be in conflict: competition among prepaid health maintenance organizations (HMOs), and patient cost sharing under fee for service (FFS). The difference between these two strategies is genuine. This chapter argues that HMO advocates overstate the merits of prepayment and underestimate the positive contribution that can be made by patient cost sharing under FFS. It is first argued, however, that a single proposal can be developed that consistently combines the main elements of the HMO strategy and the patient cost-sharing strategy. If amended to incorporate the concerns of advocates of patient cost sharing, Alain Enthoven's Consumer Choice Health Plan (CCHP) should warrant the support of advocates of both strategies. An amended CCHP offers the best practical policy for the health sector and represents a market-oriented alternative to the regulatory approach.

The first strategy being considered here was developed by Martin Feldstein, Mark Pauly, and others[1] (including this author). It stresses the role of patient cost sharing (through deductibles and coinsurance) and recommends catastrophic (major-risk) insurance that provides an out-of-pocket ceiling for each household, but at the same time requires

---

[1] Martin Feldstein, "A New Approach to National Health Insurance," *The Public Interest,* vol. 23 (Spring 1971), pp. 93–105; Mark V. Pauly, *An Analysis of National Health Insurance Proposals* (Washington, D.C.: American Enterprise Institute, 1971); Laurence Seidman, "Medical Loans and Major-Risk National Health Insurance," *Health Services Research,* vol. 12 (Summer 1977), pp. 123–28; and Laurence Seidman, "Income-Related Consumer Cost Sharing: A Strategy for the Health Sector," in Mark V. Pauly, ed., *National Health Insurance: What Now, What Later, What Never?* (Washington, D.C.: American Enterprise Institute, 1980).

most patients to bear a fraction of the cost of their own medical care. The second strategy, articulated by Alain Enthoven and others, emphasizes the role of competition between prepaid HMOs, and envisions a gradual conversion of the medical market from FFS to prepayment of providers. HMO supporters argue that prepayment will induce providers to contain cost and eliminate unnecessary service. Competition among HMOs will pressure each to provide maximum quality for a given cost.

Advocates of each of the two strategies have expressed reservations about the other approach. HMO supporters are usually skeptical of the efficacy of patient cost sharing under FFS. Proponents of patient cost sharing under FFS have questioned whether replacement of traditional FFS by prepaid HMOs for most of the population is either feasible or desirable. With a little tolerance, there is no reason why supporters of both strategies cannot unite behind a single proposal—one that consistently combines the main elements of both. Let us begin with Alain Enthoven's "Consumer Choice Health Plan (CCHP)," which is inspired primarily by a sympathy with the HMO strategy.

Consumer Choice Health Plan (CCHP) and Patient Cost Sharing: A Practical Reconciliation

In his important recent book *Health Plan*,[2] Alain Enthoven sets out the elements of CCHP. The central elements of his plan and possible amendments incorporating patient cost-sharing strategy within CCHP are as follows:

Repeal of the Current Tax Subsidy for Health Insurance. Advocates of both strategies have stressed the necessity of ending the current tax subsidy, which is a major source of inefficiency and inflation in the health sector. Currently, if an employer compensates an employee $100 in cash wage, the compensation is taxable income to the employee, so that his after-tax compensation is perhaps $70. If the employer instead compensates him by purchasing $100 of additional health insurance, the $100 is excluded from the employee's taxable income. Moreover, no limit is imposed on the amount of health insurance expense that can be excluded. This tax subsidy to health insurance has provided a powerful incentive, for it has encouraged employees to prefer, and employers and unions to negotiate, a shift in the total compensation package from cash wages to extensive "first-dollar" health insurance.

[2] Alain C. Enthoven, *Health Plan* (Reading, Mass.: Addison-Wesley Publishing Co., 1980).

451

As a result, today over 90 percent of all hospital revenues from patient care come from insurers—private or public; less than 10 percent is paid out of pocket by patients. The average hospital patient bears little or none of the cost of his own hospital care because his bill is paid by an insurer. Physicians—who decide whether hospitalization is required, select the hospital, prescribe the tests and services, and determine the length of stay—have no reason to weigh cost because their fully insured patients rationally regard hospital cost as irrelevant.

As Enthoven points out, the subsidy also implies that if an employee chooses a more costly delivery system (perhaps traditional FFS instead of an efficient HMO), he bears only a fraction of the additional cost owing to the exclusion. The subsidy has therefore weakened the ability of HMOs to attract members and has prevented a fair competition in which the full cost differential between alternative health plans is borne by the consumer who selects the costlier plan.

A Tax Credit for Health Insurance. In place of the repealed tax subsidy, CCHP would introduce a new tax credit for expense on a "qualified" health plan. The key feature of the tax credit is that for a household with given income and demographic characteristics, the credit would *not* vary with its expense on a health plan. Thus, if the household chooses plan A, which charges $200 more than plan B, its tax credit will remain the same, so that it bears the full additional cost of $200. The bearing of the full cost differential is in sharp contrast to the situation under the current tax subsidy.

The tax credit to which a given household would be entitled would vary with its expected actuarial cost, as indicated by its demographic characteristics, such as the number of persons in the household and age and sex of the members.

Enthoven would divide the population into two groups with respect to income—poor and nonpoor. He recommends that the nonpoor receive the same credit regardless of income, while the poor would receive a larger credit ("voucher"). A poor household with no income would receive the largest credit; as with a negative income tax, the credit would decline gradually until, at the border of poor-nonpoor, the poor credit would equal the nonpoor credit.

It is important to recognize that a uniform credit for all nonpoor households is not essential to the competition CCHP seeks to promote. One reason that Enthoven suggests a uniform nonpoor credit is to try to avoid any disincentive to earning a higher income. As analysis of the negative income tax has taught, any subsidy that phases out as income rises contains an implicit positive marginal tax rate that provides some discouragement to higher earnings. Despite this concern, there is a strong argument for designing the credit to decline smoothly and gradually as household income rises, from a maximum for a poor household with no income, to a small value (equal to the actuarial value of the "last-resort" credit described in the section "Catastrophic Insurance of Last Resort through a Tax Credit") for a "high" income household.[3] A gradual phase-down of credit would impose only a very small positive marginal tax rate and have little disincentive effect. It would, however, have two important advantages.

First, it would make CCHP more equitable. If, for example, $10,000 is the border between poor and nonpoor, why should the federal government provide identical credit to the $10,000 household and the $60,000 household? The purpose of the credit is to enable each household to afford a "qualified" health plan that provides adequate coverage. Since the ability to pay differs greatly among "nonpoor" households, why shouldn't the credit be adjusted accordingly? Under CCHP, the 1040 personal income tax return must provide a tax credit table that varies the credit with demographics. It can just as easily vary the credit with income.

Second, a gradual phase-down would greatly reduce the budgetary and tax cost of CCHP. The $60,000 household can afford an adequate "qualified" plan with little federal assistance. Little is gained by raising taxes on the whole population, including the $60,000 household, to finance a large credit for high-income households. Much is lost, however, because the unnecessary raising of tax rates to finance credits for the affluent discourages earning.

Phasing down the credit as income rises would not affect the central principle of CCHP: each household's credit must not vary according to its expense on a health plan, so that the household bears the full additional cost of joining a more costly plan.

A "Qualified" Health Plan. Although Enthoven is partial to prepaid HMOs and critical of FFS, he does not try to exclude FFS health plans from CCHP competition. An insurance policy that reimburses FFS providers is eligible to become "qualified." To be "qualified" for CCHP tax credit, an FFS or HMO plan must cover certain basic services (inpatient and outpatient on an equal basis, to remove the bias toward inpatient in many current plans), and to provide "catastrophic protection"—a ceiling on the out-of-pocket burden that a household must bear.

The specific magnitude of the out-of-pocket ceiling is of crucial importance to the fate of FFS plans that might rely on significant patient

---

[3] I am grateful to Alain Enthoven for his point that because of my "last-resort" credit, a complete phase-out would overdiscourage private insurance.

cost sharing. Obviously, if the required ceiling were low, patient cost sharing would be severely limited. Limited cost sharing would assure that any FFS plan would have no built-in resistance to overutilization, and cost inflation. The result would be unfair competition, biased in favor of prepaid HMOs.

A single required ceiling (Enthoven tentatively suggests $1,500, which is low—not much greater than the average premium) ignores the fact that what a household can afford depends on its income. Instead, a schedule should be developed on the basis of household budget studies in which the *maximum* tolerable burden at each income level would be approximated. For example, to obtain CCHP credit, a household with $20,000 income might be required to join a plan with a ceiling no greater than $2,500; while for a $40,000 household, the ceiling could not exceed $5,000. It should be recalled that the amendment offered in subsection (B)—that is, varying the credit inversely with income—would provide greater assistance to the $20,000 household than to the $40,000 household, so that the $20,000 household would be able to afford the higher premium policy with the lower ceiling.

It would then be essential, as Enthoven also recommends, to require health plans to display prominently the out-of-pocket ceiling and to remind potential enrollees that eligibility for CCHP credit depends on the ceiling and the household's income. Health plans may be expected to offer policies with a variety of ceilings and patient cost sharing so that each household can select a "qualified" plan.

The maximum tolerable burden for a household with a given income depends on the availability of loans. Elsewhere, I have described a medical loan program implemented by private loan institutions under contract with the government. If the loan program were incorporated in CCHP, then the ceiling schedule could be raised and the CCHP tax credit reduced without subjecting households to hardship. The result would be a reduction in the budgetary and tax cost of CCHP.

If there is to be fair competition between HMOs and FFS plans as well as patient cost sharing, it is essential that the $1,500 uniform ceiling tentatively suggested by Enthoven be replaced by a schedule that varies with income and that is set at the level of maximum tolerable burden for each income class.

Catastrophic Insurance of Last Resort through a Tax Credit. In *Health Plan,* Enthoven agrees that some provision must be made for those— for example, "migrants, derelicts, the underworld, illegal aliens, non-enrollers, others"—who do not join a health plan or who buy inadequate private coverage. Advocates of universal major-risk (catastrophic) insurance want everyone without private insurance automatically covered by a public catastrophic insurance policy. Elsewhere I have described such a policy implemented by a tax credit. The same schedule of maximum tolerable burden should be used to set the tax credit schedule.

Consider, for example, a $20,000 household without private insurance. It might be required to bear the first $1,250 of its annual medical bill. It would then be entitled to a tax credit equal to 80 percent of its medical bill in excess of $1,250 until its annual out-of-pocket burden reached $2,500—the burden that would accrue if its annual medical bill reached $7,500. It would then be entitled to a tax credit equal to 100 percent of its medical bill in excess of $7,500. Like the CCHP credit, this credit would be "refundable," so that a poor household with no tax liability would still receive a check from IRS for its medical credit.

The deductible ($1,250), the coinsurance rate (20 percent), and the ceiling ($2,500) would vary with household income. Although most households would choose to join private health plans with somewhat lower ceilings (assisted by the basic CCHP credit), the incorporation of the last-resort credit into CCHP would assure universal, income-related catastrophic protection by providing coverage for the minority who failed to join an adequate private plan.

The Problem of Adverse Selection. Enthoven's chapter of this volume expresses misgivings concerning two of my amendments—phasing down the credit as income rises and raising the out-of-pocket ceiling permitted for a qualified plan—because he is worried about adverse selection and free riders. He fears that a high-ceiling (low-premium) FFS plan will attract healthy households and that HMOs having no cost-sharing provisions will be left with unhealthy households; that is, the HMOs will be compelled to establish their own coinsurance and will become essentially fee-for-service enterprises.

Adverse selection is a problem. As Fred Kahn has said in this volume, on the one hand we want choice and competition, on the other hand we are haunted by the specter of adverse selection. It is not obvious how serious a problem it would pose. HMOs, for example, would probably respond by offering two plans—a high-premium plan with no cost sharing and a low-premium plan with patient cost sharing. Further research is surely warranted on this important aspect of the health insurance market.

Enthoven would give the benefit of the doubt to the prepayment approach. Those who believe FFS with cost sharing has an important contribution to make would give less weight to the danger of adverse selection and more weight to the benefit to consumers of wider choice. Both sides would admit that some experience with an actual CCHP competition would help us to decide where to strike the balance between choice and adverse selection.

Summary Although inspired by a sympathy for HMOs and a skepticism of patient cost sharing under FFS, CCHP would nevertheless—if the above amendments were accepted—promote fair competition between HMOs and FFS plans that should fully satisfy advocates of both HMOs and patient cost sharing.

For practical policy, unity on a modified CCHP proposal is more important than the difference in viewpoint between advocates of the two strategies. If political unity were the sole objective of this chapter, it would be prudent to omit the subsequent discussion. The assumption here, however, is that further analysis of the two competing views is in itself important and need not jeopardize a reconciliation on practical policy. As one who believes that patient cost sharing under FFS has an important role to play in the health sector, I want to challenge some assertions and analyses of HMO advocates. The following section explains why some HMO advocates have underrated the positive potential role of FFS with patient cost sharing and have overrated the virtues of prepaid HMOs.

Prepaid HMOs versus FFS with Patient Cost Sharing

Imperfect Agency: The Doctor-Patient Relationship. To place the HMOs-versus-FFS controversy in proper perspective, one must recognize the fundamental dilemma facing the consumer seeking medical care. The relationship between patient and physician may be described as "imperfect agency." The patient, lacking technical knowledge, seeks a physician who will make decisions on his behalf. Ideally, the patient wants the physician to decide exactly as the patient would if the patient possessed the physician's knowledge. If the physician behaved in this way, he would be a "perfect agent" for his patient. Physicians, however, generally weigh their own self-interest as well as the interest of their patient. It is no criticism of doctors to suggest that they, like members of virtually all other occupations, consider the financial consequences for themselves of their own behavior.

Thus, the fundamental problem of imperfect agency arises because the medical knowledge of the doctor and that of the patient are asymmetrical. The patient must therefore rely on his doctor, trusting him to be a faithful agent; yet he recognizes that the doctor has his own self-interest to consider. The patient would like to structure the incentives of his physician to be those of a perfect agent. But no structuring of incentives can accomplish this goal perfectly. Consider, first, the FFS arrangement. As Enthoven and other HMO advocates stress, under FFS the doctor is paid in proportion to the service he performs. This financial incentive in itself encourages more service.

Of course, if service were sufficiently excessive under FFS so that the patient recognized the inflation, and if the patient were subject to cost sharing, then he would resent such practice. He might not recommend the physician to friends, or refuse to return to the physician the next time he incurs a medical problem. Gradually, the "inflationary" physician might lose patients and income. In the absence of patient cost sharing, however, there would be little check on the inflationary tendency of FFS. Even if a patient recognized that his hospital bill was unnecessarily high, he would not resent his doctor as long as an insurer paid the entire bill.

Because FFS and the absence of patient cost sharing have existed simultaneously for hospital services for more than a decade, critics of hospital sector inflation have often failed to distinguish the roles of the two distinct elements. How much inefficiency is due to FFS—that is, to the fact that the hospitals are paid in proportion to service rendered? How much is due to the absence of patient cost sharing, the result of which is that each physician knows that his patient would not want cost to influence his decisions? We will return to this issue shortly.

Although HMO advocates recognize that FFS makes the agency relationship imperfect, they fail to recognize that prepayment of providers also creates a distortion in the opposite direction. Under FFS, the physician is financially rewarded if he performs more service than the patient would order if he had the physician's knowledge—provided that the patient remains unaware that the service is excessive. But under a prepaid HMO arrangement, the doctor is financially rewarded if he performs less service than the patient would want, provided, once again, that the patient remains unaware of this deficiency.

HMO advocates often emphasize exactly this tendency, and assume that it is self-evident that any cost reduction so achieved is desirable. But efficiency is not equivalent to cost reduction. Efficiency means achieving the "right" level of service and cost. Providing too little is just as inefficient as providing too much.

What is the "right" level? Ideally, it is the level that the patient (or his family) would choose if he had the technical knowledge and were faced with the true cost of service, but were assisted with a "lump-sum" income transfer so that he could afford the necessary service. The ideal involves achieving perfect agency and eliminating any problems of dual loyalty for the physician.

In practice, however, perfect agency is unattainable because of the disparity in medical knowledge; thus any arrangement—FFS or HMO—

will deviate to some extent from this ideal. As the HMO advocate is quick to emphasize, the long-run financial interest of the HMO and its physicians should limit the tendency to underserve, for if the HMO develops a reputation for such underservice, it will lose membership.

Similarly, provided there is patient cost sharing, the long-run financial interest of the FFS doctor should limit the FFS tendency to overserve, for if the physician develops a reputation for such overservice and if his patients bear the financial consequences, he will eventually lose patients.

But isn't it better to err on the side of underservice and cost reduction? Not necessarily. Each consumer will evaluate the risks differently. For one person, the FFS risk that surgery will be performed when it should not be, will lead him to prefer the HMO arrangement. For another person, the HMO risk that surgery will not be performed when it should be, will lead him to prefer the FFS arrangement.

As long as the consumer must bear the cost consequence of his choice, social welfare is promoted by permitting him to choose the arrangement he prefers. It is not correct to assert, or imply, that it is socially desirable for the consumer to choose the least costly arrangement. For many other goods or services, each consumer weighs quality, risk, and cost in making his choice. One consumer is willing to pay more to obtain a higher quality or to improve the probability that the good or service will be safe; another consumer is not, and therefore buys the less costly good or service. Economic efficiency is promoted when the subjective preference of each consumer interacts with the objective cost of the product, so that choice reflects the weighing of subjective benefit against objective cost. Choice of agency arrangement in medical care—FFS or HMO—will also promote efficiency, as long as the consumer must bear the cost consequences of his decision.

In addition to the distinction between underservice and overservice, there is another important difference between HMO and FFS that each consumer will weigh. As Enthoven concedes, under a prepaid HMO the consumer must "accept a limited choice of doctors, including only those participating in that particular system."[4] Because payment is not in proportion to service but is fixed in advance, the group of physicians who will provide service must be designated in advance. In contrast, under FFS insurance the patient can choose at the time he seeks service any physician willing to treat him.

Suppose that a person develops a particular problem unexpectedly. If he is an HMO member, he can first seek the relevant specialists within the HMO. If he is not satisfied with the treatment and wants treatment

[4] Enthoven, *Health Plan*, p. 56.

from a specialist outside his HMO, his HMO generally will not cover it.

Often, an individual who develops a particular problem wants to be treated by a physician who has successfully treated a friend or acquaintance with the same problem, or by a specialist who is recommended by a personal friend who is a physician. Under FFS, insurance will cover to the same degree any physician the person chooses. If he is an HMO member, however, he will normally be required to pay the full fee out of pocket if he selects an outside physician, despite the HMO premium he has already paid.

For some persons, the HMO's restricted choice will be outweighed by its other advantages. It should be recognized, however, that many other persons will highly value the greater flexibility and choice permitted by FFS insurance. As long as the consumer must bear any additional cost of an FFS plan, his choice of such a plan is not inefficient, or socially undesirable. Whenever a consumer, given his subjective preferences, decides that the benefit outweighs the additional cost, it would be inefficient to restrict him to the less costly good or service.

The merit of CCHP—as modified by amendments presented in this chapter—is that it would promote fair competition among health plans that would allow each household to weigh all the attributes of HMO versus FFS—cost, quality, risk, and freedom of choice of physician. Each arrangement fails to achieve perfect agency and has its pros and cons. Some HMO advocates contend that in fair competition HMOs will gradually overwhelm FFS, but such an outcome is doubtful. Whatever the result, however, what matters for consumer welfare and economic efficiency is that the competition be fair and not be improperly biased toward HMO or FFS. An amended CCHP would permit such competition. May the arrangement preferred by most consumers win.

FFS with Patient Cost Sharing. Elsewhere, I have presented at length an analysis of how consumer cost sharing (deductibles and coinsurance) is likely to affect FFS behavior. This section is a reply to the skepticism of Enthoven—whose views are similar to those of many HMO advocates—and to supporters of government regulation concerning FFS (Enthoven, of course, is a staunch opponent of regulation).

In his section "Are Deductibles and Coinsurance the Solution?"[5] Enthoven makes several points. First, that "most people show, in their political and market behavior, that they do not like heavy reliance on deductibles and coinsurance."[6] Yet Enthoven himself has correctly em-

[5] Ibid., pp. 32-36.
[6] Ibid., p. 33.

phasized the powerful stimulus of the current tax subsidy for more extensive insurance. Although he is aware that this stimulus has biased choice against HMOs, he appears to ignore the bias against patient cost sharing in FFS plans due to the same tax subsidy. Of course, consumers would rather have less cost sharing if it could be obtained without raising the premium. But it cannot. As long as the tax subsidy is repealed so that a higher premium will be fully borne by the consumer, the consumer will be compelled to weigh cost sharing against the premium, without the current distortion of the premium tax subsidy. We do not at present have evidence on how the majority would respond to such a choice because of the powerful bias of the tax subsidy.

Further, Enthoven notes that "Most of our public and private insurance now has some deductibles and/or coinsurance (though the trend is to reduce both), and that hasn't prevented inflation."[7]

This assertion is misleading. Today, more than 90 percent of all hospital revenues from patient care come from insurers, private or public.[8] This figure does not mean that every hospital patient has a coinsurance rate of perhaps 8 percent. A small number of hospital patients pay a substantial fraction of their bill, either because they have no insurance or have limited insurance, or because they experience an extremely long stay that exhausts their basic hospital coverage. The average hospital patient whose stay is eight days[9] is completely covered for hospital service (not the physician's fee), except for perhaps a small, flat-dollar deductible.

For example, one standard Blue Cross plan requires only $5 per day copayment for the first ten days; the next fifty days are completely free. In 1978 the American Hospital Association reported that average inpatient revenue per inpatient-day in community hospitals was $220.[10] Thus, hospital care was virtually free under this typical plan for the average patient. For the small minority of patients whose stay exceeds sixty days, however, cost sharing becomes significant; basic hospital insurance ends at sixty days, and "major medical coverage" requiring coinsurance of 20 percent then applies.

In contrast to hospital service, physician service is generally not fully covered. Therefore an average hospital episode, which includes physician service, is not free to the patient. In this sense, the average

[7] Ibid.

[8] Robert Gibson, "National Health Expenditures, 1978," *Health Care Financing Review*, vol. 1 (Summer 1979), p. 1.

[9] U.S. Department of Health, Education, and Welfare, National Center for Health Statistics, *Utilization of Short-Stay Hospitals*, 1978, table D.

[10] According to Dorothy Rice, director of the National Center for Health Statistics, in correspondence with the author.

patient does pay a fraction of the cost of a hospital episode. Nonetheless hospital service itself is free. When a physician, as an imperfect agent for his patient, decides whether hospitalization is necessary, which hospital to use, what tests or services to order, when discharge should occur, he has no reason to weigh cost because his patient will bear none of it. As a result, no pressure is transmitted to hospital managers to strive to provide a given quality at minimum cost because such efficiency will not influence physicians who choose for their patients. Thus, it is simply incorrect to imply that significant coinsurance has been utilized for hospital service in the last decade. It has not. Hospital service has been almost free for the average patient.

Next, Enthoven correctly notes that as long as coinsurance is less than 100 percent, it implies partial subsidization of the patient, so that utilization would still be greater than if the patient were charged 100 percent of the cost. Coinsurance is a compromise that tries to strike a balance between protection (risk reduction) and efficiency in utilization under FFS. Some inefficiency in the use of resources must therefore be accepted to limit risk. It seems plausible, however, that a significant improvement in efficiency would follow an increase in the coinsurance rate of the average hospital patient from 0 percent to 20–25 percent. The crucial fact for the physician may be whether or not his average patient bears a nontrivial fraction of any cost incurred versus none of the cost; a shift from 0 percent to 20 percent might achieve a greater change in physician behavior than any increase above 20 percent.

It is not correct to imply, as Enthoven does, that this risk-efficiency trade-off can be escaped without any disadvantage to the consumer by replacing FFS with prepayment. We have already noted pros and cons of HMOs versus FFS. A consumer with particular preferences may prefer FFS with cost sharing to an HMO, even though he must pay a higher premium to cover the somewhat greater utilization implied by cost sharing that is less than 100 percent.

Enthoven accurately notes that under major-risk insurance, an out-of-pocket burden is reached at which concern for protection outweighs concern for efficient utilization, and a ceiling is imposed; the coinsurance rate is then reduced to 0 percent. He expresses the concern that for patients who reach this range, there would be no incentive for efficient resource use.

Under cost-sharing schedules likely to be offered under a CCHP competition, only a small number of patients would reach the free-care range. For example, consider a plan with a deductible of $1,500, 20 percent coinsurance, and a ceiling of $3,000, which would be reached when the household's annual medical bill reached $9,000. If the physician's bill is $1,500, thirty-four days would be required to reach a hospital bill of $7,500. But 97 percent of hospital patients stay less than thirty-four days.[11] It is true that 3 percent of all patients constitute a larger share of total hospital cost.[12] The main point, however, remains valid: Under cost sharing, most hospital cost will be incurred by patients subject to coinsurance. Special regulation may be necessary for the few who reach the free-care range. The overwhelming majority of patients, however, will retain the incentive to care about cost, and once they have recovered will appreciate avoidance of unnecessary cost by their physician.

Enthoven's fundamental point seems to be:

> The individual episode of medical care is usually not good material for rational economic calculation. If the patient is in pain, or urgent need of care, the transaction is not entirely voluntary. The sick or worried patient is in a poor position to make an economic analysis of treatment alternatives. When my injured child is lying bleeding on the operating table is hardly the time when I want to negotiate with the doctor over fees or the number of sutures that will be used.[13]

This statement misrepresents the way in which patient cost sharing is supposed to work. The strategy of coinsurance under FFS envisions the physician as an imperfect agent for his patient making decisions concerning hospitalization: whether to admit his patient, which hospital to choose, what tests to run and procedures to follow, when to discharge the patient.

We can accept the point emphasized by critics of cost sharing that the average patient must delegate these decisions to his physician and must rely on his physician's judgment and expertise. It is unrealistic to expect the average patient, even when there is no emergency, to challenge his physician at the time of decision. When hospitalization occurs, the patient is generally preoccupied about his prospects and not disposed to dwell on financial implications.

Consider, however, the average patient two months later, recovered from his hospital stay, as he receives his hospital bill. Today, if he even receives the bill—it is often sent solely to the insurer—he is pleased to learn what he does not have to pay. Under coinsurance, however, the average patient will become concerned about the details of his bill and will reflect on his physician's choices. Should the operation have been

[11] U.S. Department of Health, Education, and Welfare, *Utilization of Short-Stay Hospitals,* table 3.

[12] Enthoven is correct when he notes that 3 percent of patients account for significantly more than 3 percent of cost.

[13] Enthoven, *Health Plan,* p. 34.

done in hospital X, instead of Y? Did he really need test Z? Was the tenth day really necessary?

Physicians who take seriously the trust relationship, as well as those who want their patients to believe they take it seriously, will soon anticipate the concern of recuperated patients who now bear an important fraction of the cost. Physicians will gradually alter their habit—developed during a decade of no patient cost sharing—of disregarding cost and will begin to weigh cost in their decision making. Such a change in behavior will enable them to satisfy cost-conscious, recuperated patients, and to avoid resentment that might otherwise arise.

Is this type of evolution in physician behavior plausible? In the few areas in which a physician's choice does affect his patient's burden, some anecdotal evidence supports the above scenario. An MD says: "I will treat you as an inpatient, not an outpatient, or in my office, so your insurance will completely cover it." Or, "I will keep you in the hospital two more days because your insurance will cover that but won't cover nursing care at home." In contrast, it should not be surprising that no physician says: "I chose this hospital instead of the other because for your problem there is no difference in quality, but this one is cheaper per day." His patient would have no reason to care about this economy under today's insurance.

Today, wherever a physician can show concern for his patient's financial burden, he generally does so. Precisely because patients must rely on their physicians, they value one who is not only highly skilled, but who also seems concerned about them. A physician who develops a reputation for disregarding the cost of hospitalization when his patients must bear a large share of that cost may gradually lose recommendations, patients, and income.

Physicians' concern for their reputation with patients, who in turn refer other patients, implies that direct participation of patients in decision making is not necessary for patient cost sharing to have a significant impact on utilization and efficiency. The emergency example given by Enthoven ignores the importance of reputation to the long-term well-being of the physician. Suppose that a physician takes the myopic view: "I'll double my fee. What choice does he have?" After an emergency is over, what will the patient think about this physician? Will he return to him for nonemergency treatment, or in a future emergency? Will he recommend him to friends?

Concern for long-term reputation prevents producers of many goods and services from attempting short-term exploitation that will backfire in the long run. A producer may be able to seduce enough buyers to purchase a shoddy product that appears to be of high quality and may earn a handsome short-run profit. But if he seeks an operation that is successful in the long run, he should think twice. Will these consumers buy his product next year? Will they recommend his brand to their friends?

Precisely this concern for long-run viability should limit the tendency of most HMOs to underserve. Enthoven and other HMO advocates are well aware of this point. Yet the same concern for long-run success should limit the tendency of FFS physicians to take advantage of emergencies or of the dependence of their patients in the short run. Similarly, it should induce most physicians to give some attention to the financial impact on their patients of decisions concerning hospitalization, provided that cost sharing applies to most of their patients.

It is often alleged that medical care differs radically from other goods and services because patients do not have the knowledge to evaluate medical services. Not many realize that the same ignorance applies to numerous other goods and services. When a person buys a car or an appliance, how often does he understand its construction or the importance of particular features to the performance he desires? How does he know whether the product is poorly made or well constructed? In fact, most consumers rely on the reputation of the company, established over years of providing products to customers. Most people rely on recommendations of friends and whether they were satisfied in retrospect with the last product they bought from that company. For many products, then, the average consumer simply cannot independently judge the quality in advance.

Despite the not uncommon ignorance of the consumer at the time he buys such a good or service, the company seeking long-term success cannot ask: "What can we get away with in the short run?" Instead, it must ask: "How will the consumer feel in retrospect? Will he want to buy the product we offer next year? Will he tell friends he was satisfied with our product and the price we charged?"

Once it is grasped that concern for the retrospective view of consumers is a fundamental motive for many producers in the economy, the difference between medical care and other goods and services becomes less pronounced. Yet failure to recognize the importance of retrospective evaluation is typical of much of the analysis of the economics of medical care. Consider another of Enthoven's examples:

> Last spring, Mrs. Smith had no idea that her child would soon come down with pneumonia. So in selecting a pediatrician, she went on the basis of the doctor's fee for a routine follow-up visit and neglected to inquire about the fee for treating a case of pneumonia. How was she to know that the doctor charged $500 for that and ordered three times as many laboratory tests as other doctors would, until she got the bill![14]

---

[14] Ibid.

464

The story does not end here, however. Will she continue to use this pediatrician? Will she recommend him to friends? If others experience the same treatment, will they recommend him to friends? If this pediatrician is of truly exceptional quality, perhaps she and others will continue to use him. As in other sectors of the economy, exceptional quality can obtain a higher price. If his quality is average, however, then over the longer term he will probably be penalized for his behavior.

If an appreciation of the role of retrospective judgment shows that the difference between medical care and other goods and services has been exaggerated, what accounts for the relative inefficiency of the hospital sector? It is, of course, primarily due to the absence of consumer cost sharing. Remove consumer cost sharing from any other product, and the symptoms of the hospital sector will quickly appear. Let stereos be free to the consumer, and the price of stereos will escalate; let long-distance calls be free, and there will soon be a national telephone cost crisis. Even the regulated sectors of the economy—the public utilities—use consumer cost sharing to restrain demand. The gradual elimination of consumer cost sharing from the hospital sector over the past two decades is sufficient to account for its symptom of inefficiency.

Fair competition under a modified CCHP will enable us to test this hypothesis. Is it FFS per se that causes exceptional inefficiency? Or is it the absence of consumer cost sharing? FFS, when tempered by significant patient cost sharing, will probably perform with much improved efficiency and will prove to be an appealing arrangement for a large fraction of consumers, despite competition from prepaid HMOs.

Conclusion

Advocates of a market-oriented, nonregulatory approach to health insurance policy are divided between two strategies that at first glance appear to be in conflict. The first strategy emphasizes competition between prepaid health maintenance organizations (HMOs) and envisions a gradual conversion of medical care from a fee-for-service (FFS) market to prepayment of providers. The second stresses major-risk (catastrophic) insurance with significant patient cost sharing under FFS and relies on the response of FFS physicians to such cost sharing to promote efficiency.

Despite the fundamental difference in viewpoint between advocates of each strategy, they should be able to unite behind a single proposal. Several amendments to Enthoven's "Consumer Choice Health Plan (CCHP)," for example, could incorporate the concerns of supporters of patient cost sharing and could assure fair competition between prepaid HMOs and FFS with cost sharing. The amendments are as follows:

1. To enable FFS plans with cost sharing to compete fairly, a plan

465

should be able to qualify for CCHP tax credit despite significant cost sharing. To achieve this end, a plan should be permitted to have an out-of-pocket ceiling as great as the estimated maximum tolerable burden for a member of a given income. If instead a low ceiling were required for "qualification," such limited cost sharing might prevent FFS plans from adequately containing costs and premiums, and might thereby bias the competition in favor of HMOs.

2. The CCHP tax credit should decline continuously with household income to a small value for high-income households. Such a gradual phase-down would be more equitable—assisting households according to their ability to afford a qualified plan—and would greatly reduce the budgetary and tax cost of CCHP.

3. CCHP should provide catastrophic insurance of last resort, implemented by a tax credit, for those without a private health plan or those whose private coverage is inadequate. The credit schedule should utilize the estimates of maximum tolerable burden cited in the first amendment.

4. CCHP should include a medical loan program that enables households to bear greater cost sharing and that reduces the necessary CCHP tax credit, and thus the budgetary and tax cost of CCHP.

An amended CCHP offers the best practical policy for the health sector and represents a market-oriented alternative to the regulatory approach. Differences in viewpoint should not prevent supporters of the two market-oriented strategies from uniting behind a single proposal: an amended Consumer Choice Health Plan.

Supply-Side Economics of Health Care and Consumer Choice Health Plan

Alain C. Enthoven

Supply-Side Economics in Health Care

Most economists who study health care services focus on the demand side, especially on the effects of coinsurance rates and prices on the use of services, because they understand and feel comfortable with these things. Most economists ignore the supply side, including important problems such as organization and choices of technology, probably in the belief that medical care is arcane and mysterious and better left to physicians. This focus produces an incomplete view, for the supply side deserves at least as much attention as the demand side. Some studies show that utilization of medical care services is strongly influenced by supply-side variables. In a study of the supply of surgeons and the demand for inhospital operations, for example, Fuchs found "other things equal, a 10 percent increase in the surgeon/population ratio results in about a 3 percent increase in per capita utilization. Moreover, differences in supply seem to have a perverse effect on fees, raising them when the surgeon/population ratio increases."[1] Supply-side behavior in medical care is far from being fully understood, however. Even in well-documented empirical studies like that of Fuchs, the findings thus far have defied satisfactory explanation by a model of rational economic behavior.

We know that there are wide variations in per capita consumption of costly health care services that are not explained by differences in insurance coverage or characteristics of the population served. The

[1] Victor R. Fuchs, "The Supply of Surgeons and the Demand for Operations," *Journal of Human Resources,* vol. 13, supplement (1978), pp. 35–56.

Health Care Financing Administration recently reported wide variations in the per capita rates of hospital admission, average length of stay, and days of care per 1,000 Medicare enrollees (aged sixty-five and over) in different geographic areas. The ten areas (designated for Professional Standards Review Organizations) with the highest days of care per 1,000 enrollees ranged from 4,644 to 5,123 (omitting one extreme case), while the ten with the lowest ranged from 2,022 to 2,443.[2] As far as investigators have been able to determine, these wide variations in resource use are not explained by differences in medical need and do not yield discernible differences in health outcomes.

Low per capita hospital use is characteristic not only of prepaid group practice health maintenance organizations (HMOs) such as the Kaiser-Permanente Medical Care Program, but also of prestigious multispecialty group practices such as the Mayo Clinic, the Palo Alto Medical Clinic, and the St. Louis Park Medical Center.[3] Thus, some systems of medical care delivery are more economical than others; in addition, there is evidence that the best systems are among the most economical. Further, it has been shown that a great deal of the extra per capita spending associated with the less economical health care systems yields no discernible marginal benefit in terms of health outcome.[4]

Resource allocation in today's health services economy is extremely inefficient. Finkler's study of open-heart surgery in California[5] estimated that in 1976, $44 million, or 24 percent of the total costs of open-heart surgery, could have been saved if all such surgery had been concentrated in thirty centers, each performing 500 operations a year, instead of the ninety-one hospitals in which the operations were performed. Another study, which examined the empirical relation between surgical volume and mortality for twelve operations including open-heart surgery,[6] found that hospitals in which fewer than 200 open-heart operations a year were

[2] Ronald Deacon et al., "Analysis of Variations in Hospital Use by Medicare Patients in PSRO Areas, 1974–1977," *Health Care Financing Review*, vol. 1 (Summer 1979), pp. 79–108.

[3] Anne Scitovsky and Nelda McCall, "Use of Hospital Services under Two Prepaid Plans," *Medical Care*, vol. 18 (January 1980), pp. 30–41. Jon B. Christianson and Walter McClure, "Competition in the Delivery of Medical Care," *New England Journal of Medicine*, vol. 301 (October 11, 1979), pp. 812–18.

[4] Alain C. Enthoven, *Health Plan: The Only Practical Solution to the Soaring Cost of Medical Care* (Reading, Mass.: Addison-Wesley, 1980).

[5] Steven A. Finkler, "Cost-Effectiveness of Regionalization: The Heart Surgery Example," *Inquiry* (Fall 1979), pp. 264–70.

[6] Harold S. Luft, John P. Bunker, and Alain C. Enthoven, "Should Operations Be Regionalized? The Empirical Relation Between Surgical Volume and Mortality," *New England Journal of Medicine*, vol. 301 (December 20, 1979), pp. 1364–69.

performed had a mortality rate 24 percent in excess of what would have been predicted for their case-mix; hospitals with more than 200 operations had a mortality rate 23 percent below the predicted rate. Thus, for these operations, mortality declined substantially with volume. Yet 44 percent of the 27,000 open-heart operations studied took place in hospitals performing fewer than 200 a year.

Some economists are convinced that all consumer behavior is rational, if only we understood it, and that demand for medical care would really be no different from the demand for other services if only people had to pay a substantial percentage of the costs. These economists would probably argue that people choose low-volume hospitals because of convenience or perhaps a preference for the bedside manner of the local heart surgeon. To characterize this type of consumer behavior as "rational" is to render empty the concept of rationality. The time and cost of travel can hardly account for the proliferation of low-volume heart-surgery suites. As Finkler pointed out, some low-volume hospitals in southern California are within walking distance of each other. I believe this illustrates the difficulty consumers have in making informed choices in their own best interest in today's system. The persistence of the low-volume hospitals is the consequence of a permissive economic environment, of referral patterns that are based on provider self-interest, and the unavailability of information to consumers.

It should not be surprising that resource allocation in our health care economy is inefficient, given the fact that our tax-subsidized system of insured fee-for-service health care finance contains no incentives for economy and actually rewards providers of care for cost-increasing behavior. This system persists, in part, because it is legally protected from fair economic competition from alternative delivery systems, and because organized medicine has worked systematically to block the development of such competition.[7]

Nonetheless, millions of people obtain their medical care from alternative health care financing and delivery plans that provide equal or better care for substantially less cost. There are several ways in which such organizations cut cost without cutting the quality of care.[8] They concentrate their surgery and other complex procedures in high-volume centers, for example, or they buy the care from such centers. This practice allows their enrolled patients to benefit from the greater proficiency and economy associated with such centers. These organizations match the resources used to the needs of the enrolled populations they

[7] Enthoven, *Health Plan*.
[8] Ibid., chap. 3.

serve. By retaining the right number of surgeons, for example, they enable their members to be served by proficient surgeons who can be kept busy and thus can make a good living at a low charge per case. Such surgeons are not under economic pressure to recommend surgery when the net benefit to the patients may be doubtful or nonexistent. On the contrary, they curtail the utilization of services yielding no discernible marginal health benefit. They also render care in less costly settings: they have pioneered in such innovations as outpatient surgery. The organizations keep unit medical records for their members so that each physician caring for a patient can easily see what diagnoses other physicians have made and what treatments have been prescribed. These records eliminate the need for duplication of costly diagnostic workups and provide opportunities for quality control through peer review. Some also eliminate vast amounts of paper work, since comprehensive capitation-financed health care plans may have little or no billing and collection of receivables for individual medical services.

Obviously these systems are not perfectly efficient. Many do not face serious competition. Luft's comprehensive review of numerous comparison studies found that "total costs (premium and out-of-pocket) for [HMO] enrollees are 10 to 40 percent lower than those for comparable people with health insurance."[9] There is strong evidence that compared with insured fee-for-service, alternative delivery systems can achieve large savings while delivering as good or better care.

In designing the Consumer Choice Health Plan (CCHP), I attempted to propose rules that would elicit a desirable supply-side response. This goal is not limited merely to motivating consumers to demand less care in the context of the present system. Rather, the goal is to transform the health care financing and delivery system from today's pattern—which is dominated by uncontrolled, insured fee for service and solo practice with built-in incentives for cost-increasing behavior—to one of competing comprehensive health care financing and delivery organizations with built-in incentives for quality, economy, and consumer satisfaction. In other words, if CCHP were to work as intended, the successful health plans would be cost-effective organized systems that served their customers well.

One of the keys to this strategy is direct incentives for providers (that is, physicians and hospital managers) to be economical in the use of health care resources. The design of CCHP is based on the recognition that physicians decide or strongly influence about 70 percent of total

---

[9] Harold S. Luft, "How Do Health Maintenance Organizations Achieve Their 'Savings'? Rhetoric and Evidence," *New England Journal of Medicine,* vol. 298 (June 15, 1978), pp. 1336–43.

health care spending. They order and perform diagnostic tests, recommend and perform surgery and other therapeutic procedures, prescribe drugs, and admit and discharge hospital inpatients. In comparison with consumers, physicians have an exceptionally large information advantage that is based on eight years of postcollege formal training plus years of experience making treatment decisions. Especially at the time of acute medical need, consumers are likely to be at a large disadvantage with respect to information. In individual cases it will probably be very difficult for them to judge whether or not their physicians are prescribing economical treatment.

Another key to the Consumer Choice strategy is the concept of a "limited provider" health care plan. In order for there to be economic competition among providers, there must be providers associated with particular health care financing plans, so that (unlike today's typical situation) the premiums people pay will be related to the cost-generating behavior of the providers they choose. In such a system, consumers may voluntarily limit their choice of provider for a year at a time to those associated with one or another health care plan in exchange for what they perceive to be lower cost and/or better benefits. This may be a loose association. While it may mean full-time employment of providers by "closed panel" health care plans, or formal contracts with participating providers, it may also include referrals to nonparticipating specialists controlled by participating physicians. Or it may mean that services rendered by participating providers are more fully covered than services rendered by nonparticipating providers. The dividing lines are imprecise. Economic competition does not have to mean a system limited to "closed panel" plans in which all physicians work full time with one or another health care plan. But it does require that health care financing plans be able to select economical providers and reward their enrolled members for obtaining care from these providers.

The essence of this strategy is (1) incentives for health care financing plans to develop *direct* cost controls and incentives for providers to be economical, and (2) incentives for consumers to choose health care financing plans that use economical providers. It differs fundamentally from a strategy that controls cost exclusively through consumer sharing in the cost of individual units of medical care received. Under the latter strategy, the provider organizations, if not the physicians, will receive a large part of their revenues on a fee-for-service basis that rewards providers for increased use of services. Providers will have *indirect* incentives to control cost: the humanitarian concern of physicians for the financial condition of their patients, and a fear of loss of patients if they are perceived as being uneconomical.

471

Changes Recommended by Seidman in Consumer Choice Health Plan

Seidman's chapter of this volume presents a distinct alternative approach within the "incentives school." If the competition strategy in general becomes accepted as the basis for public policy, then the issues raised by Seidman will have to be decided.

CCHP was meant to be one example of the application of the principles of the competition strategy to a system of universal health insurance. It was not meant to be an "all or none" proposal or the last word in health care finance. I had hoped that discussion of the proposal would bring about improvements. There were substantial reasons, however, for the design of its main features. It included, for example, a refundable tax credit equal to 60 percent of actuarial cost (average total per capita cost for covered services in each actuarial category) for every nonpoor person or family, usable only as a premium contribution to a qualified health plan. The tax credit would increase gradually to 100 percent of actuarial cost, with decreasing income, for low-income persons and families. A qualified plan is one that complies with certain rules, including (1) participation in the annual open enrollment, (2) community rating, (3) coverage of at least basic health services, (4) catastrophic expense protection (that is, a limit on out-of-pocket costs for basic health services such as $1,500 per family per year), and (5) information disclosure.

Seidman would have this tax credit phase down to a "small value" with increasing income.[10] He offers two reasons. The first is equity. In his view, higher-income families do not need the subsidy. The second is budgetary. Seidman says that phasing it down would *greatly* reduce the cost to the federal budget, but he offers no estimates to support this view. (The actuarial value of the "last resort" backup insurance Seidman proposes may not be small, in which case the difference between our proposals may not be large.)

I recommended the 60 percent tax credit for a complex set of reasons that Seidman has ignored. (Seidman's original paper for the conference made no reference to the problems of risk selection and "free riders." His chapter recognizes the possible existence of these problems, but he has not revised his proposals to take account of them.) One goal of CCHP is to reward health plans for providing better care at less cost, not for selecting preferred risks. Another goal is to reward consumers for making economical choices, not for manipulating the system to take advantage of fluctuations in their medical needs. Yet another goal is universal health insurance at prices everyone can afford. There is wide

[10] Laurence S. Seidman, "Consumer Choice Health Plan and the Patient Cost-Sharing Strategy: Can They Be Reconciled?" (this volume).

variation in the health risks of different people. I recommended a requirement of open enrollment so that high-risk persons would be able to join any health plan serving their area. I recommended community rating so that the high-risk persons within any actuarial category would pay the same premiums as low-risk persons. Since compliance with these requirements entails a substantial cost, the 60 percent tax credit available only for qualified plans would make it attractive for a health plan to qualify despite this cost. Without a substantial subsidy, health plans would find it advantageous to offer nonqualified plans to selected low-risk individuals, making insurance more costly to high-risk persons. Depending on the value of the credit under Seidman's proposal, high-income persons would have little or no incentive to join qualified plans.

With community rating, it would be advantageous for health plans to find sophisticated ways of attracting preferred risks and of discouraging enrollment of high-risk persons. To counteract this possibility, CCHP proposed a system of premium rating and subsidies by actuarial categories: health plans would receive more revenue for serving people in higher-risk categories, and such people would receive correspondingly higher subsidies. Thus, a substantial part of the subsidy of the medical expenses of the sick by the well would take place through the tax system rather than internally within health plans.

Since a great deal of medical care is for chronic conditions, the need for it is predictable. A great deal is quite elective with respect to timing. Most surgery is in this category. Suppose that we tried to organize a system of competing health plans, with annual choice of plan, in which people were free not to insure until they became ill—or what amounts to almost the same thing, they were free to buy an insurance policy with a $5,000 deductible. Low-risk people would choose the cheap plan and save money. They would take a "free ride" on the health insurance system. When they contracted a chronic disease or needed surgery, they would switch to a comprehensive insurance plan at the next annual enrollment. Comprehensive plans would attract all the poor health risks and would be driven out of business. This is not merely a theoretical possibility. The problem of adverse risk selection is of fundamental importance in the health insurance business.

I cannot predict the eventual outcome of the attempt to create such a system. It would depend on the rules. Comprehensive plans could not survive this kind of adverse selection without some form of self-protection such as requiring medical review before enrollment and exclusion of coverage of high-risk persons or those with prior medical conditions, or long-term contracts. Such devices would be incompatible with universal coverage and the competition generated by annual open enrollment.

Thus, I have concluded that the only *viable* form of economic competition in health services in a system of universal insurance—indeed the only one we observe in operation—is one in which all the plans are fairly comprehensive, in which the range of choice is narrowed so that the margin of economic advantage in switching plans with changes in health status is not large enough to make it worth switching. In a system made up predominantly of "limited provider" plans, switching health plans would generally mean switching doctors. Since most sick people would be reluctant to change doctors without some strong incentive, the margin of economic advantage from switching plans needs to be kept narrow but does not need to be eliminated to make the system workable. One purpose of the 60 percent tax credit is to narrow the range of price variation. There would be no point in offering a health plan with a premium below 60 percent of actuarial cost.

I came upon the 60 percent figure empirically. It is approximately the level of subsidy in the Federal Employees Health Benefits Program and in some other multiple-choice systems. It works. There is relatively little plan switching, and there is no evidence that any of the competitors have suffered seriously from adverse risk selection. It is possible, however, that a lower subsidy level, combined with other controls on "free riders" and preferred risk selection, might also be workable.

Both Seidman and Meyer deplore CCHP's limitations on the range of choice.[11] Meyer argues: "By setting a floor under the amount of health insurance all families or individuals must possess, we foreclose the choice of a lower option insurance package (with the concommitant risk of higher direct outlays) that would release dollars for the consumer to spend on food, housing, or education." In my view, their arguments on this point do not respond to the practical problems of creating a workable system of competition in health services. In the presence of annual choice by individuals, and in the absence of countervailing incentives or controls, the problems of adverse risk selection and "free riders" will drive the level of coverage in all plans toward the minimum allowed by law. We have to make a social decision as to what we want that level to be.

Another reason for the 60 percent tax credit is practical politics. Experience shows that attempts to remove the tax-preferred status of fringe benefits meets with intense opposition. Representative Al Ullman (Democrat, Oregon) was criticized severely for the proposed limit of $120 per family per month in his Health Cost Restraint Act. We have to recognize that the legislative process works incrementally and that

---

[11] Seidman, "Consumer Choice"; Jack A. Meyer, "Health Care Competition: Are Tax Incentives Enough?" (this volume).

it is impractical to ignore history. Recall where we are today. In 1979, the favorable tax treatment of employer-paid health benefits cost federal and state governments about $14 billion. Replacing the open-ended exclusion of employer-paid health benefits from employee taxable incomes by a tax credit of 60 percent of actuarial cost would inflict a loss on certain groups, for example, auto workers in Michigan. Transition rules would no doubt be required. In any case, retaining a refundable tax credit of 60 percent of actuarial cost for all would probably generate less opposition than the greater "take away" recommended by Seidman.

Second, Seidman objects to a single required ceiling on a household's out-of-pocket payments for covered services. He considers the $1,500 that I have suggested to be "very low" and recommends an income-related maximum that is considerably higher, for example, $5,000 per year for a household with a $40,000 income. He notes that limited cost sharing would assure that any fee-for-service plan would have no built-in resistance to overutilization and cost inflation, and he argues that the result would be unfair competition, biased in favor of prepaid HMOs.

Originally I suggested the $1,500 as an illustration, not as a firm proposal. My memorandum to Secretary of Health, Education, and Welfare, Joseph A. Califano, Jr., first proposing CCHP stated, "I would leave the amount to be set by each plan. . . . But it could be set by regulation."[12] It seemed obvious that the amount would be negotiated in the political process. I considered $1,500 not unfair to insured fee-for-service. I now believe that a limit, set by law or regulation is needed and that, if anything, $1,500 is too high. The first and sufficient reason for a lower limit is that a high limit such as $5,000 per year would allow insurance plans to design policies with high deductibles and low premiums that are especially attractive to low-risk persons and "free riders." The consequence, as we have said, would be to inundate the more comprehensive plans with adverse risks and to force them either to raise their cost sharing to meet the competition or to adopt other measures incompatible with annual open enrollment.

Second, an important goal of health insurance is for the well (low-risk persons) to help pay the medical care costs of the sick (or high-risk persons). A high coinsurance limit would make the total cost of health care services (premium and out of pocket) very high for people with high medical needs. With a $3,000 limit on cost sharing, the seriously ill will be paying $3,000 per year more for health care than the well.

Third, it is important from a supply-side point of view that every

---

[12] Alain C. Enthoven, Memorandum for Secretary of HEW Joseph Califano on National Health Insurance, Washington, D.C., September 22, 1977, p. 11.

health plan derive a substantial part—say half or more—of its revenue from premiums or capitation prepayment instead of from fees for services. This encodes a substantial part of the per capita cost of health care associated with each plan in a premium that is a price people can easily understand and act on. Estimating the actuarial value of one's cost sharing is more uncertain and complex. Such a limitation on cost sharing attenuates the cost-increasing incentives of fee for service. Moreover, as Seidman notes, limiting the extent to which health plans can rely on cost sharing puts pressure on them to develop internal cost controls and direct provider incentives for economy. This limitation would accelerate the process of delivery system reform.

While limited cost sharing at the point of medical service may be useful as an aid in controlling consumer-initiated doctor visits for care of low marginal health value—a small part of the grand total—I see little value in it when the patient is seriously ill. Seidman's argument is that knowing that the patient has to pay a share of the cost puts pressure on the doctor to be economical in the choice of services to prescribe in order to be merciful to the patient and to attract his continued business. Why use the sick patient as the fulcrum for putting leverage on the doctor? It would be more effective and more merciful to the seriously ill patient to put the leverage directly on the doctors. They have the expert knowledge and the experience of making medical decisions regularly. This is a strategic choice that we must make as a society. We cannot leave it entirely to the market to be sorted out.

Specific Comments on Seidman's Chapter

Seidman recommends fair competition between HMOs and fee-for-service insurance plans that rely exclusively on patient cost sharing for cost control. Of course, I favor a fair market test in principle. CCHP would provide a fair market test as among a large variety of alternative delivery systems, including prepaid group practices, individual practice associations, primary care networks, health care alliances, and the many hybrids that combine elements of these concepts. There are, however, some serious practical difficulties in implementing the principle of a fair market test between such alternative delivery systems and fee-for-service insurance plans with nearly unlimited cost sharing.

One problem is that we do not have, and are not likely to be able to obtain in advance, the information needed to design a strictly neutral system. A key parameter as we have noted, is the limit on consumer out-of-pocket spending for covered services. If it is set high, adverse-risk selection and "free riders" will force all competitors to use high deductibles and coinsurance rates. Most services will be purchased on

476

a fee-for-service basis. If it is set low, a high percentage of the cost will be encoded in the premium. As Seidman noted, a low limit will put health plans under competitive pressure to develop direct cost controls. We cannot know in advance what is the "neutral" or "fair" out-of-pocket expense limit. It will be different for different communities, for different income groups, and for groups with different distributions of medical risk. The out-of-pocket expense limit is only one factor in a complex ecology of incentives influencing choice of health plan. Seidman considers $1,500 "very low," but no one has identified the "neutral" out-of-pocket limit, and probably it cannot be identified in advance. In the face of this uncertainty, a policy choice will have to be made as to which approach should receive the benefit of the doubt. I think the choice should be in favor of creating some pressure on health plans to develop internal cost controls and provider incentives for economy.

Seidman's substantive reasons for recommending neutrality are that many persons will value highly the greater flexibility and choice of physician permitted by insured fee for service, and that in the face of uncertainty—for example, over the need for surgery—many people will prefer that their physicians have fee-for-service incentives. Seidman draws the dichotomy between limited choice of doctors in HMOs and unlimited choice of doctors in insured fee for service too sharply. There is less freedom than meets the eye in the insured fee-for-service system. In fact, if not in theory, people's choices are constrained by travel costs, referral patterns, and the unavailability of information as well as the cost of obtaining it. The alternative delivery systems offer some flexibility in this regard. Some, for example, cover services rendered by nonparticipating physicians but do so under less favorable financial terms. In the primary-care network model, a primary-care physician who refuses—at the patient's urging—to refer a patient to a specialist other than the one initially suggested risks losing him as a patient. Even HMO members are free to go outside their system and to obtain second opinions at their own expense. The cost of a few consultations must appear very low to people who consider $1,500 in annual out-of-pocket payments to be very low. If they find a doctor whom they prefer outside the HMO, they are free to change health plans at the next enrollment. If many persons value flexibility and choice highly in a competitive market, health plans will be under pressure to find ways to provide it. As far as fee-for-service incentives at the individual doctor level are concerned, many alternative delivery systems with built-in cost controls—for example, individual practice associations—have that feature. If patients had to pay the extra cost associated with their choice of health care financing and delivery system, I think that only the unusual patient would prefer uncontrolled fee for service, that is, a system in which the direct incentives on the physician are all cost increasing, and the only restraint is his own ability to judge the cost effectiveness of proposed treatments.

Seidman expresses concern about my apparent partiality to prepaid HMOs. My concern is not over the ability of the leading HMOs to survive as medical enterprises in the environment created by Seidman's proposals. The established HMOs could adapt and do well in such a competition—but they would have to adapt. A rational strategy for them would include high deductibles and fees for services, with markups for particular services related to the elasticity of demand for them. What does concern me is that the HMOs would have to become essentially fee-for-service enterprises. In a system of virtually unlimited cost sharing and in the absence of other countervailing incentives or controls, *the element of provider incentives for cost control arising from the capitation method of payment would be lost.* With it would be lost one of the most effective demonstrated strategies for cost control. HMOs figure prominently in my writings because they are one example, though not the only one, of medical care organizations that cut costs without cutting the quality of care. Without such examples, CCHP would be lacking in credibility as a practical strategy for cost control. The rules proposed in CCHP do not favor HMOs over other types of alternative delivery systems with built-in cost controls.

Seidman's discussion of "imperfect agency: the doctor-patient relationship" reveals far too narrow a conception of the variety of alternative financing and delivery systems that already exist, not to mention the possibilities that might evolve under a truly competitive market system. He dichotomizes the health care economy into insured fee for service and prepaid HMOs, and then explains why physicians in each must be imperfect agents for their patients—one biased to overtreatment, the other to undertreatment. He also singles out the method of payment and ignores the rest of the complex system of incentives within which physicians work (for example, professional values, malpractice threat). In fact, there exist various types of alternative delivery systems, and within each type there are endless possibilities for empirical tuning of the incentive structure. Under economic competition, such tuning would take place because the winners would be the ones that did the best job of acting as agents for their enrolled members.

Has coinsurance been tried and has it failed? Seidman says, "It is simply incorrect to imply that significant coinsurance has been utilized for hospital service in the last decade. It has not. Hospital service has been almost free for the average patient." I was thinking more of the 1960s when I wrote the statement to which Seidman objects. According to Feldstein and Taylor, consumers directly paid 29 percent of total hospital costs in 1960, 17 percent in 1970. Consumers paid 35 percent of the private costs in 1960, 27 percent in 1970.[13] Yet total health services spending increased from 5.3 percent of GNP in 1960 to 7.6 percent in 1970. Hospital spending increased from 1.97 percent of GNP in 1960 to 2.83 percent in 1970. So coinsurance was tried and health care costs rose.

Next, Seidman says, "It is not correct to imply, as Enthoven does, that this risk-efficiency trade-off can be escaped without any disadvantage to the consumer by replacing FFS with prepayment." Seidman conceptualizes the whole problem as one of insurance and of finding the best balance between risk and moral hazard. He assumes that we are on a risk-efficiency frontier that cannot be escaped, and merely advocates moving to a different point on it. I have cited evidence of great waste in the present system and of large potential efficiency gains achievable through reform of the delivery system, that is to say, through shifting the risk-efficiency frontier.

Under major-risk insurance arrangements of the type recommended by Seidman, a great deal of care would be delivered in the "free-care range," where coinsurance would not be applicable. Seidman counters that "only a small minority of patients would reach the free-care range." He estimates this number to be at 3 percent if the cost-sharing ceiling is set at $3,000. And he suggests that "special regulation may be necessary for the small minority who reach the free-care range." His method of estimation ignores the skewed distribution of cost and the pattern of repeated hospitalization among high-cost patients.

Zook and Moore recently reported that half the annual costs in a representative sample of hospitals were associated with the 13 percent of patients having the highest costs.[14] Ten percent of patients had hospital expenses above $13,700 in 1976. To this must be added physician fees, costs for outpatient care, drugs, and other charges likely to add, on average, about a third or more to the hospital bill. Seidman's proposal is not sufficiently detailed to permit cost estimation. But he should have looked at *dollars,* not *patients.* The Zook-Moore findings suggest that at least half the hospital costs would be associated with patients who are either in the free-care range or are so ill that their doctors would believe that they might end up in the free-care range in a system like the one Seidman proposes. Seidman does not make clear how his "special regulation" would apply to this half of hospital spending without

[13] Martin Feldstein and Amy Taylor, *The Rapid Rise of Hospital Costs,* Staff Report (Washington, D.C.: Council on Wage and Price Stability, January 1977).

[14] Christopher L. Zook and Francis D. Moore, "High-Cost Users of Medical Care," *New England Journal of Medicine,* vol. 302 (May 1, 1980), pp. 996–1002.

it being applied to the other half, nor does he explain what this "special regulation" would be.

Seidman and I disagree fundamentally on the probable efficacy of patient cost sharing at the time of serious illness. His argument is:

> A physician who develops a reputation for disregarding the cost of hospitalization when his patients must bear an important fraction of that cost, may gradually lose recommendations, patients, and income. . . . It is often alleged that medical care differs radically from other goods and services because patients do not have the knowledge to evaluate medical services. Not many realize that the same ignorance applies to numerous other goods and services.

For reasons already explained, I think the asymmetry between provider and customer information is especially pronounced in the case of medical care, enough to make the situation differ radically from the purchase of an automobile or automobile repair services. The professional information stored in the heads of a multispecialty team of physicians caring for a sick patient—the kind Zook and Moore found consume half of hospital resources—takes more than an order of magnitude longer to acquire than the information stored in the head of a typical automobile repairman. The education required to be able to read and understand an article in a medical journal takes many years beyond that required to understand an article on cars in *Consumer Reports*. Moreover, most people do not shop for cars when they are seriously ill.

I am not saying that substantial cost sharing would have no effect at all, simply that in many cases it would probably not be very effective. It might be effective in a routine maternity case, for example, in which the service is standard and there is ample time for the expectant mother to consider the alternatives. It might also be effective in motivating a patient with chronic renal failure to choose a less costly setting for dialysis. But it will probably be much less effective in the case of most serious illnesses requiring urgent care, especially if the patient is suffering and is emotionally impaired. We must also recognize that each patient's case will have unique elements. We should therefore question how Seidman's hypothetical physician would develop a reputation for disregarding the cost of hospitalization. By what standards would he be judged? For the most part, such standards do not exist. The appropriateness of various lengths of stay is hard enough for physicians to judge and agree on; we must also remember that they see many patients. Patients tend to see only their own case.

Consider the case of Mrs. Smith, who received a $2,000 bill for her hospital stay for pneumonia. Trying to form an opinion about her physician's sensitivity to cost, she called Mrs. Jones to find out how much she had been billed for her hospital stay. Mrs. Jones had been charged $1,000. When Mrs. Smith asked her doctor about this difference, he explained that she had had staphylococcal pneumonia while Mrs. Jones had had pneumococcal pneumonia, which is generally less serious. So the attempt to make a cost comparison failed. Mrs. Smith wondered whether she should switch doctors anyway, even though she could not be sure that her doctor hospitalized her too long. Then she realized that she had made a large investment in terms of the knowledge about her medical history contained in her doctor's head, which would be lost if she switched. She knew that it would be costly for another doctor to become equally well informed about her, so that the costs of searching for a new doctor whom she liked as well would be high.

That is not to say that consumer incentives are not important. But a more effective time to ask each consumer to consider cost would be at the annual choice of health plan, at which time he is not likely to be ill.

The principles of the competition strategy can be applied in various ways. It might be feasible to adjust CCHP marginally in some of the directions suggested by Seidman. A uniform $1,500 per family per year limit on cost sharing may not be the best way to deal with the problems of risk selection and free riders. Perhaps a better rule would be that at least half a health plan's revenue in each actuarial category must come from premiums. In any event, reconciling CCHP and major risk insurance is a considerably more complex and difficult task than Seidman thinks. Without doubt, a significant element of direct provider incentives for cost control is an essential part of an effective strategy.

Comments on Meyer's Chapter

The gist of Meyer's chapter is that CCHP is essentially sound and represents a proposed solution that is targeted to the problem. He adds, however, "There is many a slip between the cup and the lip with regard to the actual *realization* of cost savings elicited by structural modifications in tax laws or reimbursement mechanisms." I agree. What I have been recommending is a long-term strategy for fundamental reform in the health care financing and delivery system through a system of fair economic competition. This is not a quick fix!

In my September 1977 memorandum to HEW Secretary Califano proposing Consumer Choice Health Plan, I wrote:

Reorganization of health services will take a long time—a very long time by political standards—a decade or more, even under the most favorable conditions, before half the population is served by some kind of organized system with incentives for

481

economy. The Medical Profession is very resistant to organizational change. There are powerful vested interests throughout the health services industry, institutions with long traditions and deep roots in their communities. Many people will change their health plans and providers only reluctantly and slowly. There are no easy routes to health services reorganization. It will take a great deal of effort by many people in many localities.[15]

Meyer's conclusion is apt: "In a fair-choice environment, if health care expenditures continue to grow relative to other categories of spending, such an increase should be taken not as a signal for corrective government action, but as a manifestation of rational consumer preferences for more health care, for which they are willing to sacrifice other goods and services."

I think it would be useful, however, to comment in more detail on some of Meyer's specific points.

Meyer first cautions: "One of the major pitfalls for an incentives-based strategy is the possibility that cost savings significant in theory may shrink as a 'minimum benefit requirement' is expanded." I concede the force of this argument. There is a danger that special interests would force Congress to take a proposal for a lean package of essential services and turn it into a bloated bundle of special-interest provisions, with required benefits for many types of health care providers. The success of the mental health lobby in working its will on the HMO Act gives us an indication of what might occur.

I have recommended a uniform minimum package of legally defined "basic health services" as a floor under all qualified health plans for reasons that I consider compelling. Briefly, they are as follows. First, design of benefit packages is one of the main ways of selecting preferred risks and excluding bad risks. Thus, a required minimum package is needed *to curtail preferred risk selection* and to prevent effective exclusion of high-risk persons. Second, in conjunction with the limit on cost sharing for covered services, it helps to limit the "free rider" problem. Third, in order to attenuate price competition, insurers differentiate their products. Differentiation makes it harder to make comparisons, and it helps to segment the market. A uniform minimum benefit package is a tool for forcing all health plans to compete for all customers in price and quality and for reducing the information cost to consumers to make comparisons. I would welcome new ideas and proposals for institutional designs that would deal effectively with all of these considerations.

The issue is a variant of a question often asked: "How can we be

[15] Enthoven, Memorandum for Secretary Califano, p. 18.

sure the government won't mess it up?" There is no guarantee. But the situation we have today is not exactly a pristine state of natural free enterprise deserving special protection. It is the product of existing laws that can and should be improved.

We have to make a choice between market competition constrained to achieve social goals, or direct economic regulation by government. Few Americans would be prepared to accept the implications of a completely free market in health insurance. Thus the problem Meyer raises is one inherent in any viable public policy on health care finance.

Second, Meyer is concerned about the inefficient cross-subsidies generated by community rating. He distinguishes "between members of employee units covered by group health plans, Medicare and Medicaid enrollees, and those who fall between the cracks of public and private group insurance" and suggests that experience rating of employment groups would not lead to excessive premiums for high-risk individuals in those groups. Thus he suggests that we deal with the problems of nonworking people who are ineligible for federal assistance by developing a plan specially tailored for them. He finds merit in a program of risk pooling and assigned risks.

I am not aware of significant inefficient cross-subsidies generated by community rating if the size of the market areas is reasonably limited. The main cross-subsidy in community rating is that the well help to pay for the medical care of the sick, which I regard as socially desirable.

In the system created by CCHP, however, the employment basis of health insurance would disappear. (I have explained in *Health Plan* and elsewhere why the job-related system is a barrier to competition and adds to cost and complexity when we seek to achieve universal coverage). Under CCHP, everyone would be considered an individual or family from a health insurance point of view. People would no longer "fall between the cracks" for lack of membership in an employee group. Community rating by actuarial category would be needed to prevent high-risk persons from being charged enormous premiums.

Universal community rating is not mandated in Representative Ullman's Health Cost Restraint Act or in Senator David Durenberger's (Republican, Minnesota) Health Incentives Reform Act, which are incremental proposals that maintain the employment basis of health insurance but that seek to correct the perverse incentives created by today's tax laws by requiring employers to offer choices on an economically fair basis and by limiting the amount of tax-free employer contribution. In the context of such an employment-based system, Project Health of Multnomah County, Oregon, is a more promising model for the people who fall between the cracks than is the assigned risk insurance pool suggested by Meyer. Project Health acts as a broker and subsidizer for some of the families not insured through employment, and it offers them a multiple choice of alternative delivery systems. Thus it fits in with the concepts of competition and choice. Assigned risk pools are an insured fee-for-service concept. I am not aware of the successful integration of assigned risk pools with choice of HMO. The Project Health model could be used to subsidize the excess risk component of the premiums of experience-rated plans made available to high-risk nonpoor people. Universal community rating by actuarial category is, however, the most satisfactory method of protecting high-risk persons in the context of fair competition and choice. It should remain as a long-term goal.

In answer to the question, "Do HMOs produce genuine savings by delivering a comparable quality of service to a comparable population at a lower price?" Meyer relies on Luft:

> Luft has found that HMO cost savings arise not from more efficient production of a given set of services, but from changes in the number and mix of services provided. In other words, the observed differences in health care expenditures between HMOs and fee-for-service systems reflect differences in practice patterns rather than a finding that HMOs can deliver a day of hospital care or a visit to a doctor at a lower cost.

This is not to say that HMOs do not cut costs while improving the quality of care, for example, through regional concentration of complex services, matching of numbers of surgeons to the needs of the population served, and maintenance of unit medical records. Rather, it is difficult to measure and document lower unit costs with the aggregate comparison data available to Luft. The California Health Facilities Commission recently found that gross operating expenses per patient-day in Kaiser Hospitals in California ranged from 80 to 97 percent of the expenses in non-Kaiser Hospitals between 1970 and 1976.[16] The difficulty in interpreting these data is that they have not been adjusted for Kaiser utilization patterns (only more serious cases are hospitalized) or for demographics (Kaiser has a lower percentage of aged and poor). The problems lie in our data and instruments of measurement. We should not rule out the possibility that hospital-based HMOs treat a hospital case of given diagnosis and severity at substantially less cost.

"Luft finds that while HMOs have lower cost levels, there is no clear evidence that these cost levels grow more slowly over time than cost levels in conventional plans. Therefore HMOs. . .have not uncovered the key to ongoing cost control." At present HMOs are minority

---

[16] Katherine K. Carter and Allison H. Thaine, Sr., "A Comparison of Utilization and Costs in Kaiser and Non-Kaiser Hospitals in California," California Health Facilities Commission Research Report 78–2, November 1978.

enterprises in a health care economy dominated by insured fee for service and shaped by cost-increasing incentives in the tax and social security laws. Factor prices and community standards of care are set in the fee-for-service sector, and HMOs rarely face serious competition from other HMOs. Thus, what we have observed may not be a reliable indicator of what would happen if the industry were competitive and were dominated by alternative delivery systems.

Let us consider Luft's findings with respect to his four possible explanations for lower per capita hospital admissions in HMOs. The first is that HMOs avoid "discretionary" admissions. He concludes, "the data do not support the expectation that HMOs differentially reduce discretionary procedures."[17] One must be careful, however, in interpreting Luft's cautious statements. He did not say, "The data refute the hypothesis that HMOs differentially reduce discretionary admissions." Luft tested the hypothesis by comparing per capita surgery rates for eight selected procedures "suggested in several studies as being relatively discretionary" in HMOs and in comparison groups cared for under insured fee for service. For seven procedures he found that the HMOs, as often as not, reduced surgery overall as much or more than they reduced the frequency of these procedures. Luft's test is based on the unsupported assumption that his selected surgical procedures are more "discretionary" than surgery in general or medical admissions. Some hysterectomies are "necessary" because the patient has carcinoma of the uterus. In the judgment of some cardiologists, many coronary artery bypass grafts are "unnecessary" because the patients do not have diseased left main arteries and medical treatment would be just as effective. Medical admissions may be just as "discretionary." So we really have not yet found an effective way of formulating and evaluating this issue.

Luft's second explanation is that HMOs undertreat (or traditional providers overtreat) nondiscretionary cases. A good deal of evidence suggests that leading multispecialty group practices do not undertreat and that conventional providers overtreat. As we have noted, there is evidence that a great deal of health care yields no discernible marginal health benefit in the fee-for-service sector.

The third explanation is that HMOs provide preventive care. Luft is right in arguing that this explanation is not satisfactory: "Many new HMOs have started with low hospitalization rates on Day One, with no chance for their preventive services to have an effect."[18]

---

[17] Luft, "How Do Health Maintenance Organizations Achieve 'Their Savings'?" p. 1341.
[18] Harold S. Luft, "HMOs, Competition, Cost Containment, and NHI," in Mark Pauly, ed., *National Health Insurance: What Now, What Later, What Never?* (Washington D.C.: American Enterprise Institute, 1980), pp. 283–306.

The fourth explanation is the controversial one: lower HMO hospitalization rates result from self-selection among HMO enrollers. Eggers recently reported a small sample case study in which Medicare beneficiaries who joined an HMO in an open enrollment had a hospital use rate before joining that was more than 50 percent below that of a comparison group.[19] However, the study contained large potential sources of bias: for example, the groups being compared were not equal in survivorship,[20] and "new joiners" might be unrepresentative of the whole group. Other broadly based studies have found no significant differences between HMO enrollees and members of comparison groups on insured fee-for-service in health status perceived or number of chronic conditions.[21] Even Luft concludes, ". . .it is unlikely that self-selection explains fully the performance of mature HMOs."[22]

It is correct that by strict standards of scientific evidence, the hypothesis that HMO savings can be explained away by member self-selection has not been refuted. This argument is similar to caveats about the evidence on the causal link between cigarette smoking and lung cancer. In both cases, we do not have randomized controlled trials. But at the level of probable cause on which public policy must be based, the evidence that HMOs achieve substantial savings is stronger than the evidence that they do not.

To Luft's four possible explanations we might add the following fifth: physicians who are comfortable with a conservative style of practice self-select into HMOs. If that hypothesis is correct, one might conclude that no substantial savings would be gained from the nationwide spread of alternative delivery systems having built-in cost controls because the alternative delivery systems would be taking in progressively more and more costly doctors. Cost-effective organized systems, however, take care of their enrolled populations with approximately 1 to 1.2 doctors per 1,000 members. It is projected that by 1990 the United States will have 2.4 doctors per 1,000 population. Thus competition would select out the least cost-effective doctors and would direct them to occupations other than patient care.

Meyer's next caution concerns the impact of HMOs on conventional

[19] Paul Eggers, "Risk Differential between Medicare Beneficiaries Enrolled and Not Enrolled in an HMO," *Health Care Financing Review,* vol. 1 (Winter 1980), pp. 91–99.

[20] Alain C. Enthoven, "Note on Paul Eggers' December 1979 Paper on GHC Puget Sound Risk Differential." Hearings before Committee on Finance, United States Senate, Washington D.C., March 18, 1980.

[21] Clifton Gaus et al., "Contrasts in HMO and Fee-for-Service Performance," *Social Security Bulletin,* vol. 39 (May 1976), pp. 3–14; also Mark S. Blumberg, "Health Status and Health Care Use by Type of Health Care Coverage," *Milbank Memorial Fund Quarterly/Health and Society,* vol. 58 (Fall 1980).

[22] Luft, "HMOs, Competition, Cost Containment, and NHI."

providers, but that impact is probably minimal in today's noncompetitive economy. As Meyer notes, the evidence of such an impact has already been questioned. Conventional providers do not have to respond to HMO competition as long as substantial numbers of patients are covered by open-ended fee-for-service arrangements such as Medicare, Medicaid, and 100 percent employer-paid insurance. In a truly competitive market, however, doctors not in cost-effective organized systems would either have to develop similar cost controls or risk being driven out of business.

Meyer cautions us on the dangers of extrapolation. Is the successful experience with HMOs on the west coast and in Minnesota transferable to the rest of the country? Why wouldn't Kaiser and similar plans work elsewhere? Apparently Kaiser's management thinks such transfer is possible, in view of their recent entries into Colorado, Ohio, Texas, and the District of Columbia.

Part of the basis for optimism is that HMOs have achieved high market shares where they have been offered on an economically fair basis. For example, about half the federal and state employees in Kaiser's northern California service area belong to Kaiser. About 60 percent of Stanford employee families belong to the three HMOs offered them. In Minneapolis, several employee groups such as General Mills, Cargill, and Honeywell have HMO market shares above 60 percent. These market shares might be even larger if more HMOs were offered on a geographically convenient basis. The main barrier to growth of HMOs is not that most people dislike them. Most people have not been offered them on an economically fair and geographically convenient basis.

In any case, if CCHP were enacted and competition were active in some parts of the country but not in others, at least we would have stopped the present cross-subsidy in the tax and Medicare laws from the efficient to the inefficient, and we would have allowed those communities that would innovate to benefit from doing so.

We should not minimize, however, the problems of developing an alternative delivery system. Besides the ones cited by Meyer, there are problems of management, capital and "critical mass."

We have recently seen several failures among starting HMOs. Although some new HMOs have attracted excellent (but often inexperienced) managers who joined out of idealism and dedication to an idea, many have not attracted good management. New HMOs often cannot pay good salaries, they do not have the depth of positions to develop managers, and they are asking managers to take entrepreneurial risks without the possibility of an entrepreneurial reward.

Raising capital is also a difficult task, since most HMOs are nonprofit structures. We do not have much experience with investor-owned HMOs. Nonprofit HMOs cannot raise equity capital by selling stock, so they must depend on either retained earnings, government grants, or philanthropy to finance growth. Retained earnings will not finance the start-up phase. In the past, I have not favored special grants and subsidies for HMOs as I have considered it more important to emphasize the need for removal of entry barriers and for creation of conditions of fair economic competition. It would be easier to raise capital if public policy encouraged competition and made market entry easier. Nevertheless, it does appear that some means for making start-up capital available will be necessary.

The main hope for an answer to these problems lies with the large insurers and employers. After all, the Kaiser program originated in the effort to provide health care for the workers and families of Kaiser enterprises, and Ford Motor Company recently played a key role in the creation of the Health Alliance Plan in Michigan. If the economic environment were conducive, the large insurance companies would find it in their interest to create prepaid group practices, as have Prudential and INA, or to emulate United Healthcare's primary care network. The United Healthcare model could be expanded rather quickly without large front-end investments.

There is also a "critical mass" problem. Kaiser in northern California and the seven HMOs in St. Paul–Minneapolis have achieved high market penetration in some groups because their facilities are conveniently located for members of those groups. People are not really offered an HMO choice if the HMO available at work does not have a service location accessible to their homes. Thus we have a kind of "chicken and egg" problem. Perhaps many people would choose HMOs if we had many HMOs.

Meyer notes, "Making cost savings from innovative plans a reality might require changes in state and local tax (and regulatory) treatment of third-party payers *in addition* to Enthoven's proposed changes in *federal* tax rules." I agree. Procompetitive action at the state level will be needed to put all types of health care financing and delivery systems on an equal footing and to remove the last vestiges of provider dominance of the Blues, as was recently done in Ohio. If we straighten out federal financing so that a dollar saved is a dollar earned at the state level, perhaps states will be more motivated to change their laws to make competition effective.

Can antitrust be trusted? Will traditional providers use legal remedies against innovators? Since they always have, they can be expected to continue to do so. We can agree with Havighurst, as quoted by Meyer, that we need a national commitment to the competitive market strategy and a sustained effort to make it work. Havighurst's antitrust analyses and proposals are the legal counterpart to my economic analyses and proposals. The task will not be easy.

Finally, Meyer cautions,

> Consumers. . .may. . .divert resources to health care up to the point at which expected benefits approach zero, and thus may purchase individual treatments that are not "worth" their cost. . . . Nonetheless, a significant proportion of consumers might still reject innovative plans even after a change that improves the payoff in selecting a lower-cost approach.

If that is the case, let them do it with their own money. Let us not have a tax and social security system that subsidizes the choice of the more costly systems.

Over the years I doubt that many consumers would continue to choose real "flat-of-the-curve" medical care, that is, systems of care that use resources far beyond the point of zero marginal health benefit, as is the case today. I doubt that many consumers would persist in preferences for uncontrolled insured fee for service if they were given choices and had to pay the extra cost associated with it. The alternative delivery systems with built-in cost controls present themselves in a rich variety of styles. They are not limited to hospital-based prepaid group practice. Moreover, in California, the alternative delivery systems do very well among educated middle-class consumers—civil servants, professors and other teachers. They are not inferior goods. On the contrary, as many of these discerning consumers recognize, the best medical care is economical medical care. Quality and economy often go hand in hand.

Conclusion

Health Care Economics: Paths to Structural Reform

Alfred E. Kahn

The fundamental structural defect of our present system for financing and delivering health care is the absence of economic incentives at the point at which the critical decisions are made about what kind of care is to be provided. Elsewhere—reasoning that since we do not know what will ultimately prove to be the most effective set of structural arrangements for this peculiar industry, perhaps the only possible approach in the years immediately ahead is an eclectic one—I set forth the following shopping list of possible approaches to reform:[1]

- more effective use by government of its power as a buyer and subsidizer
- reimbursement in ways that give providers greater incentives to practice economy
- some hardheaded decisions by government about the kinds of health-protecting and caring services taxpayers should support
- more effective government regulation, with maximum emphasis on using incentives rather than regulatory prescription
- more effective private initiatives, by local coalitions of businesses, unions, and insurance companies, to hold the line on costs and to encourage prudent choices
- more effective competition among insurers and providers
- more cost sharing by patients

Since even economists should try to practice what they preach, I have steeled myself this time around to a greater measure of boldness—

I would like to thank Bruce Mansdorf, Rob Sedgwick, and Dennis Rapp for their help with this chapter.

[1] "Health Care and Inflation: Social Compassion and Efficient Choice," *The National Journal*, August 2, 1980, pp. 1294–97.

to try, eschewing simple eclecticism, to make some choices. I do this in the form of a series of propositions, which candor will from time to time compel me to put in the form of unresolved questions.

The Long-Term Goal of Health Care Reform

The long-run direction of structural reform of health care best suited to both our national preferences and to the particular circumstances of this industry, I suggest, is toward decentralized decision making, the ultimate form of which is the competitive market. Whenever we refer to a long-run goal, we must remind ourselves at once that in every context except microeconomic theory the long run is nothing but a succession of short runs. That means we should promptly take such initial steps in the desired direction as are feasible, and take care that whatever policies we devise for the interim do not obstruct the march toward the longer-term goal.

I will not attempt in this chapter to spell out all the familiar reasons why the decentralized, competitive model seems to me the preferable one. The case is particularly compelling here, however, because of the extraordinary complexity of the health care industry, the wide variation of circumstances from one locality to another, the inevitable distortions and arbitrariness involved in any prescriptive regulatory scheme (an arbitrariness that grows in proportion to the geographic area it encompasses), the difficulty of defining the unit of service, and the consequent ease with which regulatory prescriptions can be evaded. In these circumstances, the attractions of institutional arrangements that provide and rely upon incentives of the transacting parties to be efficient and prudent—to the extent, of course, that they can be devised—are irresistible.

There is one additional consideration counseling the greatest possible reliance on decentralized decision making that seems especially pertinent in the health care area: the political obstacles to efficient governmental planning and regulating. Such obstacles are inescapable in any system that relies heavily on the distribution of public funds and on direct governmental allocations of permissible expenditures among individual hospitals. The limited ability of governmental regulators to resist political pressures to preserve bankrupt hospitals that serve vocal constituencies, or to apply rigorously budgetary caps that cover wages as well as capital expenditures, or to withstand pressures to modify lower than desired reimbursement rates or budgets for well-connected hospitals—we may wonder, for example, whether a recent presidential directive limiting federal assistance to the construction of additional hospital capacity in areas with excessive beds will ever be applied with any bite to the Veterans Administration—all of these considerations argue against placing our central reliance on governmental direction to ensure efficient choices in this industry.

The Place of Competition

If we accept competition as the ultimate goal, we then have to confront the question of its locus. In which of the health care markets do we expect to rely on competition to do the job—the one in which the individual subscriber deals with the insurer; the employer with the insurer; or the patient or insurer with the actual providers of health care? Enthoven's plan and the Gephardt-Stockman bill appear to minimize the importance of the second of these, the employer-insurer relationship. The intention, apparently, is to remove employers as principals to these transactions, reducing them at most to the role of administering intermediaries.[2] Whatever their intention, that would be the consequence of not permitting employers to self-insure, and of requiring that premiums be community rated rather than employer experience rated.

Considering the difficulty individual subscribers are likely to have in making knowledgeable choices in this complex market and the major institutional changes that will have to take place if significantly differing competitive alternatives are to be presented, we should not be in haste to write off the possible contributions of directly interested employers to these processes. Instead, we should remember Enthoven's observation that bringing the benefits of competition to most people will not be easy, and that employers and government will have to work hard to make it happen.[3]

It seems urgent, therefore—at least in the initial stages—that we have the interested, active participation of big buyers, with millions of their own dollars at stake. They are in a position to inform themselves about the opportunities, to screen the quality of available plans, and to exert the leverage of their buying power to stimulate the emergence of alternative providing and financing institutions and of different kinds of delivery systems vying for the insurance dollar. In short we need active coalitions involving some combination of businesses, labor unions,

---

[2] Enthoven has suggested that in the world created by the Consumer Choice Health Plan (CCHP), the employment basis of health insurance would disappear and everyone would be an individual or family from a health insurance point of view. See Alain C. Enthoven, "Supply Side of Health Care and Consumer Choice Health Plan," this volume.

[3] See Alain C. Enthoven, *Health Plan* (Reading, Mass.: Addison-Wesley, 1980), p. 81.

and governments working with insurers and providers to help make it happen—as has already occurred in many localities.[4]

The Role of Local Coalitions

The potential contributions of such coalitions are not confined to the development of a competitive regime. They might choose—perhaps only as an interim cost-control technique—to work cooperatively with insurers, providers, and governments in setting limits on hospital expenditures and in apportioning among individual institutions responsibility for various services. One such experiment has been undertaken in Rochester, New York, where the Rochester Area Hospitals Corporation (RAHC), in conjunction with third-party payers—including government—sets a limit on annual expenditures for all participating hospitals, allocates that aggregate among the individual hospitals, and makes recommendations to the Health Systems Agency and state for additions to services here and cuts in existing services there, in order to reduce duplication and meet expenditure targets.

The point here is that different localities and states might essay—and assay—different institutional paths, depending on local circumstances. This possibility is a major advantage of a decentralized approach to structural reform.

The Role of the Federal Government

In what ways should the federal government encourage a movement toward decentralization and competition in the health care industry? One way that should be explored more actively than it has been is simple proselytizing.

Second, we should be taking the general approach embodied in President Carter's National Health Plan, as well as in the Gephardt-Stockman, Durenberger, and Ullman bills, of offering a choice of plans qualifying for exclusion of their cost from employees' taxable income, with employers making a uniform contribution to each, and employees receiving rebates if they select a less costly plan. We must recognize, however, that a number of technical problems with these proposals have not been resolved—for example, how they would apply to families with more than one wage earner.

Third, we should limit the size of employer contributions receiving

---

[4] One of the ways in which such coalitions might work, according to Enthoven, would be by helping finance new health maintenance organizations (HMOs). (See his "Supply-Side Economics of Health Care and Consumer Choice Health Plan," this volume.) It is not clear, however, to what extent employers would retain an incentive to help out in this way under Gephardt-Stockman or Enthoven's CCHP.

this tax preference. Unlimited exclusion is both fiscally and economically unsound. It can only encourage a greater allocation of resources into health care than would occur if incremental benefits had to be compared neutrally with incremental opportunity costs. Unlimited exclusion undoubtedly contributes, therefore, to the inflation of health care costs.

It must also weaken the pressures and incentives for cost control and the promotion of competition. So far as the employer's interest is concerned, excludability probably makes no difference. Although it causes employees to receive more of their compensation in the form of medical benefits and less in others such as wages, the costs to employers remain real in either case, and therefore their incentive to hold down such costs would appear to be undiluted.

On the workers' side, however, the nontaxability of this form of income presumably induces them to demand more lush and costly packages than they would if it were as taxable as wages. While they would in theory still be interested, in either event, in obtaining the most possible benefit per dollar of employer outlay, this tax subsidy must make them less interested than they would otherwise be in pressing for an opportunity to choose less costly plans with leaner benefits—plans that would, for example, limit their free choice of physician and all the services that fee-for-service and third-party reimbursement encourage.

A fourth component of a procompetitive government policy would be some standardization of insurance policies—not, of course, to eliminate differences among them, but to make them more readily comparable. It seems generally agreed that most subscribers are unable to make informed choices without this kind of help.

There is need, finally, for vigorous enforcement of the antitrust laws. As Joskow observes elsewhere in this volume, antitrust receives less than its deserved share of responsibility in most discussions of medical care economics. There are probably few areas of the economy in which concerted restraints, in the form of group boycotts and refusals to deal, have been as prevalent and important in discouraging the emergence of more cost-effective methods of providing service. It is distressing to observe that the vigorous efforts of the Federal Trade Commission to attack restraints like these at the local level have elicited congressional efforts to write the FTC out of this area, on the ground of states' rights.

In this connection, we should recognize that the concerted local efforts of businesses, often in collaboration with providers, to introduce a greater degree of rationality in the allocation of medical facilities in the interest of containing costs may at some point conflict with the antitrust laws. How such conflicts might be resolved remains to be seen. It should be possible, however, to devise suitable safeguards that would

497

permit such coalitions to function effectively, while also not transgressing antitrust proscriptions.

A Basic National Health Plan

As Gephardt-Stockman, Enthoven, and the Carter administration have recognized, it is probably undesirable to embark upon the competitive course without taking the one major remaining step of national health policy, namely, seeing to it that everyone in the country has minimum adequate coverage. Structural reform should be pursued, that is to say, in the context of some sort of national health plan. This course of action is desirable not merely on political and humanitarian grounds, but also because of the necessity of confronting and exorcising the specter that seems to haunt many of the contributors to this volume, namely, adverse selection.

The problem is that effective competition would require giving subscribers the widest possible range of choices of plans; but the avoidance of adverse selection counsels setting high minimum conditions for a plan to qualify for public subvention. Effective competition—particularly if it is important for employers and unions to have the strongest possible incentive to control costs—calls for experience rating, and the possibility of employer self-insurance. The avoidance of adverse selection, in contrast, suggests community rating, at least by age categories. Competition raises the prospect of cream skimming by insurance companies, appealing with low premiums to low-risk subscribers. The avoidance of adverse selection calls instead for cross-subsidization; under such a regime all plans would be required to admit high-risk subscribers at an average premium reflecting the widest possible range of experience.

I am not prepared simply to ignore the danger of adverse selection. The frequent references to the dangers of cream skimming, however, with their implicit acceptance of the desirability of internal subsidization, set an ex-regulator's antennae tingling and prompt him to ask why we should restrict competition so as to have the low-risk people—many of whom may well be poor—subsidize the high-risk—many of whom may well be rich. And why, in addition, should we follow this course when the high risks are often associated with more or less voluntary decisions to smoke cigarettes and consume large quantities of alcohol and other such delectables?

Our principal social concern should be with the people who are both high risk and poor. Why, then, would it not be most efficient to subsidize them directly? This is obviously an oversimplification, for we probably want to assume some public responsibility for assuring adequate medical coverage also for the near-poor and, indeed, the not-so-poor. Nonetheless the question remains: Why is it not more rational to do so by direct subsidies, graduated according to income, rather than by internal subsidization?

On the question of how best to take care of the poor, tax credits or vouchers seem clearly preferable to the present system of cost-based reimbursement, precisely because they open the door to competition. There also seems to be a fair measure of agreement on the desirability of giving Medicare recipients the option of selecting HMOs and receiving rebates.

Expenditure Caps

The chapters in this volume by Paul Joskow, Frank Sloan and Bruce Steinwald, and Graham Atkinson and Jack Cook suggest that budget caps can work. The real question is whether they would make economic sense. The chapter by Jack Meyer protests that a system of controls on spending "confuses budgeting and economizing." Certainly we should not minimize the dangers of budget constraints—the likelihood, for example, that they will result in a decline in supply and therefore necessitate nonprice rationing; the consequent likelihood of political pressures being exerted to relax the cap; and the irrationality of applying the same cap to all hospitals and the difficulty of devising economically efficient differentiations among them. Meyer's criticism seems to miss the point, however.

Most of the papers in this volume begin with the proposition that under our present set of institutions an uneconomically large amount of resources goes into health care. In these circumstances, budget limitations can clearly exert pressures in the right direction. Of course if they are binding, they will produce a decline in the quantity of care; but all observers seem to agree that we are purchasing an excessive quantity at present. Moreover, budget caps have the virtue of leaving the most difficult decisions about how and where to economize—presumably with the minimum degree of sacrifice—to the health care providers themselves. Meyer's problem is that his definition of economizing confuses physical efficiency with the optimal allocation of resources:

> Economizing makes it possible to obtain the same quantity and quality of services for lower total outlays. Budgeting simply makes it possible to achieve lower outlays, but not without some sacrifice in quantity and quality.[5]

On the contrary, economizing in this industry *would* presumably call for

[5] See Jack A. Meyer, "Health Care Competition: Are Tax Incentives Enough?" this volume.

"some sacrifice in quantity and quality."

It is difficult, therefore—at least in the transitional period in which we explore how much we can rely simply on more competitive arrangements to contain the alarming rise in medical costs—to forswear limits or caps on hospital expenditures, whether mandatory or voluntary, statewide or even national.

In view of the preference I have expressed for decentralized, non-bureaucratic approaches and for making the fullest use of ordinary market pressures, however, it seems desirable to explore intensively the possibility of entrusting the responsibility for setting these limits to local coalitions. These agencies have the attraction that they could at the same time pursue more fundamental structural reforms: they could, first, foster competition; second, they offer a way of introducing systems of reimbursement that will encourage providers to limit costs rather than cumulate them; and third, by planning on a regional rather than a national basis, they could attempt to allocate capital, specialized facilities, and responsibilities among individual hospitals in such a way as to take the fullest advantage of the division of labor and economies of scale. As we have noted, the Rochester experience is an apparently promising example.

State Regulation

As the preceding discussion clearly suggests, local business-labor-government coalitions can themselves function as quasi-regulators. In Michigan, for example, they have promoted rate setting by Blue Cross, as well as the development of plans to reduce excess capacity, and they have stimulated competition by supporting HMOs.

As for formal, direct state regulation, the contributors to this volume seem to agree that it can be an effective instrument for introducing more economic decision making into the provision of hospital services, and holding down rates; that it has in fact been successful in the states that have accumulated considerable experience; and that regulation is especially attractive when it takes the form of imposing not detailed regulatory prescriptions but methods of reimbursement that give providers incentives to economize. This appears to be the view of Joskow, Sloan and Steinwald, and Atkinson and Cook. Dissenters are requested to take their complaints to them. It seems also to be the case, however, that the degree of relative success of state regulation seems to have depended on how high rates and outlays were before regulation was introduced.

Finally, none of the state regulatory programs seems to confront directly the problem of turning doctors into economizers—no doubt because regulation is not the way to achieve that result. The solution seems to lie in reform of the incentives of the third-party payment system through competition, which will encourage the aggregation of physicians into organized delivery systems, and through added cost sharing for patients. After all, why should a doctor economize when his patient does not pay the bills? Seidman's argument in this volume that patient cost sharing can make an important contribution is persuasive.

One other form of regulation that deserves mention is the regulation of insurance company premiums by state commissions. This mechanism could provide a powerful supplement to the others we have discussed by requiring insurance companies to demonstrate, as a condition for obtaining rate increases, that they have attempted vigorously to introduce schemes for reimbursing providers that give them strong incentives to economize. The federal government, as the largest insurer of all, could surely do more along the same lines.

Conclusion

In view of the uncertainties about the ideal path to competition and about our ability to make progress with speed—as Jack Meyer argues convincingly here—and in view also of the limitations of attempting to apply national formulas to this diversified industry, we should not eschew a pluralistic approach to structural reform. There is a positive virtue in hedging our bets, in attempting to move along a number of lines—taking pains to see that they are not mutually frustrating—and encouraging different localities and states to lay out their own preferred paths.

I would like to see the federal government encourage the development of local purchaser coalitions aimed at stimulating the emergence of competitive alternatives, as well as bargaining with providers to introduce incentive reimbursement schemes and a rational planning of the allocation of health facilities. Others might prefer to introduce mandatory rate-setting agencies, but if so, they should take pains to emulate Maryland and emphasize incentives rather than prescriptions. In attempting to introduce measures that would encourage competition in the retail market for insurance, we should also rely on the power of the wholesale customers, who should be free to self-insure or to exert their bulk buying power in dealing directly with insurers and suppliers. State insurance commissioners should be allowed to put heavier pressure on insurance companies to exert their own influence on providers to exercise prudence. And as a very first step, governments should discard retrospective cost reimbursement for Medicare and Medicaid and should consider either a wider use of vouchers or, in conjunction with private third-party payers, should develop incentive reimbursement schemes that forestall any possibility of discrimination between the beneficiaries of public programs and private individuals. Similarly, I would like to see the federal government grant more Medicare reimbursement waivers to states and localities—as it has to Maryland and Rochester—that have effective cost control systems applicable to all third-party payers. Finally, it would be helpful to have a standby or backup mandatory federal regulatory system in order to persuade providers to persevere with their voluntary efforts.

Although I have attempted in this essay to avoid simple eclecticism, I fear, in view of the many uncertainties about what will work in containing health costs and what will not, I have still behaved like the child before a candy counter who, when asked "What will you have?" responded "All of them!" If it makes me sick, I hope my doctor will put me in the hospital, so that the costs will be covered by some anonymous third party.

A NOTE ON THE BOOK

The typeface used for the text of this book is
Times Roman, designed by Stanley Morison.
The type was set by
FotoTypesetters Incorporated, of Baltimore.
Thomson-Shore, Inc., of Dexter, Michigan, printed
and bound the book, using Glatfelter paper.
The cover and format were designed by Pat Taylor,
and the figures were drawn by Hördur Karlsson.
The manuscript was edited by Venka V. Macintyre,
and by Claire Theune of the AEI Publications staff.

SELECTED AEI PUBLICATIONS

AEI ASSOCIATES PROGRAM